Geography
Maps
Anthropology
Recreation

Library of Congress Classification
2007

Prepared by the Cataloging Policy and Support Office
Library Services

LIBRARY OF CONGRESS
Cataloging Distribution Service
Washington, D.C.

This edition cumulates all additions and changes to Classes G through Weekly List 2007/35, dated August 29, 2007. Additions and changes made subsequent to that date are published in weekly lists posted on the World Wide Web at

<http://www.loc.gov/aba/cataloging/classification/weeklylists/>

and are also available in *Classification Web*, the online Web-based edition of the Library of Congress Classification.

Library of Congress Cataloging-in-Publication Data

Library of Congress.
Library of Congress classification. G. Geography. Maps. Anthropology. Recreation / prepared by the Cataloging Policy and Support Office, Library Services. — 2007 ed.
p. cm.
"This edition cumulates all additions and changes to Class G through Weekly list 2007/35, dated August 29, 2007. Additions and changes made subsequent to that date are published in weekly lists posted on the World Wide Web ... and are also available in *Classification Web*, the online Web-based edition of the Library of Congress classification."
Includes index.
ISBN-13: 978-0-8444-1182-5 (alk. paper)
ISBN-10: 0-8444-1182-5
1. Classification, Library of Congress. 2. Classification—Books—Geography. 3. Classification—Maps. 4. Classification—Books—Anthropology. 2. Classification—Books—Recreation. I. Library of Congress. Cataloging Policy and Support Office. II. Title. III. Title: Geography. IV. Title: Maps. V. Title: Anthropology. VI. Title: Recreation.
Z696.U5G 2007 025.4'33—dc22 2007048356

For sale by the Library of Congress Cataloging Distribution Service,
101 Independence Avenue, S.E., Washington, DC 20541-4912.
Product catalog available on the Web at **www.loc.gov/cds**.

PREFACE

The first edition of Class G, with the exception of subclasses GE (*Environmental Sciences)*, GR *(Folklore)*, and GT *(Manners and Customs (General))*, was published in 1910. Subclasses GR and GT were published separately in 1915. The second edition, published in 1928, incorporated subclasses GR and GT and also included a tentative scheme for classification of atlases. The third edition, published in 1954, included for the first time a full classification scheme for maps. The fourth edition, the first to be published with the title *Geography. Maps. Anthropology. Recreation*, cumulated additions and changes made through 1975 and appeared in 1976. The 2001 edition cumulated changes made between 1976 and early 2001, and included the newly developed subclass GE. The 2005 edition cumulated changes made during the period 2001-2005. This 2007 edition cumulates changes made since the publication of the 2005 edition.

In editions of the Library of Congress classification schedules published since 2004, classification numbers or spans of numbers that appear in parentheses are formerly valid numbers that are now obsolete. Numbers or spans that appear in angle brackets are optional numbers that have never been used at the Library of Congress but are provided for other libraries that wish to use them. In most cases, a parenthesized or angle-bracketed number is accompanied by a "see" reference directing the user to the actual number that the Library of Congress currently uses, or a note explaining Library of Congress practice.

The numbers G1000-3122 (Atlases), G3160-3171 (Globes), and G3180-9980 (Maps) make use of an extensive system of geographic Cutter numbers that have been established by the Library of Congress for the classification of cartographic materials for individual regions, counties, localities, etc. Since the full list of these geographic Cutters now numbers over 100,000, it is not practical to print them in the schedule itself. The Cutters are available in separate tables that are not included in this printed edition. Although references to tables numbered G1 through G9804 appear in this schedule, only Tables G1 through G15 are actually included at the end of the volume. The remaining tables, i.e., Tables G1548 through G9804, appear in *Classification Web*, the online version of the Library of Congress Classification that is available by subscription from the Cataloging Distribution Service. Details about ordering and pricing may be obtained from the Cataloging Distribution Service at

<http://www.loc.gov/cds/>

The geographic Cutter number tables are also available in the form of a PDF file that may be downloaded at no charge from the following location:

<http://www.loc.gov/catdir/cpso/gcutter.html>

New or revised numbers and captions are added to the L.C. Classification schedules as a result of development proposals made by the cataloging staff of the Library of Congress and cooperating institutions. Upon approval of these proposals by the weekly editorial meeting of the Cataloging Policy and Support Office, new classification records are created or existing records are revised in the master classification database. Weekly lists of newly approved or revised classification numbers and captions are posted on the World Wide Web at

<http://www.loc.gov/aba/cataloging/classification/weeklylists/>

Paul Weiss, senior cataloging policy specialist in the Cataloging Policy and Support Office, is responsible for coordinating the overall intellectual and editorial content of class G. The Library of Congress Geography & Map Division oversees the content of the atlases and maps portions of subclass G as well as the geographic Cutter number tables. Kent Griffiths, assistant editor of classification schedules, creates index terms for new classification captions and maintains the master database of classification records.

Barbara B. Tillett, Chief
Cataloging Policy and Support Office

October 2007

OUTLINE

OUTLINE

	Atlases
	By region or country - Continued
G2740-2799	Australasia
G2800-3064	Oceans (General)
G3100-3102	Antarctica
G3122	Atlases of imaginary, literary, and mythological regions, etc., A-Z
G3160-3171	Globes
G3180-9980	Maps
G3180-3182	Universe. Solar system
G3190-3191	Celestial maps
G3195-3197	Moon
G3200-3202	World. Earth
G3210-3221	Northern and Southern Hemispheres
G3240-3241	Tropics. Torrid Zone
G3250-3251	Temperate Zone
G3260-3272	Polar regions. Frigid Zone
G3290-9880	By region or country
G3290-5667	America. Western Hemisphere
G3300-5184	North America
G3380-3384	Greenland
G3400-(3612)	Canada
G3700-4384	United States
G4390-4392	Caribbean area
G4410-4763	Mexico
G4800-4874	Central America
G4900-5184	West Indies
G5200-5667	South America
G5670-8904	Eastern Hemisphere. Eurasia, Africa, etc.
G5700-7342	Europe
G7000-7342	Former Soviet republics. Union of Soviet Socialist Republics (U.S.S.R.). Russia (Empire)
G7400-8198.54	Asia
G8200-8904	Africa
G8950-9084	Australasia
G9095-9794	Oceans (General)
G9800-9804	Antarctica
G9900-9980	Unlocalized maps
GA1-1776	Mathematical geography. Cartography
GA51-87	Surveys (General)
GA101-1776	Cartography
GA109	Aerial cartography

OUTLINE

OUTLINE

	Oceanography
	Physical oceanography - Continued
GC177.6-182	Optical oceanography
GC190-190.5	Ocean-atmosphere interaction
GC200-376	Dynamics of the ocean
GC205-227	Waves
GC228.5-228.6	Ocean circulation
GC229-296.8	Currents
GC297-299	Water masses and oceanic mixing
GC300-376	Tides
GC377-399	Marine sediments
GC401-881	Oceanography. By region
GC1000-1023	Marine resources. Applied oceanography
GC1080-1581	Marine pollution. Sea water pollution
GE1-350	Environmental sciences
GE70-90	Environmental education
GE170-190	Environmental policy
GE195-199	Environmentalism. Green movement
GE300-350	Environmental management
GF1-900	Human ecology. Anthropogeography
GF51	Environmental influences on humans
GF75	Human influences on the environment
GF101-127	Settlements
GF125	Cities. Urban geography
GF127	Rural settlements. Rural geography
GF500-900	By region or country
GN1-890	Anthropology
GN49-298	Physical anthropology. Somatology
GN51-59	Anthropometry
GN62.8-265	Human variation
	Including growth, physical form, skeleton, nervous system, skin, etc.
GN269-279	Race (General)
GN280.7	Man as an animal. Simian traits versus human traits
GN281-289	Human evolution
GN282-286.7	Fossil man. Human paleontology
GN296-296.5	Medical anthropology
GN301-674	Ethnology. Social and cultural anthropology
GN357-367	Culture and cultural processes
	Including social change, structuralism, diffusion, etc.

Anthropology - Continued
Ethnology. Social and cultural anthropology - Continued

GN378-396 Collected ethnographies
GN397-397.7 Applied anthropology
GN406-517 Cultural traits, customs, and institutions
GN406-442 Technology. Material culture
Including food, shelter, fire, tools, etc.
GN448-450.8 Economic organization. Economic anthropology
GN451-477.7 Intellectual life
Including communication, recreation, philosophy, religion, knowledge, etc.
GN478-491.7 Social organization
GN492-495.2 Political organization. Political anthropology
GN495.4-498 Societal groups, ethnocentrism, diplomacy, warfare, etc.
GN502-517 Psychological anthropology
GN537-674 Ethnic groups and races
GN550-674 By region or country
GN700-890 Prehistoric archaeology

GR1-950 Folklore
GR72-79 Folk literature (General)
Including folktales, legends
GR81 Folk beliefs, superstitions, etc. (General)
GR99.6-390 By region or country
GR420-950 By subject
GR420-426 Costume, jewelry
GR430-488 Folklore relating to private life
Including dreams, love, children, nursery rhymes, etc.
GR500-615 Supernatural beings, demonology, fairies, ghosts, charms, etc.
GR620-640 Cosmic phenomena, weather lore
GR650-690 Geographical topics
GR700-860 Animals, plants, and minerals
GR865-874 Transportation, travel, commerce, etc.
GR880 Medicine. Folk medicine
GR890-915 Occupations
GR931-935 Signs and symbols
GR940-941 Mythical places

GT1-7070 Manners and customs (General)
GT165-476 Houses. Dwellings
GT485 Churches and church going

	Manners and customs (General) - Continued
GT495-499	Human body and its parts. Personal beauty
GT500-2370	Costume. Dress. Fashion
GT2400-3390.5	Customs relative to private life
	Including children, marriage, eating and drinking, funeral customs, etc.
GT3400-5090	Customs relative to public and social life
	Including town life, court life, festivals, holidays, ceremonies of royalty, etc.
GT5220-5286	Customs relative to transportation and travel
GT5320-6737	Customs relative to special classes
GT5320-5690	By birth, rank, etc.
GT5750-6390	By occupation
GV1-1860	Recreation. Leisure
GV181.35-181.6	Recreation leadership. Administration of recreation services
GV182-182.5	Recreational areas and facilities. Recreation centers
GV191.2-200.66	Outdoor life. Outdoor recreation
GV191.68-198.975	Camping
GV198.945-198.975	Farm vacations, dude ranches, etc.
GV199-199.62	Hiking. Pedestrian tours
GV199.8-200.35	Mountaineering
GV200.4-200.56	Orienteering. Wilderness survival
GV200.6-200.66	Caving. Spelunking
GV201-555	Physical education and training
GV346-351.5	School and college athletics. Intramural and interscholastic athletics
GV401-433	Physical education facilities. Sports facilities
	Including gymnasiums, athletic fields, playgrounds, etc.
GV435-436.7	Physical measurements. Physical tests, etc.
GV450-451.4	Nudism. Sunbathing
GV460-555	Gymnastics. Gymnastic exercises
	Including calisthenics, heavy exercises, acrobatics, etc.
GV557-1198.995	Sports
GV711	Coaching
GV712-725	Athletic contests. Sports events
GV733-734.5	Professionalism in sports. Professional sports (General)
GV735	Umpires. Sports officiating
GV743-749	Athletic and sporting goods, supplies, etc.
GV750-770.27	Air sports: Airplane flying, kiteflying, bungee jumping, etc.

Recreation. Leisure

	Sports - Continued
GV770.3-840	Water sports: Canoeing, sailing, yachting, scuba diving, etc.
GV840.7-857	Winter sports: Ice hockey, skiing, bobsledding, snowmobiling, etc.
GV861-1017	Ball games: Baseball, football, golf, etc.
GV1020-1034	Automobile travel. Motoring. Automobile racing
GV1040-1060.4	Cycling. Bicycling. Motorcycling
GV1060.5-1098	Track and field athletics
GV1100-1150.9	Fighting sports: Bullfighting, boxing, fencing, etc.
GV1151-1190	Shooting. Archery
GV1195-1198.995	Wrestling
GV1199-1570	Games and amusements
GV1201.5	Hobbies (General)
GV1203-1220.8	Children's games and amusements
GV1218.5-1220.8	Toys
GV1221-1469.63	Indoor games and amusements
GV1232-1299	Card games: Poker, patience, whist, etc.
GV1301-1311	Gambling. Chance and banking games
GV1312-1469	Board games. Move games Including chess, go, checkers, etc.
GV1469.15-1469.62	Computer games. Video games. Fantasy games
GV1470-1511	Parties. Party games and stunts
GV1491-1507	Puzzles
GV1541-1561	Parlor magic and tricks
GV1564-1565	Darts
GV1580-1799.4	Dancing
GV1800-1860	Circuses, spectacles, etc. Including rodeos, waxworks, amusement parks, etc.

Geography (General)

For geography and description of individual countries, see D-F

For mathematical geography and cartography see GA

For physical geography see GB

1 Periodicals. Serials

Societies

2 International

3 United States

4 Canada

5 Mexico. Central America. West Indies

6 South America

7 Great Britain

8 Czechoslovakia

9 Austria

10 Hungary

11 France

13 Germany

Including West Germany

14 East Germany

15 Greece

17 Italy

19 Belgium

21 Netherlands (Holland)

23 Russia

23.5 Poland

24 Finland

25 Scandinavia

27 Spain

28 Portugal

29 Switzerland

31 Balkan States

32 Turkey

32.2 Jordan

32.5 Israel

32.7 Saudi Arabia

33 China

35 India

36 Pakistan

36.5 Bangladesh

37 Indochina

38 Indonesia

39 Japan

41 South Africa

43 Egypt

45 Algeria

47 Tanzania

49 Other African (not A-Z)

Societies -- Continued
51 Australia
53 New Zealand
55 Pacific islands
56 Congresses
Collected works (nonserial)
Cf. G159+ Collections of voyages
58 Several authors
59 Individual authors
62 Addresses, essays, lectures
63 Dictionaries. Encyclopedias
64 Directories
Geographers
65 Geography as a profession
Biography
Cf. D-F, History
Cf. GA198, GA407, GA473, etc., Cartographers
Cf. G200 Explorers
67 Collective
69.A-Z Individual, A-Z
e.g.
69.A2 Adamus Bremensis
69.B35 Barkov, Aleksandr Sergeevich
69.B4 Behaim, Martin
69.H2 Hakluyt, Richard
69.K44 Kemmerikh, Aleksandr (Aleksandr Oskarovich), 1912-
69.P4 Petermann, August
69.R4 Rennell, James
69.R6 Ritter, Karl
69.T55 Tillo, Aleksei Andreevich
Philosophy. Relation to other topics. Methodology
For relation to parapsychology see BF1045.G46
For relation to religion see BL65.G4
For relation to civilization see CB450
For relation to history. Historical geography see G141
For relation to economics. Economic geography see HF1021+
For relation to geopolitics see JC319+
Cf. HX550.G45 Geography and communism
70 General works
Special methods
70.2 Data processing
Geographic information systems
70.212 General works
70.215.A-Z By region or country, A-Z
70.23 Mathematics. Quantitative methods
70.25 Network analysis

Philosophy. Relation to other topics. Methodology
Special methods -- Continued
70.28 Simulation
70.3 Statistical methods
Remote sensing
For works on the application of remote sensing to a special field, see B-Z, e.g. GB656.2.R44 Hydrology; S494.5.R4 Agriculture
70.39 Congresses
70.4 General works
70.5.A-Z By region or country, A-Z
70.6 Equipment
71.5 Geographical perception
Cf. HQ784.G45 Geographical perception of children
Study and teaching. Research
72 Periodicals. Societies. Serials
72.5 Congresses
73 General works
74 General special
74.5 Fieldwork
75 Home geography
76 Audiovisual aids
Textbooks see G125+
76.5.A-Z By region or country, A-Z
77.A-Z Schools. By place, A-Z
Museums. Exhibitions
77.8 General works
78.A-Z By region or country, A-Z
Under each country:
.x *General works*
.x2A-.x2Z *Special. By city, A-Z*
Communication of information
79 General works
79.3 Information services
79.5 Computer network resources
Including the Internet
History of geography
Cf. G199.2+ History of voyages of discovery
80 General works
81 General special
Cf. GN476.4 Primitive geography
82 Ancient and medieval
Including Chinese
Ancient
Cf. DE22.2+ Classical geography
83 Dictionaries. Encyclopedias
Modern authors

History of geography
Ancient
Modern authors -- Continued
84 General works
86 General special
Classical authors (Greek and Roman)
87.A1 Collections
87.A3 Selections, extracts, etc.
87.A6-Z Individual authors, A-Z
Under each (unless otherwise specified):
.x Texts
Cf. subdivisions below
For original Greek and Latin texts, see PA except where authors write on geography only or texts are accompanied by translations or commentaries interpreting geography
.x2 Translations
Including texts with translations
For Latin translations, see PA if Greek texts class there; for translations into lesser known languages, see the language
.x3 Commentaries. Criticism
Including texts with commentaries
For textual criticism, see PA
Dionysius Periegetes
Orbis terrae descriptio
87.D5-.D59 Greek texts (chronologically)
Translations
87.D6 Latin. By date
87.D61-.D69 Other languages (alphabetically)
87.D7 Commentaries. Criticism
Strabo
Geographica
87.S86 Greek texts. By date
87.S87 Greek and Latin texts. By date
87.S875 Selections (Greek). By editor
Translations
87.S88 Latin. By date
87.S9 English. By date
87.S91-.S94 Other languages (alphabetically)
e.g.
87.S92 German. By translator

History of geography
Ancient
Classical authors (Greek and Roman)
Individual authors, A-Z
Strabo
Geographica -- Continued
87.S95 Commentaries. Criticism
Sources and ancient authors other than Greek and Roman
87.5 Modern works
87.7 Texts with translations
88 Voyages
88.5.A-Z Special regions, A-Z
Including works of geographical interest not provided for in D-F
Medieval to 1600/1650
Modern writers
89 General works
89.5 General special
90 Early writers (including Oriental) other than those in G91-G95
91 Early Christian
92 Viking age
93 Arabic geographers
94 Other later ("Scholastic") to 1420/1492
95 15th-16th centuries (1420/1492 to 1600/1650)
For discovery of seaway to India see G280+
Modern, 1600/1650-
96 General works
For treatises see G113+
97 17th-18th centuries
98 19th century
99 20th century
99.2 21st century
Geographical myths, folklore, etc.
see GR650+ GR940
Toponymy
Cf. GN468.45 Names and naming systems of preliterate and folk societies
100.5 General works
Gazetteers
For gazetteers of individual continents and countries, see D-F
101 Through 1800
102 1801-1870
103 1871-1974
103.5 1975-

Toponymy -- Continued
Geographic names (Universal)
For geographic names of individual continents and countries, see D-F
104 Periodicals. Societies. Serials
104.3 Congresses
104.5 Polyglot lists
By language
Including reports of national boards and commissions
105 English
106.A-Z Other languages, A-Z
107 Latin
Geographic terms
107.8 Periodicals. Societies. Serials
107.9 General works
108.A-Z By language, A-Z
e.g.
108.F7 French
108.G3 German
108.R9 Russian
108.5.A-Z Special topics and terms, A-Z
108.5.C3 Cardinal points
108.7 Geographical location codes
Tables. Distances, geographical positions, etc.
109 General works
109.5 Global Positioning System
Class here general works on the Global Positioning System.
For works on special applications of the system, see the subject, e.g. TA595.5, Satellite surveying; TL696.A77, Artificial satellites in air navigation; VK562, Artificial satellites in ship navigation. For works on the satellite component of the system, see TL798.N3. For geographic information systems see G70.2
110.A-Z By region or country, A-Z
Latitude and longitude see QB224.5+
General works, treatises, and advanced textbooks
General systematic works
113 1450-1600
Ptolemy revised, Solinus, Franck, etc.
114 1601-1800
115 1801-1974
116 1975-
Compends
120 Through 1700
121 1701-1870
122 1871-1974
123 1975-

General works, treatises, and advanced textbooks -- Continued
Textbooks
Cf. GB51+, GB55, Textbooks in physical geography
125 Through 1870
126 1871-1970 Octavos
127 1871-1970 Quartos (25 cm.+)
128 1971-
129 Outlines. Syllabi
131 Examinations, questions, etc.
133 Juvenile works
Pictorial works
136 Through 1830
137 1831-1870
138 1871-1974
138.5 1975-
140 Great cities of the world
Including capitals of the world, great streets of the world, etc.
140.5 World Heritage areas
141 Historical geography
For individual countries, see D-F
For polar regions see G575+
For individual oceans, seas, etc. see GC401+
142 Aerial geography
Cf. TR810 Aerial photography. Photographic interpretation
143 Environmental geography
Travel. Voyages and travels (General)
Cf. GT5220+ Customs relative to travel
149 Periodicals. Societies. Serials
Cf. G154 Travel agencies and clubs
Cf. GV1027 Automobile clubs
149.5 Congresses
149.7 Computer network resources
Including the Internet
Traveling instructions
Cf. G597 Polar expeditions
Cf. Q116 Scientific expeditions
Cf. RA783.5 Travel hygiene
149.9 Early works through 1800
150 1801-1974
151 1975-
Guidebooks, prospectuses, etc.
Cf. GV1024+ Automobile road guides
Cf. HE2727+ Railroad guides
Cf. HE9768 Air travel guides
Through 1974
153.A1-.Z8 General works
153.Z9 Catalogs of audiovisual materials

Travel. Voyages and travels (General)
Guidebooks, prospectuses, etc. -- Continued
1975-
153.4.A1-.Z8 General works
153.4.Z9 Catalogs of audiovisual materials
154 Travel agencies and clubs
Cf. HF5686.T73 Accounting
Biography of travel agents, publicists, etc.
154.49 Collective
154.5.A-Z Individual, A-Z
154.7 Tour guides (Persons)
Travel and the state. Tourism
Including tourist travel promotion, statistical surveys, etc.
Cf. RA638 Immunity and immunization
154.9 Congresses
155.A1 General works
155.A2-Z By region or country, A-Z
Including regulations, requirements for entry, economic studies and reports, etc.
155.5 Vocational guidance
Study and teaching. Research
155.7 General works
155.8.A-Z By region or country, A-Z
156 History of travel and touring
156.5.A-Z Special topics, A-Z
Agritourism see S565.88
156.5.B86 Business travel
(156.5.C5) Church and travel
see G156.5.R44
Cultural tourism see G156.5.H47
Education and travel see LC6681
156.5.E26 Ecotourism
For ecotourism in special regions or countries see G155.A2+
Cf. G156.5.M36 Marine ecotourism
Gay and lesbian travel see HQ75.25+
156.5.H47 Heritage tourism. Cultural tourism
For heritage tourism in special regions or countries see G155.A2+
156.5.I5 Internet and tourism
156.5.M36 Marine ecotourism
Pets and travel see SF415.45
People with physical disabilities and travel see HV3022
156.5.R44 Religious aspects
156.5.R69 Royal tourism
156.5.V64 Volunteer tourism
Wine tourism see TP548.5.T68

Travel. Voyages and travels (General)
Special topics, A-Z -- Continued
156.5.Y6 Youth travel
Travel and etiquette see BJ2137
Collected works (nonserial)
159 Through 1700
160 1701-1800
161 1801-1950
162 1951-1974
163 1975-
175 Juvenile works
180 Addresses, essays, lectures
History of discoveries, explorations, and travel
For discovery of and exploration and travel in an individual country, see D-F
For voyages to the East Indies, 1498-1761 see DS411+
For polar voyages see G575+
General works see G80
Juvenile works see G175
200 Collective biography
By nationality
For travels in individual countries, see D-F
For records of individual voyages see G370.A+
For polar exploration see G575+
American
220 Collected works (General)
222 History
Biography of explorers and travelers
225 Collective
226.A-Z Individual, A-Z
227 Arab
Austrian
227.9 History
Biography
228 Collective
228.2.A-Z Individual, A-Z
Belgian
229 Collected works (General)
229.2 History
Biography
229.5 Collective
229.52.A-Z Individual, A-Z
Chinese see G320+
Croatian
229.6 Collected works (nonserial)
229.62 History
Biography

History of discoveries, explorations, and travel
By nationality
Croatian
Biography -- Continued
229.65 Collective
229.652.A-Z Individual, A-Z
Czechoslovak
229.7 Collected works (nonserial)
229.72 History
Biography
229.75 Collective
229.752.A-Z Individual, A-Z
Danish see G300+
Dutch
230 Collected works (General)
232 History
Biography of explorers and travelers
235 Collective
236.A-Z Individual, A-Z
English
240 Collected works (General)
242 History
Biography of explorers and travelers
245 Collective
246.A-Z Individual, A-Z
Filippino see G328
French
250 Collected works (General)
252 History
Biography of explorers and travelers
255 Collective
256.A-Z Individual, A-Z
German
260 Collected works (General)
262 History
Biography of explorers and travelers
265 Collective
266.A-Z Individual, A-Z
268 Hungarian
Irish
269 Collective works (General)
269.2 History
Biography of explorers and travelers
269.5 Collective
269.52.A-Z Individual, A-Z
269.55 Israeli
Italian

History of discoveries, explorations, and travel
By nationality
Italian -- Continued
270 Collected works (General)
272 History
Biography of explorers and travelers
275 Collective
276.A-Z Individual, A-Z
Japanese see G330+
277 Jewish
Luxembourg
277.3 Collected works
277.32 History
Biography
277.35 Collective
277.36.A-Z Individual, A-Z
277.5 Polish
Portuguese and Spanish
Cf. E110 Discovery of America
278 Collected works (General)
279 History
Portuguese
Cf. DP583 Portugal, 1385-1580
280 Collected works (General)
282 History
Biography of explorers and travelers
285 Collective
286.A-Z Individual, A-Z
e.g.
286.H5 Henry the Navigator
286.M2 Magellan, Ferdinand
Spanish
287 Collected works (General)
288 History
Biography
288.8 Collective
289.A-Z Individual, A-Z
Romanian
Biography
289.5 Collective
289.52.A-Z Individual, A-Z
Russian
290 Collected works (General)
292 History
Biography
295 Collective
296.A-Z Individual, A-Z

History of discoveries, explorations, and travel
By nationality -- Continued
Scandinavian
300 Collected works (General)
302 History
Biography
305 Collective
306.A-Z Individual, A-Z
Slovenian
308 Collected works (Nonserial)
308.2 History
Biography
308.5 Collective
308.52.A-Z Individual, A-Z
Swiss
310 Collected works (General)
Biography
315 Collective
316.A-Z Individual, A-Z
Yugoslav
317 Collected works (nonserial)
317.2 History
Biography
317.5 Collective
317.52.A-Z Individual, A-Z
Chinese
320 Collected works (General)
322 History
Biography
325 Collective
326.A-Z Individual, A-Z
328 Filippino
Japanese
330 Collected works (General)
332 History
Biography
335 Collective
336.A-Z Individual, A-Z
Special voyages and travels
Ancient see G88
Medieval
369 General works
370.A-Z By explorer or traveler, or if better known, by name of ship, A-Z
e.g.

Special voyages and travels
Medieval
By explorer or traveler, or if better known, by name of ship, A-Z -- Continued
370.M2 Mandeville, Sir John. Itinerarium
For anonymous metrical version, Boke of Mawndeville see PR2065.B57+
370.S3 Schiltberger, Johannes. Reisen...
1400-1520
For voyages to America see E101+
400 General works
401.A-Z By explorer or traveler, or if better known, by name of ship, A-Z
Modern, 1521-
Circumnavigations (Expeditions)
Cf. Q115+ Scientific expeditions
Cf. R687 Medical expeditions
419 General works
420.A-Z By explorer or traveler, or if better known, by name of ship, A-Z
420.D7 Drake, Sir Francis
420.M2 Magellan
Tours around the world
439 General works
440.A-Z By explorer or traveler, or if better known, by name of ship, A-Z
445 Flights around the world
Cf. TL721.A+ Special historic flights (Aeronautics)
Travels in several parts of the world
General works
460 Through 1800
463 1801-1949
464 1950-1974
465 1975-
468 Pictorial works
Juvenile works see G570
470 America and Europe
475 America, West Indies, Africa
477 America and the Pacific
478 Atlantic to the Pacific (and vice versa) via Cape Horn
480 America and Asia
490 Europe and Asia. Africa and Asia. Europe and Africa
Tropics (General) see G910
Polar regions see G575+
492 Arctic regions and Africa, Europe, etc.
Northern Hemisphere see G916
Southern Hemisphere see G922

Special voyages and travels
Modern, 1521-
Travels in several parts of the world -- Continued
500 Islands
Cf. D-F, Description and travel
Cf. GB471+ Physical geography
Cf. VK798+ Pilot guides
503 Isolated areas
504 Hitchhiking
Walking. Tramping. Pedestrian tours see GV199+
Backpacking see GV199.6+
Mountaineering see GV199.8+
516 Adventure travel
Including safaris
Adventures, shipwrecks, buried treasures, etc.
For official reports of shipwrecks see VK1250
521 Periodicals. Societies. Serials
522 Philosophy. Motivation
Biography of adventurers see CT9970+
525 General works
Including nonserial collected narratives
530 Individual narratives. By explorer or traveler, or if better known, by name of ship, A-Z
Including sailors' yarns
For wrecks of special vessels, assign Cutter for the name of the vessel
For accounts of individual treasure sites, see CJ153 or D-F
Beachcombing. Ocean bottles
Cf. GC229+ Ocean currents
532 General works
By region or country
United States
532.4 General works
532.5.A-Z By region or state, A-Z
532.6.A-Z Other regions or countries, A-Z
Pirates, buccaneers, etc.
For works limited to one region or country, see D-F, e.g. DT201+, Barbary corsairs; F2161, Pirates in the Caribbean
535 Collective
537.A-Z Individual, A-Z
539 Filibusters. Soldiers of fortune
For works limited to one region or country, see D-F
Seafaring life, ocean travel, etc.
Cf. DE61.S43 Greek and Roman civilization
Cf. GR910 Folklore of the sea
Cf. VK149 Nautical life
540 General works

Seafaring life, ocean travel, etc. -- Continued
545 Whaling voyages
Cf. SH381+ Whale fishery
Merchant vessels see G540+
549 Men-of-war. Cruises (in time of peace)
Cf. V720+ Naval life and customs
550 Passenger life
Cf. GV710 Deck sports and games
555 Voyages touching unidentified places
e.g. Lost islands
Cf. GN751 Atlantides
Mysterious disappearances, triangles of death, etc.
557 General works
558 Bermuda Triangle
558.2 Dragon Triangle
560 Imaginary voyages
Cf. GR650+ Folklore
Cf. GR940+ Mythical places
Cf. HX806+ Utopias
570 Juvenile voyages and travels
Arctic and Antarctic regions
Including exploration, history, description, travel
Polar regions
Including both poles
575 Periodicals. Societies. Serials
576 Collected works (nonserial)
578 Congresses
Museums. Exhibitions
579 General works
579.3.A-Z By region or country, A-Z
History
580 General works
582 By nationality, A-Z
Biography
584 Collective
585.A-Z Individual, A-Z
e.g.
585.A6 Amundsen, Roald
585.B8 Byrd, Richard Evelyn
585.E6 Ellsworth, Lincoln
587 General works
590 Popular works
593 General special
Including jurisdiction, sovereignty, etc.
595 Addresses, essays, lectures
597 Instructions for polar exploration
Including equipment, hygiene, etc.

	Arctic and Antarctic regions -- Continued
599	Aircraft for polar exploration
	Arctic regions. Arctic exploration
600	Periodicals. Societies. Serials
600.5	Congresses
601	Collected works (nonserial)
606	General works
608	Popular works
610	Pictorial works
614	Juvenile works
614.5	Addresses, essays, lectures
615	General special
	Including theory of north-polar exploration, etc.
	History of exploration
620	General works
623	Early through 1800
625	19th century
	20th century
626	General works
627	1945-
630.A-Z	Exploration. By nationality, ethnic group, etc., A-Z
	e.g.
630.A5	American
630.D9	Dutch
630.S33	Scandinavian
	Biography
634	Collective
635.A-Z	Individual, A-Z
	e.g.
	Franklin see G660+
635.P4	Perry, Robert Edwin
635.R3	Rasmussen, Knud Johan Victor
635.S7	Stefansson, Vihjalmur
639	Northeast and Northwest Passages
	Western Hemisphere
639.3	General works
639.4	Juvenile works
	Northwest Passage
640	General works
650	Special expeditions (Sea and land). Narratives. By date of expedition
	Franklin Search
	Including biography of Sir John Franklin
660	General works
662	General special
665	Narratives. By date of expedition
670	Expeditions. By date of expedition

Arctic and Antarctic regions
Arctic regions. Arctic exploration
History of exploration -- Continued
Eastern Hemisphere
673 General works
674 Juvenile works
Northeast Passage
680 General works
690 Narratives. By date of expedition
700 Expeditions. By date of expedition
Special regions
American Arctic regions
Greenland
725 Periodicals. Societies. Serials
730 Collected works
General works. Description
740 Through 1821
742 1822-1900
743 1901-
750 Social life and customs
Cf. E99.E7 Eskimos
760 History
Biography
761 Collective
762.A-Z Individual, A-Z
765.A-Z Local, A-Z
e.g.
765.K5 King Christian X Land
765.P4 Peary Land
765.S35 Scoresby Sound
770.A-Z Other regions, A-Z
e.g.
For Canadian Arctic regions see F1090.5
770.S6 Smith Sound
Norwegian Arctic regions
Including Svalbard
778 General works
(780-782) Kwangsi (Autonomous region)
see G7823.K7
780 Spitsbergen
782 Jan Mayen Island
785 Bear Island. Bjørnøya
787.A-Z Other islands, etc., A-Z
e.g.
787.E33 Edge Island
787.H6 Hope Island
Barents Sea

Arctic and Antarctic regions
Arctic regions. Arctic exploration
Special regions
Barents Sea -- Continued
790 General works
800 Novaya Zemlya
810 Franz Josef Land
Siberian Arctic regions. Laptev Sea. East Siberian Sea
820 General works
825 New Siberian Islands
827 Severnaya Zemlya
830 Wrangel Island
839.A-Z Other islands, etc., A-Z
Antarctic regions. Antarctic exploration
845 Periodicals. Societies. Serials
845.5 Congresses
846 Collected works (nonserial)
850 Voyages. By date
Further divided by explorer, traveler, expedition, or ship, A-Z
855 Dictionaries. Encyclopedias. Gazetteers. Geographic names
860 General works
863 Juvenile works
Museums. Exhibitions
864 General works
865.A-Z By region or country, A-Z
Subarrange each region or country by author
History
870 General works
872.A-Z Exploration. By nationality, A-Z
Biography
874 Collective
875.A-Z Individual, A-Z
e.g.
Byrd see G585.B8
875.S35 Scott, Robert Falcon
876 Addresses, essays, lectures
877 General special
878 Jurisdiction, sovereignty, etc.
890.A-Z Special regions, A-Z
e.g.
890.A4 Terre Adélie
890.B4 Beardmore Glacier region
890.C45 Chilean areas
Graham Land see G890.P3
890.P3 Palmer Peninsula
Cf. F3031+ Falkland Islands

Arctic and Antarctic regions
Antarctic regions. Antarctic exploration
Special regions, A-Z -- Continued
890.Q4 Queen Maud Land
890.R6 Ross Dependency
890.R62 Ross Island
Tropics (General)
905 General works
907 General special
910 Special voyages and travels
Northern Hemisphere
912 General works
915 General special
916 Special voyages and travels
Southern Hemisphere
918 General works
920 General special
922 Special voyages and travels

ATLASES

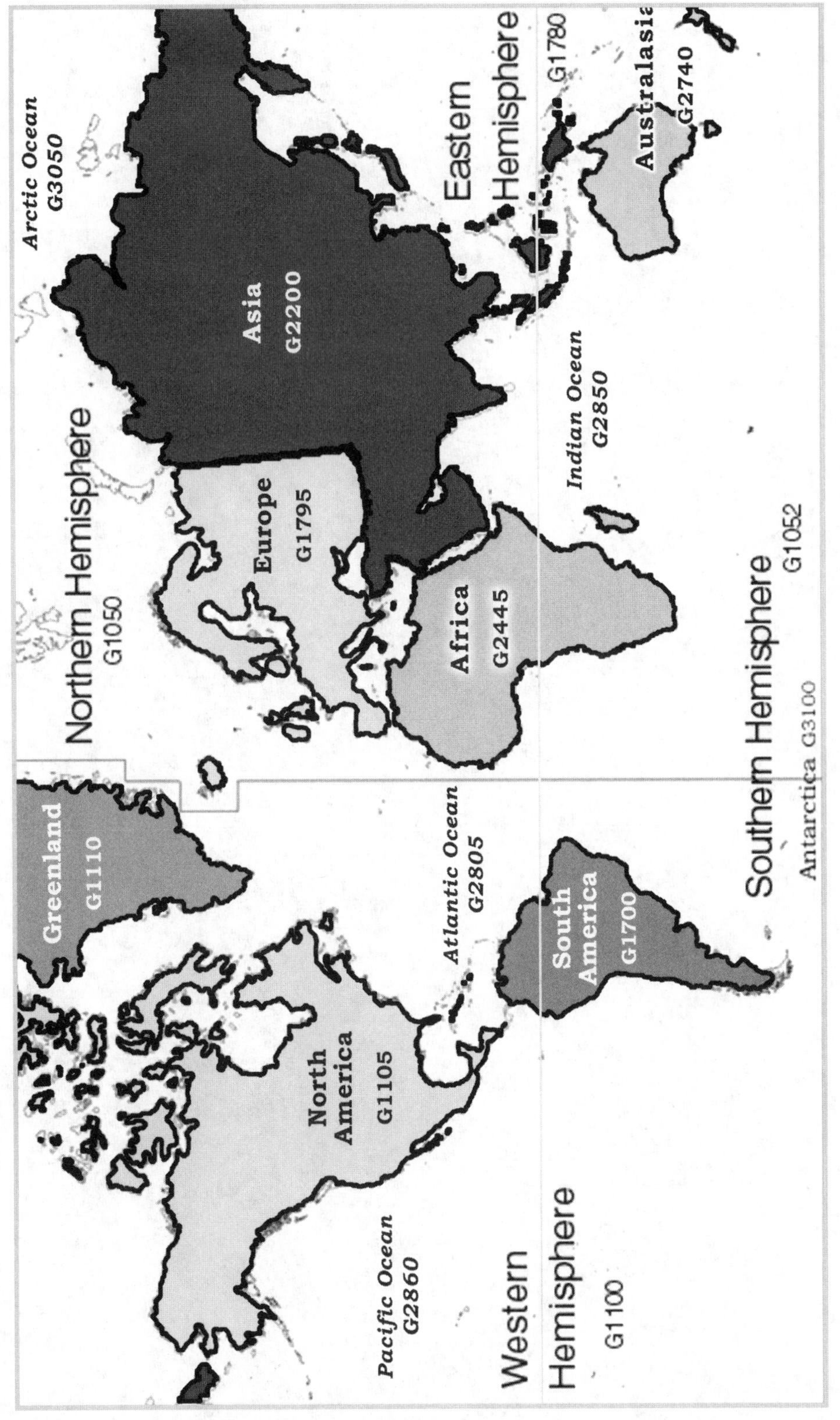

Hemispheres, Continents and Oceans

Atlases

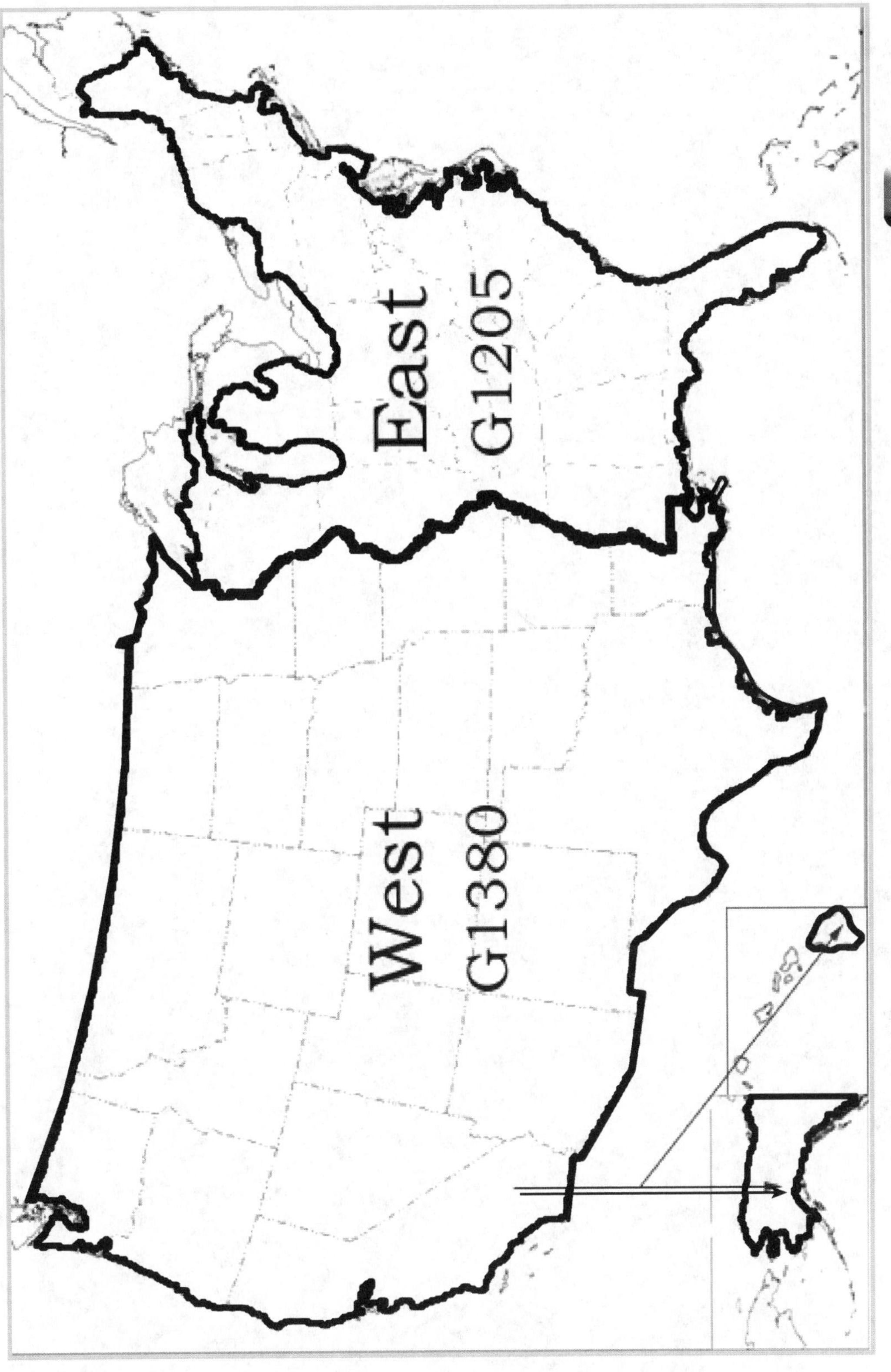

United States • *Atlases: No. 1*

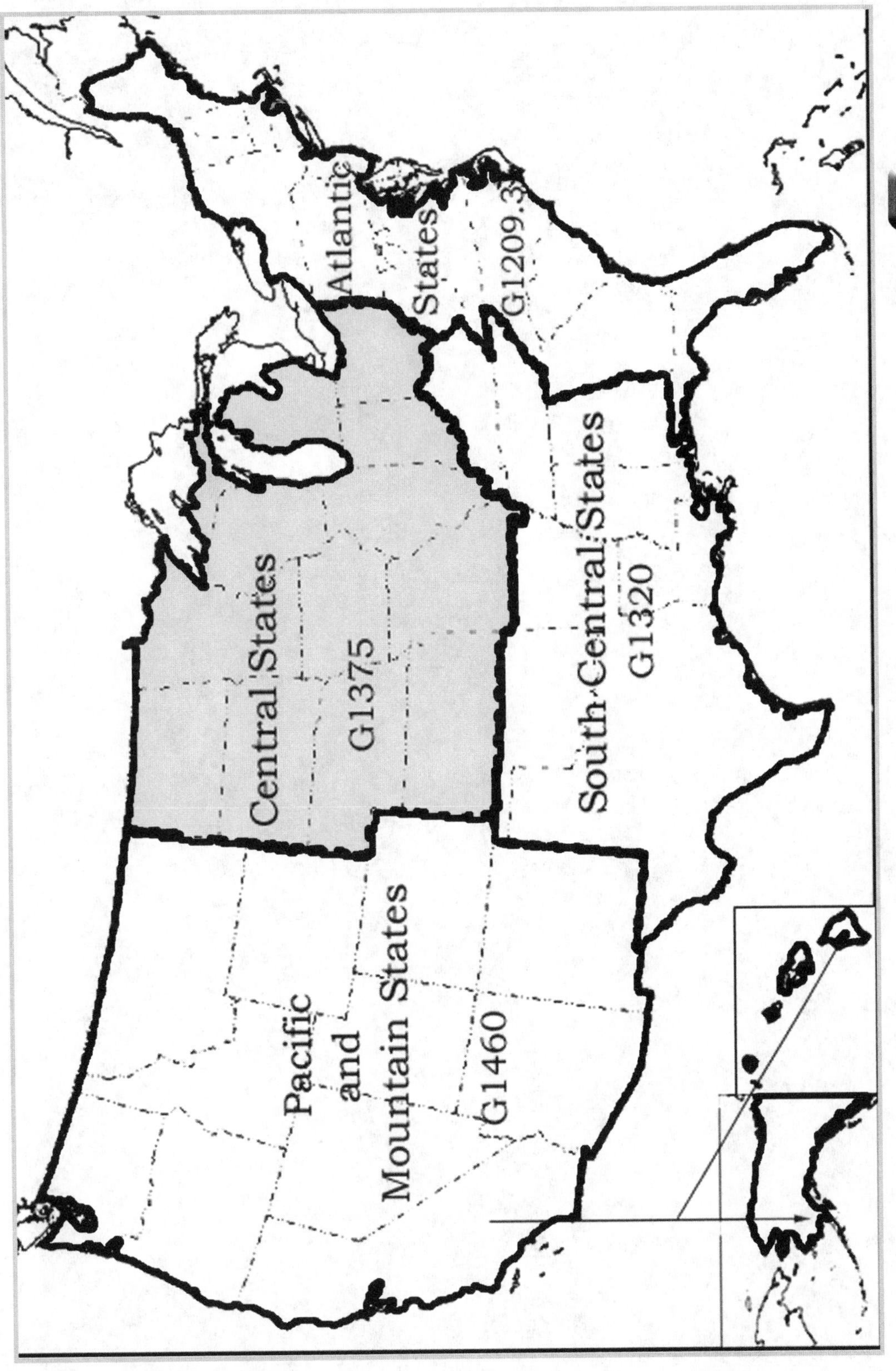

United States • *Atlases: No. 2*

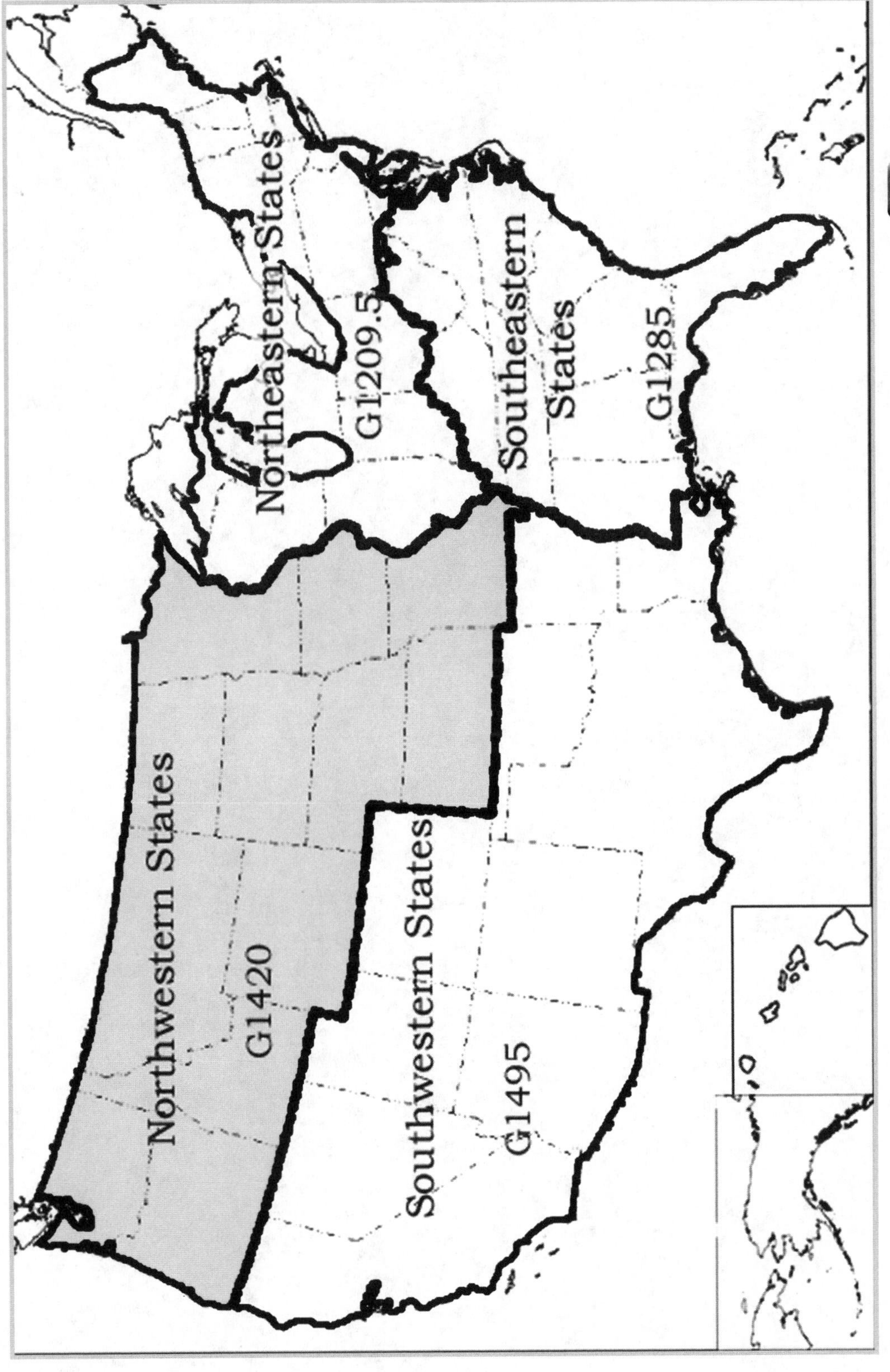

United States • *Atlases: No. 3*

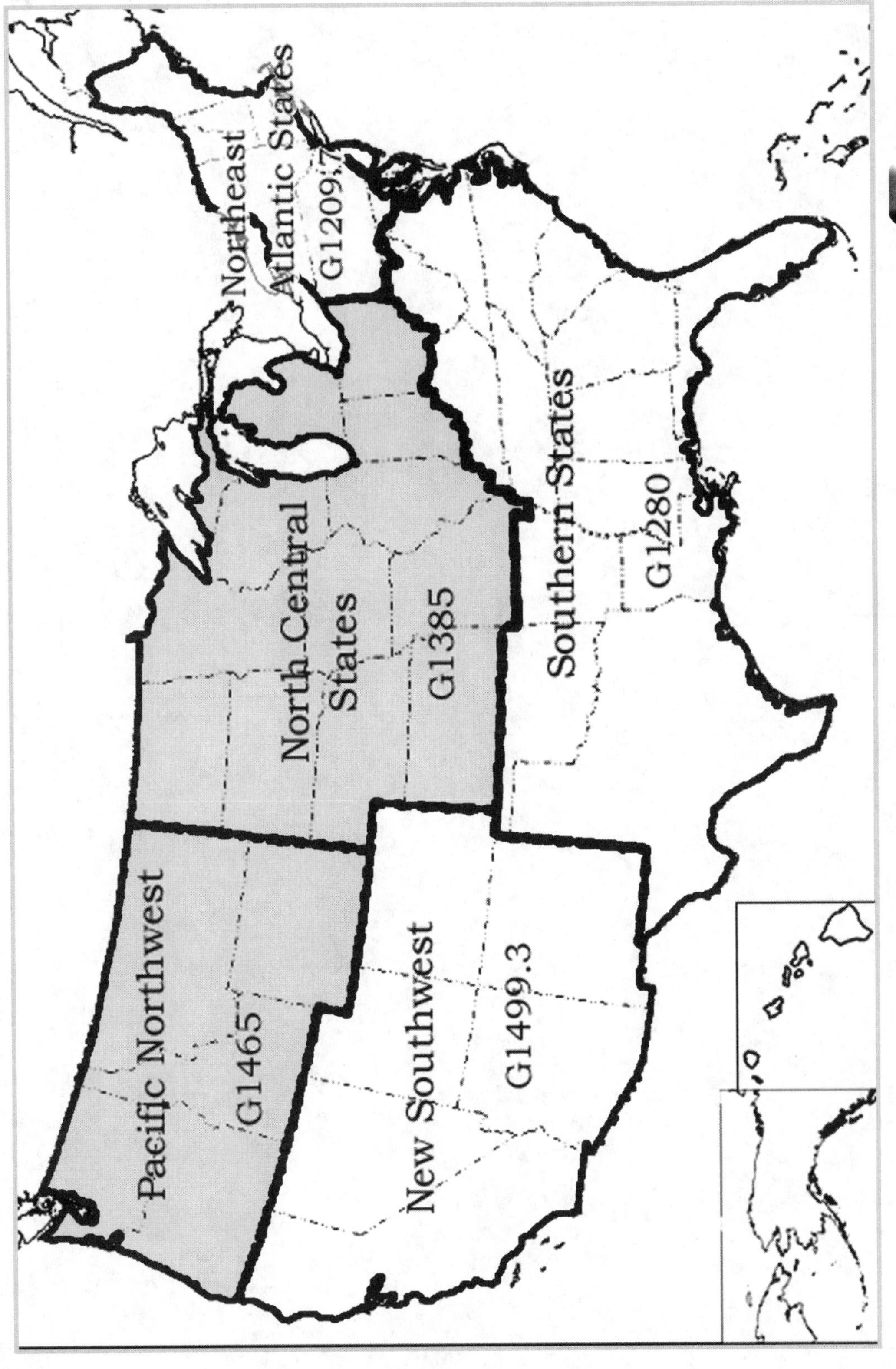

United States • *Atlases: No. 4*

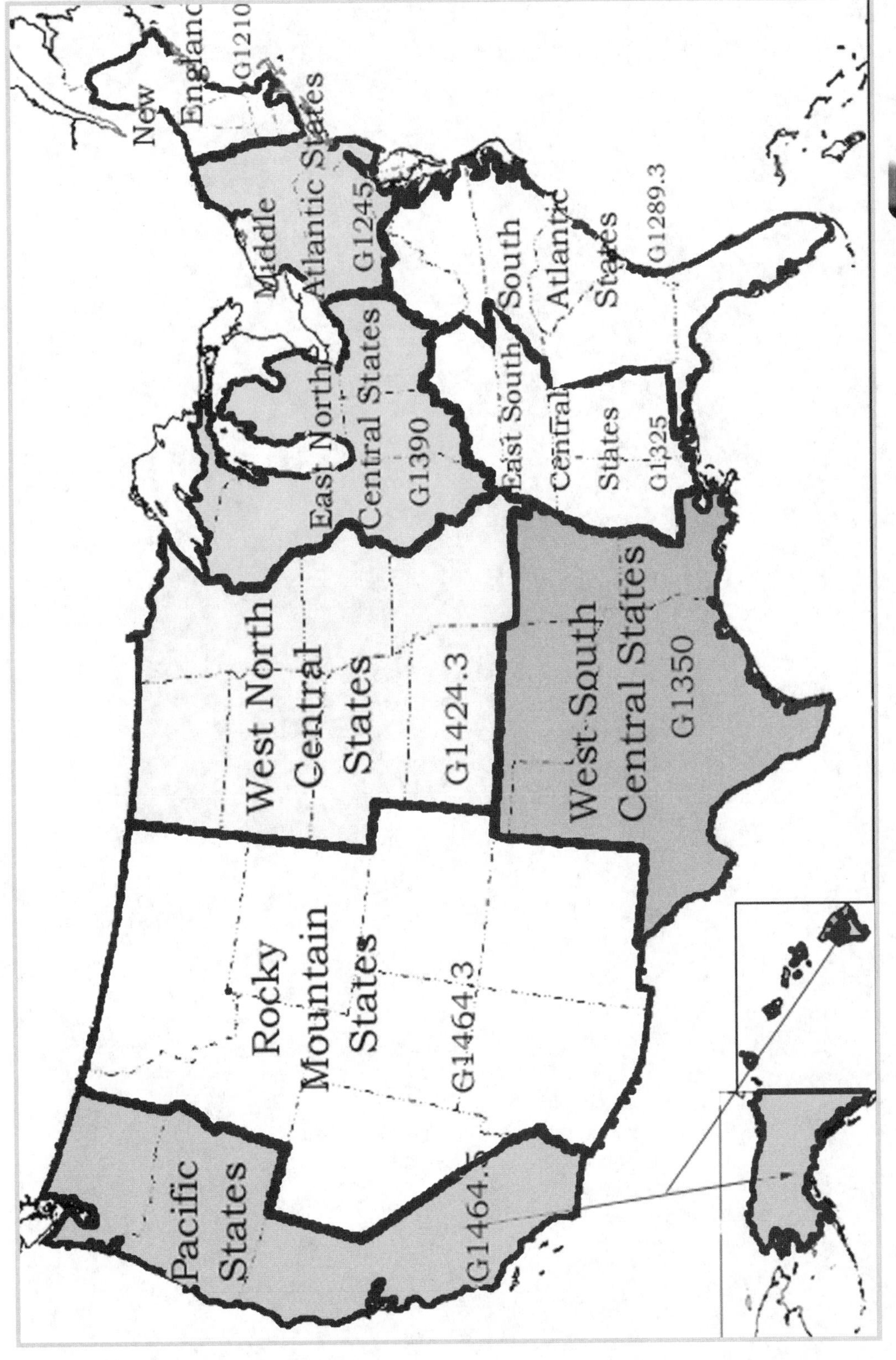
New England
G1210
Middle Atlantic States
G1245
South Atlantic States
G1289.3
East North Central States
G1390
East South Central States
G1325
West North Central States
G1424.3
West South Central States
G1350
Rocky Mountain States
G1464.3
Pacific States
G1464.5

United States • *Atlases: No. 5*

Europe • *Atlases: No. 1*

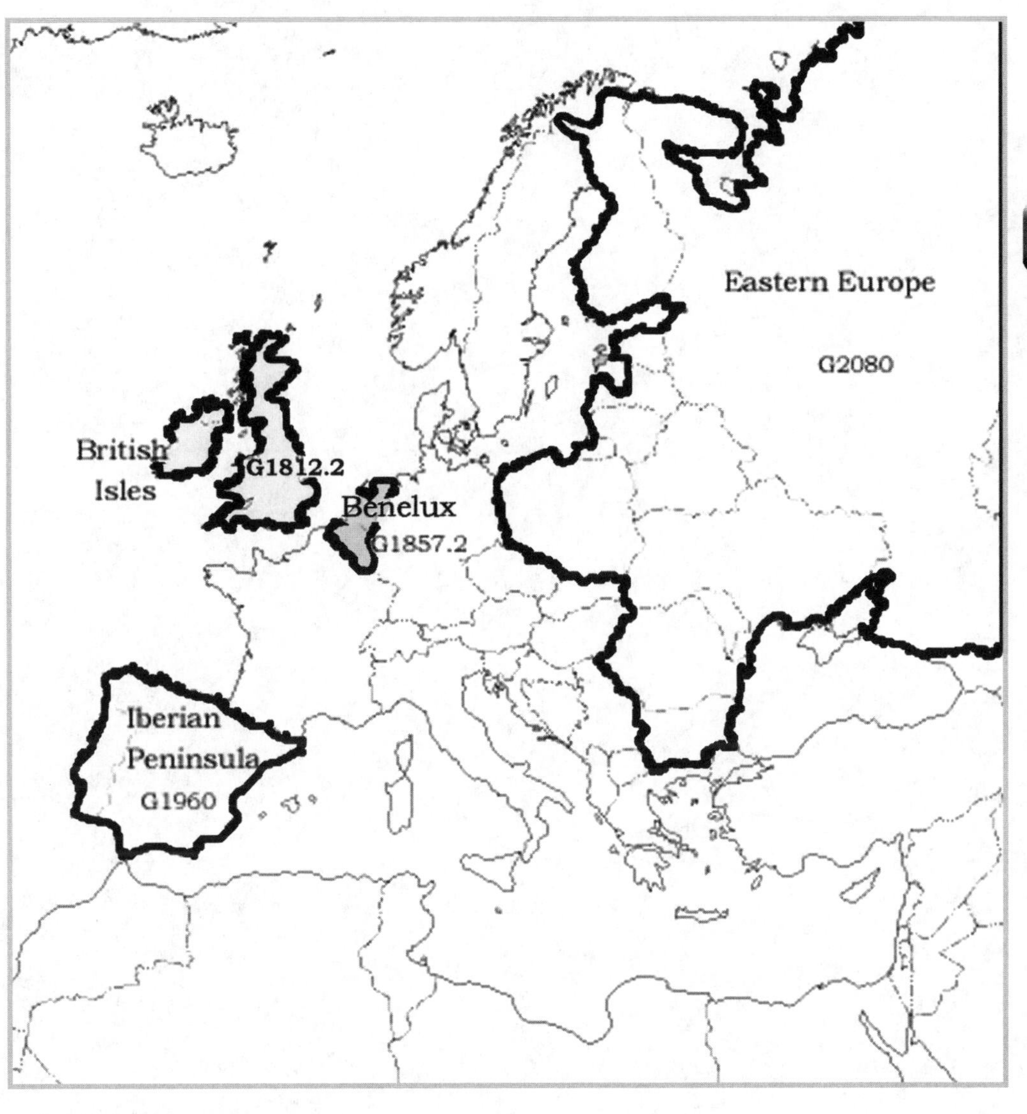

Europe • *Atlases: No. 2*

Asia • *Atlases*

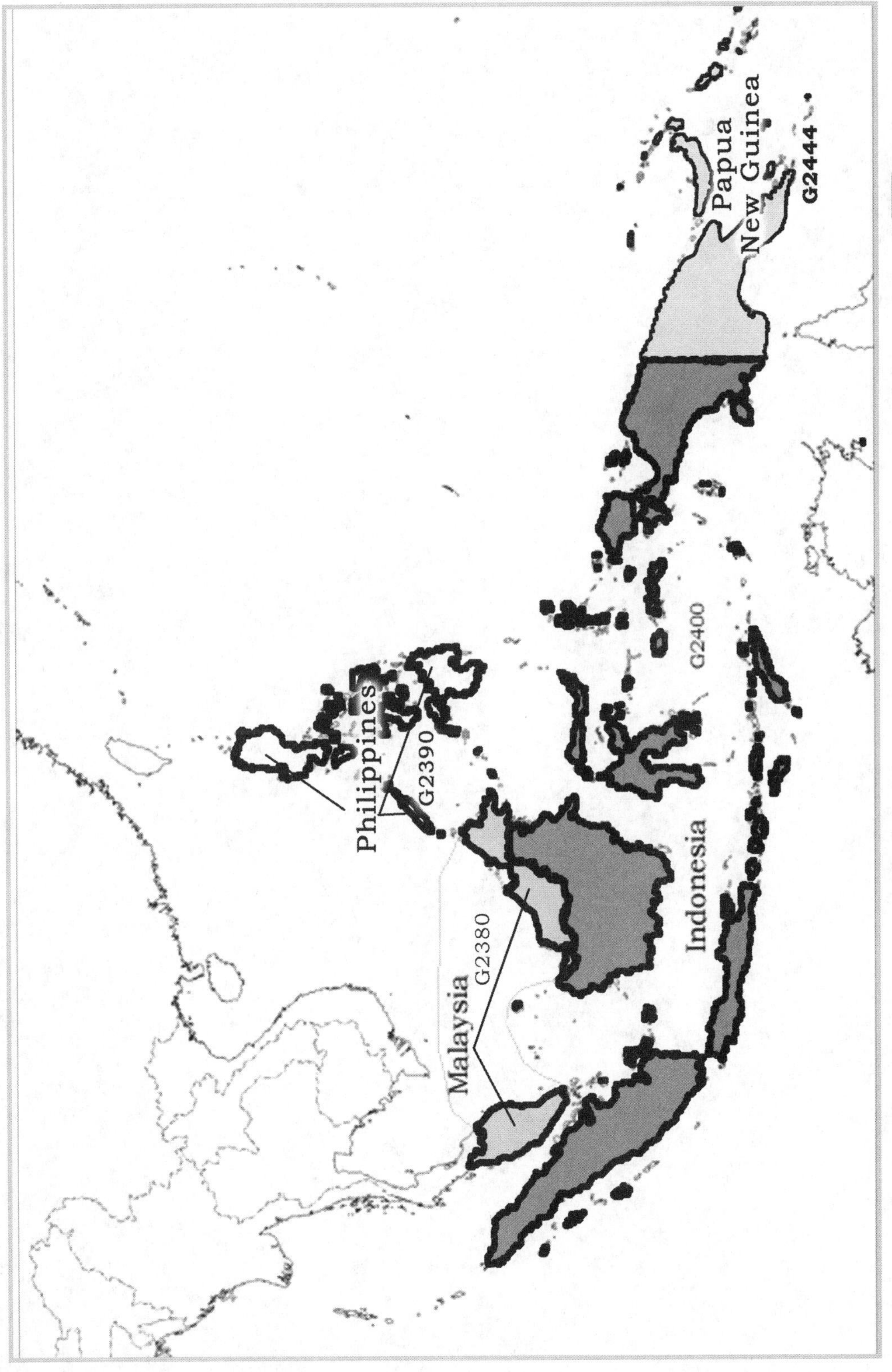

Malay Archipelago • *Atlases*

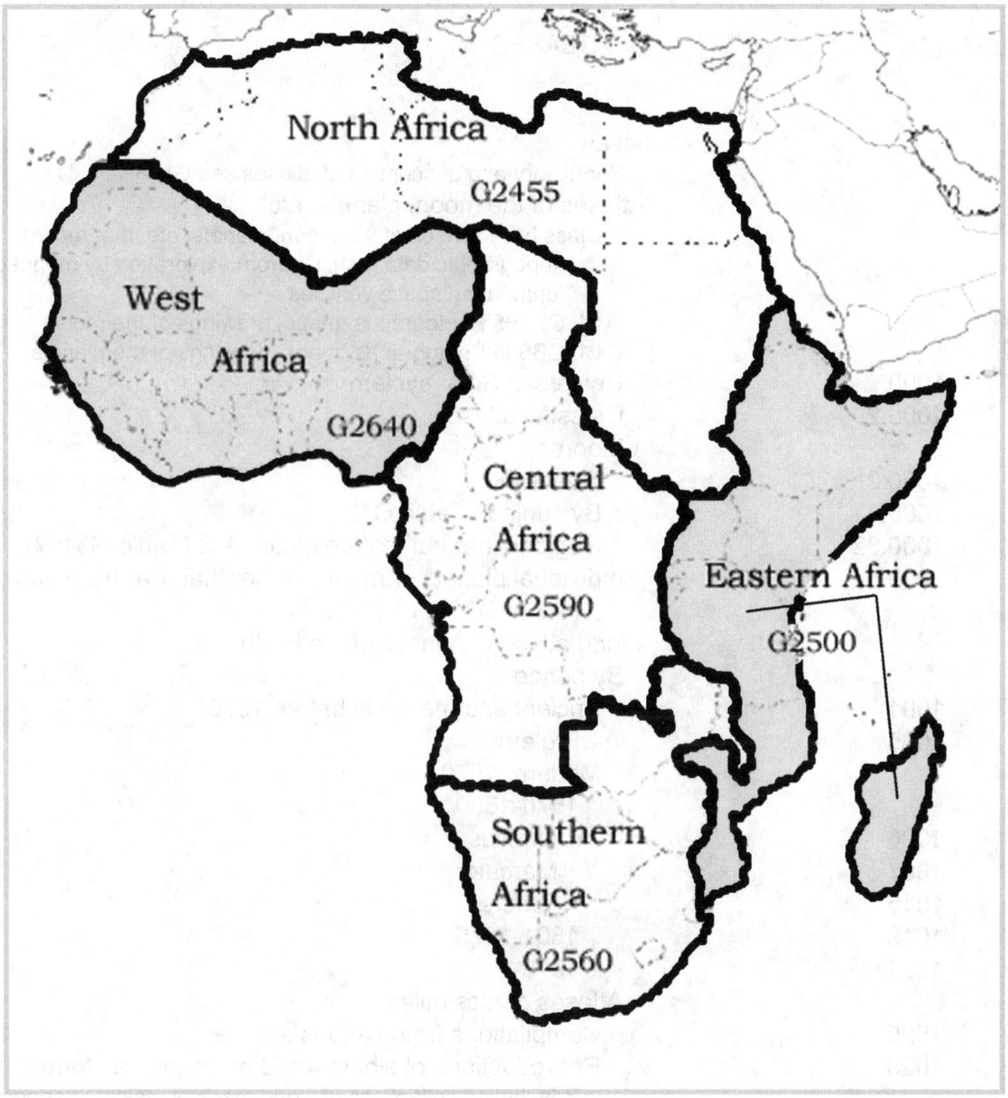

Africa • *Atlases*

Atlases
For history and description of atlases see GA1+
Atlases of the moon, planets, etc.
Class here atlases of the moon, planets, etc. that record topographic data resulting from exploration by manned or unmanned space vehicles
Cf. QB595 Photographs, maps, drawings of the moon
Cf. QB605 Photographs, maps, drawings of the planets
1000 Universe. Solar system
1000.2 Celestial atlases
Moon
1000.3 General
1000.31 By subject (Table G1)
1000.32 Regions, natural features, etc., A-Z (Table G3197)
1000.5 Individual planets or moons (other than Earth's moon), A-Z (Table G3182)
World atlases. Atlases of the Earth
By period
1001 Ancient and medieval before 1570
1005 Ptolemy
Modern, 1570-
1570-1800
1006 Ortelius
1007 Mercator
1015 Others
1019 1801-1975
1021 1976-
Atlases of facsimiles
1025 Compilations from various sources
1026 Reproductions of single world maps in atlas form
Including collections of world maps of a single cartographer
1028 Cities of the world
1029 Islands of the world
By subject
Historical atlases
Cf. G2230+ Bible atlases
1030 General works
1033 Ancient
1034 Medieval
1035 Modern
1036 Discoveries, explorations, and travel
1037 World War I
1038 World War II
1046 Other subject atlases (Table G1)
Western Hemisphere see G1100+
Eastern Hemisphere see G1780+
1050 Northern Hemisphere

1052 Southern Hemisphere
1053 Tropics. Torrid Zone
Polar regions. Frigid Zone
1054 General works
1055 Arctic regions
Maritime atlases (General)
For oceans see G2800+
For individual oceans see G2805+
1059 Early through 1800
1060 1801-1975
1061 1976-
By region or country
America. Western Hemisphere
1100 General
1101 By subject (Table G1)
1102 Regions, natural features, etc., A-Z (Table G3292)
Apply Table G1 for subject
North America
1105 General
1106 By subject (Table G1)
1107 Regions and natural features, etc., A-Z (Table G3302)
Apply Table G1 for subject
Greenland
1110 General
1111 By subject (Table G1)
1112 Regions, natural features, etc., A-Z (Table G3382)
Apply Table G1 for subject
1114 Cities and towns, etc., A-Z (Table G3384)
Apply Table G1 for subject
Canada
Including southern Canada; eastern Canada, 1870 and earlier; Rupert's Land; and Old Northwest Territories
Class regions and districts of Rupert's Land and Old Northwest Territories by specific location
1115 General
1116 By subject (Table G1 modified)
History
1116.S1 General
1116.S12 Discovery and exploration by Europeans
Including the exploration of the North and West
To 1763
1116.S2 General
1116.S26 French and Indian War, 1755-1763. Seven Years' War, 1756-1763
1763-1867
1116.S3 General

By region or country
America. Western Hemisphere
North America
Canada
By subject
History
1763-1867 -- Continued
1116.S32 American Revolution, 1775-1783
Including the American invasions of Canada
1116.S34 War of 1812
1116.S36 Rebellions in Upper and Lower Canada, 1837-1838
1116.S38 Fenian Invasions, 1866-1870
1867-1900
1116.S5 General
1116.S55 Rebellion, 1869-1870
1116.S57 Rebellion, 1885
20th century
1116.S6 General
1900-1945
1116.S62 General
1116.S65 World War I
1116.S7 World War II
1116.S73 1945-
1117 Regions, natural features, etc., A-Z (Table G3402)
Apply Table G1 for subject (except .S1-.S7, historical geography)
Apply Table G3401.S for history
1119.A1 Cities and towns collectively
For individual cities and towns see the province or territory
Eastern Canada (1871 and later)
1119.3 General
1119.31 By subject (Table G1 modified)
History
1119.31.S1 General
1119.31.S12 Discovery and exploration by Europeans
Including the exploration of the North and West
To 1763
1119.31.S2 General
1119.31.S26 French and Indian War, 1755-1763. Seven Years' War, 1756-1763
1763-1867
1119.31.S3 General
1119.31.S32 American Revolution, 1775-1783
Including the American invasions of Canada
1119.31.S34 War of 1812

By region or country
America. Western Hemisphere
North America
Canada
Eastern Canada (1871 and later)
By subject
History
1763-1867 -- Continued

1119.31.S36 Rebellions in Upper and Lower Canada, 1837-1838
1119.31.S38 Fenian Invasions, 1866-1870
1867-1900
1119.31.S5 General
1119.31.S55 Rebellion, 1869-1870
1119.31.S57 Rebellion, 1885
20th century
1119.31.S6 General
1900-1945
1119.31.S62 General
1119.31.S65 World War I
1119.31.S7 World War II
1119.31.S73 1945-
1119.32 Regions, natural features, etc., A-Z (Table G3407)
Apply Table G1 for subject (except .S1-.S7, historical geography)
Apply Table G3401.S for history
Atlantic Provinces. Atlantic Canada
1120 General
1121 By subject (Table G1 modified)
History
1121.S1 General
1121.S12 Discovery and exploration by Europeans
Including the exploration of the North and West
To 1763
1121.S2 General
1121.S26 French and Indian War, 1755-1763. Seven Years' War, 1756-1763
1763-1867
1121.S3 General
1121.S32 American Revolution, 1775-1783
Including the American invasions of Canada
1121.S34 War of 1812
1121.S36 Rebellions in Upper and Lower Canada, 1837-1838
1121.S38 Fenian Invasions, 1866-1870
1867-1900
1121.S5 General

By region or country
America. Western Hemisphere
North America
Canada
Eastern Canada (1871 and later)
Atlantic Provinces. Atlantic Canada
By subject
History
1867-1900 -- Continued
1121.S55 Rebellion, 1869-1870
1121.S57 Rebellion, 1885
20th century
1121.S6 General
1900-1945
1121.S62 General
1121.S65 World War I
1121.S7 World War II
1121.S73 1945-
1122 Regions, natural features, etc., A-Z (Table G3412)
Apply Table G1 for subject (except .S1-.S7, historical geography)
Apply Table G3401.S for history
Maritime Provinces. Acadia
1122.5 General
1122.51 By subject (Table G1 modified)
History
1122.51.S1 General
1122.51.S12 Discovery and exploration by Europeans
Including the exploration of the North and West
To 1763
1122.51.S2 General
1122.51.S26 French and Indian War, 1755-1763. Seven Years' War, 1756-1763
1763-1867
1122.51.S3 General
1122.51.S32 American Revolution, 1775-1783
Including the American invasions of Canada
1122.51.S34 War of 1812
1122.51.S36 Rebellions in Upper and Lower Canada, 1837-1838
1122.51.S38 Fenian Invasions, 1866-1870
1867-1900
1122.51.S5 General
1122.51.S55 Rebellion, 1869-1870
1122.51.S57 Rebellion, 1885
20th century
1122.51.S6 General

By region or country
America. Western Hemisphere
North America
Canada
Eastern Canada (1871 and later)
Atlantic Provinces. Atlantic Canada
Maritime Provinces. Acadia
By subject
History
20th century -- Continued
1900-1945
1122.51.S62 General
1122.51.S65 World War I
1122.51.S7 World War II
1122.51.S73 1945-
1122.52 Regions, natural features, etc., A-Z (Table G3417)
Apply Table G1 for subject (except .S1-.S7, historical geography)
Apply Table G3401.S for history
Nova Scotia
1125 General
1126 By subject (Table G1 modified)
History
1126.S1 General
1126.S12 Discovery and exploration by Europeans
Including the exploration of the North and West
To 1763
1126.S2 General
1126.S26 French and Indian War, 1755-1763. Seven Years' War, 1756-1763
1763-1867
1126.S3 General
1126.S32 American Revolution, 1775-1783
Including the American invasions of Canada
1126.S34 War of 1812
1126.S36 Rebellions in Upper and Lower Canada, 1837-1838
1126.S38 Fenian Invasions, 1866-1870
1867-1900
1126.S5 General
1126.S55 Rebellion, 1869-1870
1126.S57 Rebellion, 1885
20th century
1126.S6 General

By region or country
America. Western Hemisphere
North America
Canada
Eastern Canada (1871 and later)
Atlantic Provinces. Atlantic Canada
Maritime Provinces. Acadia
Nova Scotia
By subject
History
20th century -- Continued
1900-1945

1126.S62 General
1126.S65 World War I
1126.S7 World War II
1126.S73 1945-
1127 Regions, natural features, etc., A-Z (Table G3422)
Apply Table G1 for subject (except .S1-.S7, historical geography)
Apply Table G3401.S for history
1128 Counties, etc., A-Z (Table G3423)
Apply Table G1 for subject (except .S1-.S7, historical geography)
Apply Table G3401.S for history
1129 Cities and towns, etc., A-Z (Table G3424)
Apply Table G1 for subject (except .S1-.S7, historical geography)
Apply Table G3401.S for history

New Brunswick
1130 General
1131 By subject (Table G1 modified)
History
1131.S1 General
1131.S12 Discovery and exploration by Europeans
Including the exploration of the North and West
To 1763
1131.S2 General
1131.S26 French and Indian War, 1755-1763. Seven Years' War, 1756-1763
1763-1867
1131.S3 General
1131.S32 American Revolution, 1775-1783
Including the American invasions of Canada
1131.S34 War of 1812

By region or country
America. Western Hemisphere
North America
Canada
Eastern Canada (1871 and later)
Atlantic Provinces. Atlantic Canada
Maritime Provinces. Acadia
New Brunswick
By subject
History
1763-1867 -- Continued

1131.S36 Rebellions in Upper and Lower Canada, 1837-1838
1131.S38 Fenian Invasions, 1866-1870
1867-1900
1131.S5 General
1131.S55 Rebellion, 1869-1870
1131.S57 Rebellion, 1885
20th century
1131.S6 General
1900-1945
1131.S62 General
1131.S65 World War I
1131.S7 World War II
1131.S73 1945-
1132 Regions, natural features, etc., A-Z (Table G3432)
Apply Table G1 for subject (except .S1-.S7, historical geography)
Apply Table G3401.S for history
1133 Counties, etc., A-Z (Table G3433)
Apply Table G1 for subject (except .S1-.S7, historical geography)
Apply Table G3401.S for history
1134 Cities and towns, etc., A-Z (Table G3434)
Apply Table G1 for subject (except .S1-.S7, historical geography)
Apply Table G3401.S for history
Prince Edward Island
1135 General
1136 By subject (Table G1 modified)
History
1136.S1 General
1136.S12 Discovery and exploration by Europeans
Including the exploration of the North and West
To 1763

By region or country
America. Western Hemisphere
North America
Canada
Eastern Canada (1871 and later)
Atlantic Provinces. Atlantic Canada
Maritime Provinces. Acadia
Prince Edward Island
By subject
History
To 1763 -- Continued

1136.S2 General

1136.S26 French and Indian War, 1755-1763. Seven Years' War, 1756-1763

1763-1867

1136.S3 General

1136.S32 American Revolution, 1775-1783

Including the American invasions of Canada

1136.S34 War of 1812

1136.S36 Rebellions in Upper and Lower Canada, 1837-1838

1136.S38 Fenian Invasions, 1866-1870

1867-1900

1136.S5 General

1136.S55 Rebellion, 1869-1870

1136.S57 Rebellion, 1885

20th century

1136.S6 General

1900-1945

1136.S62 General

1136.S65 World War I

1136.S7 World War II

1136.S73 1945-

1137 Regions, natural features, etc., A-Z (Table G3427)

Apply Table G1 for subject (except .S1-.S7, historical geography)

Apply Table G3401.S for history

1139 Cities and towns, etc., A-Z (Table G3429)

Apply Table G1 for subject (except .S1-.S7, historical geography)

Apply Table G3401.S for history

Newfoundland and Labrador

Class here atlases of the island of Newfoundland as well as atlases of the province as a whole

1139.3 General

By region or country
America. Western Hemisphere
North America
Canada
Eastern Canada (1871 and later)
Atlantic Provinces. Atlantic Canada
Newfoundland and Labrador -- Continued

1139.31	By subject (Table G1 modified)
	History
1139.31.S1	General
1139.31.S12	Discovery and exploration by Europeans
	Including the exploration of the North and West
	To 1763
1139.31.S2	General
1139.31.S26	French and Indian War, 1755-1763. Seven Years' War, 1756-1763
	1763-1867
1139.31.S3	General
1139.31.S32	American Revolution, 1775-1783
	Including the American invasions of Canada
1139.31.S34	War of 1812
1139.31.S36	Rebellions in Upper and Lower Canada, 1837-1838
1139.31.S38	Fenian Invasions, 1866-1870
	1867-1900
1139.31.S5	General
1139.31.S55	Rebellion, 1869-1870
1139.31.S57	Rebellion, 1885
	20th century
1139.31.S6	General
	1900-1945
1139.31.S62	General
1139.31.S65	World War I
1139.31.S7	World War II
1139.31.S73	1945-
1139.32	Regions, natural features, etc., A-Z (Table G3437)
	Apply Table G1 for subject (except .S1-.S7, historical geography)
	Apply Table G3401.S for history
1139.34	Cities and towns, etc., A-Z (Table G3439)
	Apply Table G1 for subject (except .S1-.S7, historical geography)
	Apply Table 3401.S for history
1139.4-.42	Labrador
1139.4	General
1139.41	By subject (Table G1 modified)

By region or country
America. Western Hemisphere
North America
Canada
Eastern Canada (1871 and later)
Atlantic Provinces. Atlantic Canada
Newfoundland and Labrador
Labrador
By subject -- Continued
History

1139.41.S1 General
1139.41.S12 Discovery and exploration by Europeans
Including the exploration of the North and West
To 1763
1139.41.S2 General
1139.41.S26 French and Indian War, 1755-1763. Seven Years' War, 1756-1763
1763-1867
1139.41.S3 General
1139.41.S32 American Revolution, 1775-1783
Including the American invasions of Canada
1139.41.S34 War of 1812
1139.41.S36 Rebellions in Upper and Lower Canada, 1837-1838
1139.41.S38 Fenian Invasions, 1866-1870
1867-1900
1139.41.S5 General
1139.41.S55 Rebellion, 1869-1870
1139.41.S57 Rebellion, 1885
20th century
1139.41.S6 General
1900-1945
1139.41.S62 General
1139.41.S65 World War I
1139.41.S7 World War II
1139.41.S73 1945-
1139.42 Regions, natural features, etc., A-Z (Table G3442)
Apply Table G1 for subject (except .S1-.S7, historical geography)
Apply Table G3401.S for history

Central Provinces
Including Ontario and Quebec together
1139.7 General
1139.71 By subject (Table G1 modified)

By region or country
America. Western Hemisphere
North America
Canada
Eastern Canada (1871 and later)
Central Provinces
By subject -- Continued
History

1139.71.S1 General
1139.71.S12 Discovery and exploration by Europeans
Including the exploration of the North and West
To 1763
1139.71.S2 General
1139.71.S26 French and Indian War, 1755-1763. Seven Years' War, 1756-1763
1763-1867
1139.71.S3 General
1139.71.S32 American Revolution, 1775-1783
Including the American invasions of Canada
1139.71.S34 War of 1812
1139.71.S36 Rebellions in Upper and Lower Canada, 1837-1838
1139.71.S38 Fenian Invasions, 1866-1870
1867-1900
1139.71.S5 General
1139.71.S55 Rebellion, 1869-1870
1139.71.S57 Rebellion, 1885
20th century
1139.71.S6 General
1900-1945
1139.71.S62 General
1139.71.S65 World War I
1139.71.S7 World War II
1139.71.S73 1945-

Québec
Including the historical areas of Lower Canada and "Canada East"
1140 General
1141 By subject (Table G1 modified)
History
1141.S1 General
1141.S12 Discovery and exploration by Europeans
Including the exploration of the North and West
To 1763
1141.S2 General
1141.S26 French and Indian War, 1755-1763. Seven Years' War, 1756-1763

By region or country
America. Western Hemisphere
North America
Canada
Eastern Canada (1871 and later)
Central Provinces
Québec
By subject
History -- Continued
1763-1867
1141.S3 General
1141.S32 American Revolution, 1775-1783
Including the American invasions of Canada
1141.S34 War of 1812
1141.S36 Rebellions in Upper and Lower Canada, 1837-1838
1141.S38 Fenian Invasions, 1866-1870
1867-1900
1141.S5 General
1141.S55 Rebellion, 1869-1870
1141.S57 Rebellion, 1885
20th century
1141.S6 General
1900-1945
1141.S62 General
1141.S65 World War I
1141.S7 World War II
1141.S73 1945-
1142 Regions, natural features, etc., A-Z (Table G3452)
Apply Table G1 for subject (except .S1-.S7, historical geography)
Apply Table G3401.S for history
1143 Counties, etc., A-Z (Table G3453)
Apply Table G1 for subject (except .S1-.S7, historical geography)
Apply Table G3401.S for history
1144 Cities and towns, etc., A-Z (Table G3454)
Apply Table G1 for subject (except .S1-.S7, historical geography)
Apply Table G3401.S for history
Ontario
Including the historical areas of Upper Canada and "Canada West"
1145 General
1146 By subject (Table G1 modified)
History

By region or country
America. Western Hemisphere
North America
Canada
Eastern Canada (1871 and later)
Central Provinces
Ontario
By subject
History -- Continued

1146.S1 General
1146.S12 Discovery and exploration by Europeans
Including the exploration of the North and West
To 1763
1146.S2 General
1146.S26 French and Indian War, 1755-1763. Seven Years' War, 1756-1763
1763-1867
1146.S3 General
1146.S32 American Revolution, 1775-1783
Including the American invasions of Canada
1146.S34 War of 1812
1146.S36 Rebellions in Upper and Lower Canada, 1837-1838
1146.S38 Fenian Invasions, 1866-1870
1867-1900
1146.S5 General
1146.S55 Rebellion, 1869-1870
1146.S57 Rebellion, 1885
20th century
1146.S6 General
1900-1945
1146.S62 General
1146.S65 World War I
1146.S7 World War II
1146.S73 1945-
1147 Regions, natural features, etc., A-Z (Table G3462 modified)
Apply Table G1 for subject (except .S1-.S7, historical geography)
Apply Table G3401.S for history
Bird River see G1157.B49
Manigotagan River see G1157.M3
Saganaga Lake see G1427.S16
Winnipeg River see G1157.W56

By region or country
America. Western Hemisphere
North America
Canada
Eastern Canada (1871 and later)
Central Provinces
Ontario -- Continued

1148 Counties, etc., A-Z (Table G3463)
Apply Table G1 for subject (except .S1-.S7, historical geography)
Apply Table G3401.S for history

1149 Cities and towns, etc., A-Z (Table G3464)
Apply Table G1 for subject (except .S1-.S7, historical geography)
Apply Table G3401.S for history

Western Canada

1150 General

1151 By subject (Table G1 modified)

History

1151.S1 General

1151.S12 Discovery and exploration by Europeans
Including the exploration of the North and West

To 1763

1151.S2 General

1151.S26 French and Indian War, 1755-1763. Seven Years' War, 1756-1763

1763-1867

1151.S3 General

1151.S32 American Revolution, 1775-1783
Including the American invasions of Canada

1151.S34 War of 1812

1151.S36 Rebellions in Upper and Lower Canada, 1837-1838

1151.S38 Fenian Invasions, 1866-1870

1867-1900

1151.S5 General

1151.S55 Rebellion, 1869-1870

1151.S57 Rebellion, 1885

20th century

1151.S6 General

1900-1945

1151.S62 General

1151.S65 World War I

1151.S7 World War II

1151.S73 1945-

By region or country
America. Western Hemisphere
North America
Canada
Western Canada -- Continued

1152 Regions, natural features, etc., A-Z (Table G3472)
Apply Table G1 for subject (except .S1-.S7, historical geography)
Apply Table G3401.S for history

Prairie Provinces

1152.3 General

1152.31 By subject (Table G1 modified)

History

1152.31.S1 General

1152.31.S12 Discovery and exploration by Europeans
Including the exploration of the North and West

To 1763

1152.31.S2 General

1152.31.S26 French and Indian War, 1755-1763. Seven Years' War, 1756-1763

1763-1867

1152.31.S3 General

1152.31.S32 American Revolution, 1775-1783
Including the American invasions of Canada

1152.31.S34 War of 1812

1152.31.S36 Rebellions in Upper and Lower Canada, 1837-1838

1152.31.S38 Fenian Invasions, 1866-1870

1867-1900

1152.31.S5 General

1152.31.S55 Rebellion, 1869-1870

1152.31.S57 Rebellion, 1885

20th century

1152.31.S6 General

1900-1945

1152.31.S62 General

1152.31.S65 World War I

1152.31.S7 World War II

1152.31.S73 1945-

1152.32 Regions, natural features, etc., A-Z (Table G3472)
Apply Table G1 for subject (except .S1-.S7, historical geography)
Apply Table G3401.S for history

Manitoba

1155 General

1156 By subject (Table G1 modified)

History

By region or country
America. Western Hemisphere
North America
Canada
Western Canada
Prairie Provinces
Manitoba
By subject
History -- Continued

1156.S1 General

1156.S12 Discovery and exploration by Europeans
Including the exploration of the North and West

To 1763

1156.S2 General

1156.S26 French and Indian War, 1755-1763. Seven Years' War, 1756-1763

1763-1867

1156.S3 General

1156.S32 American Revolution, 1775-1783
Including the American invasions of Canada

1156.S34 War of 1812

1156.S36 Rebellions in Upper and Lower Canada, 1837-1838

1156.S38 Fenian Invasions, 1866-1870

1867-1900

1156.S5 General

1156.S55 Rebellion, 1869-1870

1156.S57 Rebellion, 1885

20th century

1156.S6 General

1900-1945

1156.S62 General

1156.S65 World War I

1156.S7 World War II

1156.S73 1945-

1157 Regions, natural features, etc., A-Z (Table G3482 modified)

Apply Table G1 for subject (except .S1-.S7, historical geography)

Apply Table G3401.S for history

1157.B49 Bird River [Ont. and Man.]
Subarrange by Table G1 except .S1-.S7, historical geography. For history, subarrange by Table G3401.S

By region or country
America. Western Hemisphere
North America
Canada
Western Canada
Prairie Provinces
Manitoba
Regions, natural features, etc., A-Z -- Continued

1157.M3 Manigotagan River [Ont. and Man.]
Subarrange by Table G1 except .S1-.S7, historical geography. For history, subarrange by Table G3401.S

1157.W56 Winnepeg River [Ont. and Man.]
Subarrange by Table G1 except .S1-.S7, historical geography. For history, subarrange by Table G3401.S

1159 Cities and towns, etc., A-Z (Table G3484)
Apply Table G1 for subject (except .S1-.S7, historical geography)
Apply Table G3401.S for history

Saskatchewan

1160 General

1161 By subject (Table G1 modified)
History

1161.S1 General

1161.S12 Discovery and exploration by Europeans
Including the exploration of the North and West

To 1763

1161.S2 General

1161.S26 French and Indian War, 1755-1763. Seven Years' War, 1756-1763

1763-1867

1161.S3 General

1161.S32 American Revolution, 1775-1783
Including the American invasions of Canada

1161.S34 War of 1812

1161.S36 Rebellions in Upper and Lower Canada, 1837-1838

1161.S38 Fenian Invasions, 1866-1870

1867-1900

1161.S5 General

1161.S55 Rebellion, 1869-1870

1161.S57 Rebellion, 1885

20th century

1161.S6 General

1900-1945

1161.S62 General

By region or country
America. Western Hemisphere
North America
Canada
Western Canada
Prairie Provinces
Saskatchewan
By subject
History
20th century
1900-1945 -- Continued
1161.S65 World War I
1161.S7 World War II
1161.S73 1945-
1162 Regions, natural features, etc., A-Z (Table G3492)
Apply Table G1 for subject (except .S1-.S7, historical geography)
Apply Table G3401.S for history
1164 Cities and towns, etc., A-Z (Table G3494)
Apply Table G1 for subject (except .S1-.S7, historical geography)
Apply Table G3401.S for history
Alberta
1165 General
1166 By subject (Table G1 modified)
History
1166.S1 General
1166.S12 Discovery and exploration by Europeans
Including the exploration of the North and West
To 1763
1166.S2 General
1166.S26 French and Indian War, 1755-1763. Seven Years' War, 1756-1763
1763-1867
1166.S3 General
1166.S32 American Revolution, 1775-1783
Including the American invasions of Canada
1166.S34 War of 1812
1166.S36 Rebellions in Upper and Lower Canada, 1837-1838
1166.S38 Fenian Invasions, 1866-1870
1867-1900
1166.S5 General
1166.S55 Rebellion, 1869-1870
1166.S57 Rebellion, 1885
20th century

By region or country
America. Western Hemisphere
North America
Canada
Western Canada
Prairie Provinces
Alberta
By subject
History
20th century -- Continued

1166.S6 General
1900-1945
1166.S62 General
1166.S65 World War I
1166.S7 World War II
1166.S73 1945-
1167 Regions, natural features, etc., A-Z (Table G3502)
Apply Table G1 for subject (except .S1-.S7, historical geography)
Apply Table G3401.S for history
1168 Counties, etc., A-Z (Table G3503)
Apply Table G1 for subject (except .S1-.S7, historical geography)
Apply Table G3401.S for history
1169 Cities and towns, etc., A-Z (Table G3504)
Apply Table G1 for subject (except .S1-.S7, historical geography)
Apply Table G3401.S for history
Cordilleran Provinces and Territories
Including British Columbia, Yukon, Alberta, and that portion of MacKenzie District, N.W.T. west of the Mackenzie River treated together
1169.3 General
1169.31 By subject (Table G1 modified)
History
1169.31.S1 General
1169.31.S12 Discovery and exploration by Europeans
Including the exploration of the North and West
To 1763
1169.31.S2 General
1169.31.S26 French and Indian War, 1755-1763. Seven Years' War, 1756-1763
1763-1867
1169.31.S3 General
1169.31.S32 American Revolution, 1775-1783
Including the American invasions of Canada

By region or country
America. Western Hemisphere
North America
Canada
Western Canada
Cordilleran Provinces and Territories
By subject
History
1763-1867 -- Continued

1169.31.S34 War of 1812
1169.31.S36 Rebellions in Upper and Lower Canada, 1837-1838
1169.31.S38 Fenian Invasions, 1866-1870
1867-1900
1169.31.S5 General
1169.31.S55 Rebellion, 1869-1870
1169.31.S57 Rebellion, 1885
20th century
1169.31.S6 General
1900-1945
1169.31.S62 General
1169.31.S65 World War I
1169.31.S7 World War II
1169.31.S73 1945-
British Columbia
1170 General
1171 By subject (Table G1 modified)
History
1171.S1 General
1171.S12 Discovery and exploration by Europeans
Including the exploration of the North and West
To 1763
1171.S2 General
1171.S26 French and Indian War, 1755-1763. Seven Years' War, 1756-1763
1763-1867
1171.S3 General
1171.S32 American Revolution, 1775-1783
Including the American invasions of Canada
1171.S34 War of 1812
1171.S36 Rebellions in Upper and Lower Canada, 1837-1838
1171.S38 Fenian Invasions, 1866-1870
1867-1900
1171.S5 General
1171.S55 Rebellion, 1869-1870
1171.S57 Rebellion, 1885

By region or country
America. Western Hemisphere
North America
Canada
Western Canada
Cordilleran Provinces and Territories
British Columbia
By subject
History -- Continued
20th century
1171.S6 General
1900-1945
1171.S62 General
1171.S65 World War I
1171.S7 World War II
1171.S73 1945-
1172 Regions, natural features, etc., A-Z (Table G3512)
Apply Table G1 for subject (except .S1-.S7, historical geography)
Apply Table G3401.S for history
1173 Counties, etc., A-Z (Table G3513)
Apply Table G1 for subject (except .S1-.S7, historical geography)
Apply Table G3401.S for history
1174 Cities and towns, etc., A-Z (Table G3514)
Apply Table G1 for subject (except .S1-.S7, historical geography)
Apply Table G3401.S for history
Northern Canada
Including atlases of the Northwest Territories and the Yukon together
1174.3 General
1174.31 By subject (Table G1 modified)
History
1174.31.S1 General
1174.31.S12 Discovery and exploration by Europeans
Including the exploration of the North and West
To 1763
1174.31.S2 General
1174.31.S26 French and Indian War, 1755-1763. Seven Years' War, 1756-1763
1763-1867
1174.31.S3 General
1174.31.S32 American Revolution, 1775-1783
Including the American invasions of Canada
1174.31.S34 War of 1812

By region or country
America. Western Hemisphere
North America
Canada
Northern Canada
By subject
History
1763-1867 -- Continued
1174.31.S36 Rebellions in Upper and Lower Canada, 1837-1838
1174.31.S38 Fenian Invasions, 1866-1870
1867-1900
1174.31.S5 General
1174.31.S55 Rebellion, 1869-1870
1174.31.S57 Rebellion, 1885
20th century
1174.31.S6 General
1900-1945
1174.31.S62 General
1174.31.S65 World War I
1174.31.S7 World War II
1174.31.S73 1945-
1174.32 Regions, natural features, etc., A-Z (Table G3517)
Apply Table G1 for subject (except .S1-.S7, historical geography)
Apply Table G3401.S for history
Yukon
1175 General
1176 By subject (Table G1 modified)
History
1176.S1 General
1176.S12 Discovery and exploration by Europeans
Including the exploration of the North and West
To 1763
1176.S2 General
1176.S26 French and Indian War, 1755-1763. Seven Years' War, 1756-1763
1763-1867
1176.S3 General
1176.S32 American Revolution, 1775-1783
Including the American invasions of Canada
1176.S34 War of 1812
1176.S36 Rebellions in Upper and Lower Canada, 1837-1838
1176.S38 Fenian Invasions, 1866-1870
1867-1900
1176.S5 General

By region or country
America. Western Hemisphere
North America
Canada
Northern Canada
Yukon
By subject
History
1867-1900 -- Continued
1176.S55 Rebellion, 1869-1870
1176.S57 Rebellion, 1885
20th century
1176.S6 General
1900-1945
1176.S62 General
1176.S65 World War I
1176.S7 World War II
1176.S73 1945-
1177 Regions, natural features, etc., A-Z (Table G3522)
Apply Table G1 for subject (except .S1-.S7, historical geography)
Apply Table G3401.S for history
1179 Cities and towns, etc., A-Z (Table G3524)
Apply Table G1 for subject (except .S1-.S7, historical geography)
Apply Table G3401.S for history
Northwest Territories
1180 General
1181 By subject (Table G1 modified)
History
1181.S1 General
1181.S12 Discovery and exploration by Europeans
Including the exploration of the North and West
To 1763
1181.S2 General
1181.S26 French and Indian War, 1755-1763. Seven Years' War, 1756-1763
1763-1867
1181.S3 General
1181.S32 American Revolution, 1775-1783
Including the American invasions of Canada
1181.S34 War of 1812
1181.S36 Rebellions in Upper and Lower Canada, 1837-1838
1181.S38 Fenian Invasions, 1866-1870
1867-1900
1181.S5 General

By region or country
America. Western Hemisphere
North America
Canada
Northern Canada
Northwest Territories
By subject
History
1867-1900 -- Continued

1181.S55 Rebellion, 1869-1870
1181.S57 Rebellion, 1885
20th century
1181.S6 General
1900-1945
1181.S62 General
1181.S65 World War I
1181.S7 World War II
1181.S73 1945-
1182 Regions, natural features, etc., A-Z (Table G3532)
Apply Table G1 for subject (except .S1-.S7, historical geography)
Apply Table G3401.S for history
1183 Districts, Territorial regions, etc., A-Z (Table G3533)
Apply Table G1 for subject (except .S1-.S7, historical geography)
Apply Table G3401.S for history
1184 Cities and towns, etc., A-Z (Table G3534)
Apply Table G1 for subject (except .S1-.S7, historical geography)
Apply Table G3401.S for history
Nunavut
1184.3 General
1184.31 By subject (Table G1 modified)
History
1184.31.S1 General
1184.31.S12 Discovery and exploration by Europeans
Including the exploration of the North and West
To 1763
1184.31.S2 General
1184.31.S26 French and Indian War, 1755-1763. Seven Years' War, 1756-1763
1763-1867
1184.31.S3 General
1184.31.S32 American Revolution, 1775-1783
Including the American invasions of Canada
1184.31.S34 War of 1812

By region or country
America. Western Hemisphere
North America
Canada
Northern Canada
Nunavut
By subject
History
1763-1867 -- Continued

1184.31.S36 Rebellions in Upper and Lower Canada, 1837-1838
1184.31.S38 Fenian Invasions, 1866-1870
1867-1900
1184.31.S5 General
1184.31.S55 Rebellion, 1869-1870
1184.31.S57 Rebellion, 1885
20th century
1184.31.S6 General
1900-1945
1184.31.S62 General
1184.31.S65 World War I
1184.31.S7 World War II
1184.31.S73 1945-
1184.32 Regions, natural features, etc., A-Z (Table G3537)
Apply Table G1 for subject (except .S1-.S7, historical geography)
Apply Table G3401.S for history
1184.34 Cities and towns, etc., A-Z (Table G3539)
Apply Table G1 for subject (except .S1-.S7, historical geography)
Apply Table G3401.S for history

Newfoundland
(1185-1189) General
see G1139.3-.34
(1190-1193) Labrador
see G1139.4-.42

Saint Pierre and Miquelon Islands
1195 General
1196 By subject (Table G1)
1197 Regions, natural features, etc., A-Z (Table G3652)
Apply Table G1 for subject
1199 Cities and towns, etc., A-Z (Table G3654)
Apply Table G1 for subject
Apply Table G3701.S for history

United States
1200 General
1201 By subject (Table G1a)

By region or country
America. Western Hemisphere
North America
United States -- Continued
1202 Regions, natural features, etc., A-Z (Table G3702)
Apply Table G1a for by subject
1204 Cities and towns collectively
Eastern United States, 1870 and later
Comprises the area east of the Mississippi River
1205 General
1206 By subject (Table G1a)
1207 Regions, natural features, etc., A-Z (Table G3707)
Apply Table G1a for subject
Atlantic States
1209.3 General
1209.31 By subject (Table G1a)
1209.32 Regions, natural features, etc., A-Z (Table G3709.32 modified)
Apply Table G1a for subject
Potomac River see G1247.P6
Northeastern States
1209.5 General
1209.51 By subject (Table G1a)
1209.52 Regions, natural features, etc., A-Z (Table G3712)
Apply Table G1a for subject
Northeast Atlantic States
1209.7 General
1209.71 By subject (Table G1a)
1209.72 Regions, natural features, etc., A-Z (Table G3717)
Apply Table G1a for subject
New England
1210 General
1211 By subject (Table G1a)
1212 Regions, natural features, etc., A-Z (Table G3722)
Apply Table G1a for subject
1214 Cities and towns collectively
Maine
1215 General
1216 By subject (Table G1a)
1217 Regions, natural features, etc., A-Z (Table G3732)
Apply Table G1a for subject
1218 Counties, A-Z (Table G3733)
Apply Table G1a for subject

By region or country
America. Western Hemisphere
North America
United States
Eastern United States, 1870 and later
Northeastern States
Northeast Atlantic States
New England
Maine -- Continued

1219 Cities, towns, and townships, etc., A-Z (Table G3734)
Apply Table G1a for subject

New Hampshire

1220 General

1221 By subject (Table G1a)

1222 Regions, natural features, etc., A-Z (Table G3742)
Apply Table G1a for subject

1223 Counties, A-Z (Table G3743)
Apply Table G1a for subject

1224 Cities, towns, and townships, etc., A-Z (Table G3744)
Apply Table G1a for subject

Vermont

1225 General

1226 By subject (Table G1a)

1227 Regions, natural features, etc., A-Z (Table G3752)
Apply Table G1a for subject

1228 Counties, A-Z (Table G3753)
Apply Table G1a for subject

1229 Cities, towns, and townships, etc., A-Z (Table G3754)
Apply Table G1a for subject

Massachusetts

1230 General

1231 By subject (Table G1a)

1232 Regions, natural features, etc., A-Z (Table G3762 modified)
Apply Table G1a for subject

1232.N3 Nantucket Island
Subarrange by Table G1a

1233 Counties, A-Z (Table G3763 modified)
Apply Table G1a for subject
Nantucket Island see G1232.N3

By region or country
America. Western Hemisphere
North America
United States
Eastern United States, 1870 and later
Northeastern States
Northeast Atlantic States
New England
Massachusetts -- Continued

1234 Cities, towns, and townships, etc., A-Z (Table G3764)
Apply Table G1a for subject

Rhode Island

1235 General

1236 By subject (Table G1a)

1237 Regions, natural features, etc., A-Z (Table G3772)
Apply Table G1a for subject

1238 Counties, A-Z (Table G3773)
Apply Table G1a for subject

1239 Cities, towns, and townships, etc., A-Z (Table G3774)
Apply Table G1a for subject

Connecticut

1240 General

1241 By subject (Table G1a)

1242 Regions, natural features, etc., A-Z (Table G3782)
Apply Table G1a for subject

1243 Counties, A-Z (Table G3783)
Apply Table G1a for subject

1244 Cities, towns, and townships, etc., A-Z (Table G3784)
Apply Table G1a for subject

Middle Atlantic States. Middle States
Often including Virginia and West Virginia, sometimes also Ohio and Kentucky

1245 General

1246 By subject (Table G1a)

1247 Regions, natural features, etc., A-Z (Table G3792 modified)
Apply Table G1a for subject

1247.P6 Potomac River
Subarrange by Table G1a

New York

1250 General

1251 By subject (Table G1a)

By region or country
America. Western Hemisphere
North America
United States
Eastern United States, 1870 and later
Northeastern States
Northeast Atlantic States
Middle Atlantic States. Middle States
New York -- Continued

1252 Regions, natural features, etc., A-Z (Table G3802)
Apply Table G1a for subject
Staten Island see G1254.N4:2S8
Staten Island (Staten Island Botanical Garden) see G1254.N4:2S82

1253 Counties, A-Z (Table G3803)
Apply Table G1a for subject
Bronx see G1254.N4:3B7
Kings see G1254.N4:3B8
New York see G1254.N4:2M3
Queens see G1254.N4:3Q4
Richmond see G1254.N4:2S8
Richmond (Staten Island Botanical Garden) see G1254.N4:2S82

1254 Cities, towns, and urban townships, etc., A-Z (Table G3804)
Apply Table G1a for subject

1254.N4:2M3 Manhattan [New York]
Subarrange by Table G1a

1254.N4:2S8 Staten Island [New York]
Subarrange by Table G1a

1254.N4:2S82 Staten Island Botanical Garden [New York]
Subarrange by Table G1a

1254.N4:3B7 Bronx [New York]
Subarrange by Table G1a

1254.N4:3B8 Brooklyn [New York]
Subarrange by Table G1a

1254.N4:3Q4 Queens [New York]
Subarrange by Table G1a

New Jersey

1255 General

1256 By subject (Table G1a)

1257 Regions, natural features, etc., A-Z (Table G3812)
Apply Table G1a for subject

1258 Counties, A-Z (Table G3813)
Apply Table G1a for subject

By region or country
America. Western Hemisphere
North America
United States
Eastern United States, 1870 and later
Northeastern States
Northeast Atlantic States
Middle Atlantic States. Middle States
New Jersey -- Continued

1259 Cities and towns, etc., A-Z (Table G3814)
Apply Table G1a for subject

Pennsylvania

1260 General

1261 By subject (Table G1a)

1262 Regions, natural features, etc., A-Z (Table G3822)
Apply Table G1a for subject

1263 Counties, A-Z (Table G3823)
Apply Table G1a for subject

Philadelphia (Bartram's Garden) see G1264.P5:2B3

Philadelphia (Chestnut Hill, Battle of, 1777) see G1264.P5:2C42

Philadelphia (Fabric Row) see G1264.P5:2F2

Philadelphia (Germantown, Battle of, 1777) see G1264.P5:2G433

Philadelphia (North Philadelphia) see G1264.P5:2N57

Philadelphia (Washington Square West) see G1264.P5:2W33

1264 Cities, towns, and urban townships, etc., A-Z (Table G3824 modified)
Apply Table G1a for subject

1264.P5:2B3 Bartram's Garden [Philadelphia]
Subarrange by Table G1a

1264.P5:2C42 Chestnut Hill, Battle of, 1777 [Philadelphia]
Subarrange by Table G1a

1264.P5:2F2 Fabric Row [Philadelphia]
Subarrange by Table G1a

1264.P5:2G433 Germantown, Battle of, 1777 [Philadelphia]
Subarrange by Table G1a

1264.P5:2N57 North Philadelphia [Philadelphia]
Subarrange by Table G1a

1264.P5:2W33 Washington Square West [Philadelphia]
Subarrange by Table G1a

Delaware

By region or country
America. Western Hemisphere
North America
United States
Eastern United States, 1870 and later
Northeastern States
Northeast Atlantic States
Middle Atlantic States. Middle States
Delaware -- Continued
1265 General
1266 By subject (Table G1a)
1267 Regions, natural features, etc., A-Z (Table G3832)
Apply Table G1a for subject
1268 Counties, A-Z (Table G3833)
Apply Table G1a for subject
1269 Cities and towns, etc., A-Z (Table G3834)
Apply Table G1a for subject
Maryland
1270 General
1271 By subject (Table G1a)
1272 Regions, natural features, etc., A-Z (Table G3842)
Apply Table G1a for subject
1273 Counties, A-Z (Table G3843)
Apply Table G1a for subject
1274 Cities and towns, etc., A-Z (Table G3844)
Apply Table G1a for subject
District of Columbia. Washington, D.C.
1275 General
1276 By subject (Table G1a)
1277 Regions, natural features, former towns, etc., A-Z (Table G3852)
Apply Table G1a for subject
Southern States. Confederate States of America
Including Gulf States
1280 General
1281 By subject (Table G1a)
1282 Regions, natural features, etc., A-Z (Table G3862)
Apply Table G1a for subject
Southeastern States
1285 General
1286 By subject (Table G1a)
1287 Regions, natural features, etc., A-Z (Table G3867)
Apply Table G1a for subject
South Atlantic States. Southeast Atlantic States

By region or country
America. Western Hemisphere
North America
United States
Eastern United States, 1870 and later
Southern States. Confederate States of America
Southeastern States
South Atlantic States. Southeast Atlantic States -- Continued

1289.3 General
1289.31 By subject (Table G1a)
1289.32 Regions, natural features, etc., A-Z (Table G3882)
Apply Table G1a for subject

Virginia
1290 General
1291 By subject (Table G1a)
1292 Regions, natural features, etc., A-Z (Table G3882)
Apply Table G1a for subject
1293 Counties, A-Z (Table G3883 modified)
Apply Table G1a for subject
1293.A8 Arlington
Subarrange by Table G1a
Nansemond see G1294.S9
Nansemond (Holland) see G1294.S9:2H7
Princess Anne see G1294.V8
Princess Anne (Cape Henry Life Saving Station) see G1294.V8:2C35
Warwick see G1294.N4
1294 Cities and towns, etc., A-Z (Table G3884 modified)
Apply Table G1a for subject
Arlington see G1293.A8
1294.N4 Newport News
Subarrange by Table G1a
1294.S9 Suffolk
Subarrange by Table G1a
1294.S9:2H7 Holland [Suffolk
Subarrange by Table G1a
1294.V8 Virginia Beach
Subarrange by Table G1a
1294.V8:2C35 Cape Henry Life Saving Station
Subarrange by Table G1a

West Virginia
1295 General
1296 By subject (Table G1a)

By region or country
America. Western Hemisphere
North America
United States
Eastern United States, 1870 and later
Southern States. Confederate States of America
Southeastern States
South Atlantic States. Southeast Atlantic States
West Virginia -- Continued

1297 Regions, natural features, etc., A-Z (Table G3892)
Apply Table G1a for subject

1298 Counties, A-Z (Table G3893)
Apply Table G1a for subject

1299 Cities and towns, etc., A-Z (Table G3894)
Apply Table G1a for subject

North Carolina

1300 General

1301 By subject (Table G1a)

1302 Regions, natural features, etc., A-Z (Table G3902)
Apply Table G1a for subject

1303 Counties, A-Z (Table G3903)
Apply Table G1a for subject

1304 Cities and towns, etc., A-Z (Table G3904)
Apply Table G1a for subject

South Carolina

1305 General

1306 By subject (Table G1a)

1307 Regions, natural features, etc., A-Z (Table G3912)
Apply Table G1a for subject

1308 Counties, A-Z (Table G3913)
Apply Table G1a for subject

1309 Cities and towns, etc., A-Z (Table G3914)
Apply Table G1a for subject

Georgia

1310 General

1311 By subject (Table G1a)

1312 Regions, natural features, etc., A-Z (Table G3922)
Apply Table G1a for subject

1313 Counties, A-Z (Table G3923)
Apply Table G1a for subject

1314 Cities and towns, etc., A-Z (Table G3924)
Apply Table G1a for subject

Florida

By region or country
America. Western Hemisphere
North America
United States
Eastern United States, 1870 and later
Southern States. Confederate States of America
Southeastern States
South Atlantic States. Southeast Atlantic States
Florida -- Continued

1315 General
1316 By subject (Table G1a)
1317 Regions, natural features, etc., A-Z (Table G3932)
Apply Table G1a for subject
1318 Counties, A-Z (Table G3933)
Apply Table G1a for subject
1319 Cities and towns, etc., A-Z (Table G3934)
Apply Table G1a for subject

South Central States
1320 General
1321 By subject (Table G1a)
1322 Regions, natural features, etc., A-Z (Table G3937)
Apply Table G1a for subject

East South Central States
1325 General
1326 By subject (Table G1a)
1327 Regions, natural features, etc., A-Z (Table G3942)
Apply Table G1a for subject

Kentucky
1330 General
1331 By subject (Table G1a)
1332 Regions, natural features, etc., A-Z (Table G3952)
Apply Table G1a for subject
1333 Counties, A-Z (Table G3953)
Apply Table G1a for subject
1334 Cities and towns, etc., A-Z (Table G3954)
Apply Table G1a for subject

Tennessee
1335 General
1336 By subject (Table G1a)
1337 Regions, natural features, etc., A-Z (Table G3962)
Apply Table G1a for subject

By region or country
America. Western Hemisphere
North America
United States
Eastern United States, 1870 and later
Southern States. Confederate States of America
Southeastern States
South Central States
East South Central States
Tennessee -- Continued

1338 Counties, A-Z (Table G3963)
Apply Table G1a for subject

1339 Cities and towns, etc., A-Z (Table G3964)
Apply Table G1a for subject

Alabama

1340 General

1341 By subject (Table G1a)

1342 Regions, natural features, etc., A-Z (Table G3972)
Apply Table G1a for subject

1343 Counties, A-Z (Table G3973)
Apply Table G1a for subject

1344 Cities and towns, etc., A-Z (Table G3974)
Apply Table G1a for subject

Mississippi

1345 General

1346 By subject (Table G1a)

1347 Regions, natural features, etc., A-Z (Table G3982)
Apply Table G1a for subject

1348 Counties, A-Z (Table G3983)
Apply Table G1a for subject

1349 Cities and towns, etc., A-Z (Table G3984)
Apply Table G1a for subject

West South Central States. Old Southwest

1350 General

1351 By subject (Table G1a)

1352 Regions, natural features, etc., A-Z (Table G3992)
Apply Table G1a for subject

Arkansas

1355 General

1356 By subject (Table G1a)

1357 Regions, natural features, etc., A-Z (Table G4002)
Apply Table G1a for subject

By region or country
America. Western Hemisphere
North America
United States
Eastern United States, 1870 and later
Southern States. Confederate States of America
Southeastern States
South Central States
West South Central States. Old Southwest
Arkansas -- Continued
1358 Counties, A-Z (Table G4003)
Apply Table G1a for subject
1359 Cities and towns, etc., A-Z (Table G4004)
Apply Table G1a for subject
Louisiana
1360 General
1361 By subject (Table G1a)
1362 Regions, natural features, etc., A-Z (Table G4012)
Apply Table G1a for subject
1363 Counties, A-Z (Table G4013)
Apply Table G1a for subject
1364 Cities and towns, etc., A-Z (Table G4014)
Apply Table G1a for subject
Oklahoma
1365 General
1366 By subject (Table G1a)
1367 Regions, natural features, etc., A-Z (Table G4022)
Apply Table G1a for subject
1368 Counties, A-Z (Table G4023)
Apply Table G1a for subject
1369 Cities and towns, etc., A-Z (Table G4024)
Apply Table G1a for subject
Texas
1370 General
1371 By subject (Table G1a)
1372 Regions, natural features, etc., A-Z (Table G4032)
Apply Table G1a for subject
1373 Counties, A-Z (Table G4033)
Apply Table G1a for subject
1374 Cities and towns, etc., A-Z (Table G4034)
Apply Table G1a for subject
Middle West
1375 General
1376 By subject (Table G1a)

By region or country
America. Western Hemisphere
North America
United States
Middle West -- Continued
1377 Regions, natural features, etc., A-Z (Table G4042)
Apply Table G1a for subject
The West
Comprising the area west of the Mississippi River
1380 General
1381 By subject (Table G1a)
1382 Regions, natural features, etc., A-Z (Table G4052)
Apply Table G1a for subject
North Central States
(1385) General
see G1375
(1386) By subject
see G1376
(1387) Regions, natural features, etc., A-Z
see G1377
East North Central States. Old Northwest. Northwest Territory. Territory Northwest of the River Ohio
1390 General
1391 By subject (Table G1a)
1392 Regions, natural features, etc., A-Z (Table G4072)
Apply Table G1a for subject
Ohio
1395 General
1396 By subject (Table G1a)
1397 Regions, natural features, etc., A-Z (Table G4082)
Apply Table G1a for subject
1398 Counties, A-Z (Table G4083)
Apply Table G1a for subject
1399 Cities and towns, A-Z (Table G4084)
Apply Table G1a for subject
Indiana
1400 General
1401 By subject (Table G1a)
1402 Regions, natural features, etc., A-Z (Table G4092)
Apply Table G1a for subject
1403 Counties, A-Z (Table G4093)
Apply Table G1a for subject

By region or country
America. Western Hemisphere
North America
United States
The West
North Central States
East North Central States. Old Northwest. Northwest Territory. Territory Northwest of the River Ohio
Indiana -- Continued
1404 Cities and towns, etc., A-Z (Table G4094)
Apply Table G1a for subject
Illinois
1405 General
1406 By subject (Table G1a)
1407 Regions, natural features, etc., A-Z (Table G4102)
Apply Table G1a for subject
1408 Counties, A-Z (Table G4103)
Apply Table G1a for subject
1409 Cities and towns, etc., A-Z (Table G4104)
Apply Table G1a for subject
Michigan
1410 General
1411 By subject (Table G1a)
1412 Regions, natural features, etc., A-Z (Table G4112)
Apply Table G1a for subject
1413 Counties, A-Z (Table G4113)
Apply Table G1a for subject
1414 Cities and towns, etc., A-Z (Table G4114)
Apply Table G1a for subject
Wisconsin
1415 General
1416 By subject (Table G1a)
1417 Regions, natural features, etc., A-Z (Table G4122)
Apply Table G1a for subject
1418 Counties, A-Z (Table G4123)
Apply Table G1a for subject
1419 Cities and towns, etc., A-Z (Table G4124)
Apply Table G1a for subject
Northwestern States
Comprises the area between the Great Lakes and the Pacific Ocean
1420 General
1421 By subject (Table G1a)

By region or country
America. Western Hemisphere
North America
United States
The West
Northwestern States -- Continued

1422 Regions, natural features, etc., A-Z (Table G4127)
Apply Table G1a for subject

West North Central States
Comprises the area between the Great Lakes and the Rocky Mountains

1424.3 General
1424.31 By subject (Table G1a)
1424.32 Regions, natural features, etc., A-Z (Table G4132)
Apply Table G1a for subject

Minnesota
1425 General
1426 By subject (Table G1a)
1427 Regions, natural features, etc., A-Z (Table G4142 modified)
Apply Table G1a for subject
1427.S16 Saganaga Lake [MN & Ont.]
Subarrange by Table G1a
1428 Counties, A-Z (Table G4143)
Apply Table G1a for subject
1429 Cities and towns, etc., A-Z (Table G4144)
Apply Table G1a for subject

Iowa
1430 General
1431 By subject (Table G1a)
1432 Regions, natural features, etc., A-Z (Table G4152)
Apply Table G1a for subject
1433 Counties, A-Z (Table G4153)
Apply Table G1a for subject
1434 Cities and towns, etc., A-Z (Table G4154)
Apply Table G1a for subject

Missouri
1435 General
1436 By subject (Table G1a)
1437 Regions, natural features, etc., A-Z (Table G4162)
Apply Table G1a for subject
1438 Counties, A-Z (Table G4163)
Apply Table G1a for subject

By region or country
America. Western Hemisphere
North America
United States
The West
Northwestern States
West North Central States
Missouri -- Continued
1439 Cities and towns, etc., A-Z (Table G4164)
Apply Table G1a for subject
North Dakota
1440 General
1441 By subject (Table G1a)
1442 Regions, natural features, etc., A-Z (Table G4172)
Apply Table G1a for subject
1443 Counties, A-Z (Table G4173)
Apply Table G1a for subject
1444 Cities and towns, etc., A-Z (Table G4174)
Apply Table G1a for subject
South Dakota
1445 General
1446 By subject (Table G1a)
1447 Regions, natural features, etc., A-Z (Table G4182)
Apply Table G1a for subject
1448 Counties, A-Z (Table G4183)
Apply Table G1a for subject
1449 Cities and towns, etc., A-Z (Table G4184)
Apply Table G1a for subject
Nebraska
1450 General
1451 By subject (Table G1a)
1452 Regions, natural features, etc., A-Z (Table G4192)
Apply Table G1a for subject
1453 Counties, A-Z (Table G4193)
Apply Table G1a for subject
1454 Cities and towns, etc., A-Z (Table G4194)
Apply Table G1a for subject
Kansas
1455 General
1456 By subject (Table G1a)
1457 Regions, natural features, etc., A-Z (Table G4202)
Apply Table G1a for subject

By region or country
America. Western Hemisphere
North America
United States
The West
Northwestern States
West North Central States
Kansas -- Continued
1458 Counties, A-Z (Table G4203)
Apply Table G1a for subject
1459 Cities and towns, etc., A-Z (Table G4204)
Apply Table G1a for subject
Pacific and Mountain States. Far West
1460 General
1461 By subject (Table G1a)
1462 Regions, natural features, etc., A-Z (Table G4212)
Apply Table G1a for subjecta
Rocky Mountain States
1464.3 General
1464.31 By subject (Table G1a)
1464.32 Regions, natural features, etc., A-Z (Table G4222)
Apply Table G1a for subject
Pacific States
Comprises Alaska, California, Hawaii, Oregon, and Washington
1464.5 General
1464.51 By subject (Table G1a)
1464.52 Regions, natural features, etc., A-Z (Table G4232)
Apply Table G1a for subject
Pacific Northwest
The old Oregon Country, comprising the present states of Oregon, Washington, and Idaho, parts of Montana and Wyoming, and the province of British Columbia
1465 General
1466 By subject (Table G1a)
1467 Regions, natural features, etc., A-Z (Table G4242)
Apply Table G1a for subjecta
Montana
1470 General
1471 By subject (Table G1a)
1472 Regions, natural features, etc., A-Z (Table G4252)
Apply Table G1a for subject

By region or country
America. Western Hemisphere
North America
United States
The West
Pacific and Mountain States. Far West
Pacific Northwest
Montana -- Continued

1473 Counties, A-Z (Table G4253)
Apply Table G1a for subject
1474 Cities and towns, etc., A-Z (Table G4254)
Apply Table G1a for subject

Wyoming

1475 General
1476 By subject (Table G1a)
1477 Regions, natural features, etc., A-Z (Table G4262)
Apply Table G1a for subject
1478 Counties, A-Z (Table G4263)
Apply Table G1a for subject
1479 Cities and towns, etc., A-Z (Table G4264)
Apply Table G1a for subject

Idaho

1480 General
1481 By subject (Table G1a)
1482 Regions, natural features, etc., A-Z (Table G4272)
Apply Table G1a for subject
1483 Counties, A-Z (Table G4273)
Apply Table G1a for subject
1484 Cities and towns, etc., A-Z (Table G4274)
Apply Table G1a for subject

Washington

1485 General
1486 By subject (Table G1a)
1487 Regions, natural features, etc., A-Z (Table G4282)
Apply Table G1a for subject
1488 Counties, A-Z (Table G4283)
Apply Table G1a for subject
1489 Cities and towns, etc., A-Z (Table G4284)
Apply Table G1a for subject

Oregon

1490 General
1491 By subject (Table G1a)

By region or country
America. Western Hemisphere
North America
United States
The West
Pacific and Mountain States. Far West
Pacific Northwest
Oregon -- Continued

1492 Regions, natural features, etc., A-Z (Table G4292)
Apply Table G1a for subject

1493 Counties, A-Z (Table G4293)
Apply Table G1a for subject

1494 Cities and towns, etc., A-Z (Table G4294)
Apply Table G1a for subject

Southwestern States
Including West South Central States and New Southwest

1495 General

1496 By subject (Table G1a)

1497 Regions, natural features, etc., A-Z (Table G4297)
Apply Table G1a for subject

New Southwest
Roughly corresponds with the old Spanish province of New Mexico

1499.3 General

1499.31 By subject (Table G1a)

1499.32 Regions, natural features, etc., A-Z (Table G4302)
Apply Table G1a for subject

Colorado

1500 General

1501 By subject (Table G1a)

1502 Regions, natural features, etc., A-Z (Table G4312)
Apply Table G1a for subject

1503 Counties, A-Z (Table G4313 modified)
Apply Table G1a for subject

Denver see G1504.D4

Denver (Denver International Airport) see G1504.D4:2D5

Denver (Denver Zoo) see G1504.D4:2D6

1504 Cities and towns, etc., A-Z (Table G4314 modified)
Apply Table G1a for subject

By region or country
America. Western Hemisphere
North America
United States
The West
Pacific and Mountain States. Far West
Southwestern States
New Southwest
Colorado
Cities and towns, etc., A-Z -- Continued
1504.D4 Denver
Subarrange by Table G1a
1504.D4:2D5 Denver International Airport
Subarrange by Table G1a
1504.D4:2D6 Denver Zoo
Subarrange by Table G1a
New Mexico
1505 General
1506 By subject (Table G1a)
1507 Regions, natural features, etc., A-Z (Table G4322)
Apply Table G1a for subject
1508 Counties, A-Z (Table G4323)
Apply Table G1a for subject
1509 Cities and towns, etc., A-Z (Table G4324)
Apply Table G1a for subject
Arizona
1510 General
1511 By subject (Table G1a)
1512 Regions, natural features, etc., A-Z (Table G4332)
Apply Table G1a for subject
1513 Counties, A-Z (Table G4333)
Apply Table G1a for subject
1514 Cities and towns, etc., A-Z (Table G4334)
Apply Table G1a for subject
Utah
1515 General
1516 By subject (Table G1a)
1517 Regions, natural features, etc., A-Z (Table G4342)
Apply Table G1a for subject
1518 Counties, A-Z (Table G4343)
Apply Table G1a for subject
1519 Cities and towns, etc., A-Z (Table G4344)
Apply Table G1a for subject
Nevada

By region or country
America. Western Hemisphere
North America
United States
The West
Pacific and Mountain States. Far West
Southwestern States
New Southwest
Nevada -- Continued

1520 General
1521 By subject (Table G1a)
1522 Regions, natural features, etc., A-Z (Table G4352)
Apply Table G1a for subject
1523 Counties, A-Z (Table G4353 modified)
Apply Table G1a for subject
Ormsby see G1524.C4
1524 Cities and towns, etc., A-Z (Table G4354 modified)
Apply Table G1a for subject
1524.C4 Carson City
Subarrange by Table G1a

California
1525 General
1526 By subject (Table G1a)
1527 Regions, natural features, etc., A-Z (Table G4362)
Apply Table G1a for subject
1528 Counties, A-Z (Table G4363)
Apply Table G1a for subject
1529 Cities and towns, etc., A-Z (Table G4364)
Apply Table G1a for subject

Alaska
1530 General
1531 By subject (Table G1a)
1532 Regions, natural features, etc., A-Z (Table G4372)
Apply Table G1a for subject
1533 Boroughs, census divisions, etc., A-Z (Table G4373)
Apply Table G1a for subject
1534 Cities and towns, etc., A-Z (Table G4374)
Apply Table G1a for subject

Hawaii. Sandwich Islands
1534.2 General
1534.21 By subject (Table G1a)

By region or country
America. Western Hemisphere
North America
United States
The West
Pacific and Mountain States. Far West
Hawaii -- Continued

1534.22 Regions, natural features, etc., A-Z (Table G4382)
Apply Table G1a for subject

1534.23 Counties, A-Z (Table G4383)
Apply Table G1a for subject

1534.24 Cities and towns, etc., A-Z (Table G4384)
Apply Table G1a for subject

Caribbean area

1535 General

1536 By subject (Table G1)

1537 Regions, natural features, etc., A-Z (Table G4392)
Apply Table G1 for subject

Latin America (General)

1540 General

1541 By subject (Table G1)

1542 Regions, natural features, etc., A-Z (Table G4412)
Apply Table G1 for subject

Mexico

1545 General

1546 By subject (Table G1)

1547 Regions, natural features, etc., A-Z (Table G4412)
Apply Table G1 for subject

1548 States, A-Z (Table G1548)
Apply Table G1 for subject

1549 Cities and towns, etc., A-Z (Table G4414)
Apply Table G1 for subject

Central America

1550 General

1551 By subject (Table G1)

1552 Regions, natural features, etc., A-Z (Table G4802)
Apply Table G1 for subject

Guatemala

1555 General

1556 By subject (Table G1)

1557 Regions, natural features, etc., A-Z (Table G4812)
Apply Table G1 for subject

1558 Departments, A-Z (Table G4813)
Apply Table G1 for subject

1559 Cities and towns, etc., A-Z (Table G4814)
Apply Table G1 for subject

By region or country
America. Western Hemisphere
North America
Central America -- Continued
Belize. British Honduras
1560 General
1561 By subject (Table G1)
1562 Regions, natural features, etc., A-Z (Table G4822)
Apply Table G1 for subject
1563 Districts, A-Z (Table G4823)
Apply Table G1 for subject
1564 Cities and towns, etc., A-Z (Table G4824)
Apply Table G1 for subject
Honduras
1565 General
1566 By subject (Table G1)
1567 Regions, natural features, islands, etc., A-Z (Table G4832)
Apply Table G1 for subject
1568 Departments, A-Z (Table G4833)
Apply Table G1 for subject
1569 Cities and towns, etc., A-Z (Table G4834)
Apply Table G1 for subject
El Salvador
1570 General
1571 By subject (Table G1)
1572 Regions, natural features, etc., A-Z (Table G4842)
Apply Table G1 for subject
1573 Departments, A-Z (Table G4843)
Apply Table G1 for subject
1574 Cities and towns, etc., A-Z (Table G4844)
Apply Table G1 for subject
Nicaragua
1575 General
1576 By subject (Table G1)
1577 Regions, natural features, etc., A-Z (Table G4852)
Apply Table G1 for subject
1578 Departments, A-Z (Table G4853)
Apply Table G1 for subject
1579 Cities and towns, etc., A-Z (Table G4854)
Apply Table G1 for subject
Costa Rica
1580 General
1581 By subject (Table G1)
1582 Regions, natural features, etc., A-Z (Table G4862)
Apply Table G1 for subject

By region or country
America. Western Hemisphere
North America
Central America
Costa Rica -- Continued
1583 Provinces, etc., A-Z (Table G4863)
Apply Table G1 for subject
1584 Cities and towns, etc., A-Z (Table G4864)
Apply Table G1 for subject
Panama
1585 General
1586 By subject (Table G1)
1587 Regions, natural features, etc., A-Z (Table G4872)
Apply Table G1 for subject
1588 Provinces, etc., A-Z (Table G4873)
Apply Table G1 for subject
1589 Cities and towns, etc., A-Z (Table G4874)
Apply Table G1 for subject
(1590-1594) Canal Zone
see G1587
West Indies
1600 General
1601 By subject (Table G1)
1602 Regions, natural features, islands, etc., A-Z (Table G4902)
Apply Table G1 for subject
Class here maps of West Indian islands and archipelagoes not classed or associated with G1605-G1694
Cuba
1605 General
1606 By subject (Table G1)
1607 Regions, natural features, etc., A-Z (Table G4922)
Apply Table G1 for subject
1608 Provinces, A-Z (Table G4923)
Apply Table G1 for subject
1609 Cities and towns, etc., A-Z (Table G4924)
Apply Table G1 for subject
Hispaniola
1610 General
1611 By subject (Table G1)
1612 Regions, natural features, etc., A-Z (Table G4932)
Apply Table G1 for subject
Haiti
1615 General
1616 By subject (Table G1)

By region or country
America. Western Hemisphere
North America
West Indies
Hispaniola
Haiti -- Continued
1617 Regions, natural features, etc., A-Z (Table G4942)
Apply Table G1 for subject
1618 Departments, A-Z (Table G4943)
Apply Table G1 for subject
1619 Cities and towns, etc., A-Z (Table G4944)
Apply Table G1 for subject
Dominican Republic. Santo Domingo
1620 General
1621 By subject (Table G1)
1622 Regions, natural features, etc., A-Z (Table G4952)
Apply Table G1 for subject
1623 Provinces, A-Z (Table G4953)
Apply Table G1 for subject
1624 Cities and towns, etc., A-Z (Table G4954)
Apply Table G1 for subject
Jamaica
1625 General
1626 By subject (Table G1)
1627 Regions, natural features, etc., A-Z (Table G4962)
Apply Table G1 for subject
1628 Parishes, A-Z (Table G4963)
Apply Table G1 for subject
1629 Cities and towns, etc., A-Z (Table G4964)
Apply Table G1 for subject
Puerto Rico
1630 General
1631 By subject (Table G1)
1632 Regions, natural features, etc., A-Z (Table G4972)
Apply Table G1 for subject
1634 Cities and towns, etc., A-Z (Table G4974)
Apply Table G1 for subject
Bahamas. Lucayos
1635 General
1636 By subject (Table G1)
Regions, natural features, islands, etc., A-Z (Table G4982)
Apply Table G1 for subject
Cities and towns, etc., A-Z (Table G4984)
Apply Table G1 for subject

By region or country
America. Western Hemisphere
North America
West Indies -- Continued
Virgin Islands
Including atlases of Virgin Islands of the United States and British Virgin Islands
1640 General
1641 By subject (Table G1)
1642 Regions, natural features, islands, etc., A-Z (Table G5007, G5012, G5022)
Apply Table G1 for subject
1644 Cities and towns, etc., A-Z (Table G5014, G5024)
Apply Table G1 for subject
Leeward Islands
1650 General
1651 By subject (Table G1)
1652 Regions, natural features, islands, etc., A-Z (Table G5032)
Apply Table G1 for subject
French West Indies
1660 General
1661 By subject (Table G1)
1662 Regions, natural features, islands, etc., A-Z (Table G1662)
Apply Table G1 for subject
Windward Islands
1670 General
1671 By subject (Table G1)
1672 Islands, A-Z
Trinidad and Tobago
1680 General
1681 By subject (Table G1)
1682 Regions, natural features, islands, etc., A-Z (Table G5147)
Apply Table G1 for subject
1683 Counties, wards, A-Z (Table G5148)
Apply Table G1 for subject
1684 Cities and towns, etc., A-Z (Table G5149)
Apply Table G1 for subject
Netherlands Antilles. Dutch West Indies
1690 General
1691 By subject (Table G1)
1692 Islands, A-Z (Table G1692)
Apply Table G1 for subject
South America
1700 General

By region or country
America. Western Hemisphere
South America -- Continued
1701 By subject (Table G1)
1702 Regions, natural features, etc., A-Z (Table G5202)
Apply Table G1 for subject
Guianas
1705 General
1706 By subject (Table G1)
1707 Regions, natural features, etc., A-Z (Table G5242)
Apply Table G1 for subject
Guyana. British Guiana
1710 General
1711 By subject (Table G1)
1712 Regions, natural features, etc., A-Z (Table G5252)
Apply Table G1 for subject
1713 Administrative districts, etc., A-Z (Table G5253)
Apply Table G1 for subject
1714 Cities and towns, etc., A-Z (Table G5254)
Apply Table G1 for subject
Suriname. Dutch Guiana
1715 General
1716 By subject (Table G1)
1717 Regions, natural features, etc., A-Z (Table G5262)
Apply Table G1 for subject
1718 Administrative districts, etc., A-Z (Table G5263)
Apply Table G1 for subject
1719 Cities and towns, etc., A-Z (Table G5264)
Apply Table G1 for subject
French Guiana
1720 General
1721 By subject (Table G1)
1722 Regions, natural features, etc., A-Z (Table G5272)
Apply Table G1 for subject
1723 Administrative divisions, A-Z (Table G5273)
Apply Table G1 for subject
1724 Cities and towns, etc., A-Z (Table G5274)
Apply Table G1 for subject
Venezuela
1725 General
1726 By subject (Table G1)
1727 Regions, natural features, etc., A-Z (Table G5282)
Apply Table G1 for subject
1728 States, territories, A-Z (Table G5283)
Apply Table G1 for subject
1729 Cities and towns, etc., A-Z (Table G5284)
Apply Table G1 for subject

By region or country
America. Western Hemisphere
South America -- Continued
Colombia
1730 General
1731 By subject (Table G1)
1732 Regions, natural features, etc., A-Z (Table G5292)
Apply Table G1 for subject
1733 Administrative divisions, A-Z (Table G5293)
Apply Table G1 for subject
1734 Cities and towns, etc., A-Z (Table G5294)
Apply Table G1 for subject
Ecuador
1735 General
1736 By subject (Table G1)
1737 Regions, natural features, etc., A-Z (Table G5302)
Apply Table G1 for subject
1738 Provinces, etc., A-Z (Table G5303)
Apply Table G1 for subject
1739 Cities and towns, etc., A-Z (Table G5304)
Apply Table G1 for subject
Peru
1740 General
1741 By subject (Table G1)
1742 Regions, natural features, etc., A-Z (Table G5312)
Apply Table G1 for subject
1743 Departments, A-Z (Table G5313)
Apply Table G1 for subject
1744 Cities and towns, etc., A-Z (Table G5314)
Apply Table G1 for subject
Bolivia
1745 General
1746 By subject (Table G1)
1747 Regions, natural features, etc., A-Z (Table G5322)
Apply Table G1 for subject
1748 Departments, etc., A-Z (Table G5323)
Apply Table G1 for subject
1749 Cities and towns, etc., A-Z (Table G5324)
Apply Table G1 for subject
Chile
1750 General
1751 By subject (Table G1)
1752 Regions, natural features, etc., A-Z (Table G5332)
Apply Table G1 for subject
1753 Administrative regions, etc., A-Z (Table G5333)
Apply Table G1 for subject

By region or country
America. Western Hemisphere
South America
Chile -- Continued
1754 Cities and towns, etc., A-Z (Table G5334)
Apply Table G1 for subject
Argentina
1755 General
1756 By subject (Table G1)
1757 Regions, natural features, etc., A-Z (Table G5352)
Apply Table G1 for subject
Islas Malvinas see G2835+
1758 Provinces, A-Z (Table G5353)
Apply Table G1 for subject
1759 Cities and towns, etc., A-Z (Table G5354)
Apply Table G1 for subject
Uruguay
1765 General
1766 By subject (Table G1)
1767 Regions, natural features, etc., A-Z (Table G5372)
Apply Table G1 for subject
1768 Departments, etc., A-Z (Table G5373)
Apply Table G1 for subject
1769 Cities and towns, etc., A-Z (Table G5374)
Apply Table G1 for subject
Paraguay
1770 General
1771 By subject (Table G1)
1772 Regions, natural features, etc., A-Z (Table G5382)
Apply Table G1 for subject
1773 Departments, etc., A-Z (Table G5383)
Apply Table G1 for subject
1774 Cities and towns, etc., A-Z (Table G5384)
Apply Table G1 for subject
Brazil
1775 General
1776 By subject (Table G1)
1777 Regions, natural features, etc., A-Z (Table G5402)
Apply Table G1 for subject
1778 States, territories, A-Z (Table G1778)
Apply Table G1 for subject
1779 Cities and towns, etc., A-Z (Table G5404)
Apply Table G1 for subject
Eastern Hemisphere. Eurasia, Africa, etc.
1780 General
1781 By subject (Table G1)

By region or country
Eastern Hemisphere. Eurasia, Africa, etc. -- Continued
1782 Regions, natural features, etc., A-Z (Table G5672)
Apply Table G1 for subject
Islamic Empire. Islamic countries
1785 General
1786 By subject (Table G1)
Europe
By period
1791 Ancient and medieval
1792 15th-16th centuries
1793 17th-18th centuries
1801-1975
1795 General
1796 By subject (Table G1)
1797 Regions, natural features, etc., A-Z (Table G5702)
Apply Table G1 for subject
1976-
1797.2 General
1797.21 By subject (Table G1)
1797.22 Regions, natural features, etc., A-Z (Table G5702)
Apply Table G1 for subject
1799 Cities and towns collectively
For individual cities and towns, see the country
Western Europe
1800 General
1801 By subject (Table G1)
1802 Regions, natural features, etc., A-Z (Table G1802)
Apply Table G1 for subject
British Empire. Commonwealth of Nations
Including atlases of British colonies, dependencies, etc. (Collectively)
Class individual colonies, dependencies, etc., according to location, e.g., G2560+, South Africa
1805 General
1806 By subject (Table G1)
British Isles. Great Britain
By period
1807 15th-16th centuries
1808 17th-18th centuries
1801-1975
1810 General
1811 By subject (Table G1 modified)
History
1811.S1 General
(1811.S12) This number not used
1811.S2 To 1066

By region or country
Eastern Hemisphere. Eurasia, Africa, etc.
Europe
Western Europe
British Isles. Great Britain
By period
1801-1975
By subject
History -- Continued

1811.S3 Medieval period, 1066-1485
1811.S33 Norman period, 1066-1154
1811.S35 Plantagenets, 1154-1399
1811.S37 15th century
1811.S4 Modern period, 1485-
1811.S45 16th century: Tudors, 1485-1603
1811.S5 17th century: Stuarts, 1603-1714
1811.S53 Commonwealth and protectorate, 1660-1688
1811.S54 18th century
1811.S55 19th century
1811.S6 20th century
1811.S65 World War I
1811.S7 World War II
1812 Regions, natural features, etc., A-Z (Table G5742)

Apply Table G1 for subject (except .S1-.S7, historical geography)

Apply Table G5741.S for history

1976-
1812.2 General
1812.21 By subject (Table G1 modified)
History
1812.21.S1 General
(1812.21.S12) This number not used
1812.21.S2 To 1066
1812.21.S3 Medieval period, 1066-1485
1812.21.S33 Norman period, 1066-1154
1812.21.S35 Plantagenets, 1154-1399
1812.21.S37 15th century
1812.21.S4 Modern period, 1485-
1812.21.S45 16th century: Tudors, 1485-1603
1812.21.S5 17th century: Stuarts, 1603-1714
1812.21.S53 Commonwealth and protectorate, 1660-1688
1812.21.S54 18th century
1812.21.S55 19th century
1812.21.S6 20th century

By region or country
Eastern Hemisphere. Eurasia, Africa, etc.
Europe
Western Europe
British Isles. Great Britain
By period
1976-
By subject
History
Modern period, 1485-
20th century -- Continued
1812.21.S65 World War I
1812.21.S7 World War II
1812.22 Regions, natural features, etc., A-Z (Table G5742)
Apply Table G1 for subject (except .S1-.S7, historical geography)
Apply Table G5741.S for history
1814.A1 Cities and towns collectively
Apply Table G1 for subject (except .S1-.S7, historical geography)
Apply Table G5741.S for history
For individual cities and towns, see the country
England
1815 General
1816 By subject (Table G1 modified)
History
1816.S1 General
(1816.S12) This number not used
1816.S2 To 1066
1816.S3 Medieval period, 1066-1485
1816.S33 Norman period, 1066-1154
1816.S35 Plantagenets, 1154-1399
1816.S37 15th century
1816.S4 Modern period, 1485-
1816.S45 16th century: Tudors, 1485-1603
1816.S5 17th century: Stuarts, 1603-1714
1816.S53 Commonwealth and protectorate, 1660-1688
1816.S54 18th century
1816.S55 19th century
1816.S6 20th century
1816.S65 World War I
1816.S7 World War II
1817 Regions, natural features, etc., A-Z (Table G5752)
Apply Table G1 for subject (except .S1-.S7, historical geography)
Apply Table G5741.S for history

By region or country
Eastern Hemisphere. Eurasia, Africa, etc.
Europe
Western Europe
British Isles. Great Britain
England -- Continued

1818 Counties, etc., A-Z (Table G5753 modified)
Apply Table G1 for subject (except .S1-.S7, historical geography)
Apply Table G5741.S for history
Greater London (Metropolitan county) see G1819.L7
Greater Manchester (Metropolitan county) see G1819.M3
London, Greater (Metropolitan county) see G1819.L7
Manchester, Greater (Metropolitan county) see G1819.M3

1819 Cities and towns, etc., A-Z (Table G5754 modified)
Apply Table G1 for subject (except .S1-.S7, historical geography)
Apply Table G5741.S for history

1819.L7 London
Subarrange by Table G1 except .S1-.S7, historical geography. For history, subarrange by Table G5741.S

1819.M3 Manchester
Subarrange by Table G1 except .S1-.S7, historical geography. For history, subarrange by Table G5741.S

Wales

1820 General
1821 By subject (Table G1 modified)
History
1821.S1 General
(1821.S12) This number not used
1821.S2 To 1066
1821.S3 Medieval period, 1066-1485
1821.S33 Norman period, 1066-1154
1821.S35 Plantagenets, 1154-1399
1821.S37 15th century
1821.S4 Modern period, 1485-
1821.S45 16th century: Tudors, 1485-1603
1821.S5 17th century: Stuarts, 1603-1714
1821.S53 Commonwealth and protectorate, 1660-1688
1821.S54 18th century
1821.S55 19th century

By region or country
Eastern Hemisphere. Eurasia, Africa, etc.
Europe
Western Europe
British Isles. Great Britain
Wales
By subject
History
Modern period, 1485- -- Continued

1821.S6 20th century
1821.S65 World War I
1821.S7 World War II
1822 Regions, natural features, etc., A-Z (Table G5762)
Apply Table G1 for subject (except .S1-.S7, historical geography)
Apply Table G5741.S for history
1823 Counties, A-Z (Table G5763)
Apply Table G1 for subject (except .S1-.S7, historical geography)
Apply Table G5741.S for history
1824 Cities and towns, etc., A-Z (Table G5764)
Apply Table G1 for subject (except .S1-.S7, historical geography)
Apply Table G5741.S for history

Scotland
1825 General
1826 By subject (Table G1 modified)
History
1826.S1 General
(1826.S12) This number not used
1826.S2 To 1057
1826.S3 1057-1603
1826.S34 War of Independence, 1285-1371
1826.S36 Stuarts to the Union, 1371-1707
1826.S4 17th century
1826.S45 Revolution of 1688
1826.S5 18th century
1826.S52 Jacobite Rebellion, 1715
1826.S53 Jacobite Rebellion, 1745-1746
1826.S55 19th century
1826.S6 20th century
1826.S65 World War I
1826.S7 World War II
1827 Regions, natural features, etc., A-Z (Table G5772 modified)
Apply Table G1 for subject (except .S7-.S7, history)
Apply Table G5771.S for history

By region or country
Eastern Hemisphere. Eurasia, Africa, etc.
Europe
Western Europe
British Isles. Great Britain
Scotland
Regions, natural features, etc., A-Z -- Continued

1827.O6 Orkney Islands
Subarrange by Table G1 except .S1-.S7, historical geography. For history, subarrange by Table G5771.S

1827.S5 Shetland Islands
Subarrange by Table G1 except .S1-.S7, historical geography. For history, subarrange by Table G5771.S

1827.W39 Western Isles
Subarrange by Table G1 except .S1-.S7, historical geography. For history, subarrange by Table G5771.S

1828 Administrative regions, island areas, A-Z (Table G5773 modified)
Apply Table G1 for subject (except .S7-.S7, history)
Apply Table G5771.S for history
Orkney see G1827.O6
Shetland see G1827.S5
Western Isles see G1827.W39

1829 Cities and towns, etc., A-Z (Table G5774)
Apply Table G1 for subject (except .S7-.S7, history)
Apply Table G5771.S for history

Northern Ireland

1829.2 General

1829.21 By subject (Table G1)

1829.22 Regions, natural features, etc., A-Z (Table G5792)
Apply Table G1 for subject

1829.23 Counties, etc., A-Z (Table G5793)
Apply Table G1 for subject

1829.24 Cities and towns, etc., A-Z (Table G5794)
Apply Table G1 for subject

Eire. Irish Free State
Including atlases of the island treated as a whole

1830 General

1831 By subject (Table G1)

1832 Regions, natural features, etc., A-Z (Table G5782)
Apply Table G1 for subject

1833 Counties, A-Z (Table G5783)
Apply Table G1 for subject

By region or country
Eastern Hemisphere. Eurasia, Africa, etc.
Europe
Western Europe
Eire. Irish Free State -- Continued
1834 Cities and towns, etc., A-Z (Table G5784)
Apply Table G1 for subject
1835 French Empire. French Union
Including atlases of French colonies, dependencies, etc. (Collectively)
Class individual colonies, dependencies, etc., according to location, e.g., G2645+, French West Africa
France
By period
1837 15th-16th centuries
1838 17th-18th centuries
1801-1975
1840 General
1841 By subject (Table G1 modified)
History
1841.S1 General
(1841.S12) This number not used
1841.S2 To 987
1841.S3 Medieval period, 987-1515
1841.S4 Modern period, 1515-
1841.S5 17th century
1841.S54 18th century
1841.S545 Revolution, 1789-1799
1841.S55 Consulate and Empire, 1799-1815
1841.S56 19th century
1841.S6 20th century
1841.S65 World War I
1841.S7 World War II
1841.S73 1945-
1842 Regions, natural features, etc., A-Z (Table G5832 modified)
Apply Table G1 for subject (except .S1-.S7, historical geography)
Apply Table G5831.S for history
1842.P35 Paris Region. Région parisienne
Subarrange by Table G1 except .S1-.S7, historical geography. For history, subarrange by Table G5831.S

By region or country
Eastern Hemisphere. Eurasia, Africa, etc.
Europe
Western Europe
France
By period
1801-1975 -- Continued

1843 Provinces, departments, etc., A-Z (Table G5833 modified)
Apply Table G1 for subject (except .S1-.S7, historical geography)
Apply Table G5831.S for history
Paris see G1844.P3
Paris Region see G1842.P35
Région parisienne see G1842.P35

1844 Cities and towns, etc., A-Z (Table G5834 modified)
Apply Table G1 for subject (except .S1-.S7, historical geography)
Apply Table G5831.S for history

1844.P3 Paris
Subarrange by Table G1 except .S1-.S7, historical geography. For history, subarrange by Table G5831.S

1976-

1844.2 General

1844.21 By subject (Table G1 modified)
History

1844.21.S1 General

(1844.21.S12) This number not used

1844.21.S2 To 987

1844.21.S3 Medieval period, 987-1515

1844.21.S4 Modern period, 1515-

1844.21.S5 17th century

1844.21.S54 18th century

1844.21.S545 Revolution, 1789-1799

1844.21.S55 Consulate and Empire, 1799-1815

1844.21.S56 19th century

1844.21.S6 20th century

1844.21.S65 World War I

1844.21.S7 World War II

1844.21.S73 1945-

1844.22 Regions, natural features, etc., A-Z (Table G5832 modified)
Apply Table G1 for subject (except .S1-.S7, historical geography)
Apply Table G5831.S for history

By region or country
Eastern Hemisphere. Eurasia, Africa, etc.
Europe
Western Europe
France
By period
1976-
Regions, natural features, etc., A-Z -- Continued

1844.22.P35 Paris Region. Région parisienne
Subarrange by Table G1 except .S1-.S7, historical geography. For history, subarrange by Table G5831.S

1844.23 Provinces, departments, etc., A-Z (Table G5833 modified)
Apply Table G1 for subject (except .S1-.S7, historical geography)
Apply Table G5831.S for history
Paris see G1844.24.P3
Paris Region see G1844.22.P35
Région parisienne see G1844.22.P35

1844.24 Cities and towns, etc., A-Z (Table G5834 modified)
Apply Table G1 for subject (except .S1-.S7, historical geography)
Apply Table G5831.S for history

1844.24.P3 Paris
Subarrange by Table G1 except .S1-.S7, historical geography. For history, subarrange by Table G5831.S

Monaco
1845 General
1846 By subject (Table G1)
1847 Regions, natural features, etc., A-Z (Table G5982)
Apply Table G1 for subject
1849 Cities and towns, etc., A-Z (Table G5984)
Apply Table G1 for subject

Benelux countries. Low countries
By period
1850 15th-16th centuries
1851 17th-18th centuries
1801-1975
1855 General
1856 By subject (Table G1)
1976-
1857.2 General
1857.21 By subject (Table G1)

By region or country
Eastern Hemisphere. Eurasia, Africa, etc.
Europe
Western Europe
Benelux countries. Low countries -- Continued
Netherlands Union
Including atlases of Dutch colonies, dependencies, etc. (Collectively)
Class individual colonies, dependencies, etc., according to location, e.g., G1715+, Suriname
1858 General
1859 By subject (Table G1)
Netherlands
1860 General
1861 By subject (Table G1)
1862 Regions, natural features, etc., A-Z (Table G6002)
Apply Table G1 for subject
1863 Provinces, A-Z (Table G6003)
Apply Table G1 for subject
1864 Cities and towns, etc., A-Z (Table G6004)
Apply Table G1 for subject
Belgium
1865 General
1866 By subject (Table G1 modified)
History
1866.S1 General
(1866.S12) This number not used
1866.S2 To 1555
1866.S3 1555-1648
1866.S4 Modern period, 1648-
1866.S5 18th century
1866.S55 19th century
1866.S56 Revolution, 1830-1839
1866.S6 20th century
1866.S65 World War I
1866.S7 World War II
1866.S73 1945-
1867 Regions, natural features, etc., A-Z (Table G6012)
Apply Table G1 for subject (except .S1-.S7, historical geography)
Apply Table G6011.S for history
1868 Provinces, A-Z (Table G6013)
Apply Table G1 for subject (except .S1-.S7, historical geography)
Apply Table G6011.S for history

By region or country
Eastern Hemisphere. Eurasia, Africa, etc.
Europe
Western Europe
Benelux countries. Low countries
Belgium -- Continued

1869 Cities and towns, etc., A-Z (Table G6014)
Apply Table G1 for subject (except .S1-.S7, historical geography)
Apply Table G6011.S for history

Luxembourg
1870 General
1871 By subject (Table G1)
1872 Regions, natural features, etc., A-Z (Table G6022)
Apply Table G1 for subject
1873 Districts, A-Z (Table G6023)
Apply Table G1 for subject
1874 Cities and towns, etc., A-Z (Table G6024)
Apply Table G1 for subject

Central Europe
1880 General
1881 By subject (Table G1)
1882 Regions, natural features, etc., A-Z (Table G6032 modified)
Apply Table G1 for subject
Erzegebirge see G1947.E7

Alps
1890 General
1891 By subject (Table G1)

Switzerland
1895 General
1896 By subject (Table G1 modified)
History
1896.S1 General
(1896.S12) This number not used
1896.S2 To 1648
1896.S3 1648-1789
1789-1815
1896.S4 General
1896.S45 Helvetic Republic, 1789-1803
1815-1900
1896.S5 General
1896.S55 Sonderbund, 1845-1847
1900-1945
1896.S6 General
1896.S65 World War I
1896.S7 World War II

By region or country
Eastern Hemisphere. Eurasia, Africa, etc.
Europe
Central Europe
Switzerland
By subject
History -- Continued
1896.S73 1945-
1897 Regions, natural features, etc., A-Z (Table G6042)
Apply Table G1 for subject (except .S1-.S7, historical geography)
Apply Table G6041.S for history
1898 Cantons, A-Z (Table G6043)
Apply Table G1 for subject (except .S1-.S7, historical geography)
Apply Table G6041.S for history
1899 Cities and towns, etc., A-Z (Table G6044)
Apply Table G1 for subject (except .S1-.S7, historical geography)
Apply Table G6041.S for history
Liechtenstein
1900 General
1901 By subject (Table G1)
1902 Regions, natural features, etc., A-Z (Table G6052)
Apply Table G1 for subject
Apply Table G6081.S for history
1903 Communes (Gemeindes), A-Z (Table G6053)
Apply Table G1 for subject
1904 Cities and towns, etc., A-Z (Table G6054)
Apply Table G1 for subject
German Empire
Including atlases of German colonies (Collectively)
Class individual colonies, etc., according to location, e.g., G2540+, Former German East Africa
1905 General
1906 By subject (Table G1)
Germany
Including atlases of the former East and West Germany together, Prussia as a whole, and the Holy Roman Empire
For East Prussia, see G1953.O5, G2143.K2
For Pomerania, see G1918.3+, G1952.P58
For Posen, see G1953.P6
For Silesia, see G1953.S5
For West Prussia, see G1952.P8
By period
1907 Early through 16th century

By region or country
Eastern Hemisphere. Eurasia, Africa, etc.
Europe
Central Europe
Germany
By period -- Continued
1908 17th-18th centuries
1801-1975
1910 General
1911 By subject (Table G1 modified)
History
1911.S1 General
(1911.S12) This number not used
1911.S55 19th century
20th century
1911.S6 General
1911.S65 World War I
1911.S7 World War II
1911.S73 1945-
1912 Regions, natural features, etc., A-Z (Table G6082 modified)
Apply Table G1 for subject
Apply Table G6081.Sa for history
Erzegebirge see G1947.E7
1912.F7 Franconia [Duchy]
Subarrange by Table G1 except .S1-.S7, historical geography. For history, subarrange by Table G6081.Sa
Mulde River see G1918.52.M8
1976-
1912.2 General
1912.21 By subject (Table G1 modified)
History
1912.21.S1 General
(1912.21.S12) This number not used
(1912.21.S65) This number not used
(1912.21.S7) This number not used
1912.22 Regions, natural features, etc., A-Z (Table G6082 modified)
Apply Table G1 for subject
Apply Table G6081.Sb for history
Erzegebirge see G1947.E7
1912.22.F7 Franconia [Duchy]
Subarrange by Table G1 except .S1-.S7, historical geography. For history, subarrange by Table G6081.Sb
Mulde River see G1918.52.M8

By region or country
Eastern Hemisphere. Eurasia, Africa, etc.
Europe
Central Europe
Germany -- Continued

(1914) Cities and towns
see G1924

East Germany (German Democratic Republic)

1915 General

1916 By subject (Table G1 modified)

History

1916.S1 General

(1916.S12) This number not used

1916.S2 To 843

1916.S3 Medieval period, 843-1517

Modern period, 1517-

1916.S4 General

1916.S5 17th century

1916.S54 18th century

1916.S55 19th century

20th century

1916.S6 General

1916.S65 World War I

1916.S7 World War II

1916.S73 1945-

(1917) Regions and natural features, etc., A-Z
see G1912, G1912.22

(1918) Administrative districts (Bezirke), former states (Länder), etc., A-Z
see G1918.2+

Administrative districts (Lander, Regierungsbezirke, Bezirke, Landkreise, etc.)

Brandenburg

1918.2 General

1918.21 By subject (Table G1 modified)

History

1918.21.S1 General

(1918.21.S12) This number not used

1918.21.S2 To 843

1918.21.S3 Medieval period, 843-1517

Modern period, 1517-

1918.21.S4 General

1918.21.S5 17th century

1918.21.S54 18th century

1918.21.S55 19th century

20th century

1918.21.S6 General

By region or country
Eastern Hemisphere. Eurasia, Africa, etc.
Europe
Central Europe
Germany
East Germany (German Democratic Republic)
Administrative districts (Lander, Regierungsbezirke, Bezirke, Landkreise, etc.)
Brandenburg
By subject
History
Modern period, 1517-
20th century -- Continued

1918.21.S65 World War I
1918.21.S7 World War II
1918.21.S73 1945-
1918.22 Regions, natural features, etc., A-Z (Table G6152)
Apply Table G1 for subject (except .S1-.S7, historical geography)
Apply Table G6081.S for history
1918.23 Administrative districts (Regierungsbezirke, Landkreise, etc.), A-Z (Table G6153)
Apply Table G1 for subject (except .S1-.S7, historical geography)
Apply Table G6081.S for history

Mecklenburg-Vorpommern. Mecklenburg
Including Mecklenburg-Schwerin and Mecklenburg-Strelitz

1918.3 General
1918.31 By subject (Table G1 modified)
History
1918.31.S1 General
(1918.31.S12) This number not used
1918.31.S2 To 843
1918.31.S3 Medieval period, 843-1517
Modern period, 1517-
1918.31.S4 General
1918.31.S5 17th century
1918.31.S54 18th century
1918.31.S55 19th century
20th century
1918.31.S6 General
1918.31.S65 World War I
1918.31.S7 World War II
1918.31.S73 1945-

By region or country
Eastern Hemisphere. Eurasia, Africa, etc.
Europe
Central Europe
Germany
East Germany (German Democratic Republic)
Administrative districts (Lander, Regierungsbezirke, Bezirke, Landkreise, etc.)
Mecklenburg-Vorpommern. Mecklenburg -- Continued

1918.32 Regions, natural features, etc., A-Z (Table G6197)
Apply Table G1 for subject (except .S1-.S7, historical geography)
Apply Table G6081.S for history

1918.33 Administrative districts (Regierungsbezirke, Landkreise, etc.), A-Z (Table G6198)
Apply Table G1 for subject (except .S1-.S7, historical geography)
Apply Table G6081.S for history

Saxony-Anhalt
Including Anhalt and Saxony (Prussian province)

1918.4 General
1918.41 By subject (Table G1 modified)
History
1918.41.S1 General
(1918.41.S12) This number not used
1918.41.S2 To 843
1918.41.S3 Medieval period, 843-1517
Modern period, 1517-
1918.41.S4 General
1918.41.S5 17th century
1918.41.S54 18th century
1918.41.S55 19th century
20th century
1918.41.S6 General
1918.41.S65 World War I
1918.41.S7 World War II
1918.41.S73 1945-

1918.42 Regions, natural features, etc., A-Z (Table G6232)
Apply Table G1 for subject (except .S1-.S7, historical geography)
Apply Table G6081.S for history

By region or country
Eastern Hemisphere. Eurasia, Africa, etc.
Europe
Central Europe
Germany
East Germany (German Democratic Republic)
Administrative districts (Lander, Regierungsbezirke, Bezirke, Landkreise, etc.)
Saxony-Anhalt -- Continued

1918.43 Administrative districts (Regierungsbezirke, Landkreise, etc.), A-Z (Table G6233)
Apply Table G1 for subject (except .S1-.S7, historical geography)
Apply Table G6081.S for history

Saxony

1918.5 General
1918.51 By subject (Table G1 modified)
History
1918.51.S1 General
(1918.51.S12) This number not used
1918.51.S2 To 843
1918.51.S3 Medieval period, 843-1517
Modern period, 1517-
1918.51.S4 General
1918.51.S5 17th century
1918.51.S54 18th century
1918.51.S55 19th century
20th century
1918.51.S6 General
1918.51.S65 World War I
1918.51.S7 World War II
1918.51.S73 1945-
1918.52 Regions, natural features, etc., A-Z (Table G6242 modified)
Apply Table G1 for subject (except .S1-.S7, historical geography)
Apply Table G6081.S for history
1918.52.M8 Mulde River
Subarrange by Table G1 except .S1-.S7, historical geography. For history, subarrange by G6081.S
1918.53 Administrative districts (Regierungsbezirke, Landkreise, etc.), A-Z (Table G6243)
Apply Table G1 for subject (except .S1-.S7, historical geography)
Apply Table G6081.S for history

Thuringia

By region or country
Eastern Hemisphere. Eurasia, Africa, etc.
Europe
Central Europe
Germany
East Germany (German Democratic Republic)
Administrative districts (Lander, Regierungsbezirke, Bezirke, Landkreise, etc.)
Thuringia -- Continued

1918.6 General
1918.61 By subject (Table G1 modified)
History
1918.61.S1 General
(1918.61.S12) This number not used
1918.61.S2 To 843
1918.61.S3 Medieval period, 843-1517
Modern period, 1517-
1918.61.S4 General
1918.61.S5 17th century
1918.61.S54 18th century
1918.61.S55 19th century
20th century
1918.61.S6 General
1918.61.S65 World War I
1918.61.S7 World War II
1918.61.S73 1945-
1918.62 Regions, natural features, etc., A-Z (Table G6292)
Apply Table G1 for subject (except .S1-.S7, historical geography)
Apply Table G6081.S for history
1918.63 Administrative districts (Regierungsbezirke, Landkreise, etc.), A-Z (Table G6293)
Apply Table G1 for subject (except .S1-.S7, historical geography)
Apply Table G6081.S for history
(1919) Cities and towns, A-Z
see G1924

West Germany (Federal Republic of Germany)
1920 General
1921 By subject (Table G1 modified)
History
1921.S1 General
(1921.S12) This number not used
1921.S2 To 843
1921.S3 Medieval period, 843-1517
Modern period, 1517-

By region or country
Eastern Hemisphere. Eurasia, Africa, etc.
Europe
Central Europe
Germany
West Germany (Federal Republic of Germany)
By subject
History
Modern period, 1517- -- Continued

1921.S4 General
1921.S5 17th century
1921.S54 18th century
1921.S55 19th century
20th century
1921.S6 General
1921.S65 World War I
1921.S7 World War II
1921.S73 1945-
(1922) Regions and natural features, etc., A-Z
see G1912, G1912.22
(1923) States (Länder), former states, etc., A-Z
see G1923.2+
Administrative districts (Länder, Regierungsbezirke, Bezirke, Landkreise, etc.)
Schleswig-Holstein
1923.2 General
1923.21 By subject (Table G1 modified)
History
1923.21.S1 General
(1923.21.S12) This number not used
1923.21.S2 To 843
1923.21.S3 Medieval period, 843-1517
Modern period, 1517-
1923.21.S4 General
1923.21.S5 17th century
1923.21.S54 18th century
1923.21.S55 19th century
20th century
1923.21.S6 General
1923.21.S65 World War I
1923.21.S7 World War II
1923.21.S73 1945-
1923.22 Regions, natural features, etc., A-Z (Table G6312)
Apply Table G1 for subject (except .S1-.S7, historical geography)
Apply Table G6081.S for history

By region or country
Eastern Hemisphere. Eurasia, Africa, etc.
Europe
Central Europe
Germany
West Germany (Federal Republic of Germany)
Administrative districts (Länder, Regierungsbezirke, Bezirke, Landkreise, etc.)
Schleswig-Holstein -- Continued

1923.23 Administrative districts (Regierungsbezirke, Landkreis, etc.), A-Z (Table G6313)
Apply Table G1 for subject (except .S1-.S7, historical geography)
Apply Table G6081.S for history

Lower Saxony (Niedersachsen). Hanover
1923.3 General
1923.31 By subject (Table G1 modified)
History
1923.31.S1 General
(1923.31.S12) This number not used
1923.31.S2 To 843
1923.31.S3 Medieval period, 843-1517
Modern period, 1517-
1923.31.S4 General
1923.31.S5 17th century
1923.31.S54 18th century
1923.31.S55 19th century
20th century
1923.31.S6 General
1923.31.S65 World War I
1923.31.S7 World War II
1923.31.S73 1945-
1923.32 Regions, natural features, etc., A-Z (Table G6322)
Apply Table G1 for subject (except .S1-.S7, historical geography)
Apply Table G6081.S for history
1923.33 Administrative districts (Regierungsbezirke, Landkreis, etc.), A-Z (Table G6323 modified)
Apply Table G1 for subject (except .S1-.S7, historical geography)
Apply Table G6081.S for history
Lüneburg (Province) see G1924.L9

North Rhine-Westphalia. Westphalia
1923.4 General
1923.41 By subject (Table G1 modified)

By region or country
Eastern Hemisphere. Eurasia, Africa, etc.
Europe
Central Europe
Germany
West Germany (Federal Republic of Germany)
Administrative districts (Länder, Regierungsbezirke, Bezirke, Landkreise, etc.)
North Rhine-Westphalia. Westphalia
By subject -- Continued
History

1923.41.S1 General
(1923.41.S12) This number not used
1923.41.S2 To 843
1923.41.S3 Medieval period, 843-1517
Modern period, 1517-
1923.41.S4 General
1923.41.S5 17th century
1923.41.S54 18th century
1923.41.S55 19th century
20th century
1923.41.S6 General
1923.41.S65 World War I
1923.41.S7 World War II
1923.41.S73 1945-
1923.42 Regions, natural features, etc., A-Z (Table G6362)
Apply Table G1 for subject (except .S1-.S7, historical geography)
Apply Table G6081.S for history
1923.43 Administrative districts (Regierungsbezirke, Landkreis, etc.), A-Z (Table G6363)
Apply Table G1 for subject (except .S1-.S7, historical geography)
Apply Table G6081.S for history

Hesse
Including Hesse-Darmstadt and Hesse-Nassau

1923.5 General
1923.51 By subject (Table G1 modified)
History
1923.51.S1 General
(1923.51.S12) This number not used
1923.51.S2 To 843
1923.51.S3 Medieval period, 843-1517
Modern period, 1517-
1923.51.S4 General
1923.51.S5 17th century

By region or country
Eastern Hemisphere. Eurasia, Africa, etc.
Europe
Central Europe
Germany
West Germany (Federal Republic of Germany)
Administrative districts (Länder, Regierungsbezirke, Bezirke, Landkreise, etc.)
Hesse
By subject
History
Modern period, 1517- -- Continued

1923.51.S54 18th century
1923.51.S55 19th century
20th century
1923.51.S6 General
1923.51.S65 World War I
1923.51.S7 World War II
1923.51.S73 1945-
1923.52 Regions, natural features, etc., A-Z (Table G6372)
Apply Table G1 for subject (except .S1-.S7, historical geography)
Apply Table G6081.S for history
1923.53 Administrative districts (Regierungsbezirke, Landkreis, etc.), A-Z (Table G6373)
Apply Table G1 for subject (except .S1-.S7, historical geography)
Apply Table G6081.S for history
Rhineland-Palatinate. Rhine Province
1923.6 General
1923.61 By subject (Table G1 modified)
History
1923.61.S1 General
(1923.61.S12) This number not used
1923.61.S2 To 843
1923.61.S3 Medieval period, 843-1517
Modern period, 1517-
1923.61.S4 General
1923.61.S5 17th century
1923.61.S54 18th century
1923.61.S55 19th century
20th century
1923.61.S6 General
1923.61.S65 World War I
1923.61.S7 World War II
1923.61.S73 1945-

By region or country
Eastern Hemisphere. Eurasia, Africa, etc.
Europe
Central Europe
Germany
West Germany (Federal Republic of Germany)
Administrative districts (Länder, Regierungsbezirke, Bezirke, Landkreise, etc.)
Rhineland-Palatinate. Rhine Province -- Continued

1923.62 Regions, natural features, etc., A-Z (Table G6392 modified)
Apply Table G1 for subject (except .S1-.S7, historical geography)
Apply Table G6081.S for history

1923.62.P3 Palatinate. Lower Palatinate
Subarrange by Table G1 except .S1-.S7, historical geography. For history, subarrange by G6081.S
Including atlases of Lower and Upper Palatinate together
For atlases of Upper Palatinate alone see G1923.83.O2

1923.63 Administrative districts (Regierungsbezirke, Landkreis, etc.), A-Z (Table G6393)
Apply Table G1 for subject (except .S1-.S7, historical geography)
Apply Table G6081.S for history

Saarland (Saar)
1923.7 General
1923.71 By subject (Table G1 modified)
History
1923.71.S1 General
(1923.71.S12) This number not used
1923.71.S2 To 843
1923.71.S3 Medieval period, 843-1517
Modern period, 1517-
1923.71.S4 General
1923.71.S5 17th century
1923.71.S54 18th century
1923.71.S55 19th century
20th century
1923.71.S6 General
1923.71.S65 World War I
1923.71.S7 World War II
1923.71.S73 1945-

By region or country
Eastern Hemisphere. Eurasia, Africa, etc.
Europe
Central Europe
Germany
West Germany (Federal Republic of Germany)
Administrative districts (Länder, Regierungsbezirke, Bezirke, Landkreise, etc.)
Saarland (Saar) -- Continued

1923.73 Administrative districts (Regierungsbezirke, Landkreis, etc.), A-Z (Table G6398)
Apply Table G1 for subject (except .S1-.S7, historical geography)
Apply Table G6081.S for history

Bavaria

1923.8 General

1923.81 By subject (Table G1 modified)

History

1923.81.S1 General

(1923.81.S12) This number not used

1923.81.S2 To 843

1923.81.S3 Medieval period, 843-1517

Modern period, 1517-

1923.81.S4 General

1923.81.S5 17th century

1923.81.S54 18th century

1923.81.S55 19th century

20th century

1923.81.S6 General

1923.81.S65 World War I

1923.81.S7 World War II

1923.81.S73 1945-

1923.82 Regions, natural features, etc., A-Z (Table G6422)
Apply Table G1 for subject (except .S1-.S7, historical geography)
Apply Table G6081.S for history

1923.83 Administrative districts (Regierungsbezirke, Landkreis, etc.), A-Z (Table G6423 modified)
Apply Table G1 for subject (except .S1-.S7, historical geography)
Apply Table G6081.S for history
Franconia (1801-1975) see G1912.F7
Franconia (1976-) see G1912.22.F7

By region or country
Eastern Hemisphere. Eurasia, Africa, etc.
Europe
Central Europe
Germany
West Germany (Federal Republic of Germany)
Administrative districts (Länder, Regierungsbezirke, Bezirke, Landkreise, etc.)
Bavaria
Administrative districts (Regierungsbezirke, Landkreis, etc.), A-Z -- Continued

1923.83.O2 Oberpfalz [Regierungsbezirk]. Upper Palatinate [Duchy]
Subarrange by Table G1 except .S1-.S7, historical geography. For history, subarrange by G6081.S
For atlases of Lower and Upper Palatinate together see G1923.62.P3

Baden-Württemberg
Including Baden, Württemberg-Baden, Württemberg-Hohenzollern, Hohenzollern, Württemberg

1923.9 General
1923.91 By subject (Table G1 modified)
History
1923.91.S1 General
(1923.91.S12) This number not used
1923.91.S2 To 843
1923.91.S3 Medieval period, 843-1517
Modern period, 1517-
1923.91.S4 General
1923.91.S5 17th century
1923.91.S54 18th century
1923.91.S55 19th century
20th century
1923.91.S6 General
1923.91.S65 World War I
1923.91.S7 World War II
1923.91.S73 1945-
1923.92 Regions, natural features, etc., A-Z (Table G6427)
Apply Table G1 for subject (except .S1-.S7, historical geography)
Apply Table G6081.S for history

By region or country
Eastern Hemisphere. Eurasia, Africa, etc.
Europe
Central Europe
Germany
West Germany (Federal Republic of Germany)
Administrative districts (Länder, Regierungsbezirke, Bezirke, Landkreise, etc.)
Baden-Württemberg -- Continued

1923.93 Administrative districts (Regierungsbezirke, Landkreis, etc.), A-Z (Table G6428)
Apply Table G1 for subject (except .S1-.S7, historical geography)
Apply Table G6081.S for history

1924 Cities and towns, A-Z (Table G6299 modified)
Apply Table G1 for subject
Apply Table G6081.S for history
Including East German cities and towns

1924.L9 Lüneburg
Subarrange by Table G1 except .S1-.S7, historical geography. For history, subarrange by G6081.S

Austria-Hungary

1930 General

1931 By subject (Table G1)

(1931.S12) This number not used

Austria

1935 General

1936 By subject (Table G1)

1937 Regions, natural features, etc., A-Z (Table G6492)
Apply Table G1 for subject

1938 Bundesländer, etc., A-Z (Table G6493 modified)
Apply Table G1 for subject
Vienna see G1939.V4

1939 Cities and towns, etc., A-Z (Table G6494 modified)
Apply Table G1 for subject

1939.V4 Vienna
Subarrange by Table G1

Hungary

1940 General

1941 By subject (Table G1)

1942 Regions, natural features, etc., A-Z (Table G6502)
Apply Table G1 for subject

1943 Counties (Megyék), A-Z (Table G6503)
Apply Table G1 for subject

1944 Cities and towns, etc., A-Z (Table G6504)
Apply Table G1 for subject

By region or country
Eastern Hemisphere. Eurasia, Africa, etc.
Europe
Central Europe
Austria-Hungary -- Continued
Czechoslovakia. Czech Republic

1945 General
1946 By subject (Table G1 modified)
History
1946.S1 General
(1946.S12) This number not used
1946.S2 Early and medieval through 1526
1946.S3 16th-18th centuries
1946.S4 1789-1815
1946.S5 1815-1918
1946.S65 World War I
1946.S67 1918-1945
1946.S7 World War II
1946.S8 1945-
1947 Regions, natural features, etc., A-Z (Table G6512 modified)

Apply Table G1 for subject (except .S1-.S7, historical geography)

Apply Table G6511.S for history

1947.E7 Erzegebirge

Subarrange by Table G1 except .S1-.S7, historical geography. For history, subarrange by G6512.S

1948 Provinces, etc., A-Z (Table G6513)

Apply Table G1 for subject (except .S1-.S7, historical geography)

Apply Table G6511.S for history

1949 Cities and towns, etc., A-Z (Table G6514)

Apply Table G1 for subject (except .S1-.S7, historical geography)

Apply Table G6511.S for history

Slovakia
1949.5 General
1949.51 By subject (Table G1 modified)
History
1949.51.S1 General
(1949.51.S12) This number not used
1949.51.S2 Early and medieval through 1526
1949.51.S3 16th-18th centuries
1949.51.S4 1789-1815
1815-1918
1949.51.S5 General

By region or country
Eastern Hemisphere. Eurasia, Africa, etc.
Europe
Central Europe
Austria-Hungary
Slovakia
By subject
History
1815-1918 -- Continued
1949.51.S65 World War I
1918-1945
1949.51.S67 General
1949.51.S7 World War II
1949.51.S8 1945-
1949.52 Regions, natural features, etc., A-Z (Table G6517)
Apply Table G1 for subject (except .S1-.S7, historical geography)
Apply Table G6511.S for history
1949.53 Provinces, etc., A-Z (Table G6518)
Apply Table G1 for subject (except .S1-.S7, historical geography)
Apply Table G6511.S for history
1949.54 Cities and towns, etc., A-Z (Table G6519)
Apply Table G1 for subject (except .S1-.S7, historical geography)
Apply Table G6516.S for history
Poland
1950 General
1951 By subject (Table G1 modified)
History
1951.S1 General
(1951.S12) This number not used
1951.S2 Early to 1573
1951.S3 1573-1795
1951.S4 1795-1830
1951.S5 1830-1918
1951.S65 World War I
1951.S67 1918-1945
1951.S7 World War II
1951.S73 1945-
1952 Regions, natural features, etc., A-Z (Table G6522)
Apply Table G1 for subject (except .S1-.S7, historical geography)
Apply Table G6521.S for history

By region or country
Eastern Hemisphere. Eurasia, Africa, etc.
Europe
Central Europe
Poland -- Continued

1953 Voivodeships, A-Z (Table G6523)
Apply Table G1 for subject (except .S1-.S7, historical geography)
Apply Table G6521.S for history

1954 Cities and towns, etc., A-Z (Table G6524)
Apply Table G1 for subject (except .S1-.S7, historical geography)
Apply Table G6521.S for history

Southern Europe
1955 General
1956 By subject (Table G1)
1957 Regions, natural features, etc., A-Z (Table G6532)
Apply Table G1 for subject

Iberian Peninsula
1960 General
1961 By subject (Table G1)

Spanish Empire
Including atlases of Spanish colonies, etc., (Collectively)
Class individual colonies, etc. according to location, e.g., G2605+, Spanish Guinea

1963 General
1964 By subject (Table G1)

Spain
1965 General
1966 By subject (Table G1)
1967 Regions, natural features, etc., A-Z (Table G6562 modified)
Apply Table G1 for subject

Andalusia see G1968.A55

1967.B25 Balearic Islands
Subarrange by Table G1

Basque Provinces see G1968.P15

1967.C35 Castile
Subarrange by Table G1

1968 Administrative regions, provinces, kingdoms, etc., A-Z (Table G6563 modified)
Apply Table G1 for subject

1968.A55 Andalusia
Subarrange by Table G1

Baleares see G1967.B25

Castile [Kingdom] see G1967.C35

By region or country
Eastern Hemisphere. Eurasia, Africa, etc.
Europe
Southern Europe
Iberian Peninsula
Spain
Administrative regions, provinces, kingdoms, etc., A-Z -- Continued
Las Palmas see G2828.L3
1968.P15 País Vasco
Subarrange by Table G1
Palmas, Las see G2828.L3
1969 Cities and towns, etc., A-Z (Table G6564)
Apply Table G1 for subject
Andorra
1970 General
1971 By subject (Table G1)
1973 Portuguese Empire
Including atlases of Portuguese colonies, etc., (Collectively)
Class individual colonies, etc. according to location, e.g., G2550+, Mozambique
Portugal. Lusitania
1975 General
1976 By subject (Table G1)
1977 Regions, natural features, etc., A-Z (Table G6692)
Apply Table G1 for subject
1978 Provinces, districts, etc., A-Z (Table G6693 modified)
Apply Table G1 for subject
Angra do Heroismo see G2818.A5
Horta see G2818.H6
Ponta Delgada see G2818.P6
1979 Cities and towns, etc., A-Z (Table G6694)
Apply Table G1 for subject
Italian Empire. Roman Empire
Including atlases of Italian colonies, etc., (Collectively)
Class individual colonies, etc. according to location, e.g., G2515+, Somalia (Italian Somaliland)
1980 General
1981 By subject (Table G1)
Italy
By period
1983 15th-16th centuries
1984 17th-18th centuries
1801-1975
1985 General

By region or country
Eastern Hemisphere. Eurasia, Africa, etc.
Europe
Southern Europe
Italy
By period
1801-1975 -- Continued

1986 By subject (Table G1)

1987 Regions, natural features, etc., A-Z (Table G6712)
Apply Table G1 for subject

1988 Regioni, etc., A-Z (Table G6713 modified)
Apply Table G1 for subject
Vatican see G1989.R7:3V3

1989 Cities and towns, etc., A-Z (Table G6714 modified)
Apply Table G1 for subject

1989.R7:3V3 Vatican City
Subarrange by Table G1

1976-

1989.2 General

1989.21 By subject (Table G1)

1989.22 Regions, natural features, etc., A-Z (Table G6712)
Apply Table G1 for subject

1989.23 Regioni, etc., A-Z (Table G6713 modified)
Apply Table G1 for subject
Vatican see G1989.24.R7:3V3

1989.24 Cities and towns, etc., A-Z (Table G6714 modified)
Apply Table G1 for subject

1989.24.R7:3V3 Vatican City
Subarrange by Table G1

Sicily

1989.3 General

1989.31 By subject (Table G1)

1989.32 Regions, natural features, etc., A-Z (Table G6762)
Apply Table G1 for subject

1989.33 Provinces, etc., A-Z (Table G6763)
Apply Table G1 for subject

Sardinia

1989.5 General

1989.51 By subject (Table G1)

1989.52 Regions, natural features, etc., A-Z (Table G6772)
Apply Table G1 for subject

1989.53 Provinces, etc., A-Z (Table G6773)
Apply Table G1 for subject

By region or country
Eastern Hemisphere. Eurasia, Africa, etc.
Europe
Southern Europe -- Continued
San Marino
1990 General
1991 By subject (Table G1)
Malta
1992.3 General
1992.31 By subject (Table G1)
1992.32 Regions, natural features, etc., A-Z (Table G6792)
Apply Table G1 for subject
1992.34 Cities and towns, etc., A-Z (Table G6794)
Apply Table G1 for subject
Southeastern Europe
1993 General
1994 By subject
1994.5 By region, natural feature, etc., A-Z
Balkan Peninsula
1995 General
1996 By subject (Table G1)
1997 Regions, natural features, etc., A-Z (Table G6802)
Apply Table G1 for subject
Greece
2000 General
2001 By subject (Table G1)
2002 Regions, natural features, etc., A-Z (Table G6812)
Apply Table G1 for subject
2003 Provinces (Nomoi), etc., A-Z (Table G6813)
Apply Table G1 for subject
2004 Cities and towns, etc., A-Z (Table G6814)
Apply Table G1 for subject
Albania
2005 General
2006 By subject (Table G1)
2007 Regions, natural features, etc., A-Z (Table G6832)
Apply Table G1 for subject
2008 Districts (Rrethi), etc., A-Z (Table G6833)
Apply Table G1 for subject
2009 Cities and towns, etc., A-Z (Table G6834)
Apply Table G1 for subject
Former Yugoslav republics. Yugoslavia
2010 General
2011 By subject (Table G1 modified)
History
2011.S1 General
(2011.S12) This number not used

By region or country
Eastern Hemisphere. Eurasia, Africa, etc.
Europe
Southeastern Europe
Balkan Peninsula
Former Yugoslav republics. Yugoslavia
By subject
History -- Continued

2011.S2 To 1800
2011.S4 19th century
2011.S6 20th century
2011.S65 World War I
2011.S67 1918-1941
2011.S7 World War II
2011.S73 1945-1992
2012 Regions, natural features, etc., A-Z (Table G6842)
Apply Table G1 for subject (except .S1-.S7, historical geography)
Apply Table G6841.S for history

Macedonia (Republic)
2014.5 General
2014.51 By subject (Table G1 modified)
History
2014.51.S1 General
(2014.51.S12) This number not used
2014.51.S2 To 1800
2014.51.S4 19th century
2014.51.S6 20th century
2014.51.S65 World War I
2014.51.S67 1918-1941
2014.51.S7 World War II
2014.51.S73 1945-1992
2014.52 Regions, natural features, etc., A-Z (Table G6847)
Apply Table G1 for subject (except .S1-.S7, historical geography)
Apply Table G6841.S for history
2014.54 Cities and towns, tc., A-Z (Table G6849)
Apply Table G1 for subject (except .S1-.S7, historical geography)
Apply Table G6841.S for history

Serbia
2015 General
2016 By subject (Table G1 modified)
History
2016.S1 General
(2016.S12) This number not used
2016.S2 To 1800

By region or country
Eastern Hemisphere. Eurasia, Africa, etc.
Europe
Southeastern Europe
Balkan Peninsula
Serbia
By subject
History -- Continued

2016.S4 19th century
2016.S6 20th century
2016.S65 World War I
2016.S67 1918-1941
2016.S7 World War II
2016.S73 1945-1992
2017 Regions, natural features, etc., A-Z (Table G6852)
Apply Table G1 for subject (except .S1-.S7, historical geography)
Apply Table G6841.S for history
2018 Administrative areas, provinces, etc., A-Z (Table G6853)
Apply Table G1 for subject (except .S1-.S7, historical geography)
Apply Table G6841.S for history
2019 Cities and towns, etc., A-Z (Table G6854)
Apply Table G1 for subject (except .S1-.S7, historical geography)
Apply Table G6841.S for history

Montenegro (Crna Gora)

2020 General
2021 By subject (Table G1 modified)
History
2021.S1 General
(2021.S12) This number not used
2021.S2 To 1800
2021.S4 19th century
2021.S6 20th century
2021.S65 World War I
2021.S67 1918-1941
2021.S7 World War II
2021.S73 1945-1992
2022 Regions, natural features, etc., A-Z (Table G6857)
Apply Table G1 for subject (except .S1-.S7, historical geography)
Apply Table G6841.S for history

By region or country
Eastern Hemisphere. Eurasia, Africa, etc.
Europe
Southeastern Europe
Balkan Peninsula
Montenegro (Crna Gora) -- Continued
2024 Cities and towns, etc., A-Z (Table G6859)
Apply Table G1 for subject (except .S1-.S7, historical geography)
Apply Table G6841.S for history
Bosnia and Hercegovina
2024.5 General
2024.51 By subject (Table G1 modified)
History
2024.51.S1 General
(2024.51.S12) This number not used
2024.51.S2 To 1800
2024.51.S4 19th century
2024.51.S6 20th century
2024.51.S65 World War I
2024.51.S67 1918-1941
2024.51.S7 World War II
2024.51.S73 1945-1992
2024.52 Regions, natural features, etc., A-Z (Table G6862)
Apply Table G1 for subject (except .S1-.S7, historical geography)
Apply Table G6841.S for history
2024.54 Cities and towns, etc., A-Z (Table G6864)
Apply Table G1 for subject (except .S1-.S7, historical geography)
Apply Table G6841.S for history
(2025-2027) Dalmatia
see G2032
Croatia (Hrvatska)
2030 General
2031 By subject (Table G1)
History
2031.S1 General
(2031.S12) This number not used
2031.S2 To 1800
2031.S4 19th century
2031.S6 20th century
2031.S65 World War I
2031.S67 1918-1941
2031.S7 World War II
2031.S73 1945-1992

By region or country
Eastern Hemisphere. Eurasia, Africa, etc.
Europe
Southeastern Europe
Balkan Peninsula
Croatia (Hrvatska) -- Continued

2032 Regions, natural features, etc., A-Z (Table G6872)
Apply Table G1 for subject (except .S1-.S7, historical geography)
Apply Table G6841.S for history

2033 Administrative divisions, A-Z (Table G6873)
Apply Table G1 for subject (except .S1-.S7, historical geography)
Apply Table G6841.S for history

2034 Cities and towns, etc., A-Z (Table G6874)
Apply Table G1 for subject (except .S1-.S7, historical geography)
Apply Table G6841.S for history

Slovenia

2034.5 General
2034.51 By subject (Table G1 modified)
History
2034.51.S1 General
(2034.51.S12) This number not used
2034.51.S2 To 1800
2034.51.S4 19th century
2034.51.S6 20th century
2034.51.S65 World War I
2034.51.S67 1918-1941
2034.51.S7 World War II
2034.51.S73 1945-1992

2034.52 Regions, natural features, etc., A-Z (Table G6877)
Apply Table G1 for subject (except .S1-.S7, historical geography)
Apply Table G6841.S for history

2034.53 Administrative divisions, A-Z (Table G6878)
Apply Table G1 for subject (except .S1-.S7, historical geography)
Apply Table G6841.S for history

2034.54 Cities and towns, etc., A-Z (Table G6879)
Apply Table G1 for subject (except .S1-.S7, historical geography)
Apply Table G6841.S for history

Romania

2035 General
2036 By subject (Table G1)

By region or country
Eastern Hemisphere. Eurasia, Africa, etc.
Europe
Southeastern Europe
Balkan Peninsula
Romania -- Continued
2037 Regions, natural features, etc., A-Z (Table G6882)
Apply Table G1 for subject
2038 Provinces, etc., A-Z (Table G6888)
Apply Table G1 for subject
2039 Cities and towns, etc., A-Z (Table G6884)
Apply Table G1 for subject
Bulgaria
2040 General
2041 By subject (Table G1)
2042 Regions, natural features, etc., A-Z (Table G6892)
Apply Table G1 for subject
2043 Provinces, etc., A-Z (Table G6893)
Apply Table G1 for subject
2044 Cities and towns, etc., A-Z (Table G6894)
Apply Table G1 for subject
Scandinavia. Northern Europe
2050 General
2051 By subject (Table G1)
2052 Regions, natural features, etc., A-Z (Table G6912)
Apply Table G1 for subject
Denmark and colonies
Including atlases of Danish colonies, etc., (Collectively)
Class individual colonies, etc., according to location, e.g., G1110+, Greenland
2053 General
2054 By subject (Table G1)
Denmark
2055 General
2056 By subject (Table G1)
2057 Regions, natural features, etc., A-Z (Table G6922)
Apply Table G1 for subject
2058 Provinces (Amter), etc., A-Z (Table G6923)
Apply Table G1 for subject
2059 Cities and towns, etc., A-Z (Table G6924)
Apply Table G1 for subject
Faeroe Islands
2059.2 General
2059.21 By subject (Table G1)
Iceland
2060 General
2061 By subject (Table G1)

By region or country
Eastern Hemisphere. Eurasia, Africa, etc.
Europe
Scandinavia. Northern Europe
Iceland -- Continued

2062 Regions, natural features, etc., A-Z (Table G6932)
Apply Table G1 for subject

2063 Provinces (Sýsler), kjördæmi, etc., A-Z (Table G6933)
Apply Table G1 for subject

2064 Cities and towns, etc., A-Z (Table G6934)
Apply Table G1 for subject

Norway

2065 General

2066 By subject (Table G1)

2067 Regions, natural features, etc., A-Z (Table G6942)
Apply Table G1 for subject

2068 Counties (Fylker), etc., A-Z (Table G6943 modified)
Apply Table G1 for subject
Bergen see G2069.B4
Oslo see G2069.O9
Oslo (Vigelandsparken) see G2069.O9:2V5
Oslo (Aker) see G2069.O9:3A3

2069 Cities and towns, etc., A-Z (Table G6944 modified)
Apply Table G1 for subject

2069.B4 Bergen
Subarrange by Table G1

2069.O9 Oslo
Subarrange by Table G1

2069.O9:2V5 Vigelandsparken [Oslo]
Subarrange by Table G1

2069.O9:3A3 Aker [Oslo]
Subarrange by Table G1

Sweden

2070 General

2071 By subject (Table G1)

2072 Regions, natural features, etc., A-Z (Table G6952)
Apply Table G1 for subject

2073 Provinces (Länni), etc., A-Z (Table G6953)
Apply Table G1 for subject

2074 Cities and towns, etc., A-Z (Table G6954)
Apply Table G1 for subject

Finland. Suomi

2075 General

2076 By subject (Table G1)

By region or country
Eastern Hemisphere. Eurasia, Africa, etc.
Europe
Scandinavia. Northern Europe
Finland. Suomi -- Continued

2077 Regions, natural features, etc., A-Z (Table G6962 modified)
Apply Table G1 for subject
2077.A2 Aland
Subarrange by Table G1
2077.A23 Aland Sea
Subarrange by Table G1
2078 Departments, etc., A-Z (Table G6963 modified)
Apply Table G1 for subject
Ahvenanmaa see G2077.A2
Ahvenanmaa (Aland Sea) see G2077.A23
2079 Cities and towns, etc., A-Z (Table G6964)
Apply Table G1 for subject

Eastern Europe
Includes Poland, Finland, Baltic States, European Russia, Romania, Bulgaria
2080 General
2081 By subject (Table G1)
2082 Regions, natural features, etc., A-Z (Table G6967)
Apply Table G1 for subject
Baltic States see G2120+
Estonia see G2125+
Latvia see G2130+
Lithuania see G2135+

Former Soviet republics. Union of Soviet Socialist Republics (U.S.S.R.). Russia (Empire)
2110 General
2111 By subject (Table G1 modified)
History
2111.S1 General
(2111.S12) This number not used
2111.S2 Early through 1613
2111.S3 17th century
2111.S4 18th century
2111.S5 1801-1917
2111.S54 Crimean War
2111.S57 Rebellion, 1905-1907
2111.S65 World War I
2111.S67 1917-1921
2111.S68 1921-1945
2111.S7 World War II
2111.S72 1945-1991

By region or country
Eastern Hemisphere. Eurasia, Africa, etc.
Europe
Former Soviet republics. Union of Soviet Socialist Republics (U.S.S.R.). Russia (Empire)
By subject
History -- Continued
2111.S75 1991-
2112 Regions, natural features, etc., A-Z (Table G7002 modified)
Apply Table G1 for subject (except .S1-.S7, historical geography)
Apply Table G7001.S for history
Ural Mountains see G2142.U7
(2114) Cities and towns etc., A-Z
see G2144 and other former Soviet republics
Former Soviet republics (Europe). European U.S.S.R. European Russia (Empire)
2115 General
2116 By subject (Table G1 modified)
History
2116.S1 General
(2116.S12) This number not used
2116.S2 Early through 1613
2116.S3 17th century
2116.S4 18th century
2116.S5 1801-1917
2116.S54 Crimean War
2116.S57 Rebellion, 1905-1907
2116.S65 World War I
2116.S67 1917-1921
2116.S68 1921-1945
2116.S7 World War II
2116.S72 1945-1991
2116.S75 1991-
2117 Regions, natural features, etc., A-Z (Table G7012)
Apply Table G1 for subject (except .S1-.S7, historical geography)
Apply Table G7001.S for history
Baltic States
Estonia
2125 General
2126 By subject (Table G1 modified)
History
2126.S1 General
(2126.S12) This number not used
2126.S2 Early through 1613

By region or country
Eastern Hemisphere. Eurasia, Africa, etc.
Europe
Former Soviet republics (Europe). European U.S.S.R.
European Russia (Empire)
Baltic States
Estonia
By subject
History -- Continued

2126.S3 17th century
2126.S4 18th century
2126.S5 1801-1917
2126.S54 Crimean War
2126.S57 Rebellion, 1905-1907
2126.S65 World War I
2126.S67 1917-1921
2126.S68 1921-1945
2126.S7 World War II
2126.S72 1945-1991
2126.S75 1991-
2127 Regions, natural features, etc., A-Z (Table G7032)
Apply Table G1 for subject (except .S1-.S7, historical geography)
Apply Table G7001.S for history
2128 Administrative divisions, A-Z (Table G7033)
Apply Table G1 for subject (except .S1-.S7, historical geography)
Apply Table G7001.S for history
2129 Cities and towns, etc., A-Z (Table G7034)
Apply Table G1 for subject (except .S1-.S7, historical geography)
Apply Table G7001.S for history

Latvia
2130 General
2131 By subject (Table G1 modified)
History
2131.S1 General
(2131.S12) This number not used
2131.S2 Early through 1613
2131.S3 17th century
2131.S4 18th century
2131.S5 1801-1917
2131.S54 Crimean War
2131.S57 Rebellion, 1905-1907
2131.S65 World War I
2131.S67 1917-1921
2131.S68 1921-1945

By region or country
Eastern Hemisphere. Eurasia, Africa, etc.
Europe
Former Soviet republics (Europe). European U.S.S.R.
European Russia (Empire)
Baltic States
Latvia
By subject
History
1921-1945 -- Continued

2131.S7 World War II
2131.S72 1945-1991
2131.S75 1991-
2132 Regions, natural features, etc., A-Z (Table G7042)
Apply Table G1 for subject (except .S1-.S7, historical geography)
Apply Table G7001.S for history
2133 Administrative divisions, A-Z (Table G7043)
Apply Table G1 for subject (except .S1-.S7, historical geography)
Apply Table G7001.S for history
2134 Cities and towns, etc., A-Z (Table G7044)
Apply Table G1 for subject (except .S1-.S7, historical geography)
Apply Table G7001.S for history

Lithuania

2135 General
2136 By subject (Table G1 modified)
History
2136.S1 General
(2136.S12) This number not used
2136.S2 Early through 1613
2136.S3 17th century
2136.S4 18th century
2136.S5 1801-1917
2136.S54 Crimean War
2136.S57 Rebellion, 1905-1907
2136.S65 World War I
2136.S67 1917-1921
2136.S68 1921-1945
2136.S7 World War II
2136.S72 1945-1991
2136.S75 1991-
2137 Regions, natural features, etc., A-Z (Table G7052)
Apply Table G1 for subject (except .S1-.S7, historical geography)
Apply Table G7001.S for history

By region or country
Eastern Hemisphere. Eurasia, Africa, etc.
Europe
Former Soviet republics (Europe). European U.S.S.R. European Russia (Empire)
Baltic States
Lithuania -- Continued

2138 Administrative divisions, A-Z (Table G7053)
Apply Table G1 for subject (except .S1-.S7, historical geography)
Apply Table G7001.S for history

2139 Cities and towns, etc., A-Z (Table G7054)
Apply Table G1 for subject (except .S1-.S7, historical geography)
Apply Table G7001.S for history

Russia (Federation). Russian Soviet Federated Socialist Republic (R.S.F.S.R.)

2140 General
2141 By subject (Table G1 modified)
History
2141.S1 General
(2141.S12) This number not used
2141.S2 Early through 1613
2141.S3 17th century
2141.S4 18th century
2141.S5 1801-1917
2141.S54 Crimean War
2141.S57 Rebellion, 1905-1907
2141.S65 World War I
2141.S67 1917-1921
2141.S68 1921-1945
2141.S7 World War II
2141.S72 1945-1991
2141.S75 1991-

2142 Regions, natural features, etc., A-Z (Table G7062 modified)
Apply Table G1 for subject (except .S1-.S7, historical geography)
Apply Table G7001.S for history

2142.U7 Ural Mountains
Subarrange by Table G1 except .S1-.S7, historical geography. For history, subarrange by Table G7001.S

2143 European administrative divisions, A-Z (Table G7063)
Apply Table G1 for subject (except .S1-.S7, historical geography)
Apply Table G7001.S for history

By region or country
Eastern Hemisphere. Eurasia, Africa, etc.
Europe
Russia (Federation). Russian Soviet Federated Socialist Republic (R.S.F.S.R.) -- Continued

2144 Cities and towns, etc., A-Z (Table G7064)
Apply Table G1 for subject (except .S1-.S7, historical geography)
Apply Table G7001.S for history

Belarus. Belorussia. White Russia

2145 General
2146 By subject (Table G1 modified)
History
2146.S1 General
(2146.S12) This number not used
2146.S2 Early through 1613
2146.S3 17th century
2146.S4 18th century
2146.S5 1801-1917
2146.S54 Crimean War
2146.S57 Rebellion, 1905-1907
2146.S65 World War I
2146.S67 1917-1921
2146.S68 1921-1945
2146.S7 World War II
2146.S72 1945-1991
2146.S75 1991-
2147 Regions, natural features, etc., A-Z (Table G7092)
Apply Table G1 for subject (except .S1-.S7, historical geography)
Apply Table G7001.S for history
2148 Administrative divisions, A-Z (Table G7093)
Apply Table G1 for subject (except .S1-.S7, historical geography)
Apply Table G7001.S for history
2149 Cities and towns, etc., A-Z (Table G7094)
Apply Table G1 for subject (except .S1-.S7, historical geography)
Apply Table G7001.S for history

Ukraine

2150 General
2151 By subject (Table G1 modified)
History
2151.S1 General
(2151.S12) This number not used
2151.S2 Early through 1613
2151.S3 17th century

By region or country
Eastern Hemisphere. Eurasia, Africa, etc.
Europe
Ukraine
By subject
History -- Continued

2151.S4 18th century
2151.S5 1801-1917
2151.S54 Crimean War
2151.S57 Rebellion, 1905-1907
2151.S65 World War I
2151.S67 1917-1921
2151.S68 1921-1945
2151.S7 World War II
2151.S72 1945-1991
2151.S75 1991-
2152 Regions, natural features, etc., A-Z (Table G7102)
Apply Table G1 for subject (except .S1-.S7, historical geography)
Apply Table G7001.S for history
2153 Administrative divisions, A-Z (Table G7103)
Apply Table G1 for subject (except .S1-.S7, historical geography)
Apply Table G7001.S for history
2154 Cities and towns, etc., A-Z (Table G7104)
Apply Table G1 for subject (except .S1-.S7, historical geography)
Apply Table G7001.S for history

Moldova. Moldavian S.S.R.

2155 General
2156 By subject (Table G1 modified)
History
2156.S1 General
(2156.S12) This number not used
2156.S2 Early through 1613
2156.S3 17th century
2156.S4 18th century
2156.S5 1801-1917
2156.S54 Crimean War
2156.S57 Rebellion, 1905-1907
2156.S65 World War I
2156.S67 1917-1921
2156.S68 1921-1945
2156.S7 World War II
2156.S72 1945-1991
2156.S75 1991-

By region or country
Eastern Hemisphere. Eurasia, Africa, etc.
Europe
Moldova. Moldavian S.S.R. -- Continued

2157 Regions, natural features, etc., A-Z (Table G7112)
Apply Table G1 for subject (except .S1-.S7, historical geography)
Apply Table G7001.S for history

2158 Administrative divisions, A-Z (Table G7113)

2159 Cities and towns, etc., A-Z (Table G7114)
Apply Table G1 for subject (except .S1-.S7, historical geography)
Apply Table G7001.S for history

Former Soviet republics in Asia. U.S.S.R. in Asia.
Russia (Empire) in Asia

2160 General

2161 By subject (Table G1 modified)
History
2161.S1 General
(2161.S12) This number not used
2161.S2 Early through 1613
2161.S3 17th century
2161.S4 18th century
2161.S5 1801-1917
2161.S54 Crimean War
2161.S57 Rebellion, 1905-1907
2161.S65 World War I
2161.S67 1917-1921
2161.S68 1921-1945
2161.S7 World War II
2161.S72 1945-1991
2161.S75 1991-

Transcaucasia

2163.5 General

2163.51 By subject (Table G1 modified)
History
2163.51.S1 General
(2163.51.S12) This number not used
2163.51.S2 Early through 1613
2163.51.S3 17th century
2163.51.S4 18th century
2163.51.S5 1801-1917
2163.51.S54 Crimean War
2163.51.S57 Rebellion, 1905-1907
2163.51.S65 World War I
2163.51.S67 1917-1921
2163.51.S68 1921-1945

By region or country
Eastern Hemisphere. Eurasia, Africa, etc.
Europe
Former Soviet republics in Asia. U.S.S.R. in Asia.
Russia (Empire) in Asia
Transcaucasia
By subject
History
1921-1945 -- Continued

2163.51.S7 World War II
2163.51.S72 1945-1991
2163.51.S75 1991-
2163.52 Regions, natural features, etc., A-Z (Table G7122)
Apply Table G1 for subject (except .S1-.S7, historical geography)
Apply Table G7001.S for history

Georgia (Republic)
2164.2 General
2164.21 By subject (Table G1 modified)
History
2164.21.S1 General
(2164.21.S12) This number not used
2164.21.S2 Early through 1613
2164.21.S3 17th century
2164.21.S4 18th century
2164.21.S5 1801-1917
2164.21.S54 Crimean War
2164.21.S57 Rebellion, 1905-1907
2164.21.S65 World War I
2164.21.S67 1917-1921
2164.21.S68 1921-1945
2164.21.S7 World War II
2164.21.S72 1945-1991
2164.21.S75 1991-
2164.22 Regions, natural features, etc., A-Z (Table G7132)
Apply Table G1 for subject (except .S1-.S7, historical geography)
Apply Table G7001.S for history
2164.23 Administrative divisions, A-Z (Table G7133)
Apply Table G1 for subject (except .S1-.S7, historical geography)
Apply Table G7001.S for history
2164.24 Cities and towns, etc., A-Z (Table G7134)
Apply Table G1 for subject (except .S1-.S7, historical geography)
Apply Table G7001.S for history

Azerbaijan

By region or country
Eastern Hemisphere. Eurasia, Africa, etc.
Europe
Former Soviet republics in Asia. U.S.S.R. in Asia.
Russia (Empire) in Asia
Transcaucasia
Azerbaijan -- Continued

2164.4	General
2164.41	By subject (Table G1 modified)
	History
2164.41.S1	General
(2164.41.S12)	This number not used
2164.41.S2	Early through 1613
2164.41.S3	17th century
2164.41.S4	18th century
2164.41.S5	1801-1917
2164.41.S54	Crimean War
2164.41.S57	Rebellion, 1905-1907
2164.41.S65	World War I
2164.41.S67	1917-1921
2164.41.S68	1921-1945
2164.41.S7	World War II
2164.41.S72	1945-1991
2164.41.S75	1991-
2164.42	Regions, natural features, etc., A-Z (Table G7142) *Apply Table G1 for subject (except .S1-.S7, historical geography)* *Apply Table G7001.S for history*
2164.43	Administrative divisions, A-Z (Table G7143) *Apply Table G1 for subject (except .S1-.S7, historical geography)* *Apply Table G7001.S for history*
2164.44	Cities and towns, etc., A-Z (Table G7144) *Apply Table G1 for subject (except .S1-.S7, historical geography)* *Apply Table G7001.S for history*
	Armenia (Republic)
2164.6	General
2164.61	By subject (Table G1 modified)
	History
2164.61.S1	General
(2164.61.S12)	This number not used
2164.61.S2	Early through 1613
2164.61.S3	17th century
2164.61.S4	18th century
2164.61.S5	1801-1917
2164.61.S54	Crimean War

By region or country
Eastern Hemisphere. Eurasia, Africa, etc.
Europe
Former Soviet republics in Asia. U.S.S.R. in Asia.
Russia (Empire) in Asia
Transcaucasia
Armenia (Republic)
By subject
History
1801-1917 -- Continued
2164.61.S57 Rebellion, 1905-1907
2164.61.S65 World War I
2164.61.S67 1917-1921
2164.61.S68 1921-1945
2164.61.S7 World War II
2164.61.S72 1945-1991
2164.61.S75 1991-
2164.64 Cities and towns, etc., A-Z (Table G7154)
Apply Table G1 for subject (except .S1-.S7, historical geography)
Apply Table G7001.S for history
Former Soviet Central Asia. Russian Central Asia. West Turkestan
Cf. G2202.2+ Central Asia
2165 General
2166 By subject (Table G1 modified)
History
2166.S1 General
(2166.S12) This number not used
2166.S2 Early through 1613
2166.S3 17th century
2166.S4 18th century
2166.S5 1801-1917
2166.S54 Crimean War
2166.S57 Rebellion, 1905-1907
2166.S65 World War I
2166.S67 1917-1921
2166.S68 1921-1945
2166.S7 World War II
2166.S72 1945-1991
2166.S75 1991-
2167 Regions, natural features, etc., A-Z (Table G7212)
Apply Table G1 for subject (except .S1-.S7, historical geography)
Apply Table G7001.S for history
Kazakhstan. Kazakh S.S.R.
2168.1 General

By region or country
Eastern Hemisphere. Eurasia, Africa, etc.
Europe
Former Soviet republics in Asia. U.S.S.R. in Asia.
Russia (Empire) in Asia
Former Soviet Central Asia. Russian Central Asia.
West Turkestan
Kazakhstan. Kazakh S.S.R. -- Continued

2168.11 By subject (Table G1 modified)
History
2168.11.S1 General
(2168.11.S12) This number not used
2168.11.S2 Early through 1613
2168.11.S3 17th century
2168.11.S4 18th century
2168.11.S5 1801-1917
2168.11.S54 Crimean War
2168.11.S57 Rebellion, 1905-1907
2168.11.S65 World War I
2168.11.S67 1917-1921
2168.11.S68 1921-1945
2168.11.S7 World War II
2168.11.S72 1945-1991
2168.11.S75 1991-
2168.12 Regions, natural features, etc., A-Z (Table G7222)
Apply Table G1 for subject (except .S1-.S7, historical geography)
Apply Table G7001.S for history
2168.13 Administrative divisions, A-Z (Table G7223)
Apply Table G1 for subject (except .S1-.S7, historical geography)
Apply Table G7001.S for history
2168.14 Cities and towns, etc., A-Z (Table G7224)
Apply Table G1 for subject (except .S1-.S7, historical geography)
Apply Table G7001.S for history
Uzbekistan. Uzbek S.S.R.
2168.3 General
2168.31 By subject (Table G1 modified)
History
2168.31.S1 General
(2168.31.S12) This number not used
2168.31.S2 Early through 1613
2168.31.S3 17th century
2168.31.S4 18th century
2168.31.S5 1801-1917
2168.31.S54 Crimean War

By region or country
Eastern Hemisphere. Eurasia, Africa, etc.
Europe
Former Soviet republics in Asia. U.S.S.R. in Asia. Russia (Empire) in Asia
Former Soviet Central Asia. Russian Central Asia. West Turkestan
Uzbekistan. Uzbek S.S.R.
By subject
History
1801-1917 -- Continued

2168.31.S57 Rebellion, 1905-1907
2168.31.S65 World War I
2168.31.S67 1917-1921
2168.31.S68 1921-1945
2168.31.S7 World War II
2168.31.S72 1945-1991
2168.31.S75 1991-
2168.32 Regions, natural features, etc., A-Z (Table G7232)
Apply Table G1 for subject (except .S1-.S7, historical geography)
Apply Table G7001.S for history
2168.33 Administrative divisions, A-Z (Table G7233)
Apply Table G1 for subject (except .S1-.S7, historical geography)
Apply Table G7001.S for history
2168.34 Cities and towns, etc., A-Z (Table G7234)
Apply Table G1 for subject (except .S1-.S7, historical geography)
Apply Table G7001.S for history

Turkmenistan. Turkmen S.S.R.

2168.5 General
2168.51 By subject (Table G1 modified)
History
2168.51.S1 General
(2168.51.S12) This number not used
2168.51.S2 Early through 1613
2168.51.S3 17th century
2168.51.S4 18th century
2168.51.S5 1801-1917
2168.51.S54 Crimean War
2168.51.S57 Rebellion, 1905-1907
2168.51.S65 World War I
2168.51.S67 1917-1921
2168.51.S68 1921-1945
2168.51.S7 World War II
2168.51.S72 1945-1991

By region or country
Eastern Hemisphere. Eurasia, Africa, etc.
Europe
Former Soviet republics in Asia. U.S.S.R. in Asia. Russia (Empire) in Asia
Former Soviet Central Asia. Russian Central Asia. West Turkestan
Turkmenistan. Turkmen S.S.R.
By subject
History -- Continued

2168.51.S75 1991-
2168.53 Administrative divisions, A-Z (Table G7243)
Apply Table G1 for subject (except .S1-.S7, historical geography)
Apply Table G7001.S1 for history
2168.54 Cities and towns, etc., A-Z (Table G7244)
Apply Table G1 for subject (except .S1-.S7, historical geography)
Apply Table G7001.S1 for history

Kyrgyzstan. Kirghiz S.S.R.
2168.7 General
2168.71 By subject (Table G1 modified)
History
2168.71.S1 General
(2168.71.S12) This number not used
2168.71.S2 Early through 1613
2168.71.S3 17th century
2168.71.S4 18th century
2168.71.S5 1801-1917
2168.71.S54 Crimean War
2168.71.S57 Rebellion, 1905-1907
2168.71.S65 World War I
2168.71.S67 1917-1921
2168.71.S68 1921-1945
2168.71.S7 World War II
2168.71.S72 1945-1991
2168.71.S75 1991-
2168.72 Regions, natural features, etc., A-Z (Table G7252)
Apply Table G1 for subject (except .S1-.S7, historical geography)
Apply Table G7001.S for history
2168.73 Administrative divisions, A-Z (Table G7253)
Apply Table G1 for subject (except .S1-.S7, historical geography)
Apply Table G7001.S for history

By region or country
Eastern Hemisphere. Eurasia, Africa, etc.
Europe
Former Soviet republics in Asia. U.S.S.R. in Asia.
Russia (Empire) in Asia
Former Soviet Central Asia. Russian Central Asia.
West Turkestan
Kyrgyzstan. Kirghiz S.S.R. -- Continued

2168.74 Cities and towns, etc., A-Z (Table G7254)
Apply Table G1 for subject (except .S1-.S7, historical geography)
Apply Table G7001.S for history

Tajikistan. Tajik S.S.R.

2168.9 General
2168.91 By subject (Table G1 modified)
History
2168.91.S1 General
(2168.91.S12) This number not used
2168.91.S2 Early through 1613
2168.91.S3 17th century
2168.91.S4 18th century
2168.91.S5 1801-1917
2168.91.S54 Crimean War
2168.91.S57 Rebellion, 1905-1907
2168.91.S65 World War I
2168.91.S67 1917-1921
2168.91.S68 1921-1945
2168.91.S7 World War II
2168.91.S72 1945-1991
2168.91.S75 1991-
2168.92 Regions, natural features, etc., A-Z (Table G7262)
Apply Table G1 for subject (except .S1-.S7, historical geography)
Apply Table G7001.S for history
2168.93 Administrative divisions, A-Z (Table G7263)
Apply Table G1 for subject (except .S1-.S7, historical geography)
Apply Table G7001.S for history
2168.94 Cities and towns, etc., A-Z (Table G7264)
Apply Table G1 for subject (except .S1-.S7, historical geography)
Apply Table G7001.S for history

Siberia. Northern Asia

2170 General
2171 By subject (Table G1 modified)
History
2171.S1 General

By region or country
Eastern Hemisphere. Eurasia, Africa, etc.
Europe
Former Soviet republics in Asia. U.S.S.R. in Asia.
Russia (Empire) in Asia
Siberia. Northern Asia
By subject
History -- Continued

(2171.S12) This number not used
2171.S2 Early through 1613
2171.S3 17th century
2171.S4 18th century
2171.S5 1801-1917
2171.S54 Crimean War
2171.S57 Rebellion, 1905-1907
2171.S65 World War I
2171.S67 1917-1921
2171.S68 1921-1945
2171.S7 World War II
2171.S72 1945-1991
2171.S75 1991-
2172 Regions, natural features, etc., A-Z (Table G7272)
Apply Table G1 for subject (except .S1-.S7, historical geography)
Apply Table G7001.S for history
2173 Administrative divisions, A-Z (Table G7273)
Apply Table G1 for subject (except .S1-.S7, historical geography)
Apply Table G7001.S for history

Buriat͡iia. Buryat-Mongol A.S.S.R.

2175.5 General
2175.51 By subject (Table G1 modified)
History
2175.51.S1 General
(2175.51.S12) This number not used
2175.51.S2 Early through 1613
2175.51.S3 17th century
2175.51.S4 18th century
2175.51.S5 1801-1917
2175.51.S54 Crimean War
2175.51.S57 Rebellion, 1905-1907
2175.51.S65 World War I
2175.51.S67 1917-1921
2175.51.S68 1921-1945
2175.51.S7 World War II
2175.51.S72 1945-1991
2175.51.S75 1991-

By region or country
Eastern Hemisphere. Eurasia, Africa, etc.
Europe
Former Soviet republics in Asia. U.S.S.R. in Asia.
Russia (Empire) in Asia
Buri͡atii͡a. Buryat-Mongol A.S.S.R.

2175.52 Regions, natural features, etc., A-Z (Table G7302)
Apply Table G1 for subject (except .S1-.S7, historical geography)
Apply Table G7001.S for history

Yakutia

2177.5 General
2177.51 By subject (Table G1 modified)
History
2177.51.S1 General
(2177.51.S12) This number not used
2177.51.S2 Early through 1613
2177.51.S3 17th century
2177.51.S4 18th century
2177.51.S5 1801-1917
2177.51.S54 Crimean War
2177.51.S57 Rebellion, 1905-1907
2177.51.S65 World War I
2177.51.S67 1917-1921
2177.51.S68 1921-1945
2177.51.S7 World War II
2177.51.S72 1945-1991
2177.51.S75 1991-
2177.52 Regions, natural features, etc., A-Z (Table G7312)
Apply Table G1 for subject (except .S1-.S7, historical geography)
Apply Table G7001.S for history

Russian Far East. Far Eastern Republic.
Dal'nevostochnii kraĭ

2180 General
2181 By subject (Table G1 modified)
History
2181.S1 General
(2181.S12) This number not used
2181.S2 Early through 1613
2181.S3 17th century
2181.S4 18th century
2181.S5 1801-1917
2181.S54 Crimean War
2181.S57 Rebellion, 1905-1907
2181.S65 World War I
2181.S67 1917-1921

By region or country
Eastern Hemisphere. Eurasia, Africa, etc.
Europe
Former Soviet republics in Asia. U.S.S.R. in Asia.
Russia (Empire) in Asia
Russian Far East. Far Eastern Republic.
Dal'nevostochniĭ kraĭ
By subject
History -- Continued

2181.S68 1921-1945
2181.S7 World War II
2181.S72 1945-1991
2181.S75 1991-
2182 Regions, natural features, etc., A-Z (Table G7322)
Apply Table G1 for subject (except .S1-.S7, historical geography)
Apply Table G7001.S for history
2183 Provinces, districts, etc., A-Z (Table G7323)
Apply Table G1 for subject (except .S1-.S7, historical geography)
Apply Table G7001.S for history

Sakhalin
2190 General
2191 By subject (Table G1 modified)
History
2191.S1 General
(2191.S12) This number not used
2191.S2 Early through 1613
2191.S3 17th century
2191.S4 18th century
2191.S5 1801-1917
2191.S54 Crimean War
2191.S57 Rebellion, 1905-1907
2191.S65 World War I
2191.S67 1917-1921
2191.S68 1921-1945
2191.S7 World War II
2191.S72 1945-1991
2191.S75 1991-

Kuril Islands (Chishima Retto)
2195 General
2196 By subject (Table G1 modified)
History
2196.S1 General
(2196.S12) This number not used
2196.S2 Early through 1613
2196.S3 17th century

By region or country
Eastern Hemisphere. Eurasia, Africa, etc.
Europe
Former Soviet republics in Asia. U.S.S.R. in Asia.
Russia (Empire) in Asia
Sakhalin
Kuril Islands (Chishima Retto)
By subject
History -- Continued

2196.S4 18th century
2196.S5 1801-1917
2196.S54 Crimean War
2196.S57 Rebellion, 1905-1907
2196.S65 World War I
2196.S67 1917-1921
2196.S68 1921-1945
2196.S7 World War II
2196.S72 1945-1991
2196.S75 1991-

Asia
2200 General
2201 By subject (Table G1)
2202 Regions and natural features, etc., A-Z (Table G7402 modified)
Apply Table G1 for subject
2202.M4 Mekong River
Subarrange by Table G1
Northern Asia see G2170+
Central Asia. Inner Asia. Turkestan
Including Sinkiang and Soviet Central Asia together, and often including Mongolia, Tibet, Jammu and Kashmir, and Northern Afghanistan
Cf. G2165+ Former Soviet Central Asia
2202.2 General
2202.21 By subject (Table G1)
Middle East. Near East. Levant. Western Asia. Southwestern Asia.
Often including Egypt and Sudan, and sometimes Libya, Ethiopia, Afghanistan, and Pakistan
2205 General
2206 By subject (Table G1)
2207 Regions, natural features, etc., A-Z (Table G7422)
Apply Table G1 for subject
Islamic Empire. Islamic countries see G1785+
Turkey. Ottoman Empire. Asia Minor
Including Turkey in Europe
2210 General

By region or country
Eastern Hemisphere. Eurasia, Africa, etc.
Asia
Middle East. Near East. Levant. Western Asia. Southwestern Asia
Turkey. Ottoman Empire. Asia Minor -- Continued

2211 By subject (Table G1 modified)
History
2211.S1 General
(2211.S12) This number not used
2211.S2 To 1288
2211.S4 Ottoman Empire, 1288-1918
2211.S65 World War I
2211.S67 1918-1960
2211.S7 World War II
2211.S73 1960-
2212 Regions, natural features, etc., A-Z (Table G7432)
Apply Table G1 for subject (except .S1-.S7, historical geography)
Apply Table G7431.S for history
2213 Provinces (Ili), A-Z (Table G7433)
Apply Table G1 for subject (except .S1-.S7, historical geography)
Apply Table G7431.S for history
2214 Cities and towns, etc., A-Z (Table G7434)
Apply Table G1 for subject (except .S1-.S7, historical geography)
Apply Table G7431.S for history

Cyprus
2215 General
2216 By subject (Table G1 modified)
History
2216.S1 General
(2216.S12) This number not used
2216.S2 Early to 1571
2216.S3 1571-1878, Turkish period
2216.S6 1878-1960, British period
2216.S65 World War I
2216.S7 World War II
2216.S8 1960-, Independent republic
2216.S82 1963 crisis
2216.S84 1974 crisis
2217 Regions, natural features, etc., A-Z (Table G7452)
Apply Table G1 for subject (except .S1-.S7, historical geography)
Apply Table G7451.S for history

By region or country
Eastern Hemisphere. Eurasia, Africa, etc.
Asia
Middle East. Near East. Levant. Western Asia. Southwestern Asia
Cyprus -- Continued
2218 Districts, A-Z (Table G7453)
Apply Table G1 for subject (except .S1-.S7, historical geography)
Apply Table G7451.S for history
2219 Cities and towns, etc., A-Z (Table G7454)
Apply Table G1 for subject (except .S1-.S7, historical geography)
Apply Table G7451.S for history
Syria
2220 General
2221 By subject (Table G1)
2222 Regions, natural features, etc., A-Z (Table G7462)
Apply Table G1 for subject
2224 Cities and towns, etc., A-Z (Table G7464)
Apply Table G1 for subject
Lebanon
2225 General
2226 By subject (Table G1 modified)
History
2226.S1 General
(2226.S12) This number not used
2226.S2 To 638
2226.S3 Medieval, 638-1517
2226.S4 Turkish period, 1517-1918
2226.S6 Autonomy, 1861-1918
2226.S65 World War I
2226.S67 French Mandate and occupation, 1919-1945
2226.S7 World War II
2226.S73 1946-1975
2226.S75 1975-
2227 Regions, natural features, etc., A-Z (Table G7472)
Apply Table G1 for subject (except .S1-.S7, historical geography)
Apply Table G7471.S for history
2229 Cities and towns, etc., A-Z (Table G7474)
Apply Table G1 for subject (except .S1-.S7, historical geography)
Apply Table G7471.S for history
Bible lands
2230 General
2231 By subject (Table G1)

By region or country
Eastern Hemisphere. Eurasia, Africa, etc.
Asia
Middle East. Near East. Levant. Western Asia. Southwestern Asia -- Continued
Israel. Palestine

2235 General
2236 By subject (Table G1 modified)
History
2236.S1 General
(2236.S12) This number not used
2236.S2 To 70 A.D.
2236.S3 70-1453
2236.S4 1454-1800
2236.S5 1801-1899
2236.S6 1900-1947
2236.S65 World War I
2236.S7 World War II
2236.S73 1948-
2237 Regions, natural features, etc., A-Z (Table G7502 modified)
Apply Table G1 for subject (except .S1-.S7, historical geography)
Apply Table G7501.S for history
Sinaitic Peninsula see G2492.S5
Sinaitic Peninsula (Safaga Island) see G2492.S2
2238 Districts, A-Z (Table G7503)
Apply Table G1 for subject (except .S1-.S7, historical geography)
Apply Table G7501.S for history
2239 Cities and towns, etc., A-Z (Table G7504)
Apply Table G1 for subject (except .S1-.S7, historical geography)
Apply Table G7501.S for history

Jordan

2240 General
2241 By subject (Table G1)
2242 Regions, natural features, etc., A-Z (Table G7512)
Apply Table G1 for subject
2243 Governorates, A-Z (Table G7513)
Apply Table G1 for subject
2244 Cities and towns, etc., A-Z (Table G7514)
Apply Table G1 for subject

Arabian Peninsula. Arabia

2245 General
2246 By subject (Table G1)
Saudi Arabia

By region or country
Eastern Hemisphere. Eurasia, Africa, etc.
Asia
Middle East. Near East. Levant. Western Asia.
Southwestern Asia
Arabian Peninsula. Arabia
Saudi Arabia -- Continued

2249.3 General
2249.31 By subject (Table G1)
2249.32 Regions, natural features, etc., A-Z (Table G7532)
Apply Table G1 for subject
2249.33 Emirates, etc., A-Z (Table G7533)
Apply Table G1 for subject
2249.34 Cities and towns, etc., A-Z (Table G7534)
Apply Table G1 for subject

Yemen (Republic)
Including atlases of the Yemen Arab Republic (North Yemen)

2249.5 General
2249.51 By subject (Table G1)
2249.52 Regions, natural features, etc., A-Z (Table G7542)
Apply Table G1 for subject
2249.53 Governorates (Muhafazahs), etc., A-Z (Table G7543)
Apply Table G1 for subject
2249.54 Cities and towns, etc., A-Z (Table G7544)
Apply Table G1 for subject

Yemen (People's Democratic Republic). Southern Yemen. Aden (Colony and Protectorate)

2249.55 General
2249.56 By subject (Table G1)

Oman. Muscat and Oman

2249.7 General
2249.71 By subject (Table G1)
2249.72 Regions, natural features, etc., A-Z (Table G7562)
Apply Table G1 for subject
2249.74 Cities and towns, etc., A-Z (Table G7564)
Apply Table G1 for subject

United Arab Emirates. Trucial States

2249.75 General
2249.76 By subject (Table G1)
2249.77 Regions, natural features, etc., A-Z (Table G7572)
Apply Table G1 for subject
2249.78 Sheikdoms, etc., A-Z (Table G7573)
Apply Table G1 for subject
2249.79 Cities and towns, etc., A-Z (Table G7574)
Apply Table G1 for subject

By region or country
Eastern Hemisphere. Eurasia, Africa, etc.
Asia
Middle East. Near East. Levant. Western Asia.
Southwestern Asia
Arabian Peninsula. Arabia -- Continued
Qatar
2249.8 General
2249.81 By subject (Table G1)
2249.82 Regions, natural features, etc., A-Z (Table G7582)
Apply Table G1 for subject
2249.84 Cities and towns, etc., A-Z (Table G7584)
Apply Table G1 for subject
Bahrain
2249.85 General
2249.86 By subject (Table G1)
2249.87 Regions, natural features, etc., A-Z (Table G7592)
Apply Table G1 for subject
2249.89 Cities and towns, etc., A-Z (Table G7594)
Apply Table G1 for subject
Kuwait
2249.9 General
2249.91 By subject (Table G1)
2249.92 Regions, natural features, etc., A-Z (Table G7602)
Apply Table G1 for subject
2249.93 Governorates (Muhafa-ah), A-Z (Table G7603)
Apply Table G1 for subject
2249.94 Cities and towns, etc., A-Z (Table G7604)
Apply Table G1 for subject
Iraq. Mesopotamia
2250 General
2251 By subject (Table G1)
2252 Regions, natural features, etc., A-Z (Table G7612)
Apply Table G1 for subject
2254 Cities and towns, etc., A-Z (Table G7614)
Apply Table G1 for subject
Iran. Persia
2255 General
2256 By subject (Table G1 modified)
History
2256.S1 General
(2256.S12) This number not used
2256.S2 Ancient, to 226 A.D.
2256.S23 Median Empire, 640-558 B.C.
2256.S25 Persian Empire, 558-330 B.C.
2256.S27 Parthian Empire, 246-226 B.C.
2256.S3 Modern, 226-

By region or country
Eastern Hemisphere. Eurasia, Africa, etc.
Asia
Middle East. Near East. Levant. Western Asia. Southwestern Asia
Iran. Persia
By subject
History
Modern, 226- -- Continued
2256.S34 Sassanian Empire, 226-651
2256.S37 Arab and Mongol rule, 651-1500
2256.S4 Safawids and Afhans, 1500-1736
2256.S5 Kajar dynasty, 1794-1925
2256.S6 Pahlavi dynasty, 1925-
2257 Regions, natural features, etc., A-Z (Table G7622)
Apply Table G1 for subject (except .S1-.S7, historical geography)
Apply Table G7621.S for history
2258 Provinces, governorships, etc., A-Z (Table G7623)
Apply Table G1 for subject (except .S1-.S7, historical geography)
Apply Table G7621.S for history
2259 Cities and towns, etc., A-Z (Table G7624)
Apply Table G1 for subject (except .S1-.S7, historical geography)
Apply Table G7621.S for history
South Asia. South Central Asia
2260 General
2261 By subject (Table G1)
2262 Regions, natural features, etc., A-Z (Table G7627)
Apply Table G1 for subject
Afghanistan
2265 General
2266 By subject (Table G1)
2267 Regions, natural features, etc., A-Z (Table G7632)
Apply Table G1 for subject
2268 Administrative divisions, A-Z (Table G7633)
Apply Table G1 for subject
2269 Cities and towns, etc., A-Z (Table G7634)
Apply Table G1 for subject
Pakistan
Including atlases of West and East Pakistan together
2270 General
2271 By subject (Table G1)
2272 Regions, natural features, etc., A-Z (Table G7642)
Apply Table G1 for subject

By region or country
Eastern Hemisphere. Eurasia, Africa, etc.
Asia
South Asia. South Central Asia
Pakistan -- Continued
2273 Administrative divisions, A-Z (Table G7643)
Apply Table G1 for subject
2274 Cities and towns, etc., A-Z (Table G7644)
Apply Table G1 for subject
Bangladesh. East Pakistan
2275 General
2276 By subject (Table G1)
2277 Regions, natural features, etc., A-Z (Table G7647)
Apply Table G1 for subject
2278 Provinces, etc., A-Z (Table G7648)
Apply Table G1 for subject
2279 Cities and towns, etc., A-Z (Table G7649)
Apply Table G1 for subject
India
2280 General
2281 By subject (Table G1)
2282 Regions, natural features, etc., A-Z (Table G7652)
Apply Table G1 for subject
2283 States, territories, etc., A-Z (Table G7653)
Apply Table G1 for subject
2284 Cities and towns, etc., A-Z (Table G7654)
Apply Table G1 for subject
Burma. Myanmar
2285 General
2286 By subject (Table G1)
2287 Regions, natural features, etc., A-Z (Table G7722)
Apply Table G1 for subject
2288 Divisions, states, A-Z (Table G7723)
Apply Table G1 for subject
2289 Cities and towns, etc., A-Z (Table G7724)
Apply Table G1 for subject
Sri Lanka. Ceylon
2290 General
2291 By subject (Table G1)
2292 Regions, natural features, etc., A-Z (Table G7752)
Apply Table G1 for subject
2293 Provinces, districts, A-Z (Table G7753)
Apply Table G1 for subject
2294 Cities and towns, etc., A-Z (Table G7754)
Apply Table G1 for subject
Nepal
2295 General

By region or country
Eastern Hemisphere. Eurasia, Africa, etc.
Asia
South Asia. South Central Asia
Nepal -- Continued
2296 By subject (Table G1)
2297 Regions, natural features, etc., A-Z (Table G7762)
Apply Table G1 for subject
2298 Zones, districts, etc., A-Z (Table G7763)
Apply Table G1 for subject
2299 Cities and towns, etc., A-Z (Table G7764)
Apply Table G1 for subject
Bhutan
2299.5 General
2299.51 By subject (Table G1)
2299.53 Zones, districts, etc., A-Z (Table G7783)
Apply Table G1 for subject
2299.54 Cities and towns, etc., A-Z (Table G7784)
Apply Table G1 for subject
Far East
2300 General
2301 By subject (Table G1 modified)
History
2301.S1 General
(2301.S12) This number not used
2301.S2 To 1500
2301.S3 1500-1800
2301.S4 1800-1904
2301.S5 Russo-Japanese War, 1904-1905
1904-1945
2301.S6 General
2301.S65 World War I
2301.S7 World War II
2301.S73 1945-
2302 Regions, natural features, etc., A-Z (Table G7802 modified)
Apply Table G1 for subject (except .S1-.S7, historical geography)
Apply Table G7801.S for history
Mekong River see G2202.M4
China. People's Republic of China. Chinese Empire
2305 General
2306 By subject (Table G1 modified)
History
2306.S1 General
(2306.S12) This number not used
2306.S2 To 960

By region or country
Eastern Hemisphere. Eurasia, Africa, etc.
Asia
Far East
China. People's Republic of China. Chinese Empire
By subject
History -- Continued
960-1644
2306.S3 General
2306.S33 Song dynasty, 960-1279
2306.S35 Yuan dynasty, 1260-1368
2306.S37 Ming dynasty, 1368-1644
Qing dynasty, 1644-1912
2306.S4 General
2306.S5 1861-1912
1912-1949
2306.S6 General
2306.S65 World War I
2306.S7 World War II
People's Republic of China, 1949-
2306.S73 General
2306.S75 Cultural Revolution, 1966-1976
2306.S77 1976-
2307 Regions, natural features, etc., A-Z (Table G7822)
Apply Table G1 for subject (except .S1-.S7, historical geography)
Apply Table G7821.S for history
2308 Provinces (Sheng), etc., A-Z (Table G7823)
Apply Table G1 for subject (except .S1-.S7, historical geography)
Apply Table G7821.S for history
2309 Cities and towns, etc., A-Z (Table G7824)
Apply Table G1 for subject (except .S1-.S7, historical geography)
Apply Table G7821.S for history
(2310-2311) Manchuria
see G2307
Mongolia
Class here atlases of Inner Mongolia and Outer Mongolia together. For atlases of Inner Mongolia alone,
see G2308
2315 General
2316 By subject (Table G1)
(2320-2321) Sinkiang. Chinese Turkestan. East Turkestan. Chinese Central Asia
see G2308

By region or country
Eastern Hemisphere. Eurasia, Africa, etc.
Asia
Far East
China. People's Republic of China. Chinese Empire -- Continued

(2325-2326) Tibet
see G2308

Mongolia (Mongolian People's Republic). Outer Mongolia

2329.3 General
2329.31 By subject (Table G1)
2329.32 Regions, natural features, etc., A-Z (Table G7897)
Apply Table G1 for subject
2329.33 Aymags, A-Z (Table G7898)
Apply Table G1 for subject
2329.34 Cities and towns, etc., A-Z (Table G7899)
Apply Table G1 for subject

South Korea (Republic of Korea). Chosen
Including atlases of Korea as a whole

2330 General
2331 By subject (Table G1 modified)
History
2331.S1 General
(2331.S12) This number not used
2331.S2 To 935
Koryŏ period, 935-1392
2331.S3 General
2331.S33 Mongolian invasions, 1231-1270
Chosŏn (Yi) dynasty, 1392-1910
2331.S4 General
2331.S44 Japanese invasions, 1592-1598
2331.S47 Manchu invasions, 1627-1637
2331.S5 1637-1864
2331.S55 1864-1910
Japanese occupation, 1910-1945
2331.S6 General
2331.S65 World War I
2331.S7 World War II
2331.S75 Allied occupation, 1945-1948
1948-1960
2331.S8 General
2331.S83 Korean War, 1950-1953
2331.S85 1960-1988
2331.S9 1988-

By region or country
Eastern Hemisphere. Eurasia, Africa, etc.
Asia
Far East
South Korea (Republic of Korea)
2332 Regions, natural features, etc., A-Z (Table G7902)
Apply Table G1 for subject (except .S1-.S7, historical geography)
Apply Table G7901.S for history
2333 Administrative divisions, A-Z (Table G7903)
Apply Table G1 for subject (except .S1-.S7, historical geography)
Apply Table G7901.S for history
2334 Cities and towns, etc., A-Z (Table G7904)
Apply Table G1 for subject (except .S1-.S7, historical geography)
Apply Table G7901.S for history
North Korea (Democratic People's Republic)
2334.3 General
2334.31 By subject (Table G1)
2334.32 Regions, natural features, etc., A-Z (Table G7907)
Apply Table G1 for subject
2334.33 Administrative divisions, A-Z (Table G7908)
Apply Table G1 for subject
2334.34 Cities and towns, etc., A-Z (Table G7909)
Apply Table G1 for subject
Ryukyu Islands see G2357
Taiwan. Formosa
2340 General
2341 By subject (Table G1 modified)
History
2341.S1 General
(2341.S12) This number not used
To 1895
2341.S2 General
2341.S3 Dutch rule, 1624-1661
2341.S4 Insurrection, 1895
1895-1945
2341.S5 General
2341.S65 World War I
2341.S7 World War II
2341.S73 1945-
2341.S75 1975-1988
2341.S77 1988-2000
2341.S8 2000-
2342 Regions, natural features, etc., A-Z (Table G7912)
Apply Table G1 for subject

By region or country
Eastern Hemisphere. Eurasia, Africa, etc.
Asia
Far East
Taiwan. Formosa -- Continued
2343 Provinces, municipalities, A-Z (Table G7913)
Apply Table G1 for subject
2344 Cities and towns, etc., A-Z (Table G7914)
Apply Table G1 for subject
(2353) Japanese Empire,
see G2355+
(2354) Colonies, dependencies, etc., (Collectively)
Class individual colonies, dependencies, etc., according to locations, e.g., G2330-G2334, South Korea (Former dependency)
see G2355+
Japan. Japanese Empire
2355 General
2356 By subject (Table G1 modified)
History
2356.S1 General
(2356.S12) This number not used
2356.S2 To 1185
1185-1868
2356.S3 General
2356.S32 Kamakura period, 1185-1333
2356.S34 Moromachi period, 1336-1573
2356.S36 Tokugawa period, 1600-1868
2356.S38 Meiji period, 1868-1912
Taishō period, 1912-1926
2356.S4 General
2356.S65 World War I
Shōwa period, 1926-1989
2356.S67 General
2356.S7 World War II
2356.S75 1989-
2357 Regions, natural features, islands, etc., A-Z (Table G7962)
Apply Table G1 for subject (except .S1-.S7, historical geography)
Apply Table G7961.S for history
2358 Prefectures (Ken), etc., A-Z (Table G7963)
Apply Table G1 for subject (except .S1-.S7, historical geography)
Apply Table G7961.S for for history

By region or country
Eastern Hemisphere. Eurasia, Africa, etc.
Asia
Far East
Japan -- Continued
2359 Cities and towns, etc., A-Z (Table G7964 modified)
Apply Table G1 for subject (except .S1-.S7, historical geography)
Apply Table G7961.S for history
2359.T7 Tokyo
Subarrange by Table G1 except .S1-.S7, historical geography. For history, subarrange by Table G7961.S
Southeast Asia. Indochina
Sometimes including Burma
2360 General
2361 By subject (Table G1)
2362 Regions, natural features, etc., A-Z (Table G8002)
Apply Table G1 for subject
Burma (Myanmar) see G2285+
French Indochina
2365 General
2366 By subject (Table G1)
Vietnam
Including maps of Vietnam as a whole, as well as maps of North or South Vietnam separately
2370 General
2371 By subject (Table G1)
2372 Regions, natural features, etc., A-Z (Table G8022)
Apply Table G1 for subject
2373 Provinces, former states, etc., A-Z (Table G8023)
Apply Table G1 for subject
2374 Cities and towns, etc., A-Z (Table G8024)
Apply Table G1 for subject
Cambodia. Khmer Republic
2374.3 General
2374.31 By subject (Table G1)
2374.32 Regions, natural features, etc., A-Z (Table G8012)
Apply Table G1 for subject
2374.33 Provinces (Khets), etc., A-Z (Table G8013)
Apply Table G1 for subject
2374.34 Cities and towns, etc., A-Z (Table G8014)
Apply Table G1 for subject
Laos
2374.5 General
2374.51 By subject (Table G1)

By region or country
Eastern Hemisphere. Eurasia, Africa, etc.
Asia
Southeast Asia. Indochina
Laos -- Continued

2374.52 Regions, natural features, etc., A-Z (Table G8017)
Apply Table G1 for subject

2374.53 Provinces, etc., A-Z (Table G8018)
Apply Table G1 for subject

2374.54 Cities and towns, etc., A-Z (Table G8019)
Apply Table G1 for subject

Thailand. Siam

2375 General

2376 By subject (Table G1)

2377 Regions, natural features, etc., A-Z (Table G8027)
Apply Table G1 for subject

2378 Provinces (Changwats), A-Z (Table G8028)
Apply Table G1 for subject

2379 Cities and towns, etc., A-Z (Table G8029)
Apply Table G1 for subject

Malaysia. Malaya
Including atlases of the Malay Peninsula

2380 General

2381 By subject (Table G1)

2382 Regions, natural features, etc., A-Z (Table G8032)
Apply Table G1 for subject

2383 States, A-Z (Table G8033)
Apply Table G1 for subject

2384 Cities and towns, etc., A-Z (Table G8034)
Apply Table G1 for subject

Singapore (Republic, Colony, and Island). Straits Settlements, 1826-1946
Including atlases of the city of Singapore

2384.3 General

2384.31 By subject (Table G1)

2384.32 Regions, natural features, etc., A-Z (Table G8042)
Apply Table G1 for subject

2384.34 Cities and towns, etc., A-Z (Table G8044)
Apply Table G1 for subject
For atlases of the city of Singapore see G2384.3+

Malay Archipelago

2385 General

2386 By subject (Table G1)

Philippines

2390 General

2391 By subject (Table G1)

By region or country
Eastern Hemisphere. Eurasia, Africa, etc.
Asia
Southeast Asia. Indochina
Malay Archipelago
Philippines -- Continued

2392 Islands, archipelagoes, regions, natural features, etc., A-Z (Table G8062)
Apply Table G1 for subject

2393 Province, A-Z (Table G8063)
Apply Table G1 for subject

2394 Cities and towns, etc., A-Z (Table G8064)
Apply Table G1 for subject

Indonesia. United States of Indonesia. Netherlands Indies. East Indies

2400 General

2401 By subject (Table G1)

2402 Regions, natural features, etc., A-Z (Table G8072)
Apply Table G1 for subject
For individual islands and archipelagoes, see G2405-G2437

2403 Provinces, etc., A-Z (Table G8073)
Apply Table G1 for subject

2404 Cities and towns, etc., A-Z (Table G8074)
Apply Table G1 for subject

Sumatra

2405 General

2406 By subject (Table G1)

2407 Regions, natural features, adjacent islands, etc., A-Z (Table G8082)
Apply Table G1 for subject

Java. Djawa

2410 General

2411 By subject (Table G1)

2412 Regions, natural features, adjacent islands, etc., A-Z (Table G8092)
Apply Table G1 for subject

Borneo. Kalimantan
For British North Borneo, North Borneo, and Sarawak see G2380+

2415 General

2416 By subject (Table G1)

2417 Regions, natural features, adjacent islands, etc., A-Z (Table G8102)
Apply Table G1 for subject

Sabah see G2380+

Sarawak see G2380+

By region or country
Eastern Hemisphere. Eurasia, Africa, etc.
Asia
Southeast Asia. Indochina
Malay Archipelago
Indonesia. United States of Indonesia. Netherlands Indies. East Indies -- Continued
Celebes
2420 General
2421 By subject (Table G1)
Lesser Sunda Islands
2425 General
2426 By subject (Table G1)
2427 Regions, natural features, adjacent islands, etc., A-Z (Table G8117)
Apply Table G1 for subject
Timor
2430 General
2431 By subject (Table G1)
Western Timor see G2403
East Timor. Timor Timur. Portuguese Timor
2433.2 General
2433.21 By subject (Table G1)
Cities and towns, etc., A-Z (Table G8198.24)
Moluccas. Spice Islands
2435 General
2436 By subject (Table G1)
2437 Regions, natural features, adjacent islands, etc., A-Z (Table G8132)
Apply Table G1 for subject
New Guinea
2440 General
2441 By subject (Table G1)
2442 Regions and natural features, etc., A-Z (Table G8142)
Apply Table G1 for subject
Class here regions and natural features located within Irian Barat or common to Irian Barat and Papua New Guinea
Irian Jaya. Irian Barat. Netherlands New Guinea see G2403
Papua New Guinea
Including atlases of Territory of Papua (formerly British New Guinea) and Trust Territory of New Guinea (formerly German New Guinea)
2444.4 General
2444.41 By subject (Table G1)

By region or country
Eastern Hemisphere. Eurasia, Africa, etc.
Asia
Southeast Asia. Indochina
Malay Archipelago
Papua New Guinea -- Continued
2444.42 Islands, archipelagoes, regions, natural features, etc., A-Z (Table G8162 modified)
Apply Table G1 for subject
Bougainville see G2877.B6
Buka see G2877.B8
Green Islands see G2877.G7
2444.43 Provinces, A-Z (Table G8163)
Apply Table G1 for subject
2444.44 Cities and towns, etc., A-Z (Table G8164)
Apply Table G1 for subject
Brunei
2444.8 General
2444.81 By subject (Table G1)
2444.83 Districts, A-Z (Table G8198.53)
Apply Table G1 for subject
2444.84 Cities and towns, etc., A-Z (Table G8198.54)
Apply Table G1 for subject
Africa
Including Sub-Saharan Africa
2445 General
2446 By subject (Table G1 modified)
History
2446.S1 General
2446.S12 This number not used
2446.S2 To 1884
2446.S3 19th century
2446.S4 1884-1960
2446.S6 20th century
2446.S65 World War I
2446.S7 World War II
2446.S73 1960-
2447 Regions, natural features, etc., A-Z (Table G8202 modified)
Apply Table G1 for subject (except .S1-.S7, historical geography)
Apply Table G8201.S for history
2447.N5 Nile River
Subarrange by Table G1 except .S1-.S7, historical geography. For history, subarrange by Table G8201.S

By region or country
Eastern Hemisphere. Eurasia, Africa, etc.
Africa -- Continued
North Africa
Including the Barbary States and Northeast Africa
2455 General
2456 By subject (Table G1)
2457 Regions, natural features, etc., A-Z (Table G8222)
Apply Table G1 for subject
Morocco
Including French Morocco
For atlases of Spanish Morocco, see G2462
2460 General
2461 By subject (Table G1)
2462 Regions, natural features, etc., A-Z (Table G8232)
Apply Table G1 for subject
2463 Provinces, A-Z (Table G8233)
Apply Table G1 for subject
2464 Cities and towns, etc., A-Z (Table G8234)
Apply Table G1 for subject
Algeria
2465 General
2466 By subject (Table G1)
2467 Regions, natural features, etc., A-Z (Table G8242)
Apply Table G1 for subject
2468 Provinces (Wilayas), A-Z (Table G8243)
Apply Table G1 for subject
2469 Cities and towns, etc., A-Z (Table G8244)
Apply Table G1 for subject
Tunisia. Tunis
2470 General
2471 By subject (Table G1)
2472 Regions, natural features, etc., A-Z (Table G8252)
Apply Table G1 for subject
2473 Governorates, A-Z (Table G8253)
Apply Table G1 for subject
2474 Cities and towns, etc., A-Z (Table G8254)
Apply Table G1 for subject
Libya
2475 General
2476 By subject (Table G1)
2477 Regions, natural features, etc., A-Z (Table G8262)
Apply Table G1 for subject
2478 Municipalities, A-Z (Table G8263)
Apply Table G1 for subject
2479 Cities and towns, etc., A-Z (Table G8264)
Apply Table G1 for subject

By region or country
Eastern Hemisphere. Eurasia, Africa, etc.
Africa
North Africa
Libya -- Continued

(2480-2481) Cyrenaica
see G2477

(2485-2486) Tripolitania. Tripoli
see G2477

Egypt. United Arab Republic

2490 General

2491 By subject (Table G1)

2492 Regions, natural features, etc., A-Z (Table G8302 modified)
Apply Table G1 for subject
Nile River see G2447.N5

2492.S2 Safaga Island
Subarrange by Table G1

2492.S5 Sinai
Subarrange by Table G1

2493 Governorates, etc., A-Z (Table G8303)
Apply Table G1 for subject

2494 Cities and towns, etc., A-Z (Table G8304)
Apply Table G1 for subject

Sudan. Anglo-Egyptian Sudan

2495 General

2496 By subject (Table G1)

2497 Regions, natural features, etc., A-Z (Table G8312)
Apply Table G1 for subject

2498 Provinces, A-Z (Table G8313)
Apply Table G1 for subject

2499 Cities and towns, etc., A-Z (Table G8314)
Apply Table G1 for subject

Eastern Africa

2500 General

2501 By subject (Table G1)

2502 Regions, natural features, etc., A-Z (Table G8322)
Apply Table G1 for subject

Ethiopia. Abyssinia

2505 General

2506 By subject (Table G1 modified)
History

2506.S1 General

(2506.S12) This number not used

2506.S65 World War I

2506.S7 World War II

2506.S73 1945-

By region or country
Eastern Hemisphere. Eurasia, Africa, etc.
Africa
Eastern Africa
Ethiopia. Abyssinia -- Continued
2507 Regions, natural features, etc., A-Z (Table G8332)
Apply Table G1 for subjects (except .S1-.S7, history)
Apply Table G8331.S for history
2508 Provinces, A-Z (Table G8333)
Apply Table G1 for subjects (except .S1-.S7, history)
Apply Table G8331.S for history
2509 Cities and towns, etc., A-Z (Table G8334)
Apply Table G1 for subjects (except .S1-.S7, history)
Apply Table G8331.S for history
Eritrea
2510 General
2511 By subject (Table G1)
2512 Regions, natural features, etc., A-Z (Table G8342)
Apply Table G1 for subject
2513 Provinces, A-Z (Table G8343)
Apply Table G1 for subject
2514 Cities and towns, etc., A-Z (Table G8344)
Apply Table G1 for subject
Somalia. Somaliland
For atlases of British Somaliland and Italian Somaliland, see G2517
2515 General
2516 By subject (Table G1)
2517 Regions, natural features, etc., A-Z (Table G8352)
Apply Table G1 for subject
2518 Administrative divisions, A-Z (Table G8353)
Apply Table G1 for subject
2519 Cities and towns, etc., A-Z (Table G8354)
Apply Table G1 for subject
Djibouti. French Territory of the Afars and Issas. French Somaliland
2520 General
2521 By subject (Table G1)
2522 Regions, natural features, etc., A-Z (Table G8362)
Apply Table G1 for subject
2524 Cities and towns, etc., A-Z (Table G8364)
Apply Table G1 for subject
Southeast Africa. British East Africa
2529.3 General
2529.31 By subject (Table G1)
2529.32 Regions, natural features, etc., A-Z (Table G8402)
Apply Table G1 for subject

By region or country
Eastern Hemisphere. Eurasia, Africa, etc.
Africa
Southeast Africa. British East Africa -- Continued
Kenya. East Africa Protectorate

2530 General
2531 By subject (Table G1)
2532 Regions, natural features, etc., A-Z (Table G8412)
Apply Table G1 for subject
2533 Provinces, A-Z (Table G8413)
Apply Table G1 for subject
2534 Cities and towns, etc., A-Z (Table G8414)
Apply Table G1 for subject

Uganda
2535 General
2536 By subject (Table G1)
2537 Regions, natural features, etc., A-Z (Table G8422)
Apply Table G1 for subject
2538 Districts, A-Z (Table G8423)
Apply Table G1 for subject
2539 Cities and towns, etc., A-Z (Table G8424)
Apply Table G1 for subject

Ruanda-Urundi. Belgian East Africa
2539.3 General
2539.31 By subject (Table G1)

Rwanda
2539.5 General
2539.51 By subject (Table G1)
2539.53 Prefectures, etc., A-Z (Table G8433)
Apply Table G1 for subject
2539.54 Cities and towns, etc., A-Z (Table G8434)
Apply Table G1 for subject

Burundi
2539.7 General
2539.71 By subject (Table G1)
2539.73 Provinces, A-Z (Table G8438)
Apply Table G1 for subject
2539.74 Cities and towns, etc., A-Z (Table G8439)
Apply Table G1 for subject

Tanzania. Tanganyika. German East Africa
2540 General
2541 By subject (Table G1)
2542 Regions, natural features, islands, etc., A-Z (Table G8442)
Apply Table G1 for subject
2543 Administrative divisions, A-Z (Table G8443)
Apply Table G1 for subject

By region or country
Eastern Hemisphere. Eurasia, Africa, etc.
Africa
Southeast Africa. British East Africa
Tanzania. Tanganyika. German East Africa -- Continued

2544 Cities and towns, etc., A-Z (Table G8444)
Apply Table G1 for subject

(2545-2546) Zanzibar
see G2542

Mozambique. Portuguese East Africa

2550 General

2551 By subject (Table G1)

2552 Regions, natural features, etc., A-Z (Table G8452)
Apply Table G1 for subject

2553 Provinces, A-Z (Table G8453)
Apply Table G1 for subject

2554 Cities and towns, etc., A-Z (Table G8454)
Apply Table G1 for subject

Madagascar. Malagasy Republic

2555 General

2556 By subject (Table G1)

2557 Regions, natural features, etc., A-Z (Table G8462)
Apply Table G1 for subject

2558 Provinces, A-Z (Table G8463)
Apply Table G1 for subject

2559 Cities and towns, etc., A-Z (Table G8464)
Apply Table G1 for subject

East African Islands see G2857

Southern Africa. British South Africa

2560 General

2561 By subject (Table G1)

2562 Regions, natural features, etc., A-Z (Table G8482)
Apply Table G1 for subject

Republic of South Africa. Union of South Africa

2565 General

2566 By subject (Table G1)

2567 Regions, natural features, etc., A-Z (Table G8502)
Apply Table G1 for subject

2568 Provinces, former homelands, etc., A-Z (Table G8503)
Apply Table G1 for subject

2569 Cities and towns, etc., A-Z (Table G8504)
Apply Table G1 for subject

Rhodesia
Including the Federation of Rhodesia and Nyasaland
For atlases limited to Nyasaland, see G2579.9+

By region or country
Eastern Hemisphere. Eurasia, Africa, etc.
Africa
Southern Africa. British South Africa
Rhodesia -- Continued

2570 General
2571 By subject (Table G1)
Zimbabwe. Southern Rhodesia
2574.3 General
2574.31 By subject (Table G1)
2574.32 Regions, natural features, etc., A-Z (Table G8562)
Apply Table G1 for subject
2574.34 Cities and towns, etc., A-Z (Table G8564)
Apply Table G1 for subject
Zambia. Northern Rhodesia
2575 General
2576 By subject (Table G1)
2577 Regions, natural features, etc., A-Z (Table G8572)
Apply Table G1 for subject
2578 Provinces, A-Z (Table G8573)
Apply Table G1 for subject
2579 Cities and towns, etc., A-Z (Table G8574)
Apply Table G1 for subject
Lesotho. Basutoland
2579.3 General
2579.31 By subject (Table G1)
2579.32 Regions, natural features, etc., A-Z (Table G8582)
Apply Table G1 for subject
2579.33 Districts, etc., A-Z (Table G8583)
Apply Table G1 for subject
2579.34 Cities and towns, etc., A-Z (Table G8584)
Apply Table G1 for subject
Swaziland
2579.5 General
2579.51 By subject (Table G1)
2579.52 Regions, natural features, etc., A-Z (Table G8592)
Apply Table G1 for subject
2579.53 Districts, etc., A-Z (Table G8593)
Apply Table G1 for subject
2579.54 Cities and towns, etc., A-Z (Table G8594)
Apply Table G1 for subject
Botswana. Bechuanaland
2579.7 General
2579.71 By subject (Table G1)
2579.72 Regions, natural features, etc., A-Z (Table G8602)
Apply Table G1 for subject

By region or country
Eastern Hemisphere. Eurasia, Africa, etc.
Africa
Southern Africa. British South Africa
Botswana. Bechuanaland -- Continued
2579.74 Cities and towns, etc., A-Z (Table G8604)
Apply Table G1 for subject
Malawi. Nyasaland. Central Africa Protectorate
For maps of the Federation of Rhodesia and Nyasaland see G2570+
2579.9 General
2579.91 By subject (Table G1)
2579.92 Regions, natural features, etc., A-Z (Table G8612)
Apply Table G1 for subject
2579.93 Districts, etc., A-Z (Table G8613)
Apply Table G1 for subject
2579.94 Cities and towns, etc., A-Z (Table G8614)
Apply Table G1 for subject
Namibia. Southwest Africa. German Southwest Africa
2580 General
2581 By subject (Table G1)
2582 Regions, natural features, etc., A-Z (Table G8622)
Apply Table G1 for subject
2583 Districts, etc., A-Z (Table G8623)
Apply Table G1 for subject
2584 Cities and towns, etc., A-Z (Table G8624)
Apply Table G1 for subject
Central Africa. Equatorial Africa
2590 General
2591 By subject (Table G1)
2592 Regions, natural features, etc., A-Z (Table G8632)
Apply Table G1 for subject
Angola. Portuguese West Africa
2595 General
2596 By subject (Table G1)
2597 Regions, natural features, etc., A-Z (Table G8642)
Apply Table G1 for subject
2598 Provinces, A-Z (Table G8643)
Apply Table G1 for subject
2599 Cities and towns, etc., A-Z (Table G8644)
Apply Table G1 for subject
Congo (Democratic Republic). Zaire. Belgian Congo
2600 General
2601 By subject (Table G1)
2602 Regions, natural features, etc., A-Z (Table G8652)
Apply Table G1 for subject

By region or country
Eastern Hemisphere. Eurasia, Africa, etc.
Africa
Central Africa. Equatorial Africa
Congo (Democratic Republic). Zaire. Belgian Congo -- Continued

2603 Provinces, A-Z (Table G8653)
Apply Table G1 for subject

2604 Cities and towns, etc., A-Z (Table G8654)
Apply Table G1 for subject

Equatorial Guinea. Spanish Guinea

2605 General

2606 By subject (Table G1)

2607 Regions, natural features, etc., A-Z (Table G8662)
Apply Table G1 for subject

2608 Provinces, A-Z (Table G8663)
Apply Table G1 for subject

2609 Cities and towns, etc., A-Z (Table G8664)
Apply Table G1 for subject

Sao Tome and Principe

2609.3 General

2609.31 By subject (Table G1)

2609.32 Regions, natural features, etc., A-Z (Table G8677)
Apply Table G1 for subject

2609.34 Cities and towns, etc., A-Z (Table G8679)
Apply Table G1 for subject

French Equatorial Africa. French Congo

2610 General

2611 By subject (Table G1)

Gabon

2615 General

2616 By subject (Table G1)

2617 Regions, natural features, etc., A-Z (Table G8692)
Apply Table G1 for subject

2618 Provinces, A-Z (Table G8693)
Apply Table G1 for subject

2619 Cities and towns, etc., A-Z (Table G8694)
Apply Table G1 for subject

Congo (Brazzaville). Middle Congo

2620 General

2621 By subject (Table G1)

2622 Regions, natural features, etc., A-Z (Table G8702)
Apply Table G1 for subject

2623 Administrative regions, A-Z (Table G8703)
Apply Table G1 for subject

2624 Cities and towns, etc., A-Z (Table G8704)
Apply Table G1 for subject

By region or country
Eastern Hemisphere. Eurasia, Africa, etc.
Africa
Central Africa. Equatorial Africa
French Equatorial Africa. French Congo -- Continued
Central African Republic. Ubangi-Shari
2625 General
2626 By subject (Table G1)
2627 Regions, natural features, etc., A-Z (Table G8712)
Apply Table G1 for subject
2628 Administrative divisions, A-Z (Table G8713)
Apply Table G1 for subject
2629 Cities and towns, etc., A-Z (Table G8714)
Apply Table G1 for subject
Chad (Tchad)
2630 General
2631 By subject (Table G1)
2632 Regions, natural features, etc., A-Z (Table G8722)
Apply Table G1 for subject
2633 Prefectures, A-Z (Table G8723)
Apply Table G1 for subject
2634 Cities and towns, etc., A-Z (Table G8724)
Apply Table G1 for subject
Cameroon. French Cameroons. German Cameroons (Kamerun)
2635 General
2636 By subject (Table G1)
2637 Regions, natural features, etc., A-Z (Table G8732)
Apply Table G1 for subject
2638 Provinces, A-Z (Table G8733)
Apply Table G1 for subject
2639 Cities and towns, etc., A-Z (Table G8734)
Apply Table G1 for subject
West Africa
Including the West Coast and Northwest Africa
2640 General
2641 By subject (Table G1)
2642 Regions, natural features, etc., A-Z (Table G8737)
French West Africa
2645 General
2646 By subject (Table G1)
2647 Regions, natural features, etc., A-Z (Table G8742)
Apply Table G1 for subject
Benin. Dahomey
2650 General
2651 By subject (Table G1)

By region or country
Eastern Hemisphere. Eurasia, Africa, etc.
Africa
West Africa
French West Africa
Benin. Dahomey -- Continued

2652 Regions, natural features, etc., A-Z (Table G8752)
Apply Table G1 for subject

2653 Administrative divisions, A-Z (Table G8753)
Apply Table G1 for subject

2654 Cities and towns, etc., A-Z (Table G8754)
Apply Table G1 for subject

Togo. French Togoland. Togoland

2655 General

2656 By subject (Table G1)

2657 Regions, natural features, etc., A-Z (Table G8762)
Apply Table G1 for subject

2658 Circonscriptions, A-Z (Table G8763)
Apply Table G1 for subject

2659 Cities and towns, etc., A-Z (Table G8764)
Apply Table G1 for subject

Niger

2660 General

2661 By subject (Table G1)

2662 Regions, natural features, etc., A-Z (Table G8772)
Apply Table G1 for subject

2663 Departments, A-Z (Table G8773)
Apply Table G1 for subject

2664 Cities and towns, etc., A-Z (Table G8774)
Apply Table G1 for subject

Côte d'Ivoire. Ivory Coast

2665 General

2666 By subject (Table G1)

2667 Regions, natural features, etc., A-Z (Table G8782)
Apply Table G1 for subject

2668 Departments, A-Z (Table G8783)
Apply Table G1 for subject

2669 Cities and towns, etc., A-Z (Table G8784)
Apply Table G1 for subject

Guinea. French Guinea

2670 General

2671 By subject (Table G1)

2672 Regions, natural features, etc., A-Z (Table G8792)
Apply Table G1 for subject

2673 Administrative regions, A-Z (Table G8793)
Apply Table G1 for subject

By region or country
Eastern Hemisphere. Eurasia, Africa, etc.
Africa
West Africa
French West Africa
Guinea. French Guinea -- Continued

2674 Cities and towns, etc., A-Z (Table G8794)
Apply Table G1 for subject

Mali. French Sudan

2675 General

2676 By subject (Table G1)

2677 Regions, natural features, etc., A-Z (Table G8802)
Apply Table G1 for subject

2678 Administrative regions, A-Z (Table G8803)
Apply Table G1 for subject

2679 Cities and towns, etc., A-Z (Table G8804)
Apply Table G1 for subject

Burkina Faso. Upper Volta

2679.3 General

2679.31 By subject (Table G1)

2679.32 Regions, natural features, etc., A-Z (Table G8807)
Apply Table G1 for subject

2679.34 Cities and towns, etc., A-Z (Table G8809)
Apply Table G1 for subject

Senegal

2680 General

2681 By subject (Table G1)

2682 Regions, natural features, etc., A-Z (Table G8812)
Apply Table G1 for subject

2683 Administrative regions, A-Z (Table G8813)
Apply Table G1 for subject

2684 Cities and towns, etc., A-Z (Table G8814)
Apply Table G1 for subject

Mauritania

2685 General

2686 By subject (Table G1)

2687 Regions, natural features, etc., A-Z (Table G8822)
Apply Table G1 for subject

2689 Cities and towns, etc., A-Z (Table G8824)
Apply Table G1 for subject

British West Africa

2690 General

2691 By subject (Table G1)

Nigeria

2695 General

2696 By subject (Table G1)

By region or country
Eastern Hemisphere. Eurasia, Africa, etc.
Africa
West Africa
British West Africa
Nigeria -- Continued

2697 Regions, natural features, etc., A-Z (Table G8842)
Apply Table G1 for subject

2698 States, administrative regions, A-Z (Table G8843)
Apply Table G1 for subject

2699 Cities and towns, etc., A-Z (Table G8844)
Apply Table G1 for subject

Ghana. Gold Coast

2700 General

2701 By subject (Table G1)

2702 Regions, natural features, etc., A-Z (Table G8852)
Apply Table G1 for subject

2703 Administrative regions, A-Z (Table G8853)
Apply Table G1 for subject

2704 Cities and towns, etc., A-Z (Table G8854)
Apply Table G1 for subject

Sierra Leone

2705 General

2706 By subject (Table G1)

2707 Regions, natural features, etc., A-Z (Table G8862)
Apply Table G1 for subject

2708 Provinces, A-Z (Table G8863)
Apply Table G1 for subject

2709 Cities and towns, etc., A-Z (Table G8864)
Apply Table G1 for subject

Gambia

2710 General

2711 By subject (Table G1)

2712 Regions, natural features, etc., A-Z (Table G8872)
Apply Table G1 for subject

2713 Administrative divisions, A-Z (Table G8873)
Apply Table G1 for subject

2714 Cities and towns, etc., A-Z (Table G8874)
Apply Table G1 for subject

Liberia

2720 General

2721 By subject (Table G1)

2722 Regions, natural features, etc., A-Z (Table G8882)
Apply Table G1 for subject

2723 Counties, A-Z (Table G8883)
Apply Table G1 for subject

By region or country
Eastern Hemisphere. Eurasia, Africa, etc.
Africa
West Africa
Liberia -- Continued
2724 Cities and towns, etc., A-Z (Table G8884)
Apply Table G1 for subject
Guinea-Bissau. Portuguese Guinea
2730 General
2731 By subject (Table G1)
2732 Regions, natural features, etc., A-Z (Table G8892)
Apply Table G1 for subject
2733 Administrative regions, A-Z (Table G8893)
Apply Table G1 for subject
2734 Cities and towns, etc., A-Z (Table G8894)
Apply Table G1 for subject
Western Sahara. Spanish Sahara
Including Spanish West Africa as a whole
For atlases limited to Ifni see G2462
2735 General
2736 By subject (Table G1)
2737 Regions, natural features, etc., A-Z (Table G8902)
Apply Table G1 for subject
2738 Administrative areas, A-Z (Table G8903)
Apply Table G1 for subject
2739 Cities and towns, etc., A-Z (Table G8904)
Apply Table G1 for subject
Australasia
2740 General
2741 By subject (Table G1)
2742 Regions, natural features, etc., A-Z (Table G8952)
Apply Table G1 for subject
Australia
2750 General
2751 By subject (Table G1 modified)
History
2751.S1 General
2751.S12 Discovery and exploration
2751.S2 To 1788
2751.S3 1788-1900
2751.S4 1901-1945
(2751.S65) This number not used
2751.S7 World War II
2751.S73 1945-

By region or country
Australasia
Australia -- Continued
2752 Regions, natural features, etc., A-Z (Table G8962)
Apply Table G1 for subject (except .S1-.S7, historical geography)
Apply Table G8961.S for history
2754 Cities and towns, etc., A-Z (Table G8964)
Apply Table G1 for subject (except .S1-.S7, historical geography)
Apply Table G8961.S for history
New South Wales
2755 General
2756 By subject (Table G1 modified)
History
2756.S1 General
2756.S12 Discovery and exploration
2756.S2 To 1788
2756.S3 1788-1900
2756.S4 1901-1945
(2756.S65) This number not used
2756.S7 World War II
2756.S73 1945-
2757 Regions, natural features, etc., A-Z (Table G8972)
Apply Table G1 for subject (except .S1-.S7, historical geography)
Apply Table G8961.S for history
2758 Shires, etc., A-Z (Table G8973)
Apply Table G1 for subject (except .S1-.S7, historical geography)
Apply Table G8961.S for history
Australian Capital Territory
For Canberra, see G2754
2760 General
2761 By subject (Table G1 modified)
History
2761.S1 General
2761.S12 Discovery and exploration
2761.S2 To 1788
2761.S3 1788-1900
2761.S4 1901-1945
(2761.S65) This number not used
2761.S7 World War II
2761.S73 1945-

By region or country
Australasia
Australia
Australian Capital Territory -- Continued
2762 Regions, natural features, etc., A-Z (Table G8982)
Apply Table G1 for subject (except .S1-.S7, historical geography)
Apply Table G8961.S for history
Victoria
2765 General
2766 By subject (Table G1 modified)
History
2766.S1 General
2766.S12 Discovery and exploration
2766.S2 To 1788
2766.S3 1788-1900
2766.S4 1901-1945
(2766.S65) This number not used
2766.S7 World War II
2766.S73 1945-
2767 Regions, natural features, etc., A-Z (Table G8992)
Apply Table G1 for subject (except .S1-.S7, historical geography)
Apply Table G8961.S for history
2768 Shires, etc., A-Z (Table G8993)
Apply Table G1 for subject (except .S1-.S7, historical geography)
Apply Table G8961.S for history
Queensland
2770 General
2771 By subject (Table G1 modified)
History
2771.S1 General
2771.S12 Discovery and exploration
2771.S2 To 1788
2771.S3 1788-1900
2771.S4 1901-1945
(2771.S65) This number not used
2771.S7 World War II
2771.S73 1945-
2772 Regions, natural features, etc., A-Z (Table G9002)
Apply Table G1 for subject (except .S1-.S7, historical geography)
Apply Table G8961.S for history

By region or country
Australasia
Australia
Queensland -- Continued
2773 Shires, etc., A-Z (Table G9003)
Apply Table G1 for subject (except .S1-.S7, historical geography)
Apply Table G8961.S for history
South Australia
2775 General
2776 By subject (Table G1 modified)
History
2776.S1 General
2776.S12 Discovery and exploration
2776.S2 To 1788
2776.S3 1788-1900
2776.S4 1901-1945
(2776.S65) This number not used
2776.S7 World War II
2776.S73 1945-
2777 Regions, natural features, etc., A-Z (Table G9012)
Apply Table G1 for subject (except .S1-.S7, historical geography)
Apply Table G8961.S for history
2778 Counties, etc., A-Z (Table G9013)
Apply Table G1 for subject (except .S1-.S7, historical geography)
Apply Table G8961.S for history
Western Australia
2780 General
2781 By subject (Table G1 modified)
History
2781.S1 General
2781.S12 Discovery and exploration
2781.S2 To 1788
2781.S3 1788-1900
2781.S4 1901-1945
(2781.S65) This number not used
2781.S7 World War II
2781.S73 1945-
2782 Regions, natural features, etc., A-Z (Table G9022)
Apply Table G1 for subject (except .S1-.S7, historical geography)
Apply Table G8961.S for history

By region or country
Australasia
Australia
Western Australia -- Continued
2783 Shires, etc., A-Z (Table G9023)
Apply Table G1 for subject (except .S1-.S7, historical geography)
Apply Table G8961.S for history
Northern Territory
2785 General
2786 By subject (Table G1 modified)
History
2786.S1 General
2786.S12 Discovery and exploration
2786.S2 To 1788
2786.S3 1788-1900
2786.S4 1901-1945
(2786.S65) This number not used
2786.S7 World War II
2786.S73 1945-
2787 Regions, natural features, etc., A-Z (Table G9042)
Apply Table G1 for subject (except .S1-.S7, historical geography)
Apply Table G8961.S for history
Tasmania
2790 General
2791 By subject (Table G1 modified)
History
2791.S1 General
2791.S12 Discovery and exploration
2791.S2 To 1788
2791.S3 1788-1900
2791.S4 1901-1945
(2791.S65) This number not used
2791.S7 World War II
2791.S73 1945-
2792 Regions, natural features, etc., A-Z (Table G9062)
Apply Table G1 for subject (except .S1-.S7, historical geography)
Apply Table G8961.S for history
New Zealand
2795 General
2796 By subject (Table G1)
2797 Regions, natural features, etc., A-Z (Table G9082)
Apply Table G1 for subject
2798 Counties, A-Z (Table G9083)
Apply Table G1 for subject

By region or country
Australasia
New Zealand -- Continued
2799 Cities and towns, etc., A-Z (Table G9084)
Apply Table G1 for subject
Oceans (General)
Cf. G1059+ Maritime atlases (General)
2800 General
2801 By subject (Table G1)
Atlantic Ocean
2805 General
2806 By subject (Table G1)
2807 Regions, natural features, etc., A-Z (Table G2807)
Apply Table G1 for subject
Bermuda
2810 General
2811 By subject (Table G1)
2812 Regions, natural features, islands, etc., A-Z (Table G9122)
Apply Table G1 for subject
2813 Counties, A-Z (Table G9123)
Apply Table G1 for subject
2814 Cities and towns, etc., A-Z (Table G9124)
Apply Table G1 for subject
Azores
2815 General
2816 By subject (Table G1)
2817 Regions, natural features, islands, etc., A-Z (Table G9132)
Apply Table G1 for subject
2818 Districts, etc., A-Z (Table G9133 modified)
Apply Table G1 for subject
2818.A5 Angra do Heroismo
Subarrange by Table G1
2818.H6 Horta
Subarrange by Table G1
2818.P6 Ponta Delgada
Subarrange by Table G1
2819 Cities and towns, etc., A-Z (Table G9134)
Apply Table G1 for subject
Madeira Islands. Funchal (District of Portugal)
2820 General
2821 By subject (Table G1)
2822 Regions, natural features, archipelagoes, islands, etc., A-Z (Table G9142)
Apply Table G1 for subject

By region or country
Oceans (General)
Atlantic Ocean
Madeira Islands -- Continued
2824 Cities and towns, etc., A-Z (Table G9144)
Apply Table G1 for subject
Canary Islands
Including two provinces of Spain: Las Palmas (Las Palmas de Gran Canaria) and Santa Cruz de Tenerife
2825 General
2826 By subject (Table G1)
2827 Regions, natural features, islands, etc., A-Z (Table G9152)
Apply Table G1 for subject
2828 Provinces, etc., A-Z (Table G9153 modified)
Apply Table G1 for subject
2828.L3 Las Palmas
Subarrange by Table G1
2829 Cities and towns, etc., A-Z (Table G9154)
Apply Table G1 for subject
Cape Verde Islands
2830 General
2831 By subject (Table G1)
2832 Regions, natural features, archipelagoes, islands, etc., A-Z (Table G9162)
Apply Table G1 for subject
2834 Cities and towns, etc., A-Z (Table G9164)
Apply Table G1 for subject
Falkland Islands
2835 General
2836 By subject (Table G1)
2837 Regions, natural features, archipelagoes, islands, etc., A-Z (Table G9177)
Apply Table G1 for subject
2839 Cities and towns, etc., A-Z (Table G9179)
Apply Table G1 for subject
Indian Ocean
2850 General
2851 By subject (Table G1)
2852 Regions, natural features, archipelagoes, islands, etc., A-Z (Table G9182)
Apply Table G1 for subject
2857 Islands or groups of islands, A-Z (Table G2857)
Apply Table G1 for subject
Pacific Ocean
2860 General
2861 By subject (Table G1)

By region or country
Oceans (General)
Pacific Ocean -- Continued
2862 Regions, natural features, etc., A-Z (Table G2862)
Apply Table G1 for subject
2867 Islands or groups of islands, A-Z
Class here islands and archipelagoes not classed in or associated with G2870-G3012
Melanesia
Class here islands or archipelagoes not classed in or associated with G2875-G2892
2870 General
2871 By subject (Table G1)
2872 Regions, natural features, archipelagoes, islands, etc., A-Z (Table G9262)
Apply Table G1 for subject
Solomon Islands
2875 General
2876 By subject (Table G1)
2877 Regions, natural features, archipelagoes, islands, etc., A-Z (Table G9282 modified)
Apply Table G1 for subject
2877.B6 Bougainville Island
Subarrange by Table G1
2877.B8 Buka Island
Subarrange by Table G1
2877.G7 Green Islands
Subarrange by Table G1
Vanuatu. New Hebrides
2880 General
2881 By subject (Table G1)
2882 Regions, natural features, archipelagoes, islands, etc., A-Z (Table G9302)
Apply Table G1 for subject
2884 Cities and towns, etc., A-Z (Table G9304)
Apply Table G1 for subject
New Caledonia
2885 General
2886 By subject (Table G1)
2887 Regions, natural features, archipelagoes, islands, dependencies, etc., A-Z (Table G9342)
Apply Table G1 for subject
2889 Cities and towns, etc., A-Z (Table G9344)
Apply Table G1 for subject
Fiji
2890 General
2891 By subject (Table G1)

By region or country
Oceans (General)
Pacific Ocean
Melanesia
Fiji -- Continued
2892 Regions, natural features, archipelagoes, islands, dependencies, etc., A-Z (Table G9382)
Apply Table G1 for subject
2894 Cities and towns, etc., A-Z (Table G9384)
Apply Table G1 for subject
Micronesia
Class here islands of Micronesian islands or archipelagoes not classed in or associated with G2905-G2934
2900 General
2901 By subject (Table G1)
2902 Regions, natural features, archipelagoes, islands, etc., A-Z (Table G9402)
Apply Table G1 for subject
Mariana Islands. Ladrone Islands
2905 General
2906 By subject (Table G1)
2907 Regions, natural features, archipelagoes, islands, etc., A-Z (Table G9412)
Apply Table G1 for subject
2909 Cities and towns, etc., A-Z (Table G9414)
Apply Table G1 for subject
Guam
2910 General
2911 By subject (Table G1)
2912 Regions, natural features, archipelagoes, islands, etc., A-Z (Table G9417)
Apply Table G1 for subject
2914 Cities and towns, etc., A-Z (Table G9419)
Apply Table G1 for subject
Caroline Islands
2920 General
2921 By subject (Table G1)
2922 Regions, natural features, archipelagoes, islands, etc., A-Z (Table G9422)
Apply Table G1 for subject
Marshall Islands
2930 General
2931 By subject (Table G1)
2932 Regions, natural features, archipelagoes, islands, etc., A-Z (Table G9462)
Apply Table G1 for subject

By region or country
Oceans (General)
Pacific Ocean -- Continued
Polynesia
Class here islands or archipelagoes not classed in or associated with Samoa Islands
2970 General
2971 By subject (Table G1)
2972 Regions, natural features, archipelagoes, islands, etc., A-Z (Table G2972)
Apply Table G1 for subject
Samoan Islands
2980 General
2981 By subject (Table G1)
Hawaii see G1534.2+
3012 East Pacific islands, A-Z (Table G9762)
Apply Table G1 for subject
Arctic Ocean
Class here islands or archipelagoes not classed in or associated with G3055-G3064
Cf. G1055 Arctic regions
3050 General
3051 By subject (Table G1)
3052 Regions, natural features, archipelagoes, islands, etc., A-Z (Table G9782)
Apply Table G1 for subject
Franz Josef Land
3055 General
3056 By subject (Table G1)
Svalbard. Spitsbergen
3060 General
3061 By subject (Table G1)
3062 Regions, natural features, archipelagoes, islands, etc., A-Z (Table G9792)
Apply Table G1 for subject
3064 Cities and towns, etc., A-Z (Table G9794)
Apply Table G1 for subject
Antarctica
3100 General
3101 By subject (Table G1)
3102 Regions, natural features, archipelagoes, islands, etc., A-Z (Table G9802)
Apply Table G1 for subject
3122.A-Z Atlases of imaginary, literary, and mythological regions, etc., A-Z

Globes

3160 Celestial globes

3165-3167 Planetary and lunar globes

3165 General

3166 By subject (Table G1)

3167 Individual planets and moons, A-Z (Table G3167)

3170-3171 Terrestrial globes

3170 General

3171 By subject (Table G1)

For history and description of maps see GA1+

MAPS

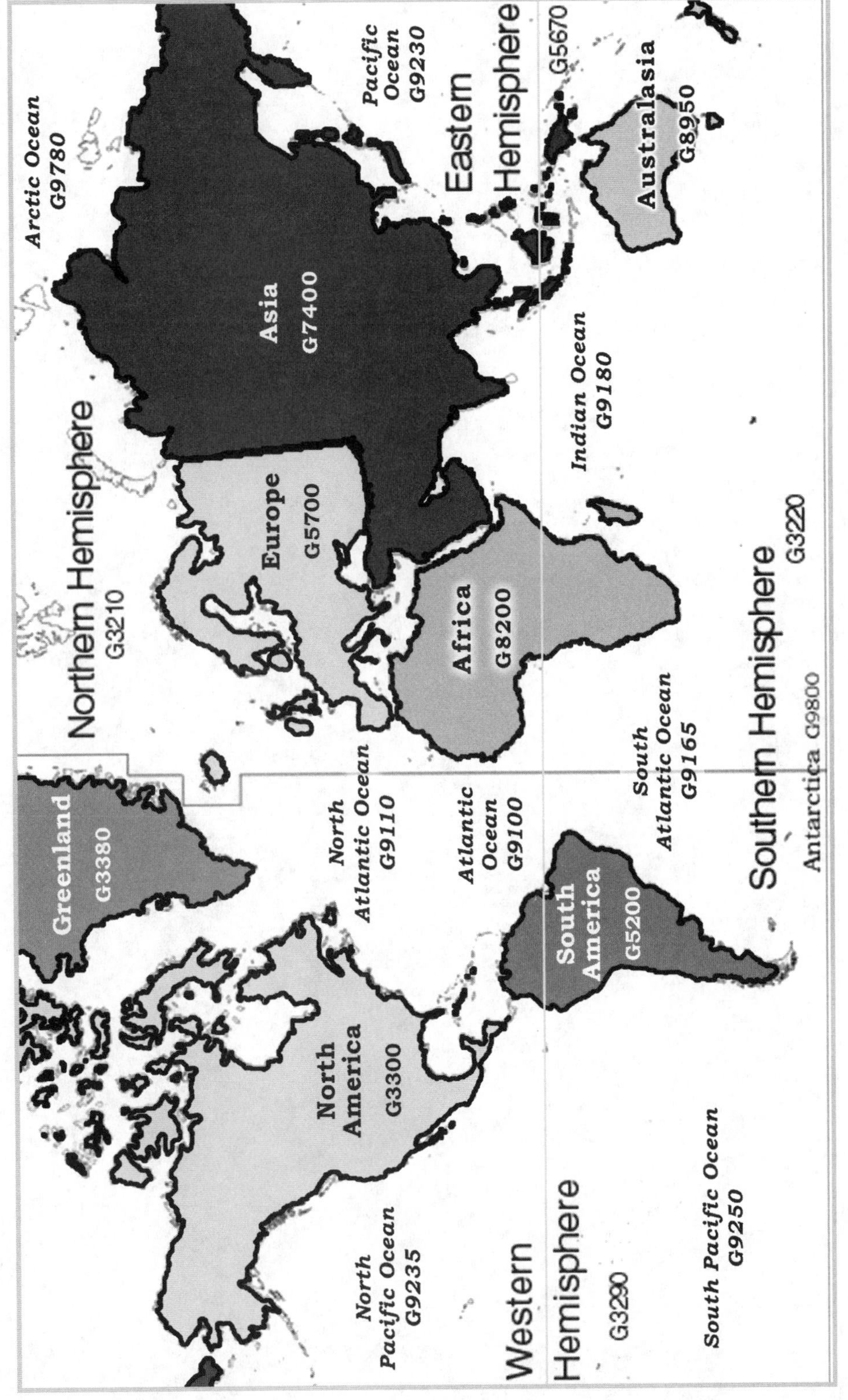

Hemispheres, Continents and Oceans

Maps

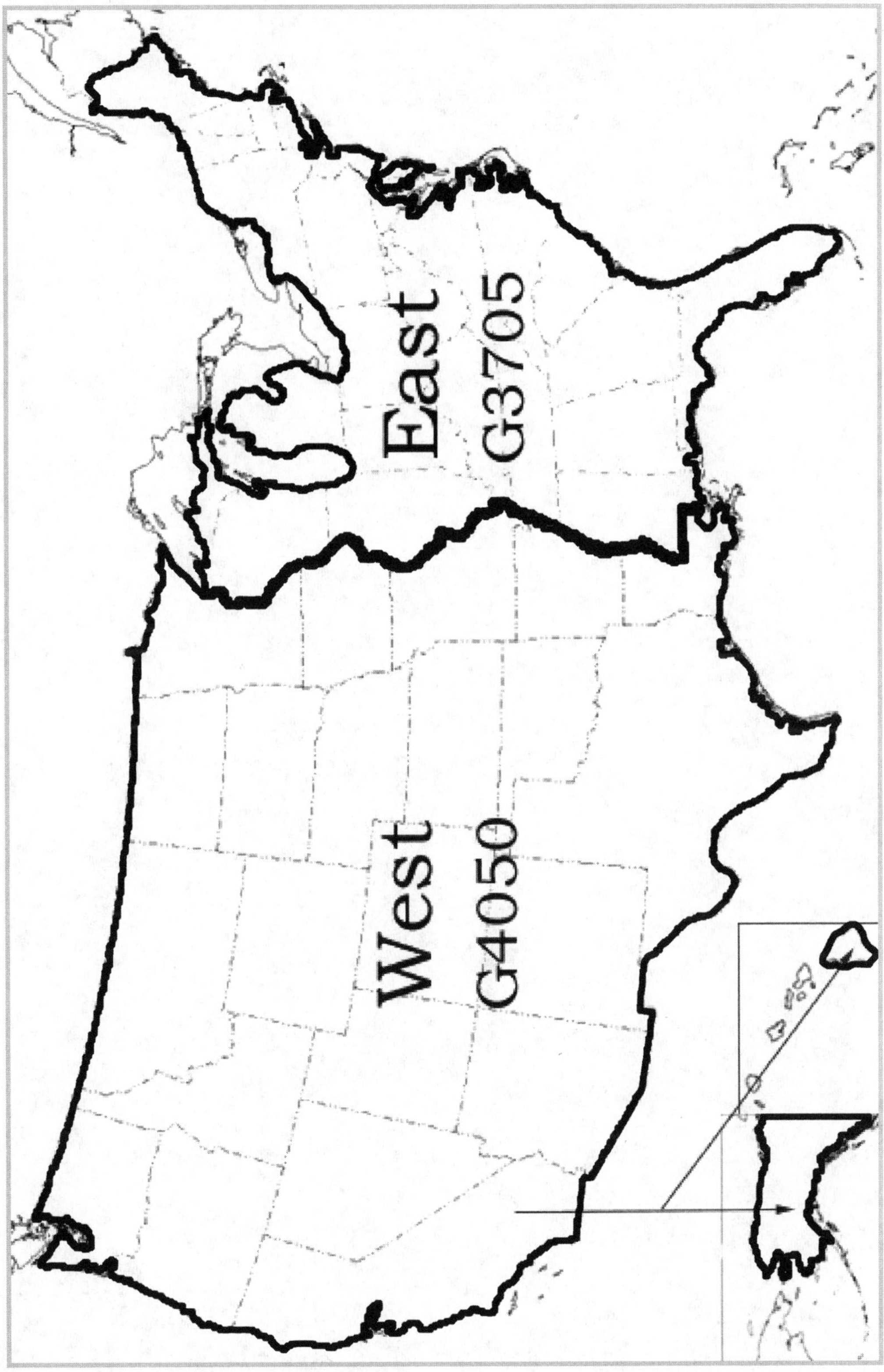

East
G3705

West
G4050

United States • *Maps: No. 1*

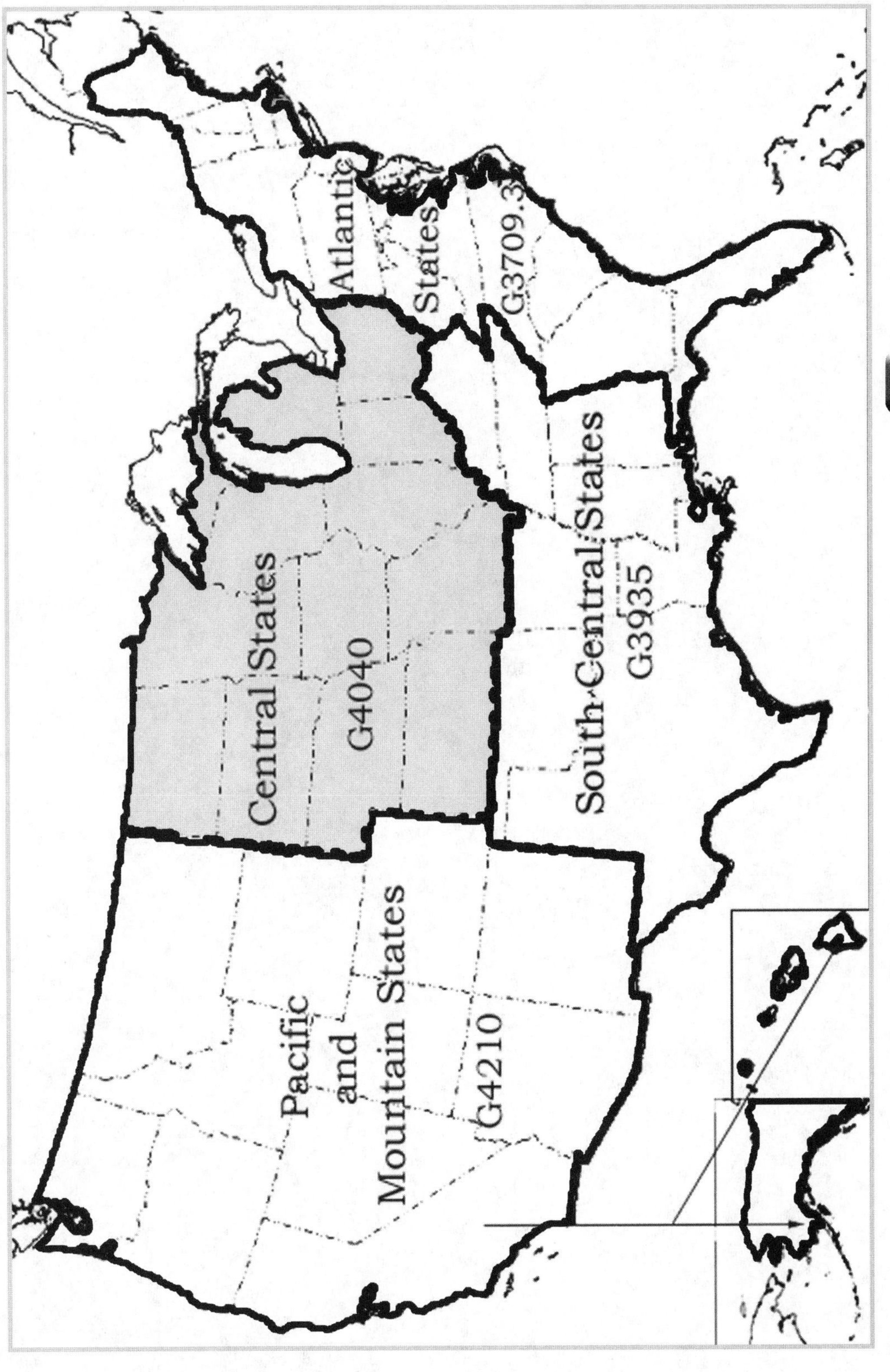

United States • *Maps: No. 2*

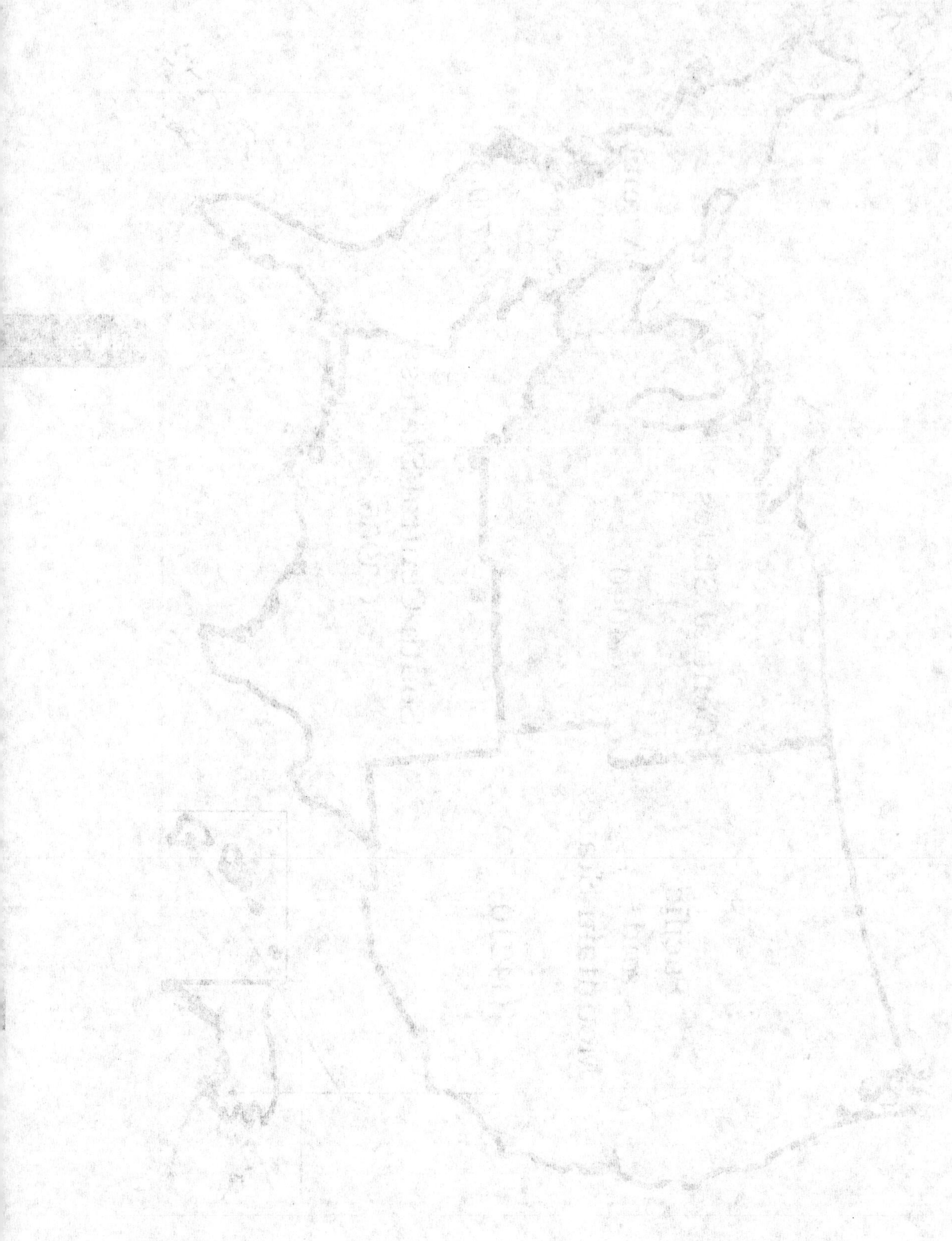

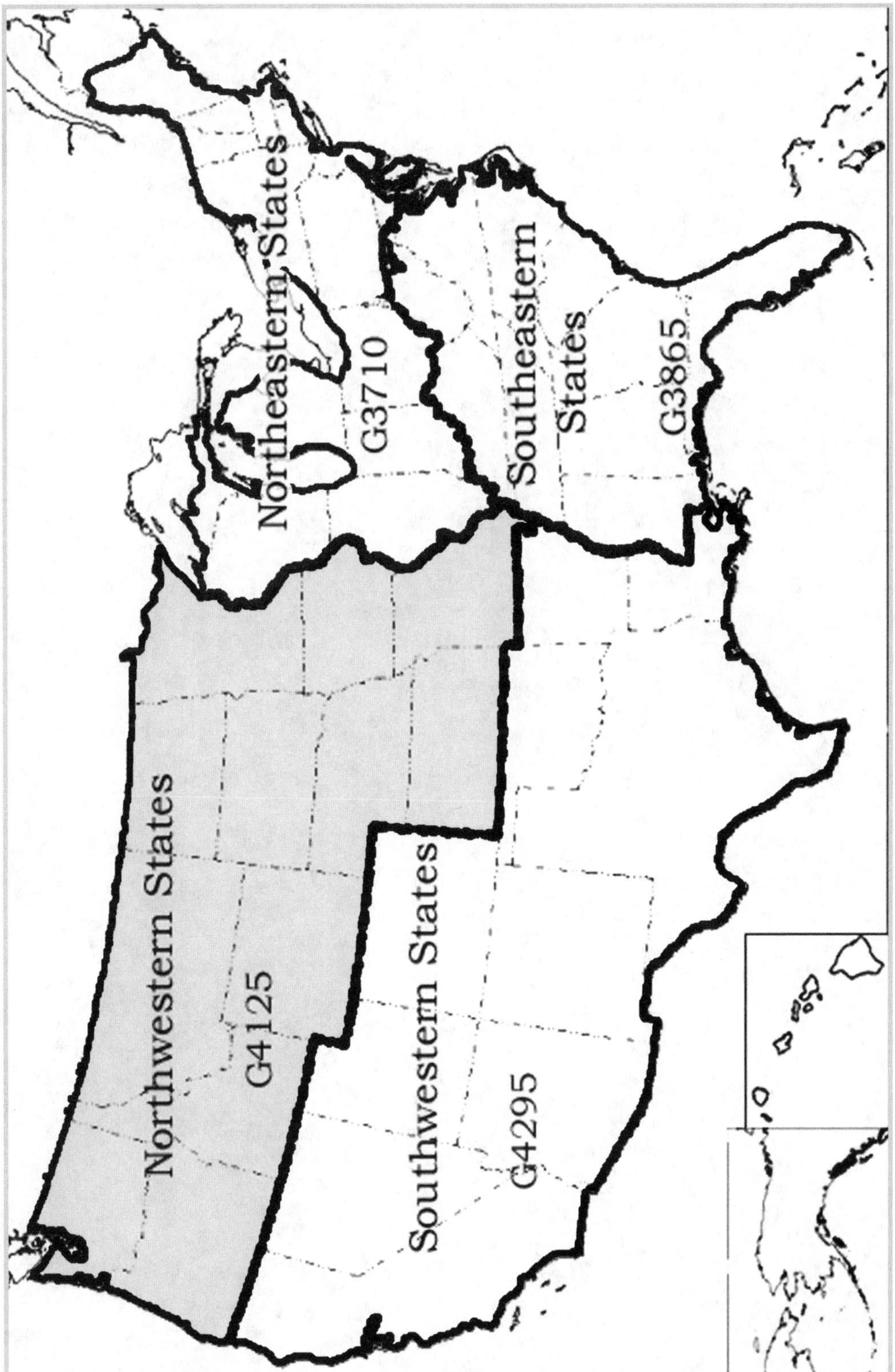

United States • *Maps: No. 3*

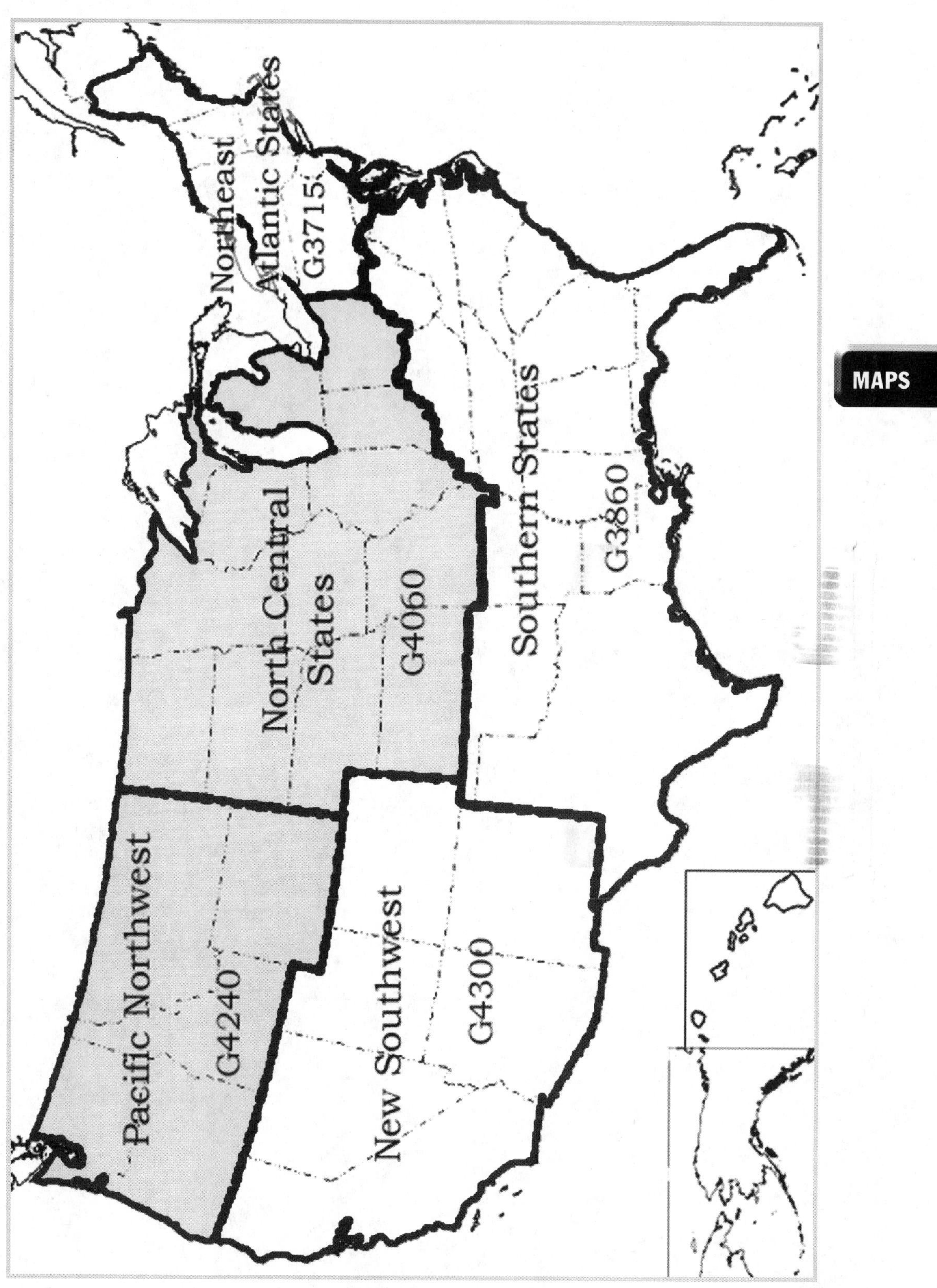

United States • *Maps: No. 4*

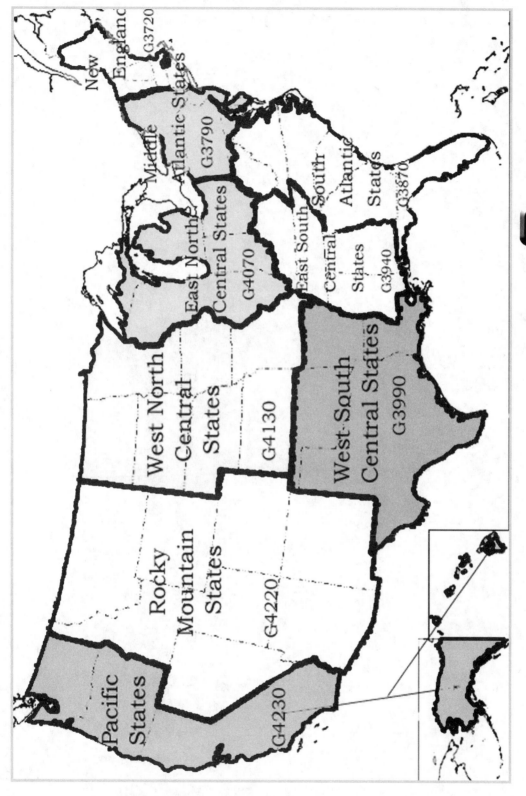

New England
G3720
Middle Atlantic States
G3790
South Atlantic States
G3870
East North Central States
G4070
East South Central States
G3940
West North Central States
G4130
West South Central States
G3990
Rocky Mountain States
G4220
Pacific States
G4230

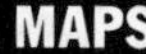

United States • *Maps: No. 5*

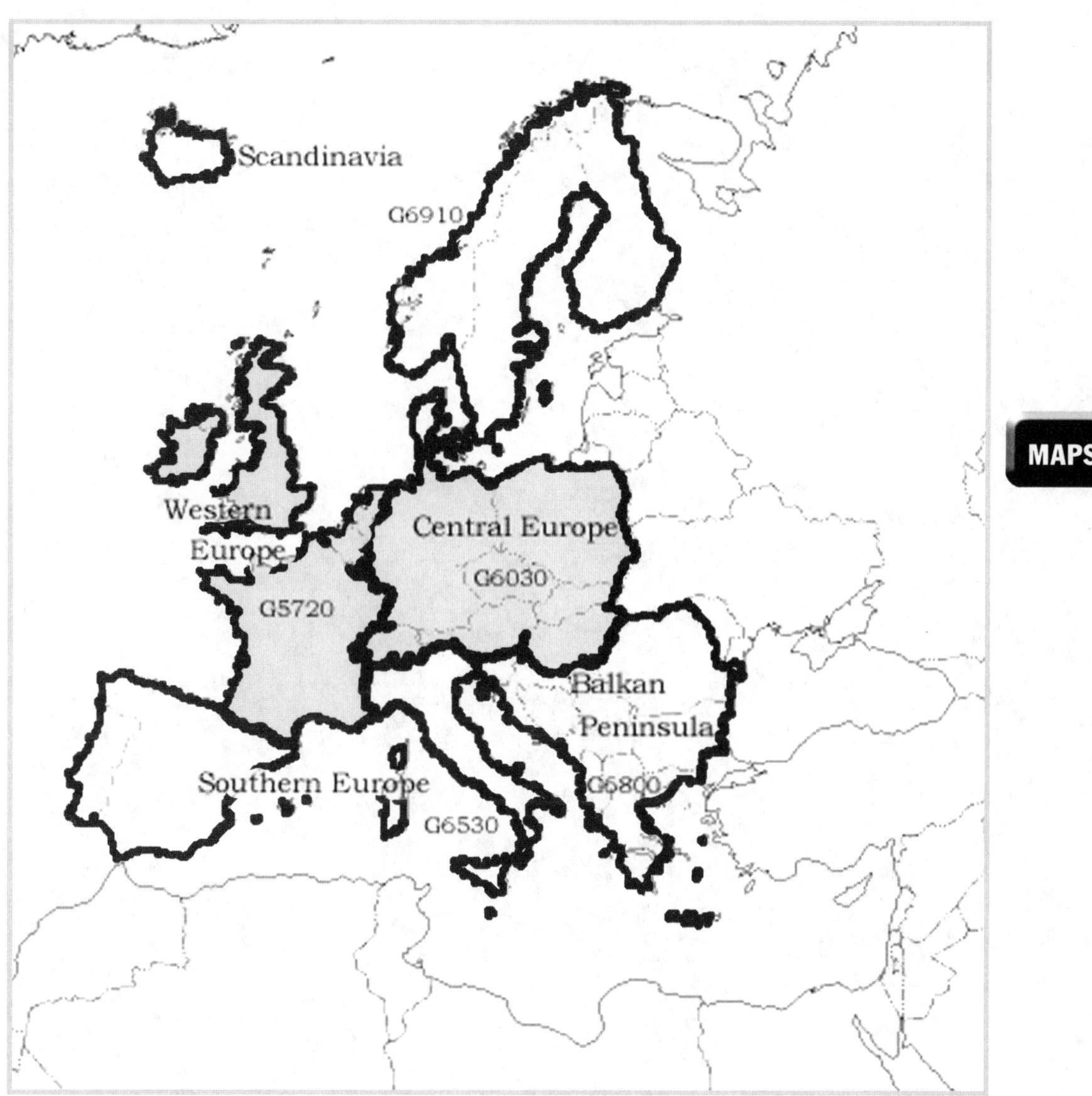

Europe • *Maps: No. 1*

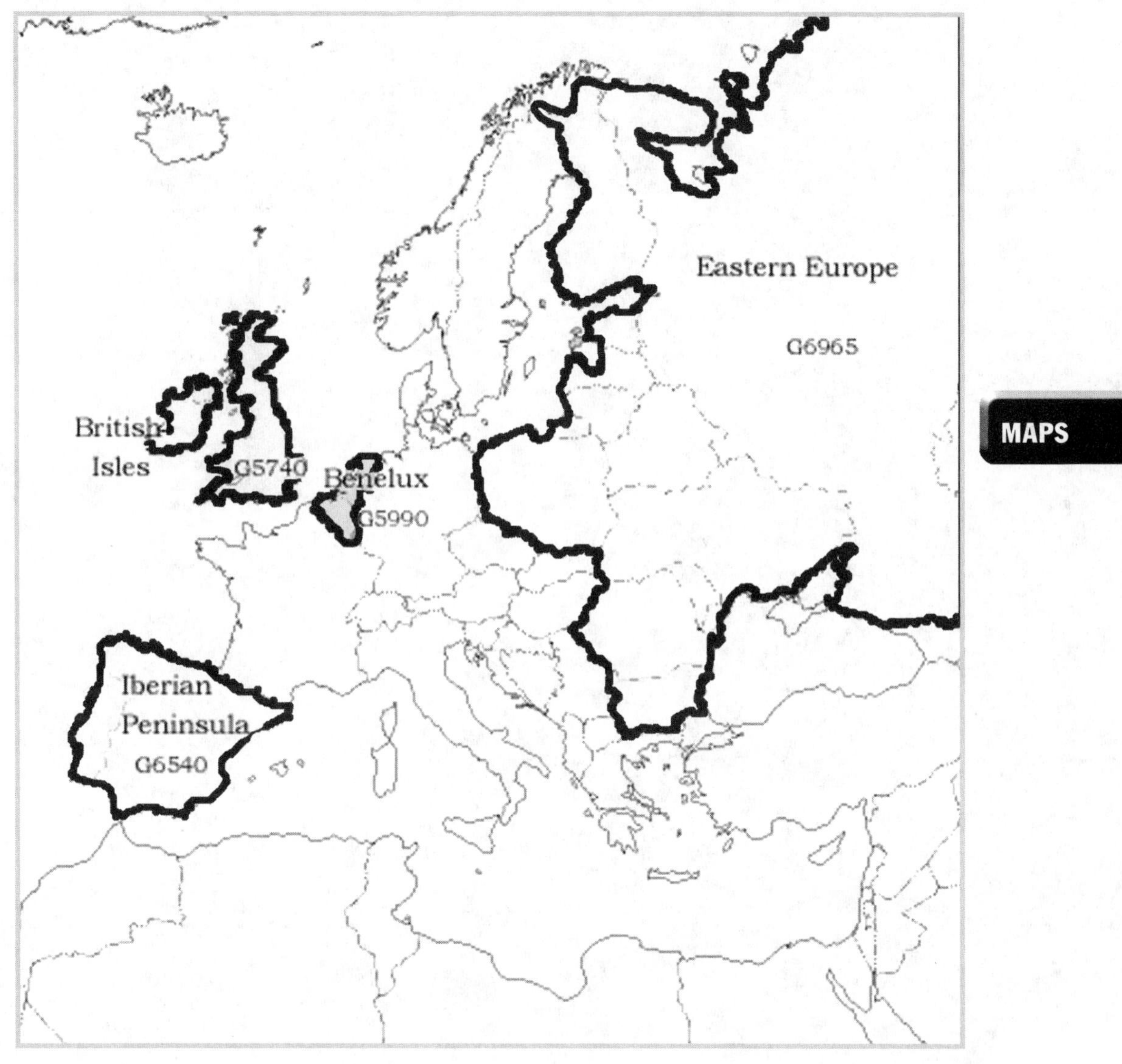

MAPS

Europe • *Maps: No. 2*

Far East
G7800

Middle East
G7420

South Asia
G7625

Southeast Asia
G8000

Asia • *Maps*

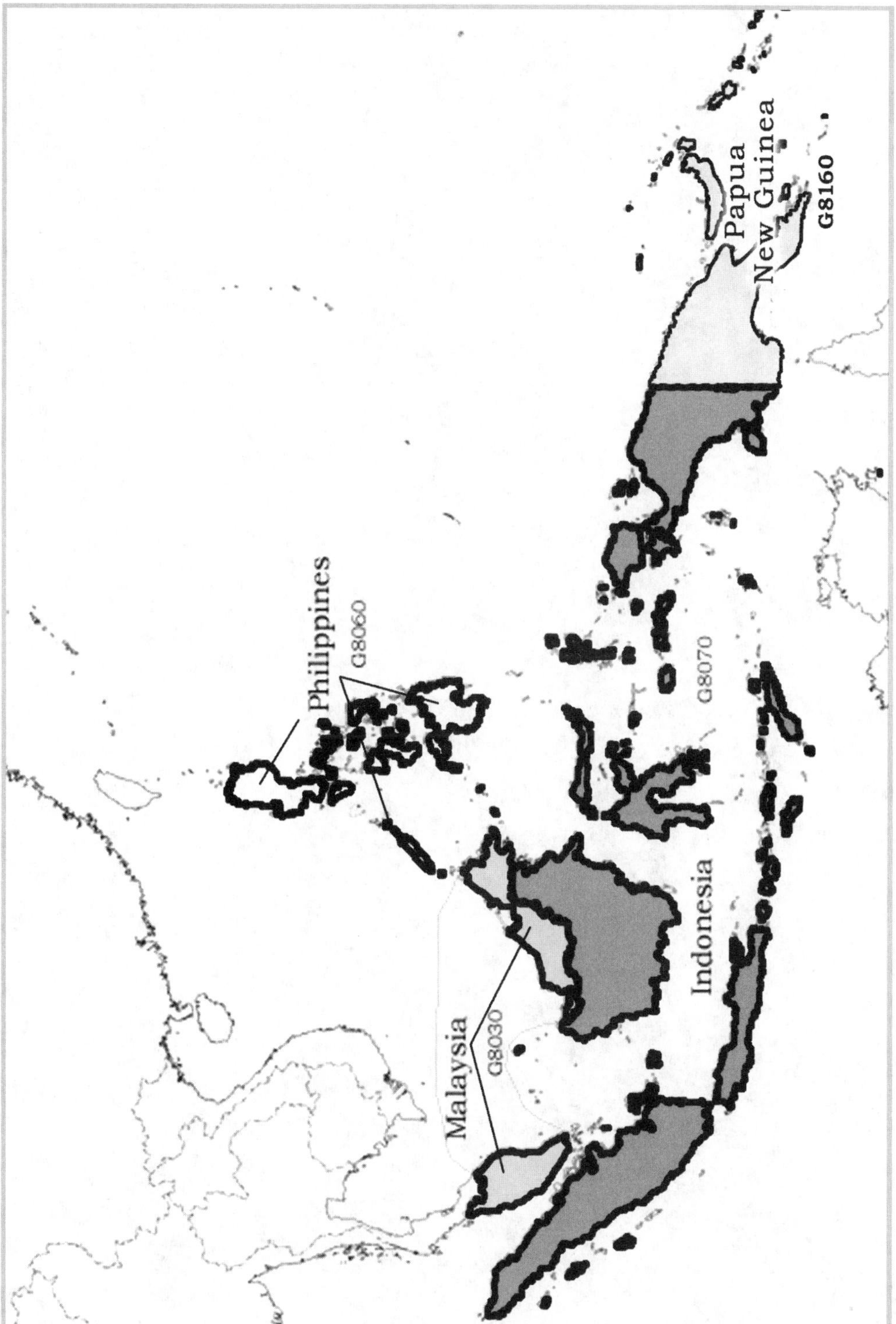

Papua
New Guinea
G8160
Philippines
G8060
G8070
Indonesia
Malaysia
G8030

Malay Archipelago • *Maps*

North Africa
G8220
West
Africa
G8735
Central
Africa
G8630
Eastern Africa
G8320
Southern
Africa
G8480

Africa • *Maps*

Maps
Universe. Solar system
3180 General
3181 By subject (Table G1)
3182 Individual planets or moons (other than Earth's moon), A-Z (Table G3182)
Apply Table G1
Celestial maps
3190 General
3191 By subject (Table G1)
Moon
3195 General
3196 By subject (Table G1)
3197 Regions, natural features, etc., A-Z (Table G3197)
Apply Table G1 for subject
World. Earth
Including maps of the known world prior to 1500 confined to the Eastern Hemisphere
Cf. G9095+ Oceans (General)
3200 General
3201 By subject (Table G1 modified)
History
3201.S1 General
3201.S12 Discovery and exploration
3201.S2 Ancient and classical history
3201.S3 Medieval history, 476-1453
3201.S33 Early medieval history
3201.S36 11th-15th centuries
3201.S4 Modern history
3201.S5 17th-19th centuries
3201.S6 20th century
3201.S65 World War I
3201.S7 World War II
3201.S73 1945-
3202 Regions, natural features, etc., A-Z (Table G3202)
Apply Table G1 for subject (except .S1-.S7, historical geography)
Apply Table G3201.S for history
Western Hemisphere see G3290+
Eastern Hemisphere see G5670+
Northern Hemisphere
3210 General
3211 By subject (Table G1)
Southern Hemisphere
3220 General
3221 By subject (Table G1)
Tropics. Torrid Zone
3240 General

Tropics. Torrid Zone -- Continued
3241 By subject (Table G1)
Temperate Zone
3250 General
3251 By subject (Table G1)
Polar regions. Frigid Zone
3260 General
3261 By subject (Table G1)
Arctic regions
Cf. G9780+ Arctic Ocean
3270 General
3271 By subject (Table G1)
Antarctica see G9800+
By region or country
America. Western Hemisphere
3290 General
3291 By subject (Table G1)
3292 Regions, natural features, etc. (Table G3292)
Apply Table G1 for subject
North America
3300 General
3301 By subject (Table G1)
3302 Regions, natural features, etc., A-Z (Table G3302)
Apply Table G1 for subject
Great Lakes Aggregation
The chain of five lakes and seaway located within the land area of North America on or near the Canadian-U.S. border. Includes and extends through the St. Lawrence but does not include the Gulf of St. Lawrence
Maps of individual physical features associated with the Great Lakes but located wholly within the United States or Canada should be classed according to location
3310 General
3311 By subject (Table G1)
3312 Regions, natural features, etc., A-Z (Table G3312)
Apply Table G1 for subject
Atlantic coast and continental shelf
3320 General
3321 By subject (Table G1)
Gulf coast and continental shelf
For maps of Gulf of Mexico as a whole see G9112
3330 General
3331 By subject (Table G1)
Pacific coast and continental shelf
3350 General
3351 By subject (Table G1)
Greenland

By region or country
America. Western Hemisphere
North America
Greenland -- Continued

3380 General
3381 By subject (Table G1)
3382 Regions, natural features, etc., A-Z (Table G3382)
Apply Table G1 for subject
3384 Cities and towns, etc., A-Z (Table G3384)
Apply Table G1 for subject

Canada
Including southern Canada; eastern Canada, 1870 and earlier; Rupert's Land; and Old Northwest Territories
Class regions and districts of Rupert's Land and Old Northwest Territories by specific location

3400 General
3401 By subject (Table G1 modified)
History
3401.S1 General
3401.S12 Discovery and exploration by Europeans
Including the exploration of the North and West
To 1763
3401.S2 General
3401.S26 French and Indian War, 1755-1763. Seven Years' War, 1756-1763
1763-1867
3401.S3 General
3401.S32 American Revolution, 1775-1783
Including the American invasions of Canada
3401.S34 War of 1812
3401.S36 Rebellions in Upper and Lower Canada, 1837-1838
3401.S38 Fenian Invasions, 1866-1870
1867-1900
3401.S5 General
3401.S55 Rebellion, 1869-1870
3401.S57 Rebellion, 1885
20th century
3401.S6 General
1900-1945
3401.S62 General
3401.S65 World War I
3401.S7 World War II
3401.S73 1945-

By region or country
America. Western Hemisphere
North America
Canada -- Continued
3402 Regions, natural features, etc., A-Z (Table G3402)
Apply Table G1 for subject (except .S1-.S7, historical geography)
Apply Table G3401.S for history
3404.A1 Cities and towns collectively
For individual cities and towns see the province or territory
Eastern Canada (1871 and later)
3405 General
3406 By subject (Table G1 modified)
History
3406.S1 General
3406.S12 Discovery and exploration by Europeans
Including the exploration of the North and West
To 1763
3406.S2 General
3406.S26 French and Indian War, 1755-1763. Seven Years' War, 1756-1763
1763-1867
3406.S3 General
3406.S32 American Revolution, 1775-1783
Including the American invasions of Canada
3406.S34 War of 1812
3406.S36 Rebellions in Upper and Lower Canada, 1837-1838
3406.S38 Fenian Invasions, 1866-1870
1867-1900
3406.S5 General
3406.S55 Rebellion, 1869-1870
3406.S57 Rebellion, 1885
20th century
3406.S6 General
1900-1945
3406.S62 General
3406.S65 World War I
3406.S7 World War II
3406.S73 1945-
3407 Regions, natural features, etc. (Table G3407)
Apply Table G1 for subject (except .S1-.S7, historical geography)
Apply Table G3401.S for history
Atlantic Provinces. Atlantic Canada
3410 General

By region or country
America. Western Hemisphere
North America
Canada
Eastern Canada (1871 and later)
Atlantic Provinces. Atlantic Canada -- Continued
3411 By subject (Table G1 modified)
History
3411.S1 General
3411.S12 Discovery and exploration by Europeans
Including the exploration of the North and West
To 1763
3411.S2 General
3411.S26 French and Indian War, 1755-1763. Seven Years' War, 1756-1763
1763-1867
3411.S3 General
3411.S32 American Revolution, 1775-1783
Including the American invasions of Canada
3411.S34 War of 1812
3411.S36 Rebellions in Upper and Lower Canada, 1837-1838
3411.S38 Fenian Invasions, 1866-1870
1867-1900
3411.S5 General
3411.S55 Rebellion, 1869-1870
3411.S57 Rebellion, 1885
20th century
3411.S6 General
1900-1945
3411.S62 General
3411.S65 World War I
3411.S7 World War II
3411.S73 1945-
3412 Regions, natural features, etc., A-Z (Table G3412)
Apply Table G1 for subject (except .S1-.S7, historical geography)
Apply Table G3401.S for history
Maritime Provinces. Acadia
3415 General
3416 By subject (Table G1 modified)
History
3416.S1 General
3416.S12 Discovery and exploration by Europeans
Including the exploration of the North and West
To 1763
3416.S2 General

By region or country
America. Western Hemisphere
North America
Canada
Eastern Canada (1871 and later)
Atlantic Provinces. Atlantic Canada
Maritime Provinces. Acadia
By subject
History
To 1763 -- Continued

3416.S26 French and Indian War, 1755-1763. Seven Years' War, 1756-1763

1763-1867

3416.S3 General

3416.S32 American Revolution, 1775-1783

Including the American invasions of Canada

3416.S34 War of 1812

3416.S36 Rebellions in Upper and Lower Canada, 1837-1838

3416.S38 Fenian Invasions, 1866-1870

1867-1900

3416.S5 General

3416.S55 Rebellion, 1869-1870

3416.S57 Rebellion, 1885

20th century

3416.S6 General

1900-1945

3416.S62 General

3416.S65 World War I

3416.S7 World War II

3416.S73 1945-

3417 Regions, natural features, etc., A-Z (Table G3417)

Apply Table G1 for subject (except .S1-.S7, historical geography)

Apply Table G3401.S for history

Nova Scotia

3420 General

3421 By subject (Table G1 modified)

History

3421.S1 General

3421.S12 Discovery and exploration by Europeans

Including the exploration of the North and West

To 1763

3421.S2 General

By region or country
America. Western Hemisphere
North America
Canada
Eastern Canada (1871 and later)
Atlantic Provinces. Atlantic Canada
Maritime Provinces
Nova Scotia
By subject
History
To 1763 -- Continued

3421.S26 French and Indian War, 1755-1763. Seven Years' War, 1756-1763

1763-1867

3421.S3 General

3421.S32 American Revolution, 1775-1783

Including the American invasions of Canada

3421.S34 War of 1812

3421.S36 Rebellions in Upper and Lower Canada, 1837-1838

3421.S38 Fenian Invasions, 1866-1870

1867-1900

3421.S5 General

3421.S55 Rebellion, 1869-1870

3421.S57 Rebellion, 1885

20th century

3421.S6 General

1900-1945

3421.S62 General

3421.S65 World War I

3421.S7 World War II

3421.S73 1945-

3422 Regions, natural features, etc., A-Z (Table G3422)

Apply Table G1 for subject (except .S1-.S7, historical geography)

Apply Table G3401.S for history

3423 Counties, etc., A-Z (Table G3423)

Apply Table G1 for subject (except .S1-.S7, historical geography)

Apply Table G3401.S for history

3424 Cities and towns, etc., A-Z (Table G3424)

Apply Table G1 for subject (except .S1-.S7, historical geography)

Apply Table G3401.S for history

Prince Edward Island

By region or country
America. Western Hemisphere
North America
Canada
Eastern Canada (1871 and later)
Atlantic Provinces. Atlantic Canada
Maritime Provinces. Acadia
Prince Edward Island -- Continued

3425 General
3426 By subject (Table G1 modified)
History
3426.S1 General
3426.S12 Discovery and exploration by Europeans
Including the exploration of the North and West
To 1763
3426.S2 General
3426.S26 French and Indian War, 1755-1763. Seven Years' War, 1756-1763
1763-1867
3426.S3 General
3426.S32 American Revolution, 1775-1783
Including the American invasions of Canada
3426.S34 War of 1812
3426.S36 Rebellions in Upper and Lower Canada, 1837-1838
3426.S38 Fenian Invasions, 1866-1870
1867-1900
3426.S5 General
3426.S55 Rebellion, 1869-1870
3426.S57 Rebellion, 1885
20th century
3426.S6 General
1900-1945
3426.S62 General
3426.S65 World War I
3426.S7 World War II
3426.S73 1945-
3427 Regions, natural features, etc., A-Z (Table G3427)
Apply Table G1 for subject (except .S1-.S7, historical geography)
Apply Table G3401.S for history

By region or country
America. Western Hemisphere
North America
Canada
Eastern Canada (1871 and later)
Atlantic Provinces. Atlantic Canada
Maritime Provinces. Acadia
Prince Edward Island -- Continued

3429 Cities and towns, etc., A-Z (Table G3429)
Apply Table G1 for subject (except .S1-.S7, historical geography)
Apply Table G3401.S for history

New Brunswick

3430 General
3431 By subject (Table G1 modified)
History
3431.S1 General
3431.S12 Discovery and exploration by Europeans
Including the exploration of the North and West
To 1763
3431.S2 General
3431.S26 French and Indian War, 1755-1763. Seven Years' War, 1756-1763
1763-1867
3431.S3 General
3431.S32 American Revolution, 1775-1783
Including the American invasions of Canada
3431.S34 War of 1812
3431.S36 Rebellions in Upper and Lower Canada, 1837-1838
3431.S38 Fenian Invasions, 1866-1870
1867-1900
3431.S5 General
3431.S55 Rebellion, 1869-1870
3431.S57 Rebellion, 1885
20th century
3431.S6 General
1900-1945
3431.S62 General
3431.S65 World War I
3431.S7 World War II
3431.S73 1945-

By region or country
America. Western Hemisphere
North America
Canada
Eastern Canada (1871 and later)
Atlantic Provinces. Atlantic Canada
Maritime Provinces. Acadia
New Brunswick
3432 Regions, natural features, etc., A-Z (Table G3432)
Apply Table G1 for subject (except .S1-.S7, historical geography)
Apply Table G3401.S for history
3433 Counties, etc., A-Z (Table G3433)
Apply Table G1 for subject (except .S1-.S7, historical geography)
Apply Table G3401.S for history
3434 Cities and towns, etc., A-Z (Table G3434)
Apply Table G1 for subject (except .S1-.S7, historical geography)
Apply Table G3401.S for history
Newfoundland and Labrador
Class here maps of the island of Newfoundland as well as maps of the province as a whole
3435 General
3436 By subject (Table G1 modified)
History
3436.S1 General
3436.S12 Discovery and exploration by Europeans
Including the exploration of the North and West
To 1763
3436.S2 General
3436.S26 French and Indian War, 1755-1763. Seven Years' War, 1756-1763
1763-1867
3436.S3 General
3436.S32 American Revolution, 1775-1783
Including the American invasions of Canada
3436.S34 War of 1812
3436.S36 Rebellions in Upper and Lower Canada, 1837-1838
3436.S38 Fenian Invasions, 1866-1870
1867-1900
3436.S5 General
3436.S55 Rebellion, 1869-1870
3436.S57 Rebellion, 1885
20th century

By region or country
America. Western Hemisphere
North America
Canada
Eastern Canada (1871 and later)
Atlantic Provinces. Atlantic Canada
Newfoundland and Labrador and Labrador
By subject
History
20th century -- Continued

3436.S6 General
1900-1945
3436.S62 General
3436.S65 World War I
3436.S7 World War II
3436.S73 1945-
3437 Regions, natural features, etc., A-Z (Table G3437)
Apply Table G1 for subject (except .S1-.S7, historical geography)
Apply Table G3401.S for history
3439 Cities and towns, etc., A-Z (Table G3439)
Apply Table G1 for subject (except .S1-.S7, historical geography)
Apply Table G3401.S for history
Labrador
3440 General
3441 By subject (Table G1 modified)
History
3441.S1 General
3441.S12 Discovery and exploration by Europeans
Including the exploration of the North and West
To 1763
3441.S2 General
3441.S26 French and Indian War, 1755-1763. Seven Years' War, 1756-1763
1763-1867
3441.S3 General
3441.S32 American Revolution, 1775-1783
Including the American invasions of Canada
3441.S34 War of 1812
3441.S36 Rebellions in Upper and Lower Canada, 1837-1838
3441.S38 Fenian Invasions, 1866-1870
1867-1900

By region or country
America. Western Hemisphere
North America
Canada
Eastern Canada (1871 and later)
Atlantic Provinces. Atlantic Canada
Newfoundland and Labrador and Labrador
Labrador
By subject
History
1867-1900 -- Continued
3441.S5 General
3441.S55 Rebellion, 1869-1870
3441.S57 Rebellion, 1885
20th century
3441.S6 General
1900-1945
3441.S62 General
3441.S65 World War I
3441.S7 World War II
3441.S73 1945-
3442 Regions, natural features, etc., A-Z (Table G3442)
Apply Table G1 for subject (except .S1-.S7, historical geography)
Apply Table G3401.S for history
Central Provinces
Including Ontario and Québec together
3445 General
3446 By subject (Table G1 modified)
History
3446.S1 General
3446.S12 Discovery and exploration by Europeans
Including the exploration of the North and West
To 1763
3446.S2 General
3446.S26 French and Indian War, 1755-1763. Seven Years' War, 1756-1763
1763-1867
3446.S3 General
3446.S32 American Revolution, 1775-1783
Including the American invasions of Canada
3446.S34 War of 1812
3446.S36 Rebellions in Upper and Lower Canada, 1837-1838
3446.S38 Fenian Invasions, 1866-1870
1867-1900

By region or country
America. Western Hemisphere
North America
Canada
Eastern Canada (1871 and later)
Central Provinces
By subject
History
1867-1900 -- Continued

3446.S5 General
3446.S55 Rebellion, 1869-1870
3446.S57 Rebellion, 1885
20th century
3446.S6 General
1900-1945
3446.S62 General
3446.S65 World War I
3446.S7 World War II
3446.S73 1945-

Québec

Including the historical areas of Lower Canada and "Canada East"

3450 General
3451 By subject (Table G1)
Apply Table G3401.S1 for history
3452 Regions, natural features, etc., A-Z (Table G3452)
Apply Table G1 for subject
Apply Table G3401.S1 for history
3453 Counties, etc., A-Z (Table G3453)
Apply Table G1 for subject
Apply Table G3401.S1 for history
3454 Cities and towns, etc., A-Z (Table G3454)
Apply Table G1 for subject
Apply Table G3401.S1 for history

Ontario

Including the historical areas of Upper Canada and "Canada West"

3460 General
3461 By subject (Table G1 modified)
History
3461.S1 General
3461.S12 Discovery and exploration by Europeans
Including the exploration of the North and West
To 1763
3461.S2 General

By region or country
America. Western Hemisphere
North America
Canada
Eastern Canada (1871 and later)
Central Provinces
Ontario
By subject
History
To 1763 -- Continued

3461.S26 French and Indian War, 1755-1763. Seven Years' War, 1756-1763

1763-1867

3461.S3 General

3461.S32 American Revolution, 1775-1783

Including the American invasions of Canada

3461.S34 War of 1812

3461.S36 Rebellions in Upper and Lower Canada, 1837-1838

3461.S38 Fenian Invasions, 1866-1870

1867-1900

3461.S5 General

3461.S55 Rebellion, 1869-1870

3461.S57 Rebellion, 1885

20th century

3461.S6 General

1900-1945

3461.S62 General

3461.S65 World War I

3461.S7 World War II

3461.S73 1945-

3462 Regions, natural features, etc., A-Z (Table G3462 modified)

Apply Table G1 for subject (except .S1-.S7, historical geography)

Apply Table G3401.S for history

Bird River see G3482.B49

Manigotagan River see G3482.M3

Saganaga Lake see G4142.S16

Winnipeg River see G3482.W56

3463 Counties, etc., A-Z (Table G3463)

Apply Table G1 for subject (except .S1-.S7, historical geography)

Apply Table G3401.S for history

By region or country
America. Western Hemisphere
North America
Canada
Eastern Canada (1871 and later)
Central Provinces
Ontario -- Continued

3464 Cities and towns, etc., A-Z (Table G3464)
Apply Table G1 for subject (except .S1-.S7, historical geography)
Apply Table G3401.S for history

Western Canada

3465 General

3466 By subject (Table G1 modified)

History

3466.S1 General

3466.S12 Discovery and exploration by Europeans
Including the exploration of the North and West

To 1763

3466.S2 General

3466.S26 French and Indian War, 1755-1763. Seven Years' War, 1756-1763

1763-1867

3466.S3 General

3466.S32 American Revolution, 1775-1783
Including the American invasions of Canada

3466.S34 War of 1812

3466.S36 Rebellions in Upper and Lower Canada, 1837-1838

3466.S38 Fenian Invasions, 1866-1870

1867-1900

3466.S5 General

3466.S55 Rebellion, 1869-1870

3466.S57 Rebellion, 1885

20th century

3466.S6 General

1900-1945

3466.S62 General

3466.S65 World War I

3466.S7 World War II

3466.S73 1945-

3467 Regions, natural features, etc., A-Z (Table G3467)
Apply Table G1 for subject (except .S1-.S7, historical geography)
Apply Table G3401.S for history

Prairie Provinces

3470 General

By region or country
America. Western Hemisphere
North America
Canada
Western Canada
Prairie Provinces -- Continued

3471 By subject (Table G1 modified)
History
3471.S1 General
3471.S12 Discovery and exploration by Europeans
Including the exploration of the North and West
To 1763
3471.S2 General
3471.S26 French and Indian War, 1755-1763. Seven Years' War, 1756-1763
1763-1867
3471.S3 General
3471.S32 American Revolution, 1775-1783
Including the American invasions of Canada
3471.S34 War of 1812
3471.S36 Rebellions in Upper and Lower Canada, 1837-1838
3471.S38 Fenian Invasions, 1866-1870
1867-1900
3471.S5 General
3471.S55 Rebellion, 1869-1870
3471.S57 Rebellion, 1885
20th century
3471.S6 General
1900-1945
3471.S62 General
3471.S65 World War I
3471.S7 World War II
3471.S73 1945-
3472 Regions, natural features, etc., A-Z (Table G3472)
Apply Table G1 for subject (except .S1-.S7, historical geography)
Apply Table G3401.S for history
Manitoba
3480 General
3481 By subject (Table G1 modified)
History
3481.S1 General
3481.S12 Discovery and exploration by Europeans
Including the exploration of the North and West
To 1763
3481.S2 General

By region or country
America. Western Hemisphere
North America
Canada
Western Canada
Prairie Provinces
Manitoba
By subject
History
To 1763 -- Continued

3481.S26 French and Indian War, 1755-1763. Seven Years' War, 1756-1763

1763-1867

3481.S3 General

3481.S32 American Revolution, 1775-1783

Including the American invasions of Canada

3481.S34 War of 1812

3481.S36 Rebellions in Upper and Lower Canada, 1837-1838

3481.S38 Fenian Invasions, 1866-1870

1867-1900

3481.S5 General

3481.S55 Rebellion, 1869-1870

3481.S57 Rebellion, 1885

20th century

3481.S6 General

1900-1945

3481.S62 General

3481.S65 World War I

3481.S7 World War II

3481.S73 1945-

3482 Regions, natural features, etc., A-Z (Table G3482 modified)

Apply Table G1 for subject (except .S1-.S7, historical geography)

Apply Table G3401.S for history

3482.B49 Bird River [Ont. and Man.]

Subarrange by Table G1 except .S1-.S7, historical geography. For history, subarrange by Table G3401.S

3482.M3 Manigotagan River [Ont. and Man.]

Subarrange by Table G1 except .S1-.S7, historical geography. For history, subarrange by Table G3401.S

By region or country
America. Western Hemisphere
North America
Canada
Western Canada
Prairie Provinces
Manitoba
Regions, natural features, etc., A-Z -- Continued

3482.W56 Winnipeg River [Ont. and Man.]
Subarrange by Table G1 except .S1-.S7, historical geography. For history, subarrange by Table G3401.S

3484 Cities and towns, etc., A-Z (Table G3484)
Apply Table G1 for subject (except .S1-.S7, historical geography)
Apply Table G3401.S for history

Saskatchewan
3490 General
3491 By subject (Table G1 modified)
History
3491.S1 General
3491.S12 Discovery and exploration by Europeans
Including the exploration of the North and West
To 1763
3491.S2 General
3491.S26 French and Indian War, 1755-1763. Seven Years' War, 1756-1763
1763-1867
3491.S3 General
3491.S32 American Revolution, 1775-1783
Including the American invasions of Canada
3491.S34 War of 1812
3491.S36 Rebellions in Upper and Lower Canada, 1837-1838
3491.S38 Fenian Invasions, 1866-1870
1867-1900
3491.S5 General
3491.S55 Rebellion, 1869-1870
3491.S57 Rebellion, 1885
20th century
3491.S6 General
1900-1945
3491.S62 General
3491.S65 World War I
3491.S7 World War II
3491.S73 1945-

By region or country
America. Western Hemisphere
North America
Canada
Western Canada
Prairie Provinces
Saskatchewan -- Continued

3492 Regions, natural features, etc., A-Z (Table G3492)
Apply Table G1 for subject (except .S1-.S7, historical geography)
Apply Table G3401.S for history

3494 Cities and towns, etc., A-Z (Table G3494)
Apply Table G1 for subject (except .S1-.S7, historical geography)
Apply Table G3401.S for history

Alberta

3500 General

3501 By subject (Table G1 modified)

History

3501.S1 General

3501.S12 Discovery and exploration by Europeans
Including the exploration of the North and West

To 1763

3501.S2 General

3501.S26 French and Indian War, 1755-1763. Seven Years' War, 1756-1763

1763-1867

3501.S3 General

3501.S32 American Revolution, 1775-1783
Including the American invasions of Canada

3501.S34 War of 1812

3501.S36 Rebellions in Upper and Lower Canada, 1837-1838

3501.S38 Fenian Invasions, 1866-1870

1867-1900

3501.S5 General

3501.S55 Rebellion, 1869-1870

3501.S57 Rebellion, 1885

20th century

3501.S6 General

1900-1945

3501.S62 General

3501.S65 World War I

3501.S7 World War II

3501.S73 1945-

By region or country
America. Western Hemisphere
North America
Canada
Western Canada
Prairie Provinces
Alberta -- Continued

3502 Regions, natural features, etc., A-Z (Table G3502)
Apply Table G1 for subject (except .S1-.S7, historical geography)
Apply Table G3401.S for history

3503 Counties, etc., A-Z (Table G3503)
Apply Table G1 for subject (except .S1-.S7, historical geography)
Apply Table G3401.S for history

3504 Cities and towns, etc., A-Z (Table G3504)
Apply Table G1 for subject (except .S1-.S7, historical geography)
Apply Table G3401.S for history

Cordilleran Provinces and Territories
Including British Columbia, Yukon, Alberta, and that portion of MacKenzie District, N.W.T. west of the MacKenzie River treated together

3505 General
3506 By subject (Table G1)
3507 Regions, natural features, etc., A-Z (Table G3507)
Apply Table G1 for subject
Apply Table G3401.S for history

British Columbia
3510 General
3511 By subject (Table G1 modified)
History
3511.S1 General
3511.S12 Discovery and exploration by Europeans
Including the exploration of the North and West

To 1763
3511.S2 General
3511.S26 French and Indian War, 1755-1763. Seven Years' War, 1756-1763

1763-1867
3511.S3 General
3511.S32 American Revolution, 1775-1783
Including the American invasions of Canada
3511.S34 War of 1812
3511.S36 Rebellions in Upper and Lower Canada, 1837-1838

By region or country
America. Western Hemisphere
North America
Canada
Western Canada
Cordilleran Provinces and Territories
British Columbia
By subject
History
1763-1867 -- Continued
3511.S38 Fenian Invasions, 1866-1870
1867-1900
3511.S5 General
3511.S55 Rebellion, 1869-1870
3511.S57 Rebellion, 1885
20th century
3511.S6 General
1900-1945
3511.S62 General
3511.S65 World War I
3511.S7 World War II
3511.S73 1945-
3512 Regions, natural features, etc., A-Z (Table G3512)
Apply Table G1 for subject (except .S1-.S7, historical geography)
Apply Table G3401.S for history
3513 Regional districts, A-Z (Table G3513)
Apply Table G1 for subject (except .S1-.S7, historical geography)
Apply Table G3401.S for history
3514 Cities and towns, etc., A-Z (Table G3514)
Apply Table G1 for subject (except .S1-.S7, historical geography)
Apply Table G3401.S for history
Northern Canada
Including maps of the Northwest Territories and the Yukon together
3515 General
3516 By subject (Table G1 modified)
History
3516.S1 General
3516.S12 Discovery and exploration by Europeans
Including the exploration of the North and West
To 1763
3516.S2 General

By region or country
America. Western Hemisphere
North America
Canada
Northern Canada
By subject
History
To 1763 -- Continued

3516.S26 French and Indian War, 1755-1763. Seven Years' War, 1756-1763

1763-1867

3516.S3 General

3516.S32 American Revolution, 1775-1783

Including the American invasions of Canada

3516.S34 War of 1812

3516.S36 Rebellions in Upper and Lower Canada, 1837-1838

3516.S38 Fenian Invasions, 1866-1870

1867-1900

3516.S5 General

3516.S55 Rebellion, 1869-1870

3516.S57 Rebellion, 1885

20th century

3516.S6 General

1900-1945

3516.S62 General

3516.S65 World War I

3516.S7 World War II

3516.S73 1945-

3517 Regions, natural features, etc., A-Z (Table G3517)

Apply Table G1 for subject (except .S1-.S7, historical geography)

Apply Table G3401.S for history

Yukon

3520 General

3521 By subject (Table G1 modified)

History

3521.S1 General

3521.S12 Discovery and exploration by Europeans

Including the exploration of the North and West

To 1763

3521.S2 General

3521.S26 French and Indian War, 1755-1763. Seven Years' War, 1756-1763

1763-1867

3521.S3 General

By region or country
America. Western Hemisphere
North America
Canada
Northern Canada
Yukon
By subject
History
1763-1867 -- Continued
3521.S32 American Revolution, 1775-1783
Including the American invasions of Canada
3521.S34 War of 1812
3521.S36 Rebellions in Upper and Lower Canada, 1837-1838
3521.S38 Fenian Invasions, 1866-1870
1867-1900
3521.S5 General
3521.S55 Rebellion, 1869-1870
3521.S57 Rebellion, 1885
20th century
3521.S6 General
1900-1945
3521.S62 General
3521.S65 World War I
3521.S7 World War II
3521.S73 1945-
3522 Regions, natural features, etc., A-Z (Table G3522)
Apply Table G1 for subject (except .S1-.S7, historical geography)
Apply Table G3401.S for history
3524 Cities and towns, etc., A-Z (Table G3524)
Apply Table G1 for subject (except .S1-.S7, historical geography)
Apply Table G3401.S for history
Northwest Territories
3530 General
3531 By subject (Table G1 modified)
History
3531.S1 General
3531.S12 Discovery and exploration by Europeans
Including the exploration of the North and West
To 1763
3531.S2 General
3531.S26 French and Indian War, 1755-1763. Seven Years' War, 1756-1763
1763-1867
3531.S3 General

By region or country
America. Western Hemisphere
North America
Canada
Northern Canada
Northwest Territories
By subject
History
1763-1867 -- Continued

3531.S32 American Revolution, 1775-1783
Including the American invasions of Canada
3531.S34 War of 1812
3531.S36 Rebellions in Upper and Lower Canada, 1837-1838
3531.S38 Fenian Invasions, 1866-1870
1867-1900
3531.S5 General
3531.S55 Rebellion, 1869-1870
3531.S57 Rebellion, 1885
20th century
3531.S6 General
1900-1945
3531.S62 General
3531.S65 World War I
3531.S7 World War II
3531.S73 1945-
3532 Regions, natural features, etc., A-Z (Table G3532)
Apply Table G1 for subject (except .S1-.S7, historical geography)
Apply Table G3401.S for history
3533 Districts, territorial regions, etc., A-Z (Table G3533)
Apply Table G1 for subject (except .S1-.S7, historical geography)
Apply Table G3401.S for history
3534 Cities and towns, etc., A-Z (Table G3534)
Apply Table G1 for subject (except .S1-.S7, historical geography)
Apply Table G3401.S for history
Nunavut
3535 General
3536 By subject (Table G1 modified)
History
3536.S1 General
3536.S12 Discovery and exploration by Europeans
Including the exploration of the North and West
To 1763
3536.S2 General

By region or country
America. Western Hemisphere
North America
Canada
Northern Canada
Nunavut
By subject
History
To 1763 -- Continued

3536.S26 French and Indian War, 1755-1763. Seven Years' War, 1756-1763

1763-1867

3536.S3 General

3536.S32 American Revolution, 1775-1783

Including the American invasions of Canada

3536.S34 War of 1812

3536.S36 Rebellions in Upper and Lower Canada, 1837-1838

3536.S38 Fenian Invasions, 1866-1870

1867-1900

3536.S5 General

3536.S55 Rebellion, 1869-1870

3536.S57 Rebellion, 1885

20th century

3536.S6 General

1900-1945

3536.S62 General

3536.S65 World War I

3536.S7 World War II

3536.S73 1945-

3537 Regions, natural features, etc., A-Z (Table G3537)

Apply Table G1 for subject (except .S1-.S7, historical geography)

3539 Cities and towns, etc., A-Z (Table G3539)

Apply Table G1 for subject (except .S1-.S7, historical geography)

Newfoundland

(3600-3604) General

see G3435+

(3610-3612) Labrador

see G3440+

Saint Pierre and Miquelon Islands

3650 General

3651 By subject (Table G1)

3652 Regions, natural features, etc., A-Z (Table G3652)

Apply Table G1 for subject

By region or country
America. Western Hemisphere
North America
Saint Pierre and Miquelon Islands -- Continued
3654 Cities and towns, etc., A-Z (Table G3654)
Apply Table G1 for subject
3691 United States possessions (Collectively)
Class individual possessions by location, e.g., G9415, Guam
United States
3700 General
3701 By subject (Table G1a)
3702 Regions, natural features, etc., A-Z (Table G3702)
Apply Table G1a for subject
3704.A1 Cities and towns (Collectively)
For individual cities and towns, see the state
Eastern United States, 1870 and later
Comprises the area east of the Mississippi River
3705 General
3706 By subject (Table G1a)
3707 Regions, natural features, etc., A-Z (Table G3707)
Apply Table G1a for subject
Atlantic States
3709.3 General
3709.31 By subject (Table G1a)
3709.32 Regions, natural features, etc., A-Z (Table G3709.32 modified)
Apply Table G1a for subject
Potomac River see G3792.P6
Northeastern States
3710 General
3711 By subject (Table G1a)
3712 Regions, natural features, etc., A-Z (Table G3712)
Apply Table G1a for subject
Northeast Atlantic States
3715 General
3716 By subject (Table G1a)
3717 Regions, natural features, etc., A-Z (Table G3717)
Apply Table G1a for subject
New England
3720 General
3721 By subject (Table G1a)
3722 Regions, natural features, etc., A-Z (Table G3722)
Apply Table G1a for subject
Maine

By region or country
America. Western Hemisphere
North America
United States
Eastern United States, 1870 and later
Northeastern States
Northeast Atlantic States
New England
Maine -- Continued

3730 General
3731 By subject (Table G1a)
3732 Regions, natural features, etc., A-Z (Table G3732)
Apply Table G1a for subject
3733 Counties, A-Z (Table G3733)
Apply Table G1a for subject
3734 Cities, towns, and townships, etc., A-Z (Table G3734)
Apply Table G1a for subject

New Hampshire

3740 General
3741 By subject (Table G1a)
3742 Regions, natural features, etc., A-Z (Table G3742)
Apply Table G1a for subject
3743 Counties, A-Z (Table G3743)
Apply Table G1a for subject
3744 Cities, towns, and townships, etc., A-Z (Table G3744)
Apply Table G1a for subject

Vermont

3750 General
3751 By subject (Table G1a)
3752 Regions, natural features, etc., A-Z (Table G3752)
Apply Table G1a for subject
3753 Counties, A-Z (Table G3753)
Apply Table G1a for subject
3754 Cities, towns, and townships, etc., A-Z (Table G3754)
Apply Table G1a for subject

Massachusetts

3760 General
3761 By subject (Table G1a)
3762 Regions, natural features, etc., A-Z (Table G3762 modified)
Apply Table G1a for subject

By region or country
America. Western Hemisphere
North America
United States
Eastern United States, 1870 and later
Northeastern States
Northeast Atlantic States
New England
Massachusetts
Regions, natural features, etc., A-Z -- Continued

3762.N3 Nantucket Island
Subarrange by Table G1a

3763 Counties, A-Z (Table G3763 modified)
Apply Table G1a for subject
Nantucket Island see G3762.N3

3764 Cities, towns, and townships, etc., A-Z (Table G3764)
Apply Table G1a for subject

Rhode Island

3770 General

3771 By subject (Table G1a)

3772 Regions, natural features, etc., A-Z (Table G3772)
Apply Table G1a for subject

3773 Counties, A-Z (Table G3773)
Apply Table G1a for subject

3774 Cities, towns, and townships, etc., A-Z (Table G3774)
Apply Table G1a for subject

Connecticut

3780 General

3781 By subject (Table G1a)

3782 Regions, natural features, etc., A-Z (Table G3782)
Apply Table G1a for subject

3783 Counties, A-Z (Table G3783)
Apply Table G1a for subject

3784 Cities, towns, and townships, etc., A-Z (Table G3784)
Apply Table G1a for subject

Middle Atlantic States. Middle States
Often including Virginia and West Virginia, sometimes also Ohio and Kentucky

3790 General

3791 By subject (Table G1a)

By region or country
America. Western Hemisphere
North America
United States
Eastern United States, 1870 and later
Northeastern States
Northeast Atlantic States
Middle Atlantic States. Middle States -- Continued

3792 Regions, natural features, etc., A-Z (Table G3792 modified)
Apply Table G1a for subject

3792.P6 Potomac River
Subarrange by Table G1a

New York (State)

3800 General

3801 By subject (Table G1a)

3802 Regions, natural features, etc., A-Z (Table G3802 modified)
Apply Table G1a for subject
Staten Island see G3804.N4:2S8
Staten Island (Staten Island Botanical Garden) see G3804.N4:2S82

3803 Counties, A-Z (Table G3803 modified)
Apply Table G1a for subject
Bronx see G3804.N4:3B7
Kings see G3804.N4:3B8
New York see G3804.N4:2M3
Queens see G3804.N4:3Q4
Richmond see G3804.N4:2S8
Richmond (Staten Island Botanical Garden) see G3804.N4:2S82

3804 Cities, towns, and urban townships, etc., A-Z (Table G3804 modified)
Apply Table G1a for subject

3804.N4:2M3 Manhattan [New York]
Subarrange by Table G1a

3804.N4:2S8 Staten Island [New York]
Subarrange by Table G1a

3804.N4:2S82 Staten Island Botanical Garden [New York]
Subarrange by Table G1a

3804.N4:3B7 Bronx [New York]
Subarrange by Table G1a

3804.N4:3B8 Brooklyn [New York]
Subarrange by Table G1a

3804.N4:3Q4 Queens [New York]
Subarrange by Table G1a

By region or country
America. Western Hemisphere
North America
United States
Eastern United States, 1870 and later
Northeastern States
Northeast Atlantic States
Middle Atlantic States. Middle States -- Continued
New Jersey
3810 General
3811 By subject (Table G1a)
3812 Regions, natural features, etc., A-Z (Table G3812)
Apply Table G1a for subject
3813 Counties, A-Z (Table G3813)
Apply Table G1a for subject
3814 Cities and towns, etc., A-Z (Table G3814)
Apply Table G1a for subject
Pennsylvania
3820 General
3821 By subject (Table G1a)
3822 Regions, natural features, etc., A-Z (Table G3822)
Apply Table G1a for subject
3823 Counties, A-Z (Table G3823)
Apply Table G1a for subject
Philadelphia see G3824.P5
Philadelphia (Bartrams's Garden) see G3824.P5:2B3
Philadelphia (Chestnut Hill, Battle of, 1777) see G3824.P5:2C42
Philadelphia (Fabric Row) see G3824.P5:2F2
Philadelphia (Germantown, Battle of, 1777) see G3824.P5:2G433
Philadelphia (North Philadelphia) see G3824.P5:2N57
Philadelphia (Washington Square West) see G3824.P5:2W33
3824 Cities and towns, etc., A-Z (Table G3824 modified)
Apply Table G1a for subject
3824.P5 Philadelphia
Subarrange by Table G1a
3824.P5:2B3 Bartram's Garden [Philadelphia]
Subarrange by Table G1a

By region or country
America. Western Hemisphere
North America
United States
Eastern United States, 1870 and later
Northeastern States
Northeast Atlantic States
Middle Atlantic States. Middle States
Pennsylvania
Cities and towns, etc., A-Z -- Continued

3824.P5:2C42 Chestnut Hill, Battle of, 1777 [Philadelphia]
Subarrange by Table G1a

3824.P5:2F2 Fabric Row [Philadelphia]
Subarrange by Table G1a

3824.P5:2G433 Germantown, Battle of, 1777 [Philadelphia]
Subarrange by Table G1a

3824.P5:2N57 North Philadelphia [Philadelphia]
Subarrange by Table G1a

3824.P5:2W33 Washington Square West [Philadelphia]
Subarrange by Table G1a

Delaware

3830 General

3831 By subject (Table G1a)

3832 Regions, natural features, etc., A-Z (Table G3832)
Apply Table G1a for subject

3833 Counties, A-Z (Table G3833)
Apply Table G1a for subject

3834 Cities and towns, etc., A-Z (Table G3834)
Apply Table G1a for subject

Maryland

3840 General

3841 By subject (Table G1a)

3842 Regions, natural features, etc., A-Z (Table G3842)
Apply Table G1a for subject

3843 Counties, A-Z (Table G3843)
Apply Table G1a for subject

3844 Cities and towns, etc., A-Z (Table G3844)
Apply Table G1a for subject

District of Columbia. Washington, D.C.

3850 General

3851 By subject (Table G1a)

3852 Buildings, sections, former towns, streets, etc., A-Z (Table G3852)
Apply Table G1a for subject

By region or country
America. Western Hemisphere
North America
United States
Eastern United States, 1870 and later -- Continued
Southern States. Confederate States of America
Including Gulf States

3860 General
3861 By subject (Table G1a)
3862 Regions, natural features, etc., A-Z (Table G3862)
Apply Table G1a for subject

Southeastern States
3865 General
3866 By subject (Table G1a)
3867 Regions, natural features, etc., A-Z (Table G3867)
Apply Table G1a for subject

South Atlantic States. Southeast Atlantic States
3870 General
3871 By subject (Table G1a)
3872 Regions, natural features, etc., A-Z (Table G3872)
Apply Table G1a for subject

Virginia
3880 General
3881 By subject (Table G1a)
3882 Regions, natural features, etc., A-Z (Table G3882)
Apply Table G1a for subject
3883 Counties, A-Z (Table G3883 modified)
Apply Table G1a for subject
3883.A8 Arlington
Subarrange by Table G1a
Nansemond see G3884.S9
Nansemond (Holland) see G3884.S9:2H7
Princess Anne see G3884.V8
Princess Anne (Cape Henry Life Saving Station) see G3884.V8:2C35
Warwick see G3884.N4
3884 Cities and towns, etc., A-Z (Table G3884 modified)
Apply Table G1a for subject
Arlington see G3883.A8
3884.N4 Newport News
Subarrange by Table G1a
3884.S9 Suffolk
Subarrange by Table G1a

By region or country
America. Western Hemisphere
North America
United States
Eastern United States, 1870 and later
Southern States. Confederate States of America
Southeastern States
South Atlantic States. Southeast Atlantic States
Virginia
Cities and towns, etc., A-Z -- Continued

3884.S9:2H7 Holland [Suffolk]
Subarrange by Table G1a

3884.V8 Virginia Beach
Subarrange by Table G1a

3884.V8:2C35 Cape Henry Life Saving Station
Subarrange by Table G1a

West Virginia

3890 General

3891 By subject (Table G1a)

3892 Regions, natural features, etc., A-Z (Table G3892)
Apply Table G1a for subject

3893 Counties, A-Z (Table G3893)
Apply Table G1a for subject

3894 Cities and towns, etc., A-Z (Table G3894)
Apply Table G1a for subject

North Carolina

3900 General

3901 By subject (Table G1a)

3902 Regions, natural features, etc., A-Z (Table G3902)
Apply Table G1a for subject

3903 Counties, A-Z (Table G3903)
Apply Table G1a for subject

3904 Cities and towns, etc., A-Z (Table G3904)
Apply Table G1a for subject

South Carolina

3910 General

3911 By subject (Table G1a)

3912 Regions, natural features, etc., A-Z (Table G3912)
Apply Table G1a for subject

3913 Counties, A-Z (Table G3913)
Apply Table G1a for subject

3914 Cities and towns, etc., A-Z (Table G3914)
Apply Table G1a for subject

Georgia

By region or country
America. Western Hemisphere
North America
United States
Eastern United States, 1870 and later
Southern States. Confederate States of America
Southeastern States
South Atlantic States. Southeast Atlantic States
Georgia -- Continued

3920 General
3921 By subject (Table G1a)
3922 Regions, natural features, etc., A-Z (Table G3922)
Apply Table G1a for subject
3923 Counties, A-Z (Table G3923)
Apply Table G1a for subject
3924 Cities and towns, etc., A-Z (Table G3924)
Apply Table G1a for subject

Florida

3930 General
3931 By subject (Table G1a)
3932 Regions, natural features, etc., A-Z (Table G3932)
Apply Table G1a for subject
3933 Counties, A-Z (Table G3933)
Apply Table G1a for subject
3934 Cities and towns, etc., A-Z (Table G3934)
Apply Table G1a for subject

South Central States

3935 General
3936 By subject (Table G1a)
3937 Regions, natural features, etc., A-Z (Table G3937)
Apply Table G1a for subject

East South Central States

3940 General
3941 By subject (Table G1a)
3942 Regions, natural features, etc., A-Z (Table G3942)
Apply Table G1a for subject

Kentucky

3950 General
3951 By subject (Table G1a)
3952 Regions, natural features, etc., A-Z (Table G3952)
Apply Table G1a for subject

By region or country
America. Western Hemisphere
North America
United States
Eastern United States, 1870 and later
Southern States. Confederate States of America
Southeastern States
South Central States
East South Central States
Kentucky -- Continued

3953 Counties, A-Z (Table G3953)
Apply Table G1a for subject

3954 Cities and towns, etc., A-Z (Table G3954)
Apply Table G1a for subject

G3180-G9980

Tennessee

3960 General

3961 By subject (Table G1a)

3962 Regions, natural features, etc., A-Z (Table G3962)
Apply Table G1a for subject

3963 Counties, A-Z (Table G3963)
Apply Table G1a for subject

3964 Cities and towns, etc., A-Z (Table G3964)
Apply Table G1a for subject

Alabama

3970 General

3971 By subject (Table G1a)

3972 Regions, natural features, etc., A-Z (Table G3972)
Apply Table G1a for subject

3973 Counties, A-Z (Table G3973)
Apply Table G1a for subject

3974 Cities and towns, etc., A-Z (Table G3974)
Apply Table G1a for subject

Mississippi

3980 General

3981 By subject (Table G1a)

3982 Regions, natural features, etc., A-Z (Table G3982)
Apply Table G1a for subject

3983 Counties, A-Z (Table G3983)
Apply Table G1a for subject

3984 Cities and towns, etc., A-Z (Table G3984)
Apply Table G1a for subject

West South Central States. Old Southwest

3990 General

3991 By subject (Table G1a)

By region or country
America. Western Hemisphere
North America
United States
Eastern United States, 1870 and later
Southern States. Confederate States of America
Southeastern States
South Central States
West South Central States. Old Southwest -- Continued

3992 Regions, natural features, etc., A-Z (Table G3992)
Apply Table G1a for subject

Arkansas

4000 General
4001 By subject (Table G1a)
4002 Regions, natural features, etc., A-Z (Table G4002)
Apply Table G1a for subject
4003 Counties, A-Z (Table G4003)
Apply Table G1a for subject
4004 Cities and towns, etc., A-Z (Table G4004)
Apply Table G1a for subject

Louisiana

4010 General
4011 By subject (Table G1a)
4012 Regions, natural features, etc., A-Z (Table G4012)
Apply Table G1a for subject
4013 Counties, A-Z (Table G4013)
Apply Table G1a for subject
4014 Cities and towns, etc., A-Z (Table G4014)
Apply Table G1a for subject

Oklahoma

4020 General
4021 By subject (Table G1a)
4022 Regions, natural features, etc., A-Z (Table G4022)
Apply Table G1a for subject
4023 Counties, A-Z (Table G4023)
Apply Table G1a for subject
4024 Cities and towns, etc., A-Z (Table G4024)
Apply Table G1a for subject

Texas

4030 General
4031 By subject (Table G1a)

By region or country
America. Western Hemisphere
North America
United States
Eastern United States, 1870 and later
Southern States. Confederate States of America
Southeastern States
South Central States
West South Central States. Old Southwest
Texas -- Continued
4032 Regions, natural features, etc., A-Z (Table G4032)
Apply Table G1a for subject
4033 Counties, A-Z (Table G4033)
Apply Table G1a for subject
4034 Cities and towns, etc., A-Z (Table G4034)
Apply Table G1a for subject
Middle West
4040 General
4041 By subject (Table G1a)
4042 Regions, natural features, etc., A-Z (Table G4042)
Apply Table G1a for subject
The West
Comprising the area west of the Mississippi River
4050 General
4051 By subject (Table G1a)
4052 Regions, natural features, etc., A-Z (Table G4052)
Apply Table G1a for subject
North Central States
(4060) General
see G4040
(4061) By subject
see G4041
(4062) Regions, natural features, etc., A-Z
see G4042
East North Central States. Old Northwest. Northwest Territory
4070 General
4071 By subject (Table G1a)
4072 Regions, natural features, etc., A-Z (Table G4072)
Apply Table G1a for subject
Ohio
4080 General
4081 By subject (Table G1a)

By region or country
America. Western Hemisphere
North America
United States
The West
North Central States
East North Central States. Old Northwest.
Northwest Territory
Ohio -- Continued

4082 Regions, natural features, etc., A-Z (Table G4082)
Apply Table G1a for subject

4083 Counties, A-Z (Table G4083)
Apply Table G1a for subject

4084 Cities and towns, etc., A-Z (Table G4084)
Apply Table G1a for subject

Indiana

4090 General

4091 By subject (Table G1a)

4092 Regions, natural features, etc., A-Z (Table G4092)
Apply Table G1a for subject

4093 Counties, A-Z (Table G4093)
Apply Table G1a for subject

4094 Cities and towns, etc., A-Z (Table G4094)
Apply Table G1a for subject

Illinois

4100 General

4101 By subject (Table G1a)

4102 Regions, natural features, etc., A-Z (Table G4102)
Apply Table G1a for subject

4103 Counties, A-Z (Table G4103)
Apply Table G1a for subject

4104 Cities and towns, etc., A-Z (Table G4104)
Apply Table G1a for subject

Michigan

4110 General

4111 By subject (Table G1a)

4112 Regions, natural features, etc., A-Z (Table G4112)
Apply Table G1a for subject

4113 Counties, A-Z (Table G4113)
Apply Table G1a for subject

4114 Cities and towns, etc., A-Z (Table G4114)
Apply Table G1a for subject

Wisconsin

By region or country
America. Western Hemisphere
North America
United States
The West
North Central States
East North Central States. Old Northwest. Northwest Territory
Wisconsin -- Continued
4120 General
4121 By subject (Table G1a)
4122 Regions, natural features, etc., A-Z (Table G4122)
Apply Table G1a for subject
4123 Counties, A-Z (Table G4123)
Apply Table G1a for subject
4124 Cities and towns, etc., A-Z (Table G4124)
Apply Table G1a for subject
Northwestern States
Comprises the area between the Great Lakes and the Pacific Ocean
4125 General
4126 By subject (Table G1a)
4127 Regions, natural features, etc., A-Z (Table G4127)
Apply Table G1a for subject
West North Central States
The area between the Great Lakes and the Rocky Mountains
4130 General
4131 By subject (Table G1a)
4132 Regions, natural features, etc., A-Z (Table G4132)
Apply Table G1a for subject
Minnesota
4140 General
4141 By subject (Table G1a)
4142 Regions, natural features, etc., A-Z (Table G4142 modified)
Apply Table G1a for subject
4142.S16 Saganaga Lake [MN & Ont.]
Subarrange by Table G1a
4143 Counties, A-Z (Table G4143)
Apply Table G1a for subject
4144 Cities and towns, etc., A-Z (Table G4144)
Apply Table G1a for subject
Iowa
4150 General

By region or country
America. Western Hemisphere
North America
United States
The West
Northwestern States
West North Central States
Iowa -- Continued
4151 By subject (Table G1a)
4152 Regions, natural features, etc., A-Z (Table G4152)
Apply Table G1a for subject
4153 Counties, A-Z (Table G4153)
Apply Table G1a for subject
4154 Cities and towns, etc., A-Z (Table G4154)
Apply Table G1a for subject
Missouri
4160 General
4161 By subject (Table G1a)
4162 Regions, natural features, etc., A-Z (Table G4162)
Apply Table G1a for subject
4163 Counties, A-Z (Table G4163)
Apply Table G1a for subject
4164 Cities and towns, etc., A-Z (Table G4164)
Apply Table G1a for subject
North Dakota
4170 General
4171 By subject (Table G1a)
4172 Regions, natural features, etc., A-Z (Table G4172)
Apply Table G1a for subject
4173 Counties, A-Z (Table G4173)
Apply Table G1a for subject
4174 Cities and towns, etc., A-Z (Table G4174)
Apply Table G1a for subject
South Dakota
4180 General
4181 By subject (Table G1a)
4182 Regions, natural features, etc., A-Z (Table G4182)
Apply Table G1a for subject
4183 Counties, A-Z (Table G4183)
Apply Table G1a for subject
4184 Cities and towns, etc., A-Z (Table G4184)
Apply Table G1a for subject
Nebraska

By region or country
America. Western Hemisphere
North America
United States
The West
Northwestern States
West North Central States
Nebraska -- Continued
4190 General
4191 By subject (Table G1a)
4192 Regions, natural features, etc., A-Z (Table G4192)
Apply Table G1a for subject
4193 Counties, A-Z (Table G4193)
Apply Table G1a for subject
4194 Cities and towns, etc., A-Z (Table G4194)
Apply Table G1a for subject
Kansas
4200 General
4201 By subject (Table G1a)
4202 Regions, natural features, etc., A-Z (Table G4202)
Apply Table G1a for subject
4203 Counties, A-Z (Table G4203)
Apply Table G1a for subject
4204 Cities and towns, etc., A-Z (Table G4204)
Apply Table G1a for subject
Pacific and Mountain States. Far West
4210 General
4211 By subject (Table G1a)
4212 Regions, natural features, etc., A-Z (Table G4212)
Apply Table G1a for subject
Rocky Mountain States
4220 General
4221 By subject (Table G1a)
4222 Regions, natural features, etc., A-Z (Table G4222)
Apply Table G1a for subject
Pacific States
Comprises Alaska, California, Hawaii, Oregon, and Washington
4230 General
4231 By subject (Table G1a)
4232 Regions, natural features, etc., A-Z (Table G4232)
Apply Table G1a for subject

By region or country
America. Western Hemisphere
North America
United States
The West
Pacific and Mountain States. Far West -- Continued
Pacific Northwest
The old Oregon country, comprising the present states of Oregon, Washington, and Idaho, parts of Montana and Wyoming, and the province of British Columbia

4240 General
4241 By subject (Table G1a)
4242 Regions, natural features, etc., A-Z (Table G4242)
Apply Table G1a for subject

Montana
4250 General
4251 By subject (Table G1a)
4252 Regions, natural features, etc., A-Z (Table G4252)
Apply Table G1a for subject
4253 Counties, A-Z (Table G4253)
Apply Table G1a for subject
4254 Cities and towns, etc., A-Z (Table G4254)
Apply Table G1a for subject

Wyoming
4260 General
4261 By subject (Table G1a)
4262 Regions, natural features, etc., A-Z (Table G4262)
Apply Table G1a for subject
4263 Counties, A-Z (Table G4263)
Apply Table G1a for subject
4264 Cities and towns, etc., A-Z (Table G4264)
Apply Table G1a for subject

Idaho
4270 General
4271 By subject (Table G1a)
4272 Regions, natural features, etc., A-Z (Table G4272)
Apply Table G1a for subject
4273 Counties, A-Z (Table G4273)
Apply Table G1a for subject
4274 Cities and towns, etc., A-Z (Table G4274)
Apply Table G1a for subject

Washington

By region or country
America. Western Hemisphere
North America
United States
The West
Pacific and Mountain States. Far West
Pacific Northwest
Washington -- Continued

4280 General

4281 By subject (Table G1a)

4282 Regions, natural features, etc., A-Z (Table G4282)
Apply Table G1a for subject

4283 Counties, A-Z (Table G4283)
Apply Table G1a for subject

4284 Cities and towns, etc., A-Z (Table G4284)
Apply Table G1a for subject

Oregon

4290 General

4291 By subject (Table G1a)

4292 Regions, natural features, etc., A-Z (Table G4292)
Apply Table G1a for subject

4293 Counties, A-Z (Table G4293)
Apply Table G1a for subject

4294 Cities and towns, etc., A-Z (Table G4294)
Apply Table G1a for subject

Southwestern States
Including West South Central States and New Southwest

4295 General

4296 By subject (Table G1a)

4297 Regions, natural features, etc., A-Z (Table G4297)
Apply Table G1a for subject

New Southwest
Roughly corresponds with the old Spanish province of New Mexico

4300 General

4301 By subject (Table G1a)

4302 Regions, natural features, etc., A-Z (Table G4302)
Apply Table G1a for subject

Colorado

4310 General

4311 By subject (Table G1a)

By region or country
America. Western Hemisphere
North America
United States
The West
Pacific and Mountain States. Far West
Southwestern States
New Southwest
Colorado -- Continued

4312 Regions, natural features, etc., A-Z (Table G4312)
Apply Table G1a for subject

4313 Counties, A-Z (Table G4313 modified)
Apply Table G1a for subject
Denver see G4314.D4
Denver (Denver International Airport) see G4314.D4:2D5
Denver (Denver Zoo) see G4314.D4:2D6

4314 Cities and towns, etc., A-Z (Table G4314 modified)
Apply Table G1a for subject

4314.D4 Denver
Subarrange by Table G1a

4314.D4:2D5 Denver International Airport
Subarrange by Table G1a

4314.D4:2D6 Denver Zoo
Subarrange by Table G1a

New Mexico

4320 General

4321 By subject (Table G1a)

4322 Regions, natural features, etc., A-Z (Table G4322)
Apply Table G1a for subject

4323 Counties, A-Z (Table G4323)
Apply Table G1a for subject

4324 Cities and towns, etc., A-Z (Table G4324)
Apply Table G1a for subject

Arizona

4330 General

4331 By subject (Table G1a)

4332 Regions, natural features, etc., A-Z (Table G4332)
Apply Table G1a for subject

4333 Counties, A-Z (Table G4333)
Apply Table G1a for subject

4334 Cities and towns, etc., A-Z (Table G4334)
Apply Table G1a for subject

By region or country
America. Western Hemisphere
North America
United States
The West
Pacific and Mountain States. Far West
Southwestern States
New Southwest -- Continued
Utah
4340 General
4341 By subject (Table G1a)
4342 Regions, natural features, etc., A-Z (Table G4342)
Apply Table G1a for subject
4343 Counties, A-Z (Table G4343)
Apply Table G1a for subject
4344 Cities and towns, etc., A-Z (Table G4344)
Apply Table G1a for subject
Nevada
4350 General
4351 By subject (Table G1a)
4352 Regions, natural features, etc., A-Z (Table G4352)
Apply Table G1a for subject
4353 Counties, A-Z (Table G4353 modified)
Apply Table G1a for subject
Ormsby see G4354.C4
4354 Cities and towns, etc., A-Z (Table G4354 modified)
Apply Table G1a for subject
4354.C4 Carson City
Subarrange by Table G1a
California
4360 General
4361 By subject (Table G1a)
4362 Regions, natural features, etc., A-Z (Table G4362)
Apply Table G1a for subject
4363 Counties, A-Z (Table G4363)
Apply Table G1a for subject
4364 Cities and towns, etc., A-Z (Table G4364)
Apply Table G1a for subject
Alaska
4370 General
4371 By subject (Table G1a)

By region or country
America. Western Hemisphere
North America
United States
The West
Pacific and Mountain States. Far West
Alaska -- Continued
4372 Regions, natural features, etc., A-Z (Table G4372)
Apply Table G1a for subject
4373 Counties, A-Z (Table G4373)
Apply Table G1a for subject
4374 Cities and towns, etc., A-Z (Table G4374)
Apply Table G1a for subject
Hawaii. Sandwich Islands
4380 General
4381 By subject (Table G1a)
4382 Regions, natural features, etc., A-Z (Table G4382)
Apply Table G1a for subject
4383 Counties, A-Z (Table G4383)
Apply Table G1a for subject
4384 Cities and towns, etc., A-Z (Table G4384)
Apply Table G1a for subject
Caribbean area
4390 General
4391 By subject (Table G1)
4392 Regions, natural features, etc., A-Z (Table G4392)
Apply Table G1 for subject
Latin America see G3292
Mexico
4410 General
4411 By subject (Table G1)
4412 Regions, natural features, etc., A-Z (Table G4412)
Apply Table G1 for subject
4414 Cities and towns, etc., A-Z (Table G4414)
Apply Table G1 for subject
Northern States
4420 General
4421 By subject (Table G1)
4422 Regions, natural features, etc., A-Z (Table G4422)
Apply Table G1 for subject
Tamaulipas
4430 General
4431 By subject (Table G1)
4432 Regions, natural features, etc., A-Z (Table G4432)
Apply Table G1 for subject

By region or country
America. Western Hemisphere
North America
Mexico
Northern States -- Continued
Nuevo León
4440 General
4441 By subject (Table G1)
4442 Regions, natural features, etc., A-Z (Table G4442)
Apply Table G1 for subject
Coahuila
4450 General
4451 By subject (Table G1)
4452 Regions, natural features, etc., A-Z (Table G4452)
Apply Table G1 for subject
Chihuahua
4460 General
4461 By subject (Table G1)
4462 Regions, natural features, etc., A-Z (Table G4462)
Apply Table G1 for subject
Sonora
4470 General
4471 By subject (Table G1)
4472 Regions, natural features, etc., A-Z (Table G4472)
Baja California (Region)
4475 General
4476 By subject (Table G1)
4477 Regions, natural features, etc., A-Z (Table G4477)
Apply Table G1 for subject
Baja California (State). Baja California Norte
4480 General
4481 By subject (Table G1)
4482 Regions, natural features, etc., A-Z (Table G4482)
Apply Table G1 for subject
Baja California Sur
4485 General
4486 By subject (Table G1)
4487 Regions, natural features, etc., A-Z (Table G4487)
Apply Table G1 for subject
Sinaloa
4490 General
4491 By subject (Table G1)
4493 Administrative divisions, A-Z (Table G4493)
Apply Table G1 for subject
Durango

By region or country
America. Western Hemisphere
North America
Mexico
Northern States
Durango -- Continued
4500 General
4501 By subject (Table G1)
Zacatecas
4510 General
4511 By subject (Table G1)
San Luis Potosî
4520 General
4521 By subject (Table G1)
Central States
4530 General
4531 By subject (Table G1)
4532 Regions, natural features, etc., A-Z (Table G4532)
Apply Table G1 for subject
Veracruz
4540 General
4541 By subject (Table G1)
4542 Regions, natural features, etc., A-Z (Table G4542)
Apply Table G1 for subject
Puebla
4550 General
4551 By subject (Table G1)
4552 Regions, natural features, etc., A-Z (Table G4552)
Apply Table G1 for subject
Tlaxcala
4560 General
4561 By subject (Table G1)
Hidalgo
4570 General
4571 By subject (Table G1)
Mexico (State)
4580 General
4581 By subject (Table G1)
4582 Regions, natural features, etc., A-Z (Table G4582)
Apply Table G1 for subject
Mexico (Federal District)
4590 General
4591 By subject (Table G1)
4592 Regions, natural features, etc., A-Z (Table G4592)
Apply Table G1 for subject
Morelos
4600 General

By region or country
America. Western Hemisphere
North America
Mexico
Central States
Morelos -- Continued
4601 By subject (Table G1)
Michoacán de Ocampo
4610 General
4611 By subject (Table G1)
4612 Regions, natural features, etc., A-Z (Table G4612)
Apply Table G1 for subject
Querétaro
4620 General
4621 By subject (Table G1)
4622 Regions, natural features, etc., A-Z (Table G4622)
Apply Table G1 for subject
Guanajuato
4630 General
4631 By subject (Table G1)
Jalisco
4640 General
4641 By subject (Table G1)
Aguascalientes
4650 General
4651 By subject (Table G1)
Nayarit
4660 General
4661 By subject (Table G1)
Colima
4670 General
4671 By subject (Table G1)
4672 Regions, natural features, etc., A-Z (Table G4672)
Apply Table G1 for subject
Southern States
4680 General
4681 By subject (Table G1)
4682 Regions, natural features, etc., A-Z (Table G4682)
Apply Table G1 for subject
Guerrero
4690 General
4691 By subject (Table G1)
4692 Regions, natural features, etc., A-Z (Table G4692)
Apply Table G1 for subject
Oaxaca
4700 General
4701 By subject (Table G1)

By region or country
America. Western Hemisphere
North America
Mexico
Southern States
Oaxaca -- Continued
4702 Regions, natural features, etc., A-Z (Table G4702)
Apply Table G1 for subject
Chiapas
4720 General
4721 By subject (Table G1)
Tabasco
4730 General
4731 By subject (Table G1)
Campeche
4740 General
4741 By subject (Table G1)
4742 Regions, natural features, etc., A-Z (Table G4742)
Apply Table G1 for subject
Yucatán
4750 General
4751 By subject (Table G1)
4752 Regions, natural features, etc., A-Z (Table G4752)
Apply Table G1 for subject
Quintana Roo
4760 General
4761 By subject (Table G1)
4762 Regions, natural features, etc., A-Z (Table G4762)
Apply Table G1 for subject
Central America
4800 General
4801 By subject (Table G1)
4802 Regions, natural features, etc., A-Z (Table G4802)
Apply Table G1 for subject
Guatemala
4810 General
4811 By subject (Table G1)
4812 Regions, natural features, etc., A-Z (Table G4812)
Apply Table G1 for subject
4813 Departments, A-Z (Table G4813)
Apply Table G1 for subject
4814 Cities and towns, etc., A-Z (Table G4814)
Apply Table G1 for subject
Belize. British Honduras
4820 General
4821 By subject (Table G1)

By region or country
America. Western Hemisphere
North America
Central America
Belize. British Honduras -- Continued

4822 Regions, natural features, etc., A-Z (Table G4822)
Apply Table G1 for subject

4823 Districts, A-Z (Table G4823)
Apply Table G1 for subject

4824 Cities and towns, etc., A-Z (Table G4824)
Apply Table G1 for subject

Honduras

4830 General

4831 By subject (Table G1)

4832 Regions, natural features, islands, etc., A-Z (Table G4832)
Apply Table G1 for subject

4833 Departments, A-Z (Table G4833)
Apply Table G1 for subject

4834 Cities and towns, etc., A-Z (Table G4834)
Apply Table G1 for subject

El Salvador

4840 General

4841 By subject (Table G1)

4842 Regions, natural features, etc., A-Z (Table G4842)
Apply Table G1 for subject

4843 Departments, A-Z (Table G4843)
Apply Table G1 for subject

4844 Cities and towns, etc., A-Z (Table G4844)
Apply Table G1 for subject

Nicaragua

4850 General

4851 By subject (Table G1)

4852 Regions, natural features, etc., A-Z (Table G4852)
Apply Table G1 for subject

4853 Departments, A-Z (Table G4853)
Apply Table G1 for subject

4854 Cities and towns, etc., A-Z (Table G4854)
Apply Table G1 for subject

Costa Rica

4860 General

4861 By subject (Table G1)

4862 Regions, natural features, etc., A-Z (Table G4862)
Apply Table G1 for subject

4863 Provinces, etc., A-Z (Table G4863)
Apply Table G1 for subject

By region or country
America. Western Hemisphere
North America
Central America
Costa Rica -- Continued
4864 Cities and towns, etc., A-Z (Table G4864)
Apply Table G1 for subject
Panama
4870 General
4871 By subject (Table G1)
4872 Regions, natural features, etc., A-Z (Table G4872)
Apply Table G1 for subject
4873 Provinces, etc., A-Z (Table G4873)
Apply Table G1 for subject
4874 Cities and towns, etc., A-Z (Table G4874)
Apply Table G1 for subject
West Indies
4900 General
4901 By subject (Table G1)
4902 Regions, natural features, islands, etc., A-Z (Table G4902)
Apply Table G1 for subject
Class here maps of West Indian islands and archipelagoes not classed in or associated with G4910-G5184
Greater Antilles
4910 General
4911 By subject (Table G1)
4912 Regions, natural features, islands, etc., A-Z (Table G4912)
Apply Table G1 for subject
Cuba
4920 General
4921 By subject (Table G1)
4922 Regions, natural features, etc., A-Z (Table G4922)
Apply Table G1 for subject
4923 Provinces, A-Z (Table G4923)
Apply Table G1 for subject
4924 Cities and towns, etc., A-Z (Table G4924)
Apply Table G1 for subject
Hispaniola
4930 General
4931 By subject (Table G1)
4932 Regions, natural features, etc., A-Z (Table G4932)
Apply Table G1 for subject
Haiti
4940 General

By region or country
America. Western Hemisphere
North America
West Indies
Greater Antilles
Hispaniola
Haiti -- Continued
4941 By subject (Table G1)
4942 Regions, natural features, etc., A-Z (Table G4942)
Apply Table G1 for subject
4943 Departments, A-Z (Table G4943)
Apply Table G1 for subject
4944 Cities and towns, etc., A-Z (Table G4944)
Apply Table G1 for subject
Dominican Republic. Santo Domingo
4950 General
4951 By subject (Table G1)
4952 Regions, natural features, etc., A-Z (Table G4952)
Apply Table G1 for subject
4953 Provinces, A-Z (Table G4953)
Apply Table G1 for subject
4954 Cities and towns, etc., A-Z (Table G4954)
Apply Table G1 for subject
Jamaica
4960 General
4961 By subject (Table G1)
4962 Regions, natural features, etc., A-Z (Table G4962)
Apply Table G1 for subject
4963 Parishes, A-Z (Table G4963)
Apply Table G1 for subject
4964 Cities and towns, etc., A-Z (Table G4964)
Apply Table G1 for subject
Cayman Islands
4965 General
4966 By subject (Table G1)
4967 Regions, natural features, islands, etc., A-Z (Table G4967)
Apply Table G1 for subject
4969 Cities and towns, etc., A-Z (Table G4969)
Apply Table G1 for subject
Puerto Rico
4970 General
4971 By subject (Table G1)
4972 Regions, natural features, etc., A-Z (Table G4972)
Apply Table G1 for subject

By region or country
America. Western Hemisphere
North America
West Indies
Greater Antilles
Puerto Rico -- Continued
4974 Cities and towns, etc., A-Z (Table G4974)
Apply Table G1 for subject
Bahamas. Lucayos
4980 General
4981 By subject (Table G1)
4982 Regions, natural features, islands, etc., A-Z (Table G4982)
Apply Table G1 for subject
4984 Cities and towns, etc., A-Z (Table G4984)
Apply Table G1 for subject
Turks and Caicos Islands
4985 General
4986 By subject (Table G1)
4987 Regions, natural features, islands, etc., A-Z (Table G4987)
Apply Table G1 for subject
4989 Cities and towns, etc., A-Z (Table G4989)
Apply Table G1 for subject
Lesser Antilles. Caribbees
5000 General
5001 By subject (Table G1)
Virgin Islands (General)
5005 General
5006 By subject (Table G1)
Virgin Islands of the United States
5010 General
5011 By subject (Table G1)
5012 Regions, natural features, islands, etc., A-Z (Table G5012)
Apply Table G1 for subject
5014 Cities and towns, etc., A-Z (Table G5014)
Apply Table G1 for subject
British Virgin Islands
5020 General
5021 By subject (Table G1)
5022 Regions, natural features, islands, etc., A-Z (Table G5022)
Apply Table G1 for subject
5024 Cities and towns, etc., A-Z (Table G5024)
Apply Table G1 for subject
Leeward Islands

By region or country
America. Western Hemisphere
North America
West Indies
Lesser Antilles. Caribbees
Leeward Islands
5030 General
5031 By subject (Table G1)
5032 Regions, natural features, islands, etc., A-Z (Table G5032)
Apply Table G1 for subject
Saint Kitts and Nevis
5040 General
5041 By subject (Table G1)
5042 Regions, natural features, islands, etc., A-Z (Table G5042)
Apply Table G1 for subject
5044 Cities and towns, etc., A-Z (Table G5044)
Apply Table G1 for subject
Anguilla
5045 General
5046 By subject (Table G1)
Antigua and Barbuda
5050 General
5051 By subject (Table G1)
5052 Regions, natural features, islands, etc., A-Z (Table G5052 modified)
Apply Table G1 for subject
5052.B3 Barbuda
Subarrange by Table G1
5053 Parishes, A-Z (Table G5053 modified)
Apply Table G1 for subject
Barbuda see G5052.B3
5054 Cities and towns, etc., A-Z (Table G5054)
Apply Table G1 for subject
Montserrat
5055 General
5056 By subject (Table G1)
5059 Cities and towns, etc., A-Z (Table G5059)
Apply Table G1 for subject
French West Indies
5060 General
5061 By subject (Table G1)
Guadeloupe
5070 General
5071 By subject (Table G1)

By region or country
America. Western Hemisphere
North America
West Indies
French West Indies
Guadeloupe -- Continued
5072 Regions, natural features, islands, etc., A-Z (Table G5072)
Apply Table G1 for subject
5074 Cities and towns, etc., A-Z (Table G5074)
Apply Table G1 for subject
Martinique
5080 General
5081 By subject (Table G1)
5082 Regions, natural features, islands, etc., A-Z (Table G5082)
Apply Table G1 for subject
5084 Cities and towns, etc., A-Z (Table G5084)
Apply Table G1 for subject
Windward Islands
5090 General
5091 By subject (Table G1)
Dominica
5100 General
5101 By subject (Table G1)
5102 Regions, natural features, islands, etc., A-Z (Table G5102)
Apply Table G1 for subject
5104 Cities and towns, etc., A-Z (Table G5104)
Apply Table G1 for subject
Saint Lucia
5110 General
5111 By subject (Table G1)
5112 Regions, natural features, islands, etc., A-Z (Table G5112)
Apply Table G1 for subject
5114 Cities and towns, etc., A-Z (Table G5114)
Apply Table G1 for subject
Saint Vincent (Island and independent State)
5120 General
5121 By subject (Table G1)
5122 Regions, natural features, islands, etc., A-Z (Table G5122)
Apply Table G1 for subject
5124 Cities and towns, etc., A-Z (Table G5124)
Apply Table G1 for subject
Grenada (Island and independent State)

By region or country
America. Western Hemisphere
North America
West Indies
Windward Islands
Grenada (Island and independent State) -- Continued
5130 General
5131 By subject (Table G1)
5132 Regions, natural features, islands, etc., A-Z (Table G5132)
Apply Table G1 for subject
5133 Administrative divisions, A-Z (Table G5133)
Apply Table G1 for subject
5134 Cities and towns, etc., A-Z (Table G5134)
Apply Table G1 for subject
Barbados
5140 General
5141 By subject (Table G1)
5144 Cities and towns, etc., A-Z (Table G5144)
Apply Table G1 for subject
Trinidad and Tobago
5145 General
5146 By subject (Table G1)
5147 Regions, natural features, islands, etc., A-Z (Table G5147)
Apply Table G1 for subject
5148 Counties, wards, A-Z (Table G5148)
Apply Table G1 for subject
5149 Cities and towns, etc., A-Z (Table G5149)
Apply Table G1 for subject
Trinidad
5150 General
5151 By subject (Table G1)
5152 Regions, natural features, islands, etc., A-Z (Table G5152)
Apply Table G1 for subject
Tobago
5160 General
5161 By subject (Table G1)
5162 Regions, natural features, islands, etc., A-Z (Table G5162)
Apply Table G1 for subject
Netherlands Antilles. Dutch West Indies
5165 General
5166 By subject (Table G1)

By region or country
America. Western Hemisphere
North America
West Indies
Windward Islands
Netherlands Antilles. Dutch West Indies -- Continued
5167 Regions, natural features, islands, etc., A-Z (Table G5167)
Apply Table G1 for subject
Aruba
5170 General
5171 By subject (Table G1)
5172 Regions, natural features, islands, etc., A-Z (Table G5172)
5174 Cities and towns, etc., A-Z (Table G5174)
Bonaire
5175 General
5176 By subject (Table G1)
Curaçao
5180 General
5181 By subject (Table G1)
5182 Regions, natural features, islands, etc., A-Z (Table G5182)
Apply Table G1 for subject
5184 Cities and towns, etc., A-Z (Table G5184)
Apply Table G1 for subject
South America
5200 General
5201 By subject (Table G1)
5202 Regions, natural features, etc., A-Z (Table G5202)
Apply Table G1 for subject
Atlantic coast and continental shelf
5220 General
5221 By subject (Table G1)
Pacific coast and continental shelf
5230 General
5231 By subject (Table G1)
Guianas
5240 General
5241 By subject (Table G1)
5242 Regions, natural features, etc., A-Z (Table G5242)
Apply Table G1 for subject
Guyana. British Guiana
5250 General
5251 By subject (Table G1)
5252 Regions, natural features, etc., A-Z (Table G5252)
Apply Table G1 for subject

By region or country
America. Western Hemisphere
South America
Guianas
Guyana. British Guiana -- Continued
5253 Administrative districts, etc., A-Z (Table G5253)
Apply Table G1 for subject
5254 Cities and towns, etc., A-Z (Table G5254)
Apply Table G1 for subject
Suriname. Dutch Guiana
5260 General
5261 By subject (Table G1)
5262 Regions, natural features, etc., A-Z (Table G5262)
Apply Table G1 for subject

5263 Administrative districts, etc., A-Z (Table G5263)
Apply Table G1 for subject
5264 Cities and towns, etc., A-Z (Table G5264)
Apply Table G1 for subject
French Guiana
5270 General
5271 By subject (Table G1)
5272 Regions, natural features, etc., A-Z (Table G5272)
Apply Table G1 for subject
5273 Administrative divisions, A-Z (Table G5273)
Apply Table G1 for subject
5274 Cities and towns, etc., A-Z (Table G5274)
Apply Table G1 for subject
Venezuela
5280 General
5281 By subject (Table G1)
5282 Regions, natural features, etc., A-Z (Table G5282)
Apply Table G1 for subject
5283 States, territories, A-Z (Table G5283)
Apply Table G1 for subject
5284 Cities and towns, etc., A-Z (Table G5284)
Apply Table G1 for subject
Colombia
5290 General
5291 By subject (Table G1)
5292 Regions, natural features, etc., A-Z (Table G5292)
Apply Table G1 for subject
5293 Administrative divisions, A-Z (Table G5293)
Apply Table G1 for subject
5294 Cities and towns, etc., A-Z (Table G5294)
Apply Table G1 for subject
Ecuador
5300 General

By region or country
America. Western Hemisphere
South America
Ecuador -- Continued
5301 By subject (Table G1)
5302 Regions, natural features, etc., A-Z (Table G5302)
Apply Table G1 for subject
5303 Provinces, etc., A-Z (Table G5303)
Apply Table G1 for subject
5304 Cities and towns, etc., A-Z (Table G5304)
Apply Table G1 for subject
Peru
5310 General
5311 By subject (Table G1)
5312 Regions, natural features, etc., A-Z (Table G5312)
Apply Table G1 for subject
5313 Departments, A-Z (Table G5313)
Apply Table G1 for subject
5314 Cities and towns, etc., A-Z (Table G5314)
Apply Table G1 for subject
Bolivia
5320 General
5321 By subject (Table G1)
5322 Regions, natural features, etc., A-Z (Table G5322)
Apply Table G1 for subject
5323 Departments, etc., A-Z (Table G5323)
Apply Table G1 for subject
5324 Cities and towns, etc., A-Z (Table G5324)
Apply Table G1 for subject
Chile
5330 General
5331 By subject (Table G1)
5332 Regions, natural features, etc., A-Z (Table G5332)
Apply Table G1 for subject
Easter Islands see G9665+
5333 Administrative regions, etc., A-Z (Table G5333)
Apply Table G1 for subject
5334 Cities and towns, etc., A-Z (Table G5334)
Apply Table G1 for subject
Argentina
5350 General
5351 By subject (Table G1)
5352 Regions, natural features, etc., A-Z (Table G5352)
Apply Table G1 for subject
Islas Malvinas see G9175+
5353 Provinces, A-Z (Table G5353)
Apply Table G1 for subject

By region or country
America. Western Hemisphere
South America
Argentina -- Continued
5354 Cities and towns, etc., A-Z (Table G5354)
Apply Table G1 for subject
Uruguay
5370 General
5371 By subject (Table G1)
5372 Regions, natural features, etc., A-Z (Table G5372)
Apply Table G1 for subject
5373 Departments, etc., A-Z (Table G5373)
Apply Table G1 for subject
5374 Cities and towns, etc., A-Z (Table G5374)
Apply Table G1 for subject
Paraguay
5380 General
5381 By subject (Table G1)
5382 Regions, natural features, etc., A-Z (Table G5382)
Apply Table G1 for subject
5383 Departments, etc., A-Z (Table G5383)
Apply Table G1 for subject
5384 Cities and towns, etc., A-Z (Table G5384)
Apply Table G1 for subject
Brazil
5400 General
5401 By subject (Table G1)
5402 Regions, natural features, etc., A-Z (Table G5402)
Apply Table G1 for subject
5404 Cities and towns, etc., A-Z (Table G5404)
Apply Table G1 for subject
North Brazil. Amazon Brazil
5410 General
5411 By subject (Table G1)
5412 Regions, natural features, etc., A-Z (Table G5412)
Rondônia. Guaporé
5420 General
5421 By subject (Table G1)
5422 Regions, natural features, etc., A-Z (Table G5422)
Apply Table G1 for subject
Acre
5430 General
5431 By subject (Table G1)
Amazonas
5440 General
5441 By subject (Table G1)

By region or country
America. Western Hemisphere
South America
Brazil
North Brazil. Amazon Brazil
Amazonas -- Continued
5442 Regions, natural features, etc., A-Z (Table G5442)
Apply Table G1 for subject
Roraima. Rio Branco
5460 General
5461 By subject (Table G1)
5462 Regions, natural features, etc., A-Z (Table G5462)
Apply Table G1 for subject
Pará
5470 General
5471 By subject (Table G1)
5472 Regions, natural features, etc., A-Z (Table G5472)
Apply Table G1 for subject
Amapá
5490 General
5491 By subject (Table G1)
Northeast Brazil
5500 General
5501 By subject (Table G1)
Maranhão
5505 General
5506 By subject (Table G1)
5507 Regions, natural features, etc., A-Z (Table G5507)
Apply Table G1 for subject
Piauî (Piauhy)
5510 General
5511 By subject (Table G1)
5512 Regions, natural features, etc., A-Z (Table G5512)
Apply Table G1 for subject
Ceará
5515 General
5516 By subject (Table G1)
5517 Regions, natural features, etc., A-Z (Table G5517)
Apply Table G1 for subject
Rio Grande do Norte
5520 General
5521 By subject (Table G1)
Paraîba
5525 General
5526 By subject (Table G1)
Pernambuco
5530 General

By region or country
America. Western Hemisphere
South America
Brazil
Northeast Brazil
Pernambuco -- Continued
5531 By subject (Table G1)
Alagôas
5540 General
5541 By subject (Table G1)
Fernando de Noronha
5545 General
5546 By subject (Table G1)
East Brazil. Southeastern States
5550 General
5551 By subject (Table G1)
5552 Regions, natural features, etc., A-Z (Table G5552)
Apply Table G1 for subject
Sergipe
5555 General
5556 By subject (Table G1)
Bahia
5560 General
5561 By subject (Table G1)
5562 Regions, natural features, etc., A-Z (Table G5562)
Apply Table G1 for subject
Minas Gerais
5570 General
5571 By subject (Table G1)
5572 Regions, natural features, etc., A-Z (Table G5572)
Apply Table G1 for subject
5573 Administrative divisions, A-Z (Table G5573)
Apply Table G1 for subject
Espírito Santo
5580 General
5581 By subject (Table G1)
5582 Regions, natural features, etc., A-Z (Table G5582)
Apply Table G1 for subject
Rio de Janeiro (State)
5590 General
5591 By subject (Table G1)
5592 Regions, natural features, etc., A-Z (Table G5592)
Apply Table G1 for subject
Guanabara
Until April 1960 known as Distrito Federal
5595 General
5596 By subject (Table G1)

By region or country
America. Western Hemisphere
South America
Brazil -- Continued
South Brazil
5600 General
5601 By subject (Table G1)
5602 Regions, natural features, etc., A-Z (Table G5602)
Apply Table G1 for subject
São Paulo
5605 General
5606 By subject (Table G1)
5607 Regions, natural features, etc., A-Z (Table G5607)
Apply Table G1 for subject
Paraná
5610 General
5611 By subject (Table G1)
5612 Regions, natural features, etc., A-Z (Table G5612)
Apply Table G1 for subject
Santa Catarina
5615 General
5616 By subject (Table G1)
5617 Regions, natural features, etc., A-Z (Table G5617)
Apply Table G1 for subject
5618 Administrative divisions, A-Z (Table G5618)
Apply Table G1 for subject
Rio Grande do Sul
5620 General
5621 By subject (Table G1)
5622 Regions, natural features, etc., A-Z (Table G5622)
Apply Table G1 for subject
Central West Brazil
5630 General
5631 By subject (Table G1)
Mato Grosso
5640 General
5641 By subject (Table G1)
5642 By region (Table G5642)
Apply Table G1 for subject
5643 Administrative divisions, A-Z (Table G5643)
Apply Table G1 for subject
Mato Grosso do Sul (1977-)
5645 General
5646 By subject (Table G1)
Tocantins (1988-)
5655 General
5656 By subject (Table G1)

By region or country
America. Western Hemisphere
South America
Brazil
Central West Brazil -- Continued
Goìas
5660 General
5661 By subject (Table G1)
Distrito Federal (1960-)
5665 General
5666 By subject (Table G1)
5667 Regions, natural features, etc., A-Z (Table G5667)
Apply Table G1 for subject
Eastern Hemisphere. Eurasia, Africa, etc.
For maps of the known world prior to 1500, that are confined to the Eastern Hemisphere see G3200+
5670 General
5671 By subject (Table G1)
5672 Regions, natural features, etc., A-Z (Table G5672)
Apply Table G1 for subject
Islamic Empire. Islamic countries
Including maps of Arab countries together, Islamic Empire, etc.
5680 General
5681 By subject (Table G1)
5685-5687 Asia and Africa
5685 General
5686 By subject (Table G1)
5687 Regions, natural features, etc., A-Z (Table G5687)
Apply Table G1 for subject
5690-5692 Eurasia
5690 General
5691 By subject (Table G1)
5692 Regions, natural features, etc., A-Z (Table G5692)
Apply Table G1 for subject
5695-5697 Europe and Africa
5695 General
5696 By subject (Table G1)
Europe
5700 General
5701 By subject (Table G1)
5702 Regions, natural features, etc., A-Z (Table G5702)
Apply Table G1 for subject
Western Europe
5720 General
5721 By subject (Table G1)

By region or country
Eastern Hemisphere. Eurasia, Africa, etc.
Europe
Western Europe -- Continued
5722 Regions, natural features, etc., A-Z (Table G5722)
Apply Table G1 for subject
British Empire. Commonwealth of Nations
Including maps of British colonies, dependencies, etc. (Collectively)
Class individual colonies, dependencies, etc. according to location, e.g., G9120+, Bermuda
5730 General
5731 By subject (Table G1)
British Isles. Great Britain
5740 General
5741 By subject (Table G1 modified)
History
5741.S1 General
(5741.S12) This number not used
5741.S2 To 1066
5741.S3 Medieval period, 1066-1485
5741.S33 Norman period, 1066-1154
5741.S35 Plantagenets, 1154-1399
5741.S37 15th century
5741.S4 Modern period, 1485-
5741.S45 16th century: Tudors, 1485-1603
5741.S5 17th century: Stuarts, 1603-1714
5741.S53 Commonwealth and protectorate, 1660-1688
5741.S54 18th century
5741.S55 19th century
5741.S6 20th century
5741.S65 World War I
5741.S7 World War II
5742 Regions, natural features, etc., A-Z (Table G5742)
Apply Table G1 for subject (except .S1-.S7, historical geography)
Apply Table G5741.S for history
England
Including maps of England and Wales depicted together
5750 General
5751 By subject (Table G1 modified)
History
5751.S1 General
(5751.S12) This number not used
5751.S2 To 1066
5751.S3 Medieval period, 1066-1485

By region or country
Eastern Hemisphere. Eurasia, Africa, etc.
Europe
Western Europe
British Isles. Great Britain
England
By subject
History
Medieval period, 1066-1485 -- Continued
5751.S33 Norman period, 1066-1154
5751.S35 Plantagenets, 1154-1399
5751.S37 15th century
5751.S4 Modern period, 1485-
5751.S45 16th century: Tudors, 1485-1603
5751.S5 17th century: Stuarts, 1603-1714
5751.S53 Commonwealth and protectorate, 1660-1688
5751.S54 18th century
5751.S55 19th century
5751.S6 20th century
5751.S65 World War I
5751.S7 World War II
5752 Regions, natural features, etc., A-Z (Table G5752)
Apply Table G1 for subject (except .S1-.S7, historical geography)
Apply Table G5741.S for history
5753 Counties, etc., A-Z (Table G5753 modified)
Apply Table G1 for subject (except .S1-.S7, historical geography)
Apply Table G5741.S for history
Greater London (Metropolitan county) see G5754.L7
Greater Manchester (Metropolitan county) see G5754.M3
London, Greater (Metropolitan county) see G5754.L7
Manchester, Greater (Metropolitan county) see G5754.M3
5754 Cities and towns, etc., A-Z (Table G5754 modified)
Apply Table G1 for subject (except .S1-.S7, historical geography)
Apply Table G5741.S for history
5754.L7 London
Subarrange by Table G1 except .S1-.S7, historical geography. For history, subarrange by Table G5741.S

By region or country
Eastern Hemisphere. Eurasia, Africa, etc.
Europe
Western Europe
British Isles. Great Britain
England
Cities and towns, etc., A-Z -- Continued
5754.M3 Manchester
Subarrange by Table G1 except .S1-.S7, historical geography. For history, subarrange by Table G5741.S
Wales
5760 General
5761 By subject (Table G1 modified)
History
5761.S1 General
(5761.S12) This number not used
5761.S2 To 1066
5761.S3 Medieval period, 1066-1485
5761.S33 Norman period, 1066-1154
5761.S35 Plantagenets, 1154-1399
5761.S37 15th century
5761.S4 Modern period, 1485-
5761.S45 16th century: Tudors, 1485-1603
5761.S5 17th century: Stuarts, 1603-1714
5761.S53 Commonwealth and protectorate, 1660-1688
5761.S54 18th century
5761.S55 19th century
5761.S6 20th century
5761.S65 World War I
5761.S7 World War II
5762 Regions, natural features, etc., A-Z (Table G5762)
Apply Table G1 for subject (except .S1-.S7, historical geography)
Apply Table G5741.S for history
5763 Counties, A-Z (Table G5763)
Apply Table G1 for subject (except .S1-.S7, historical geography)
Apply Table G5741.S for history
5764 Cities and towns, etc., A-Z (Table G5764)
Apply Table G1 for subject (except .S1-.S7, historical geography)
Apply Table G5741.S for history
Scotland
5770 General
5771 By subject (Table G1 modified)
History

By region or country
Eastern Hemisphere. Eurasia, Africa, etc.
Europe
Western Europe
British Isles. Great Britain
Scotland
By subject
History -- Continued

5771.S1 General
(5771.S12) This number not used
5771.S2 To 1057
5771.S3 1057-1603
5771.S34 War of Independence, 1285-1371
5771.S36 Stuarts to the Union, 1371-1707
5771.S4 17th century
5771.S45 Revolution of 1688
5771.S5 18th century
5771.S52 Jacobite Rebellion, 1715
5771.S53 Jacobite Rebellion, 1745-1746
5771.S55 19th century
5771.S6 20th century
5771.S65 World War I
5771.S7 World War II
5772 Regions, natural features, etc., A-Z (Table G5772 modified)
Apply Table G1 for subject (except .S7-.S7, history)
Apply Table G5771.S for history
5772.O6 Orkney Islands
Subarrange by Table G1 except .S1-.S7, historical geography. For history, subarrange by Table G5771.S
5772.S5 Shetland Islands
Subarrange by Table G1 except .S1-.S7, historical geography. For history, subarrange by Table G5771.S
5772.W39 Western Isles
Subarrange by Table G1 except .S1-.S7, historical geography. For history, subarrange by Table G5771.S
5773 Administrative regions, island areas, A-Z (Table G5773 modified)
Apply Table G1 for subject (except .S7-.S7, history)
Apply Table G5771.S for history
Orkney see G5772.O6
Shetland see G5772.S5
Western Isles see G5772.W39

By region or country
Eastern Hemisphere. Eurasia, Africa, etc.
Europe
Western Europe
British Isles. Great Britain
Scotland -- Continued
5774 Cities and towns, etc., A-Z (Table G5774)
Apply Table G1 for subject (except .S7-.S7, history)
Apply Table G5771.S for history
Eire. Irish Free State
Including maps of the island of Ireland treated as a whole
5780 General
5781 By subject (Table G1)
5782 Regions, natural features, etc., A-Z (Table G5782)
Apply Table G1 for subject
5783 Counties, A-Z (Table G5783)
Apply Table G1 for subject
5784 Cities and towns, etc., A-Z (Table G5784)
Apply Table G1 for subject
Northern Ireland
5790 General
5791 By subject (Table G1)
5792 Regions, natural features, etc., A-Z (Table G5792)
Apply Table G1 for subject
5793 Counties, etc., A-Z (Table G5793)
Apply Table G1 for subject
5794 Cities and towns, etc., A-Z (Table G5794)
Apply Table G1 for subject
Isle of Man
5800 General
5801 By subject (Table G1)
5802 Regions, natural features, etc., A-Z (Table G5802)
Apply Table G1 for subject
5804 Cities and towns, etc., A-Z (Table G5804)
Apply Table G1 for subject
Channel Islands
5810 General
5811 By subject (Table G1)
5812 Regions, natural features, etc., A-Z (Table G5812)
Apply Table G1 for subject
5814 Cities and towns, etc., A-Z (Table G5814)
Apply Table G1 for subject

By region or country
Eastern Hemisphere. Eurasia, Africa, etc.
Europe
Western Europe -- Continued
French Empire. French Union
Including maps of French colonies, dependencies, etc. (Collectively)
Class individual colonies, dependencies, etc. according to location, e.g., G8680+, French Equatorial Africa
5820 General
5821 By subject (Table G1)
France
5830 General
5831 By subject (Table G1 modified)

History
5831.S1 General
(5831.S12) This number not used
5831.S2 To 987
5831.S3 Medieval period, 987-1515
5831.S4 Modern period, 1515-
5831.S5 17th century
5831.S545 Revolution, 1789-1799
5831.S55 Consulate and Empire, 1799-1815
5831.S56 19th century
5831.S6 20th century
5831.S65 World War I
5831.S7 World War II
5831.S73 1945-
5832 Regions, natural features, etc., A-Z (Table G5832 modified)
Apply Table G1 for subject (except .S1-.S7, historical geography)
Apply Table G5831.S for history
5832.P35 Paris Region. Région parisienne
Subarrange by Table G1 except .S1-.S7, historical geography. For history, subarrange by Table G5831.S
5833 Provinces, departments, etc., A-Z (Table G5833 modified)
Apply Table G1 for subject (except .S1-.S7, historical geography)
Apply Table G5831.S for history
Corse
see G5970+
Corsica
see G5970+
Paris see G5834.P3

By region or country
Eastern Hemisphere. Eurasia, Africa, etc.
Europe
Western Europe
France
Provinces, departments, etc., A-Z -- Continued
Paris Region see G5832.P35
Région parisienne see G5832.P35
5834 Cities and towns, etc., A-Z (Table G5834 modified)
Apply Table G1 for subject (except .S1-.S7, historical geography)
Apply Table G5831.S for history
5834.P3 Paris
Subarrange by Table G1 except .S1-.S7, historical geography. For history, subarrange by Table G5831.S
Corsica
5970 General
5971 By subject (Table G1)
5972 Regions, natural features, etc., A-Z (Table G5972)
Apply Table G1 for subject
Monaco
5980 General
5981 By subject (Table G1)
5982 Regions, natural features, etc., A-Z (Table G5982)
Apply Table G1 for subject
5984 Cities and towns, etc., A-Z (Table G5984)
Apply Table G1 for subject
Benelux countries. Low countries
5990 General
5991 By subject (Table G1)
Netherlands Union
Including maps of Dutch colonies, dependencies, et. (Collectively)
Class individual colonies, dependencies, etc. according to location, e.g., G5165+, Netherlands Antilles
5995 General
5996 By subject (Table G1)
Netherlands
6000 General
6001 By subject (Table G1)
6002 Regions, natural features, etc., A-Z (Table G6002)
Apply Table G1 for subject
6003 Provinces, A-Z (Table G6003)
Apply Table G1 for subject
6004 Cities and towns, etc., A-Z (Table G6004)
Apply Table G1 for subject

By region or country
Eastern Hemisphere. Eurasia, Africa, etc.
Europe
Western Europe
Benelux countries. Low countries -- Continued
Belgium
6010 General
6011 By subject (Table G1 modified)
History
6011.S1 General
(6011.S12) This number not used
6011.S2 To 1555
6011.S3 1555-1648
6011.S4 Modern period, 1648-
6011.S5 18th century
6011.S55 19th century
6011.S56 Revolution, 1830-1839
6011.S6 20th century
6011.S65 World War I
6011.S7 World War II
6011.S73 1945-
6012 Regions, natural features, etc., A-Z (Table G6012)
Apply Table G1 for subject (except .S1-.S7, historical geography)
Apply Table G6011.S for history
6013 Provinces, A-Z (Table G6013)
Apply Table G1 for subject (except .S1-.S7, historical geography)
Apply Table G6011.S for history
6014 Cities and towns, etc., A-Z (Table G6014)
Apply Table G1 for subject (except .S1-.S7, historical geography)
Apply Table G6011.S for history
Luxembourg
6020 General
6021 By subject (Table G1)
6022 Regions, natural features, etc., A-Z (Table G6022)
Apply Table G1 for subject
6023 Districts, A-Z (Table G6023)
Apply Table G1 for subject
6024 Cities and towns, etc., A-Z (Table G6024)
Apply Table G1 for subject
Central Europe
6030 General
6031 By subject (Table G1)

By region or country
Eastern Hemisphere. Eurasia, Africa, etc.
Europe
Central Europe -- Continued
6032 Regions, natural features, etc., A-Z (Table G6032 modified)
Apply Table G1 for subject
Erzegebirge see G6512.E7
Alps
Class here maps of the Alps as a whole
For regions and natural features within the Alps see the country or region in which they are located
6035 General
6036 By subject (Table G1)
Switzerland
6040 General
6041 By subject (Table G1 modified)
History
6041.S1 General
(6041.S12) This number not used
6041.S2 To 1648
6041.S3 1648-1789
1789-1815
6041.S4 General
6041.S45 Helvetic Republic, 1789-1803
1815-1900
6041.S5 General
6041.S55 Sonderbund, 1845-1847
1900-1945
6041.S6 General
6041.S65 World War I
6041.S7 World War II
6041.S73 1945-
6042 Regions, natural features, etc., A-Z (Table G6042)
Apply Table G1 for subject (except .S1-.S7, historical geography)
Apply Table G6041.S for history
6043 Cantons, A-Z (Table G6043)
Apply Table G1 for subject (except .S1-.S7, historical geography)
Apply Table G6041.S for history
6044 Cities and towns, etc., A-Z (Table G6044)
Apply Table G1 for subject (except .S1-.S7, historical geography)
Apply Table G6041.S for history
Liechtenstein
6050 General

By region or country
Eastern Hemisphere. Eurasia, Africa, etc.
Europe
Central Europe
Liechtenstein -- Continued
6051 By subject (Table G1)
6052 Regions, natural features, etc., A-Z (Table G6052)
Apply Table G1 for subject
6053 Communes (Gemeindes), A-Z (Table G6053)
Apply Table G1 for subject
6054 Cities and towns, etc., A-Z (Table G6054)
Apply Table G1 for subject
German Empire
Including maps of German colonies, dependencies, etc. (Collectively)
Class individual colonies according to location, e.g., G8620+, Southwest Africa. German Southwest Africa
6070 General
6071 By subject (Table G1)
Germany
Including maps of the former East and West Germany together, Prussia as a whole, and the Holy Roman Empire
For East Prussia, see G6523.O5, G7063.K2
For Pomerania, see G6195+, G6522.P58
For Posen, see G6523
For Silesia, see G6523
For West Prussia, see G6522
6080 General
6081 By subject (Table G1 modified)
History
6081.S1 General
(6081.S12) This number not used
6081.S2 To 843
6081.S3 Medieval period, 843-1517
Modern period, 1517-
6081.S4 General
6081.S5 17th century
6081.S54 18th century
6081.S55 19th century
20th century
6081.S6 General
6081.S65 World War I
6081.S7 World War II
6081.S73 1945-

By region or country
Eastern Hemisphere. Eurasia, Africa, etc.
Europe
Central Europe
Germany -- Continued
6082 Regions, natural features, etc., A-Z (Table G6082 modified)
Apply Table G1 for subject (except .S1-.S7, historical geography)
Apply Table G6081.S for history
Erzegebirge see G6512.E7
6082.F7 Franconia [Duchy]
Subarrange by Table G1 except .S1-.S7, historical geography. For history, subarrange by Table G6081.S
Mulde River see G6242.M8
Administrative districts (Länder, Regierungsbezirke, Bezirke, Landkreise, etc.)
see G6150+
East Germany (German Democratic Republic)
6090 General
6091 By subject (Table G1 modified)
History
6091.S1 General
(6091.S12) This number not used
6091.S2 To 843
6091.S3 Medieval period, 843-1517
Modern period, 1517-
6091.S4 General
6091.S5 17th century
6091.S54 18th century
6091.S55 19th century
20th century
6091.S6 General
6091.S65 World War I
6091.S7 World War II
6091.S73 1945-
(6092) Regions, natural features, etc., A-Z
see G6082
(6093) Administrative districts (Länder, Regierungsbezirke, Bezirke, Landkreise, etc.)
see G6150+
(6094) Cities and towns, A-Z
see G6299
(6105-6108) Cottbus
see G6150+

By region or country
Eastern Hemisphere. Eurasia, Africa, etc.
Europe
Central Europe
Germany
East Germany (German Democratic Republic) -- Continued

(6115-6118) Dresden
see G6240+

East Berlin (Bezirk) see G6299

(6125-6128) Erfurt
see G6290+

(6135-6138) Frankfurt
see G6150+

(6145-6148) Gera
see G6290+

Brandenburg

6150 General

6151 By subject (Table G1 modified)

History

6151.S1 General

(6151.S12) This number not used

6151.S2 To 843

6151.S3 Medieval period, 843-1517

Modern period, 1517-

6151.S4 General

6151.S5 17th century

6151.S54 18th century

6151.S55 19th century

20th century

6151.S6 General

6151.S65 World War I

6151.S7 World War II

6151.S73 1945-

6152 Regions, natural features, etc., A-Z (Table G6152)

Apply Table G1 for subject (except .S1-.S7, historical geography)

Apply Table G6081.S for history

6153 Administrative districts (Regierungsbezirke, Landkreise, etc.), A-Z (Table G6153)

Apply Table G1 for subject (except .S1-.S7, historical geography)

Apply Table G6081.S for history

(6155-6158) Halle
see G6230+

By region or country
Eastern Hemisphere. Eurasia, Africa, etc.
Europe
Central Europe
Germany
East Germany (German Democratic Republic) -- Continued

(6165-6168) Karl-Marx-Stadt (Bezirk). Chemnitz
see G6240+

(6175-6178) Leipzig
see G6240+

(6185-6188) Magdeburg
see G6230+

Meckenburg-Vorpommern. Mecklenburg
Including Mecklenburg-Schwerin and Mecklenburg-Strelitz

6195 General

6196 By subject (Table G1 modified)

History

6196.S1 General

(6196.S12) This number not used

6196.S2 To 843

6196.S3 Medieval period, 843-1517

Modern period, 1517-

6196.S4 General

6196.S5 17th century

6196.S54 18th century

6196.S55 19th century

20th century

6196.S6 General

6196.S65 World War I

6196.S7 World War II

6196.S73 1945-

6197 Regions, natural features, etc., A-Z (Table G6197)
Apply Table G1 for subject (except .S1-.S7, historical geography)
Apply Table G6081.S for history

6198 Administrative districts (Regierungsbezirke, Landkreis, etc.), A-Z (Table G6198)
Apply Table G1 for subject (except .S1-.S7, historical geography)
Apply Table G6081.S for history

(6205-6208) Neubrandenburg
see G6195+

(6215-6218) Potsdam
see G6150+

By region or country
Eastern Hemisphere. Eurasia, Africa, etc.
Europe
Central Europe
Germany
East Germany (German Democratic Republic) -- Continued

(6225-6228) Rostock
see G6195+

Saxony-Anhalt
Including Anhalt and Saxony (Prussian province)

6230 General
6231 By subject (Table G1 modified)
History
6231.S1 General
(6231.S12) This number not used
6231.S2 To 843
6231.S3 Medieval period, 843-1517
Modern period, 1517-
6231.S4 General
6231.S5 17th century
6231.S54 18th century
6231.S55 19th century
20th century
6231.S6 General
6231.S65 World War I
6231.S7 World War II
6231.S73 1945-
6232 Regions, natural features, etc., A-Z (Table G6232)
Apply Table G1 for subject (except .S1-.S7, historical geography)
Apply Table G6081.S for history
6233 Administrative districts (Regierungsbezirke, Landkreis, etc.), A-Z (Table G6233)
Apply Table G1 for subject (except .S1-.S7, historical geography)
Apply Table G6081.S for history

Saxony
6240 General
6241 By subject (Table G1 modified)
History
6241.S1 General
(6241.S12) This number not used
6241.S2 To 843
6241.S3 Medieval period, 843-1517
Modern period, 1517-

By region or country
Eastern Hemisphere. Eurasia, Africa, etc.
Europe
Central Europe
Germany
East Germany (German Democratic Republic)
Saxony
By subject
History
Modern period, 1517- -- Continued

6241.S4 General
6241.S5 17th century
6241.S54 18th century
6241.S55 19th century
20th century
6241.S6 General
6241.S65 World War I
6241.S7 World War II
6241.S73 1945-
6242 Regions, natural features, etc., A-Z (Table G6242 modified)
Apply Table G1 for subject (except .S1-.S7, historical geography)
Apply Table G6081.S for history
6242.M8 Mulde River
Subarrange by Table G1 except .S1-.S7, historical geography. For history, subarrange by G6081.S
6243 Administrative districts (Regierungsbezirke, Landkreis, etc.), A-Z (Table G6243)
Apply Table G1 for subject (except .S1-.S7, historical geography)
Apply Table G6081.S for history
(6260-6265) Schwerin
see G6195+
(6280-6283) Suhl
see G6290+
Thuringia
6290 General
6291 By subject (Table G1 modified)
History
6291.S1 General
(6291.S12) This number not used
6291.S2 To 843
6291.S3 Medieval period, 843-1517
Modern period, 1517-
6291.S4 General

By region or country
Eastern Hemisphere. Eurasia, Africa, etc.
Europe
Central Europe
Germany
East Germany (German Democratic Republic)
Thuringia
By subject
History
Modern period, 1517- -- Continued

6291.S5 17th century
6291.S54 18th century
6291.S55 19th century
20th century
6291.S6 General
6291.S65 World War I
6291.S7 World War II
6291.S73 1945-
6292 Regions, natural features, etc., A-Z (Table G6292)
Apply Table G1 for subject (except .S1-.S7, historical geography)
Apply Table G6081.S for history
6293 Administrative districts (Regierungsbezirke, Landkreis, etc.), A-Z (Table G6293)
Apply Table G1 for subject (except .S1-.S7, historical geography)
Apply Table G6081.S for history
Cities and towns see G6299

West Germany (Federal Republic of Germany)
6295 General
6296 By subject (Table G1 modified)
History
6296.S1 General
(6296.S12) This number not used
6296.S2 To 843
6296.S3 Medieval period, 843-1517
Modern period, 1517-
6296.S4 General
6296.S5 17th century
6296.S54 18th century
6296.S55 19th century
20th century
6296.S6 General
6296.S65 World War I
6296.S7 World War II
6296.S73 1945-

By region or country
Eastern Hemisphere. Eurasia, Africa, etc.
Europe
Central Europe
Germany
West Germany (Federal Republic of Germany) -- Continued

(6297) Regions, natural features, etc., A-Z
see G6082

(6298) Administrative districts (Länder, Regierungsbezirke, Bezirke, Landkreise, etc.)
see G6310+

6299 Cities and towns, etc., A-Z (Table G6299 modified)
Apply Table G1 for subject (except .S1-.S7, historical geography)
Apply Table G6081.S for history
Including East German cities and towns

6299.L9 Lüneburg
Subarrange by Table G1 except .S1-.S7, historical geography. For history, subarrange by G6081.S

Schleswig-Holstein
6310 General
6311 By subject (Table G1 modified)
History
6311.S1 General
(6311.S12) This number not used
6311.S2 To 843
6311.S3 Medieval period, 843-1517
Modern period, 1517-
6311.S4 General
6311.S5 17th century
6311.S54 18th century
6311.S55 19th century
20th century
6311.S6 General
6311.S65 World War I
6311.S7 World War II
6311.S73 1945-

6312 Regions, natural features, etc., A-Z (Table G6312)
Apply Table G1 for subject (except .S1-.S7, historical geography)
Apply Table G6081.S for history

By region or country
Eastern Hemisphere. Eurasia, Africa, etc.
Europe
Central Europe
Germany
West Germany (Federal Republic of Germany)
Schleswig-Holstein -- Continued

6313 Administrative districts (Regierungsbezirke, Landkreis, etc.), A-Z (Table G6313)
Apply Table G1 for subject (except .S1-.S7, historical geography)
Apply Table G6081.S for history

Lower Saxony (Niedersachsen). Hanover

6320 General
6321 By subject (Table G1 modified)
History
6321.S1 General
(6321.S12) This number not used
6321.S2 To 843
6321.S3 Medieval period, 843-1517
Modern period, 1517-
6321.S4 General
6321.S5 17th century
6321.S54 18th century
6321.S55 19th century
20th century
6321.S6 General
6321.S65 World War I
6321.S7 World War II
6321.S73 1945-
6322 Regions, natural features, etc., A-Z (Table G6322)
Apply Table G1 for subject (except .S1-.S7, historical geography)
Apply Table G6081.S for history
6323 Administrative districts (Regierungsbezirke, Landkreis, etc.), A-Z (Table G6323 modified)
Apply Table G1 for subject (except .S1-.S7, historical geography)
Apply Table G6081.S for history
Lüneburg (Province) see G6299.L9

North Rhine-Westphalia. Westphalia

6360 General
6361 By subject (Table G1 modified)
History
6361.S1 General
(6361.S12) This number not used

By region or country
Eastern Hemisphere. Eurasia, Africa, etc.
Europe
Central Europe
Germany
West Germany (Federal Republic of Germany)
North Rhein-Westphalia. Westphalia
By subject
History -- Continued

6361.S2 To 843
6361.S3 Medieval period, 843-1517
Modern period, 1517-
6361.S4 General
6361.S5 17th century
6361.S54 18th century
6361.S55 19th century
20th century
6361.S6 General
6361.S65 World War I
6361.S7 World War II
6361.S73 1945-
6362 Regions, natural features, etc., A-Z (Table G6362)
Apply Table G1 for subject (except .S1-.S7, historical geography)
Apply Table G6081.S for history
6363 Administrative districts (Regierungsbezirke, Landkreise, etc.), A-Z (Table G6363)
Apply Table G1 for subject (except .S1-.S7, historical geography)
Apply Table G6081.S for history

Hesse
Including Hesse-Darmstadt and Hesse-Nassau
6370 General
6371 By subject (Table G1 modified)
History
6371.S1 General
(6371.S12) This number not used
6371.S2 To 843
6371.S3 Medieval period, 843-1517
Modern period, 1517-
6371.S4 General
6371.S5 17th century
6371.S54 18th century
6371.S55 19th century
20th century
6371.S6 General

By region or country
Eastern Hemisphere. Eurasia, Africa, etc.
Europe
Central Europe
Germany
West Germany (Federal Republic of Germany)
Hesse
By subject
History
Modern period, 1517-
20th century -- Continued
6371.S65 World War I
6371.S7 World War II
6371.S73 1945-
6372 Regions, natural features, etc., A-Z (Table G6372)
Apply Table G1 for subject (except .S1-.S7, historical geography)
Apply Table G6081.S for history
6373 Administrative districts (Regierungsbezirke, Landkreise, etc.), A-Z (Table G6373)
Apply Table G1 for subject (except .S1-.S7, historical geography)
Apply Table G6081.S for history
Rhineland-Palatinate. Rhine Province
6390 General
6391 By subject (Table G1 modified)
History
6391.S1 General
(6391.S12) This number not used
6391.S2 To 843
6391.S3 Medieval period, 843-1517
Modern period, 1517-
6391.S4 General
6391.S5 17th century
6391.S54 18th century
6391.S55 19th century
20th century
6391.S6 General
6391.S65 World War I
6391.S7 World War II
6391.S73 1945-
6392 Regions, natural features, etc., A-Z (Table G6392 modified)
Apply Table G1 for subject (except .S1-.S7, historical geography)
Apply Table G6081.S for history

By region or country
Eastern Hemisphere. Eurasia, Africa, etc.
Europe
Central Europe
Germany
West Germany (Federal Republic of Germany)
Rhineland-Palatinate. Rhine Province
Regions, natural features, etc., A-Z -- Continued

6392.P3 Palatinate. Lower Palatinate
Subarrange by Table G1 except .S1-.S7, historical geography. For history, subarrange by G6081.S
Including maps of Lower and Upper Palatinate together
For maps of upper Palatinate alone see G6423.O2

6393 Administrative districts (Regierungsbezirke, Landkreise, etc.), A-Z (Table G6393)
Apply Table G1 for subject (except .S1-.S7, historical geography)
Apply Table G6081.S for history

Saarland (Saar)
6395 General
6396 By subject (Table G1 modified)
History
6396.S1 General
(6396.S12) This number not used
6396.S2 To 843
6396.S3 Medieval period, 843-1517
Modern period, 1517-
6396.S4 General
6396.S5 17th century
6396.S54 18th century
6396.S55 19th century
20th century
6396.S6 General
6396.S65 World War I
6396.S7 World War II
6396.S73 1945-

6398 Administrative districts (Regierungsbezirke, Landkreise, etc.), A-Z (Table G6398)
Apply Table G1 for subject (except .S1-.S7, historical geography)
Apply Table G6081.S for history

Bavaria
6420 General
6421 By subject (Table G1 modified)

By region or country
Eastern Hemisphere. Eurasia, Africa, etc.
Europe
Central Europe
Germany
West Germany (Federal Republic of Germany)
Bavaria
By subject -- Continued
History
6421.S1 General
(6421.S12) This number not used
6421.S2 To 843
6421.S3 Medieval period, 843-1517
Modern period, 1517-
6421.S4 General
6421.S5 17th century
6421.S54 18th century
6421.S55 19th century
20th century
6421.S6 General
6421.S65 World War I
6421.S7 World War II
6421.S73 1945-
6422 Regions, natural features, etc., A-Z (Table G6422)
Apply Table G1 for subject (except .S1-.S7, historical geography)
Apply Table G6081.S for history
6423 Administrative districts (Regierungsbezirk, Landkreise, etc.), A-Z (Table G6423 modified)
Apply Table G1 for subject (except .S1-.S7, historical geography)
Apply Table G6081.S for history
Franconia see G6082.F7
6423.O2 Oberpfalz [Regierungsbezirk]. Upper Palatinate [Duchy]
Subarrange each by Table G1 except .S1-.S7, historical geography. For history, subarrange by G6081.S
For maps of Lower and Upper Palatinate together see G6392.P3
Baden-Württemberg
Including Baden, Württemberg-Baden, Württemberg-Hohenzollern, Hohenzollern, Württemberg
6425 General
6426 By subject (Table G1 modified)
History

By region or country
Eastern Hemisphere. Eurasia, Africa, etc.
Europe
Central Europe
Germany
West Germany (Federal Republic of Germany)
Baden-Württemberg
By subject
History -- Continued

6426.S1 General
(6426.S12) This number not used
6426.S2 To 843
6426.S3 Medieval period, 843-1517
Modern period, 1517-
6426.S4 General
6426.S5 17th century
6426.S54 18th century
6426.S55 19th century
20th century
6426.S6 General
6426.S65 World War I
6426.S7 World War II
6426.S73 1945-
6427 Regions, natural features, etc., A-Z (Table G6427)
Apply Table G1 for subject (except .S1-.S7, historical geography)
Apply Table G6081.S for history
6428 Administrative districts (Regierungsbezirke, Landkreise, etc.), A-Z (Table G6428)
Apply Table G1 for subject (except .S1-.S7, historical geography)
Apply Table G6081.S for history

Austria-Hungary
6480 General
6481 By subject (Table G1)
Austria
6490 General
6491 By subject (Table G1)
6492 Regions, natural features, etc., A-Z (Table G6492)
Apply Table G1 for subject
6493 Bundesländer, etc., A-Z (Table G6493 modified)
Apply Table G1 for subject
Vienna see G6494.V4
6494 Cities and towns, etc., A-Z (Table G6494 modified)
Apply Table G1 for subject

By region or country
Eastern Hemisphere. Eurasia, Africa, etc.
Europe
Central Europe
Austria-Hungary
Austria
Cities and towns, etc., A-Z -- Continued
6494.V4 Vienna
Subarrange by Table G1
Hungary
6500 General
6501 By subject (Table G1)
6502 Regions, natural features, etc., A-Z (Table G6502)
Apply Table G1 for subject
6503 Counties (Megyék), A-Z (Table G6503)
Apply Table G1 for subject
6504 Cities and towns, etc., A-Z (Table G6504)
Apply Table G1 for subject
Czechoslovakia. Czech Republic
6510 General
6511 By subject (Table G1 modified)
History
6511.S1 General
(6511.S12) This number not used
6511.S2 Early and medieval through 1526
6511.S3 16th-18th centuries
6511.S4 1789-1815
6511.S5 1815-1918
6511.S65 World War I
6511.S67 1918-1945
6511.S7 World War II
6511.S8 1945-
6512 Regions, natural features, etc., A-Z (Table G6512 modified)
Apply Table G1 for subject (except .S1-.S7, historical geography)
Apply Table G6511.S for history
6512.E7 Erzegebirge
Subarrange by Table G1 except .S1-.S7, historical geography. For history, subarrange by G6511.S
6513 Provinces, A-Z (Table G6513)
Apply Table G1 for subject (except .S1-.S7, historical geography)
Apply Table G6511.S for history

By region or country
Eastern Hemisphere. Eurasia, Africa, etc.
Europe
Central Europe
Austria-Hungary
Czechoslovakia. Czech Republic -- Continued
6514 Cities and towns, etc., A-Z (Table G6514)
Apply Table G1 for subject (except .S1-.S7, historical geography)
Apply Table G6511.S for history
Slovakia
6515 General
6516 By subject (Table G1 modified)
History
6516.S1 General
(6516.S12) This number not used
6516.S2 Early and medieval through 1526
6516.S3 16th-18th centuries
6516.S4 1789-1815
1815-1918
6516.S5 General
6516.S65 World War I
1918-1945
6516.S67 General
6516.S7 World War II
6516.S8 1945-
6517 Regions, natural features, etc., A-Z (Table G6517)
Apply Table G1 for subject (except .S1-.S7, historical geography)
Apply Table G6516.S for history
6518 Provinces, A-Z (Table G6518)
Apply Table G1 for subject (except .S1-.S7, historical geography)
Apply Table G6516.S for history
6519 Cities and towns, etc., A-Z (Table G6519)
Apply Table G1 for subject (except .S1-.S7, historical geography)
Apply Table G6516.S for history
Poland
6520 General
6521 By subject (Table G1 modified)
History
6521.S1 General
(6521.S12) This number not used
6521.S2 Early to 1573
6521.S3 1573-1795
6521.S4 1795-1830

By region or country
Eastern Hemisphere. Eurasia, Africa, etc.
Europe
Central Europe
Poland
By subject
History -- Continued

6521.S5 1830-1918
6521.S65 World War I
6521.S67 1918-1945
6521.S7 World War II
6521.S73 1945-
6522 Regions, natural features, etc., A-Z (Table G6522)
Apply Table G1 for subject (except .S1-.S7, historical geography)
Apply Table G6521.S for history
6523 Voivodeships, etc., A-Z (Table G6523)
Apply Table G1 for subject (except .S1-.S7, historical geography)
Apply Table G6521.S for history
6524 Cities and towns, etc., A-Z (Table G6524)
Apply Table G1 for subject (except .S1-.S7, historical geography)
Apply Table G6521.S for history

Southern Europe
Cf. G5672 Mediterranean region
6530 General
6531 By subject (Table G1)
6532 Regions, natural features, etc., A-Z (Table G6532)
Apply Table G1 for subject

Iberian Peninsula
6540 General
6541 By subject (Table G1)

Spanish Empire
Including maps of Spanish colonies, etc. (Collectively)
Class individual colonies, etc., according to location, e.g., G8232, Spanish Morocco
6550 General
6551 By subject (Table G1)

Spain
6560 General
6561 By subject (Table G1)
6562 Regions, natural features, etc., A-Z (Table G6562 modified)
Apply Table G1 for subject
Andalusia see G6563.A55

By region or country
Eastern Hemisphere. Eurasia, Africa, etc.
Europe
Southern Europe
Iberian Peninsula
Spain
Regions, natural features, etc., A-Z -- Continued
6562.B25 Balearic Islands
Subarrange by Table G1
Basque Provinces see G6563.P15
6562.C35 Castile
Subarrange by Table G1
6563 Administrative regions, provinces, kingdoms, etc., A-Z (Table G6563 modified)
Apply Table G1 for subject
6563.A55 Andalusia
Subarrange by Table G1
Baleares see G6562.B25
Castile [Kindgom] see G6562.C35
Las Palmas see G9153.L3
6563.P15 País Vasco
Subarrange by Table G1
Palmas, Las see G9153.L3
6564 Cities and towns, etc., A-Z (Table G6564)
Apply Table G1 for subject
Andorra
6660 General
6661 By subject (Table G1)
6662 Regions, natural features, etc., A-Z (Table G6662)
Apply Table G1 for subject
6663 Parishes, A-Z (Table G6663)
Apply Table G1 for subject
6664 Cities and towns, etc., A-Z (Table G6664)
Apply Table G1 for subject
Gibraltar
6670 General
6671 By subject (Table G1)
Portuguese Empire
Including maps of Portuguese colonies, etc. (Collectively)
Class individual colonies, etc., according to location, e.g., G8640+, Angola
6680 General
6681 By subject (Table G1)
Portugal. Lusitania
6690 General
6691 By subject (Table G1)

By region or country
Eastern Hemisphere. Eurasia, Africa, etc.
Europe
Southern Europe
Iberian Peninsula
Portugal. Lusitania -- Continued

6692 Regions, natural features, etc., A-Z (Table G6692)
Apply Table G1 for subject

6693 Provinces, districts, etc., A-Z (Table G6693 modified)
Apply Table G1 for subject
Angra do Heroismo see G9133.A5
Horta see G9133.H6
Ponta Delgada see G9133.P6

6694 Cities and towns, etc., A-Z (Table G6694)
Apply Table G1 for subject

Roman Empire
6700 General
6701 By subject (Table G1)

Italian Empire
Including maps of Italian colonies, etc. (Collectively)
Class individual colonies, etc., according to location, e.g., G8352, Italian Somaliland
6705 General
6706 By subject (Table G1)

Italy
6710 General
6711 By subject (Table G1)
6712 Regions, natural features, etc., A-Z (Table G6712)
Apply Table G1 for subject

6713 Regioni, etc., A-Z (Table G6713 modified)
Apply Table G1 for subject
Vatican see G6714.R7:3V3

6714 Cities and towns, etc., A-Z (Table G6714 modified)
Apply Table G1 for subject

6714.R7:3V3 Vatican City
Subarrange by Table G1

Sicily
6760 General
6761 By subject (Table G1)
6762 Regions, natural features, etc., A-Z (Table G6762)
Apply Table G1 for subject

6763 Provinces, etc., A-Z (Table G6763)
Apply Table G1 for subject

Sardinia
6770 General
6771 By subject (Table G1)

By region or country
Eastern Hemisphere. Eurasia, Africa, etc.
Europe
Southern Europe
Italy
Sardinia -- Continued
6772 Regions, natural features, etc., A-Z (Table G6772)
Apply Table G1 for subject
6773 Provinces, etc., A-Z (Table G6773)
Apply Table G1 for subject
San Marino
6780 General
6781 By subject (Table G1)
6782 Regions, natural features, etc., A-Z (Table G6782)
Apply Table G1 for subject
6784 Cities and towns, etc., A-Z (Table G6784)
Apply Table G1 for subject
Malta
6790 General
6791 By subject (Table G1)
6792 Regions, natural features, etc., A-Z (Table G6792)
Apply Table G1 for subject
6794 Cities and towns, etc., A-Z (Table G6794)
Apply Table G1 for subject
Balkan Peninsula. Southeastern Europe
6800 General
6801 By subject (Table G1)
6802 Regions, natural features, etc., A-Z (Table G6802)
Apply Table G1 for subject
Greece
6810 General
6811 By subject (Table G1)
6812 Regions, natural features, etc., A-Z (Table G6812)
Apply Table G1 for subject
6813 Provinces (Nomoi), etc., A-Z (Table G6813)
Apply Table G1 for subject
6814 Cities and towns, etc., A-Z (Table G6814)
Apply Table G1 for subject
Albania
6830 General
6831 By subject (Table G1)
6832 Regions, natural features, etc., A-Z (Table G6832)
Apply Table G1 for subject
6833 Districts (Rrethi), etc., A-Z (Table G6833)
Apply Table G1 for subject
6833.T5 Tirana (Rrethi)

By region or country
Eastern Hemisphere. Eurasia, Africa, etc.
Europe
Balkan Peninsula. Southeastern Europe
Albania -- Continued
6834 Cities and towns, etc., A-Z (Table G6834)
Apply Table G1 for subject
Former Yugloslav republics. Yugoslavia
6840 General
6841 By subject (Table G1 modified)
History
6841.S1 General
(6841.S12) This number not used
6841.S2 To 1800
6841.S4 19th century
6841.S6 20th century
6841.S65 World War I
6841.S67 1918-1941
6841.S7 World War II
6841.S73 1945-1992
6842 Regions, natural features, etc., A-Z (Table G6842)
Apply Table G1 for subject (except .S1-.S7, historical geography)
Apply Table G6841.S for history
Macedonia (Republic)
6845 General
6846 By subject (Table G1 modified)
History
6846.S1 General
(6846.S12) This number not used
6846.S2 To 1800
6846.S4 19th century
6846.S6 20th century
6846.S65 World War I
6846.S67 1918-1941
6846.S7 World War II
6846.S73 1945-1992
6847 Regions, natural features, etc., A-Z (Table G6847)
Apply Table G1 for subject (except .S1-.S7, historical geography)
Apply Table G6841.S for history
6849 Cities and towns, etc., A-Z (Table G6849)
Apply Table G1 for subject (except .S1-.S7, historical geography)
Apply Table G6841.S for history
Serbia
6850 General

By region or country
Eastern Hemisphere. Eurasia, Africa, etc.
Europe
Balkan Peninsula. Southeastern Europe
Serbia -- Continued

6851 By subject (Table G1 modified)
History
6851.S1 General
(6851.S12) This number not used
6851.S2 To 1800
6851.S4 19th century
6851.S6 20th century
6851.S65 World War I
6851.S67 1918-1941
6851.S7 World War II
6851.S73 1945-1992
6852 Regions, natural features, etc., A-Z (Table G6852)
Apply Table G1 for subject (except .S1-.S7, historical geography)
Apply Table G6841.S for history
6853 Administrative areas, provinces, etc., A-Z (Table G6853)
Apply Table G1 for subject (except .S1-.S7, historical geography)
Apply Table G6841.S for history
6854 Cities and towns, etc., A-Z (Table G6854)
Apply Table G1 for subject (except .S1-.S7, historical geography)
Apply Table G6841.S for history

Montenegro (Crna Gora)
6855 General
6856 By subject (Table G1 modified)
History
6856.S1 General
(6856.S12) This number not used
6856.S2 To 1800
6856.S4 19th century
6856.S6 20th century
6856.S65 World War I
6856.S67 1918-1941
6856.S7 World War II
6856.S73 1945-1992
6857 Regions, natural features, etc., A-Z (Table G6857)
Apply Table G1 for subject (except .S1-.S7, historical geography)
Apply Table G6841.S for history

By region or country
Eastern Hemisphere. Eurasia, Africa, etc.
Europe
Balkan Peninsula. Southeastern Europe
Montenegro (Crna Gora) -- Continued

6859 Cities and towns, etc., A-Z (Table G6859)
Apply Table G1 for subject (except .S1-.S7, historical geography)
Apply Table G6841.S for history

Bosnia and Hercegovina

6860 General

6861 By subject (Table G1 modified)
History
6861.S1 General
(6861.S12) This number not used
6861.S2 To 1800
6861.S4 19th century
6861.S6 20th century
6861.S65 World War I
6861.S67 1918-1941
6861.S7 World War II
6861.S73 1945-1992

6862 Regions, natural features, etc., A-Z (Table G6862)
Apply Table G1 for subject (except .S1-.S7, historical geography)
Apply Table G6841.S for history

6863 Administrative divisions, etc., A-Z (Table G6863)
Apply Table G1 for subject (except .S1-.S7, historical geography)
Apply Table G6841.S for history

6864 Cities and towns, etc., A-Z (Table G6864)
Apply Table G1 for subject (except .S1-.S7, historical geography)
Apply Table G6841.S for history

Croatia (Hrvatska)

6870 General

6871 By subject (Table G1 modified)
History
6871.S1 General
(6871.S12) This number not used
6871.S2 To 1800
6871.S4 19th century
6871.S6 20th century
6871.S65 World War I
6871.S67 1918-1941
6871.S7 World War II
6871.S73 1945-1992

By region or country
Eastern Hemisphere. Eurasia, Africa, etc.
Europe
Balkan Peninsula. Southeastern Europe
Croatia (Hrvatska) -- Continued

6872 Regions, natural features, etc., A-Z (Table G6872)
Apply Table G1 for subject (except .S1-.S7, historical geography)
Apply Table G6841.S for history

6873 Administrative divisions, etc., A-Z (Table G6873)
Apply Table G1 for subject (except .S1-.S7, historical geography)
Apply Table G6841.S for history

6874 Cities and towns, etc., A-Z (Table G6874)
Apply Table G1 for subject (except .S1-.S7, historical geography)
Apply Table G6841.S for history

Slovenia
6875 General
6876 By subject (Table G1 modified)
History
6876.S1 General
(6876.S12) This number not used
6876.S2 To 1800
6876.S4 19th century
6876.S6 20th century
6876.S65 World War I
6876.S67 1918-1941
6876.S7 World War II
6876.S73 1945-1992

6877 Regions, natural features, etc., A-Z (Table G6877)
Apply Table G1 for subject (except .S1-.S7, historical geography)
Apply Table G6841.S for history

6878 Administrative divisions, etc., A-Z (Table G6878)
Apply Table G1 for subject (except .S1-.S7, historical geography)
Apply Table G6841.S for history

6879 Cities and towns, etc., A-Z (Table G6879)
Apply Table G1 for subject (except .S1-.S7, historical geography)
Apply Table G6841.S for history

Romania
6880 General
6881 By subject (Table G1)
6882 Regions, natural features, etc., A-Z (Table G6882)
Apply Table G1 for subject

By region or country
Eastern Hemisphere. Eurasia, Africa, etc.
Europe
Balkan Peninsula. Southeastern Europe
Romania -- Continued
6883 Provinces, etc., A-Z (Table G6883)
Apply Table G1 for subject
6884 Cities and towns, etc., A-Z (Table G6884)
Apply Table G1 for subject
Bulgaria
6890 General
6891 By subject (Table G1)
6892 Regions, natural features, etc., A-Z (Table G6892)
Apply Table G1 for subject
6893 Provinces, etc., A-Z (Table G6893)
Apply Table G1 for subject
6894 Cities and towns, etc., A-Z (Table G6894)
Apply Table G1 for subject
Scandinavia. Northern Europe
6910 General
6911 By subject (Table G1)
6912 Regions, natural features, etc., A-Z (Table G6912)
Apply Table G1 for subject
Denmark and colonies
Including maps of Danish colonies, etc. (Collectively)
Class individual colonies, etc., according to location, e.g., G3380+, Greenland
6915 General
6916 By subject (Table G1)
Denmark
6920 General
6921 By subject (Table G1)
6922 Regions, natural features, etc., A-Z (Table G6922)
Apply Table G1 for subject
6923 Provinces (Amter), etc., A-Z (Table G6923)
Apply Table G1 for subject
6924 Cities and towns, etc., A-Z (Table G6924)
Apply Table G1 for subject
Faeroe Islands
6925 General
6926 By subject (Table G1)
6927 Regions, natural features, etc., A-Z (Table G6927)
Apply Table G1 for subject
6929 Cities and towns, etc., A-Z (Table G6929)
Apply Table G1 for subject
Greenland see G3380+
Iceland

By region or country
Eastern Hemisphere. Eurasia, Africa, etc.
Europe
Scandinavia. Northern Europe
Iceland -- Continued
6930 General
6931 By subject (Table G1)
6932 Regions, natural features, etc., A-Z (Table G6932)
Apply Table G1 for subject
6933 Provinces (Sýsler), kjördæmi, etc., A-Z (Table G6933)
Apply Table G1 for subject
6934 Cities and towns, etc., A-Z (Table G6934)
Apply Table G1 for subject
Norway
6940 General
6941 By subject (Table G1)
6942 Regions, natural features, etc., A-Z (Table G6942)
Apply Table G1 for subject
6943 Counties (Fylker), etc., A-Z (Table G6943 modified)
Apply Table G1 for subject
Bergen see G6944.B4
Oslo see G6944.O9
Oslo (Vigelandsparken) see G6944.O9:2V5
Oslo (Aker) see G6944.O9:3A3
6944 Cities and towns, etc., A-Z (Table G6944 modified)
Apply Table G1 for subject
6944.B4 Bergen
Subarrange by Table G1
6944.O9 Oslo
Subarrange by Table G1
6944.O9:2V5 Vigelandsparken [Oslo]
Subarrange by Table G1
6944.O9:3A3 Aker [Oslo]
Subarrange by Table G1
Sweden
6950 General
6951 By subject (Table G1)
6952 Regions, natural features, etc., A-Z (Table G6952)
Apply Table G1 for subject
6953 Provinces (Länni), etc., A-Z (Table G6953)
Apply Table G1 for subject
6954 Cities and towns, etc., A-Z (Table G6954)
Apply Table G1 for subject
Finland. Suomi
6960 General
6961 By subject (Table G1)

By region or country
Eastern Hemisphere. Eurasia, Africa, etc.
Europe
Scandinavia. Northern Europe
Finland. Suomi -- Continued

6962 Regions, natural features, etc., A-Z (Table G6962 modified)
Apply Table G1 for subject
6962.A2 Aland
Subarrange by Table G1
6962.A23 Aland Sea
Subarrange by Table G1
6963 Departments, etc., A-Z (Table G6963 modified)
Apply Table G1 for subject
Ahvenanmaa see G6962.A2
Ahvenanmaa (Aland Sea) see G6962.A23
6964 Cities and towns, etc., A-Z (Table G6964)
Apply Table G1 for subject

Eastern Europe
Including Poland, Finland, Baltic States, European Russia, Romania, Bulgaria, Soviet zone of influence, 1946-1991
For Poland see G6520+
For Finland see G6960+
For the Baltic States collectively see G7020+
For Estonia see G7030+
For Latvia see G7040+
For Lithuania see G7050+
6965 General
6966 By subject (Table G1)
6967 Regions, natural features, etc., A-Z (Table G6967)
Apply Table G1 for subject

Former Soviet republics. Union of Soviet Socialist Republics (U.S.S.R.). Russia (Empire)
7000 General
7001 By subject (Table G1 modified)
History
7001.S1 General
(7001.S12) This number not used
7001.S2 Early through 1613
7001.S3 17th century
7001.S4 18th century
7001.S5 1801-1917
7001.S54 Crimean War
7001.S57 Rebellion, 1905-1907
7001.S65 World War I
7001.S67 1917-1921

By region or country
Eastern Hemisphere. Eurasia, Africa, etc.
Europe
Former Soviet republics. Union of Soviet Socialist Republics (U.S.S.R.). Russia (Empire)
By subject
History -- Continued

7001.S68 1921-1945
7001.S7 World War II
7001.S72 1945-1991
7001.S75 1991-
7002 Regions, natural features, etc., A-Z (Table G7002 modified)
Apply Table G1 for subject (except .S1-.S7, historical geography)
Apply Table G7001.S for history
Ural Mountains see G7062.U7
(7004) Cities and towns
see G7064 and other former Soviet republics

Former Soviet republics (Europe). European U.S.S.R. European Russia (Empire)

7010 General
7011 By subject (Table G1 modified)
History
7011.S1 General
(7011.S12) This number not used
7011.S2 Early through 1613
7011.S3 17th century
7011.S4 18th century
7011.S5 1801-1917
7011.S54 Crimean War
7011.S57 Rebellion, 1905-1907
7011.S65 World War I
7011.S67 1917-1921
7011.S68 1921-1945
7011.S7 World War II
7011.S72 1945-1991
7011.S75 1991-
7012 Regions, natural features, etc., A-Z (Table G7012)
Apply Table G1 for subject (except .S1-.S7, historical geography)
Apply Table G7001.S for history

Baltic States

7020 General
7021 By subject (Table G1 modified)
History
7021.S1 General

By region or country
Eastern Hemisphere. Eurasia, Africa, etc.
Europe
Baltic States
By subject
History -- Continued

(7021.S12) This number not used
7021.S2 Early through 1613
7021.S3 17th century
7021.S4 18th century
7021.S5 1801-1917
7021.S54 Crimean War
7021.S57 Rebellion, 1905-1907
7021.S65 World War I
7021.S67 1917-1921
7021.S68 1921-1945
7021.S7 World War II
7021.S72 1945-1991
7021.S75 1991-
7022 Regions, natural features, etc., A-Z (Table G7022)
Apply Table G1 for subject (except .S1-.S7, historical geography)
Apply Table G7001.S for history

Estonia
7030 General
7031 By subject (Table G1 modified)
History
7031.S1 General
(7031.S12) This number not used
7031.S2 Early through 1613
7031.S3 17th century
7031.S4 18th century
7031.S5 1801-1917
7031.S54 Crimean War
7031.S57 Rebellion, 1905-1907
7031.S65 World War I
7031.S67 1917-1921
7031.S68 1921-1945
7031.S7 World War II
7031.S72 1945-1991
7031.S75 1991-
7032 Regions, natural features, etc., A-Z (Table G7032)
Apply Table G1 for subject (except .S1-.S7, historical geography)
Apply Table G7001.S for history

By region or country
Eastern Hemisphere. Eurasia, Africa, etc.
Europe
Baltic States
Estonia -- Continued

7033 Administrative divisions, A-Z (Table G7033)
Apply Table G1 for subject (except .S1-.S7, historical geography)
Apply Table G7001.S for history

7034 Cities and towns, A-Z (Table G7034)
Apply Table G1 for subject (except .S1-.S7, historical geography)
Apply Table G7001.S for history

Latvia

7040 General

7041 By subject (Table G1 modified)

History

7041.S1 General

(7041.S12) This number not used

7041.S2 Early through 1613

7041.S3 17th century

7041.S4 18th century

7041.S5 1801-1917

7041.S54 Crimean War

7041.S57 Rebellion, 1905-1907

7041.S65 World War I

7041.S67 1917-1921

7041.S68 1921-1945

7041.S7 World War II

7041.S72 1945-1991

7041.S75 1991-

7042 Regions, natural features, etc., A-Z (Table G7042)
Apply Table G1 for subject (except .S1-.S7, historical geography)
Apply Table G7001.S for history

7043 Administrative divisions, A-Z (Table G7043)
Apply Table G1 for subject (except .S1-.S7, historical geography)
Apply Table G7001.S for history

7044 Cities and towns, A-Z (Table G7044)
Apply Table G1 for subject (except .S1-.S7, historical geography)
Apply Table G7001.S for history

Lithuania

7050 General

7051 By subject (Table G1 modified)

History

By region or country
Eastern Hemisphere. Eurasia, Africa, etc.
Europe
Baltic States
Lithuania
By subject
History -- Continued

7051.S1 General
(7051.S12) This number not used
7051.S2 Early through 1613
7051.S3 17th century
7051.S4 18th century
7051.S5 1801-1917
7051.S54 Crimean War
7051.S57 Rebellion, 1905-1907
7051.S65 World War I
7051.S67 1917-1921
7051.S68 1921-1945
7051.S7 World War II
7051.S72 1945-1991
7051.S75 1991-
7052 Regions, natural features, etc., A-Z (Table G7052)
Apply Table G1 for subject (except .S1-.S7, historical geography)
Apply Table G7001.S for history
7053 Administrative divisions, A-Z (Table G7053)
Apply Table G1 for subject (except .S1-.S7, historical geography)
Apply Table G7001.S for history
7054 Cities and towns, A-Z (Table G7054)
Apply Table G1 for subject (except .S1-.S7, historical geography)
Apply Table G7001.S for history

Russia (Federation). Russian Soviet Federated Socialist Republic (R.S.F.S.R.)
Asian provinces, districts, etc. see G7270+

7060 General
7061 By subject (Table G1 modified)
History
7061.S1 General
(7061.S12) This number not used
7061.S2 Early through 1613
7061.S3 17th century
7061.S4 18th century
7061.S5 1801-1917
7061.S54 Crimean War
7061.S57 Rebellion, 1905-1907

By region or country
Eastern Hemisphere. Eurasia, Africa, etc.
Europe
Russia (Federation). Russian Soviet Federated Socialist Republic (R.S.F.S.R.)
By subject
History
1801-1917 -- Continued
7061.S65 World War I
7061.S67 1917-1921
7061.S68 1921-1945
7061.S7 World War II
7061.S72 1945-1991
7061.S75 1991-
7062 Regions, natural features, etc., A-Z (Table G7062 modified)
Apply Table G1 for subject (except .S1-.S7, historical geography)
Apply Table G7001.S for history
7062.U7 Ural Mountains
Subarrange by Table G1 except .S1-.S7, historical geography. For history, subarrange by Table G7001.S
7063 European administrative divisions, A-Z (Table G7063)
Apply Table G1 for subject (except .S1-.S7, historical geography)
Apply Table G7001.S for history
7064 Cities and towns, A-Z (Table G7064)
Apply Table G1 for subject (except .S1-.S7, historical geography)
Apply Table G7001.S for history
Including those in Siberia, Buri͡ati͡a, Yakutia, Russian Far East, and Sakhalin
Belarus. Belorussia. White Russia
7090 General
7091 By subject (Table G1 modified)
History
7091.S1 General
(7091.S12) This number not used
7091.S2 Early through 1613
7091.S3 17th century
7091.S4 18th century
7091.S5 1801-1917
7091.S54 Crimean War
7091.S57 Rebellion, 1905-1907
7091.S65 World War I
7091.S67 1917-1921

By region or country
Eastern Hemisphere. Eurasia, Africa, etc.
Europe
Belarus. Belorussia. White Russia
By subject
History -- Continued

7091.S68 1921-1945
7091.S7 World War II
7091.S72 1945-1991
7091.S75 1991-
7092 Regions, natural features, etc., A-Z (Table G7092)
Apply Table G1 for subject (except .S1-.S7, historical geography)
Apply Table G7001.S for history
7093 Administrative divisions, A-Z (Table G7093)
Apply Table G1 for subject (except .S1-.S7, historical geography)
Apply Table G7001.S for history
7094 Cities and towns, A-Z (Table G7094)
Apply Table G1 for subject (except .S1-.S7, historical geography)
Apply Table G7001.S for history

Ukraine

7100 General
7101 By subject (Table G1 modified)
History
7101.S1 General
(7101.S12) This number not used
7101.S2 Early through 1613
7101.S3 17th century
7101.S4 18th century
7101.S5 1801-1917
7101.S54 Crimean War
7101.S57 Rebellion, 1905-1907
7101.S65 World War I
7101.S67 1917-1921
7101.S68 1921-1945
7101.S7 World War II
7101.S72 1945-1991
7101.S75 1991-
7102 Regions, natural features, etc., A-Z (Table G7102)
Apply Table G1 for subject (except .S1-.S7, historical geography)
Apply Table G7001.S for history

By region or country
Eastern Hemisphere. Eurasia, Africa, etc.
Europe
Ukraine -- Continued

7103 Administrative divisions, A-Z (Table G7103)
Apply Table G1 for subject (except .S1-.S7, historical geography)
Apply Table G7001.S for history

7104 Cities and towns, A-Z (Table G7104)
Apply Table G1 for subject (except .S1-.S7, historical geography)
Apply Table G7001.S for history

Moldova. Moldavian S.S.R.

7110 General
7111 By subject (Table G1 modified)
History
7111.S1 General
(7111.S12) This number not used
7111.S2 Early through 1613
7111.S3 17th century
7111.S4 18th century
7111.S5 1801-1917
7111.S54 Crimean War
7111.S57 Rebellion, 1905-1907
7111.S65 World War I
7111.S67 1917-1921
7111.S68 1921-1945
7111.S7 World War II
7111.S72 1945-1991
7111.S75 1991-

7112 Regions, natural features, etc., A-Z (Table G7112)
Apply Table G1 for subject (except .S1-.S7, historical geography)
Apply Table G7001.S for history

7113 Administrative divisions, A-Z (Table G7113)
Apply Table G1 for subject (except .S1-.S7, historical geography)
Apply Table G7001.S for history

7114 Cities and towns, A-Z (Table G7114)
Apply Table G1 for subject (except .S1-.S7, historical geography)
Apply Table G7001.S for history

Former Soviet republics in Asia. U.S.S.R. in Asia. Russia (Empire) in Asia

7115 General
7116 By subject (Table G1 modified)
History

By region or country
Eastern Hemisphere. Eurasia, Africa, etc.
Europe
Former Soviet republics in Asia. U.S.S.R. in Asia.
Russia (Empire) in Asia
By subject
History -- Continued

7116.S1 General
(7116.S12) This number not used
7116.S2 Early through 1613
7116.S3 17th century
7116.S4 18th century
7116.S5 1801-1917
7116.S54 Crimean War
7116.S57 Rebellion, 1905-1907
7116.S65 World War I
7116.S67 1917-1921
7116.S68 1921-1945
7116.S7 World War II
7116.S72 1945-1991
7116.S75 1991-

Transcaucasia

7120 General
7121 By subject (Table G1 modified)

History

7121.S1 General
(7121.S12) This number not used
7121.S2 Early through 1613
7121.S3 17th century
7121.S4 18th century
7121.S5 1801-1917
7121.S54 Crimean War
7121.S57 Rebellion, 1905-1907
7121.S65 World War I
7121.S67 1917-1921
7121.S68 1921-1945
7121.S7 World War II
7121.S72 1945-1991
7121.S75 1991-
7122 Regions, natural features, etc., A-Z (Table G7122)

Apply Table G1 for subject (except .S1-.S7, historical geography)

Apply Table G7001.S for history

Georgia (Republic)

7130 General
7131 By subject (Table G1 modified)

History

By region or country
Eastern Hemisphere. Eurasia, Africa, etc.
Europe
Former Soviet republics in Asia. U.S.S.R. in Asia. Russia (Empire) in Asia
Transcaucasia
Georgia (Republic)
By subject
History -- Continued

7131.S1 General
(7131.S12) This number not used
7131.S2 Early through 1613
7131.S3 17th century
7131.S4 18th century
7131.S5 1801-1917
7131.S54 Crimean War
7131.S57 Rebellion, 1905-1907
7131.S65 World War I
7131.S67 1917-1921
7131.S68 1921-1945
7131.S7 World War II
7131.S72 1945-1991
7131.S75 1991-
7132 Regions, natural features, etc., A-Z (Table G7132)
Apply Table G1 for subject (except .S1-.S7, historical geography)
Apply Table G7001.S for history
7133 Administrative divisions, A-Z (Table G7133)
Apply Table G1 for subject (except .S1-.S7, historical geography)
Apply Table G7001.S for history
7134 Cities and towns, A-Z (Table G7134)
Apply Table G1 for subject (except .S1-.S7, historical geography)
Apply Table G7001.S for history

Azerbaijan
7140 General
7141 By subject (Table G1 modified)
History
7141.S1 General
(7141.S12) This number not used
7141.S2 Early through 1613
7141.S3 17th century
7141.S4 18th century
7141.S5 1801-1917
7141.S54 Crimean War
7141.S57 Rebellion, 1905-1907

By region or country
Eastern Hemisphere. Eurasia, Africa, etc.
Europe
Former Soviet republics in Asia. U.S.S.R. in Asia.
Russia (Empire) in Asia
Transcaucasia
Azerbaijan
By subject
History
1801-1917 -- Continued
7141.S65 World War I
7141.S67 1917-1921
7141.S68 1921-1945
7141.S7 World War II
7141.S72 1945-1991
7141.S75 1991-
7142 Regions, natural features, etc., A-Z (Table G7142)
Apply Table G1 for subject (except .S1-.S7, historical geography)
Apply Table G7001.S for history
7143 Administrative divisions, A-Z (Table G7143)
Apply Table G1 for subject (except .S1-.S7, historical geography)
Apply Table G7001.S for history
7144 Cities and towns, A-Z (Table G7144)
Apply Table G1 for subject (except .S1-.S7, historical geography)
Apply Table G7001.S for history
Armenia (Republic)
7150 General
7151 By subject (Table G1 modified)
History
7151.S1 General
(7151.S12) This number not used
7151.S2 Early through 1613
7151.S3 17th century
7151.S4 18th century
7151.S5 1801-1917
7151.S54 Crimean War
7151.S57 Rebellion, 1905-1907
7151.S65 World War I
7151.S67 1917-1921
7151.S68 1921-1945
7151.S7 World War II
7151.S72 1945-1991
7151.S75 1991-

By region or country
Eastern Hemisphere. Eurasia, Africa, etc.
Europe
Former Soviet republics in Asia. U.S.S.R. in Asia.
Russia (Empire) in Asia
Transcaucasia
Armenia (Republic) -- Continued
7154 Cities and towns, A-Z (Table G7154)
Apply Table G1 for subject (except .S1-.S7, historical geography)
Apply Table G7001.S for history
Former Soviet Central Asia. Russian Central Asia. West Turkestan
Cf. G7405+ Central Asia
7210 General
7211 By subject (Table G1 modified)
History
7211.S1 General
(7211.S12) This number not used
7211.S2 Early through 1613
7211.S3 17th century
7211.S4 18th century
7211.S5 1801-1917
7211.S54 Crimean War
7211.S57 Rebellion, 1905-1907
7211.S65 World War I
7211.S67 1917-1921
7211.S68 1921-1945
7211.S7 World War II
7211.S72 1945-1991
7211.S75 1991-
7212 Regions, natural features, etc., A-Z (Table G7212)
Apply Table G1 for subject (except .S1-.S7, historical geography)
Apply Table G7001.S for history
Kazakhstan
7220 General
7221 By subject (Table G1 modified)
History
7221.S1 General
(7221.S12) This number not used
7221.S2 Early through 1613
7221.S3 17th century
7221.S4 18th century
7221.S5 1801-1917
7221.S54 Crimean War
7221.S57 Rebellion, 1905-1907

By region or country
Eastern Hemisphere. Eurasia, Africa, etc.
Europe
Former Soviet republics in Asia. U.S.S.R. in Asia. Russia (Empire) in Asia
Former Soviet Central Asia. Russian Central Asia. West Turkestan
Kazakhstan
By subject
History
1801-1917 -- Continued

7221.S65 World War I
7221.S67 1917-1921
7221.S68 1921-1945
7221.S7 World War II
7221.S72 1945-1991
7221.S75 1991-
7222 Regions, natural features, etc., A-Z (Table G7222)
Apply Table G1 for subject (except .S1-.S7, historical geography)
Apply Table G7001.S for history
7223 Administrative divisions, A-Z (Table G7223)
Apply Table G1 for subject (except .S1-.S7, historical geography)
Apply Table G7001.S for history
7224 Cities and towns, A-Z (Table G7224)
Apply Table G1 for subject (except .S1-.S7, historical geography)
Apply Table G7001.S for history

Uzbekistan
7231 By subject (Table G1 modified)
History
7231.S1 General
(7231.S12) This number not used
7231.S2 Early through 1613
7231.S3 17th century
7231.S4 18th century
7231.S5 1801-1917
7231.S54 Crimean War
7231.S57 Rebellion, 1905-1907
7231.S65 World War I
7231.S67 1917-1921
7231.S68 1921-1945
7231.S7 World War II
7231.S72 1945-1991
7231.S75 1991-

By region or country
Eastern Hemisphere. Eurasia, Africa, etc.
Europe
Former Soviet republics in Asia. U.S.S.R. in Asia.
Russia (Empire) in Asia
Former Soviet Central Asia. Russian Central Asia.
West Turkestan
Uzbekistan -- Continued

7232 Regions, natural features, etc., A-Z (Table G7232)
Apply Table G1 for subject (except .S1-.S7, historical geography)
Apply Table G7001.S for history

7233 Administrative divisions, A-Z (Table G7233)
Apply Table G1 for subject (except .S1-.S7, historical geography)
Apply Table G7001.S for history

7234 Cities and towns, A-Z (Table G7234)
Apply Table G1 for subject (except .S1-.S7, historical geography)
Apply Table G7001.S for history

Turkmenistan
7240 General
7241 By subject (Table G1 modified)
History
7241.S1 General
(7241.S12) This number not used
7241.S2 Early through 1613
7241.S3 17th century
7241.S4 18th century
7241.S5 1801-1917
7241.S54 Crimean War
7241.S57 Rebellion, 1905-1907
7241.S65 World War I
7241.S67 1917-1921
7241.S68 1921-1945
7241.S7 World War II
7241.S72 1945-1991
7241.S75 1991-

7242 Region, natural features, etc., A-Z (Table G7242)
Apply Table G1 for subject (except .S1-.S7, historical geography)
Apply Table G7001.S for history

7243 Administrative divisions, A-Z (Table G7243)
Apply Table G1 for subject (except .S1-.S7, historical geography)
Apply Table G7001.S for history

By region or country
Eastern Hemisphere. Eurasia, Africa, etc.
Europe
Former Soviet republics in Asia. U.S.S.R. in Asia.
Russia (Empire) in Asia
Former Soviet Central Asia. Russian Central Asia.
West Turkestan
Turkmenistan -- Continued
7244 Cities and towns, A-Z (Table G7244)
Apply Table G1 for subject (except .S1-.S7, historical geography)
Apply Table G7001.S for history
Kyrgyzstan. Kirghiz S.S.R.
7250 General
7251 By subject (Table G1 modified)
History
7251.S1 General
(7251.S12) This number not used
7251.S2 Early through 1613
7251.S3 17th century
7251.S4 18th century
7251.S5 1801-1917
7251.S54 Crimean War
7251.S57 Rebellion, 1905-1907
7251.S65 World War I
7251.S67 1917-1921
7251.S68 1921-1945
7251.S7 World War II
7251.S72 1945-1991
7251.S75 1991-
7252 Regions, natural features, etc., A-Z (Table G7252)
Apply Table G1 for subject (except .S1-.S7, historical geography)
Apply Table G7001.S for history
7253 Administrative divisions, A-Z (Table G7253)
Apply Table G1 for subject (except .S1-.S7, historical geography)
Apply Table G7001.S for history
7254 Cities and towns, A-Z (Table G7254)
Apply Table G1 for subject (except .S1-.S7, historical geography)
Apply Table G7001.S for history
Tajikistan. Tadzhik S.S.R.
7261 By subject (Table G1 modified)
History
7261.S1 General
(7261.S12) This number not used

By region or country
Eastern Hemisphere. Eurasia, Africa, etc.
Europe
Former Soviet republics in Asia. U.S.S.R. in Asia.
Russia (Empire) in Asia
Former Soviet Central Asia. Russian Central Asia.
West Turkestan
Tajikistan. Tadzhik S.S.R.
By subject
History -- Continued

7261.S2 Early through 1613
7261.S3 17th century
7261.S4 18th century
7261.S5 1801-1917
7261.S54 Crimean War
7261.S57 Rebellion, 1905-1907
7261.S65 World War I
7261.S67 1917-1921
7261.S68 1921-1945
7261.S7 World War II
7261.S72 1945-1991
7261.S75 1991-
7262 Regions, natural features, etc., A-Z (Table G7262)
Apply Table G1 for subject (except .S1-.S7, historical geography)
Apply Table G7001.S for history
7263 Administrative divisions, A-Z (Table G7263)
Apply Table G1 for subject (except .S1-.S7, historical geography)
Apply Table G7001.S for history
7264 Cities and towns, A-Z (Table G7264)
Apply Table G1 for subject (except .S1-.S7, historical geography)
Apply Table G7001.S for history

Siberia. Northern Asia
7270 General
7271 By subject (Table G1 modified)
History
7271.S1 General
(7271.S12) This number not used
7271.S2 Early through 1613
7271.S3 17th century
7271.S4 18th century
7271.S5 1801-1917
7271.S54 Crimean War
7271.S57 Rebellion, 1905-1907
7271.S65 World War I

By region or country
Eastern Hemisphere. Eurasia, Africa, etc.
Europe
Former Soviet republics in Asia. U.S.S.R. in Asia.
Russia (Empire) in Asia
Siberia. Northern Asia
By subject
History -- Continued

7271.S67 1917-1921
7271.S68 1921-1945
7271.S7 World War II
7271.S72 1945-1991
7271.S75 1991-
7272 Regions, natural features, etc., A-Z (Table G7272)
Apply Table G1 for subject (except .S1-.S7, historical geography)
Apply Table G7001.S for history
7273 Administrative divisions, A-Z (Table G7273)
Apply Table G1 for subject (except .S1-.S7, historical geography)
Apply Table G7001.S for history

Buri͡atii͡a. Buryat-Mongol A.S.S.R.

7300 General
7301 By subject (Table G1 modified)
History
7301.S1 General
(7301.S12) This number not used
7301.S2 Early through 1613
7301.S3 17th century
7301.S4 18th century
7301.S5 1801-1917
7301.S54 Crimean War
7301.S57 Rebellion, 1905-1907
7301.S65 World War I
7301.S67 1917-1921
7301.S68 1921-1945
7301.S7 World War II
7301.S72 1945-1991
7301.S75 1991-
7302 Regions, natural features, etc., A-Z (Table G7302)
Apply Table G1 for subject (except .S1-.S7, historical geography)
Apply Table G7001.S for history

Sakha. Yakutia

7310 General
7311 By subject (Table G1 modified)
History

By region or country
Eastern Hemisphere. Eurasia, Africa, etc.
Europe
Former Soviet republics in Asia. U.S.S.R. in Asia. Russia (Empire) in Asia
Sakha. Yakutia
By subject
History -- Continued

7311.S1 General
(7311.S12) This number not used
7311.S2 Early through 1613
7311.S3 17th century
7311.S4 18th century
7311.S5 1801-1917
7311.S54 Crimean War
7311.S57 Rebellion, 1905-1907
7311.S65 World War I
7311.S67 1917-1921
7311.S68 1921-1945
7311.S7 World War II
7311.S72 1945-1991
7311.S75 1991-
7312 Regions, natural features, etc., A-Z (Table G7312)
Apply Table G1 for subject (except .S1-.S7, historical geography)
Apply Table G7001.S for history

Russian Far East. Far Eastern Republic. Dal'nevostochniĭ kraĭ

7320 General
7321 By subject (Table G1 modified)
History
7321.S1 General
(7321.S12) This number not used
7321.S2 Early through 1613
7321.S3 17th century
7321.S4 18th century
7321.S5 1801-1917
7321.S54 Crimean War
7321.S57 Rebellion, 1905-1907
7321.S65 World War I
7321.S67 1917-1921
7321.S68 1921-1945
7321.S7 World War II
7321.S72 1945-1991
7321.S75 1991-

By region or country
Eastern Hemisphere. Eurasia, Africa, etc.
Europe
Former Soviet republics in Asia. U.S.S.R. in Asia.
Russia (Empire) in Asia
Russian Far East. Far Eastern Republic.
Dal'nevostochnīĭ kraĭ -- Continued

7322 Regions, natural features, etc., A-Z (Table G7322)
Apply Table G1 for subject (except .S1-.S7, historical geography)
Apply Table G7001.S for history

7323 Provinces, districts, etc., A-Z (Table G7323)
Apply Table G1 for subject (except .S1-.S7, historical geography)
Apply Table G7001.S for history

Sakhalin
7330 General
7331 By subject (Table G1 modified)
History
7331.S1 General
(7331.S12) This number not used
7331.S2 Early through 1613
7331.S3 17th century
7331.S4 18th century
7331.S5 1801-1917
7331.S54 Crimean War
7331.S57 Rebellion, 1905-1907
7331.S65 World War I
7331.S67 1917-1921
7331.S68 1921-1945
7331.S7 World War II
7331.S72 1945-1991
7331.S75 1991-

Kuril Islands (Chishima Retto)
7340 General
7341 By subject (Table G1 modified)
History
7341.S1 General
(7341.S12) This number not used
7341.S2 Early through 1613
7341.S3 17th century
7341.S4 18th century
7341.S5 1801-1917
7341.S54 Crimean War
7341.S57 Rebellion, 1905-1907
7341.S65 World War I
7341.S67 1917-1921

By region or country
Eastern Hemisphere. Eurasia, Africa, etc.
Europe
Former Soviet republics in Asia. U.S.S.R. in Asia.
Russia (Empire) in Asia
Sakhalin
Kuril Islands (Chishima Retto)
By subject
History -- Continued
7341.S68 1921-1945
7341.S7 World War II
7341.S72 1945-1991
7341.S75 1991-
7342 By region (Table G7342)
Apply Table G1 (except .S1-.S7, historical geography)
Apply Table G7001.S for history
Asia
7400 General
7401 By subject (Table G1)
7402 Regions, natural features, etc., A-Z (Table G7402 modified)
Apply Table G1 for subject
7402.M4 Mekong River
Subarrange by Table G1
Northern Asia see G7270+
Central Asia. Inner Asia. Turkestan
Including Sinkiang and Soviet Central Asia together, and often including Mongolia, Tibet, Jammu and Kashmir, and Northern Afghanistan
Cf. G7210+ Former Soviet Central Asia
7405 General
7406 By subject (Table G1)
Middle East. Near East. Levant. Western Asia. Southwestern Asia
Often including Egypt and Sudan, and sometimes Libya, Ethiopia, Afghanistan, and Pakistan
7420 General
7421 By subject (Table G1)
7422 Regions, natural features, etc., A-Z (Table G7422)
Apply Table G1 for subject
Islamic Empire. Islamic countries see G5680+
Turkey. Ottoman Empire. Asia Minor
Including Turkey in Europe (Eastern Thrace)
7430 General
7431 By subject (Table G1 modified)
History
7431.S1 General

By region or country
Eastern Hemisphere. Eurasia, Africa, etc.
Asia
Middle East. Near East. Levant. Western Asia. Southwestern Asia
Turkey. Ottoman Empire. Asia Minor
By subject
History -- Continued

(7431.S12) This number not used
7431.S2 To 1288
7431.S4 Ottoman Empire, 1288-1918
7431.S65 World War I
7431.S67 1918-1960
7431.S7 World War II
7431.S73 1960-
7432 Regions, natural features, etc., A-Z (Table G7432)
Apply Table G1 for subject (except .S1-.S7, historical geography)
Apply Table G7431.S for history
7433 Provinces (Ili), A-Z (Table G7433)
Apply Table G1 for subject (except .S1-.S7, historical geography)
Apply Table G7431.S for history
7434 Cities, towns, etc., A-Z (Table G7434)
Apply Table G1 for subject (except .S1-.S7, historical geography)
Apply Table G7431.S for history

Cyprus
7450 General
7451 By subject (Table G1 modified)
History
7451.S1 General
(7451.S12) This number not used
7451.S2 Early to 1571
7451.S3 1571-1878, Turkish period
7451.S6 1878-1960, British period
7451.S65 World War I
7451.S7 World War II
7451.S8 1960-, Independent republic
7451.S82 1963 crisis
7451.S84 1974 crisis
7452 Regions, natural features, etc., A-Z (Table G7452)
Apply Table G1 for subject (except .S1-.S7, historical geography)
Apply Table G7451.S for history

By region or country
Eastern Hemisphere. Eurasia, Africa, etc.
Asia
Middle East. Near East. Levant. Western Asia. Southwestern Asia
Cyprus -- Continued

7453 Districts, A-Z (Table G7453)
Apply Table G1 for subject (except .S1-.S7, historical geography)
Apply Table G7451.S for history

7454 Cities and towns, etc., A-Z (Table G7454)
Apply Table G1 for subject (except .S1-.S7, historical geography)
Apply Table G7451.S for history

Syria

7460 General

7461 By subject (Table G1)

7462 Regions, natural features, etc., A-Z (Table G7462)
Apply Table G1 for subject

7463 Provinces, etc., A-Z (Table G7463)
Apply Table G1 for subject

7464 Cities and towns, etc., A-Z (Table G7464)
Apply Table G1 for subject

Lebanon

7470 General

7471 By subject (Table G1 modified)

History

7471.S1 General

(7471.S12) This number not used

7471.S2 To 638

7471.S3 Medieval, 638-1517

7471.S4 Turkish period, 1517-1918

7471.S6 Autonomy, 1861-1918

7471.S65 World War I

7471.S67 French Mandate and occupation, 1919-1945

7471.S7 World War II

7471.S73 1946-1975

7471.S75 1975-

7472 Regions, natural features, etc., A-Z (Table G7472)
Apply Table G1 for subject (except .S1-.S7, historical geography)
Apply Table G7471.S for history

7473 Districts, A-Z (Table G7473)
Apply Table G1 for subject (except .S1-.S7, historical geography)
Apply Table G7471.S for history

By region or country
Eastern Hemisphere. Eurasia, Africa, etc.
Asia
Middle East. Near East. Levant. Western Asia. Southwestern Asia
Lebanon

7474 Cities and towns, etc., A-Z (Table G7474)
Apply Table G1 for subject (except .S1-.S7, historical geography)
Apply Table G7471.S for history

Bible lands

7480 General

7481 By subject (Table G1)

7481.2 Old Testament
Including maps of special aspects of the Old Testament, e.g., Exodus, the Kingdom of David and Solomon, etc.

7481.3 New Testament
Including maps of special aspects of the New Testament, e.g., the life of Jesus, Paul's journeys, etc.

Israel. Palestine

7500 General

7501 By subject (Table G1 modified)
History

7501.S1 General

(7501.S12) This number not used

7501.S2 To 70 A.D.

7501.S3 70-1453

7501.S4 1454-1800

7501.S5 1801-1899

7501.S6 1900-1947

7501.S65 World War I

7501.S7 World War II

7501.S73 1948-

7502 Regions, natural features, etc., A-Z (Table G7502 modified)
Apply Table G1 for subject (except .S1-.S7, historical geography)
Apply Table G7501.S for history
Sinaitic Peninsula see G8302.S5
Sinaitic Peninsula (Safaga Island) see G8302.S2

7503 Districts, A-Z (Table G7503)
Apply Table G1 for subject (except .S1-.S7, historical geography)
Apply Table G7501.S for history

By region or country
Eastern Hemisphere. Eurasia, Africa, etc.
Asia
Middle East. Near East. Levant. Western Asia. Southwestern Asia
Israel. Palestine -- Continued
7504 Cities and towns, etc., A-Z (Table G7504)
Apply Table G1 for subject (except .S1-.S7, historical geography)
Apply Table G7501.S for history
Jordan
7510 General
7511 By subject (Table G1)
7512 Regions, natural features, etc., A-Z (Table G7512)
Apply Table G1 for subject
7513 Governorates, A-Z (Table G7513)
Apply Table G1 for subject
7514 Cities and towns, etc., A-Z (Table G7514)
Apply Table G1 for subject
Arabian Peninsula. Arabia
7520 General
7521 By subject (Table G1)
Saudi Arabia
7530 General
7531 By subject (Table G1)
7532 Regions, natural features, etc., A-Z (Table G7532)
Apply Table G1 for subject
7533 Emirates, etc., A-Z (Table G7533)
Apply Table G1 for subject
7534 Cities and towns, etc., A-Z (Table G7534)
Apply Table G1 for subject
Yemen (Republic)
Including maps of the Yemen Arab Republic (North Yemen)
7540 General
7541 By subject (Table G1)
7542 Regions, natural features, etc., A-Z (Table G7542)
Apply Table G1 for subject
7543 Governorates (Muhafazahs), etc., A-Z (Table G7543)
Apply Table G1 for subject
7544 Cities and towns, etc., A-Z (Table G7544)
Apply Table G1 for subject
Yemen (People's Democratic Republic). Southern Yemen. Aden
7550 General
7551 By subject (Table G1)

By region or country
Eastern Hemisphere. Eurasia, Africa, etc.
Asia
Middle East. Near East. Levant. Western Asia. Southwestern Asia
Arabian Peninsula. Arabia -- Continued
Oman. Muscat and Oman
7560 General
7561 By subject (Table G1)
7562 Regions, natural features, etc., A-Z (Table G7562)
Apply Table G1 for subject
7564 Cities and towns, etc., A-Z (Table G7564)
Apply Table G1 for subject

United Arab Emirates. Trucial States
7570 General
7571 By subject (Table G1)
7572 Regions, natural features, etc., A-Z (Table G7572)
Apply Table G1 for subject
7573 Sheikdoms, etc., A-Z (Table G7573)
Apply Table G1 for subject
7574 Cities and towns, etc., A-Z (Table G7574)
Apply Table G1 for subject
Qatar
7580 General
7581 By subject (Table G1)
7582 Regions, natural features, etc., A-Z (Table G7582)
Apply Table G1 for subject
7584 Cities and towns, etc., A-Z (Table G7584)
Apply Table G1 for subject
Bahrain
7590 General
7591 By subject (Table G1)
7592 Regions, natural features, etc., A-Z (Table G7592)
Apply Table G1 for subject
7594 Cities and towns, etc., A-Z (Table G7594)
Apply Table G1 for subject
Kuwait
7600 General
7601 By subject (Table G1)
7602 Regions, natural features, etc., A-Z (Table G7602)
Apply Table G1 for subject
7603 Governorates (Muhafa-ah), A-Z (Table G7603)
Apply Table G1 for subject
7604 Cities and towns, etc., A-Z (Table G7604)
Apply Table G1 for subject
Iraq. Mesopotamia
7610 General

By region or country
Eastern Hemisphere. Eurasia, Africa, etc.
Asia
Middle East. Near East. Levant. Western Asia. Southwestern Asia
Iraq. Mesopotamia -- Continued

7611 By subject (Table G1)
7612 Regions, natural features, etc., A-Z (Table G7612)
Apply Table G1 for subject
7613 Governorates, etc., A-Z (Table G7613)
Apply Table G1 for subject
7614 Cities and towns, etc., A-Z (Table G7614)
Apply Table G1 for subject

Iran. Persia
7620 General
7621 By subject (Table G1 modified)
History
7621.S1 General
(7621.S12) This number not used
7621.S2 Ancient, to 226 A.D.
7621.S23 Median Empire, 640-558 B.C.
7621.S25 Persian Empire, 558-330 B.C.
7621.S27 Parthian Empire, 246-226 B.C.
7621.S3 Modern, 226-
7621.S34 Sassanian Empire, 226-651
7621.S37 Arab and Mongol rule, 651-1500
7621.S4 Safawids and Afhans, 1500-1736
7621.S5 Kajar dynasty, 1794-1925
7621.S6 Pahlavi dynasty, 1925-
7622 Regions, natural features, etc., A-Z (Table G7622)
Apply Table G1 for subject (except .S1-.S7, historical geography)
Apply Table G7621.S for history
7623 Provinces, governorships, etc., A-Z (Table G7623)
Apply Table G1 for subject (except .S1-.S7, historical geography)
Apply Table G7621.S for history
7624 Cities and towns, etc., A-Z (Table G7624)
Apply Table G1 for subject (except .S1-.S7, historical geography)
Apply Table G7621.S for history

South Asia
7625 General
7626 By subject (Table G1)
7627 Regions, natural features, etc., A-Z (Table G7627)
Apply Table G1 for subject
Afghanistan

By region or country
Eastern Hemisphere. Eurasia, Africa, etc.
Asia
South Asia
Afghanistan -- Continued
7630 General
7631 By subject (Table G1)
7632 Regions, natural features, etc., A-Z (Table G7632)
Apply Table G1 for subject
7633 Administrative divisions, A-Z (Table G7633)
Apply Table G1 for subject
7634 Cities and towns, etc., A-Z (Table G7634)
Apply Table G1 for subject
Pakistan
Including maps of West and East Pakistan together
7640 General
7641 By subject (Table G1)
7642 Regions, natural features, etc., A-Z (Table G7642)
Apply Table G1 for subject
7643 Administrative divisions, A-Z (Table G7643)
Apply Table G1 for subject
7644 Cities and towns, etc., A-Z (Table G7644)
Apply Table G1 for subject
Bangladesh. East Pakistan
7645 General
7646 By subject (Table G1)
7647 Regions, natural features, etc., A-Z (Table G7647)
Apply Table G1 for subject
7648 Provinces, etc., A-Z (Table G7648)
Apply Table G1 for subject
7649 Cities and towns, etc., A-Z (Table G7649)
Apply Table G1 for subject
India
7650 General
7651 By subject (Table G1)
7652 Regions, natural features, etc., A-Z (Table G7652)
Apply Table G1 for subject
7653 States, territories, etc., A-Z (Table G7653)
Apply Table G1 for subject
7654 Cities and towns, etc., A-Z (Table G7654)
Apply Table G1 for subject
Burma. Myanmar
7720 General
7721 By subject (Table G1)
7722 Regions, natural features, etc., A-Z (Table G7722)
Apply Table G1 for subject

By region or country
Eastern Hemisphere. Eurasia, Africa, etc.
Asia
South Asia
Burma. Myanmar -- Continued
7723 Divisions, states, A-Z (Table G7723)
Apply Table G1 for subject
7724 Cities and towns, etc., A-Z (Table G7724)
Apply Table G1 for subject
Sri Lanka. Ceylon
7750 General
7751 By subject (Table G1)
7752 Regions, natural features, etc., A-Z (Table G7752)
Apply Table G1 for subject
7753 Provinces, districts, A-Z (Table G7753)
Apply Table G1 for subject
7754 Cities and towns, etc., A-Z (Table G7754)
Apply Table G1 for subject
Nepal
7760 General
7761 By subject (Table G1)
7762 Regions, natural features, etc., A-Z (Table G7762)
Apply Table G1 for subject
7763 Zones, districts, etc., A-Z (Table G7763)
Apply Table G1 for subject
7764 Cities and towns, etc., A-Z (Table G7764)
Apply Table G1 for subject
Bhutan
7780 General
7781 By subject (Table G1)
7783 Zones, districts, etc., A-Z (Table G7783)
Apply Table G1 for subject
7784 Cities and towns, etc., A-Z (Table G7784)
Apply Table G1 for subject
Far East
7800 General
7801 By subject (Table G1 modified)
History
7801.S1 General
(7801.S12) This number not used
7801.S2 To 1500
7801.S3 1500-1800
7801.S4 1800-1904
7801.S5 Russo-Japanese War, 1904-1905
1904-1945
7801.S6 General
7801.S65 World War I

By region or country
Eastern Hemisphere. Eurasia, Africa, etc.
Asia
Far East
By subject
History
1904-1945 -- Continued
7801.S7 World War II
7801.S73 1945-
7802 Regions, natural features, etc., A-Z (Table G7802 modified)
Apply Table G1 for subject (except .S1-.S7, historical geography)
Apply Table G7801.S for history
Mekong River see G7402.M4
Chinese Empire
Including maps of Chinese dependencies, etc. (Collectively)
Class individual dependencies, etc. according to location, e.g., G7830+, Manchuria
7810 General
7811 By subject (Table G1)
China. People's Republic of China
7820 General
7821 By subject (Table G1 modified)
History
7821.S1 General
(7821.S12) This number not used
7821.S2 To 960
960-1644
7821.S3 General
7821.S33 Song dynasty, 960-1279
7821.S35 Yuan dynasty, 1260-1368
7821.S37 Ming dynasty, 1368-1644
Qing dynasty, 1644-1912
7821.S4 General
7821.S5 1861-1912
1912-1949
7821.S6 General
7821.S65 World War I
7821.S7 World War II
People's Republic of China, 1949-
7821.S73 General
7821.S75 Cultural Revolution, 1966-1976
7821.S77 1976-

By region or country
Eastern Hemisphere. Eurasia, Africa, etc.
Asia
Far East
China. People's Republic of China -- Continued
7822 Regions, natural features, etc., A-Z (Table G7822)
Apply Table G1 for subjects (except .S1-.S7, history)
Apply Table G7821.S for history
7823 Provinces (Sheng), etc., A-Z (Table G7823)
Apply Table G1 for subjects (except .S1-.S7, history)
Apply Table G7821.S for history
7824 Cities and towns, etc., A-Z (Table G7824)
Apply Table G1 for subjects (except .S1-.S7, history)
Apply Table G7821.S for history
(7830-7831) Manchuria
see G7822
(7850-7852) Inner Mongolia (Autonomous region)
see G7823
Guangxi Zhuangzu Zizhiqu. Kwangsi (Autonomous region)
see G7823
Ningxia Huizu Zizhiqu. Nianghsia (Autonomous region)
see G7823
Tuva. Tannu Tuva
see G7273
(7880-7882) Sinkiang (Autonomous region). Chinese Turkestan. East Turkestan
see G7823
(7890-7892) Tibet (Autonomous region)
see G7823
Mongolia (Mongolian People's Republic). Outer Mongolia
Including maps of Inner and Outer Mongolia together
7895 General
7896 By subject (Table G1)
7897 Regions, natural features, etc., A-Z (Table G7897)
Apply Table G1 for subject
7898 Aymags, A-Z (Table G7898)
Apply Table G1 for subject
7899 Cities and towns, etc., A-Z (Table G7899)
Apply Table G1 for subject
South Korea (Republic of Korea). Chosen
Including maps of Korea as a whole
7900 General
7901 By subject (Table G1 modified)
History

By region or country
Eastern Hemisphere. Eurasia, Africa, etc.
Asia
Far East
South Korea (Republic of Korea). Chosen
By subject
History -- Continued

7901.S1 General
(7901.S12) This number not used
7901.S2 To 935
Koryŏ period, 935-1392
7901.S3 General
7901.S33 Mongolian invasions, 1231-1270
Chosŏn (Yi) dynasty, 1392-1910
7901.S4 General
7901.S44 Japanese invasions, 1592-1598
7901.S47 Manchu invasions, 1627-1637
7901.S5 1637-1864
7901.S55 1864-1910
Japanese occupation, 1910-1945
7901.S6 General
7901.S65 World War I
7901.S7 World War II
7901.S75 Allied occupation, 1945-1948
1948-1960
7901.S8 General
7901.S83 Korean War, 1950-1953
7901.S85 1960-1988
7901.S9 1988-
7902 Regions, natural features, etc., A-Z (Table G7902)
Apply Table G1 for subject (except .S1-.S7, historical geography)
Apply Table G7901.S for history
7903 Administrative divisions, A-Z (Table G7903)
Apply Table G1 for subject (except .S1-.S7, historical geography)
Apply Table G7901.S for history
7904 Cities and towns, etc., A-Z (Table G7904)
Apply Table G1 for subject (except .S1-.S7, historical geography)
Apply Table G7901.S for history
North Korea (Democratic People's Republic)
7905 General
7906 By subject (Table G1)
7908 Administrative divisions, A-Z (Table G7908)
Apply Table G1 for subject

G3180-G9980

By region or country
Eastern Hemisphere. Eurasia, Africa, etc.
Asia
Far East
North Korea (Democratic People's Republic) -- Continued
7909 Cities and towns, etc., A-Z (Table G7909)
Apply Table G1 for subject
Taiwan. Formosa
7910 General
7911 By subject (Table G1 modified)
History
7911.S1 General
(7911.S12) This number not used
To 1895
7911.S2 General
7911.S3 Dutch rule, 1624-1661
7911.S4 Insurrection, 1895
1895-1945
7911.S5 General
7911.S65 World War I
7911.S7 World War II
7911.S73 1945-
7911.S75 1975-1988
7911.S77 1988-2000
7911.S8 2000-
7912 Regions, natural features, etc., A-Z (Table G7912)
Apply Table G1 for subject
7913 Provinces, municipalities, A-Z (Table G7913)
Apply Table G1 for subject
7914 Cities and towns, etc., A-Z (Table G7914)
Apply Table G1 for subject
(7940-7944) Hong Kong
see G7823
(7945-7947) Macau
see G7823
(7950-7951) Japanese Empire
Including maps of Japanese colonies, dependencies, etc. (Collectively)
see G7960+
Class individual colonies, dependencies, etc. according to location, e.g. G7335+, Karafuto
Japan
7960 General
7961 By subject (Table G1 modified)
History
7961.S1 General

By region or country
Eastern Hemisphere. Eurasia, Africa, etc.
Asia
Far East
Japan
By subject
History -- Continued

(7961.S12) This number not used
7961.S2 To 1185
1185-1868
7961.S3 General
7961.S32 Kamakura period, 1185-1333
7961.S34 Moromachi period, 1336-1573
7961.S36 Tokugawa period, 1600-1868
7961.S38 Meiji period, 1868-1912
Taishō period, 1912-1926
7961.S4 General
7961.S65 World War I
Shōwa period, 1926-1989
7961.S67 General
7961.S7 World War II
7961.S75 1989-
7962 Regions, natural features, islands, etc., A-Z (Table G7962)
Apply Table G1 for subject (except .S1-.S7, historical geography)
Apply Table G7961.S for history
7963 Prefectures (Ken), etc., A-Z (Table G7963)
Apply Table G1 for subject (except .S1-.S7, historical geography)
Apply Table G7961.S for history
7964 Cities and towns, etc., A-Z (Table G7964 modified)
Apply Table G1 for subject (except .S1-.S7, historical geography)
Apply Table G7961.S for history
7964.T7 Tokyo
Subarrange by Table G1 except .S1-.S7, historical geography. For history, subarrange by Table G7961.S

Southeast Asia. Indochina
Sometimes including Burma
8000 General
8001 By subject (Table G1)
8002 Regions, natural features, etc., A-Z (Table G8002)
Apply Table G1 for subject
Burma (Myanmar) see G7720+
French Indochina

By region or country
Eastern Hemisphere. Eurasia, Africa, etc.
Asia
Southeast Asia. Indochina
French Indochina -- Continued

8005 General

8006 By subject (Table G1)

Cambodia. Khmer Republic

8010 General

8011 By subject (Table G1)

8012 Regions, natural features, etc., A-Z (Table G8012)
Apply Table G1 for subject

8013 Provinces (Khets), etc., A-Z (Table G8013)
Apply Table G1 for subject

8014 Cities and towns, etc., A-Z (Table G8014)
Apply Table G1 for subject

Laos

8015 General

8016 By subject (Table G1)

8017 Regions, natural features, etc., A-Z (Table G8017)
Apply Table G1 for subject

8018 Provinces, etc., A-Z (Table G8018)
Apply Table G1 for subject

8019 Cities and towns, etc., A-Z (Table G8019)
Apply Table G1 for subject

Vietnam
Including maps of Vietnam as a whole, as well as maps of North or South Vietnam separately

8020 General

8021 By subject (Table G1)

8022 Regions, natural features, etc., A-Z (Table G8022)
Apply Table G1 for subject

8023 Provinces, former states, etc., A-Z (Table G8023)
Apply Table G1 for subject

8024 Cities and towns, etc., A-Z (Table G8024)
Apply Table G1 for subject

Thailand. Siam

8025 General

8026 By subject (Table G1)

8027 Regions, natural features, etc., A-Z (Table G8027)
Apply Table G1 for subject

8028 Provinces (Changwats), A-Z (Table G8028)
Apply Table G1 for subject

8029 Cities and towns, etc., A-Z (Table G8029)
Apply Table G1 for subject

Malaysia. Malaya
Including maps of the Malay Peninsula

By region or country
Eastern Hemisphere. Eurasia, Africa, etc.
Asia
Southeast Asia. Indochina
Malaysia. Malaya -- Continued
8030 General
8031 By subject (Table G1)
8032 Regions, natural features, etc., A-Z (Table G8032)
Apply Table G1 for subject
8033 States, A-Z (Table G8033)
Apply Table G1 for subject
8034 Cities and towns, etc., A-Z (Table G8034)
Apply Table G1 for subject
Singapore (Republic, Colony, and Island). Straits Settlements, 1826-1946
Including maps of the city of Singapore
8040 General
8041 By subject (Table G1)
8042 Regions, natural features, etc., A-Z (Table G8042)
Apply Table G1 for subject
8044 Cities and towns, etc., A-Z (Table G8044)
Apply Table G1 for subject
For maps of Singapore see G8040+
Malay Archipelago
8050 General
8051 By subject (Table G1)
8052 Islands, archipelagoes, regions, natural features, etc., A-Z (Table G8052)
Philippines
8060 General
8061 By subject (Table G1)
8062 Islands, archipelagoes, regions, natural features, etc., A-Z (Table G8062)
Apply Table G1 for subject
8063 Provinces, A-Z (Table G8063)
Apply Table G1 for subject
8064 Cities and towns, etc., A-Z (Table G8064)
Apply Table G1 for subject
Indonesia. United States of Indonesia. Netherlands Indies. East Indies
8070 General
8071 By subject (Table G1)
8072 Regions, natural features, etc., A-Z (Table G8072)
Apply Table G1 for subject
For individual islands and archipelagoes, see G8080-G8132

By region or country
Eastern Hemisphere. Eurasia, Africa, etc.
Asia
Southeast Asia. Indochina
Indonesia. United States of Indonesia. Netherlands Indies. East Indies -- Continued

8073 Provinces, etc., A-Z (Table G8073)
Apply Table G1 for subject

8074 Cities and towns, etc., A-Z (Table G8074)
Apply Table G1 for subject

Sumatra

8080 General

8081 By subject (Table G1)

8082 Regions, natural features, adjacent islands, etc., A-Z (Table G8082)
Apply Table G1 for subject

Java. Djawa

8090 General

8091 By subject (Table G1)

8092 Regions, natural features, adjacent islands, etc., A-Z (Table G8092)
Apply Table G1 for subject

Borneo. Kalimantan
For British North Borneo, North Borneo, Sarawak see G8033
For Brunei see G8198.5+

8100 General

8101 By subject (Table G1)

8102 Regions, natural features, adjacent islands, etc., A-Z (Table G8102)
Apply Table G1 for subject

Celebes. Sulawesi

8110 General

8111 By subject (Table G1)

Lesser Sunda Islands

8115 General

8116 By subject (Table G1)

8117 Regions, natural features, adjacent islands, etc., A-Z (Table G8117)
Apply Table G1 for subject

Moluccas. Spice Islands

8130 General

8131 By subject (Table G1)

8132 Regions, natural features, adjacent islands, etc., A-Z (Table G8132)
Apply Table G1 for subject

New Guinea

By region or country
Eastern Hemisphere. Eurasia, Africa, etc.
Asia
Southeast Asia. Indochina
New Guinea -- Continued
8140 General
8141 By subject (Table G1)
8142 Regions, natural features, etc., A-Z (Table G8142)
Apply Table G1 for subject
Class here regions and natural features located within Irian Barat or common to Irian Barat and Papua New Guinea
Irian Jaya. Irian Barat. Netherlands New Guinea
see G8073
Papua New Guinea
Including maps of Territory of Papua (formerly British New Guinea) and Trust Territory of New Guinea (formerly German New Guinea)
8160 General
8161 By subject (Table G1)
8162 Islands, regions, natural features, etc., A-Z (Table G8162 modified)
Apply Table G1 for subject
Class here works of individual islands or island groups not classed in or associated with G8180-G8182
Bougainville see G9282.B6
Buka see G9282.B8
Green Islands see G9282.G7
8163 Provinces, A-Z (Table G8163)
Apply Table G1 for subject
8164 Cities and towns, etc., A-Z (Table G8164)
Apply Table G1 for subject
Bismarck Archipelago
8180 General
8181 By subject (Table G1)
8182 Islands, archipelagoes, regions, natural features, etc., A-Z (Table G8182)
Apply Table G1 for subject
Louisiade Archipelago
8185 General
8186 By subject (Table G1)
8187 Islands, archipelagoes, regions, natural features, etc., A-Z (Table G8187)
Apply Table G1 for subject
D'Entrecasteaux Islands
8190 General

By region or country
Eastern Hemisphere. Eurasia, Africa, etc.
Asia
Southeast Asia. Indochina
New Guinea
D'Entrecasteaux Islands -- Continued
8191 By subject (Table G1)
8192 Islands, archipelagoes, regions, natural features, etc., A-Z (Table G8192)
Apply Table G1 for subject
Timor
8195 General
8196 By subject (Table G1)
Western Timur
see G8073
East Timor. Timor Timur. Portuguese Timor
8198.2 General
8198.21 By subject (Table G1)
8198.24 Cities and towns, etc., A-Z (Table G8198.24)
Brunei
8198.5 General
8198.51 By subject (Table G1)
8198.52 Regions, natural features, etc., A-Z (Table G8198.52)
Apply Table G1 for subject
8198.53 Districts, A-Z (Table G8198.53)
Apply Table G1 for subject
8198.54 Cities and towns, etc., A-Z (Table G8198.54)
Apply Table G1 for subject
Africa
Including Sub-Saharan Africa
8200 General
8201 By subject (Table G1 modified)
History
8201.S1 General
8201.S12 This number not used
8201.S2 To 1884
8201.S3 19th century
8201.S4 1884-1960
8201.S6 20th century
8201.S65 World War I
8201.S7 World War II
8201.S73 1960-
8202 Regions, natural features, etc., A-Z (Table G8202 modified)
Apply Table G1 for subject (except .S1-.S7, historical geography)
Apply Table G8201.S for history

By region or country
Eastern Hemisphere. Eurasia, Africa, etc.
Africa
Regions, natural features, etc., A-Z -- Continued
8202.N5 Nile River
Subarrange by Table G1 except .S1-.S7, historical geography. For history, subarrange by Table G8201.S
North Africa
Including the Barbary States and Northeast Africa
8220 General
8221 By subject (Table G1)
8222 Regions, natural features, etc., A-Z (Table G8222)
Apply Table G1 for subject
Morocco
Including French Morocco
For maps of Spanish Morocco see G8232
8230 General
8231 By subject (Table G1)
8232 Regions, natural features, etc., A-Z (Table G8232)
Apply Table G1 for subject
8233 Provinces, A-Z (Table G8233)
Apply Table G1 for subject
8234 Cities and towns, etc., A-Z (Table G8234)
Apply Table G1 for subject
Algeria
8240 General
8241 By subject (Table G1)
8242 Regions, natural features, etc., A-Z (Table G8242)
Apply Table G1 for subject
8243 Provinces, A-Z (Table G8243)
Apply Table G1 for subject
8244 Cities and towns, etc., A-Z (Table G8244)
Apply Table G1 for subject
Tunisia. Tunis
8250 General
8251 By subject (Table G1)
8252 Regions, natural features, etc., A-Z (Table G8252)
Apply Table G1 for subject
8253 Governorates, A-Z (Table G8253)
Apply Table G1 for subject
8254 Cities and towns, etc., A-Z (Table G8254)
Apply Table G1 for subject
Libya
8260 General
8261 By subject (Table G1)

By region or country
Eastern Hemisphere. Eurasia, Africa, etc.
Africa
North Africa
Libya -- Continued
8262 Regions, natural features, etc., A-Z (Table G8262)
Apply Table G1 for subject
8263 Municipalities, A-Z (Table G8263)
Apply Table G1 for subject
8264 Cities and towns, etc., A-Z (Table G8264)
Apply Table G1 for subject
Egypt. United Arab Republic
8300 General
8301 By subject (Table G1)
8302 Regions, natural features, etc., A-Z (Table G8302 modified)
Apply Table G1 for subject
Nile River see G8202.N5
8302.S2 Safaga Island
Subarrange by Table G1
8302.S5 Sinai
Subarrange by Table G1
8303 Governorates, etc., A-Z (Table G8303)
Apply Table G1 for subject
8304 Cities and towns, etc., A-Z (Table G8304)
Apply Table G1 for subject
Sudan. Anglo-Egyptian Sudan
8310 General
8311 By subject (Table G1)
8312 Regions, natural features, etc., A-Z (Table G8312)
Apply Table G1 for subject
8313 Provinces, A-Z (Table G8313)
Apply Table G1 for subject
8314 Cities and towns, etc., A-Z (Table G8314)
Apply Table G1 for subject
Eastern Africa
8320 General
8321 By subject (Table G1)
8322 Regions, natural features, etc., A-Z (Table G8322)
Apply Table G1 for subject
Ethiopia. Abyssinia
8330 General
8331 By subject (Table G1 modified)
History
8331.S1 General
(8331.S12) This number not used
8331.S65 World War I

By region or country
Eastern Hemisphere. Eurasia, Africa, etc.
Africa
Eastern Africa
Ethiopia. Abyssinia
By subject
History -- Continued
8331.S7 World War II
8331.S73 1945-
8332 Regions, natural features, etc., A-Z (Table G8332)
Apply Table G1 for subjects (except .S1-.S7, history)
Apply Table G8331.S for history
8333 Provinces, A-Z (Table G8333)
Apply Table G1 for subjects (except .S1-.S7, history)
Apply Table G8331.S for history
8334 Cities and towns, etc., A-Z (Table G8334)
Apply Table G1 for subjects (except .S1-.S7, history)
Apply Table G8331.S for history
Eritrea
8340 General
8341 By subject (Table G1)
8342 Regions, natural features, etc., A-Z (Table G8342)
Apply Table G1 for subject
8343 Provinces, A-Z (Table G8343)
Apply Table G1 for subject
8344 Cities and towns, etc., A-Z (Table G8344)
Apply Table G1 for subject
Somalia. Somaliland
For maps of British Somaliland and Italian Somaliland see G8352
8350 General
8351 By subject (Table G1)
8352 Regions, natural features, etc., A-Z (Table G8352)
Apply Table G1 for subject
8353 Administrative regions, A-Z (Table G8353)
Apply Table G1 for subject
8354 Cities and towns, etc., A-Z (Table G8354)
Apply Table G1 for subject
Djibouti. French Territory of the Afars and Issas. French Somaliland
8360 General
8361 By subject (Table G1)
8362 Regions, natural features, etc., A-Z (Table G8362)
Apply Table G1 for subject
8364 Cities and towns, etc., A-Z (Table G8364)
Apply Table G1 for subject
Southeast Africa. British East Africa

By region or country
Eastern Hemisphere. Eurasia, Africa, etc.
Africa
Eastern Africa
Southeast Africa. British East Africa -- Continued
8400 General
8401 By subject (Table G1)
8402 Regions, natural features, etc., A-Z (Table G8402)
Apply Table G1 for subject
Kenya. East Africa Protectorate
8410 General
8411 By subject (Table G1)
8412 Regions, natural features, etc., A-Z (Table G8412)
8413 Provinces, A-Z (Table G8413)
8414 Cities and towns, etc., A-Z (Table G8414)
Uganda
8420 General
8421 By subject (Table G1)
8422 Regions, natural features, etc., A-Z (Table G8422)
Apply Table G1 for subject
8423 Districts, A-Z (Table G8423)
Apply Table G1 for subject
8424 Cities and towns, etc., A-Z (Table G8424)
Apply Table G1 for subject
Ruanda-Urundi. Belgian East Africa
8425 General
8426 By subject (Table G1)
Rwanda
8430 General
8431 By subject (Table G1)
8433 Prefectures, etc., A-Z (Table G8433)
Apply Table G1 for subject
8434 Cities and towns, etc., A-Z (Table G8434)
Apply Table G1 for subject
Burundi
8435 General
8436 By subject (Table G1)
8438 Provinces, A-Z (Table G8438)
8439 Cities and towns, etc., A-Z (Table G8439)
Tanzania. Tanganyika. German East Africa
8440 General
8441 By subject (Table G1)
8442 Regions, natural features, etc., A-Z (Table G8442)
Apply Table G1
8443 Administrative divisions, A-Z (Table G8443)
Apply Table G1

By region or country
Eastern Hemisphere. Eurasia, Africa, etc.
Africa
Eastern Africa
Southeast Africa. British East Africa
Tanzania. Tanganyika. German East Africa -- Continued
8444 Cities and towns, etc., A-Z (Table G8444)
Apply Table G1
Mozambique. Portuguese East Africa
8450 General
8451 By subject (Table G1)
8452 Regions, natural features, etc., A-Z (Table G8452)
Apply Table G1 for subject
8453 Provinces, A-Z (Table G8453)
Apply Table G1 for subject
8454 Cities and towns, etc., A-Z (Table G8454)
Apply Table G1 for subject
Madagascar. Malagasy Republic
8460 General
8461 By subject (Table G1)
8462 Regions, natural features, etc., A-Z (Table G8462)
Apply Table G1 for subject
8463 Provinces, A-Z (Table G8463)
Apply Table G1 for subject
8464 Cities and towns, etc., A-Z (Table G8464)
Apply Table G1 for subject
Southern Africa. British South Africa
8480 General
8481 By subject (Table G1)
8482 Regions, natural features, etc., A-Z (Table G8482)
Apply Table G1 for subject
Republic of South Africa. Union of South Africa
8500 General
8501 By subject (Table G1)
8502 Regions, natural features, etc., A-Z (Table G8502)
Apply Table G1 for subject
8503 Provinces, former homelands, etc., A-Z (Table G8503)
Apply Table G1 for subject
8504 Cities and towns, etc., A-Z (Table G8504)
Apply Table G1 for subject
Rhodesia
Including the Federation of Rhodesia and Nyasaland
For maps limited to Nyasaland see G8610+
8550 General
8551 By subject (Table G1)

By region or country
Eastern Hemisphere. Eurasia, Africa, etc.
Africa
Southern Africa. British South Africa
Rhodesia -- Continued
Zimbabwe. Southern Rhodesia
8560 General
8561 By subject (Table G1)
8562 Regions, natural features, etc., A-Z (Table G8562)
Apply Table G1 for subject
8564 Cities and towns, etc., A-Z (Table G8564)
Apply Table G1 for subject
Zambia. Northern Rhodesia
8570 General
8571 By subject (Table G1)
8572 Regions, natural features, etc., A-Z (Table G8572)
Apply Table G1 for subject
8573 Provinces, A-Z (Table G8573)
Apply Table G1 for subject
8574 Cities and towns, etc., A-Z (Table G8574)
Apply Table G1 for subject
Lesotho. Basutoland
8580 General
8581 By subject (Table G1)
8582 Regions, natural features, etc., A-Z (Table G8582)
Apply Table G1 for subject
8583 Districts, etc., A-Z (Table G8583)
Apply Table G1 for subject
8584 Cities and towns, etc., A-Z (Table G8584)
Apply Table G1 for subject
Swaziland
8590 General
8591 By subject (Table G1)
8592 Regions, natural features, etc., A-Z (Table G8592)
Apply Table G1 for subject
8593 Districts, etc., A-Z (Table G8593)
Apply Table G1 for subject
8594 Cities and towns, etc., A-Z (Table G8594)
Apply Table G1 for subject
Botswana. Bechuanaland
8600 General
8601 By subject (Table G1)
8602 Regions, natural features, etc., A-Z (Table G8602)
Apply Table G1 for subject
8604 Cities and towns, etc., A-Z (Table G8604)
Apply Table G1 for subject

By region or country
Eastern Hemisphere. Eurasia, Africa, etc.
Africa
Southern Africa. British South Africa -- Continued
Malawi. Nyasaland. Central Africa Protectorate
For maps of the Federation of Rhodesia and Nyasaland see G8550+

8611 By subject (Table G1)
8612 Regions, natural features, etc., A-Z (Table G8612)
Apply Table G1 for subject
8613 Districts, A-Z (Table G8613)
Apply Table G1 for subject
8614 Cities and towns, etc., A-Z (Table G8614)
Apply Table G1 for subject

Namibia. Southwest Africa. German Southwest Africa
8620 General
8621 By subject (Table G1)
8622 Regions, natural features, etc., A-Z (Table G8622)
Apply Table G1 for subject
8623 Districts, etc., A-Z (Table G8623)
Apply Table G1 for subject
8624 Cities and towns, etc., A-Z (Table G8624)
Apply Table G1 for subject

Central Africa. Equatorial Africa
8630 General
8631 By subject (Table G1)
8632 Regions, natural features, etc., A-Z (Table G8632)
Apply Table G1 for subject

Angola. Portuguese West Africa
8640 General
8641 By subject (Table G1)
8642 Regions, natural features, etc., A-Z (Table G8642)
Apply Table G1 for subject
8643 Provinces, A-Z (Table G8643)
Apply Table G1 for subject
8644 Cities and towns, etc., A-Z (Table G8644)
Apply Table G1 for subject

Congo (Democratic Republic). Zaire. Belgian Congo
8650 General
8651 By subject (Table G1)
8652 Regions, natural features, etc., A-Z (Table G8652)
Apply Table G1 for subject
8653 Provinces, A-Z (Table G8653)
Apply Table G1 for subject
8654 Cities and towns, etc., A-Z (Table G8654)
Apply Table G1 for subject

Equatorial Guinea. Spanish Guinea

By region or country
Eastern Hemisphere. Eurasia, Africa, etc.
Africa
Central Africa. Equatorial Africa
Equatorial Guinea. Spanish Guinea -- Continued
8660 General
8661 By subject (Table G1)
8662 Regions, natural features, etc., A-Z (Table G8662)
Apply Table G1 for subject
8663 Provinces, A-Z (Table G8663)
Apply Table G1 for subject
8664 Cities and towns, etc., A-Z (Table G8664)
Apply Table G1 for subject
Sao Tome and Principe
8675 General
8676 By subject (Table G1)
8677 Regions, natural features, etc., A-Z (Table G8677)
Apply Table G1 for subject
8679 Cities and towns, etc., A-Z (Table G8679)
Apply Table G1 for subject
French Equatorial Africa. French Congo
8680 General
8681 By subject (Table G1)
Gabon
8690 General
8691 By subject (Table G1)
8692 Regions, natural features, etc., A-Z (Table G8692)
Apply Table G1 for subject
8693 Provinces, A-Z (Table G8693)
Apply Table G1 for subject
8694 Cities and towns, etc., A-Z (Table G8694)
Apply Table G1 for subject
Congo (Brazzaville). Middle Congo
8700 General
8701 By subject (Table G1)
8702 Regions, natural features, etc., A-Z (Table G8702)
Apply Table G1 for subject
8703 Administrative regions, A-Z (Table G8703)
Apply Table G1 for subject
8704 Cities and towns, etc., A-Z (Table G8704)
Apply Table G1 for subject
Central African Republic. Ubangi-Shari
8710 General
8711 By subject (Table G1)
8712 Regions, natural features, etc., A-Z (Table G8712)
Apply Table G1 for subject

By region or country
Eastern Hemisphere. Eurasia, Africa, etc.
Africa
Central Africa. Equatorial Africa
French Equatorial Africa. French Congo
Central African Republic. Ubangi-Shari -- Continued
8713 Administrative divisions, A-Z (Table G8713)
Apply Table G1 for subject
8714 Cities and towns, etc., A-Z (Table G8714)
Apply Table G1 for subject
Chad (Tchad)
8720 General
8721 By subject (Table G1)
8722 Regions, natural features, etc., A-Z (Table G8722)
Apply Table G1 for subject
8723 Prefectures, A-Z (Table G8723)
Apply Table G1 for subject
8724 Cities and towns, etc., A-Z (Table G8724)
Apply Table G1 for subject
Cameroon. French Cameroons. German Cameroons (Kamerun)
For maps of British Cameroons see G8842
8730 General
8731 By subject (Table G1)
8732 Regions, natural features, etc., A-Z (Table G8732)
Apply Table G1 for subject
8733 Provinces, A-Z (Table G8733)
Apply Table G1 for subject
8734 Cities and towns, etc., A-Z (Table G8734)
Apply Table G1 for subject
West Africa
Including the West Coast and Northwest Africa
8735 General
8736 By subject (Table G1)
8737 Regions, natural features, etc., A-Z (Table G8737)
Apply Table G1 for subject
French West Africa
8740 General
8741 By subject (Table G1)
8742 Regions, natural features, etc., A-Z (Table G8742)
Apply Table G1 for subject
Benin. Dahomey
8750 General
8751 By subject (Table G1)
8752 Regions, natural features, etc., A-Z (Table G8752)
Apply Table G1 for subject

By region or country
Eastern Hemisphere. Eurasia, Africa, etc.
Africa
West Africa
French West Africa
Benin. Dahomey -- Continued

8753 Administrative divisions, A-Z (Table G8753)
Apply Table G1 for subject

8754 Cities and towns, etc., A-Z (Table G8754)
Apply Table G1 for subject

Togo. French Togoland. Togoland
For maps of British Togoland (Trans-Volta Togoland) see G8853

8760 General

8761 By subject (Table G1)

8762 Regions, natural features, etc., A-Z (Table G8762)
Apply Table G1 for subject

8763 Circonscriptions, A-Z (Table G8763)
Apply Table G1 for subject

8764 Cities and towns, etc., A-Z (Table G8764)
Apply Table G1 for subject

Niger

8770 General

8771 By subject (Table G1)

8772 Regions, natural features, etc., A-Z (Table G8772)
Apply Table G1 for subject

8773 Departments, A-Z (Table G8773)
Apply Table G1 for subject

8774 Cities and towns, etc., A-Z (Table G8774)
Apply Table G1 for subject

Côte d'Ivoire. Ivory Coast

8780 General

8781 By subject (Table G1)

8782 Regions, natural features, etc., A-Z (Table G8782)
Apply Table G1 for subject

8783 Departments, A-Z (Table G8783)
Apply Table G1 for subject

8784 Cities and towns, etc., A-Z (Table G8784)
Apply Table G1 for subject

Guinea. French Guinea

8790 General

8791 By subject (Table G1)

8792 Regions, natural features, etc., A-Z (Table G8792)
Apply Table G1 for subject

8793 Administrative regions, A-Z (Table G8793)
Apply Table G1 for subject

By region or country
Eastern Hemisphere. Eurasia, Africa, etc.
Africa
West Africa
French West Africa
Guinea. French Guinea -- Continued
8794 Cities and towns, etc., A-Z (Table G8794)
Apply Table G1 for subject
Mali. French Sudan
8800 General
8801 By subject (Table G1)
8802 Regions, natural features, etc., A-Z (Table G8802)
Apply Table G1 for subject
8803 Administrative regions, A-Z (Table G8803)
Apply Table G1 for subject
8804 Cities and towns, etc., A-Z (Table G8804)
Apply Table G1 for subject
Burkina Faso. Upper Volta
8805 General
8806 By subject (Table G1)
8807 Regions, natural features, etc., A-Z (Table G8807)
Apply Table G1 for subject
8809 Cities and towns, etc., A-Z (Table G8809)
Apply Table G1 for subject
Senegal
8810 General
8811 By subject (Table G1)
8812 Regions, natural features, etc., A-Z (Table G8812)
Apply Table G1 for subject
8813 Administrative regions, A-Z (Table G8813)
Apply Table G1 for subject
8814 Cities and towns, etc., A-Z (Table G8814)
Apply Table G1 for subject
Mauritania
8820 General
8821 By subject (Table G1)
8822 Regions, natural features, etc., A-Z (Table G8822)
Apply Table G1 for subject
8824 Cities and towns, etc., A-Z (Table G8824)
Apply Table G1 for subject
British West Africa
8830 General
8831 By subject (Table G1)
Nigeria
8840 General
8841 By subject (Table G1)

By region or country
Eastern Hemisphere. Eurasia, Africa, etc.
Africa
West Africa
British West Africa
Nigeria -- Continued

8842 Regions, natural features, etc., A-Z (Table G8842)
Apply Table G1 for subject
8843 States, administrative regions, A-Z (Table G8843)
Apply Table G1 for subject
8844 Cities and towns, etc., A-Z (Table G8844)
Apply Table G1 for subject

Ghana. Gold Coast

8850 General
8851 By subject (Table G1)
8852 Regions, natural features, etc., A-Z (Table G8852)
Apply Table G1 for subject
8853 Administrative regions, A-Z (Table G8853)
Apply Table G1 for subject
8854 Cities and towns, etc., A-Z (Table G8854)
Apply Table G1 for subject

Sierra Leone

8860 General
8861 By subject (Table G1)
8862 Regions, natural features, etc., A-Z (Table G8862)
Apply Table G1 for subject
8863 Provinces, A-Z (Table G8863)
Apply Table G1 for subject
8864 Cities and towns, etc., A-Z (Table G8864)
Apply Table G1 for subject

Gambia

8870 General
8871 By subject (Table G1)
8872 Regions, natural features, etc., A-Z (Table G8872)
Apply Table G1 for subject
8873 Administrative divisions, A-Z (Table G8873)
Apply Table G1 for subject
8874 Cities and towns, etc., A-Z (Table G8874)
Apply Table G1 for subject

Liberia

8880 General
8881 By subject (Table G1)
8882 Regions, natural features, etc., A-Z (Table G8882)
Apply Table G1 for subject
8883 Counties, A-Z (Table G8883)
Apply Table G1 for subject

By region or country
Eastern Hemisphere. Eurasia, Africa, etc.
Africa
West Africa
Liberia -- Continued
8884 Cities and towns, etc., A-Z (Table G8884)
Apply Table G1 for subject
Guinea-Bissau. Portuguese Guinea
8890 General
8891 By subject (Table G1)
8892 Regions, natural features, etc., A-Z (Table G8892)
Apply Table G1 for subject
8893 Administrative regions, A-Z (Table G8893)
Apply Table G1 for subject
8894 Cities and towns, etc., A-Z (Table G8894)
Apply Table G1 for subject
Western Sahara. Spanish Sahara
Including Spanish West Africa as a whole
For maps limited to Ifni see G8232
For Zona Sur del Protectorado de Marruecos (Southern Protectorate of Morocco) see G8233
8900 General
8901 By subject (Table G1)
8902 Regions, natural features, etc., A-Z (Table G8902)
Apply Table G1 for subject
8903 Administrative areas, A-Z (Table G8903)
Apply Table G1 for subject
8904 Cities and towns, etc., A-Z (Table G8904)
Apply Table G1 for subject
Australasia
Cf. G9250+ South Pacific
8950 General
8951 By subject (Table G1)
8952 Regions, natural features, etc., A-Z (Table G8952)
Apply Table G1 for subject
Australia
8960 General
8961 By subject (Table G1 modified)
History
8961.S1 General
8961.S12 Discovery and exploration
8961.S2 To 1788
8961.S3 1788-1900
8961.S4 1901-1945
(8961.S65) This number not used
8961.S7 World War II
8961.S73 1945-

By region or country
Australasia
Australia -- Continued

8962 Regions, natural features, etc., A-Z (Table G8962)
Apply Table G1 for subjects (except .S1-.S7, history)
Apply Table G8961.S for history

8964 Cities and towns, A-Z (Table G8964)
Apply Table G1 for subjects (except .S1-.S7, history)
Apply Table G8961.S for history

8970-8973 New South Wales
8970 General
8971 By subject (Table G1 modified)
History
8971.S1 General
8971.S12 Discovery and exploration
8971.S2 To 1788
8971.S3 1788-1900
8971.S4 1901-1945
(8971.S65) This number not used
8971.S7 World War II
8971.S73 1945-

8972 Regions, natural features, etc., A-Z (Table G8972)
Apply Table G1 for subject (except .S1-.S7, historical geography)
Apply Table G8961.S for subject

8973 Shires, etc., A-Z (Table G8973)
Apply Table G1 for subject (except .S1-.S7, historical geography)
Apply Table G8961.S for history

8980-8983 Australian Capital Territory
For Canberra see G8964
8980 General
8981 By subject (Table G1 modified)
History
8981.S1 General
8981.S12 Discovery and exploration
8981.S2 To 1788
8981.S3 1788-1900
8981.S4 1901-1945
(8981.S65) This number not used
8981.S7 World War II
8981.S73 1945-

8982 Regions, natural features, etc., A-Z (Table G8982)
Apply Table G1 for subject (except .S1-.S7, historical geography)
Apply Table G8961.S for history

8990-8993 Victoria

By region or country
Australasia
Australia
Victoria -- Continued

8990 General

8991 By subject (Table G1 modified)

History

8991.S1 General

8991.S12 Discovery and exploration

8991.S2 To 1788

8991.S3 1788-1900

8991.S4 1901-1945

(8991.S65) This number not used

8991.S7 World War II

8991.S73 1945-

8992 Regions, natural features, etc., A-Z (Table G8992)

Apply Table G1 for subject (except .S1-.S7, historical geography)

Apply Table G8961.S for history

8993 Shires, etc., A-Z (Table G8993)

Apply Table G1 for subject (except .S1-.S7, historical geography)

Apply Table G8961.S for history

9000-9003 Queensland

9000 General

9001 By subject (Table G1 modified)

History

9001.S1 General

9001.S12 Discovery and exploration

9001.S2 To 1788

9001.S3 1788-1900

9001.S4 1901-1945

(9001.S65) This number not used

9001.S7 World War II

9001.S73 1945-

9002 Regions, natural features, etc., A-Z (Table G9002)

Apply Table G1 for subject (except .S1-.S7, historical geography)

Apply Table G8961.S for history

9003 Shires, etc., A-Z (Table G9003)

Apply Table G1 for subject (except .S1-.S7, historical geography)

Apply Table G8961.S for history

9010-9013 South Australia

9010 General

9011 By subject (Table G1 modified)

History

By region or country
Australasia
Australia
South Australia
By subject
History -- Continued
9011.S1 General
9011.S12 Discovery and exploration
9011.S2 To 1788
9011.S3 1788-1900
9011.S4 1901-1945
(9011.S65) This number not used
9011.S7 World War II
9011.S73 1945-
9012 Regions, natural features, etc., A-Z (Table G9012)
Apply Table G1 for subject (except .S1-.S7, historical geography)
Apply Table G8961.S for history
9013 Counties, etc., A-Z (Table G9013)
Apply Table G1 for subject (except .S1-.S7, historical geography)
Apply Table G8961.S for history
9020-9023 Western Australia
9020 General
9021 By subject (Table G1 modified)
History
9021.S1 General
9021.S12 Discovery and exploration
9021.S2 To 1788
9021.S3 1788-1900
9021.S4 1901-1945
(9021.S65) This number not used
9021.S7 World War II
9021.S73 1945-
9022 Regions, natural features, etc., A-Z (Table G9022)
Apply Table G1 for subject (except .S1-.S7, historical geography)
Apply Table G8961.S for history
9023 Shires, etc., A-Z (Table G9023)
Apply Table G1 for subject (except .S1-.S7, historical geography)
Apply Table G8961.S for history
9040-9043 Northern Territory
9040 General
9041 By subject (Table G1 modified)
History
9041.S1 General

By region or country
Australasia
Australia
Northern Territory
By subject
History -- Continued
9041.S12 Discovery and exploration
9041.S2 To 1788
9041.S3 1788-1900
9041.S4 1901-1945
(9041.S65) This number not used
9041.S7 World War II
9041.S73 1945-
9042 Regions, natural features, etc., A-Z (Table G9042)
Apply Table G1 for subject (except .S1-.S7, historical geography)
Apply Table G8961.S for history
9060-9063 Tasmania
9060 General
9061 By subject (Table G1 modified)
History
9061.S1 General
9061.S12 Discovery and exploration
9061.S2 To 1788
9061.S3 1788-1900
9061.S4 1901-1945
(9061.S65) This number not used
9061.S7 World War II
9061.S73 1945-
9062 Regions, natural features, etc., A-Z (Table G9062)
Apply Table G1 for subject (except .S1-.S7, historical geography)
Apply Table G8961.S for history
New Zealand
9080 General
9081 By subject (Table G1)
9082 Regions, natural features, etc., A-Z (Table G9082)
Apply Table G1 for subject
9083 Counties, A-Z (Table G9083)
Apply Table G1 for subject
9084 Cities and towns, etc., A-Z (Table G9084)
Apply Table G1 for subject
Oceans (General)
Class an island or group of islands not provided with classification numbers and situated close to a continent, larger island, or group of islands with the neighboring land area

By region or country
Oceans (General) -- Continued
9095 General
9096 By subject (Table G1)
Atlantic Ocean
9100 General
9101 By subject (Table G1)
9102 Regions, natural features, etc., A-Z (Table G9102)
Apply Table G1 for subject
North Atlantic
9110 General
9111 By subject (Table G1)
9112 Regions, bays, etc., A-Z (Table G9112)
Apply Table G1 for subject
For maps of Gulf of Mexico coast or continental shelf see G3330+
Bermuda
9120 General
9121 By subject (Table G1)
9122 Regions, natural features, islands, etc., A-Z (Table G9122)
Apply Table G1 for subject
9123 Counties, A-Z (Table G9123)
Apply Table G1 for subject
9124 Cities and towns, etc., A-Z (Table G9124)
Apply Table G1 for subject
Azores
9130 General
9131 By subject (Table G1)
9132 Regions, natural features, islands, etc., A-Z (Table G9132)
Apply Table G1 for subject
9133 Districts, etc., A-Z (Table G9133 modified)
Apply Table G1 for subject
9133.A5 Angra do Heroismo
Subarrange by Table G1
9133.H6 Horta
Subarrange by Table G1
9133.P6 Ponta Delgada
Subarrange by Table G1
9134 Cities and towns, etc., A-Z (Table G9134)
Apply Table G1 for subject
Madiera Islands. Funchal (District of Portugal)
9140 General
9141 By subject (Table G1)

By region or country
Oceans (General)
Atlantic Ocean
North Atlantic
Madiera Islands. Funchal (District of Portugal) -- Continued
9142 Regions, natural features, archipelagoes, islands, etc., A-Z (Table G9142)
Apply Table G1 for subject
9144 Cities and towns, etc., A-Z (Table G9144)
Apply Table G1 for subject
Canary Islands
Including two provinces of Spain: Las Palmas (Las Palmas de Gran Canaria) and Santa Cruz de Tenerife
9150 General
9151 By subject (Table G1)
9152 Regions, natural features, islands, etc., A-Z (Table G9152)
Apply Table G1 for subject
9153 Provinces, etc., A-Z (Table G9153 modified)
Apply Table G1 for subject
9153.L3 Las Palmas
Subarrange by Table G1
9154 Cities and towns, etc., A-Z (Table G9154)
Apply Table G1 for subject
Cape Verde Islands
9160 General
9161 By subject (Table G1)
9162 Regions, natural features, archipelagoes, islands, etc., A-Z (Table G9162)
Apply Table G1 for subject
9164 Cities and towns, etc., A-Z (Table G9164)
Apply Table G1 for subject
South Atlantic
9165 General
9166 By subject (Table G1)
9167 Regions, natural features, archipelagoes, islands, etc., A-Z (Table G9167)
Apply Table G1 for subject
Class here maps of South Atlantic islands and archipelagoes not classed in or associated with G9170-G9179
Saint Helena (Colony)
9170 General
9171 By subject (Table G1)

By region or country
Oceans (General)
Atlantic Ocean
South Atlantic
Saint Helena (Colony) -- Continued
9172 Regions, natural features, archipelagoes, islands, etc., A-Z (Table G9172)
Apply Table G1 for subject
Falkland Islands
9175 General
9176 By subject (Table G1)
9177 Regions, natural features, archipelagoes, islands, etc., A-Z (Table G9177)
Apply Table G1 for subject
9179 Cities and towns, etc., A-Z (Table G9179)
Apply Table G1 for subject
Indian Ocean
9180 General
9181 By subject (Table G1)
9182 Regions, natural features, archipelagoes, islands, etc., A-Z (Table G9182)
Apply Table G1 for subject
Class here maps of Indian Ocean islands and archipelagoes not classed in or associated with G9185-G9219
Mauritius
Cf. G9182 Mascarene Islands
9185 General
9186 By subject (Table G1)
9187 Regions, natural features, archipelagoes, islands, etc., A-Z (Table G9187)
Apply Table G1 for subject
9189 Cities and towns, etc., A-Z (Table G9189)
Apply Table G1 for subject
Réunion. Isle de Bourbon
Cf. G9182 Mascarene Islands
9190 General
9191 By subject (Table G1)
9192 Regions, natural features, archipelagoes, islands, dependencies, etc., A-Z (Table G9192)
Apply Table G1 for subject
9194 Cities and towns, etc., A-Z (Table G9194)
Apply Table G1 for subject
British Indian Ocean Territory
9195 General
9196 By subject (Table G1)

By region or country
Oceans (General)
Indian Ocean
British Indian Ocean Territory -- Continued

9197 Regions, natural features, archipelagoes, islands, etc., A-Z (Table G9197)
Apply Table G1 for subject

Seychelles

9200 General

9201 By subject (Table G1)

9202 Regions, natural features, archipelagoes, islands, dependencies, etc., A-Z (Table G9202)
Apply Table G1 for subject

9204 Cities and towns, etc., A-Z (Table G9204)
Apply Table G1 for subject

Cocos Islands. Keeling Islands

9205 General

9206 By subject (Table G1)

9207 Regions, natural features, archipelagoes, islands, etc., A-Z (Table G9207)
Apply Table G1 for subject

Comoros

9210 General

9211 By subject (Table G1)

9212 Regions, natural features, archipelagoes, islands, etc., A-Z (Table G9212)
Apply Table G1 for subject

9214 Cities and towns, etc., A-Z (Table G9214)
Apply Table G1 for subject

Maldives

9215 General

9216 By subject (Table G1)

9217 Regions, atolls, archipelagoes, islands, etc., A-Z (Table G9217)
Apply Table G1 for subject

9218 Administrative divisions, A-Z (Table G9218)
Apply Table G1 for subject

9219 Cities and towns, etc., A-Z (Table G9219)
Apply Table G1 for subject

Pacific Ocean

9230 General

9231 By subject (Table G1)

9232 Regions, natural features, archipelagoes, islands, etc., A-Z (Table G9232)
Apply Table G1 for subject

North Pacific

9235 General

By region or country
Oceans (General)
Pacific Ocean
North Pacific -- Continued
9236 By subject (Table G1)
9237 Regions, atolls, archipelagoes, islands, etc., A-Z (Table G9237)
Apply Table G1 for subject
South Pacific. Oceania
Cf. G8950+ Australasia
9250 General
9251 By subject (Table G1)
9252 Regions, natural features, archipelagoes, islands, etc., A-Z (Table G9252)
Apply Table G1 for subject
Melanesia
9260 General
9261 By subject (Table G1)
9262 Regions, natural features, archipelagoes, islands, etc., A-Z (Table G9262)
Apply Table G1 for subject
Class here maps of Melanesian islands and archipelagoes not classed in or associated with G9275-G9384
British Solomon Islands Protectorate
9275 General
9276 By subject (Table G1)
Solomon Islands
9280 General
9281 By subject (Table G1)
9282 Regions, natural features, archipelagoes, islands, etc., A-Z (Table G9282 modified)
Apply Table G1 for subject
9282.B6 Bougainville Island
Subarrange by Table G1
9282.B8 Buka Island
Subarrange by Table G1
9282.G7 Green Islands
Subarrange by Table G1
Santa Cruz Islands. Queen Charlotte Islands
9290 General
9291 By subject (Table G1)
9292 Regions, natural features, archipelagoes, islands, etc., A-Z (Table G9292)
Apply Table G1 for subject
New Hebrides. Anglo-French Condominium of the New Hebrides

By region or country
Oceans (General)
Pacific Ocean
South Pacific. Oceania
Melanesia
New Hebrides. Anglo-French Condominium of the New Hebrides -- Continued
9295 General
9296 By subject (Table G1)
New Hebrides Islands
9300 General
9301 By subject (Table G1)
9302 Regions, natural features, archipelagoes, islands, etc., A-Z (Table G9302)
Apply Table G1 for subject
9304 Cities and towns, etc., A-Z (Table G9304)
Apply Table G1 for subject
Banks Islands
9310 General
9311 By subject (Table G1)
New Caledonia (Island or territory)
9340 General
9341 By subject (Table G1)
9342 Regions, natural features, archipelagoes, islands, etc., A-Z (Table G9342)
Apply Table G1 for subject
9344 Cities and towns, etc., A-Z (Table G9344)
Apply Table G1 for subject
Loyalty Islands
9350 General
9351 By subject (Table G1)
Chesterfield Archipelago
9370 General
9371 By subject (Table G1)
Futuna Islands see G9525+
Wallis Islands see G9520+
Fiji
9380 General
9381 By subject (Table G1)
9382 Regions, natural features, archipelagoes, islands, dependencies, etc., A-Z (Table G9382)
Apply Table G1 for subject
9384 Cities and towns, etc., A-Z (Table G9384)
Apply Table G1 for subject
Micronesia
9400 General
9401 By subject (Table G1)

By region or country
Oceans (General)
Pacific Ocean
South Pacific. Oceania
Micronesia -- Continued

9402 Regions, natural features, archipelagoes, islands, etc., A-Z (Table G9402)
Apply Table G1 for subject
Class here maps of Micronesian islands or archipelagoes not classed in or associated with G9405-G9486

Trust Territory of the Pacific Islands
Including the Caroline, Marshall, and Mariana Islands, except Guam
Class here maps of the Trust Territory as a whole

9405 General
9406 By subject (Table G1)

Mariana Islands. Ladrone Islands
9410 General
9411 By subject (Table G1)
9412 Regions, natural features, archipelagoes, islands, etc., A-Z (Table G9412)
Apply Table G1 for subject
9414 Cities and towns, etc., A-Z (Table G9414)
Apply Table G1 for subject

Guam
9415 General
9416 By subject (Table G1)
9417 Regions, natural features, archipelagoes, islands, etc., A-Z (Table G9417)
Apply Table G1 for subject
9419 Cities and towns, etc., A-Z (Table G9419)
Apply Table G1 for subject

Caroline Islands
9420 General
9421 By subject (Table G1)
9422 Regions, natural features, atolls, islands, etc., A-Z (Table G9422)
Apply Table G1 for subject
Class here maps of the islands or atolls in the Carolines not classed in or associated with G9425-G9452
9423 Administrative regions, A-Z (Table G9423)
Apply Table G1 for subject

Palau Islands. Pelew Islands
9425 General
9426 By subject (Table G1)

By region or country
Oceans (General)
Pacific Ocean
South Pacific. Oceania
Micronesia
Trust Territory of the Pacific Islands
Caroline Islands
Palau Islands. Pelew Islands -- Continued
9427 Regions, natural features, archipelagoes, islands, etc., A-Z (Table G9427)
Apply Table G1 for subject
Yap
9430 General
9431 By subject (Table G1)
9432 Regions, natural features, archipelagoes, islands, etc., A-Z (Table G9432)
Apply Table G1 for subject
Hall Islands. Horu Shoto
9435 General
9436 By subject (Table G1)
Chuuk. Hogoleu Islands. Mototokko Shoto
9440 General
9441 By subject (Table G1)
9442 Regions, atolls, archipelagoes, islands, etc., A-Z (Table G9442)
Apply Table G1 for subject
Losap Atoll
9445 General
9446 By subject (Table G1)
Mortlock Islands. Nomoi Islands
9450 General
9451 By subject (Table G1)
Marshall Islands
9460 General
9461 By subject (Table G1)
9462 Regions, atolls, archipelagoes, islands, etc., A-Z (Table G9462)
Apply Table G1 for subject
Ralik Chain
9465 General
9466 By subject (Table G1)
9467 Regions, atolls, archipelagoes, islands, etc., A-Z (Table G9467)
Apply Table G1 for subject
Ratak Chain
9470 General
9471 By subject (Table G1)

By region or country
Oceans (General)
Pacific Ocean
South Pacific. Oceania
Micronesia
Trust Territory of the Pacific Islands
Marshall Islands
Ratak Chain -- Continued

9472 Regions, atolls, archipelagoes, islands, etc., A-Z (Table G9472)
Apply Table G1 for subject

Gilbert and Ellice Islands Colony
Including the Gilbert Islands, Ellice Islands, Ocean Island, and islands claimed by the United Kingdom in the Phoenix and Line Islands
Class here maps of the entire colony
For maps of component islands, regions, etc., see G9480-G9489, G9510-G9514, G9530-G9544

9475 General
9476 By subject (Table G1)

Kiribati. Gilbert Islands. Kingsmill Islands

9480 General
9481 By subject (Table G1)
9482 Regions, atolls, archipelagoes, islands, etc., A-Z (Table G9482)
Apply Table G1
For maps of the colony as a whole see G9475+

Ocean Island. Banaba
Administered by Gilbert and Ellice Islands Colony

9485 General
9486 By subject (Table G1)

Polynesia. Western Polynesia

9500 General
9501 By subject (Table G1)
9502 Regions, atolls, archipelagoes, islands, etc., A-Z
Class here maps of Western Polynesia islands not classed in or associated with G9510-G9604

Tuvalu. Ellice Islands. Lagoon Islands
Administered by Gilbert and Ellice Islands Colony
For maps of the colony as a whole see G9475+

9510 General
9511 By subject (Table G1)
9512 Regions, atolls, archipelagoes, islands, etc., A-Z (Table G9512)
Apply Table G1 for subject

Territory of Wallis and Futuna

9515 General

By region or country
Oceans (General)
Pacific Ocean
South Pacific. Oceania
Polynesia. Western Polynesia
Territory of Wallis and Futuna -- Continued
9516 By subject (Table G1)
Wallis Islands
9520 General
9521 By subject (Table G1)
Futuna Islands. Hoorn Islands
9525 General
9526 By subject (Table G1)
Line Islands. Equatorial Islands
Christmas, Fanning, Washington, Caroline, Flint, Malden, and Vostock Islands are administered by Gilbert and Ellice Islands Colony
For maps of the colony as a whole see G9475+
9530 General
9531 By subject (Table G1)
Phoenix Islands
Birnie, Gardner, Hull, McKean, Phoenix, and Sydney Islands are administered by Gilbert and Ellice Islands Colony
For maps of the colony as a whole see G9475+
9540 General
9541 By subject (Table G1)
Tokelau Islands. Union Islands
9550 General
9551 By subject (Table G1)
9552 Regions, atolls, archipelagoes, islands, etc., A-Z (Table G9552)
Apply Table G1 for subject
Samoan Islands. Navigators Islands
9555 General
9556 By subject (Table G1)
American Samoa
9560 General
9561 By subject (Table G1)
9562 Regions, atolls, archipelagoes, islands, etc., A-Z (Table G9562)
Apply Table G1 for subject
9564 Cities and towns, etc., A-Z (Table G9564)
Apply Table G1 for subject
Samoa. Western Samoa
9565 General
9566 By subject (Table G1)

By region or country
Oceans (General)
Pacific Ocean
South Pacific. Oceania
Polynesia. Western Polynesia
Samoan Islands. Navigators Islands
Samoa. Western Samoa -- Continued

9567 Regions, atolls, archipelagoes, islands, etc., A-Z (Table G9567)
Apply Table G1 for subject

9569 Cities and towns, etc., A-Z (Table G9569)
Apply Table G1 for subject

Tonga. Friendly Islands

9570 General

9571 By subject (Table G1)

9572 Regions, natural features, archipelagoes, islands, etc., A-Z (Table G9572)
Apply Table G1 for subject

9573 Administrative divisions, A-Z (Table G9573)
Apply Table G1 for subject

9574 Cities and towns, etc., A-Z (Table G9574)
Apply Table G1 for subject

Niue. Savage Island

9580 General

9581 By subject (Table G1)

Kermadec Islands

9590 General

9591 By subject (Table G1)

9592 Regions, natural features, archipelagoes, islands, etc., A-Z (Table G9592)
Apply Table G1 for subject

Cook Islands

9600 General

9601 By subject (Table G1)

9602 Regions, atolls, archipelagoes, islands, etc., A-Z (Table G9602)
Apply Table G1 for subject

French Oceania (Territory of French Polynesia)

9610 General

9611 By subject (Table G1)

9612 Regions, atolls, archipelagoes, islands, etc., A-Z
Class here maps of miscellaneous French Polynesia islands not classed in or associated with G9620-G9654

Clipperton see G9762

Marquesas Islands

9620 General

By region or country
Oceans (General)
Pacific Ocean
South Pacific. Oceania
Polynesia. Western Polynesia
French Oceania (Territory of French Polynesia)
Marquesas Islands -- Continued
9621 By subject (Table G1)
9622 Regions, natural features, archipelagoes, islands, etc., A-Z (Table G9622)
Apply Table G1 for subject
Tuamoto Archipelago (Îles Tuamoto et Gambier. Paumotu Islands). Low Archipelago
9630 General
9631 By subject (Table G1)
9632 Regions, atolls, archipelagoes, islands, etc., A-Z (Table G9632)
Apply Table G1 for subject
Society Islands
9640 General
9641 By subject (Table G1)
9642 Regions, atolls, archipelagoes, islands, etc., A-Z (Table G9642)
Apply Table G1 for subject
9644 Cities and towns, etc., A-Z (Table G9644)
Apply Table G1 for subject
Tubuai Islands. Austral Islands
9650 General
9651 By subject (Table G1)
9652 Regions, natural features, archipelagoes, islands, etc., A-Z (Table G9652)
Apply Table G1 for subject
Pitcairn (Island and colony)
9660 General
9661 By subject (Table G1)
9662 Regions, atolls, archipelagoes, etc., A-Z (Table G9662)
Apply Table G1 for subject
Easter Island
9665 General
9666 By subject (Table G1)
9667 Regions, natural features, archipelagoes, islands, etc., A-Z (Table G9667)
Apply Table G1 for subject
Hawaiian Islands see G4380+

By region or country
Oceans (General)
Pacific Ocean -- Continued
East Pacific
Class maps of islands relatively close to the American continents with the country or subdivision of the country to which they belong
9760 General
9761 By subject (Table G1)
9762 Regions, archipelagoes, islands, etc., A-Z (Table G9762)
Apply Table G1 for subject
Arctic Ocean
9780 General
9781 By subject (Table G1)
9782 Regions, natural features, archipelagoes, islands, etc., A-Z (Table G9782)
Apply Table G1 for subject
Class here maps of Arctic islands and archipelagoes not classed in or associated with G9785-G9794
Franz Josef Land. Fridtjof Nansen Land
9785 General
9786 By subject (Table G1)
Svalbard. Spitsbergen
9790 General
9791 By subject (Table G1)
9792 Regions, natural features, archipelagoes, islands, etc., A-Z (Table G9792)
Apply Table G1 for subject
Antarctica
9800 General
9801 By subject (Table G1)
9802 Regions, natural features, archipelagoes, islands, etc., A-Z (Table G9802)
Apply Table G1 for subject
9803 Territories, administrative districts, etc., A-Z (Table G9803)
Apply Table G1 for subject
9804 Cities and towns, etc., A-Z (Table G9804)
Apply Table G1 for subject
9880 Collections of geographically dispersed material

Unlocalized maps

9900 Theoretical maps

Class here maps whose primary intent is the illustration or definition of terms and concepts and maps designed to illustrate methods of map making. Class maps of a determinable geographic area with the area

9930 Maps of imaginary places

9980 Maps of unidentified places

Mathematical geography. Cartography
Cf. QB275+ Geodesy
Cf. QB630+ Astronomical geography
Mathematical geography
1 Periodicals. Societies. Serials
Collected works (nonserial)
2 Several authors
2.5 Individual authors
Study and teaching. Research
2.7 General works
By region or country
2.8 United States
2.9.A-Z Other regions or countries, A-Z
3 History
Cf. GA201+ Cartography
Cf. GA260+ Globes
4 Handbooks, tables, etc.
General works, treatises, and textbooks
5 Early through 1500
6 16th century. Cosmographies
7 17th-18th centuries
1801-1974
9 Comprehensive works
12 Compends
Cf. GA260+ History, description and construction of globes
13 1975-
23 General special (Special aspects of the subject as a whole)
Including calculation of geographical areas
Surveys (General)
Cf. QB301+ Geodetic surveys
Cf. QE61 Geological surveys
Cf. TA590 Topographical surveying (Engineering)
Cf. VK588+ Hydrographic surveys
History, organization, methods, etc.
51 General works
Individual regions or countries
see GA55+
53 General special
55 International surveys
56 Several countries (not limited to one continent)
America
57 General works
United States
59 General works
61.A-.W By state, A-W
63.A-Z Other American countries, A-Z

Mathematical geography
Surveys (General) -- Continued
Europe
65 General works
66.A-Z By country, A-Z
Asia
70 General works
71.A-Z By country, A-Z
Africa
75 General works
76.A-Z By country, A-Z
Australia and Pacific islands
80 General works
Australia
85 General works
86.A-Z By state or territory, A-Z
86.5 New Zealand
87.A-Z Pacific islands, A-Z

Cartography

Class here works on map making and works about maps (General)

For works on the construction, use, and reading of maps in a special field, see the subject, e.g. QC878 Construction of weather maps; UG470 Military mapping; S494.5.C3 Agricultural cartography; etc.

For maps themselves see G3180+

Cf. GN476.5 Primitive cartography

101 Periodicals. Societies. Serials
101.2 Congresses
Collected works (nonserial)
101.5 Several authors
101.7 Individual authors
102 Dictionaries. Encyclopedias
102.2 Terminology. Abbreviations. Notation
Cf. GA155 Map symbols
102.25 Directories
Philosophy. Relation to other topics. Methodology
102.3 General works
102.4.A-Z Special methods, A-Z
102.4.E4 Electronic data processing
102.4.R44 Remote sensing
Study and teaching. Research
102.5 General works
By region or country
102.6 United States
102.7.A-Z Other regions or countries, A-Z

Cartography -- Continued
General works, treatises, and advanced textbooks
Including thematic cartography (General)
103 Early through 1800
105 1801-1974
105.3 1975-
Elementary textbooks see GA130
105.5 Popular works
105.6 Juvenile works
108 Addresses, essays, lectures
108.5 Handbooks, tables, etc.
108.7 General special (Special aspects of the subject as a whole)
109 Aerial cartography
Cf. TA592+ Aerial surveying
Cf. TL587 Aeronautical charts
109.5 Cadastral mapping
109.8 Statistical mapping
Projection
110 General works
115 Special types (not A-Z)
Including orthomorphic, equal area, perspective, as well as individual methods, e. g. Mercator's, Lambert's, etc.
116 Grids
Latitude and longitude see QB224.5+
118 Map scales
125 Topographic drawing
Cf. TA616 Surveying
130 Elementary map drawing and reading
Including juvenile textbooks
135 Maps for people with visual disabilities
138 Block diagrams
139 Digital mapping
139.5 Multimedia cartography
140 Relief maps
145 Modeling
Map printing, engraving, etc.
150 General works
150.5 Equipment, machinery, supplies
150.7 Reproduction, photocopying,etc.
151 Map reading (General)
For military map reading see UG470+
Cf. G107.8+ Geographic terms
Cf. GA102.2 Cartographic terms
Cf. GA130 Elementary map drawing and reading
155 Conventional signs and symbols
190 Museums. Exhibitions
Arrange by author

Cartography -- Continued
Collections of maps, globes, etc. Map libraries
Cf. GA361 Collections of marine charts
Cf. Z692.M3 Handling of maps in libraries
Cf. Z695.6 Cataloging of maps
192 Periodicals. Societies. Serials
193.A-Z By region or country, A-Z
Biography
194 Collective
194.2.A-Z Individual, A-Z
195.A-Z Individual public collections. By place, A-Z
e.g.
195.W64 Wolfenbüttel. Herzog-August-Bibliothek
197.A-Z Individual private collections. By collector, A-Z
197.3 Collector's manuals. History of collecting
Cartographers
Including cartographic historians
197.5 Cartography as a profession
198 Biography (General)
Including biography (General) of globe makers
For biography of cartographers by country, see GA407; GA473; GA483 etc.
For biography of globe makers by country see GA281+
History
201 General
203 General special
Including cartographical sources, value of maps in boundary disputes, popes as geographers
By period
Ancient
Cf. G83+ History of geography
205 General
Special
207 Chinese
209 Egyptian
211 Indian
213 Greek and Roman
221 Medieval
231 16th century (1450-1600)
236 17th-18th centuries
241 19th century
246 20th century
By country see GA401+
Globe making. Globes
For globes themselves see G3160+
Cf. GA192+ Collections of globes
Cf. GA198 Biography of globe makers

Cartography
Globe making. Globes -- Continued

260 General works
263 General special
265 Manuals for the use of globes
By period
267 Before 16th century
271 16th century
273 17th century
275 18th century
277 19th century
278 20th century
By country
281 United States
282 Canada
283.A-Z Other American countries, A-Z
284.A-Z Europe, A-Z

Under each country (unless otherwise specified):

.x	*General works*
.x2A-.x2Z	*Individual biography, A-Z*
.x3	*Special globes. By date or approximate date* *Subarrange by globe maker and author*

Italy
284.I7 General works
284.I8A-.I8Z Individual biography, A-Z
284.I9 Special globes. By date and then by maker
Netherlands
284.N2 General works
284.N3A-.N3Z Individual biography, A-Z
284.N4 Special globes. By date and then by maker
285.A-Z Asia, A-Z

Under each country:

.x	*General works*
.x2A-.x2Z	*Individual biography, A-Z*
.x3	*Special globes. By date or approximate date* *Subarrange by globe maker and author*

286.A-Z Africa, A-Z
287 Australia
287.5 New Zealand
288.A-Z Pacific islands, A-Z

Cartography -- Continued
World maps, general atlases, etc.
Class here works on the history and description of atlases and maps
For the atlases and maps themselves see G1001+

300 General works
Early Oriental
301 Identified. By date
Subarrange: (1) by cartographer or title, (2) by author or editor
302 Not identified
Subarrange by author of history or description
Date and cartographer unknown
Ancient and medieval to 1400
303 By date
Subarrange: (1) by cartographer or title, (2) by author or editor
Undated
304.A1-.Z4 By cartographer or title of map
Subarrange by author or editor
304.Z5-.Z99 Anonymous maps arranged by approximate date
Subarrange by author or editor
304.Z5 Before 1000
304.Z6 11th century
304.Z7 12th century
304.Z8 13th century
304.Z9 14th century
15th century
307 By date
Subarrange: (1) by cartography or title, (2) by author or editor
Undated
308.A1-.Z4 By cartographer or title of map
Subarrange by author or editor
Anonymous maps arranged by approximate date
Subarrange by author or editor
308.Z5 Before 1425
308.Z6 1425-1450
308.Z7 1450-1475
308.Z8 1475-1500
16th century
311 By date
Subarrange: (1) by cartographer or title, (2) by author or editor
312 Undated
312.A1-.Z4 By cartographer or title of map
Subarrange by author or editor

Cartography
World maps, general atlases, etc.
16th century
Undated -- Continued
Anonymous maps arranged by approximate date
Subarrange by author or editor

312.Z5 Before 1525
312.Z6 1525-1550
312.Z7 1550-1575
312.Z8 1575-1600

17th century
315 By date
Subarrange: (1) by cartographer or title, (2) by author or editor
316 Undated
316.A1-.Z4 By cartographer or title of map
Subarrange by author or editor
Anonymous maps arranged by approximate date
Subarrange by author or editor
316.Z5 Before 1625
316.Z6 1625-1650
316.Z7 1650-1675
316.Z8 1675-1700

18th century
317 By date
Subarrange: (1) by cartographer or title, (2) by author or editor
318 Undated
318.A1-.Z4 By cartographer or title of map
Subarrange by author or editor
Anonymous maps arranged by approximate date
Subarrange by author or editor
318.Z5 Before 1725
318.Z6 1725-1750
318.Z7 1750-1775
318.Z8 1775-1800

19th century
319 By date
Subarrange: (1) by cartographer or title, (2) by author or editor
320 Undated
320.A1-.Z4 By cartographer or title of map
Subarrange by author or editor
Anonymous maps arranged by approximate date
Subarrange by author or editor
320.Z5 Before 1825
320.Z6 1825-1850

Cartography
World maps, general atlases, etc.
19th century
Undated
Anonymous maps arranged by approximate date -- Continued

320.Z7 1850-1875
320.Z8 1875-1900
320.5.A-Z Series of maps by special publishers, A-Z
e.g.
320.5.S7 Society for the Diffusion of Useful Knowledge
20th century
321 By date
Subarrange: (1) by cartographer or title, (2) by author or editor
322 Undated
322.A1-.Z4 By cartographer or title of map
Subarrange by author or editor
Anonymous maps arranged by approximate date
Subarrange by author or editor
322.Z5 Before 1925
322.Z6 1925-1950
322.Z7 1950-1975
322.Z8 1975-2000
323 International Map Committee
325.A-Z Series of maps by special publishers, A-Z
Maps. By region or country
Class here works on the history of map production in particular regions or countries and works on the history and description of maps of special regions or countries
341 Eastern Hemisphere
Western Hemisphere see GA401+
345 Northern Hemisphere
347 Southern Hemisphere
Polar regions
351 General works
355 Arctic regions
357 Antarctic regions. Antarctica
Oceans. Seas. Marine cartography
359 General works
361 Collections of nautical charts
For collections issued by individual countries see GA401+
Arctic Ocean
364 General works
365.A-Z Special parts, A-Z
Atlantic Ocean

Cartography
Maps. By region or country
Oceans. Seas. Marine cartography
Atlantic Ocean -- Continued
368 General works
North Atlantic
369 General works
370 North Sea
371 Baltic Sea
372 English Channel. Saint George's Channel
373 Biscay, Bay of
374 Gibraltar, Strait of
Mediterranean Sea
375 General works
376.A-Z Special parts, A-Z
378 Black Sea
380 South Atlantic
381 Caribbean Sea and Gulf of Mexico
Pacific Ocean
383 General works
North Pacific
384 General works
385 Bering Sea. Sea of Okhotsk
386 Japan Sea
387 Yellow Sea
388 China Sea
390 South Pacific
Indian Ocean
392 General works
394 Red Sea
395 Persian Gulf
396 Arabian Sea
397 Bengal, Bay of
America. Western Hemisphere
Including North and South America together or North America alone
401 General works
402 Individual maps. By date or approximate date
Subarrange: (1) by cartographer or title, (2) by author or editor
United States
405 General works. General history of cartography in the United States
405.5 General special
406 Official works. Documents
Biography of cartographers
Cf. GA281 Biography of globe makers

Cartography
Maps. By region or country
United States
Biography of cartographers -- Continued

407.A1 Collective
407.A2-Z Individual, A-Z
408 Individual maps. By date or approximate date
Subarrange: (1) by cartographer or title, (2) by author or editor
By region or state
408.5.A-Z Individual regions, A-Z
Individual states
409 Alabama
410 Alaska
411 Arizona
412 Arkansas
413 California
414 Colorado
415 Connecticut
416 Delaware
417 District of Columbia
418 Florida
419 Georgia
419.5 Hawaii
420 Idaho
421 Illinois
422 Indian Territory
423 Indiana
424 Iowa
425 Kansas
426 Kentucky
427 Louisiana
428 Maine
429 Maryland
430 Massachusetts
431 Michigan
432 Minnesota
433 Mississippi
434 Missouri
435 Montana
436 Nebraska
437 Nevada
438 New Hampshire
439 New Jersey
440 New Mexico
441 New York
442 North Carolina

Cartography
Maps. By region or country
United States
By region or state
Individual states -- Continued

443 North Dakota
444 Ohio
445 Oklahoma
446 Oregon
447 Pennsylvania
448 Rhode Island
449 South Carolina
450 South Dakota
451 Tennessee
452 Texas
453 Utah
454 Vermont
455 Virginia
456 Washington
457 West Virginia
458 Wisconsin
459 Wyoming
460.A-Z Individual cities and towns, A-Z

Other regions or countries
471-475 Canada. British North America (Table G7)
481-485 Mexico (Table G7)

Central America
491 General works
501-505 Belize. British Honduras (Table G7)
511-515 Costa Rica (Table G7)
521-525 Guatemala (Table G7)
531-535 Honduras (Table G7)
541-545 Nicaragua (Table G7)
546-550 Panama (Table G7)
551-555 El Salvador (Table G7)

West Indies
561 General works
571-575 Bahamas (Table G7)
581-585 Cuba (Table G7)
591-595 Haiti (Table G7)
601-605 Jamaica (Table G7)
611-615 Puerto Rico (Table G7)
621.A-Z Other islands, A-Z
631-635 Bermudas (Table G7)

South America
641 General works
651-655 Argentina (Table G7)

Cartography
Maps. By region or country
Other regions or countries
South America -- Continued

661-665 Bolivia (Table G7)
671-675 Brazil (Table G7)
681-685 Chile (Table G7)
691-695 Colombia (Table G7)
701-705 Ecuador (Table G7)
Guianas
711 General works
716-720 Guyana (Table G7)
721-725 Suriname (Table G7)
726-730 French Guiana (Table G7)
741-745 Paraguay (Table G7)
751-755 Peru (Table G7)
761-765 Uruguay (Table G7)
771-775 Venezuela (Table G7)
Europe
781 General works
787 Alps
Not confined to one country
Great Britain. England (General)
791-794 General works (Table G7 modified)
795.A-Z England (Local), A-Z
801-805 Northern Ireland (Table G7)
811-815 Scotland (Table G7)
821-825 Wales (Table G7)
826-830 Ireland (Table G7)
831-835 Austria (Table G7)
Including Austria-Hungary
841-845 Czechoslovakia (Table G7)
851-855 Hungary (Table G7)
861-865 France (Table G7)
871-875 Germany (Table G7)
Including West Germany
876-880 East Germany (Table G7)
881-885 Greece (Table G7)
891-895 Italy (Table G7)
Low countries. Benelux
901 General works
911-915 Belgium (Table G7)
921-925 Netherlands (Holland) (Table G7)
931-935 Russia (Federation) (Table G7)
941-945 Poland (Table G7)
Scandinavia
For Finland see GA1077.F5

Cartography
Maps. By region or country
Other regions or countries
Europe
Scandinavia -- Continued

951 General works
961-965 Denmark (Table G7)
971-975 Iceland (Table G7)
981-985 Norway (Table G7)
991-995 Sweden (Table G7)

Spain and Portugal. Spain (General)

1001-1004 General works (Table G7 modified)
1005.A-Z Spain (Local), A-Z
1011-1015 Portugal (Table G7)
1021-1025 Switzerland (Table G7)

Balkan States

1031 General works
1036-1040 Albania (Table G7)
1041-1045 Bulgaria (Table G7)
1061-1065 Romania (Table G7)
1071-1075 Yugoslavia (Table G7)
1077.A-Z Other European regions or countries, A-Z

e. g.

1077.C87 Croatia
1077.F5 Finland
1077.L35 Latvia
1077.L5 Lithuania
1077.L9 Luxembourg
1077.M43 Malta
1077.U47 Ukraine

Asia

1081 General works
1091-1095 Afghanistan (Table G7)
1101-1105 Arabia (Table G7)
1121-1125 China (Table G7)
1131-1135 India (Table G7)
1136-1140 Pakistan (Table G7)

Indochina

1141 General works
1151-1155 Vietnam. Annam (Table G7)
1161-1165 Cambodia (Table G7)
1191-1195 Thailand. Siam (Table G7)
1201-1205 Malaysia (Table G7)
1211 East Indies
1221-1225 Indonesia (Table G7)
1231-1235 Philippines (Table G7)
1241-1245 Japan (Table G7)

Cartography
Maps. By region or country
Other regions or countries
Asia -- Continued
1251-1255 Korea (Table G7)
1261-1265 Iran. Persia (Table G7)
Russia in Asia
1271 General works
1281-1285 Central Asia (Table G7)
1291-1295 Siberia (Table G7)
1301-1305 Turkey (Table G7)
Armenia
see GA935.A7
1321-1325 Israel. Palestine (Table G7)
1331-1335 Syria (Table G7)
1340.A-Z Other Asian regions or countries, A-Z
Africa
1341 General works
North Africa
Including Northeast Africa
1346 General works
1348-1352 Morocco (Table G7)
1358-1362 Algeria (Table G7)
1368-1372 Tunisia (Table G7)
1378-1382 Libya (Table G7)
1388-1392 Egypt (Table G7)
1398-1402 Sudan (Table G7)
1408-1412 Canary Islands (Table G7)
1414.A-Z Other regions or countries, A-Z
1418 Sudan region and the Sahara
East Africa
1428 General works
1434-1438 Ethiopia (Table G7)
1439-1443 Afars and Issas (Table G7)
1444-1448 Somalia (Table G7)
1454-1458 Kenya (Table G7)
1464-1468 Uganda (Table G7)
1474-1478 Rwanda (Table G7)
1484-1488 Burundi (Table G7)
1494-1498 Tanzania (Table G7)
1499.A-Z Other regions or countries, A-Z
Central Africa
1500 General works
1508-1512 Central African Republic (Table G7)
1518-1522 Gabon (Table G7)
1528-1532 Congo (Brazzaville) (Table G7)
1538-1542 Zaire. Congo (Democratic Republic) (Table G7)

Cartography
Maps. By region or country
Other regions or countries
Africa
Central Africa -- Continued

1543.A-Z	Other regions or countries, A-Z
	West Africa
1550	General works
1558-1562	Mauritania (Table G7)
1568-1572	Senegal (Table G7)
1578-1582	Liberia (Table G7)
1588-1592	Nigeria (Table G7)
1598-1602	Cameroon (Table G7)
1603.A-Z	Other regions or countries, A-Z
	Southern Africa
1604	General works
1608-1612	Zambia (Table G7)
1618-1622	Malawi (Table G7)
1628-1632	Mozambique (Table G7)
1638-1642	Namibia. South-West Africa (Table G7)
1648-1652	Zimbabwe. Rhodesia (Table G7)
1658-1662	South Africa (Table G7)
1668-1672	Madagascar (Table G7)
1673.A-Z	Other regions or countries, A-Z
1681-1685	Australia (Table G7)
1765-1769	New Zealand (Table G7)
	Pacific islands
1771	General works
1776	Marshall Islands

Physical geography
Cf. GC1+ Oceanography
Cf. QC851+ Meteorology. Climatology
Cf. QE1+ Geology
Cf. QH1+ Natural history
Cf. QK1+ Botany
Cf. QL1+ Zoology
Cf. S590+ Soils
Periodicals see G1
Societies see G2+
3 Congresses
Collected works (nonserial)
5 Several authors
9 Individual authors
10 Dictionaries. Encyclopedias
11 History
Philosophy. Relation to other topics. Methodology
21 General works
21.5.A-Z Special methods, A-Z
21.5.E44 Electronic data processing
21.5.M33 Mathematics
21.5.R43 Remote sensing
21.5.S55 Simulation methods
21.5.S7 Statistical methods
Study and teaching. Research
23 General works
24 Problems, exercises, examinations
25 Fieldwork
25.5 Laboratory manuals
By region or country
26 United States
26.2.A-Z Other regions or countries, A-Z
27 Museums. Exhibitions
Arrange by author
General works, treatises, and advanced textbooks
51 Early through 1800
53 1801-1974
54.5 1975-
55 Elementary textbooks
55.5 Outlines, syllabi
55.6 Pictorial works
58 Juvenile works
59 Popular works
59.5 Addresses, essays, lectures
59.6 Handbooks, tables, etc.
60 General special (Special aspects of the subject as a whole)
By region or country

By region or country -- Continued
America
111 General works
North America
115 General works
United States
121 General works
124.A-Z By region, A-Z
e.g.
124.N4 New England
126.A-.W By state, A-W
Canada
131 General works
132.A-Z By region, island, province, or state, A-Z
Mexico
133 General works
134.A-Z By region, island, province, or state, A-Z
Central America
136 General works
139.A-Z By country, A-Z
West Indies. Caribbean Area
142 General works
143.A-Z By island or country, A-Z
South America
144 General works
151 Argentina
153 Bolivia
155 Brazil
156 Chile
157 Colombia
158 Ecuador
Guianas
159 General works
160 Guyana (British Guiana)
161 Suriname (Dutch Guiana)
162 French Guiana
163 Paraguay
165 Peru
167 Uruguay
169 Venezuela
South Atlantic islands
170 General works
170.2.A-Z By region, island, province, or state, A-Z
Europe
171 General works
174 Northern Europe
178 Mediterranean Basin

By region or country
Europe -- Continued
Great Britain. England
181 General works
184.A-Z England. By region or county, A-Z
Northern Ireland
186 General works
189.A-Z By region, island, province, or state, A-Z
Scotland
191 General works
194.A-Z By region, island, province, or state, A-Z
Wales
196 General works
199.A-Z By region, island, province, or state, A-Z
Ireland (Eire)
200 General works
200.2.A-Z By region, island, province, or state, A-Z
Austria
201 General works
204.A-Z By region, island, province, or state, A-Z
Bulgaria
205 General works
205.2.A-Z By region, island, province, or state, A-Z
Czechoslovakia
205.4 General works
205.5.A-Z By region, island, province, or state, A-Z
Finland
205.7 General works
205.8.A-Z By region, island, province, or state, A-Z
France
206 General works
209.A-Z By region, island, province, or state, A-Z
Germany
Including West Germany
211 General works
214.A-Z By region, island, province, or state, A-Z
East Germany
215 General works
215.2.A-Z By region, island, province, or state, A-Z
Greece
216 General works
219.A-Z By region, island, province, or state, A-Z
Hungary
220 General works
220.2.A-Z By region, island, province, or state, A-Z
Italy
221 General works

By region or country
Europe
Italy -- Continued
224.A-Z By region, island, province, or state, A-Z
Low countries
225 General works
Belgium
226 General works
229.A-Z By region, island, province, or state, A-Z
Netherlands
231 General works
234.A-Z By region, island, province, or state, A-Z
235 Luxemburg
Poland
235.4 General works
235.5.A-Z By region, island, province, or state, A-Z
Romania
235.7 General works
235.8.A-Z By region, island, province, or state, A-Z
Russia
236 General works
239.A-Z By region, island, province, or state, A-Z
Scandinavia
240 General works
Denmark
241 General works
244.A-Z By region, island, province, or state, A-Z
Norway
246 General works
249.A-Z By region, island, province, or state, A-Z
Sweden
251 General works
254.A-Z By region, island, province, or state, A-Z
Spain
256 General works
259.A-Z By region, island, province, or state, A-Z
Portugal
261 General works
264.A-Z By region, island, province, or state, A-Z
Switzerland
266 General works
269.A-Z By region, island, province, or state, A-Z
Yugoslavia
275 General works
275.2.A-Z By region, island, province, or state, A-Z
276.A-Z Other regions or countries, A-Z
e.g.

By region or country
Europe
Other regions or countries, A-Z -- Continued
276.A35 Alps
Asia
280 General works
Near East. Middle East
281 General works
283 Syria
284 Israel
285 Saudi Arabia. Arabian Peninsula
286 Iraq
287 Jordan
288 Iran
289 Lebanon
289.2 Turkey
289.4.A-Z Other regions or countries, A-Z
290 Central Asia
293 Himalaya Mountains
Southern Asia. Southeast Asia
295 General works
297 Afghanistan
299 Pakistan
India
301 General works
302.A-Z By region, island, province, or state, A-Z
303 Sri Lanka
304 Burma. Myanmar
305 Vietnam
306 Thailand
Malaysia
308 General works
309.A-Z By region, island, province, or state, A-Z
Indonesia
311 General works
312.A-Z By region, island, province, or state, A-Z
313 Philippines
314.A-Z Other regions or countries, A-Z
Eastern Asia. Far East
315 General works
China
316 General works
317 Tibet
For Himalaya Mountains see GB293
318.A-Z Other regions or provinces, A-Z
e.g.
318.S5 Sinkiang. East Turkestan

GB

By region or country
Asia
Eastern Asia. Far East -- Continued
318.3 Mongolia
318.5 Taiwan
319 Korea
Including South Korea
319.5 North Korea
322 Japan
Northern Asia. Siberia. Russia in Asia
325 General works
326 Soviet Central Asia
327.A-Z Other regions or republics, A-Z
328.A-Z Islands of the Pacific, A-Z
Africa
330 General works
331 North Africa
331.5 Algeria
332 Egypt
334 Libya
336 Morocco
337 Tunisia
338 Sahara
349 Sub-Saharan Africa
Central Africa
350 General works
351 Congo (Brazzaville)
352 Zaire. Congo (Democratic Republic)
West Africa
355 General works
356 Nigeria
359.A-Z Other regions or countries, A-Z
e.g.
359.A5 Angola
359.L5 Liberia
359.S6 Spanish Sahara. Rio de Oro
Southern Africa
360 General works
362 Mozambique
363 South Africa
365.A-Z Other regions or countries, A-Z
e.g.
365.S55 Southern Rhodesia. Zimbabwe
365.S6 South-West Africa. Namibia
365.Z3 Zambia
Eastern Africa. East Africa
370 General works

By region or country
Africa
Eastern Africa. East Africa -- Continued
375.A-Z By region or country, A-Z
e.g.
375.E8 Ethiopia
375.K4 Kenya
375.T3 Tanzania
375.U3 Uganda
378.A-Z Islands, A-Z
e.g.
378.C3 Canary Islands
378.M3 Madagascar
Australia
381 General works
384.A-Z By region, island, province, or state, A-Z
New Zealand
385 General works
386.A-Z By region, island, province, or state, A-Z
Pacific islands
391 General works
394.A-Z By island or group of islands, A-Z
395 Arctic regions
397 Antarctica
398 Arid regions
Cf. GB611+ Geomorphology
Cf. GB841 Hydrology
398.5 Cold regions
Cf. GB641+ Geomorphology
Cf. GB2401+ Ice, glaciers, ice sheets, sea ice
398.7 Tropics
Cf. GB446 Geomorphology
Geomorphology. Landforms. Terrain
Cf. QE500+ Dynamic and structural geology
400 Periodicals. Societies. Serials
400.2 Congresses
400.3 Dictionaries. Encyclopedias
Methodology
400.4 General works
400.42.A-Z Special methods, A-Z
400.42.A35 Aerial photography in geomorphology
400.42.A8 Astronautics in geomorphology
400.42.E4 Electronic data processing
400.42.M3 Mapping
400.42.M33 Mathematical models
400.42.M34 Mathematics
400.42.R4 Remote sensing

Geomorphology. Landforms. Terrain
Methodology
Special methods, A-Z -- Continued

400.42.S7	Statistical methods
400.42.T73	Tracers
	Study and teaching. Research
400.5	General works
	By region or country
400.6	United States
400.65.A-Z	Other regions or countries, A-Z
400.7	History
	General works, treatises, and advanced textbooks
401	1801-1974
401.5	1975-
402	Elementary textbooks
403	Pictorial works
405	Addresses, essays, lectures
406	General special
	By region or country
	America
425	General works
	North America
427	General works
	United States
427.5	General works
428.A-Z	By region or state, A-Z
428.5.A-Z	Other regions or countries, A-Z
	Central America
429	General works
430.A-Z	By region or country, A-Z
	South America
431	General works
432.A-Z	By region or country, A-Z
434.A-Z	South Atlantic islands, A-Z
	Europe
435	General works
436.A-Z	By region or country, A-Z
	Asia
437	General works
438.A-Z	By region or country, A-Z
	Africa
439	General works
440.A-Z	By region or country, A-Z
441	Australia
442	New Zealand
444	Arctic regions
445	Antarctica

Geomorphology. Landforms. Terrain
By region or country -- Continued
446 Tropics
447 Climatic geomorphology
447.3 Environmental geomorphology
448 Slopes
Coasts
Including beaches, coast changes, and shorelines
Cf. D-F, History and description of individual countries
Cf. GC1+ Oceanography
Cf. QE39 Submarine geology
Cf. TC330+ Shore protection
450 Periodicals. Societies. Serials
450.2 Congresses
450.4 Dictionaries. Encyclopedias
450.6 Terminology. Abbreviations. Notations
450.8 Instruments and apparatus
General works, treatises, and textbooks
451 1801-1974
451.2 1975-
452 Pictorial works
452.2 Handbooks, tables, etc.
453 Juvenile works
454.A-Z By special coastal landform, A-Z
For landforms of special regions see GB455+
454.B3 Beach cusps
454.F5 Fjords
454.I54 Inlets
454.P46 Peninsulas
454.R5 Ripple marks
454.S3 Sand
454.S66 Spits
454.W3 Washover fans
By region
Cf. GB460.A1+ Coasts, shorelines, etc. By continent or country
Arctic Ocean
455 General works
455.2 Alaska
455.3 Canada
455.4 Greenland
455.6 Norway
455.7 Finland
455.8 Russia. Siberia
456 Antarctica
Atlantic Ocean
457 General works

Geomorphology. Landforms. Terrain
Coasts
By region
Atlantic Ocean -- Continued
Western Atlantic see GB459+
Northeastern Atlantic Ocean
457.115 General works
457.12 Iceland. Faroe Islands
North Sea. Skagerrak
457.2 General works
British Isles. England
Including coasts on the Atlantic Ocean and Irish Sea
457.21 General works
457.22 Scotland
457.24 Hebrides
457.25 Wales
457.26 Isle of Man
457.27 Northern Ireland
457.28 Channel Islands
457.285 Ireland (Eire)
457.3 Norway
457.4 Denmark
457.5 Germany
457.53 Netherlands
457.54 Belgium
Baltic Sea. Cattegat
457.545 General works
457.55 Denmark
457.56 Bornholm
457.57.A-Z Other islands of the Baltic, A-Z
457.58 Germany
457.59 Poland
457.6 Russia. Baltic States
457.62 Finland
457.63 Sweden
457.64 English Channel
For Channel Islands see GB457.28
457.66 France
457.68 Biscay, Bay of
457.69 Spain
457.695 Portugal
Mediterranean Sea
457.71 General works
457.72 Spain
457.73 France
457.74 Italy
457.75 Balkan Peninsula

Geomorphology. Landforms. Terrain
Coasts
By region
Atlantic Ocean
Northeastern Atlantic Ocean
Mediterranean Sea -- Continued

457.755 Black Sea. Azov, Sea of
457.76 Turkey. Near East
457.78 North Africa
457.79.A-Z Islands of the Mediterranean, A-Z
457.8 African coast
457.82.A-Z Eastern Atlantic Islands, A-Z
e.g.
457.82.C3 Cape Verde Islands
457.82.M3 Madeira Islands
457.822 Caspian Sea

Indian Ocean
457.825 General works
457.83 African coast
457.84.A-Z Islands, A-Z
457.85 Red Sea. Gulf of Aden
457.86 Persian Gulf. Gulf Of Oman
457.87 Arabian Sea
457.88 Bengal, Bay of

Pacific Ocean
458 General works
Northwestern Pacific Ocean
458.1 General works
458.15 Gulf of Siam
458.2 China Sea
458.25 Yellow Sea
458.3 Japan Sea
458.33 Okhotsk, Sea of. Western Bering Sea
458.35.A-Z North Pacific islands, A-Z
South Pacific
458.4 General works
458.5 Australia
458.55 New Zealand
South Pacific islands
458.6 General works
458.62.A-Z By island or group of islands, A-Z
Eastern Pacific Ocean
458.67 General works
458.7 Alaska. Eastern Bering Sea
British Columbia
458.73 General works
458.75 Vancouver Island

Geomorphology. Landforms. Terrain
Coasts
By region
Pacific Ocean
Eastern Pacific Ocean -- Continued
458.8 United States
458.85 Mexico
458.87 Central America
458.9 South America
Western Atlantic Ocean
459 General works
459.15 South America
459.17 Caribbean Sea
459.2.A-Z West Indies, A-Z
Gulf of Mexico
459.25 General works
459.3 Florida Keys
United States
459.4 General works
459.5.A-Z Inland waters, A-Z
459.6 Nova Scotia. New Brunswick. Quebec
459.7 Newfoundland and Labrador
By continent or country
Class here only works dealing with the coast or coasts of a continent or country that borders more than one of the water areas in GB455+
For works dealing with a coast bordering on only one of these water areas see GB455+
America
460.A1 General works
North America
460.A2 General works
460.A25 Central America
460.A3 South America
460.A4 Europe
460.A5 Asia
460.A6 Africa
Australia see GB458.5
Antarctica see GB456
460.A7-Z By country, A-Z
Reefs
Cf. QE565+ Geology
461 General works
America
463 General works
United States
464 General works

Geomorphology. Landforms. Terrain
Reefs
America
United States -- Continued
465.A-.W By state, A-W
466.A-Z By reef, A-Z
468.112-.995 Other countries (Table G2b)
Add country number in table to GB468
Islands
Cf. G500 Voyages and travels
471 General works
472.5.A-Z Special types of islands, A-Z
472.5.F55 Floating islands
America
473 General works
United States
474 General works
475.A-.W By state, A-W
476.A-Z By island, A-Z
478.112-.995 Other countries (Table G2b)
Add country number in table to GB478
Earth movements, subsidences, etc. see QE598+
Hypsometry. Tables of heights see QC895
Leveling see TA606+
Mountains. Orography
Cf. GV199.8+ Mountaineering
Cf. QE521.5+ Volcanoes
Cf. QE621+ Mountain building
500 Periodicals. Societies. Serials
500.5 Dictionaries. Encyclopedias
General works
500.9 Early through 1800
501 1801-1974
501.2 1975-
511 Popular works
512 Juvenile works
515 Mountain passes
By region or country
America
521 General works
United States
525 General works
525.5.A-Z By region, state, or mountain range, A-Z
530.A-Z Other countries, A-Z
531.A-Z By region or mountain range, A-Z (except United States)
Europe

Geomorphology. Landforms. Terrain
Mountains. Orography
By region or country
Europe -- Continued
541 General works
542.A-Z By country, A-Z
543.A-Z By region or mountain range, A-Z
e.g.
Alps
543.A4 General works
543.A5A-.A5Z Special, A-Z
e.g.
543.A5J8 Jungfrau
Asia
544 General works
545.A-Z By country, A-Z
546.A-Z By region or mountain range, A-Z
e.g.
Himalaya
546.H5 General works
546.H6A-.H6Z Special, A-Z
e.g.
546.H6E84 Everest
Africa
547 General works
548.A-Z By country, A-Z
549.A-Z By region or mountain range, A-Z
551 Australia
552 New Zealand
553 Pacific islands
554 Arctic regions
555 Antarctica
Other natural landforms
Fluvial geomorphology
Including floodplains, river channels, valleys, watersheds, arroyos, canyons, and wadis
561 General works
562 General special
563 America
United States
564 General works
565.A-.W By state, A-W
566.A-Z Special, A-Z
568.112-.995 Other countries (Table G2b)
Add country number in table to GB568
Peneplains, piedmonts, plains, plateaus, steppes, tundras
Including cuestas, grasslands, llanos, prairies, and savannas

Geomorphology. Landforms. Terrain
Other natural landforms
Peneplains, piedmonts, plains, plateaus, steppes, tundras -- Continued

571 General works
572 General special
573 America
United States
574 General works
575.A-.W By state, A-W
576.A-Z Special, A-Z
578.112-.995 Other countries (Table G2b)
Add country number in table to GB578

Glacial landforms
Including drumlins
581 General works
582 General special
583 America
United States
584 General works
585.A-.W By state, A-W
586.A-Z Special, A-Z
588.112-.995 Other countries (Table G2b)
Add country number in table to GB588

Alluvial fans, deltas, terraces
591 General works
592 General special
593 America
United States
594 General works
595.A-.W By state, A-W
596.A-Z Special, A-Z
598.112-.995 Other countries (Table G2b)
Add country number in table to GB598

Karst landforms
599 Periodicals. Societies. Serials
599.2 Congresses
600 General works
By region or country
United States
600.2 General works
600.3.A-Z By region or state, A-Z
600.4.A-Z Other regions or countries, A-Z
600.5 Juvenile works
600.6 Addresses, essays, lectures

Geomorphology. Landforms. Terrain
Other natural landforms
Karst landforms -- Continued
Caves. Speleology
Cf. GN783+ Prehistoric archaeology
Cf. GV200.6+ Caves and caving

601.A1	Periodicals. Societies. Serials
601.A2	Congresses
601.A4	History
601.A6-Z	General works
601.2	Juvenile works
601.3	Popular works
601.4	Pictorial works
	Methodology
601.5	General works
601.52.A-Z	Special methods, A-Z
601.52.M34	Mapping
601.52.S95	Surveying
	Biography
601.58	Collective
601.6.A-Z	Individual, A-Z
601.8	Marine caves
	Cave exploration (Recreation) see GV200.6+
	Cave exploration (Technical) see GB601+
	By region or country
	America
603	General works
	United States
604	General works
605.A-Z	By region or state, A-Z
606.A-Z	By cave, A-Z
608.112-.995	Other (Table G2b) Add country number in table to GB608
609	Polje. Interior valleys
609.2	Sinkholes
609.4	Karren
	Deserts. Arid regions
611	General works
612	General special
613	America
	United States
614	General works
615.A-.W	By state, A-W
616.A-Z	Special, A-Z
618.112-.995	Other countries (Table G2b) Add country number in table to GB618

Geomorphology. Landforms. Terrain
Other natural landforms -- Continued
Wetlands
Including bogs, heaths, marshes, moors, peatbogs, swamps, etc.

621 General works
622 General special
623 America
United States
624 General works
625.A-.W By state, A-W
626.A-Z Special, A-Z
628.112-.995 Other countries (Table G2b)
Add country number in table to GB628

Dunes
631 General works
632 General special
633 America
United States
634 General works
635.A-.W By state, A-W
636.A-Z Special, A-Z
638.112-.995 Other countries (Table G2b)
Add country number in table to GB638

Frozen ground. Cold regions
Including aufeis, frost heaving, ice-wedge polygons, patterned ground, rock glaciers, and thermokarst

641 General works
642 General special
643 America
United States
644 General works
645.A-.W By state, A-W
646.A-Z Special, A-Z
648.112-.995 Other countries (Table G2b)
Add country number in table to GB648

649.A-Z Other, A-Z
649.D8 Duricrusts
649.E3 Earth pyramids
649.L3 Lava tubes
649.S3 Sand waves

Hydrology. Water
Cf. HD1690+ Water rights
Cf. QC920 Water in meteorology
Cf. QE39.5.P27 Paleohydrology
Cf. QE581 Aqueous erosion
Cf. QH541.15.E19 Ecohydrology
Cf. S494.5.W3 Water in agriculture
Cf. TC1+ Hydraulic engineering
Cf. TD201+ Water supply

651 Periodicals. Societies. Serials
652 Congresses
Collected works (nonserial)
653 Several authors
653.2 Individual authors
655 Dictionaries. Encyclopedias
655.5 Terminology. Abbreviations. Notation
Methodology
656 General works
656.2.A-Z Special methods, A-Z
656.2.A37 Aerial photography in meteorology
656.2.A9 Automation
656.2.C63 Computer programs
656.2.E42 Electromechanical analogies
656.2.E43 Electronic data processing
656.2.H9 Hydrologic models
656.2.M29 Mapping
656.2.M33 Mathematical models
656.2.M34 Mathematics
656.2.R3 Radar in hydrology
656.2.R34 Radioisotopes in hydrology
656.2.R44 Remote sensing
656.2.S7 Statistical methods
Communication of information
657 General works
657.2 Information services
Study and teaching. Research
658 General works
658.3 Problems, exercises, examinations
658.35 Activity programs
658.4 Fieldwork
658.5 Laboratory manuals
By region or country
658.7 United States
658.8.A-Z Other regions or countries, A-Z
659 Instruments and apparatus
Museums. Exhibitions
659.4 General works

Hydrology. Water
Museums. Exhibitions -- Continued
659.5.A-Z By region or country, A-Z
Under each country:
.x General works
.x2A-.x2Z Special. By city, A-Z
659.6 History
Biography
659.7 Collective
659.72.A-Z Individual, A-Z
General works, treatises, and advanced textbooks
659.9 Early through 1800
661 1801-1974
661.2 1975-
662 Outlines, syllabi
662.3 Juvenile works
662.4 Addresses, essays, lectures
662.5 Handbooks, tables, etc.
665 General special
671 Popular works
By region or country
Class here works on general hydrology
For groundwater and special types of bodies of water see GB1001+
Cf. GC1+ Oceanography
Cf. VK1+ Hydrography and navigation
North America
700 General works
United States
701 General works
705.A-Z By region or state, A-Z
For Hawaii see GB832
Canada
707 General works
708.A-Z By region or province, A-Z
Mexico
711 General works
712.A-Z By region or state, A-Z
Central America
714 General works
715.A-Z By region or country, A-Z
717 West Indies
South America
718 General works
719.A-Z By region or country, A-Z
Europe
720 General works

Hydrology. Water
By region or country
Europe -- Continued
Great Britain
721 General works
722.A-Z By region or country, A-Z
e.g.
722.S3 Scotland
Austria
725 General works
725.2.A-Z By region, etc., A-Z
Bulgaria
726 General works
726.2.A-Z By region, etc., A-Z
Czechoslovakia
727 General works
727.2.A-Z By region, etc., A-Z
Finland
727.4 General works
727.5.A-Z By region, etc., A-Z
France
728 General works
729.A-Z By region, etc., A-Z
Germany
Including West Germany
731 General works
732.A-Z By region, etc., A-Z
East Germany
733.5 General works
733.6.A-Z By region, etc., A-Z
Greece
734 General works
735.A-Z By region, etc., A-Z
Hungary
736 General works
736.2.A-Z By region, etc., A-Z
Italy
737 General works
738.A-Z By region, etc., A-Z
Low countries
739 General works
Belgium
740 General works
741.A-Z By region, etc., A-Z
Netherlands
743 General works
744.A-Z By region, etc., A-Z

Hydrology. Water
By region or country
Europe -- Continued
Poland
745 General works
745.2.A-Z By region, etc., A-Z
Romania
745.4 General works
745.5.A-Z By region, etc., A-Z
Russia
746 General works
747.A-Z By region, etc., A-Z
Scandinavia
748.5 General works
Denmark
749 General works
750.A-Z By region, etc., A-Z
Norway
752 General works
753.A-Z By region, etc., A-Z
Sweden
755 General works
756.A-Z By region, etc., A-Z
Spain
758 General works
759.A-Z By region, etc., A-Z
Portugal
761 General works
762.A-Z By region, etc., A-Z
Switzerland
767 General works
768.A-Z By region, etc., A-Z
Yugoslavia
771 General works
771.2.A-Z By region, etc., A-Z
772.A-Z Other European regions or countries, A-Z

Under each country:

.x	*General works*
.x2A-.x2Z	*Local, A-Z*

e.g.
772.C7-.C72 Crete
772.L8-.L82 Luxemburg
Asia
773 General works
Eastern Asia. Far East
773.2 General works
773.4 Burma. Myanmar

Hydrology. Water
By region or country
Asia
Eastern Asia. Far East -- Continued

773.6 Cambodia
773.8 Sri Lanka
China
774 General works
775.A-Z By region, etc., A-Z
776 Taiwan
India
777 General works
778.A-Z By region, etc., A-Z
Indonesia
779 General works
779.2.A-Z By region, etc., A-Z
Japan
781 General works
782.A-Z By region, etc., A-Z
783 Korea
783.5 Laos
784 Malaysia
785 Pakistan
Philippines
786 General works
786.2.A-Z By region, etc., A-Z
Russia in Asia. Siberia
787 General works
788.A-Z By region, etc., A-Z
790 Thailand
790.5 Vietnam
Middle East. Near East
791 General works
791.5 Cyprus
792 Iran
792.5 Iraq
793 Israel. Palestine
793.5 Jordan
794 Lebanon
794.5 Syria
794.6 Turkey
Arabian Peninsula. Arabia. Persian Gulf Region
795 General works
795.2 Bahrain
795.3 Kuwait
795.4 Oman
795.5 Qatar

Hydrology. Water
By region or country
Asia
Middle East. Near East
Arabian Peninsula. Arabia. Persian Gulf Region -- Continued

795.6 Saudi Arabia
795.7 United Arab Emirates
795.8 Yemen (Yemen Arab Republic)
795.85 Yemen (People's Democratic Republic). Southern Yemen
796.A-Z Other regions or countries, A-Z
797 Arab countries

Africa

800 General works

North Africa

800.2 General works
800.4 Algeria
801 Egypt
801.5 Libya
802 Morocco
802.5 Tunisia
803 Sahara
803.5.A-Z Other regions or countries, A-Z

Eastern Africa

804 General works
804.5 Ethiopia
805 Kenya
805.5 Somalia
806 Sudan
806.5 Tanzania
807 Uganda
807.5.A-Z Other regions or countries, A-Z

Central Africa

808 General works
808.5 Zaire. Congo (Democratic Republic)
809.A-Z Other regions or countries, A-Z

West Africa

812 General works
812.5 Ghana
813 Niger
813.5 Nigeria
814 Senegal
814.5 Upper Volta
815.A-Z Other regions or countries, A-Z

Southern Africa

817 General works

Hydrology. Water
By region or country
Africa
Southern Africa -- Continued
817.5 Malawi
818 Mozambique
818.5 South Africa
819 South-West Africa. Namibia
819.5 Zambia
820.A-Z Other regions or countries, A-Z
Australia
821 General works
822.A-Z By region, etc., A-Z
823 New Zealand
Pacific islands
831 General works
832 Hawaii
833.A-Z Other islands or groups of islands, A-Z
835 Arctic regions
839 Antarctica
840 Tropics
841 Arid regions
842 Forest hydrology
For local see GB700+
Cf. SD425 Forests and water supply
843 Karst hydrology
For local see GB700+
844 Rangeland hydrology
For local see GB700+
845 Hydrological forecasting
848 Hydrologic cycle
850 Water transport phenomena
Natural water chemistry
Cf. GC100+ Properties of sea water
Cf. GC109+ Chemical oceanography
Cf. QD142 Water analysis
Cf. QH90+ Hydrobiology
855 General works
By region or country
United States
857 General works
857.2.A-Z By region or state, A-Z
857.3.A-Z Other regions or countries, A-Z
860 Color
Ground and surface waters
Watersheds. Runoff. Drainage
Cf. TD657+ Sanitary engineering

Hydrology. Water
Ground and surface waters
Watersheds. Runoff. Drainage -- Continued
980 General works
By region or country
United States
990 General works
991.A-Z By region or state, A-Z
992.A-Z Other regions or countries, A-Z
Groundwater. Hydrogeology
Cf. QE640+ Stratigraphy
1001 Periodicals. Societies. Serials
1001.2 Congresses
1001.4 Dictionaries. Encyclopedias
1001.5 Terminology. Abbreviations. Notations
Methodology
1001.7 General works
1001.72.A-Z Special methods, A-Z
1001.72.A37 Aerial photography
1001.72.A38 Aeronautics
1001.72.A83 Astronautics
1001.72.A9 Automation
1001.72.C55 Classification
1001.72.E42 Electromechanical analogies
1001.72.E45 Electronic data processsing
1001.72.F67 Forecasting
1001.72.G44 Geophysical well logging
1001.72.M32 Mapping
1001.72.M35 Mathematical models
1001.72.M37 Mathematics
1001.72.R32 Radar
1001.72.R34 Radioisotopes
1001.72.R42 Remote sensing
1001.72.S3 Sampling
1001.72.S7 Statistical methods
Communication of information
1001.8 General works
1001.82 Information services
Study and teaching. Research
1002 General works
1002.2 Problems, exercises, examinations
1002.25 Activity programs
1002.3 Fieldwork
1002.4 Laboratory manuals
By region or country
1002.5 United States
1002.6.A-Z Other regions or countries, A-Z

Hydrology. Water
Ground and surface waters
Groundwater. Hydrogeology -- Continued
1002.7 Instruments and apparatus
Biography
1002.73 Collective
1002.74.A-Z Individual, A-Z
General works
1002.8 Early through 1800
1003 1801-1974
1003.2 1975-
1003.6 Pictorial works
1003.7 Popular works
1003.8 Juvenile works
1004 Addresses, essays, lectures
1004.2 Handbooks, tables, etc.
1005 General special
By region or country
1011 America
1012 North America
United States
1015 General works
East. Atlantic coast
1016 General works
1016.3 New England
1016.5 Appalachian region
1016.6 Middle Atlantic States
1016.7 Lake region
1017 Mississippi Valley
1018 South. Gulf States
West
1019 General works
1020 Northwest
1021 Pacific Coast
1022 Southwest
1023 Yellowstone National Park
1025.A-.W By state, A-W
1027.A-Z By spring, river, etc., A-Z
1029-1198 Other regions or countries (Table G3 modified)
Add country number in table to GB1000
Antarctic regions
1197 General works
1197.5.A-Z Local, A-Z
1197.6 Groundwater exploration
1197.7 Groundwater flow
Cf. TC176 Underground flow
1197.77 Groundwater recharge

Hydrology. Water
Ground and surface waters
Groundwater. Hydrogeology
Saltwater encroachment. Salinity
1197.8 General works
By region or country
United States
1197.82 General works
1197.83.A-Z By region or state, A-Z
1197.84.A-Z Other regions or countries, A-Z
Springs. Hot springs
Cf. RA794 Health resorts, spas, etc.
Cf. TN923+ Mineral waters
1198 General works
By region or country
United States
1198.2 General works
1198.3.A-Z By region or state, A-Z
1198.4.A-Z Other regions or countries, A-Z
Geysers
1198.5 General works
By region or country
United States
1198.6 General works
1198.7.A-Z By region or state, A-Z
1198.8.A-Z Other regions or countries, A-Z
Aquifers
1199 General works
By region or country
United States
1199.2 General works
1199.3.A-Z By region or state, A-Z
1199.4.A-Z Other regions or countries, A-Z
Geothermal resources
Cf. TK1041+ Production of electric energy from heat
1199.5 General works
By region or country
United States
1199.6 General works
1199.7.A-Z By region or state, A-Z
1199.8.A-Z Other regions or countries, A-Z
Rivers. Stream measurements
Including bayous
For technique of stream measuring see TC175+
Cf. GB561+ Floodplains, river channels, valleys, watersheds, etc.
1201 Periodicals. Societies. Serials

Hydrology. Water
Ground and surface waters
Rivers. Stream measurements -- Continued

1201.2	Congresses
1201.4	Dictionaries. Encyclopedias.
1201.5	Terminology. Abbreviations. Notations
	Methodology
1201.7	General works
1201.72.A-Z	Special methods, A-Z
1201.72.A37	Aerial photography
1201.72.A38	Aeronautics
1201.72.A83	Astronautics
1201.72.A9	Automation
1201.72.C55	Classification
1201.72.E42	Electromechanical analogies
1201.72.E45	Electronic data processsing
1201.72.F67	Forecasting
1201.72.G44	Geophysical well logging
1201.72.M32	Mapping
1201.72.M35	Mathematical models
1201.72.M37	Mathematics
1201.72.R32	Radar
1201.72.R34	Radioisotopes
1201.72.R42	Remote sensing
1201.72.S3	Sampling
1201.72.S7	Statistical methods
	Communication of information
1201.8	General works
1201.82	Information services
	Study and teaching. Research
1202	General works
1202.2	Problems, exercises, examinations
1202.25	Activity programs
1202.3	Fieldwork
1202.4	Laboratory manuals
	By region or country
1202.5	United States
1202.6.A-Z	Other regions or countries, A-Z
1202.7	Instruments and apparatus
	General works
1202.8	Early through 1800
1203	1801-1974
1203.2	1975-
1203.6	Pictorial works
1203.7	Popular works
1203.8	Juvenile works
1204	Addresses, essays, lectures

Hydrology. Water
Ground and surface waters
Rivers. Stream measurements -- Continued
1204.2 Handbooks, tables, etc.
1205 General special
1207 Streamflow
By region or country
1211 America
1212 North America
United States
1215 General works
East. Atlantic coast
1216 General works
1216.3 New England
1216.5 Appalachian region
1216.6 Chesapeake Bay Watershed
1216.7 Lake region
1217 Great Lakes watershed
1218 South. Gulf States
West
1219 General works
1220 Northwest
1221 Pacific Coast
1222 Southwest
1223 Yellowstone National Park
1225.A-.W By state, A-W
1227.A-Z By spring, river, etc., A-Z
1229-1398 Other regions or countries (Table G3)
Add country number in table to GB1200
Ice on rivers
1398.2 General works
By region or country
United States
1398.3 General works
1398.4.A-Z By region or state, A-Z
1398.5.A-Z Other regions or countries, A-Z
River temperatures
1398.6 General works
By region or country
United States
1398.7 General works
1398.8.A-Z By region or state, A-Z
1398.9.A-Z Other regions or countries, A-Z
Floods
Cf. TC530+ Flood control
1399 General works
1399.2 Flood forecasting

Hydrology. Water
 Ground and surface waters
  Rivers. Stream measurements
   Floods -- Continued
    By region or country
     United States

1399.3 General works
1399.4.A-Z By region or state, A-Z
1399.5.A-Z Other regions or countries, A-Z

River sediments

1399.6 General works

By region or country
 United States

1399.7 General works
1399.8.A-Z By region or state, A-Z
1399.9.A-Z Other regions or countries, A-Z

Waterfalls

1401 Periodicals. Societies. Serials
1401.2 Congresses
1401.4 Dictionaries. Encyclopedias.
1401.5 Terminology. Abbreviations. Notations

Methodology

1401.7 General works
1401.72.A-Z Special methods, A-Z
1401.72.A37 Aerial photography
1401.72.A38 Aeronautics
1401.72.A83 Astronautics
1401.72.A9 Automation
1401.72.C55 Classification
1401.72.E42 Electromechanical analogies
1401.72.E45 Electronic data processsing
1401.72.F67 Forecasting
1401.72.G44 Geophysical well logging
1401.72.M32 Mapping
1401.72.M35 Mathematical models
1401.72.M37 Mathematics
1401.72.R32 Radar
1401.72.R34 Radioisotopes
1401.72.R42 Remote sensing
1401.72.S3 Sampling
1401.72.S7 Statistical methods

Communication of information

1401.8 General works
1401.82 Information services

Study and teaching. Research

1402 General works
1402.2 Problems, exercises, examinations

Hydrology. Water
Ground and surface waters
Rivers. Stream measurements
Waterfalls
Study and teaching. Research -- Continued

1402.25 Activity programs
1402.3 Fieldwork
1402.4 Laboratory manuals
By region or country
1402.5 United States
1402.6.A-Z Other regions or countries, A-Z
1402.7 Instruments and apparatus
General works
1402.8 Early through 1800
1403 1801-1974
1403.2 1975-
1403.6 Pictorial works
1403.7 Popular works
1403.8 Juvenile works
1404 Addresses, essays, lectures
1405 General special
By region or country
1411 America
1412 North America
United States
1415 General works
East. Atlantic coast
1416 General works
1416.3 New England
1416.5 Appalachian region
1416.7 Lake region
1417 Mississippi Valley
1418 South. Gulf States
West
1419 General works
1420 Northwest
1421 Pacific Coast
1422 Southwest
1423 Yellowstone National Park
1425.A-.W By state, A-W
1427.A-Z By spring, river, etc., A-Z
1429-1598 Other regions or countries (Table G3)
Add country number in table to GB1400

Lakes. Limnology
For freshwater biology of lakes see QH98
Cf. QE39.5.P3 Paleolimnology

1601 Periodicals. Societies. Serials

Hydrology. Water
Ground and surface waters
Lakes. Limnology -- Continued

1601.2 Congresses
1601.4 Dictionaries. Encyclopedias.
1601.5 Terminology. Abbreviations. Notations
Methodology
1601.7 General works
1601.72.A-Z Special methods, A-Z
1601.72.A37 Aerial photography
1601.72.A38 Aeronautics
1601.72.A83 Astronautics
1601.72.A9 Automation
1601.72.C55 Classification
1601.72.E42 Electromechanical analogies
1601.72.E45 Electronic data processsing
1601.72.F67 Forecasting
1601.72.G44 Geophysical well logging
1601.72.M32 Mapping
1601.72.M35 Mathematical models
1601.72.M37 Mathematics
1601.72.R32 Radar
1601.72.R34 Radioisotopes
1601.72.R42 Remote sensing
1601.72.S3 Sampling
1601.72.S7 Statistical methods
Communication of information
1601.8 General works
1601.82 Information services
Study and teaching. Research
1602 General works
1602.2 Problems, exercises, examinations
1602.25 Activity programs
1602.3 Fieldwork
1602.4 Laboratory manuals
By region or country
1602.5 United States
1602.6.A-Z Other regions or countries, A-Z
1602.7 Instruments and apparatus
General works
1602.8 Early through 1800
1603 1801-1974
1603.2 1975-
1603.6 Pictorial works
1603.7 Popular works
1603.8 Juvenile works
1604 Addresses, essays, lectures

Hydrology. Water
Ground and surface waters
Lakes. Limnology -- Continued

1604.2	Handbooks, tables, etc.
1605	General special
	By region or country
1611	America
1612	North America
	United States
1615	General works
	East. Atlantic coast
1616	General works
1616.3	New England
1616.5	Appalachian region
1616.7	Lake region
1617	Mississippi Valley
1618	South. Gulf States
	West
1619	General works
1620	Northwest
1621	Pacific Coast
1622	Southwest
1623	Yellowstone National Park
1625.A-.W	By state, A-W
1627.A-Z	By spring, river, etc., A-Z
	Great Lakes
1627.G8	General works
	Lake Ontario
1627.G81	General works
1627.G82A-.G82Z	By region, A-Z
	Lake Erie
1627.G83	General works
1627.G84A-.G84Z	By region, A-Z e.g.
1627.G84S2	Sandusky Bay
	Lake Huron
1627.G85	General works
1627.G86A-.G86Z	By region, A-Z
	Lake Michigan
1627.G87	General works
1627.G88A-.G88Z	By region, A-Z
	Lake Superior
1627.G89	General works
1627.G895A-.G895Z	By region, A-Z
1629-1798	Other regions or countries (Table G3) Add country number in table to GB1600
	Ice on lakes

GB

Hydrology. Water
Ground and surface waters
Lakes. Limnology
Ice on lakes -- Continued
1798.2 General works
By region or country
United States
1798.3 General works
1798.4.A-Z By region or state, A-Z
1798.5.A-Z Other regions or countries, A-Z
Lake temperatures
1798.6 General works
By region or country
United States
1798.7 General works
1798.8.A-Z By region or state, A-Z
1798.9.A-Z Other regions or countries, A-Z
Ponds
For freshwater biology see QH98
1801 Periodicals. Societies. Serials
1801.2 Congresses
1801.4 Dictionaries. Encyclopedias.
1801.5 Terminology. Abbreviations. Notations
Methodology
1801.7 General works
1801.72.A-Z Special methods, A-Z
1801.72.A37 Aerial photography
1801.72.A38 Aeronautics
1801.72.A83 Astronautics
1801.72.A9 Automation
1801.72.C55 Classification
1801.72.E42 Electromechanical analogies
1801.72.E45 Electronic data processsing
1801.72.F67 Forecasting
1801.72.G44 Geophysical well logging
1801.72.M32 Mapping
1801.72.M35 Mathematical models
1801.72.M37 Mathematics
1801.72.R32 Radar
1801.72.R34 Radioisotopes
1801.72.R42 Remote sensing
1801.72.S3 Sampling
1801.72.S7 Statistical methods
Communication of information
1801.8 General works
1801.82 Information services
Study and teaching. Research

Hydrology. Water
Ground and surface waters
Ponds
Study and teaching. Research -- Continued

1802 General works
1802.2 Problems, exercises, examinations
1802.25 Activity programs
1802.3 Fieldwork
1802.4 Laboratory manuals
By region or country
1802.5 United States
1802.6.A-Z Other regions or countries, A-Z
1802.7 Instruments and apparatus
General works
1802.8 Early through 1800
1803 1801-1974
1803.2 1975-
1803.6 Pictorial works
1803.7 Popular works
1803.8 Juvenile works
1804 Addresses, essays, lectures
1804.2 Handbooks, tables, etc.
1805 General special
By region or country
1811 America
1812 North America
United States
1815 General works
East. Atlantic coast
1816 General works
1816.3 New England
1816.5 Appalachian region
1816.7 Lake region
1817 Mississippi Valley
1818 South. Gulf States
West
1819 General works
1820 Northwest
1821 Pacific Coast
1822 Southwest
1823 Yellowstone National Park
1825.A-.W By state, A-W
1827.A-Z By spring, river, etc., A-Z
1829-1998 Other regions or countries (Table G3)
Add country number in table to GB1800

Lagoons
For freshwater biology see QH98

Hydrology. Water
Ground and surface waters
Lagoons -- Continued

2201 Periodicals. Societies. Serials
2201.2 Congresses
2201.4 Dictionaries. Encyclopedias.
2201.5 Terminology. Abbreviations. Notations
Methodology
2201.7 General works
2201.72.A-Z Special methods, A-Z
2201.72.A37 Aerial photography
2201.72.A38 Aeronautics
2201.72.A83 Astronautics
2201.72.A9 Automation
2201.72.C55 Classification
2201.72.E42 Electromechanical analogies
2201.72.E45 Electronic data processsing
2201.72.F67 Forecasting
2201.72.G44 Geophysical well logging
2201.72.M32 Mapping
2201.72.M35 Mathematical models
2201.72.M37 Mathematics
2201.72.R32 Radar
2201.72.R34 Radioisotopes
2201.72.R42 Remote sensing
2201.72.S3 Sampling
2201.72.S7 Statistical methods
Communication of information
2201.8 General works
2201.82 Information services
Study and teaching. Research
2202 General works
2202.2 Problems, exercises, examinations
2202.25 Activity programs
2202.3 Fieldwork
2202.4 Laboratory manuals
By region or country
2202.5 United States
2202.6.A-Z Other regions or countries, A-Z
2202.7 Instruments and apparatus
General works
2202.8 Early through 1800
2203 1801-1974
2203.2 1975-
2203.6 Pictorial works
2203.7 Popular works
2203.8 Juvenile works

Hydrology. Water
Ground and surface waters
Lagoons -- Continued
2204 Addresses, essays, lectures
2204.2 Handbooks, tables, etc.
2205 General special
By region or country
2211 America
2212 North America
United States
2215 General works
East. Atlantic coast
2216 General works
2216.3 New England
2216.5 Appalachian region
2216.7 Lake region
2217 Mississippi Valley
2218 South. Gulf States
West
2219 General works
2220 Northwest
2221 Pacific Coast
2222 Southwest
2223 Yellowstone National Park
2225.A-.W By state, A-W
2227.A-Z By spring, river, etc., A-Z
2229-2398 Other regions or countries (Table G3)
Add country number in table to GB2200
Ice. Glaciers. Ice sheets. Sea ice
Cf. GB581+ Glacial landforms
Cf. GB1398.2+ Ice on rivers
Cf. GB1798.2+ Ice on lakes
Cf. QC981.8.I23 Climatology
Cf. QE575+ Glacial erosion
Cf. QE697+ Pleistocene. Glacial epoch
Cf. TA714 Avalanche control
Cf. VK1299 Icebergs and navigation
2401 Periodicals. Societies. Serials
2401.2 Congresses
2401.4 Dictionaries. Encyclopedias.
2401.5 Terminology. Abbreviations. Notations
Methodology
2401.7 General works
2401.72.A-Z Special methods, A-Z
2401.72.A37 Aerial photography
2401.72.A38 Aeronautics
2401.72.A83 Astronautics

Hydrology. Water
Ground and surface waters
Ice. Glaciers. Ice sheets. Sea ice
Methodology
Special methods, A-Z -- Continued

2401.72.A9 Automation
2401.72.C55 Classification
2401.72.E42 Electromechanical analogies
2401.72.E45 Electronic data processsing
2401.72.F67 Forecasting
2401.72.G44 Geophysical well logging
2401.72.M32 Mapping
2401.72.M35 Mathematical models
2401.72.M37 Mathematics
2401.72.R32 Radar
2401.72.R34 Radioisotopes
2401.72.R42 Remote sensing
2401.72.S3 Sampling
2401.72.S7 Statistical methods

Communication of information
2401.8 General works
2401.82 Information services

Study and teaching. Research
2402 General works
2402.2 Problems, exercises, examinations
2402.25 Activity programs
2402.3 Fieldwork
2402.4 Laboratory manuals
By region or country
2402.5 United States
2402.6.A-Z Other regions or countries, A-Z

2402.7 Instruments and apparatus

General works
2402.8 Early through 1800
2403 1801-1974
2403.2 1975-

2403.6 Pictorial works
2403.7 Popular works
2403.8 Juvenile works
2404 Addresses, essays, lectures
2404.2 Handbooks, tables, etc.
2405 General special

By region or country
2411 America
2412 North America
United States
2415 General works

Hydrology. Water
Ground and surface waters
Ice. Glaciers. Ice sheets. Sea ice
By region or country
United States -- Continued
East. Atlantic coast

2416 General works
2416.3 New England
2416.5 Appalachian region
2416.7 Lake region
2417 Mississippi Valley
2418 South. Gulf States
West
2419 General works
2420 Northwest
2421 Pacific Coast
2422 Southwest
2423 Yellowstone National Park
2425.A-.W By state, A-W
2427.A-Z By spring, river, etc., A-Z
2429-2598 Other regions or countries (Table G3)
Add country number in table to GB2400

Snow. Snow surveys
Cf. TA714 Snow mechanics. Avalanche control
2601 Periodicals. Societies. Serials
2601.2 Congresses
2601.4 Dictionaries. Encyclopedias.
2601.5 Terminology. Abbreviations. Notations
Methodology
2601.7 General works
2601.72.A-Z Special methods, A-Z
2601.72.A37 Aerial photography
2601.72.A38 Aeronautics
2601.72.A83 Astronautics
2601.72.A9 Automation
2601.72.C55 Classification
2601.72.E42 Electromechanical analogies
2601.72.E45 Electronic data processsing
2601.72.F67 Forecasting
2601.72.G44 Geophysical well logging
2601.72.M32 Mapping
2601.72.M35 Mathematical models
2601.72.M37 Mathematics
2601.72.R32 Radar
2601.72.R34 Radioisotopes
2601.72.R42 Remote sensing
2601.72.S3 Sampling

Hydrology. Water
Ground and surface waters
Snow. Snow surveys
Methodology
Special methods, A-Z -- Continued
2601.72.S7 Statistical methods
Communication of information
2601.8 General works
2601.82 Information services
Study and teaching. Research
2602 General works
2602.2 Problems, exercises, examinations
2602.25 Activity programs
2602.3 Fieldwork
2602.4 Laboratory manuals
By region or country
2602.5 United States
2602.6.A-Z Other regions or countries, A-Z
2602.7 Instruments and apparatus
General works
2602.8 Early through 1800
2603 1801-1974
2603.2 1975-
2603.6 Pictorial works
2603.7 Popular works
2603.8 Juvenile works
2604 Addresses, essays, lectures
2604.2 Handbooks, tables, etc.
2605 General special
By region or country
2611 America
2612 North America
United States
2615 General works
East. Atlantic coast
2616 General works
2616.3 New England
2616.5 Appalachian region
2616.7 Lake region
2617 Mississippi Valley
2618 South. Gulf States
West
2619 General works
2620 Northwest
2621 Pacific Coast
2622 Southwest
2623 Yellowstone National Park

Hydrology. Water
Ground and surface waters
Snow. Snow surveys
By region or country
United States -- Continued

2625.A-.W By state, A-W
2627.A-Z By spring, river, etc., A-Z
2629-2798 Other regions or countries (Table G3)
Add country number in table to GB2600

Hydrometeorology
Cf. QC851+ Meteorology. Climatology

2801 Periodicals. Societies. Serials
2801.2 Congresses
2801.4 Dictionaries. Encyclopedias.
2801.5 Terminology. Abbreviations. Notations

Methodology
2801.7 General works
2801.72.A-Z Special methods, A-Z
2801.72.A37 Aerial photography
2801.72.A38 Aeronautics
2801.72.A83 Astronautics
2801.72.A9 Automation
2801.72.C55 Classification
2801.72.E42 Electromechanical analogies
2801.72.E45 Electronic data processsing
2801.72.F67 Forecasting
2801.72.G44 Geophysical well logging
2801.72.M32 Mapping
2801.72.M35 Mathematical models
2801.72.M37 Mathematics
2801.72.R32 Radar
2801.72.R34 Radioisotopes
2801.72.R42 Remote sensing
2801.72.S3 Sampling
2801.72.S7 Statistical methods

Communication of information
2801.8 General works
2801.82 Information services

Study and teaching. Research
2802 General works
2802.2 Problems, exercises, examinations
2802.25 Activity programs
2802.3 Fieldwork
2802.4 Laboratory manuals

By region or country
2802.5 United States
2802.6.A-Z Other regions or countries, A-Z

Hydrology. Water
Ground and surface waters
Hydrometeorology -- Continued

2802.7 Instruments and apparatus
General works
2802.8 Early through 1800
2803 1801-1974
2803.2 1975-
2803.6 Pictorial works
2803.7 Popular works
2803.8 Juvenile works
2804 Addresses, essays, lectures
2804.2 Handbooks, tables, etc.
2805 General special
By region or country
2811 America
2812 North America
United States
2815 General works
East. Atlantic coast
2816 General works
2816.3 New England
2816.5 Appalachian region
2816.7 Lake region
2817 Mississippi Valley
2818 South. Gulf States
West
2819 General works
2820 Northwest
2821 Pacific Coast
2822 Southwest
2823 Yellowstone National Park
2825.A-.W By state, A-W
2827.A-Z By spring, river, etc., A-Z
2829-2998 Other regions or countries (Table G3)
Add country number in table to GB2800

Natural disasters
For specific disasters treated as historic events in individual countries, see the country in D-F
For works that discuss natural disasters in general as historic events see D24
Cf. GB1399+ Floods
Cf. GC219+ Tidal waves
Cf. GC225+ Storm surges
Cf. GF85 Hazardous environments (Human ecology)
Cf. HV8080.D5 Disaster operations (Police work)
Cf. QC929.A8 Avalanches
Cf. QC940.6+ Storms
Cf. QE521+ Volcanoes and earthquakes
Cf. QE598+ Earth movements
Cf. QH545.N3 Effect on plants and animals
Cf. SD420.5+ Forest fires
Cf. TF539 Damage to railroads

5000 Periodicals. Societies. Serials
5001 Congresses
Study and teaching. Research
5005 General works
By region or country
5007 United States
5008.A-Z Other regions or countries, A-Z
By region or country
5010 United States
5011.112-.995 Other regions or countries (Table G2b)
Add country number in table to GB5011
5014 General works
5018 Popular works
5019 Juvenile works
5020 Addresses, essays, lectures
5030 Natural disaster warning systems

Oceanography
Cf. GB651+ Hydrology
Cf. QC801+ Geophysics
Cf. QE39 Submarine geology
Cf. QE39.5.P25 Paleoceanography
Cf. QE350.2+ Geology of the Atlantic Ocean
Cf. QE350.4+ Geology of the Pacific Ocean
Cf. QH91+ Marine biology
Cf. QK103 Marine flora
Cf. QL120+ Marine fauna

1 Periodicals. Societies. Serials
2 Congresses
Collected works (nonserial)
6 Several authors
7 Individual authors
9 Dictionaries. Encyclopedias
9.2 Terminology. Abbreviations. Notation
10 Directories
Philosophy. Relation to other topics. Methodology
10.2 General works
10.4.A-Z Special methods, A-Z
10.4.A3 Aeronautics
10.4.A8 Astronautics
10.4.E38 Electromechanical analogies
10.4.E4 Electronic data processing
10.4.M33 Mapping
10.4.M36 Mathematical models
10.4.N8 Nuclear energy
10.4.P5 Photography
10.4.R3 Radioactive tracers
10.4.R4 Remote sensing
10.4.S5 Simulation methods
10.4.S7 Statistical methods
General works, treatises, and advanced textbooks
10.9 Early works through 1800
11 1801-1974
11.2 1975-
16 Elementary textbooks
20 Outlines, syllabi
21 Popular works
21.5 Juvenile works
24 Handbooks, tables, etc.
26 Addresses, essays, lectures
28 General special (Special aspects of the subject as a whole)
History
29 General works
29.2.A-Z By region or country, A-Z

Biography
30.A1 Collective
30.A2-Z Individual, A-Z
30.5 Oceanography as a profession
Study and teaching
For research see GC57+
31 General works
31.2 Audiovisual aids
31.3 Problems, exercises, examinations
31.35 Activity programs
31.4 Observations
31.5 Laboratory manuals
By region or country
31.6 United States
31.7.A-Z Other regions or countries, A-Z
Museums. Exhibitions
35 General works
35.2.A-Z By region or country, A-Z
Under each country:
.x General works
.x2A-.x2Z Special. By city, A-Z
Communication of oceanographic information
37 General works
37.5 Information services
38 Exchange of oceanographic information
38.5 Marine geographic information systems
41 Instruments and apparatus
For special instruments, etc., see GC78, GC155, GC177, GC306, etc.
For hydrographic instruments and methods of observation in navigation see VK593.5
Oceanographic research
For results of oceanographic research, see the topic studied
Cf. VM453 Oceanographic research ships
57 General works
By region or country
58 United States
59.112-.995 Other regions or countries (Table G2b)
Add country number in table to GC59
Oceanographic expeditions
63.A1 Collective
63.A2-Z By name of expedition, or name of ship
64 Oceanography and state. Oceanographic policy

Underwater exploration
Cf. CC1+ Archaeology
Cf. G521+ Buried treasure
Cf. GV200.63 Cave diving
Cf. QH91+ Marine biology
Cf. TR800 Underwater photography
Cf. VM975+ Diving (Marine engineering)
65 General works
66 Manned underwater stations
66.5 Undersea colonies
67 Oceanographic submersibles
Deep-sea soundings
For soundings in special regions, see GC84+
75 General works
78.A-Z Special instruments, A-Z
Cf. VK584.S6 Sounding apparatus in navigation
Submarine topography
Cf. QE39 Submarine geology
83 General works
83.2.A-Z Local, A-Z
Continental margins
84 General works
84.2.A-Z Local, A-Z
Continental shelves
85 General works
85.2.A-Z Local, A-Z
Continental slopes
86 General works
86.2.A-Z Local, A-Z
Ocean bottom. Ocean basin
87 General works
87.2.A-Z Local, A-Z
87.6.A-Z Special ocean bottom features, A-Z
87.6.O25 Oceanic plateaus
Plateaus see GC87.6.O25
87.6.S4 Seamounts
87.6.S92 Submarine fans
87.6.T76 Troughs
Sea level
89 General works
90.A-Z By region or country, A-Z
Estuarine oceanography
For oceanography of special estuaries see GC401+
96 Periodicals. Societies. Serials
96.5 Congresses
97 General works
Estuarine sediments

	Estuarine oceanography
	Estuarine sediments -- Continued
97.7	General works
97.8.A-Z	Local, A-Z
	Straits
	For oceanography of special straits see GC401+
98	Periodicals. Societies. Serials
98.5	Congresses
99	General works
	Seawater
	For seawater in special regions see GC401+
100	Congresses
	General works
100.8	Early through 1800
101	1801-1974
101.2	1975-
103	Addresses, essays, lectures
	Chemical oceanography
	For chemical oceanography in special regions see GC401+
109	Periodicals. Societies. Serials
110	Congresses
	General works
111	1801-1974
111.2	1975-
113	Addresses, essays, lectures
116	General special
117.A-Z	Inorganic substances and their inorganic compounds, A-Z
	For organic substances and compounds see GC118+
117.C34	Calcium
117.C37	Carbon
117.C47	Chromium
117.I76	Iron
117.M44	Mercury
117.M46	Metals
117.N5	Nitrogen
117.R37	Rare earth metals
117.S5	Silica
117.S8	Sulfur
117.T7	Trace elements
	Organic substances and compounds
118	General works
118.2.A-Z	Special, A-Z
118.2.C37	Carbohydrates
118.2.O73	Organometallic compounds
	Salinity
120	Congresses
	General works

Chemical oceanography
Salinity
General works -- Continued
121 1801-1974
121.2 1975-
122 Methodology
Distribution of salinity
123 General works
125 Surface
127 Deep sea
130.A-Z Local, A-Z
141 Absorbed gases
149 Radioactivity
Physical oceanography
For physical oceanography (General) in special regions see GC401+
150 Periodicals. Societies. Serials
150.2 Congresses
General works
150.4 1801-1974
150.5 1975-
150.7 Addresses, essays, lectures
Density
151 General works
155 Methodology. Hydrometers
Temperature
160 Congresses
General works
161 1801-1974
161.2 1975-
166 General special
166.5 Charts, diagrams
167.A-Z Local, A-Z
Distribution of temperatures
171 General works
173 Surface
175 Deep sea
177 Methodology
Optical oceanography
177.6 Congresses
General works
178 1801-1974
178.2 1975-
179 Addresses, essays, lectures
180 General special
181 Underwater light
182 Ocean color

Ocean-atmosphere interaction
General works
190 1801-1974
190.2 1975-
190.3 Addresses, essays, lectures
190.5 Methodology
Dynamics of the ocean
For dynamics of the ocean (General) in special regions see GC401+
Cf. QA911+ Hydrodynamics
200 Congresses
General works
201 1801-1974
201.2 1975-
202 Addresses, essays, lectures
203 General special
Waves
Cf. QA927 Mathematical theory
Cf. QC157 Mechanics
205 Periodicals. Societies. Serials
206 Congresses
General works
211 1801-1974
211.2 1975-
211.6 Juvenile works
213 Addresses, essays, lectures
Methodology
213.5 General works
213.7.A-Z Special methods, A-Z
213.7.M3 Mathematical models
214.A-Z Local, A-Z
215 Waves in inland waters
Seiches
217 General works
218.A-Z Local, A-Z
Tsunamis. Tidal waves
219 Congresses
220 Study and teaching. Research
By region or country
220.3 United States
220.4.A-Z Other regions or countries, A-Z
General works
221 1801-1974
221.2 1975-
221.5 Juvenile works
221.7 Addresses, essays, lectures
221.8 Handbooks, tables, etc.

Dynamics of the ocean
Waves
Tsunamis. Tidal waves -- Continued
222.A-Z Local, A-Z
223 Warning systems
Storm surges
225 General works
226.A-Z By region or country, A-Z
227 Rogue waves
Ocean circulation
228.5 General works
228.6.A-Z Local, A-Z
Currents
Cf. G532+ Ocean bottles
229 Congresses
229.2 Dictionaries. Encyclopedias
General works
229.8 Early through 1800
231 1801-1974
231.2 1975-
232 Juvenile works
233 Addresses, essays, lectures
236 Handbooks, tables, etc.
239 General special
Methodology
239.2 General works
239.3.A-Z Special methods, A-Z
239.3.M3 Mathematical models
239.5 Causes of currents
By region
Polar
240 General works
Arctic
Including Arctic Ocean
241 General works
Barents Sea
241.2 General works
241.3 White Sea
241.5 Greenland Sea
Antarctic
Including Antarctic Ocean
245 General works
245.2 Weddell Sea
245.3 Ross Sea
Temperate
251 General works
253 North Temperate

Dynamics of the ocean
Currents
By region
Temperate -- Continued
255 South Temperate
261 Tropical. Equatorial
By ocean
Atlantic Ocean
271 General works
272 North Atlantic
Cf. GC241+ Arctic regions
273 South Atlantic
Cf. GC245+ Antarctic region
By sea or other body of water
274 Baltic Sea
274.2 English Channel
274.3 Irish Sea
274.4 Irminger Sea
275 North Sea
Including Skagerrak and Cattegat
275.2 Norwegian Sea
276 Biscay, Bay of
Mediterranean Sea
277 General works
277.2.A-Z Individual parts, A-Z
e.g.
277.2.M4 Messina, Strait of
278 Black Sea
278.5 Caribbean Sea
Coastal waters
279.A-Z Europe and Africa, A-Z
e.g.
279.D8 Dover, Strait of
281.A-Z North America, A-Z
e.g.
281.F9 Fundy, Bay of
281.M5 Miami Beach, Fla.
281.S2 Saint Lawrence, Gulf of
282.A-Z South America, A-Z
Indian Ocean
283 General works
284 Red Sea
285 Persian Gulf
Pacific Ocean
286 General works
287 North Pacific
288 South Pacific

Dynamics of the ocean
Currents
By ocean
Pacific Ocean -- Continued
By sea
288.15 Bering Sea
288.2 Coral Sea
288.5 Japan Sea
288.7 Tasman Sea
Currents on inland waters
290 General works
Great Lakes
291 General works
292.A-Z Individual lakes, A-Z
e.g.
292.E7 Erie, Lake
293.A-Z Other lakes, A-Z
e.g.
293.M4 Mead, Lake
By individual current
296 Gulf Stream
296.2 Kuroshio
296.8.A-Z Other, A-Z
296.8.A38 Agulhas Current
296.8.E4 El Niño Current
296.8.G8 Guinea Current
296.8.L3 La Niña Current
296.8.P33 Pacific Equatorial Countercurrent
296.8.P47 Peru Current
296.8.T78 Tsushima Current
Water masses
297 General works
298.A-Z Local, A-Z
299 Oceanic mixing
Tides
Cf. QB414+ Theory of tides
Cf. VK600+ Tide and current tables
300 Periodicals. Societies. Serials
300.2 Congresses
300.3 Dictionaries. Encyclopedias
General works
300.8 Early through 1800
301 1801-1974
301.2 1975-
302 Juvenile works
302.2 Addresses, essays, lectures
302.3 Handbooks, tables, etc. Observers' manuals

Dynamics of the ocean
Tides -- Continued
303 General special
Methodology
305 General works
305.5.A-Z Special methods, A-Z
305.5.E4 Electronic data processing
305.5.M3 Mathematical models
306 Instruments and apparatus
Including tide predictors, gauges
307 Tide stations
Tidal currents
308 General works
309.A-Z Local. By region, A-Z
e.g.
309.B6 Boston Harbor
309.C5 Chesapeake Bay
309.M3 Massachusetts
e.g. Narragansett Bay to Nantucket Sound
309.N7 New York Harbor
309.S27 Saint Johns River
By region
311 Arctic
Including Arctic Ocean
313 Antarctic
Including Antarctic Ocean
316 Temperate
321 Tropical. Equatorial
Atlantic Ocean
331 General works
334 North Atlantic
335 South Atlantic
By sea or other body of water
337 Baltic Sea
341 North Sea
Including Skagerrak and Cattegat
343 English Channel
346 Biscay, Bay of
Mediterranean Sea
347 General works
348.A-Z Special parts, A-Z
e.g.
348.I7 Italy
European coast
350 General works
351.A-Z By country, A-Z
African coast

Dynamics of the ocean
Tides
By region
Atlantic Ocean
African coast -- Continued
352 General works
353.A-Z By country, A-Z
American coast
United States
356.A1 General works
356.A3-.W By state, A-W
357.A-Z By city, A-Z
358.A-Z Other special, A-Z
e.g.
358.C2 Canada. Canadian coast
358.F8 Fundy, Bay of
Indian Ocean
359 General works
361 Red Sea
364 Persian Gulf
Pacific Ocean
367 General works
369 North Pacific
371 South Pacific
Tides of inland waters
373 General works
374 Tides of the Great Lakes
375.A-Z Tides on other lakes, A-Z
376 Tidal bores
Marine sediments
Cf. GC75+ Deep-sea soundings
Cf. GC97.7+ Estuarine sediments
Cf. QE471+ Sedimentary rocks
Cf. QE471.2 Sediments
Cf. QE571+ Sedimentation
377 Congresses
General works
380 1801-1974
380.15 1975-
380.2.A-Z Special topics, A-Z
380.2.A25 Acoustic properties
380.2.A52 Analysis
380.2.G3 Gas content
Microbiology see QR106+
380.2.S28 Sampling
380.2.S4 Sediment transport
380.2.T4 Testing

Marine sediments -- Continued
By region
380.3 Tropical. Equatorial
380.5 Arctic
Including Arctic Ocean
380.6 Antarctic
Including Antarctic Ocean
Atlantic Ocean
381 General works
North Atlantic
383 General works
383.2 Caribbean Sea
383.5 Gulf of Mexico
385 Baltic Sea
387 North Sea
389 Mediterranean Sea
389.5 Black Sea
South Atlantic
391 General works
392 Scotia Sea
Indian Ocean
393 General works
393.5 Arabian Sea
394 Red Sea
395 Persian Gulf
Pacific Ocean
397 General works
North Pacific
398 General works
398.3 Puget Sound
398.4 Sea of Japan
398.5 Bering Sea
398.6 Okhotsk, Sea of
398.7 Yellow Sea
399 South Pacific
Oceanography. By region
Arctic Ocean
401 General works
Western
411 General works
413 Beaufort Sea
421 Baffin Bay
431 Davis Strait
436 Denmark Strait
439 Greenland Sea
441 Hudson Bay
443 Hudson Strait

Oceanography. By region
Arctic Ocean -- Continued
Eastern
451 General works
452 Barents Sea
453 Kara Sea
454 East Siberian Sea
455 Chukchi Sea
456 Laptev Sea
Coast of Antarctica. Antarctic Ocean
461 General works
462 Weddell Sea
463 Ross Sea
Atlantic Ocean
481 General works
North Atlantic
491 General works
492 Norwegian Sea
Western Atlantic
501 General works
502 Grand Banks of Newfoundland
503 Labrador Sea
506 Georges Bank
Coast of North America
511 General works
512.A-Z By state or province, A-Z
e.g.
512.M3 Maine
521 Gulf of Mexico
531 Caribbean Sea
535 Sargasso Sea
541 Coast of South America
Eastern Atlantic
551 General works
561 Scandinavian coasts
571 Baltic Sea. Coast of Finland
581 German coast
591 North Sea
593 Dutch coast
597 Belgian coast
601 British coast
603 Irish Sea
611 English Channel
621 French coast
631 Biscay, Bay of
641 Spanish and Portuguese coasts
645 Gibraltar, Strait of

Oceanography. By region
Atlantic Ocean
Eastern Atlantic -- Continued
Mediterranean Sea
651 General works
661 Adriatic Sea
671 Aegean Sea
681 Black Sea
685.A-Z Other parts, A-Z
e.g.
685.A9 Azov, Sea of
685.B58 Bocca Piccola
685.B6 Bosporus
685.M4 Messina, Strait of
685.S8 Suez Canal
685.T3 Taranto, Gulf of
South Atlantic
691 General works
701 Gulf of Guinea
711 Cape of Good Hope
715 Caspian Sea
Indian Ocean
721 General works
731 Arabian Sea
741 Red Sea
751 Persian Gulf
761 Bengal, Bay of
765 Australian coast
Pacific Ocean
771 General works
North Pacific
781 General works
Western Pacific
791 General works
801 China Sea
Including East China Sea, South China Sea
811 Yellow Sea
821 Japan Sea
831 Okhotsk, Sea of
841 Bering Sea
845.A-Z Other, A-Z
e.g.
845.Y6 Yŏsu Bay
Eastern Pacific
851 General works
852 Alaskan coast
854 Canadian coast

Oceanography. By region
Pacific Ocean
North Pacific
Eastern Pacific -- Continued
856 United States coast
858 Mexican coast
859 Central American coast
860.A-Z Other, A-Z
e.g.
860.C8 Costa Rica
Central Pacific. Equatorial Pacific
860.5 General works
860.7 Line Islands
South Pacific
861 General works
862 Coral Sea
863 Java Sea
865 Tasman Sea
871 South American coast
875 Australia
For coasts on specific bodies of water, see the body, e.g. GC765, Indian Coast of Australia
877 Polar regions
880 Tropical. Equatorial
881 Temperate
Marine resources. Applied oceanography
For applied oceanography, see the field of application, e.g. TD898 Radioactive waste disposal in the sea; VK588+ Marine hydrography
Cf. HC92 Economic geography
Cf. SH1+ Fish culture and fisheries
Cf. TC147 Tidal power as a source of energy
Cf. TD478+ Fresh water from seawater
Cf. V396+ Military oceanography
1000 Periodicals. Societies. Serials
1001 Congresses
Study and teaching. Research
1005 General works
By region or country
1005.2 United States
1005.3.A-Z Other regions or countries, A-Z
General works
1015 1801-1974
1015.2 1975-
1016 Popular works
1016.5 Juvenile works
1017 General special

Marine resources. Applied oceanography -- Continued
1018 Conservation
1018.5 Management
Including ocean zoning
By region or country
United States
1020 General works
1021.A-Z By region or state, A-Z
1023.112-.995 Other regions or countries (Table G2b)
Add country number in table to GC1023
Mineral resources see TN264
Marine pollution. Sea water pollution
Cf. QH91.8.O4 Oil pollution (Marine biology)
Cf. TD195.O25 Environmental effects of ocean mining
1080 Periodicals. Societies. Serials
1081 Congresses
1085 General works
1090 Juvenile works
By region
Arctic Ocean
1101 General works
Western
1111 General works
1113 Beaufort Sea
1121 Baffin Bay
1131 Davis Strait
1136 Denmark Strait
1139 Greenland Sea
1141 Hudson Bay
1143 Hudson Strait
Eastern
1151 General works
1152 Barents Sea
1153 Kara Sea
1154 East Siberian Sea
1155 Chukchi Sea
Coast of Antarctica. Antarctic Ocean
1161 General works
1162 Weddell Sea
Atlantic Ocean
1181 General works
North Atlantic
1191 General works
1192 Norwegian Sea
Western Atlantic
1201 General works
1202 Grand Banks of Newfoundland

Marine pollution. Sea water pollution
By region
Atlantic Ocean
Western Atlantic -- Continued
1203 Labrador Sea
Coast of North America
1211 General works
1212.A-Z By state or province, A-Z
e.g.
1212.M3 Maine
1221 Gulf of Mexico
1231 Caribbean Sea
1235 Sargasso Sea
1241 Coast of South America
Eastern Atlantic
1251 General works
1261 Scandinavian coasts
1271 Baltic Sea. Coast of Finland
1281 German coast
1291 North Sea
1293 Dutch coast
1297 Belgian coast
1301 British coast
1303 Irish Sea
1311 English Channel
1321 French coast
1331 Biscay, Bay of
1341 Spanish and Portuguese coasts
1345 Gibraltar, Strait of
Mediterranean Sea
1351 General works
1361 Adriatic Sea
1371 Aegean Sea
1381 Black Sea
1385.A-Z Other parts, A-Z
e.g.
1385.A9 Azov, Sea of
1385.B58 Bocca Piccola
1385.B6 Bosporus
1385.M4 Messina, Strait of
1385.S8 Suez Canal
1385.T3 Taranto, Gulf of
South Atlantic
1391 General works
1401 Gulf of Guinea
1411 Cape of Good Hope
1415 Caspian Sea

Marine pollution. Sea water pollution
By region -- Continued
Indian Ocean

1421	General works
1431	Arabian Sea
1441	Red Sea
1451	Persian Gulf
1461	Bengal, Bay of
	Pacific Ocean
1471	General works
	North Pacific
1481	General works
	Western Pacific
1491	General works
1501	China Sea Including East China Sea, South China Sea
1511	Yellow Sea
1521	Japan Sea
1531	Okhotsk, Sea of
1541	Bering Sea
1545.A-Z	Other, A-Z
1545.Y6	Yŏsu Bay
	Eastern Pacific
1551	General works
1552	Alaskan coast
1554	Canadian coast
1556	United States coast
1558	Mexican coast
1559	Central American coast
1560.A-Z	Other, A-Z
	South Pacific
1561	General works
1562	Coral Sea
1565	Tasman Sea
1571	South American coast
1580	Tropical. Equatorial
1581	Temperate

Environmental sciences
Cf. BF353 Environmental psychology
Cf. BH301.E58 Aesthetics
Cf. CC81 Environmental archaeology
Cf. GF1+ Human ecology
Cf. HC1+ Natural resources
Cf. HC79.E5 Environmental policy and economic development
Cf. K3581+ Environmental law
Cf. QE38 Environmental geology
Cf. QH540+ Ecology
Cf. RA565+ Environmental health
Cf. S900+ Conservation of natural resources
Cf. TA170+ Environmental engineering (Civil engineering)
Cf. TD1+ Environmental technology
Cf. TD169+ Environmental protection
Cf. TD172+ Environmental pollution

1 Periodicals. Societies. Serials
5 Congresses
10 Dictionaries. Encyclopedias
15 Terminology. Abbreviations. Notation
20 Directories
Communication in environmental sciences
25 General works
Information services
30 General works
30.5.A-Z By region or country, A-Z
32 Computer networks
Including the Internet
35 Environmental literature
Philosophy. Relation to other topics. Methodology
40 General works
42 Environmental ethics
Cf. GE220+ Environmental justice
43 Bioregionalism
45.A-Z Special methods, A-Z
45.D37 Data processing. Computer applications
45.M35 Mapping
45.M37 Mathematical models
45.M38 Mathematics
45.R44 Remote sensing
45.S25 Sampling
45.S73 Statistical methods
50 History
Biography
55 Collective
56.A-Z Individual, A-Z

GE

60 Vocational guidance
Environmental education. Study and teaching. Research
70 General works
75.A-.Z8 Audio-visual aids
75.Z9 Catalogs of audiovisual materials
76 Problems, exercises, examinations
76.5 Interdisciplinary research
77 Activity programs
By region or country
United States
80 General works
85.A-Z By region or state, A-Z
90.A-Z Other regions or countries, A-Z
Museums. Exhibitions
95 General works
100.A-Z By region or country, A-Z
105 General works
110 Popular works
115 Juvenile works
120 Pictorial works
123 Handbooks, manuals, etc.
125 Public opinion
Environmental conditions. Environmental quality. Environmental indicators. Environmental degradation
140 General works
140.5 Juvenile works
Environmental risk assessment
145 General works
By region or country see GE150+
146 Environmental disasters
149 Global environmental change
Cf. QC903 Global temperature changes
Cf. QC981.8.G56 Global warming
By region or country
United States
150 General works
155.A-Z By region or state, A-Z
160.A-Z Other regions or countries, A-Z
Environmental policy
Cf. HC79.E5 Environmental policy and economic development
170 General works
By region or country
United States
180 General works
185.A-Z By region or state, A-Z
190.A-Z Other regions or countries, A-Z

GE

Environmentalism. Green movement
Cf. JA75.8 Political science
195 General works
195.5 Juvenile works
195.7 Environmental responsibility
195.9 Women in the environmental movement
Cf. HQ1194 Ecofeminism
By region or country
United States
197 General works
198.A-Z By region or state, A-Z
199.A-Z Other regions or countries, A-Z
Environmental justice
220 General works
By region or country
United States
230 General works
235.A-Z By region or state, A-Z
240.A-Z Other regions or countries, A-Z
Environmental management
For environmental management in specific fields, see the field, e.g. HD30.255, Industrial management
Cf. QH75+ Ecosystem management
300 General works
By region or country
United States
310 General works
315.A-Z By region or state, A-Z
320.A-Z Other regions or countries, A-Z
350 Ecological engineering

Human ecology. Anthropogeography
Including human geography
For environmental sciences, see GE
For environmental archaeology see CC81
For conservation of natural resources see S900+
For environmental protection and pollution see TD1+
Cf. HM861 Social ecology

1	Periodicals. Societies. Serials
3	Congresses
4	Dictionaries. Encyclopedias
4.5	Terminology. Notations. Abbreviations
5	Directories
	Collected works (nonserial)
8	Several authors
9.A-Z	Individual authors, A-Z
	History. Environmental history
13	General works
13.3.A-Z	By region or country, A-Z
	Biography
15	Collective
16.A-Z	Individual, A-Z
	Philosophy. Relation to other topics. Methodology Cf. HX550.E25 Communism and ecology
21	General works
21.5	Relation to archaeology Cf. CC81 Environmental archaeology
23.A-Z	Special methods, A-Z
23.C35	Cartography
23.E4	Electronic data processing
23.G7	Graphic methods
(23.I53)	Indexes see GE140-GE160
23.M35	Mathematics. Quantitative methods
23.N47	Network analysis
24	Applied human geography
	Study and teaching. Research
26	General works
26.3.A-.Z8	Audiovisual aids
26.3.Z9	Catalogs of audiovisual materials
26.5	Problems, exercises, examinations
	By region or country
	United States
27	General works

Study and teaching. Research
By region or country
United States -- Continued
27.5.A-Z By region or state, A-Z
Under each state:
.x General works
.x2A-.x2Z Individual schools or universities. By place, A-Z
28.A-Z Other regions or countries, A-Z
Under each country:
.x General works
.x2A-.x2Z Individual schools or universities. By place, A-Z
General works, treatises, and textbooks
Early through 1969
31 Comprehensive works
33 Elementary textbooks
37 Popular works
1970-
41 Comprehensive works
43 Elementary textbooks
45 Outlines, syllabi
46 Pictorial works
47 Popular works
48 Juvenile works
49 Addresses, essays, lectures
50 General special (Special aspects of the subject as a whole)
50.5 Public opinion
51 Environmental influences on humans
Class here general works only
Cf. GN386+ Ethnology
Cf. BF353 Environmental psychology
Cf. GE1+ Environmental sciences
Cf. GN406.5 Technology, material culture
Cf. HB849.415 Demography
Humans and specific environments
Arctic regions
see GF891
53 Frontiers
54 Jungles
54.5 Forests
Cf. SD416+ Forestry
55 Deserts. Arid regions
Cf. GB611+ Desertification (general and natural aspects)
57 Mountains
58 Volcanoes. Volcanic activity
59 Plains. Grasslands. Steppes

Humans and specific environments -- Continued
61 Islands
Bodies of water
63 Rivers
65 Oceans
67 Lakes
71 Climatic influences on humans
75 Human influences on the environment
Cf. HB849.415 Population and the environment
77 Organic living
Cf. RA773+ Personal health
Cf. S605.5 Organic farming
Cf. SB453.5+ Organic gardening
Cf. TX369 Natural foods
Cf. TX392+ Vegetarianism
78 Self-reliant living
80 Ethical, moral and religious aspects
For works on environmental ethics see GE42
85 Hazardous aspects of the environment
Cf. TD172+ Environmental pollution
86 Survival skills
Cf. HQ2035+ Life skills
Landscape assessment
90 General works
91.A-Z By region or country, A-Z
95 Spatial studies
98 Chronogeography. Time-geography
Settlements
Including limits of land settlement, natural boundaries, etc.
For human migrations see GN370
For demography, theory of population, etc. see HB848+
For geopolitics see JC319+
101 General works
By region or country see GF500+
125 Cities. Urban geography
For urban geography of individual cities, see D-F
Cf. HT101+ Urban sociology
127 Rural settlements. Rural geography
Cf. HT401+ Rural sociology
By region or country
America
500 General works
501 North America
United States
503 General works
504.A-Z By region or state, A-Z
Canada

GF

By region or country
America
Canada -- Continued
511 General works
512.A-Z By region or province, A-Z
514 Latin America
Mexico
516 General works
517.A-Z By region or state, A-Z
Central America
521 General works
522.A-Z By region or country, A-Z
524 Caribbean Area
West Indies
526 General works
527.A-Z By region, country, island, etc., A-Z
South America
531 General works
532.A-Z By region or country, A-Z
Europe
540 General works
541 Mediterranean Region
545 Alps
547 Baltic region
Great Britain. England (General)
551 General works
552.A-Z England (Local), A-Z
Scotland
555 General works
556.A-Z By region, county, etc., A-Z
Wales
557 General works
558.A-Z By region, county, etc., A-Z
Northern Ireland
561 General works
562.A-Z By region, county, etc., A-Z
563 Ireland
Austria
565 General works
567.A-Z Local, A-Z
568 Czechoslovakia. Czech Republic
568.5 Slovakia
569 Hungary
France
571 General works
574.A-Z By region, state, etc., A-Z

By region or country
Europe -- Continued
Germany
Including West Germany
576 General works
578.A-Z Local, A-Z
579 East Germany
Greece
581 General works
582.A-Z By region, state, etc., A-Z
Italy
586 General works
587.A-Z By region, state, etc., A-Z
591 Low countries
Netherlands
593 General works
594.A-Z By region, state, etc., A-Z
Belgium
596 General works
597.A-Z By region, state, etc., A-Z
Russia. Soviet Union. Former Soviet republics
For individual states, see GF602.2+ and GF676+
601 General works
(602) By region, state, etc.,
see GF602.2+ and GF676+
Baltic States
602.2 General works
602.3 Estonia
602.4 Latvia
602.5 Lithuania
602.6 Belarus
602.7 Russia (Federation)
For Siberia see GF676
602.8 Moldova
602.9 Ukraine
604 Finland
611 Scandinavia
Norway
612 General works
613.A-Z By region, state, etc., A-Z
Sweden
614 General works
615.A-Z By region, state, etc., A-Z
Denmark
616 General works
617.A-Z By region, state, etc., A-Z
Spain

By region or country
Europe
Spain -- Continued
621 General works
622.A-Z By region, state, etc., A-Z
Portugal
623 General works
624.A-Z By region, state, etc., A-Z
Switzerland
631 General works
632.A-Z By region, state, etc., A-Z
641 Balkan Peninsula (General)
642.A-Z Individual Balkan states, A-Z
Under each:
.x General works
.x2A-.x2Z Local, A-Z
645.A-Z Other regions or countries of Europe, A-Z
645.A53 Andorra
645.C36 Central Europe
645.E92 Eastern Europe
645.I25 Iceland
645.L9 Luxembourg
645.P7 Poland
651 Asia
China
656 General works
657.A-Z By region, state, etc., A-Z
658 Hong Kong
659 Korea
India
661 General works
662.A-Z By region, state, etc., A-Z
(664) Pakistan
see GF696.P34
Japan
666 General works
667.A-Z By region, state, etc., A-Z
668 Southeast Asia
Including Malay Archipelago
669 Malaysia
669.2 Indonesia
669.3 Thailand
669.4 Philippines
669.5 Vietnam
670 Middle East (General)
Iran
671 General works

By region or country
Asia
Iran -- Continued
672.A-Z By region, state, etc., A-Z
674 Afghanistan
675 Iraq. Mesopotamia
676 Siberia
Central Asia
677.2 General works
677.3 Kazakhstan
677.4 Kyrgyzstan
677.5 Tajikistan
677.6 Turkmenistan
677.7 Uzbekistan
Turkey. Asia Minor
678 General works
679.A-Z By region, state, etc., A-Z
Arabian Peninsula
680 General works
Saudi Arabia
681 General works
682.A-Z By region, state, etc., A-Z
Palestine. Israel
685 General works
686.A-Z By region, state, etc., A-Z
Syria
687 General works
688.A-Z By region, state, etc., A-Z
696.A-Z Other regions or countries of Asia, A-Z
696.B26 Bahrain
696.B3 Bangladesh
696.B67 Borneo
696.H55 Himalaya Mountains Region
696.K87 Kurdistan
696.L42 Lebanon
Mesopotamia see GF675
696.N35 Nepal
696.P34 Pakistan
696.S75 Sri Lanka
696.U5 United Arab Emirates
698 Arab countries
Africa
701 General works
702 North Africa
703 Morocco
704 Algeria
706 Libya

By region or country
Africa -- Continued
Egypt
711 General works
712.A-Z By region, state, etc., A-Z
715 Sahara
Eastern Africa
720 General works
721 Ethiopia
724 Kenya
725 Madagascar
726 Mozambique
726.5 Rwanda
728 Sudan
729 Tanzania
729.5 Uganda
730 Central Africa
West Africa
740 General works
742 Benin
743 Burkina Faso
744 Cameroon
746 Gabon
746.2 Guinea
746.3 Mali
746.4 Nigeria
746.5 Senegal
746.7 Sierra Leone
747 Zaire. Congo (Democratic Republic)
Southern Africa
750 General works
753 Botswana
754 Namibia
758 South Africa
Atlantic Ocean islands
765 General works
766 Bermuda
Indian Ocean islands
769 General works
770 Réunion
Pacific area
Including coastal regions of Asia and America
798 General works
Australia
801 General works
802.A-Z By region, state, etc., A-Z
New Zealand

By region or country
Pacific area
New Zealand -- Continued
805 General works
806.A-Z By region, state, etc., A-Z
Pacific islands
851 General works
852.A-Z By region, country, island, etc., A-Z
891 Arctic regions
Cf. G600+ Geography
895 Tropics
900 Developing countries

	Anthropology
1	Periodicals. Serials
2	Societies
3	Congresses
	Collected works (nonserial)
4	Several authors
6	Individual authors
11	Dictionaries. Encyclopedias
11.5	Directories
12	Terminology. Abbreviations. Notation
	Communication of information
12.8	General works
13	Information services
13.5	Computer network resources. Computer networks Including the Internet
14	Anthropological archives
17	History
17.3.A-Z	By region or country, A-Z
	Biography
20	Collective
21.A-Z	Individual, A-Z
	General works, treatises, and textbooks
23	Early through 1870
24	1871-1974
25	1975-
27	General special (Special aspects of the subject as a whole)
29	Addresses, essays, lectures
	Popular works
30	Early through 1870
31	1871-1974
31.2	1975-
31.5	Juvenile works
32	Pictorial works
	Philosophy. Relation to other topics. Methodology Cf. BD450 Philosophical anthropology
33	General works
33.5	Relation to demography
	Relation to parapsychology see BF1045.A65
	Relation to psychology see GN502+
	Relation to theater see PN2041.A57
33.6	Anthropological ethics
33.8	Feminist anthropology
34	Classification
34.2	Irony in anthropology
34.3.A-Z	Other special methods, A-Z
34.3.A35	Aerial photography
	Artificial intelligence see GN34.3.I53

Philosophy. Relation to other topics. Methodology
Other special methods, A-Z -- Continued
34.3.C6 Componential analysis
34.3.D36 Data processing
34.3.F53 Fieldwork
34.3.I53 Information technology
Including artificial intelligence
34.3.M3 Mathematical anthropology
34.3.P45 Photography
34.3.S7 Statistical methods
Museums. Exhibitions
Class here general collections only. For special collections, see the subject
35 General works
36.A-Z By region or country, A-Z
Under each country:
.x *General works*
.x2A-.x2Z *Special. By city, A-Z*
e.g.
Cuba
36.C9 General works
36.C92H38 Havana. Universidad. Museo anthropológico Montané
41 Private collections
Anthropologists
41.6 General works
41.8 Anthropology as a profession
Biography see GN20+
Study and teaching. Research
42 General works
42.3.A-.Z8 Audiovisual aids
42.3.Z9 Catalogs of audiovisual materials
42.5 Computers. Data processing
By region or country
Class individual institutions by state or country without further subdivision
United States
43 General works
43.2.A-Z By region or state, A-Z
44.A-Z Other American regions or countries, A-Z
45.A-Z Europe. By region or country, A-Z
46.A-Z Other regions or countries, A-Z
Physical anthropology. Somatology
Cf. GF51 Environmental influences on humans
Cf. QM1+ Human anatomy
Cf. QP34+ Human physiology
49 Periodicals. Societies. Serials
50 Congresses

Physical anthropology. Somatology -- Continued
50.2 Collected works (nonserial)
50.3 Dictionaries. Encyclopedias
History
50.4 General works
50.45.A-Z By region or country, A-Z
Biography
50.5 Collective
50.6.A-Z Individual, A-Z
Philosophy. Relation to other topics. Methodology
50.8 General works
Anthropometry
General works
51.A2 Early works through 1800
51.A3-Z 1801-
53 Instruments
54 Special methods
56 Compilations of statistical data, tables, etc. (General)
For compilations of data on special topics, see the topic
Special anthropometric studies
Including results of studies
For works on a specific ethnic group or race, regardless of topic see GN57.A+
For studies limited to special topics, without regard to ethnic groups or races see GN62.9
57.A-Z By race, ethnic group, etc., A-Z
e.g.
Aboriginal Australians see GN57.A9
57.A35 African Americans
57.A9 Australians, Aboriginal
57.B5 Blacks
Cf. GN57.A35 African Americans
Indians see E98.A55
58.A-Z By region or country, A-Z
59.A-Z By class of persons, A-Z
59.A35 Aged. Older people
Athletes see GV435
Children (Physical anthropology) see GN63
Children (School hygiene) see LB3421+
59.M4 Men
Older people see GN59.A35
59.S7 Soldiers
Including all military personnel
59.S8 Students
59.W6 Women
59.6 Study and teaching. Research
Museums. Exhibitions

Physical anthropology. Somatology
Museums. Exhibitions -- Continued
59.8 General works
59.82.A-Z By region or country, A-Z
Subarrange each region or country by author
60 General works
62 General special
Cf. GN269+ Race (General)
Man as an animal see GN280.7
Human variation
Cf. GN269+ Race (General)
62.8 General works
62.85 Sex differences
Including bio-cultural studies
Human growth
Cf. QP84 Physiology of growth
62.9 General works
63 Children. Adolescents
Cf. LB1101+ Child development for teachers
Cf. LB3421+ Physical measurements of school children
Cf. RJ1+ Pediatrics
63.6 Twins, triplets, etc.
For works on human variation in the physiology of multiple births see GN236.5
Cf. BF723.T9 Child psychology
Cf. HQ777.35 Child rearing
Physical form and dimensions
Head. Cephalometry
Cf. GN71+ Craniometry
63.8 General works
64 Face form and profile. Physiognomy
Including shape of special features, e.g. nose, lips, etc.
For works on the shape of the ear see GN201
Cf. BF840+ Physiognomy and phrenology
64.2 Facial expression
Body dimensions and proportions
Cf. NC765 Proportions in art
66 General works
66.5 Somatotypes
67 Climate and body build
67.5 Women
Special variations
Cf. RB140+ Growth disorders
Giants
69 General works
Biography

Physical anthropology. Somatology
Human variation
Physical form and dimensions
Body dimensions and proportions
Special variations
Giants
Biography -- Continued
69.2 Collective
69.22.A-Z Individual, A-Z
69.3 Dwarfs. Midgets
Cf. CT9992 Biography
Cf. RB140.3 Growth disorders
The skeleton. Osteology
For works on the skeletal remains of fossil man see GN281+
Cf. QM101+ Anatomy of the skeleton
Philosophy. Relations to other topics
69.8 Forensic anthropology
Cf. RA1059 Forensic osteology
70 General works
By continent
America
70.5.A1 General works
70.5.A2-Z Individual countries, A-Z
Europe
70.6.A1 General works
70.6.A2-Z Individual countries, A-Z
Asia
70.7.A1 General works
70.7.A2-Z Individual countries, A-Z
Africa
70.8.A1 General works
70.8.A2-Z Individual countries, A-Z
Australia and Pacific islands
70.9.A1 General works
70.9.A2-Z Individual countries, A-Z
The skull. Craniology. Craniometry
71 General works
72 General special
Including identification of skulls, artificial deformation of skulls, etc.
74 Facial reconstruction
By period
Pleistocene skulls see GN282+
Ancient skulls
Including post-Pleistocene to medieval periods
84 General works

Physical anthropology. Somatology
Human variation
The skeleton. Osteology
The skull. Craniology. Craniometry
By period
Ancient skulls -- Continued

85.A-Z By region or country, A-Z

Medieval and modern skulls

87 General works

Including description of skulls from several parts of the world

By continent

America

90 General works

93.A-Z Individual countries, A-Z

Europe

100 General works

103.A-Z Individual countries, A-Z

Asia

110 General works

113.A-Z Individual countries, A-Z

Africa

120 General works

123.A-Z Individual countries, A-Z

Australia and Pacific islands

125 General works

128.A-Z Individual countries, A-Z

130.A-Z By race, A-Z

e.g.

130.B56 Black

130.M7 Mongolian

Negro see GN130.B56

131 Special details (not A-Z)

e.g. Exotosis, eye sockets, hard palate, prognathism

For teeth see GN209

141 Vertebra

145 Shoulder girdle, scapula, etc.

151 Pelvis

161 Extremities

Including hand, foot, etc.

171 Muscular system

Nervous system. Brain (Convolutions, etc.)

Cf. QM455 Anatomy of the brain

181 General works

By continent

America

182 General works

Physical anthropology. Somatology
Human variation
Nervous system. Brain (Convolutions, etc.)
By continent
America -- Continued
183.A-Z Individual countries, A-Z
Europe
184 General works
185.A-Z Individual countries, A-Z
Asia
186 General works
187.A-Z Individual countries, A-Z
Africa
188 General works
189.A-Z Individual countries, A-Z
Australia and Pacific islands
190 General works
190.5.A-Z Individual countries, A-Z
Skin
191 General works
192 Dermatoglyphics. Fingerprints
Including classification, directories, information, use, etc.
Cf. HV6074 Criminal anthropology
193 Hair
197 Color. Pigmentation
Including hair and eyes
199 Albinism
201 Sense organs
Including the shape of the external ear
Cf. QM501+ Anatomy of the sense organs
206 Internal organs
Including individual organs, e.g. heart, lungs, etc.
209 Teeth. Dental anthropology
211 Sex organs
Physiological anthropology
Cf. QP1+ Physiology
221 General works
223 Basal metabolism
Physical traits
229 Strength
Posture. Movement
231 General works
232 Sitting position

Physical anthropology. Somatology
Human variation
Physiological anthropology
Physical traits -- Continued
233 Left- and right-handedness
Including significance, measurement and determination of hand preferences, etc.
Cf. LB1123 Left- and right-handedness in education
Cf. QP385+ Localization of functions (Brain)
Reproduction. Sexual functions
235 General works
Birth
236 General works
236.5 Multiple births (Twins, triplets, etc.)
For works on the twins, triplets, etc., themselves see GN63.6
Cf. RG567 Multiple pregnancy
Cf. RG696+ Obstetrics
238 Puberty
241 Fertility
Hereditary functions
Cf. GN289+ Population genetics
Cf. QH431 Human genetics
247 General works
251 Atavism
252 Inbreeding
Cf. HQ1026 Consanguineous marriages
Cf. HV4981 Social pathology
254 Racial crossing. Miscegenation
Cf. HQ1031 Mixed marriages
256 Degeneration
Cf. HQ750+ Eugenics
Blood
260 General works
263 Blood groups
264 Hemoglobin polymorphisms
265 Immunoglobulin allotypes
Race (General)
For anthropometric works on particular races see GN57+
For works on particular races see GN537
269 General works
Race psychology
Cf. BF431+ Racial intelligence
Cf. BF699+ Genetic psychology
Cf. CB195+ Civilization and race
Cf. GN502+ Psychological anthropology
Cf. QP351+ Physiological psychology

Physical anthropology. Somatology
Race (General)
Race psychology -- Continued
270 General works
273 General special
Senses and sensation
274 General works
275 Hearing
277 Vision
279.A-Z Other senses, A-Z
280.7 Man as an animal. Simian traits versus human traits
Including man's place in nature
Cf. GF1+ Human ecology
Human evolution
Including the origin of man
Cf. BF698.95 Evolutionary psychology
Cf. BL263 Natural theology
Cf. QH359+ Biology
281 General works
281.4 General special
Fossil man. Human paleontology
Class here works on physical remains only, including particular parts of the skeleton.
For works on physical remains and associated cultural remains see GN768+
282 General works
282.5 General special
e.g. Piltdown man
282.6 Gigantopithecus
Australopithecines
283 General works
283.25 Australopithecus afarensis
283.3 Australopithecus prometheus
283.5 Meganthropus paleojavanicus
283.6 Paranthropus crassidens
283.7 Plesianthropus transvaalensis
283.8 Zinjanthropus boisei
283.9 Homo habilis
Homo erectus. Pithecanthropines
284 General works
284.4 Homo soloensis
284.6 Java man. Pithecanthropus erectus. Homo erectus javensis
284.7 Peking man. Homo erectus pekinensis. Sinanthropus pekinensis
284.8 Heidelberg man. Homo heidelbergensis
285 Homo neanderthalensis

Physical anthropology. Somatology
Human evolution
Fossil man. Human paleontology
Homo erectus. Pithecanthropines -- Continued
Homo sapiens
286 General works
286.2 Boskop man
286.3 Cro-Magnon man
Including Proto Cro-Magnon
286.7 Swanscombe
Population genetics
Including mechanics of evolution and continuing evolution
Cf. GN247+ Hereditary functions
Cf. HB848+ Population (Economic theory)
Cf. QH455 Genetics (General)
289 General works
290.A-Z By region or country, A-Z
293 Mummies
Medical anthropology
Cf. GN477+ Traditional medicine (Ethnology)
Cf. GR880 Traditional medicine (Folklore)
296 General works
296.5.A-Z By region or country, A-Z
298 Social aspects of the human body
Cf. GR489+ Human body in folklore
Cf. GT495+ Manners and customs about the human body
Ethnology. Social and cultural anthropology
Many topics provided for here represent concepts also encompassed by the discipline of sociology in HM. In cases of overlap, the following principle should normally apply, unless specific instructions are made to the contrary. Class here those works that deal with the nature of human societies in general, as well as those works that deal specifically with preliterate and/or folk societies. For those works that deal principally with modern civilization, see HM
Cf. CB3+ History of civilization
Cf. GF1+ Human ecology
Cf. GT1+ Manners and customs (General)
Cf. HM401+ Sociology
301 Periodicals. Societies. Serials
302 Congresses
Collected works (nonserial)
303 Several authors
304 Individual authors
307 Dictionaries. Encyclopedias
307.3 Directories

Ethnology. Social and cultural anthropology -- Continued
Communication of information
307.5 General works
307.6 Information services
307.65 Computer network resources. Computer networks
Including the Internet
307.7 Writing of ethnographies
Study and teaching
307.8 General works
307.82 Audiovisual aids
307.85.A-Z By region or country, A-Z
Museums. Exhibitions see GN35+
History
For the history of specific schools of thought, see the subject, e.g. GN365+ German diffusionists
308 General works
308.3.A-Z By region or country, A-Z
Ethnologists see GN41.6+
General works, treatises, and textbooks
310 Through 1870
315 1871-1974
316 1975-
320 General special (Special aspects of the subject as a whole)
323 Outlines, syllabi
325 Addresses, essays, lectures
330 Popular works
333 Juvenile works
340 Pictorial works
Philosophy. Relation to other topics. Methodology
345 General works
Relation to archaeology. Ethnoarchaeology see CC79.E85
345.15 Relation to communism. Marxist anthropology
345.2 Relation to history. Ethnohistory
Relation to linguistics see P35+
Relation to religion see BL256
345.3 Classification
345.5 Cultural relativism
Cf. GN469 Value systems
Cf. GN495.8 Ethnocentrism
Cf. GN517 Culture shock
345.6 Intercultural communication
345.65 Cross-cultural orientation
Special methods
345.7 Cross cultural studies
Fieldwork
346 General works
346.3 Interviews

Ethnology. Social and cultural anthropology
Philosophy. Relation to other topics. Methodology
Special methods
Fieldwork -- Continued
346.4 Participant observation
346.5 Data processing
346.6 Life histories
346.7 Cartography. Mapping
346.8 Mathematical models
346.85 Statistical methods
347 Visual anthropology. Photography. Motion pictures
348 Sound recordings in ethnology
Culture and cultural processes
357 General works
357.5 Origin of culture
358 Culture change. Social change
Cultural evolution. Evolutionism
360 General works
360.4 Neo-evolutionism
362 Structuralism. Structural anthropology
363 Functionalism
Culture diffusion
365 General works
Culture history
365.4 General works
365.6 Kulturkreis theory
365.8 Cultural determinism
365.9 Biological determinism. Sociobiology
Cf. QL775 Social behavior in animals
Psychoanalytic approach see GN508
Acculturation. Culture contact
Cf. GN380 Threatened societies
366 General works
367 Assimilation
368 First contact with Western civilization
370 Migrations of peoples (General)
372 Feral studies. Wolf children
378 Collected ethnographies
Class here works that describe two or more ethnic groups not confined to one geographic region or country. For works on specific groups in specific regions or countries, see the appropriate number for the group in D-F
For works on individual groups not confined to one region or country see GN537+
For comprehensive works on the groups of specific regions or countries see GN550+
Ethnographies of special categories of peoples

Ethnology. Social and cultural anthropology
Collected ethnographies
Ethnographies of special categories of peoples -- Continued

380 Threatened societies
Class here ethnographies that discuss collectively the nonliterate peoples of the world whose particular way of life is being shattered by Western encroachments

386 Oceanic peoples. Maritime anthropology
Cf. CB458 History of civilization
Cf. CB465 History of civilization
Cf. GF65 Oceanic influences of humans
Cf. GN440+ Transportation by water

387 Nomadic peoples

388 Hunting and gathering peoples
Cf. GN407 Food and food production

389 Fishing peoples

390 Desert people

391 Island people

392 Mountain people

393 Grassland people

394 Rain forest people

395 City dwellers. Urban anthropology

396 Peaceful societies

Applied anthropology

397 Periodicals. Societies. Serials

397.5 General works

397.7.A-Z By region or country, A-Z

Cultural traits, customs, and institutions
Class here general works on specific topics only
For works on specific topics pertaining to special groups or races see GN537+
For works on topics pertaining to one region or country see GN550+

Technology. Material culture

406 General works

406.5 Influence of the environment

Food and food production. Subsistence. Nutritional anthropology

407 General works

Hunting and gathering

407.3 General works

407.33.A-Z Special, A-Z

Arrows see GN498.B78

Caribou hunting see GN407.33.R45

407.33.H55 Harpoons

407.33.R45 Reindeer and caribou hunting

Ethnology. Social and cultural anthropology
Cultural traits, customs, and institutions
Technology. Material culture
Food and food production. Subsistence. Nutritional anthropology
Hunting and gathering
Special, A-Z -- Continued

407.33.T7 Traps
407.35 Fishing
Including fishing implements
Agriculture
407.4 General works
Domesticated plants
407.5 General works
407.55 Horticulture
Domesticted animals
407.6 General works
407.7 Pastoralism. Herding
407.8 Irrigation
408 Geophagy. Dirt eating
409 Cannibalism
409.5 Insects
Including entomophagy
410 Food preparation
410.5 Beverages
Stimulants and narcotics
411 General works
411.5 Alcohol
Shelter. Habitation
413 General works
413.5 Village patterns
Dwellings
Cf. GT165+ Manners and customs
414 General works
414.3.A-Z Special types, A-Z
414.3.C38 Cave-dwellings
414.3.G7 Grass huts
414.3.T45 Tents
Furniture
415 General works
415.3.A-Z Special, A-Z
415.3.H35 Hammocks
Fire. Light and heat
416 General works
416.5 Light and heat
417 Fire-making
Including fire-making implements

Ethnology. Social and cultural anthropology
Cultural traits, customs, and institutions
Technology. Material culture -- Continued
Clothing and adornment
Cf. GT500+ Manners and customs

418	General works
	Ornaments. Jewelry
418.4	General works
419.A-Z	Special, A-Z
419.B4	Beads
419.13	Hairstyles. Headdresses
419.15	Cosmetics. Body markings. Body painting
419.2	Mutilations
419.25	Body piercing
419.3	Tattooing
419.5	Masks
	Arts and crafts. Industries
429	General works
430	General special
	Special crafts
431	Basketmaking
432	Weaving and spinning. Textile fabrics
433	Pottery making
433.5	Beadwork
	Special materials
	Stone
434	General works
434.2.A-Z	Special, A-Z
434.2.A45	Amber
434.2.F55	Flint
	Plant materials
434.3	General works
434.5	Bark
434.6	Gourds
434.7	Wood
	Animal materials
435	General works
435.3	Bone, tooth, horn
435.5	Leather. Skin dressing
435.7	Shell
435.9	Feathers
	Metals. Metallurgy
436	General works
436.2	Copper. Bronze
436.3	Gold
436.4	Iron
	Tools. Implements

Ethnology. Social and cultural anthropology
Cultural traits, customs, and institutions
Technology. Material culture
Arts and crafts. Industries
Tools. Implements -- Continued

436.8 General works

437.A-Z Special, A-Z

Class here works on tools made of various materials
For works on tools used in a particular activity see GN406+
For works on tools made of a special material see GN434+
For prehistoric tools see GN700+

437.A35 Adzes

437.A9 Axes

437.D7 Drilling implements

437.K55 Knives

437.P65 Pounders

Transportation

Cf. GN407.6+ Domesticated animals

438 General works

438.2 General special

439 Routes of communication

Including trails, roads, bridges, etc.

Transportation by water. Navigation

440 General works

440.1 Boats

440.2 Canoes

441 Vehicles. Wheels

442 Snowshoes. Skis

Economic organization. Economic anthropology

448 General works

448.2 General special

448.3 Allocation of natural resources

Division of labor. Organization of work

448.5 General works

448.6 Specialization

448.8 Cooperation. Competition

Property. Ownership

449 General works

449.3 Land tenure

Distribution of goods and services

449.6 General works

449.8 Ceremonial exchange

Commerce and trade

450 General works

GN

Ethnology. Social and cultural anthropology
Cultural traits, customs, and institutions
Economic organization. Economic anthropology
Distribution of goods and services
Commerce and trade -- Continued

450.2 Markets
Cf. HF5470 Business (General)
450.4 Barter
450.5 Money
450.7 Reciprocity
450.8 Business anthropology
Cf. HD58.7 Corporate culture

Intellectual life
For works on the arts, see the specific subject
Cf. GN502+ Psychological anthropology
451 General works
Communication
Cf. P1+ Linguistics
452 General works
452.5 Symbolism. Signs and symbols
453 Creativity. Creative ability
Recreation. Sports
454 General works
454.5 General special
454.55 Wit and humor
Cf. PN6147 Wit and humor (General)
454.6 Gambling
454.7 Children's play
Games and toys
454.8 General works
455.A-Z Special, A-Z
455.D64 Dolls
455.S9 String figures
Philosophy. World view
468 General works
468.2 General special
Classification systems
Cf. GN476+ Science and knowledge
468.4 General works
468.45 Names. Naming systems
468.5 Folk models
468.7 Ethics
469 Values
469.5 Time concepts. Cross-cultural studies of time

Ethnology. Social and cultural anthropology
Cultural traits, customs, and institutions
Intellectual life -- Continued
Religion and ritual. Belief systems
For works on the religion of a particular ethnic group or religion see BL1+
For works on mythology see BL300+

470 General works
470.2 General special
470.5 Origin of religion
470.7 Religion and society
471 Nature worship. Animism
471.4 Mana. Taboo
472 Fetishism
Totemism see GN489
472.4 Religious experience. Trances. Vision and ecstasy
Including the use of hallucinogenic drugs
472.5 Supernatural beings
472.6 Soul concept
Nativistic movements
472.7 General works
472.75 Cargo cults
472.8 Ancestor worship
Rites and ceremonies
473 General works
473.3 Head hunting
Sacrifice
473.4 General works
473.5 Blood sacrifice
473.6 Rain-making rites
474 Religious specialists, priests, etc.
Magic. Witchcraft
Cf. BF1403.2+ Occultism
Cf. GR525+ Folklore
475 General works
475.3 Magic
475.5 Witchcraft. Black magic. Sorcery
475.6 Evil eye
Cf. BF1553 Occult sciences
475.7 Divination
Cf. BF1745+ Occult sciences
Cf. BL613 Religions
475.8 Curing. Medicine men. Shamanism
Science and knowledge
476 General works
476.15 Mathematics. Counting and number systems
476.3 Astronomy. Calendars

Ethnology. Social and cultural anthropology
Cultural traits, customs, and institutions
Intellectual life
Science and knowledge -- Continued
Geography
476.4 General works
476.5 Cartography
476.6 History
Biology. Ethnobiology
476.7 General works
476.73 Ethnobotany
Ethnozoology
476.76 General works
476.78 Ethnoentomology. Insects
Cf. GN409.5 Edible insects
Medicine
Cf. GN296+ Medical anthropology
Cf. GN475.8 Medicine men
Cf. GR880 Folk medicine
477 General works
Surgery
477.5 General works
Mutilation see GN419.2
477.7 Trepanation
Social organization
Cf. HM401+ Sociology
478 General works
479 General special
479.5 Matriarchy
479.6 Patriarchy
Social roles
Sex roles
Cf. BF692.2+ Psychology
Cf. GN62.85 Physical anthropology and biocultural studies
Cf. GN490.7 Sex-based groups
Cf. HQ1075+ Sociology
479.65 General works
479.7 Women
Age roles see GN490.5
Leadership roles see GN492.25
479.8 Social groups (General)
Domestic groups. Family. Forms of marriage
Cf. GN484.4+ Marriage customs
Cf. HQ1+ Sociology
480 General works
480.2 General special

Ethnology. Social and cultural anthropology
Cultural traits, customs, and institutions
Social organization
Domestic groups. Family. Forms of marriage -- Continued

480.25 Incest. Consanguinity
480.3 Endogamy and exogamy
Polygamy
480.33 General works
480.35 Polygyny
480.36 Polyandry
480.4 Cross-cousin marriage
480.43 Levirate
480.5 Nuclear families
480.55 Extended families
Residence rules
480.6 General works
480.63 Matrilocal. Uxorilocal
480.65 Patrilocal. Virilocal
Life cycle
Childhood
482 General works
Birth. Infancy
482.1 General works
482.3 Adoption
482.4 Birth control. Abortion
482.5 Infanticide
Adolescence. Youth
483 General works
483.3 Initiations. Puberty rites
484 Circumcision. Female circumcision
Including clitoridectomy and infibulation
Adulthood
484.2 General works
Sexual behavior. Sex customs
484.3 General works
484.35 Homosexuality
484.38 Menstruation
Marriage
484.4 General works
484.43 Betrothal
484.45 Bridewealth. Dowry
484.47 Virginity. Defloration
484.7 Divorce
485 Old age
Death
485.5 General works

Ethnology. Social and cultural anthropology
Cultural traits, customs, and institutions
Social organization
Life cycle
Death -- Continued

486 Funeral and mourning customs
Cf. GT3150+ Manners and customs

486.3 Friendship
Cf. GN490.2 Institutionalized friendships

Kinship systems. Regulation of descent

486.5 Dictionaries. Encyclopedias

487 General works

Unilineal descent

487.3 General works

487.4 Matrilineal

487.5 Patrilineal

487.6 Double descent

487.7.A-Z Special kinship groups, A-Z

487.7.C55 Clans. Sibs

487.7.M6 Moieties

487.7.P45 Phratries

Cognatic descent. Nonunilineal descent

488 General works

488.2 Ambilineal. Ramages

488.4 Bilateral. Kindreds

489 Totemism

Associations

490 General works

490.2 Institutionalized friendships. Blood brothers. Bond friends

490.3 God parents

490.5 Age groups
Cf. GN483.3 Puberty rites

490.7 Sex-based groups

490.8 Secret societies

Social stratification

491 General works

491.4 Castes

491.45 Classes

491.5 Professional distinctions
Cf. GN448.6 Economic specialization

491.7 Territorial groups. Human territoriality

Political organization. Political anthropology

492 General works

492.2 General special

492.25 Leadership. Authority

492.3 Political customs and rites

Ethnology. Social and cultural anthropology
Cultural traits, customs, and institutions
Political organization. Political anthropology -- Continued
Types of political organizations

492.4 Bands
492.44 Segmentary systems
492.5 Tribes
492.55 Chieftainships
States
492.6 General works
492.7 Kingships. Kings

Social control
Cf. GN471.4 Taboo
Cf. K190+ Primitive law

493 General works
493.3 Social norms. Behavioral conformity
493.5 Deviance
494 Violation of norms. Crime
494.3 Punishment. Ordeals
Disputes
494.5 General works
495 Retaliation. Vendetta
495.2 Violence

Societal groups. Ethnic groups
Cf. GN506 Patterns of culture
Cf. HT1501+ Races

495.4 General works
495.6 Ethnicity. Ethnic identity
495.8 Ethnocentrism
Cf. GN345.5 Cultural relativism

Intergroup relations. Diplomacy. Ethnic relations. Ethnic conflict
Cf. GN345.6 Intercultural communication

496 General works
496.5 Feuds
Warfare
497 General works
Weapons and armor
497.5 General works
498.A-Z Special, A-Z
498.B5 Blowguns
498.B6 Boomerangs
Cf. GV1097.B65 Throwing sports
498.B78 Bows and arrows
Including arrowheads
498.C6 Clubs
498.S5 Shields

Ethnology. Social and cultural anthropology
Cultural traits, customs, and institutions
Societal groups. Ethnic groups
Intergroup relations. Diplomacy
Warfare
Weapons and armor
Special, A-Z -- Continued

498.S55 Slings
498.S68 Spears
498.T5 Throwing sticks

Psychological anthropology
Cf. GN270+ Race psychology

502 General works
504 Culture and personality
Cf. BF698.9.C8 Psychology (General)
506 Culture patterns. Cultural configurations
Cf. BF751 National characteristics
508 Psychoanalytic interpretations
510 Socialization. Enculturation
Cf. HQ783 Sociology
Cf. LC189+ Educational sociology
512 Self concept. Self identity
Cf. GN495.6 Ethnic identity
514 Psychology and social change
Cf. RC451.5.A2 Ethnopsychiatry
517 Culture shock

Ethnic groups and races
Cf. CB195+ Civilization and race
Cf. GN269+ Race (General)

Groups not limited to particular regions
Including works on certain European groups found in several countries

537 Caucasian. White races (General)
539 Indo-European
Cf. DS15+ Indo-Europeans in Asia
543 Mediterranean
547 Semitic. Jewish
548 Mongolian races (General)
Negro races (General) see GN645
549.A-Z Other, A-Z
549.A7 Arabs
549.B3 Basques
549.B9 Budini
549.C3 Celts
For works on Celtic antiquities see D70
549.C73 Creoles
549.F5 Finno-Ugrians

Ethnology. Social and cultural anthropology
Ethnic groups and races
Groups not limited to particular regions
Other, A-Z -- Continued

549.G4 Germanic tribes

Gypsies see DX101+

549.P3 Pelasgi

549.P9 Pygmies

Romanies see DX101+

549.S6 Slavs

549.T4 Teutonic peoples. Nordic peoples

549.U7 Uralic peoples

By region or country

Class here comprehensive works on the preliterate or folk societies of particular regions or countries (including works on certain individual large groupings, e.g. Bantus, Melanesians, Aboriginal Australians, etc.) even in the case of works limited to special topics or aspects

Class catalogs of audiovisual material under the appropriate subject number with the cutter ".Z9"

For works on particular societies or groups, including works on specific topics pertaining to those groups, see the society or group in D-F

For works on prehistoric archaeology including prehistoric remains of particular regions or countries see GN700+

North America

For local works on Indians of North America, see F

For works on Indians of North America see E51+

550 General works

560.A-Z By region or country, A-Z

Central and South America. Latin America (General)

For works on Indians of Central America, the West Indies, and South America, see E65 etc.

For local works on Indians of Central and South America, see F

562 General works

564.A-Z By region or country, A-Z

Europe

575 General works

Class here works on special topics in the anthropology of Europe, such as material culture, kinship, etc.

For general works on the ethnic groups of Europe see D990

GN

Ethnology. Social and cultural anthropology
Ethnic groups and races
By region or country
Europe -- Continued

585.A-Z By region or country, A-Z

Class here works on special topics in the anthropology of individual countries in Europe, such as material culture, kinship, etc.

For general works on the ethnic groups of individual countries in Europe, see the numbers for ethnography under those countries, e.g. DC34+ , France

588 Mediterranean Region
590 Parts of Asia, Africa, and Oceania (Collectively)

Asia

625 General works
635.A-Z By region or country, A-Z

e.g.

635.B6 Borneo
635.I4 India
635.I65 Indonesia
635.M35 Malay Archipelago
635.M4 Malaysia
635.M43 Maldives
635.N42 Near East. Middle East. Southwestern Asia

New Guinea see GN671.N5

Philippines see GN671.P5

635.R9 Ryukyu Islands
635.S5 Siberia
635.S58 Southeast Asia
635.S64 Soviet Central Asia
635.T4 Thailand
640 Arab countries
641 Islamic countries

Africa

Including Blacks in general

643 Periodicals. Societies. Serials
645 General works

North Africa

646 General works
648 Egypt
649.A-Z Other regions or countries, A-Z
649.A4 Algeria
649.L53 Libya
649.M65 Morocco

Northeast Africa

650 General works

	Ethnology. Social and cultural anthropology
	Ethnic groups and races
	By region or country
	Africa
	Northeast Africa -- Continued
650.5.A-Z	By region or country, A-Z
650.5.D55	Djibouti
650.5.E8	Ethiopia
650.5.S65	Somalia
	Sahara. Sahel
	Including French-speaking West Africa and the Sudan region
651	General works
652.A-Z	By region or country, A-Z
652.C44	Central African Republic
652.C5	Chad
652.M25	Mali
652.M28	Mauritania
652.N54	Niger
652.S93	Sudan
652.T63	Togo
652.U65	Upper Volta
	West Africa
	Including Central Africa
	For works on French-speaking West Africa see GN651+
652.5	General works
653	Nigeria
	Including the Niger area (General)
	Zaire
	Including the Congo area (General)
654.A1	Periodicals. Societies. Serials
654.A5-Z	General works
655.A-Z	Other regions or countries, A-Z
655.A5	Angola
655.B46	Benin
655.C3	Cameroon
	Central African Republic see GN652.C44
655.C65	Congo (Brazzaville)
	Côte d'Ivoire see GN655.I9
655.G3	Gabon
655.G35	Gambia
655.G45	Ghana
655.G74	Equatorial Guinea
655.G76	Portuguese Guinea
655.I9	Ivory Coast. Côte d'Ivoire
655.L5	Liberia

Ethnology. Social and cultural anthropology
Ethnic groups and races
By region or country
Africa
West Africa
Other regions or countries, A-Z -- Continued

655.S3 Senegal
655.S5 Sierra Leone
Southern Africa. South Africa
656 General works
657.A-Z By region or country, A-Z
657.B64 Botswana
657.M15 Malawi
657.N35 Namibia. South-West Africa
657.O36 Okavango River
657.R4 Northern Rhodesia. Zambia
657.R5 Southern Rhodesia. Zimbabwe
South-West Africa see GN657.N35
Zimbabwe see GN657.R5
Eastern Africa
658 General works
659.A-Z By region or country, A-Z
659.B78 Burundi
Ethiopia see GN650.5.E8
659.K4 Kenya
659.M6 Mozambique
659.R85 Rwanda
659.T3 Tanzania
659.U3 Uganda
661.A-Z Islands, A-Z
661.A95 Azores
661.C2 Canary Islands
661.C65 Comoros
661.M2 Madagascar
661.M38 Mauritius
661.R48 Réunion
661.S49 Seychelles
Australia and Pacific islands
662 General works
663 General special
By country, island, or island group

Ethnology. Social and cultural anthropology
Ethnic groups and races
By region or country
Australia and Pacific islands
By country, island, or island group -- Continued
Australia
Until 2004, the Library of Congress classed general works on Aboriginal Australians in GN665+
Beginning in 2004, newly cataloged works on Aboriginal Australians are classed in DU123.2+ except works limited to particular regions or states, which are classed in GN667.A+

665 General works
666 General special
667.A-Z By region or state, A-Z
For works on Tasmania see DU189
667.5 New Zealand
For works on Maori see DU422.8+
668 Melanesia (General)
669 Micronesia (General)
670 Polynesia (General)
671.A-Z Other countries, islands, or island groups, A-Z
Where possible, class individual islands or small island groups with the country or island territory in which they are located. For example, class the Loyalty Islands, which are a part of the territory of New Caledonia, in GN671.N35
Bismarck Archipelago see GN671.N5
Bougainville Island see GN671.N5
671.C3 Caroline Islands
Including the Federated States of Micronesia and Kapingamarangi and Manihiki Atolls
671.C5 Chatham Islands
671.C6 Cook Islands
Including Manihiki Atoll
671.E2 Easter Island
Federated States of Micronesia see GN671.C3
671.F5 Fiji
671.G35 Gambier Islands. Mangareva
671.H3 Hawaii
Kapingamarangi Atoll see GN671.C3
671.K57 Kiribati
Manihiki Atoll see GN671.C3
Loyalty Islands see GN671.N35
671.M27 Mariana Islands. Northern Mariana Islands
671.M3 Marquesas Islands
671.M33 Marshall Islands

Ethnology. Social and cultural anthropology
Ethnic groups and races
By region or country
Australia and Pacific islands
By country, island, or island group
Other countries, islands, or island groups, A-Z -- Continued

671.N27 Nauru
671.N35 New Caledonia
Including the Loyalty Islands
671.N5 New Guinea. Papua New Guinea
Including Bismarck Archipelago, Bougainville Island
671.N6 New Hebrides. Vanuatu
671.P5 Philippines
Portuguese Timor see GN635.I65
671.S2 Samoan Islands
671.S55 Society Islands
671.S6 Solomon Islands
671.T46 Tokelau Islands
671.T5 Tonga
671.T6 Torres Strait Islands
671.T76 Truk Islands
671.T77 Tuamotu Islands
671.T8 Tubuai Islands
671.T88 Tuvalu
Vanuatu see GN671.N6
671.W3 Wallis and Futuna Islands
673 Arctic regions
For works on Eskimos see E99.E7
674 Tropics

Prehistoric archaeology
Class here works on cultures without writing. Class archaeological studies of historic or proto-historic cultures with written records, including those limited to the Bronze age or Iron age, in D-F
For works dealing with a particular period, including works dealing with a particular period also limited in coverage to a particular topic and/or geographic area see GN768+
For works on a particular topic and geographic area without regard to the period see GN803+

700 Periodicals. Societies. Serials
701 Congresses
705 Collected works (nonserial)
710 Dictionaries. Encyclopedias
Philosophy. Relation to other topics. Methodology see CC73+

Prehistoric archaeology -- Continued
Study and teaching. Research see GN761
Museums. Exhibitions see GN800+
History
720 General works
722.A-Z By region or country, A-Z
Biography see CC110+
General works, treatises, and textbooks
733 Early through 1800
735 1801-1869
738 1870-1950
739 1951-1974
740 1975-
741 General special
743 Popular works
744 Juvenile works
746 Pictorial works
Lost continents
Including Atlantis, Lemuria, Mu, etc.
750 Periodicals. Societies. Serials
751 General works
755 Subterranean civilization
761 Study and teaching. Research
766 Addresses, essays, lectures
By period division
For works that are limited in scope to the physical remains of Early man see GN282+
Stone age
768 General works
Archeolithic. Eolithic
769 General works
770 General special
By continent
For America, see E-F
Europe
770.2.A1 General works
770.2.A5-Z Special cultures, peoples, etc., A-Z
770.22.A-Z By region or country, A-Z
Prefer classification by special cultures
770.25 Mediterranean Region (General)
770.28 Eurasia
Asia
770.3.A1 General works
770.3.A5-Z Special cultures, peoples, etc., A-Z
For list of cultures see GN770.2.A5+
770.32.A-Z By region or country, A-Z
Prefer classification by special cultures

Prehistoric archaeology
By period division
Stone age
Archeolithic. Eolithic
By continent
Asia
By region or country, A-Z -- Continued

770.32.N4 Near East. Middle East

Africa

770.4.A1 General works

770.4.A5-Z Special cultures, peoples, etc., A-Z
For list of cultures see GN770.2.A5+

770.42.A-Z By region or country, A-Z
Prefer classification by special cultures

Australia and Pacific islands

770.5.A1 General works

770.5.A5-Z Special cultures, peoples, etc.
For list of cultures see GN770.2.A5+

770.52.A-Z By region or country, A-Z
Prefer classification by special cultures

Paleolithic

771 General works

772 General special

By continent
For America, see E-F

Europe

772.2.A1 General works

772.2.A5-Z Special cultures, peoples, etc., A-Z
Establish here all paleolithic cultures regardless of continent

772.2.A53 Acheulian

772.2.A78 Aterien

772.2.A8 Aurignacian

772.2.C3 Capsian

772.2.C48 Chatelperronien

772.2.C53 Clactonian

772.2.H36 Hamburgian

772.2.M3 Magdalenian

772.2.M6 Mousterian

772.2.P32 Patjitan

772.2.P4 Perigordian
Including Gravettian

Reindeer see GN772.2.M3

772.2.S6 Solutrean

772.22.A-Z By region or country, A-Z
Prefer classification by special cultures

772.25 Mediterranean Region (General)

Prehistoric archaeology
By period division
Stone age
Paleolithic
By continent -- Continued

772.28 Eurasia
Asia
772.3.A1 General works
772.3.A5-Z Special cultures, peoples, etc., A-Z
For list of cultures see GN772.2.A5+
772.32.A-Z By region or country, A-Z
Prefer classification by special cultures
772.32.N4 Near East
Africa
772.4.A1 General works
772.4.A5-Z Special cultures, peoples, etc., A-Z
For list of cultures see GN772.2.A5+
772.42.A-Z By region or country, A-Z
Prefer classification by special cultures
Australia and Pacific islands
772.5.A1 General works
772.5.A5-Z Special cultures, peoples, etc., A-Z
For list of cultures see GN772.2.A5+
772.52.A-Z By region or country, A-Z
Prefer classification by special cultures
Mesolithic
773 General works
774 General special
By continent
For America, see E-F
Europe
774.2.A1 General works
774.2.A5-Z Special cultures, peoples, etc., A-Z
Establish here all mesolithic cultures regardless of continent
774.2.A85 Asturian
774.2.A97 Azilian
774.2.M33 Maglemosean
774.2.N38 Natufian
774.2.S6 Smithfield
774.2.T3 Tardenoisian
774.2.W5 Wilton
774.22.A-Z By region or country, A-Z
Prefer classification by special cultures
774.25 Mediterranean Region (General)
774.28 Eurasia
Asia

GN

Prehistoric archaeology
By period division
Stone age
Mesolithic
By continent
Asia -- Continued

774.3.A1 General works
774.3.A5-Z Special cultures, peoples, etc., A-Z
For list of cultures see GN774.2.A5+
774.32.A-Z By region or country, A-Z
Prefer classification by special cultures
774.32.N4 Near East

Africa

774.4.A1 General works
774.4.A5-Z Special cultures, peoples, etc., A-Z
For list of cultures see GN774.2.A5+
774.42.A-Z By region or country, A-Z
Prefer classification by special cultures

Australia and Pacific islands

774.5.A1 General works
774.5.A5-Z Special cultures, peoples, etc., A-Z
For list of cultures see GN774.2.A5+
774.52.A-Z By region or country, A-Z
Prefer classification by special cultures

Neolithic

775 General works
776 General special

By continent
For America, see E-F
Europe

776.2.A1 General works
776.2.A5-Z Special cultures, peoples, etc., A-Z
Establish here all neolithic cultures regardless of continent
776.2.B3 Bandkeramik
776.2.B4 Beaker
776.2.B47 Bernburg
776.2.B64 Boisman culture
776.2.C6 Corded ware
776.2.C68 Cotofeni
776.2.C83 Cucuteni-Tripolye
776.2.D3 Danilo
776.2.F8 Funnel-beaker
Ghassul see GN778.2.G48
776.2.H34 Halaf
776.2.H6 Horgen
776.2.H75 Hsi-t'uan shan

Prehistoric archaeology
By period division
Stone age
Neolithic
By continent
Europe
Special cultures, peoples, etc., A-Z -- Continued
776.2.J6 Jōmon
776.2.L4 Lengyel-Jordansmühl
776.2.L52 Liangzhu
776.2.M5 Michelsberg
776.2.O35 Okhotsk
776.2.P3 Passage Graves
776.2.P43 P'ei-li-kang
776.2.P47 Pfyn
776.2.S27 Satsumon
776.2.S55 Single grave culture
776.2.S73 Starčevo
776.2.V5 Vinča
776.2.Y27 Yang-shao
776.2.Y3 Yayoi
776.22.A-Z By region or country, A-Z
Prefer classification by special cultures
776.25 Mediterranean Region (General)
776.28 Eurasia
Asia
776.3.A1 General works
776.3.A5-Z Special cultures, peoples, etc., A-Z
For list of cultures see GN776.2.A5+
776.32.A-Z By region or country, A-Z
Prefer classification by special cultures
776.32.N4 Near East
Africa
776.4.A1 General works
776.4.A5-Z Special cultures, peoples, etc., A-Z
For list of cultures see GN776.2.A5+
776.42.A-Z By region or country, A-Z
Prefer classification by special cultures
Australia and Pacific islands
776.5.A1 General works
776.5.A5-Z Special cultures, peoples, etc., A-Z
For list of cultures see GN776.2.A5+
776.52.A-Z By region or country, A-Z
Prefer classification by special cultures
Copper and bronze ages
777 General works
778 General special

Prehistoric archaeology
By period division
Copper and bronze ages -- Continued
By continent
For America, see E-F
Europe
778.2.A1 General works
778.2.A2-Z Special cultures, peoples, etc., A-Z
Establish here all copper and bronze age cultures regardless of continent
778.2.A22 Abashev
778.2.B3 Baden
778.2.B44 Bell beaker
778.2.C37 Castelluccian culture
778.2.G48 Ghassul
778.2.K5 Knoviz
778.2.K87 Kura-Araxes culture
778.2.L3 Lausitz
778.2.M35 Maikop culture
778.2.M53 Mierzanowice
778.2.N87 Nuraghi
778.2.T86 Tumulus
778.2.U22 Ubaid
778.2.U43 Unetice
778.2.U76 Urnfield
778.2.V83 Vučedol
778.22.A-Z By region or country, A-Z
Prefer classification by special cultures
778.25 Mediterranean Region (General)
778.28 Eurasia
Asia
778.3.A1 General works
778.3.A5-Z Special cultures, peoples, etc., A-Z
For list of cultures see GN778.2.A2+
778.32.A-Z By region or country, A-Z
Prefer classification by special cultures
778.32.N4 Near East
Africa
778.4.A1 General works
778.4.A5-Z Special cultures, peoples, etc., A-Z
For list of cultures see GN778.2.A2+
778.42.A-Z By region or country, A-Z
Prefer classification by special cultures
Australia and Pacific islands
778.5.A1 General works
778.5.A5-Z Special cultures, peoples, etc., A-Z
For list of cultures see GN778.2.A2+

Prehistoric archaeology
By period division
Copper and bronze ages
By continent
Australia and Pacific islands -- Continued
778.52.A-Z By region or country, A-Z
Prefer classification by special cultures
Iron age
779 General works
780 General special
By continent
For America, see E-F
Europe
780.2.A1 General works
780.2.A5-Z Special cultures, peoples, etc., A-Z
Establish here all iron age cultures regardless of continent
780.2.H3 Hallstatt
780.2.J38 Jastorf culture
780.2.L3 La Tène period
780.2.P39 Pazyryk culture
780.2.P79 Przeworsk
780.2.S27 Sargat
780.2.V5 Villanovan culture
780.22.A-Z By region or country, A-Z
Prefer classification by special cultures
780.25 Mediterranean Region (General)
780.28 Eurasia
Asia
780.3.A1 General works
780.3.A5-Z Special cultures, peoples, etc., A-Z
For list of cultures see GN780.2.A5+
780.32.A-Z By region or country, A-Z
Prefer classification by special cultures
780.32.N4 Near East
Africa
780.4.A1 General works
780.4.A5-Z Special cultures, peoples, etc., A-Z
For list of cultures see GN780.2.A5+
780.42.A-Z By region or country, A-Z
Prefer classification by special cultures
Australia and Pacific islands
780.5.A1 General works
780.5.A5-Z Special cultures, peoples, etc., A-Z
For list of cultures see GN780.2.A5+
780.52.A-Z By region or country, A-Z
Prefer classification by special cultures

Prehistoric archaeology -- Continued
By special topic
For works on special topics in special geographic areas see GN803+
Caves and cave dwellers
Cf. GB601+ Caves (Physical geography)
783 General works
General special
783.3 Artificial caves
783.5 Other (not A-Z)
784 Coastal sites. Coastal archaeology
785 Lake dwellings and lake dwellers
786 Wetland sites. Water-saturated sites
787 Kitchen middens
789 Fortifications. Earthworks
790 Megolithic monuments
Including menhirs, dolmens, cromlechs, etc.
795 Mounds, tumuli, etc.
796 Leys. Straight tracks
799.A-Z Other special topics, A-Z
799.A4 Agriculture
Including agricultural implements and the origin of domestic plants and animals
Cf. S419+ History of agriculture
799.A5 Amber
Architecture see GN799.B8
Art see N5310+
799.A76 Artisans
799.A8 Astronomy
799.A9 Axes
799.B62 Boats
799.B65 Bone implements. Bone carving
799.B7 Bronzes
799.B8 Buildings. Architecture
799.C25 Cannibalism
799.C35 Chemistry
799.C38 Children
799.C45 Commerce
799.C49 Cordage
799.C5 Costume
799.C9 Cyclons
Demography see GN33.5
799.E4 Economics
799.E63 Engineering
Including irrigation engineering and hydraulic engineering
799.F48 Fire
Including hearths

Prehistoric archaeology
By special topic
Other special topics, A-Z -- Continued

799.F5 Fishing
799.F6 Food
799.G6 Gold
Hearths see GN799.F48
799.H84 Hunting
799.M4 Metallurgy
799.N3 Navigation
799.P4 Petroglyphs. Rock paintings
799.P5 Pins and needles
799.P6 Pottery
799.P74 Psychology
799.Q83 Quarries
799.R4 Religion
Rock paintings see GN799.P4
799.S4 Sculpture
799.S43 Settlement patterns
799.S45 Sex role
799.S5 Skis
799.S9 Symbolism
799.T43 Textile fabrics
799.T6 Tools
799.T7 Toys
799.T73 Transportation
799.W26 Warfare
799.W3 Weapons
Including arrowheads, daggers, spearheads, swords
799.W4 Weaving
799.W66 Women

Museums. Exhibitions (General)
Class here works on general collections or exhibitions only. For works on collections or exhibitions representative of particular periods, topics, or places, or combinations thereof, see the period, topic, or place

800 General works
802 Private collections
By region or country
Europe
803 General works
Great Britain
805.A1 Periodicals. Societies
805.A2 Congresses
805.A3A-.A3Z Museums. Exhibitions. By city, A-Z
805.A5-Z General works
806.A-Z Local, A-Z

Prehistoric archaeology
By region or country
Europe -- Continued
Ireland

806.5.A1 Periodicals. Societies
806.5.A2 Congresses
806.5.A3A-.A3Z Museums. Exhibitions. By city, A-Z
806.5.A5-Z General works
806.6.A-Z Local, A-Z

Austria

807.A1 Periodicals. Societies
807.A2 Congresses
807.A3A-.A3Z Museums. Exhibitions. By city, A-Z
807.A5-Z General works
808.A-Z Local, A-Z

France

811.A1 Periodicals. Societies
811.A2 Congresses
811.A3A-.A3Z Museums. Exhibitions. By city, A-Z
811.A5-Z General works
812.A-Z Local, A-Z

Germany
Including West Germany

813.A1 Periodicals. Societies
813.A2 Congresses
813.A3A-.A3Z Museums. Exhibitions. By city, A-Z
813.A5-Z General works
814.A-Z Local, A-Z

East Germany

814.5.A1 Periodicals. Societies
814.5.A2 Congresses
814.5.A3A-.A3Z Museums. Exhibitions. By city, A-Z
814.5.A5-Z General works
814.6.A-Z Local, A-Z

Greece

815.A1 Periodicals. Societies
815.A2 Congresses
815.A3A-.A3Z Museums. Exhibitions. By city, A-Z
815.A5-Z General works
816.A-Z Local, A-Z

Italy

817.A1 Periodicals. Societies
817.A2 Congresses
817.A3A-.A3Z Museums. Exhibitions. By city, A-Z
817.A5-Z General works
818.A-Z Local, A-Z

Netherlands

Prehistoric archaeology
By region or country
Europe
Netherlands -- Continued

819.A1	Periodicals. Societies
819.A2	Congresses
819.A3A-.A3Z	Museums. Exhibitions. By city, A-Z
819.A5-Z	General works
820.A-Z	Local, A-Z
	Belgium
821.A1	Periodicals. Societies
821.A2	Congresses
821.A3A-.A3Z	Museums. Exhibitions. By city, A-Z
821.A5-Z	General works
822.A-Z	Local, A-Z
	Russia. Soviet Union. Russia (Federation) Including former Soviet republics (collectively) For individual European states see GN845.A+ For individual Asian regions or states see GN855.A+
823.A1	Periodicals. Societies
823.A2	Congresses
823.A3A-.A3Z	Museums. Exhibitions. By city, A-Z
823.A5-Z	General works
824.A-Z	Local, A-Z
825	Scandinavia
	Denmark
826.A1	Periodicals. Societies
826.A2	Congresses
826.A3A-.A3Z	Museums. Exhibitions. By city, A-Z
826.A5A-Z	General works
827.A-Z	Local, A-Z
	Norway
828.A1	Periodicals. Societies
828.A2	Congresses
828.A3A-.A3Z	Museums. Exhibitions. By city, A-Z
828.A5-Z	General works
829.A-Z	Local, A-Z
	Sweden
830.A1	Periodicals. Societies
830.A2	Congresses
830.A3A-.A3Z	Museums. Exhibitions. By city, A-Z
830.A5-Z	General works
831.A-Z	Local, A-Z
	Spain
835.A1	Periodicals. Societies
835.A2	Congresses
835.A3A-.A3Z	Museums. Exhibitions. By city, A-Z

GN

Prehistoric archaeology
By region or country
Europe
Spain -- Continued

835.A5-Z General works
836.A-Z Local, A-Z
Portugal
837.A1 Periodicals. Societies
837.A2 Congresses
837.A3A-.A3Z Museums. Exhibitions. By city, A-Z
837.A5-Z General works
838.A-Z Local, A-Z
Switzerland
841.A1 Periodicals. Societies
841.A2 Congresses
841.A3A-.A3Z Museums. Exhibitions. By city, A-Z
841.A5-Z General works
842.A-Z Local, A-Z
845.A-Z Other regions or countries, A-Z
845.A3 Adriatic Sea Region
845.A34 Aegean Sea Region
845.A56 Alps
845.B28 Balkan Peninsula
845.B3 Baltic States
845.B4 Belarus
845.B5 Bosnia and Hercegovina
845.B8 Bulgaria
(845.C3) Caucasus
see GN855.C35
845.C7 Croatia
(845.C93) Cyprus
see GN855.C93
845.C95 Czechoslovakia. Czech Republic
845.E15 Eastern Europe
845.E5 Estonia
845.F5 Finland
845.H8 Hungary
845.L3 Latvia
845.L5 Lithuania
845.M2 Macedonia (Republic)
845.M3 Malta
845.M7 Moldova
845.P7 Poland
845.R8 Romania
845.S3 Slovakia
845.S5 Slovenia
845.U37 Ukraine

Prehistoric archaeology
By region or country
Europe
Other regions or countries, A-Z -- Continued

845.W47 Western Mediterranean
845.Y8 Yugoslavia
848 Mediterranean Region
849 Eurasia
Asia
851 General works
855.A-Z By region or country, A-Z
855.A3 Afghanistan
855.A72 Arabian Peninsula
855.A74 Armenia (Republic)
855.A78 Azerbaijan
855.B34 Baluchistan
855.B35 Bangladesh
855.C35 Caucasus
855.C4 Asia, Central
855.C6 China
855.C65 Chukchi Peninsula
855.C93 Cyprus
855.E27 East Asia
855.E3 Egypt
855.G4 Georgia (Republic)
855.I4 India
855.I5 Indochina
855.I6 Indonesia
855.I72 Iraq
855.I75 Israel
855.J2 Japan
855.J67 Jordan
855.K2 Kazakhstan
855.K6 Korea
855.K8 Kyrgyzstan
855.M25 Macau
855.M4 Malaysia
855.M65 Mongolia
(855.N35) Near East
see GN857
855.O43 Oman
855.P18 Pakistan
855.P3 Palestine
855.P5 Philippines
855.Q2 Qatar
855.R9 Russian Far East
Including Siberia

Prehistoric archaeology
By region or country
Asia
By region or country, A-Z -- Continued

855.S33 Saudi Arabia

Siberia see GN855.R9

855.S74 Sri Lanka

855.S95 Syria

855.T28 Taiwan

855.T4 Tajikistan

855.T45 Thailand

855.T47 Thar Desert

855.T5 Tibet

855.T83 Turkey

855.U5 Uzbekistan

855.V5 Vietnam

857 Middle East (General)

For individual countries see GN855.A+

Africa

861 General works

865.A-Z By region or country, A-Z

Atlantic Ocean islands

868 General works

869.A-Z By island or group of islands, A-Z

Australia and Pacific islands

871 General works

875.A-Z By country, island, or island group, A-Z

For individual islands or small island groups, see, whenever possible, the country or island territory in which they are located, e.g. class Moen Island with Micronesia (Federated States), not with Truk Islands

885 Arctic regions (General)

890 Tropics

Folklore
Cf. GN301+ Ethnology
Cf. GT1+ Manners and customs
Cf. GV1743 Folk dancing
Cf. M1627+ Folk music
Cf. ML3544+ Folk music
Cf. NK607+ Folk art

1	Periodicals. Societies. Serials
10	Congresses
	Collected works (nonserial)
15	Several authors
20	Individual authors
35	Dictionaries. Encyclopedias
37	Directories
	Philosophy. Relation to other topics. Methodology
40	General works
41	Relation to history
41.3	Relation to literature For specific literatures, see the literature in P Cf. PN56.F58 Folklore in literature
41.5	Relation to politics
42	Relation to psychology
42.5	Relation to social history
42.6	Relation to sociology
43.A-Z	Relation to special classes of persons, A-Z
43.C4	Children
44.A-Z	Special methods, A-Z
44.C3	Cartography
44.E43	Electronic data processing
44.O72	Oral-formulaic analysis
44.S7	Structural analysis
	Communication in folklore Including intercultural communication
44.4	General works
44.5	Folkloristic writing
	Study and teaching. Research
45	General works
45.5	Fieldwork
	By region or country
46	United States
47.A-Z	Other regions or countries, A-Z
	Museums. Exhibitions see GN35+
48	History
	Folklorists
49	Folklore as a profession
	Biography
50	Collective

GR

Folklorists
Biography -- Continued
55.A-Z Individual, A-Z
58 Applied folklore
General works, treatises, and textbooks
60 Early through 1800
65 1801-1974
66 1975-
67 General special (Special aspects of the subject as a whole)
68 Outlines, syllabi
68.5 Popular works
69 Juvenile works
71 Addresses, essays, lectures
For studies or collections of folk literature from a particular region, country, or ethnic group, including folk literature from a particular region, etc., on a specific topic see GR91.2+
For folk literature on a specific topic not limited to a particular region, etc. see GR430+
For medieval literature (general) see PN661+
Folk literature (General)
For medieval literature by language, see PQ-PT
72 General works
72.3 Performance
Including the performance of folktales, i.e. storytelling
72.5 Themes, motives, etc.
72.56 Classification, indexes, etc.
73 Collection of texts
By form
Fable see PN980+
Folk drama see PN6120.F6
Folktales
For fairy tales see GR550+
For juvenile folktales see PZ8
74 General works
Themes, motives, etc.
74.4 General works
74.6 Classification, indexes, etc.
75.A-Z Individual folktale themes and motives, A-Z
Including collections of variant tales found in more than one region or country
75.A42 Aladdin
75.A53 Anansi
75.B22 Baba Yaga
75.B3 Basil maiden
75.B38 Beauty and the beast
75.B4 Befana

Folk literature (General)
By form
Folktales
Themes, motives, etc.
Individual folktale themes and motives, A-Z -- Continued

75.B53 Black ox
75.B57 Bluebeard
75.B6 Book of the book
75.B76 Brother and Sister
75.C4 Cinderella
75.C8 Cupid and Psyche
75.D72 Dragon slayer
75.F4 Ferdinand the Faithful and Ferdinand the Unfaithful
75.F58 Flying Dutchman
75.F72 Frau Holle
75.F75 Frog Prince
75.G45 Giufà
75.G6 Grateful dead
75.G64 Green Man
75.H3 Halfchick
The kids and wolf see GR75.W64
75.J32 Jackal
75.L56 Little Red Riding Hood
75.M3 Maiden without hands
75.M44 Melusine
75.M92 Mushkil Gusha
75.O3 Oedipus
75.O4 Oldenburger Horn
75.O9 Our Lady's child
75.P5 Pent Cuckoo
75.P53 Perseus
75.P55 Pied Piper of Hamelin
75.P6 Polyphemus
75.P73 Pregnant man
75.P74 Prince and the arm bands
Psyche and Cupid see GR75.C8
75.P85 Puss in Boots
75.R35 Rapunzel
75.S44 Servant's good counsels
75.S55 Sleeping Beauty
75.S6 Snow White
75.S67 Sorcerer's apprentice
75.S69 Spinning women by the spring
75.S8 Swan maidens
75.T35 Taming of the Shrew
75.T48 Three oranges

Folk literature (General)
By form
Folktales
Themes, motives, etc.
Individual folktale themes and motives, A-Z -- Continued
75.T5 Three stolen princesses
75.T64 Tom Thumb
75.T66 Tooth Fairy
75.T93 Two Brothers
75.U45 Uglier foot
75.W3 Wandering Jew
Cf. PN57.W3 Wandering Jew as theme in literature
75.W55 Wild huntsman
75.W64 Wolf and the kids
76 Collections of texts
For collections of tales on a single theme from more than one region or country see GR75.A+
Jokes see PN6147
Nursery rhymes see GR487
Proverbs see PN6400+
Riddles see PN6366+
Legends
78 General works
79 Collections of texts
Memorates
79.5 General works
79.6 Collections of texts
81 Folk beliefs, superstitions, etc. (General)
By race or group not limited to special places
For folklore of individual races or groups in specific regions or countries see GR99.6+
Celtic see GR137
Christian see BR135+
Gypsy see DX157
93.5 Finno-Ugrian
95 Indo-European
96 Portuguese in foreign countries
Romani see DX157
Semitic
97 General works
Jewish
97.8 Periodicals. Societies. Serials
98 General works
By hemisphere
99 Northern

By hemisphere -- Continued
99.2 Southern
99.4 Eastern
Western see GR100
By region or country
Class here works on the folklore of specific places, including the folklore of specific places on specific topics
99.6 Pacific area
100 America
North America
101 General works
American Indians see E98.F6
United States
105 General works
Themes, motives, etc.
105.3 General works
105.34 Classification, indexes, etc.
105.37.A-Z Individual themes and motives, A-Z
Including collections of variant tales found in more than one region or state
105.37.C63 Cockaigne
105.37.D3 Davy Crockett
105.37.J32 Jack tales
105.37.M54 Mike Fink
105.37.P38 Paul Bunyan
105.5 Collections of texts (General)
106 New England
106.5 Middle Atlantic
107 Middle West
107.5 Mississippi River
108 The South
108.15 Appalachian Region
108.2 Shenandoah Valley
108.3 Ozark Mountains
108.5 Southwest
108.6 Rio Grande Valley
109 The West
For Mexican Americans see GR111.M49
109.5 Northwest, Pacific
110.A-.W By state, A-W
e.g.
110.H38 Hawaii
111.A-Z By ethnic group, A-Z
111.A47 African Americans
Including Gullahs
American Indians see E98.F6
111.C55 Chinese Americans

By region or country
North America
United States
By ethnic group, A-Z -- Continued

111.F55 Filipino Americans
111.F56 Finnish Americans
111.F73 French Americans
Including Cajun
111.G47 German Americans
Including Pennsylvania Dutch
111.G74 Greek Americans
111.H57 Hispanic Americans
111.I73 Italian Americans
111.M49 Mexican Americans
111.P65 Polish Americans
111.R65 Romanian Americans
111.S33 Scandinavian Americans
111.S65 Spanish Americans (Spain)
111.S84 Swedish Americans
112 Insular possessions (General)

Canada
113 General works
113.5.A-Z Local, A-Z
113.7.A-Z By ethnic group, A-Z
Acadians see GR113.7.F73
113.7.F73 French-Canadians
113.7.M34 Macedonians
113.7.M45 Mennonites
113.7.U57 Ukrainians

Latin America
114 General works
Mexico
115 General works
115.5 Local, A-Z
Central America
117 General works
118.A-Z By region or country, A-Z
West Indies. Caribbean Area
120 General works
121.A-Z By island, etc., A-Z
121.B3 Bahamas
121.C37 Carriacou
121.C8 Cuba
121.D6 Dominican Republic
121.G8 Guadeloupe
121.H3 Haiti
121.J2 Jamaica

By region or country
Latin America
West Indies. Caribbean Area
By island, etc., A-Z -- Continued

121.M36 Martinique
121.N42 Netherlands Antilles
121.P8 Puerto Rico
121.S24 Saint Lucia
121.T7 Trinidad and Tobago

South America

130 General works
133.A-Z By region or country, A-Z

Under each country:

.x	*General works*
.x2A-.x2Z	*Local, A-Z*
.x3A-.x3Z	*By ethnic group, A-Z*

Europe

135 General works

By people not limited to one country

136 Miscellaneous combinations of peoples
e.g. Slavs and Magyars
137 Celtic peoples
137.5 Frisian peoples
137.6 Mennonites
137.7 Basque peoples
138 Slavic peoples
138.3 Szeklers
138.5 Sami
139 Nordic peoples. Germanic peoples
139.2 Walser peoples

By region not limited to one country

139.3 Alps
139.4 Ardennes
Balkan Peninsula see GR250+
139.45 Baltic region
Cf. GR204+ Baltic States
139.47 Carpathian Mountains
139.48 Danube River Valley
139.5 Eastern Europe
139.6 Fichtelgebirge
139.7 Macedonia
Cf. GR255+ Macedonia (Republic)
139.78 Pyrenees
Mediterranean Region see GR264
139.8 Rhine River Valley
Scandinavia see GR205+

Great Britain. England

	By region or country
	Europe
	Great Britain. England -- Continued
140	Periodicals. Societies. Serials
141	General works
142.A-Z	England (Local), A-Z
	Scotland
143	Periodicals. Societies. Serials
144	General works
145.A-Z	Local, A-Z
	Northern Ireland
146	Periodicals. Societies. Serials
147	General works
148.A-Z	Local, A-Z
	Wales
149	Periodicals. Societies. Serials
150	General works
151.A-Z	Local, A-Z
153.A-Z	Other divisions, A-Z
	e.g.
153.G9	Guernsey
153.M3	Man, Isle of
	Ireland
153.4	Periodicals. Societies. Serials
153.5	General works
153.6.A-Z	Local, A-Z
	Czechoslovakia. Czech Republic
154	General works
154.2.A-Z	Local, A-Z
154.3.A-Z	By ethnic group, A-Z
154.3.G47	Germans
154.3.P64	Poles
154.3.U47	Ukrainians
	Slovakia
154.4	General works
154.43.A-Z	Local, A-Z
154.47.A-Z	By ethnic group, A-Z
	Hungary
154.5	General works
154.7.A-Z	Local, A-Z
154.8.A-Z	By ethnic group, A-Z
154.8.G47	Germans
154.8.S56	Slovaks
	Austria
155	Periodicals. Societies. Serials
156	General works
159.A-Z	Local, A-Z

	By region or country
	Europe -- Continued
	France
160	Periodicals. Societies. Serials
161	General works
162.A-Z	Local, A-Z
162.5.A-Z	By ethnic group, A-Z
162.5.C38	Catalans
163	Andorra
	Germany
	Including West Germany
165	Periodicals. Societies. Serials
166	General works
167.A-Z	Local (West Germany), A-Z
	Cf. DD801.R7+ Rhine legends, etc.
	East Germany
168	General works
169.A-Z	Local, A-Z
169.2.A-Z	By tribe or ethnic group, A-Z
169.2.S6	Sorbs
	Greece (Modern)
	For ancient Greek folk literature see PA3285
170	General works
170.2.A-Z	Local, A-Z
170.3.A-Z	By ethnic group, A-Z
170.3.A76	Aromanians
170.3.M33	Macedonians
	Italy
175	Periodicals. Societies. Serials
176	General works
177.A-Z	Local, A-Z
177.2.A-Z	By ethnic group, A-Z
177.2.A42	Albanians
177.2.C38	Catalans
177.2.F74	Friulians
177.2.G47	Germans
177.2.G74	Greeks
178	Malta
179	Monaco
	Netherlands
180	Periodicals. Societies. Serials
181	General works
182.A-Z	Local, A-Z
	Belgium
185	General works
186.A-Z	Local, A-Z
187.A-Z	By ethnic group, A-Z

By region or country
Europe
Belgium
By ethnic group, A-Z -- Continued
187.F54 Flemish
187.W35 Walloons
188 Luxemburg
Poland
195 General works
196.A-Z Local, A-Z
196.2.A-Z By ethnic group, A-Z
196.2.G47 Germans
196.2.U47 Ukrainians
Finland
200 General works
201.A-Z Local, A-Z
201.2.A-Z By ethnic group, A-Z
201.2.S94 Swedes
Russia. Soviet Union. Former Soviet republics
For former republics of the Caucasus see GR276+
For Armenia (Republic) see GR277
For former republics of central Asia see GR300+
202 General works
202.5.A-Z By ethnic group, A-Z
Russia (Federation)
203.17 General works
203.19.A-Z Local, A-Z
For Siberia see GR345
203.2.A-Z By ethnic group, A-Z
203.2.A2 Abaza
203.2.A48 Altais
203.2.C45 Chechens
203.2.C5 Chukchi
203.2.C57 Circassian
203.2.D64 Dolgans
203.2.E83 Even
203.2.E84 Evenki
203.2.G47 Germans
203.2.G55 Gilyaks
203.2.I54 Ingush
203.2.K45 Kets
203.2.K53 Khanty
203.2.K65 Komi
203.2.K86 Kumyk
203.2.M25 Mansi
203.2.M37 Mari
203.2.M67 Mordvins

By region or country
Europe
Russia (Federation)
By ethnic group, A-Z -- Continued

203.2.N4 Nentsy
203.2.N53 Nganasani
203.2.N64 Nogai
203.2.O2 Ob-Ugrians
203.2.S54 Shor
203.2.T36 Tat
203.2.T37 Tatars
203.2.U34 Udekhe
203.2.V46 Veps
203.2.V67 Votes

Belarus

203.4 General works
203.5.A-.Z Local, A-Z
203.6 Moldova

Ukraine

203.8 General works
203.9.A-.Z Local, A-Z
203.95.A-.Z By ethnic group, A-Z

Baltic States

204 General works
204.2 Estonia
204.5 Latvia
204.8 Lithuania

Scandinavia

For works on Lapp folklore see GR138.5

205 General works

Denmark

209 Periodicals. Societies. Serials
210 General works
211.A-Z Local, A-Z
213 Faeroe Islands
214 Greenland

For works on Eskimo folklore see E99.E7

215 Iceland

Norway

220 Periodicals. Societies. Serials
221 General works
222.A-Z Local, A-Z

Sweden

224 Periodicals. Societies. Serials
225 General works
226.A-Z Local, A-Z

Spain

GR

By region or country
Europe
Spain -- Continued
229 Periodicals. Societies. Serials
230 General works
233 Moorish folklore
237.A-Z Local, A-Z
Portugal
238 General works
239.A-Z Local, A-Z
239.2.A-Z By ethnic group, A-Z
Switzerland
Cf. DQ92 Tell and Rütli legends
240 Periodicals. Societies. Serials
241 General works
242.A-Z Local, A-Z
Balkan States. Southern Slavs
250 General works
250.5.A-Z By group not limited to one country, A-Z
250.5.M33 Macedonians
For Macedonians in a particular country, see the country
250.5.T87 Turks
For Turks in a particular country, see the country
251 Albania
252 Bosnia and Hercegovina
253 Bulgaria
254 Croatia
Macedonia (Republic)
Cf. GR139.7 Macedonia as a region
255 General works
256.A-Z Local, A-Z
256.2.A-Z By ethnic group, A-Z
256.2.A75 Aromanians
256.2.T87 Turks
Romania
257 General works
258.A-Z Local, A-Z
258.2.A-Z By ethnic group, A-Z
258.2.A74 Armenians
258.2.A75 Aromanians
258.2.C73 Csangos
258.2.G47 Germans
258.2.H86 Hungarians
258.2.S56 Slovaks
258.2.T37 Tatars
258.7 Slovenia
Yugoslavia

By region or country
Europe
Balkan States. Southern Slavs
Yugoslavia -- Continued
259 General works
260.A-Z Local, A-Z
260.2.A-Z By ethnic group, A-Z
260.2.A43 Albanians
260.2.H86 Hungarians
260.2.M33 Macedonians
260.2.S44 Serbs
260.2.U37 Ukrainians
263.A-Z Other European countries, A-Z
264 Mediterranean Region
Asia. The Orient
265 General works
268.A-Z By race or group not limited to one country, A-Z
268.A73 Arabs
268.D85 Dungans
268.K2 Kalmyks
(268.M57) Miris (Hill tribe)
see GR305.7.M57
268.T86 Turkic peoples
268.T89 Tuvinians
268.U5 Uighur (Turkic people)
Middle East
For Arab countries collectively see GR268.A73
270 General works
271.A-Z By group not limited to one country, A-Z
271.A75 Armenians
For Armenians in a particular country, see the country
271.B44 Bedouins
For Bedouins in a particular country, see the country
271.K85 Kurds
For Kurds in a particular country, see the country
275 Arabian Peninsula. Saudi Arabia. Persian Gulf States
For other countries of the Arabian Peninsula see GR295.A+
Caucasus
276 General works
277 Armenia (Republic)
278 Azerbaijan
279 Georgia (Republic)
Turkey
280 General works
281.A-Z Local, A-Z
281.2.A-Z By ethnic group, A-Z

By region or country
Asia. The Orient
Middle East
Turkey
By ethnic group, A-Z -- Continued

281.2.A39 Adygei
281.2.A75 Armenians
281.2.G46 Georgians (Transcaucasians)
281.2.G74 Greeks
281.2.J48 Jews
281.2.K87 Kurds

Israel. Palestine
285 General works
286.A-Z Local, A-Z
286.2.A-Z By ethnic group, A-Z
286.2.A72 Arabs

Iran
290 General works
291.A-Z Local, A-Z
291.2.A-Z By ethnic group, A-Z
291.2.A94 Azerbaijanis. Azeris
291.2.K47 Khalaj
291.2.K87 Kurds
291.2.T87 Turkmen

293 Syria
295.A-Z Other, A-Z
e.g.
295.C9 Cyprus

Central Asia
300 General works
300.2.A-Z By ethnic group not limited to one republic or country, A-Z
300.2.D86 Dungans
300.2.K39 Kazakhs
300.2.K57 Kirghiz
300.2.T33 Tajiks
300.2.T87 Turkmen
300.2.U9 Uzbeks

Kazakh S.S.R. Kazakhstan
300.3 General works
300.32.A-Z Local, A-Z

Kirghiz S.S.R. Kirghizistan
300.4 General works
300.42.A-Z Local, A-Z

Tajik S.S.R. Tajikistan
300.5 General works
300.52.A-Z Local, A-Z

By region or country
Asia. The Orient
Central Asia -- Continued
Turkmen S.S.R. Turkmenistan
300.6 General works
300.62.A-Z Local, A-Z
Uzbek S.S.R. Uzbekistan
300.7 General works
300.72.A-Z Local, A-Z
South Asia
302 General works
302.2.A-Z By ethnic group not limited to one country, A-Z
302.2.A35 Akha
302.2.B44 Bengali
302.2.B55 Bhojpuri
302.2.C53 Chakma
302.2.D63 Dogri
302.2.P34 Panjabis
302.2.P85 Pushtuns
302.2.T34 Tamil
Afghanistan
302.5 General works
302.7.A-Z Local, A-Z
302.9.A-Z By ethnic group, A-Z
Pakistan
303 General works
304.A-Z Local, A-Z
304.3.A-Z By ethnic group, A-Z
304.3.B35 Baluchi
304.3.B73 Brahui
Bangladesh
304.5 General works
304.7.A-Z Local, A-Z
304.9.A-Z By ethnic group, A-Z
India
305 General works
305.5.A-Z Local, A-Z
305.7.A-Z By ethnic group, A-Z
305.7.A38 Adivasis
305.7.A44 Ahirs
305.7.A54 Angami
305.7.B34 Badaga
305.7.B46 Bengali
305.7.B54 Bhojpuri
305.7.B56 Bhotia
305.7.B87 Buxas
305.7.D67 Dorla

By region or country
Asia. The Orient
South Asia
India
By ethnic group, A-Z -- Continued

305.7.G83	Gujaratis
305.7.G84	Gujars
305.7.H35	Hajong
305.7.H62	Ho
305.7.J48	Jews
305.7.K32	Kadar
305.7.K34	Kachari
305.7.K36	Kanarese
305.7.K43	Kharia
305.7.K84	Kuki
305.7.K86	Kumauni
305.7.L45	Lepcha
305.7.L52	Liangmai
305.7.L85	Lushai
305.7.M34	Maram
305.7.M35	Maratha
305.7.M37	Maria
305.7.M39	Marwaris
305.7.M45	Meitheis
305.7.M57	Miri
305.7.M85	Munda
305.7.N33	Naga
305.7.N44	Nepalese
305.7.O72	Oraon
305.7.P34	Paite
305.7.P37	Panjabis
305.7.R32	Rabaris
305.7.R34	Rajput
305.7.S36	Santal
305.7.S54	Sikhs
305.7.S56	Sindhi
305.7.T35	Tamil
305.7.T44	Telugu
305.7.T66	Toto
305.7.T84	Tulu
305.7.W35	Warli
	Sri Lanka
306	General works
306.5.A-Z	Local, A-Z
306.7.A-Z	By ethnic group, A-Z
306.7.V43	Veddah
307.A-Z	Other, A-Z

By region or country
Asia. The Orient -- Continued
Southeast Asia

308	General works
308.5.A-Z	By ethnic group not limited to one country, A-Z
308.5.C52	Cham
308.5.H67	Hmong
308.5.J37	Jarai
308.5.K45	Khmu'
308.5.L34	Lahu
308.5.L58	Lisu
308.5.M34	Malays
308.5.T34	Tai
308.5.Y36	Yao
	Burma. Myanmar
309	General works
309.2.A-Z	Local, A-Z
309.5.A-Z	By ethnic group, A-Z
310	Cambodia
	Laos
311	General works
311.2.A-Z	Local, A-Z
311.5.A-Z	By ethnic group, A-Z
311.5.K38	Katu
311.5.Y36	Yao
	Thailand
312	General works
312.2.A-Z	Local, A-Z
312.5.A-Z	By ethnic group, A-Z
312.5.B55	Black Tai
312.5.K37	Karen
312.5.K45	Khmer
	Vietnam
313	General works
313.2.A-Z	Local, A-Z
313.5.A-Z	By ethnic group, A-Z
313.5.B35	Bana
313.5.C83	Cua
313.5.H56	Hmong
313.5.H7	Hrê
313.5.J37	Jarai
313.5.K36	Katu
313.5.K73	Krem
313.5.L38	Lawa
313.5.L64	Lolo
313.5.M3	Maa
313.5.M36	Mang

By region or country
Asia. The Orient
Southeast Asia
Vietnam
By ethnic group, A-Z -- Continued

313.5.M57	Mnong
313.5.M65	Montagnards
313.5.M86	Muong
313.5.N86	Nung
313.5.R53	Rhade
313.5.R65	Roglai
313.5.T34	Tai
313.5.T38	Tay Nung
313.5.T45	Tho
313.5.U66	Upper Ta'oih
313.5.V35	Vân Kiêu
	Malaysia
315	General works
316.A-Z	Local, A-Z
316.5.A-Z	By ethnic group, A-Z
316.5.B83	Bugis
316.5.C45	Chewong
316.5.C46	Chinese
316.5.D39	Dayak
316.5.D87	Dusun
316.5.I23	Iban
316.5.M34	Mah Meri
316.5.P45	Penan
316.5.S46	Senoi
	Singapore
316.7	General works
316.72.A-Z	Local, A-Z
316.75.A-Z	By ethnic group, A-Z
	Brunei
317	General works
317.2.A-Z	Local, A-Z
317.5.A-Z	By ethnic group, A-Z
	Indonesia
320	General works
323	Borneo. Kalimantan
324.A-Z	Other local, A-Z
324.5.A-Z	By ethnic group, A-Z
324.5.A25	Achinese
324.5.B34	Banjarese
324.5.B38	Betawi
324.5.B55	Bima
324.5.B83	Bugis

By region or country
Asia. The Orient
Southeast Asia
Indonesia
By ethnic group, A-Z -- Continued

324.5.B86 Bunak
324.5.D35 Dairi Pakpak
324.5.D39 Dayak
324.5.D65 Donggo
324.5.D85 Dusun
324.5.G38 Gayo
324.5.I2 Iban
324.5.K37 Karo-Batak
324.5.K58 Kluet
324.5.M46 Mentawi
324.5.M55 Minangkabau
324.5.P47 Petalangan
324.5.S39 Sawai
324.5.S56 Simelungun
324.5.S94 Sundanese
324.5.T45 Tengger
324.5.T47 Tetum
324.5.T6 Toba-Batak
324.5.T62 Tobelo
324.5.W64 Wolio

Philippines
325 General works
326.A-Z Local, A-Z
326.2.A-Z By ethnic group, A-Z
326.2.C43 Cebuano
326.2.I35 Ifugao
326.2.I73 Itbayat
326.2.M33 Mandaya
326.2.M35 Manobos
326.2.M36 Mansaka
326.2.M37 Maranao
326.2.P34 Palawan
326.2.P35 Pampangan

Eastern Asia. Far East
330 General works

China
334 Periodicals. Societies. Serials
335 General works

Themes, motives, etc.
335.3 General works
335.4.A-Z Individual folktale themes and motives, A-Z

Daoji, 1148-1209 see GR335.4.T35

By region or country
Asia. The Orient
Eastern Asia. Far East
China
Themes, motives, etc.
Individual folktale themes and motives, A-Z -- Continued

335.4.H83 Hua, Mulan (Legendary character)
335.4.M45 Mengjiangnü (Legendary character)
335.4.M56 Ming Taizu, Emperor of China, 1328-1398
335.4.T35 Tao-chi, 1148-1209. Daoji, 1148-1209
336.A-Z Local, A-Z
e.g.
336.M66 Mongolia. Inner Mongolia
337 Tibet
337.5 Outer Mongolia
338 Taiwan
Japan
339 Periodicals. Societies. Serials
340 General works
341.A-Z Local, A-Z
Korea
342 General works
342.5.A-Z Local, A-Z
345 Siberia (Russia)
Africa
350 General works
By group not limited to one region or country
350.2 Bantu-speaking peoples
By region or country
West Africa
350.3 General works
350.32.A-Z By group not limited to one country, A-Z
350.32.B28 Baka (West African people)
350.32.B3 Bambara
350.32.D98 Dyula
350.32.F35 Fang
350.32.F82 Fula
350.32.M33 Mandingo
350.32.S65 Soninke
350.32.T45 Tenda
350.32.Z37 Zarma
Equatorial Guinea
350.4 General works
350.42.A-Z Local or individual groups, A-Z
350.42.B83 Bubi
350.42.N35 Ndowe

By region or country
Africa
By region or country
West Africa -- Continued
Cameroon

351 General works
351.2.A-Z Local or individual groups, A-Z
351.2.B34 Bali
351.2.B35 Bamileke
351.2.B38 Basa
351.2.B46 Beti
351.2.D82 Duala
351.2.E86 Ewondo
351.2.K65 Kom
351.2.L55 Limbum
Mafa see GR351.2.M37
351.2.M34 Maka
351.2.M37 Matakam. Mafa
351.2.M55 Mongo
351.2.N75 Nso
351.2.U43 Uldeme

Nigeria

351.3 General works
351.32.A-Z Local or individual groups, A-Z
351.32.B56 Bini
351.32.E45 Emai
351.32.G35 Gbagyi
351.32.H34 Hausa
351.32.I34 Igbo
351.32.K35 Kanuri
351.32.K54 Kilba
351.32.N53 Niger River Delta
351.32.T35 Tangale
351.32.Y47 Yergum
351.32.Y56 Yoruba

Benin

351.4 General works
351.42.A-Z Local or individual groups, A-Z
351.42.A35 Aja
351.42.F65 Fon

Togo

351.5 General works
351.52.A-Z Local or individual groups, A-Z
351.52.C45 Chokossi
351.52.E83 Ewe
351.52.K32 Kabiye
351.52.T45 Tem

	By region or country
	Africa
	By region or country
	West Africa -- Continued
	Ghana
351.6	General works
351.62.A-Z	Local or individual groups, A-Z
351.62.A83	Ashanti
351.62.B85	Builsa
351.62.E83	Ewe
351.62.F36	Fanti
351.62.G32	Gã
351.62.G83	Gurma
351.62.M33	Mamprusi
351.62.N94	Nzima
351.62.T85	Twi
	Burkina Faso. Upper Volta
351.7	General works
351.72.A-Z	Local or individual groups, A-Z
351.72.D34	Dagaaba
351.72.M63	Mossi
351.72.S24	Samo
351.72.T87	Tusia
	Ivory Coast. Côte d'Ivoire
351.8	General works
351.82.A-Z	Local or individual groups, A-Z
351.82.A27	Abron
351.82.A59	Akye
351.82.A62	Anyi
351.82.B35	Bambara
351.82.B36	Baoule
351.82.S46	Senufo
	Niger
351.9	General works
351.92.A-Z	Local or individual groups, A-Z
351.92.B69	Bozo
351.92.F84	Fula
351.92.H38	Hausa
351.92.S65	Songhai
351.92.Z37	Zarma
	Liberia
352	General works
352.2.A-Z	Local or individual groups, A-Z
352.2.G34	Gbandi
	Sierra Leone
352.3	General works
352.32.A-Z	Local or individual groups, A-Z

By region or country
Africa
By region or country
West Africa
Sierra Leone
Local or individual groups, A-Z -- Continued

352.32.K74	Krio
352.32.K87	Kuranko
352.32.L35	Limba
352.32.M35	Mandingo
352.32.M46	Mende
352.32.S94	Susu
	Guinea-Bissau
352.5	General works
352.52.A-Z	Local or individual groups, A-Z
352.52.B35	Badyara
	Guinea
352.6	General works
352.62.A-Z	Local or individual groups, A-Z
352.62.K65	Kono
	Senegal
352.7	General works
352.72.A-Z	Local or individual groups, A-Z
352.72.D54	Diola
352.72.M35	Mandingo
352.72.W64	Wolof
	Mali
352.8	General works
352.82.A-Z	Local or individual groups, A-Z
352.82.B35	Bambara
352.82.M34	Mandingo
	Gambia
352.9	General works
352.92.A-Z	Local or individual groups, A-Z
	Mauritania
352.95	General works
352.97.A-Z	Local or individual groups, A-Z
352.97.F84	Fula
352.97.W64	Wolof
	North Africa
353	General works
353.2.A-Z	By group not limited to one country, A-Z
353.2.B39	Bedouins
353.2.B43	Berbers
353.2.K33	Kabyles
353.2.T8	Tuaregs
	Morocco

GR

By region or country
Africa
By region or country
North Africa
Morocco -- Continued
353.3 General works
353.32.A-Z Local or individual groups, A-Z
Algeria
353.4 General works
353.42.A-Z Local or individual groups, A-Z
Tunisia
353.5 General works
353.52.A-Z Local or individual groups, A-Z
Libya
353.6 General works
353.62.A-Z Local or individual groups, A-Z
Egypt
355 General works
355.2.A-Z Local or individual groups, A-Z
Chad
355.5 General works
355.52.A-Z Local or individual groups, A-Z
355.52.G35 Gambaye
355.52.M27 Masa
355.52.S25 Sara
355.52.Z33 Zaghawa
Eastern Africa
355.6 General works
355.62.A-Z By group not limited to one country, A-Z
355.62.E27 East Indians
355.62.M47 Meru
355.62.S93 Swahili-speaking peoples
Sudan
355.8 General works
355.82.A-Z Local or individual groups, A-Z
355.82.D53 Dinka
355.82.M37 Masiriyah
355.82.N82 Nubians
355.82.Z35 Zande
Ethiopia
356 General works
356.2.A-Z Local or individual groups, A-Z
356.2.B67 Boran
356.2.F34 Falashas. Ethiopian Jews
356.2.G35 Gamo
356.2.G87 Gurage
Jews see GR356.2.F34

By region or country
Africa
By region or country
Eastern Africa
Ethiopia
Local or individual groups, A-Z -- Continued

356.2.O75	Oromo
	Djibouti. French Somaliland
356.24	General works
356.25.A-Z	Local or individual groups, A-Z
	Somalia
356.3	General works
356.32.A-Z	Local or individual groups, A-Z
	Kenya
356.4	General works
356.42.A-Z	Local or individual groups, A-Z
356.42.B83	Bukusu
356.42.E45	Embu
356.42.G87	Gusii
356.42.K36	Kamba
356.42.K53	Kikuyu
(356.42.K87)	Kusu see GR356.42.B83
356.42.L83	Luo
356.42.M37	Masai
356.42.P64	Pokomo
356.42.S25	Samburu
356.42.W33	Wachaga
	Uganda
356.5	General works
356.52.A-Z	Local or individual groups, A-Z
356.52.B33	Bairo
356.52.L34	Lango
	Burundi
356.58	General works
356.582.A-Z	Local or individual groups, A-Z
	Rwanda
356.6	General works
356.62.A-Z	Local or individual groups, A-Z
356.62.B38	Batwa
356.62.H87	Hutu
	Tanzania
356.7	General works
356.72.A-Z	Local or individual groups, A-Z
356.72.B84	Burungi
356.72.C45	Chaga
356.72.F58	Fipa

By region or country
Africa
By region or country
Eastern Africa
Tanzania
Local or individual groups, A-Z -- Continued

356.72.H36 Hatsa
356.72.H38 Haya
356.72.M38 Matengo
356.72.M85 Mwera
356.72.N47 Ngonde
356.72.S95 Swahili-speaking peoples
356.72.W33 Wachaga
356.72.W34 Wambulu
356.72.W35 Wanyatura

Mozambique
356.9 General works
356.92.A-Z Local or individual groups, A-Z
356.92.M34 Makonde
356.92.T56 Thonga

Madagascar
357 General works
357.2.A-Z Local or individual groups, A-Z
357.2.A57 Antandroy
357.2.B48 Betsimisaraka
357.2.M35 Mahafaly
357.2.M47 Merina
357.2.T35 Tanala

Central Africa
357.3 General works
357.32.A-Z By group not limited to one country, A-Z
357.32.B36 Banziri
357.32.L88 Luvale
357.32.M34 Mandja
357.32.M66 Mongombo

Central African Republic
357.4 General works
357.42.A-Z Local or individual groups, A-Z
357.42.K37 Kara (Gbayan people)
357.42.M38 Manja
357.42.N55 Ngbaka-Ma'bo

Congo (Brazzaville)
357.5 General works
357.52.A-Z Local or individual groups, A-Z
357.52.K66 Kota
357.52.L33 Laadi
357.52.M34 Mbosi

By region or country
Africa
By region or country
Central Africa -- Continued
Gabon

357.6	General works
357.62.A-Z	Local or individual groups, A-Z
357.62.F34	Fang
	Congo (Democratic Republic). Zaire
357.8	General works
357.82.A-Z	Local or individual groups, A-Z
357.82.B33	Bakongo
357.82.B35	Balese
357.82.B57	Bira
357.82.B65	Boma
357.82.H83	Hungana
357.82.K57	Kituba
357.82.K64	Kongo
357.82.L82	Luba
357.82.L84	Lulua
357.82.M42	Mbala
357.82.M64	Mongo
357.82.M78	Mputu
357.82.N45	Ngongo
357.82.N57	Nkundu
357.82.P46	Pende
357.82.R53	Rega
357.82.R84	Rundi
357.82.R88	Ruund
357.82.S24	Sakata
357.82.S95	Suku
(357.82.W35)	Warega see GR357.82.R53
357.82.Y36	Yanzi
	Southern Africa
358	General works
358.2.A-Z	By group not limited to one country, A-Z
	Bantu-speaking peoples see GR350.2
358.2.B83	Bushmen. San
	Hottentot see GR358.2.K45
358.2.K45	Khoikhoi
358.2.L86	Lunda, Southern
	San see GR358.2.B83
	Angola
358.3	General works
358.32.A-Z	Local or individual groups, A-Z
358.32.C45	Chokwe

By region or country
  Africa
    By region or country
      Southern Africa
        Angola
          Local or individual groups, A-Z -- Continued

358.32.L88	Luvale
358.32.M35	Mbundu
	Zambia
358.4	General works
358.42.A-Z	Local or individual groups, A-Z
358.42.B43	Bemba
358.42.T66	Tonga
	Malawi
358.5	General works
358.52.A-Z	Local or individual groups, A-Z
358.52.Y36	Yao
	Zimbabwe. Southern Rhodesia
358.6	General works
358.62.A-Z	Local or individual groups, A-Z
358.62.K37	Karanga
358.62.M3	Mashona. Shona
358.62.N34	Ndebele
	Botswana
358.7	General works
358.72.A-Z	Local or individual groups, A-Z
	Namibia
358.8	General works
358.82.A-Z	Local or individual groups, A-Z
358.82.H45	Herero
358.82.H55	Himba
358.82.J83	Ju/'hoan
358.82.K94	Kxoe
358.82.N32	Nama
358.82.N35	Ndonga
	South Africa
359	General works
359.2.A-Z	Local or individual groups, A-Z
359.2.A47	Afrikaners
359.2.L62	Lobedu
359.2.M34	Malay
359.2.P44	Pedi
359.2.P65	Pondo
359.2.S95	Swazi
359.2.T78	Tswana
359.2.V43	Venda
359.2.X64	Xhosa

By region or country
Africa
By region or country
Southern Africa
South Africa
Local or individual groups, A-Z -- Continued

359.2.Z83	Zulu
	Lesotho
359.5	General works
359.52.A-Z	Local or individual groups, A-Z
	Basuto see GR359.52.S68
359.52.S68	Sotho. Basuto
	Swaziland
359.55	General works
359.56.A-Z	Local or individual groups, A-Z
359.56.S95	Swazi
360.A-Z	Atlantic and Indian Ocean islands, A-Z
360.A95	Azores
360.C27	Canary Islands
360.C3	Cape Verde Islands
360.C58	Comoros
360.F4	Fernando Po
360.M343	Mauritius
360.R48	Réunion
360.S3	Sao Tome
360.S44	Seychelles
	Australia
365	General works
366.A-Z	Local or individual groups, A-Z
	Aboriginal Australians see GR366.A87
366.A87	Australians, Aboriginal
366.K84	Kukatja
366.K86	Kumbainggar
366.W35	Walbiri
370	Tasmania
	New Zealand
	Including Maori tales, etc.
375	General works
376.A-Z	Local or individual groups, A-Z
376.N45	Ngaitahu
376.T65	Tokelauans
	Pacific islands
380	General works
383	Micronesia (General)

GR

By region or country
Pacific islands -- Continued
385.A-Z By country, island, or island group, A-Z
Class where possible individual islands or small island groups with the country or island territory in which they are located, e.g., class the Loyalty Islands, which are a part of the territory of New Caledonia, with New Caledonia
385.C66 Cook Islands
385.E2 Easter Island
385.F5 Fiji
385.G85 Guam
Hawaii see GR110.H38
385.K5 Kiribati
385.M29 Mariana Islands
385.M3 Marquesas Islands
385.M37 Marshall Islands
385.M625 Micronesia (Federated States)
Including Nukuoro Atoll, Ulithi
New Britain Island see GR385.P36
385.N5 New Caledonia
New Guinea see GR385.P36
New Hebrides see GR385.V35
Nukuoro Atoll see GR385.M625
385.P33 Palau
385.P36 Papua New Guinea. New Guinea
Including Bismarck Archipelago, New Britain Island
Philippines see GR325+
385.S3 Samoan Islands
Including American Samoa and Western Samoa
385.S575 Society Islands
385.S6 Solomon Islands
385.T6 Tonga
385.T63 Torres Strait Islands
Ulithi see GR385.M625
385.V35 Vanuatu. New Hebrides
385.W34 Wallis and Futuna Islands
390 Arctic regions (General)
By subject
For works on special subjects limited to a special region or country see GR99.6+
Costume. Dress
420 General works
425 Jewelry. Rings
Cf. GR805 Gems
426 Crowns. Wreaths
Folklore relating to private life
430 General works

By subject
Folklore relating to private life -- Continued
435 Dreams
Cf. BF1074+ Parapsychology
Birth, love, marriage, and death, etc.
440 General works
450 Birth
452 Aging
455 Death
460 Love. Love potions
462 Sex
465 Marriage
Including family life
467 Rebirth
469 Men
Women
470 General works
471 Mothers. Stepmothers
472 Twins
473 Brothers and sisters
Children and childhood
475 General works
Games
Including collections and discussion of rhyming games
480 General works
481 Hand games. Hand-clapping games
485 Counting-out rhymes
486 Alphabet rhymes
487 Nursery rhymes
For collections of nursery rhymes, see PZ, e.g., for collections of American and English nursery rhymes see PZ8.3
488 Older people. Old age
Human body and its parts
489 General works
489.2 Blood
489.25 Navel
489.3 Teeth
489.4 Heart
489.45 Generative organs. Penis. Vagina
489.5 People with disabilities
Dwellings
490 General works
495 Fire. Hearths
496 Lanterns
497 Beds
498 Eating. Drinking

By subject -- Continued
Supernatural beings and forces
Cf. BL473 Religions
Cf. GR825+ Mythical monsters
500 General works
Sacred places. Churches
Cf. BL580+ Worship (Religions)
505 General works
506 Cemeteries
507 Sepulchral and perpetual lamps
510 Gods
512 Devils
515 Heroes
Cf. BL325.H46 Mythology
517 Soldiers
520 Kings
Cf. BL325.K5 Mythology
Cf. DG124 Cult of emperors
Cf. JC375+ Origins, myth, magic, etc., of monarchy
523 Fools. Jesters
524 Trickster
Demonology
Cf. BF1501+ Occultism
Cf. BL480 Religious doctrines (General)
525 General works
530 Witches
535 Sorcerers
540 Incantations. Invocations. Exorcisms
Fairies
Including brownies, elves, gnomes, jinn, etc.
Cf. BF1552 Occultism
Cf. GR785 Wood nymphs, dryads
549 General works
Fairy tales
For fairy tales of special regions or countries see GR99.6+
Cf. PN3437 Fairy tales (Fiction genre)
Cf. PN6071.F15 Literary collections
550 General works
552 Collections of texts (General)
Cf. PZ8 American and English juvenile literature
555 Dwarfs
560 Ogres. Giants
580 Ghosts. Specters. Apparitions
Cf. BF1444+ Occultism
581 Zombies
Evil eye see GN475.6

By subject -- Continued
Charms. Talismans. Amulets. Spells
Cf. BF1561 Occultism
Cf. GN475+ Primitive religion
600 General works
Special topics
605 Elixirs. Elixir of life
Love potions see GR460
610 Pentacles
615 Wishes
Nature
618 General works
Cosmic phenomena
620 General works
625 Sun. Moon. Stars
(630) Thunder and lightning
see GR640
Weather lore. Meteorology
635 General works
Cf. QC998 Weather forecasting
638 Wind. Air. Breezes
640 Thunder and lightning
Astrology see BF1651+
Alchemy, History of see QD13
Alchemy (General) see QD23.3+
Geographical topics
650 General works
655 Earth
660 Mountains
Cf. GR940+ Mythical mountains
665 Caves
Seas see GR910
675 Islands
Cf. GR940+ Mythical islands
Waters
678 General works
680 Rivers. Streams
685 Floods
690 Springs. Wells
Animals, plants, and minerals
700 General works
Animals. Animal lore
705 General works
710 Language of animals
Special kinds of animals
712 Poisonous animals
Including venom

By subject
Nature
Animals, plants, and minerals
Animals. Animal lore
Special kinds of animals -- Continued

715 Horses
720 Dogs
725 Cats
730.A-Z Other mammals, A-Z
730.A6 Apes
730.A8 Asses
730.B3 Badgers
730.B4 Bears
730.B8 Bulls
730.C38 Cattle
730.D4 Deer
730.E44 Elephants
730.F6 Foxes
730.G6 Goats
730.H3 Hares
730.L55 Lions
730.M5 Mice
730.M57 Moles
730.M6 Monkeys
730.R3 Rams
730.S4 Seals
730.S9 Swine
730.W5 Wild boar
730.W6 Wolves
735 Birds. Eggs
740 Reptiles
745 Fishes
Insects
750 General works
751 Butterflies
752.A-Z Other insects, A-Z
752.B44 Bees
755 Spiders
760.A-Z Other animals, A-Z
760.B3 Barnacles
760.M65 Mollusks. Shells
760.O27 Octopuses
Shells see GR760.M65
760.T6 Toads
Plants. Plant lore
Cf. QK83 Botany
780 General works

By subject
Nature
Animals, plants, and minerals
Plants. Plant lore -- Continued
785 Trees
Including wood nymphs, dryads
790.A-Z Special kinds of plants and plant parts, A-Z
790.A65 Apple
790.A78 Artemisia vulgaria
790.E3 Edelweiss
790.F5 Fig
790.F78 Fruit
790.G3 Garlic
790.G5 Ginseng
790.J35 Japanese flowering cherry
790.L33 Leaves
790.L4 Lemon
790.M3 Mandrakes
790.M35 Marijuana
790.M37 Mate plant
790.M88 Mushrooms
790.N88 Nuts
790.O45 Olive
790.P45 Psychotropic plants
790.R6 Roses
790.S4 Sesame
790.S55 Shamrock (Emblem)
790.S94 Sweet woodruff
790.W54 Wild flowers
Minerals and rocks. Folklore of stones
800 General works
805 Precious stones. Gems
810 Metals
Mythical animals, plants, and minerals
820 General works
Mythical animals. Monsters
Cf. BF1484 Animal ghosts
825 General works
830.A-Z Special, A-Z
830.B3 Basilisk
830.D7 Dragons
830.J3 Jayhawk
Mermaids see GR910
830.P4 Phoenix
830.S3 Salamanders
Sea monsters see GR910
830.T3 Tengu

By subject
Nature
Animals, plants, and minerals
Mythical animals, plants, and minerals
Mythical animals. Monsters
Special, A-Z -- Continued
830.U6 Unicorns
830.V3 Vampires
Cf. BF1556 Occultism
830.W4 Werewolves
Mythical plants
840 General works
845.A-Z Special, A-Z
860 Mythical minerals
Cf. QD25 Philosopher's stone
Transportation and travel
Cf. GR910 Seafaring
865 General works
866 Crossroads
Vehicles
867 General works
869 Automobiles
870 Railroads
Commerce
872 General works
873 Markets
874 Money
877 Law. Justice
880 Medicine. Folk medicine
Cf. GN477+ Ethnology
Cf. GR489+ Folklore of the body, blood, etc.
Cf. R706 Curiosities, delusions
Music. Dance
885 General works
885.4 Drums
887 Recreation. Sports
Cf. GR480+ Children's games
Occupations
890 General works
895 Agriculture
Including planting, harvesting, etc.
896 Blacksmithing
897 Executioners. Executions
897.5 Fire fighting
898 Hunting
900 Mining. Mines
903 Office work. Office practice

By subject
Occupations -- Continued

904 Potters. Pottery making
905 Sandmen
910 Seafaring. Folklore of the sea
Including mermaids and sea monsters
Cf. PN57.F6 Flying Dutchman as a theme in literature
915 Textile industry. Weaving
930 Special days, months, seasons, etc.
Signs and symbols
Cf. AZ108 Symbols and their use
931 General works
932.A-Z Special, A-Z
932.C5 Circle
932.S66 Square
932.T45 Three monkeys
933 Special numbers
935 Color
Mythical places
Including mythical islands, mountains, etc.
Cf. G555 Voyages touching unidentified places
Cf. GN750+ Lost continents
940 General works
941.A-Z By place, A-Z
941.C58 Ciudad de los Césares
941.I82 Is (Legendary city)
941.S26 San Borondon
941.S52 Shambhala
943 Treasure troves
950.A-Z Miscellaneous implements, utensils, etc., A-Z
950.B3 Balance (Scales)
950.G5 Girdle. Cincture
950.K6 Knots
950.S9 Swords

Manners and customs (General)

Class here comprehensive works on social life and customs, as well as works on certain specific customs

For general works on the broader topic of civilization, i.e., the aggregate of characteristics displayed in the collective life of literate peoples, including intellectual life, the arts, etc., as well as social life and customs, see CB

For general works on the social life and customs of literate peoples in specific countries, see D-F

For works on the social life and customs of particular ethnic groups, see the name of the group in D-F

Cf. HM+ Sociology

For general works on the social life and customs of pre-literate and folk cultures see GN301+

Cf. BJ1801+ Social usages. Etiquette

Cf. GR1+ Folklore

1 Periodicals. Societies. Serials

3 Congresses

Collected works (nonserial)

19 Several authors

23 Individual authors

31 Dictionaries. Encyclopedias

Museums. Exhibitions

see GN35+; D-F

41 History of the study of manners and customs

Biography

51 Collective

53.A-Z Individual, A-Z

61 Philosophy. Relation to other topics. Methodology

General works, treatises, and textbooks

70 Early through 1850

75 1851-1974

76 1975-

80 Pictorial works

85 Juvenile works

90 Addresses, essays, lectures

95 General special (Special aspects of the subject as a whole)

By period

Class here works on Europe as a whole for the period ending with 1944

For works on Europe dealing with later periods and works on other regions or countries of any period, see D-F

110 Ancient

For classical period, see DE-DG

120 Medieval

Modern

129 General works

By period
Modern -- Continued
130 Renaissance
135 16th century
140 17th century
143 18th century
146 19th century
150 20th century
Houses. Dwellings
Including the history of dwellings
Cf. GT3550 Castle life
Cf. NA7100+ Domestic architecture
Philosophy. Relation to other topics
165 General works
165.5 Relation to psychology
Cf. BF353 Environmental psychology
170 General works
171 Popular works
172 Juvenile works
By period
175 Ancient
Cf. DF99 Greek dwellings
Cf. DG97+ Roman dwellings
180 Medieval
185 Renaissance
190 16th-18th centuries
195 1801-
By region or country
201 America
North America
203 General works
United States
205 General works
By period
206 Colonial period. 18th and early 19th century
207 19th century
208 20th century
By region
210 New England
211 South
214 Central
217 West
219 Pacific States
225.A-.W By state, A-W
227.A-Z By city, A-Z
Canada
228 General works

Houses. Dwellings
By region or country
North America
Canada -- Continued
229.A-Z Local, A-Z
Latin America
230 General works
Mexico
231 General works
232.A-Z Local, A-Z
Central America
233 General works
Belize. British Honduras
235 General works
236.A-Z Local, A-Z
Costa Rica
237 General works
238.A-Z Local, A-Z
Guatemala
239 General works
240.A-Z Local, A-Z
Honduras
241 General works
242.A-Z Local, A-Z
Nicaragua
243 General works
244.A-Z Local, A-Z
Panama
245 General works
245.5.A-Z Local, A-Z
El Salvador
246 General works
246.5.A-Z Local, A-Z
West Indies
247 General works
Bahamas
249 General works
250.A-Z Local, A-Z
Cuba
251 General works
252.A-Z Local, A-Z
Haiti
253 General works
254.A-Z Local, A-Z
Jamaica
255 General works
256.A-Z Local, A-Z

Houses. Dwellings
By region or country
Latin America
West Indies -- Continued
Puerto Rico
257 General works
257.5.A-Z Local, A-Z
258.A-Z Other, A-Z
South America
259 General works
Argentina
261 General works
262.A-Z Local, A-Z
Bolivia
263 General works
264.A-Z Local, A-Z
Brazil
265 General works
266.A-Z Local, A-Z
Chile
267 General works
268.A-Z Local, A-Z
Colombia
269 General works
270.A-Z Local, A-Z
Ecuador
271 General works
272.A-Z Local, A-Z
Guianas
273 General works
274.A-Z Local, A-Z
Paraguay
275 General works
276.A-Z Local, A-Z
Peru
277 General works
278.A-Z Local, A-Z
Uruguay
279 General works
280.A-Z Local, A-Z
Venezuela
281 General works
282.A-Z Local, A-Z
Europe
283 General works
Great Britain. England (General)
285 General works

Houses. Dwellings
By region or country
Europe
Great Britain. England (General) -- Continued
287.A-Z England (Local), A-Z
Scotland
289 General works
290.A-Z Local, A-Z
Northern Ireland
291 General works
292.A-Z Local, A-Z
Wales
293 General works
294.A-Z Local, A-Z
Ireland
294.5 General works
294.6.A-Z Local, A-Z
Austria
295 General works
296.A-Z Local, A-Z
Hungary
296.5 General works
296.6.A-Z Local, A-Z
France
297 General works
298.A-Z Local, A-Z
298.5 North Sea Region
Germany
Including West Germany
298.9 General works
299.A-Z West Germany (Local, A-Z)
East Germany
300 General works
300.5.A-Z Local, A-Z
Greece
301 General works
302.A-Z Local, A-Z
Italy
303 General works
304.A-Z Local, A-Z
Low Countries
305 General works
Netherlands
307 General works
308.A-Z Local, A-Z
Belgium
309 General works

Houses. Dwellings
By region or country
Europe
Low Countries
Belgium -- Continued
310.A-Z Local, A-Z
311 Russia. Soviet Union. Former Soviet republics
Cf. GT349+ Central Asia
Cf. GT371+ Siberia (Russia)
Russia (Federation)
312.2 General works
312.22.A-Z Local, A-Z
Belarus
312.3 General works
312.32.A-Z Local, A-Z
Moldova
312.4 General works
312.42.A-Z Local, A-Z
Ukraine
312.5 General works
312.52.A-Z Local, A-Z
Scandinavia
313 General works
Denmark
315 General works
316.A-Z Local, A-Z
Iceland
317 General works
318.A-Z Local, A-Z
Norway
319 General works
320.A-Z Local, A-Z
Sweden
321 General works
322.A-Z Local, A-Z
Spain
323 General works
324.A-Z Local, A-Z
Portugal
325 General works
326.A-Z Local, A-Z
Switzerland
327 General works
328.A-Z Local, A-Z
Balkan States
331 General works
Albania

Houses. Dwellings
By region or country
Europe
Balkan States
Albania -- Continued
332 General works
332.5.A-Z Local, A-Z
Bulgaria
333 General works
334.A-Z Local, A-Z
Romania
337 General works
338.A-Z Local, A-Z
Yugoslavia
339 General works
340.A-Z Local, A-Z
341.A-Z Other, A-Z
342.A-Z Other European regions or countries, A-Z
e.g.
342.F5 Finland
Asia. The Orient
343 General works
Middle East
343.5 General works
Israel
343.7 General works
343.72.A-Z Local, A-Z
Syria
344 General works
344.2.A-Z Local, A-Z
Turkey
345 General works
346.A-Z Local, A-Z
Caucasus
346.2 General works
Armenia (Republic)
346.3 General works
346.32.A-Z Local, A-Z
Azerbaijan
346.4 General works
346.42.A-Z Local, A-Z
Georgia (Republic)
346.45 General works
346.46.A-Z Local, A-Z
Iraq
346.5 General works
346.6.A-Z Local, A-Z

Houses. Dwellings
By region or country
Asia. The Orient -- Continued
Iran
347 General works
348.A-Z Local, A-Z
Central Asia
349 General works
Kazakhstan
350.2 General works
350.22.A-Z Local, A-Z
Kyrgyzstan
350.23 General works
350.24.A-Z Local, A-Z
Tajikistan
350.3 General works
350.32.A-Z Local, A-Z
Turkmenistan
350.4 General works
350.42.A-Z Local, A-Z
Uzbekistan
350.45 General works
350.46.A-Z Local, A-Z
South Asia
350.5 General works
India
351 General works
352.A-Z Local, A-Z
Nepal
352.2 General works
352.3.A-Z Local, A-Z
Sri Lanka
352.5 General works
352.6.A-Z Local, A-Z
Southeast Asia
353 General works
Thailand
355 General works
356.A-Z Local, A-Z
Malaysia
357 General works
358.A-Z Local, A-Z
Indonesia
359 General works
360.A-Z Local, A-Z
Philippines
361 General works

GT

Houses. Dwellings
By region or country
Asia. The Orient
Southeast Asia
Philippines -- Continued

362.A-Z	Local, A-Z
	Vietnam
362.5	General works
362.6.A-Z	Local, A-Z
	East Asia
363	General works
	China
365	General works
366.A-Z	Local, A-Z
	Taiwan
366.5	General works
366.6.A-Z	Local, A-Z
	Japan
367	General works
368.A-Z	Local, A-Z
	Korea
369	General works
370.A-Z	Local, A-Z
	Siberia (Russia)
371	General works
(372.A-Z)	Local, A-Z
	Africa
373	General works
	Egypt
375	General works
376.A-Z	Local, A-Z
377.A-Z	Other regions or countries, A-Z
	Australia
379	General works
380.A-Z	Local, A-Z
	New Zealand
381	General works
382.A-Z	Local, A-Z
	Pacific islands
383	General works
384.A-Z	By island or group of islands, A-Z
	Special topics
	Heating. Hearths. Fireplaces. Stoves
420	General works
425.A-Z	By region or country, A-Z
	Lighting
440	General works

Houses. Dwellings
Special topics
Lighting -- Continued
445 Lamps, lanterns, etc.
446.A-Z By region or country, A-Z
Furniture
450 General works
455.A-Z By region or country, A-Z
456 Chairs
457 Beds
460 Wall hangings
461 Locks and keys
470 House marks
471 House names
472 Sanitation
474 Sanding. Sandhouses
476 Toilets
Household arts. Households
Cf. TT700+ Sewing, needlework
Cf. TX641.2+ Cookery
480 General works
481 By region or country, A-Z
482 Laundering
Cf. TT980+ Laundry work
485 Churches and church going
Cf. BR1+ Christianity
Cf. BV4523 Christian life
Cf. NA4790+ Christian architecture
Human body and its parts
Cf. GT2290+ Hairdressing, cosmetics, tattooing, etc.
Cf. GN418+ Clothing and adornment
Cf. GT2845+ Bathing
495 General works
497.A-Z By region or country, A-Z
498.A-Z Specific parts of the body, A-Z
498.B55 Blood
498.B74 Breast
498.B87 Buttocks
498.F66 Foot
Hair see GT2290+
498.H34 Hand
498.H43 Head
498.H45 Heart
498.P45 Penis
498.S56 Skin
498.S65 Stomach
498.T47 Testis

499 Personal beauty
Class here historical and descriptive works on personal beauty
Cf. RA776.98+ Practical works on grooming and appearance
Cf. HQ1219+ Beauty in women
Costume. Dress. Fashion
Class here descriptive and historical studies, and publications of historical interest
Cf. NK4700+ Costume and its accessories (Art)
Cf. TT490+ Clothing manufacture
500 Periodicals. Societies. Serials
For current fashion periodicals see TT500.A2+
503 Exhibitions
505 Collections of costumes (General)
Cf. NK4701.8+ Museums and collections (Art)
507 Dictionaries. Encyclopedias
General works
509 Early through 1800
510 1801-1974
511 1975-
513 Pictorial works
518 Juvenile works
520 Addresses, essays, lectures
Philosophy. Relation to other topics
521 General works
522 Relation to aesthetics
523 Relation to art
Relation to ethics see BJ1697
523.9 Relation to politics
524 Relation to psychology
525 Relation to sociology. Social aspects
(527) Laws, regulations, etc., concerning dress
see class K
529 Cold weather clothing
Cf. GT1605 Arctic regions
529.2 Hot weather clothing
By class (age, sex, etc.) see GT1710+
By occupation (trades, etc.) see GT5910+
By period
Ancient
530 General works
533 Egyptian
535 Other Near Eastern: Babylonian, Assyrian, Persian, etc.
537 South Asian
538 Far Eastern
Including Japanese and Chinese
540 Hebrew
Classical

Costume. Dress. Fashion
By period
Ancient
Classical -- Continued
545 General works
550 Greek
555 Roman
560 Other ancient
575 Medieval
Modern
580 General works
585 1500-1789
589 1790-1815
595 1816-1899
596 1900-
By region or country
601 America
North America
603 General works
United States
605 General works
607 Colonial period. 18th and early 19th century
610 19th century
615 20th century
617.A-Z Local, A-Z
Canada
620 General works
621.A-Z Local, A-Z
Latin America
623 General works
625 Mexico
Central America
630 General works
633 Belize. British Honduras
636 Costa Rica
639 Guatemala
641 Honduras
644 Nicaragua
646 Panama
648 El Salvador
West Indies
655 General works
658 Bahamas
661 Cuba
664 Haiti
667 Jamaica
670 Puerto Rico

Costume. Dress. Fashion
By region or country
Latin America
West Indies -- Continued
673.A-Z Other, A-Z
South America
675 General works
678 Argentina
681 Bolivia
684 Brazil
687 Chile
690 Colombia
693 Ecuador
Guianas
695 General works
698 Guyana
701 Suriname
704 French Guiana
707 Paraguay
710 Peru
713 Uruguay
716 Venezuela
Europe
720 General works
By ethnic group not limited to one country
721 Basque
725 Slavic
Great Britain. England (General)
730 General works
By period
731 Ancient
732 Medieval
Modern
733 General works
734 15th-16th centuries
735 17th century
736 18th century
737 19th century
738 20th century
England (Local)
741.A-Z By region or county, A-Z
742.A-Z By city, A-Z
750-762 Scotland (Table G5)
770-782 Northern Ireland (Table G5)
790-802 Wales (Table G5)
805.A-Z Other local, A-Z
e.g.

Costume. Dress. Fashion
By region or country
Europe
Great Britain. England (General)
Other local, A-Z -- Continued
805.J4 Jersey
Ireland
806 General works
807.A-Z Local, A-Z
Austria
810 General works
By period
811 Ancient
812 Medieval
Modern
813 General works
814 15th-16th centuries
815 17th century
816 18th century
817 19th century
818 20th century
Local
820.A-Z By division, A-Z
821.A-Z By city, A-Z
Hungary
825 General works
831.A-Z By division, A-Z
833.A-Z By city, A-Z
Czechoslovakia. Czech Republic
835 General works
841.A-Z By division, A-Z
843.A-Z By city, A-Z
Slovakia
845 General works
847.A-Z By division, A-Z
849.A-Z By city, A-Z
France
850 General works
By period
851 Ancient
852 Medieval
Modern
853 General works
855 15th-16th centuries
857 17th century. Reign of Louis XIV
18th century. Early 19th century
860 General works

Costume. Dress. Fashion
By region or country
Europe
France
By period
Modern
18th century. Early 19th century -- Continued
863 Reign of Louis XV
865 Reign of Louis XVI
867 French Revolution
19th century
871 General works
873 First Empire
875 Second Empire
880 20th century
885.A-Z By region or department, A-Z
By city
887 Paris
889.A-Z Other cities, A-Z
Germany
Including general works on West Germany
900 General works
By period
901 Ancient
902 Medieval
Modern
903 General works
905 15th-16th centuries
907 17th century
909 18th century
910 19th century
911 20th century
By region or state
915 East Germany (General)
918 Baden-Württemberg
919 Bavaria
920 Black Forest
920.5 Eastphalia
921 Hesse
923 Lower Saxony
924 North Rhine-Westphalia
925 Rhineland-Palatinate
926 Saarland
928 Schleswig-Holstein
930 Swabia
931.A-Z By city, A-Z
East Germany

Costume. Dress. Fashion
By region or country
Europe
East Germany -- Continued

(932) General works
see GT915

(933) Local, A-Z
see GT918+

940-952 Greece (Modern) (Table G5)

960-972 Italy (Table G5)

975 Vatican

Low Countries

980 General works

1000-1012 Netherlands (Table G5)

1020-1032 Belgium (Table G5)

Russia. Soviet Union. Former Soviet republics collectively
Cf. GT1444+ Former Soviet Central Asia

1040 General works

By period

1041 Ancient

1042 Medieval

Modern

1043 General works

1044 15th-16th centuries

1045 17th century

1046 18th century

1047 19th century

1048 20th century

Russia (Federation)
Cf. GT1570 Siberia (Russia)

1050 General works

1051.A-Z By division, A-Z

1052.A-Z By city, A-Z

Ukraine

1053 General works

1053.2.A-Z By division, A-Z

1053.3.A-Z By city, A-Z

Belarus

1054 General works

1054.2.A-Z By division, A-Z

1054.3.A-Z By city, A-Z

Moldova

1055 General works

1055.2.A-Z By division, A-Z

1055.3.A-Z By city, A-Z

Lithuania

Costume. Dress. Fashion
By region or country
Europe
Lithuania -- Continued

1056 General works
1056.2.A-Z By division, A-Z
1056.22.A-Z By city, A-Z

Latvia

1056.3 General works
1056.32.A-Z By division, A-Z
1056.33.A-Z By city, A-Z

Estonia

1056.4 General works
1056.42.A-Z By division, A-Z
1056.43.A-Z By city, A-Z

(1057) Armenia (Republic)
see GT1402

(1057.3) Georgia (Republic)
see GT1403

(1057.4) Azerbaijan
see GT1404

1060 Poland
1080 Finland

Scandinavia

1100 General works
1120-1132 Denmark (Table G5)
1140 Iceland
1150-1162 Norway (Table G5)
1170-1182 Sweden (Table G5)

Spain and Portugal

1190 General works
1200-1212 Spain (Table G5)
1220-1232 Portugal (Table G5)

1240-1252 Switzerland (Table G5)

Balkan States

1280 General works
1285 Albania

Bosnia and Hercegovina

1287 General works
1288.A-Z Local, A-Z

Bulgaria

1290 General works
1291.A-Z Local, A-Z

Croatia

1295 General works
1296.A-Z Local, A-Z

Macedonia (Republic)

Costume. Dress. Fashion
By region or country
Europe
Balkan States
Macedonia (Republic) -- Continued
1305 General works
1306.A-Z Local, A-Z
Montenegro
1307 General works
1308.A-Z Local, A-Z
Romania
1310 General works
1311.A-Z Local, A-Z
Serbia
1312 General works
1313.A-Z Local, A-Z
Slovenia
1315 General works
1316.A-Z Local, A-Z
Yugoslavia
1325 General works
1326.A-Z Local, A-Z
1330.A-Z Other European regions or countries, A-Z
e.g.
1330.A44 Alps
Mediterranean islands
For islands belonging to particular Mediterranean countries, see the local divisions of those countries
1350 Cyprus
1360 Malta
Asia
1370 General works
Middle East
1380 General works
1390 Arabia
1400 Turkey
Caucasus
1401 General works
1402 Armenia (Republic)
1403 Azerbaijan
1404 Georgia (Republic)
1405 Iraq
1410 Syria
1420 Iran
1430.A-Z Other regions or countries, A-Z
Western and Central Asia
1440 General works

Costume. Dress. Fashion
By region or country
Asia
Western and Central Asia -- Continued
1443 Afghanistan
Former Soviet Central Asia
1444 General works
1445 Kazakhstan
1446 Kyrgyzstan
1447 Tajikistan
1448 Turkmenistan
1449 Uzbekistan
1450.A-Z Other regions or countries, A-Z
South Asia. Southeast Asia
1455 General works
India
1460 General works
1470.A-Z By region or state, A-Z
1475.A-Z By city, A-Z
1476 Nepal
1478 Pakistan
1479 Sri Lanka
Indochina
1490 General works
1495 Vietnam
1498 Cambodia
1501 Laos
1520 Thailand
1522 Burma. Myanmar
1530 Malaysia
Indonesia
1535 General works
1539.A-Z By island, A-Z
Philippines
1540 General works
1544.A-Z By island, A-Z
1545.A-Z Other regions or countries, A-Z
East Asia
1550 General works
1555 China
1555.5 Mongolia
1556 Taiwan
1560 Japan
1565 Korea
1570 Siberia (Russia)
Africa
1580 General works

Costume. Dress. Fashion
By region or country
Africa -- Continued
North Africa
1581 General works
1582 Morocco
1583 Algeria
1585 Egypt
1585.5 Ethiopia
1586 Kenya
1586.5 Tanzania
1587 Zaire. Congo (Democratic Republic)
1588 South Africa
1589.A-Z Other African regions or countries, A-Z
1589.5.A-Z Atlantic and Indian Ocean islands, A-Z
1589.5.C33 Canary Islands
1589.5.C34 Cape Verde Islands
Australia
1590 General works
1593.A-Z By state or territory, A-Z
1595 New Zealand
Pacific islands
1597 General works
1599.A-Z By island or group of islands, A-Z
1605 Arctic regions
By class (Age, sex, birth, etc.)
For clothing of industries and trades see GT5910+
For clothing of professional classes see GT6110+
For sports uniforms see GV749.U53
For academic dress see LB2389
1710 Men
1720 Women
1730 Children
(1740) Theatrical costumes
see PN2067
Masks. Disguise. Masquerade
Including costumes based on masks
Cf. TT898 Decorative crafts
1747 General works
1748.A-Z By region or country, A-Z
Under each country:
.x *General works*
.x2A-.x2Z *Local, A-Z*
1749 Mannequins (Figures)
1750 Fancy dress
Including evening gowns and formal wear
For works limited to one region or country see GT601+

GT

Costume. Dress. Fashion
By class (Age, sex, birth, etc.) -- Continued
Wedding costumes
1752 General works
1753.A-Z By region or country, A-Z
Court costumes
Cf. GT975 Pontifical court dress
1754 General works
1755.A-Z By region or country, A-Z
Christening gowns
1756 General works
1757.A-Z By region or country, A-Z
1759 Heroes. Heroines
1760 Nobility
Cf. CR4480+ Insignia
1800 Burghers
1850 Peasants
1855 Sportswear. Sport clothes
For riding costumes see GT5885+
For sports uniforms see GV749.U53
Work clothes
1860 General works
1865.A-Z By region or country, A-Z
1900 Uniforms (General)
For soldiers' uniforms see UC480+
For seamen's uniforms see VC300+
1950 Religious and military orders (General)
For religious costume in general, see BL+ for religious orders alone see BX for military orders alone see CR
Burial clothing
1955 General works
1956.A-Z By region or country, A-Z
Materials and articles of clothing. Details and accessories
For materials and articles of particular places see GT601+
2050 General works
2060 Dresses
2070 Fur
2071 Lace and lace making
Underwear
2073 General works
2075 Crinolines. Corsets
2077 Bathing suits
2079 Coats. Jackets. Suits
2080 Shirts
Trousers. Pants. Slacks
2082 General works

Costume. Dress. Fashion
Materials and articles of clothing. Details and accessories
Trousers. Pants. Slacks -- Continued
2085 Jeans. Blue jeans
Headgear
Including hats, hoods, etc.
2110 General works
2111 Headbands
2111.5 Ornamental combs
2112 Veils
Cf. BP190.5.H44 Islam
2113 Scarves
2114 Shawls
2117 Aprons
2120 Neckwear. Ties
2125 Sashes
2128 Hosiery. Stockings. Garters
2130 Footwear
Including shoes, sandals, etc.
Cf. TS989+ Boot and shoe making
2135 Handkerchiefs
2150 Fans
2170 Gloves
2180 Handbags
2190 Muffs
2210 Umbrellas. Parasols
2220 Walking sticks. Canes
2225 Wrapping cloths
Ornaments. Jewelry
Cf. TS740+ Jewelry manufacture
2250 General works
2252.A-Z By region or country, A-Z
2255 Pearls
2260 Necklaces, torques, etc.
2265 Earrings
2270 Rings, bracelets, armillae, etc.
2280 Pins, clasps, brooches, etc.
2281 Buckles
2282 Cuff links
Hair. Hairdressing. Hairstyles
2290 General works
2295.A-Z By region or country, A-Z
2310 Use of false hair. Wigs
2318 Mustaches
2320 Beards

GT

Costume. Dress. Fashion
Materials and articles of clothing. Details and accessories -- Continued
Cosmetics, perfumes, etc.
Cf. RA776.98 Grooming
Cf. TP983+ Chemical technology
2340 General works
2341.A-Z By region or country, A-Z
Body markings
Including body painting and mehndi
Cf. GN419.15 Ethnology
2343 General works
2344.A-Z By region or country, A-Z
Tattooing
Cf. GN419.3 Ethnology
Cf. GT5960.T36+ Tattoo artists
2345 General works
2346.A-Z By region or country, A-Z
2347 Tribal tattoos
2350 Other (not A-Z)
2370 Spectacles, eyeglasses, opera glasses, etc.
Customs relating to private life
Including family customs, traditions, and festivals
Cf. GR430+ Folklore
Cf. HQ1+ Sociology
2400 General works
2402.A-Z By region or country, A-Z
2405 Privacy
2420 Family life. Home life
Family reunions
2423 General works
2424.A-Z By region or country, A-Z
2430 Birthdays
Cf. GV1472.7.B5 Birthday parties
Cf. PN6084.B5 Birthday books
2435 Naming ceremonies
Cf. GT2460+ Birth customs, baptism, adoption rites, etc.
Children
2450 General works
Birth customs, baptism, adoption rites, etc.
Cf. GT2435 Naming ceremonies
Cf. GT5080 Ceremonies of royalty
2460 General works
By period
Ancient
2462 General works
Classical

Customs relative to private life
Children
Birth customs, baptism, adoption rites, etc.
By period
Ancient
Classical -- Continued
2462.3 General works
2462.5 Roman
2465.A-Z By region or country, A-Z
2467 Infant carriers
2470 Circumcision
Cf. BM705 Judaism
Cf. GN484 Ethnology
2480 Amusements. Games. Play
Cf. GV182.9 Recreation for children
Cf. GV1202.92+ Children's amusements
Adolescence. Maturation
Including coming of age rites and ceremonies, initiations
Cf. GN483.3 Coming of age rites (Ethnology)
2485 General works
2486 General special (Special aspects of the subject as a whole)
2487.A-Z By region or country, A-Z
2490 Quinceañera
Women
2520 General works
2540 Young women. Girls
Love. Courtship. Marriage. Sex customs
For works on sex customs (ethnology) see GN484.3+
For works on sex customs (social) see HQ12+
2600 General works
By period
2610 Ancient
2620 Medieval
2630 Modern
2637 Hugging
Including spooning
2640 Kissing
Courtship. Betrothal
2650 General works
2651 Bundling
Marriage customs
Cf. GT1752+ Wedding costumes
Cf. GT5070 Royal marriages
General works
2660 Early through 1800
2665 1801-
By period

Customs relative to private life
Love. Courtship. Marriage. Sex customs
Marriage customs
By period -- Continued
2670 Ancient
2680 Medieval
2690 Modern
2695.A-Z By ethnic group, A-Z
Class here only individual groups not located in particular regions or countries.
For groups located in particular regions or countries, see the group in classes D-F
2695.J4 Jews
Cf. BM713 Judaism
2695.K87 Kurds
2695.M8 Muslims
2695.S5 Slavs
2701-2796 By region or country (Table G6)
2796.5 Brides
2797 Wedding cakes
2798 Honeymoons
2800 Wedding anniversaries
2810 Girdles of chastity
Celibacy (General) see HQ800.15
Celibacy of the clergy see BV4390
Eliminative behavior
2830 General works
2831.A-Z By region or country, A-Z
Defecation
2835 General works
2838.A-Z By region or country, A-Z
2840 Flatulence
Bathing customs
Cf. RA780 Bathing (Personal hygiene)
Cf. RM819+ Baths (Physical therapy)
2845 General works
2846.A-Z By region or country, A-Z
2846.5 Sauna
2847 Odors. Smell
Eating and drinking customs
Cf. GT3770+ Inns and taverns
2850 General works
2853.A-Z By region or country, A-Z
Foods and beverages
Cf. BJ2021+ Etiquette of entertaining
Cf. TX15+ History and antiquities of home economics
Cf. TX631+ Gastronomy

Customs relative to private life
Eating and drinking customs
Foods and beverages -- Continued

2855	General works
	Foods
	Cf. TX341+ Home economics
2860	General works
	Animal food
	Cf. TX743+ Cookery
2865	General works
2866.A-Z	By region or country, A-Z
	Bread
2868	General works
2868.2.A-Z	By region or country, A-Z
	Wedding cakes see GT2797
	Meat
2868.5	General works
2868.6.A-Z	By region or country, A-Z
2869	Sugar
2870	Condiments. Salt, etc.
	Cf. TX819.A1+ Cookery
	Beverages
	Cf. TX815+ Cookery
2880	General works
2883.A-Z	By region or country, A-Z
	Alcoholic beverages
2884	General works
2885	Wine
2887	Rice wines. Sake
2890	Ale and beer
	Distilled liquors
2893	General works
2894	Brandy
2895	Whiskey
2896	Gin
2897	Rum
2898	Absinthe
	Tea
	Cf. RM240+ Diet therapy
2905	General works
2907.A-Z	By region or country, A-Z
	Japanese tea ceremony
2910	General works
	Tea masters
2911.A1	Collective
2911.A2-Z	Individual, A-Z
2912.A-Z	Special schools, A-Z

Customs relative to private life
Eating and drinking customs
Foods and beverages
Beverages
Tea
Japanese tea ceremony
Special schools, A-Z -- Continued
2912.E35 Edo Senke school
2912.E57 Enshū school
2912.M8 Mushanokōji Senke
2912.O4 Omote Senke
2912.O73 Oribe Senke
2912.S42 Sekishū school
2912.S55 Sōhen school
2912.U7 Ura Senke
Japanese style gardens see SB458
Gardens in Japan see SB466.J3+
2915 Utensils, etc.
2916 Aesthetics, psychology, etc.
Kaiseki see TX724.5.J3
Coffee
Cf. RM240+ Diet therapy
2918 General works
2919.A-Z By region or country, A-Z
2920.A-Z Other, A-Z
2920.C3 Chocolate
2920.M3 Mate (Tea)
2930 Drinking of healths. Toasts
Drinking vessels
Cf. NK4895+ Decorative arts
2940 General works
Special
2945.A-Z By form, material, etc., A-Z
Cf. NK7218 Gold and silver plate
2947.A-Z By region or country, A-Z
Tables. Table settings. Tableware
2948 General works
2949 Chopsticks
2950 Spoons
2952 Toothpicks
Picnics
Including clambakes
2955 General works
2956.A-Z By region or country, A-Z
2960 Luncheons
2995 Lying down customs
Sleeping customs

Customs relative to private life
Sleeping customs -- Continued
3000.3 General works
3000.4.A-Z By region or country, A-Z
3000.5.A-Z Special topics, A-Z
3000.5.B43 Bedrooms
3000.5.B44 Beds
3000.5.C67 Co-sleeping
3000.5.P54 Pillows
Morning customs
3002 General works
3002.3.A-Z By region or country, A-Z
Sitting customs
3005.3 General works
3005.4.A-Z By region or country, A-Z
3010 Narcotics. Psychotropic drugs
3015 Betel. Betel nut
Tobacco. Smoking
3020 General works
3021.A-Z By region or country, A-Z
3030 Snuff
Incense
3031 General works
3032 Japanese incense ceremony
Exchange of gifts. Gift wrapping
3040 General works
3041.A-Z By region or country, A-Z
Salutations, farewells, courtesies, etc.
Cf. GT2640 Kissing
3050 General works
3050.5.A-.Z By region or country, A-Z
3055 Scatology
3070 Insult. Invective
3080 Swearing. Profanity
3085 Oaths. Vows
3100 Treatment of older people
Burial and funeral customs. Treatment of the dead
Cf. BF789.F8 Funerals (Psychology)
Cf. GT1955+ Burial clothes
Cf. RA619+ Public health
3150 General works
3170 Ancient
3180 Medieval
3190 Modern
3201-3296 By region or country (Table G6)
Interment. Burial
3320 General works

Customs relative to private life
Burial and funeral customs. Treatment of the dead
Interment. Burial -- Continued
3325 Coffins
Incineration. Cremation
3330 General works
3331.A-Z By region or country, A-Z
3335 Urns
3340 Embalming. Mummies
For works limited to Egyptian mummies see DT62.M7
3350 Exposure
3353 Body snatching
Special funeral customs
3360 Wakes
3370 Suttee. Widow suicide
Cf. GT3276 India
Cf. GT3330+ Incineration, cremation
3380 Ship burial
For works on specific ship burials, see D-F
Mourning customs
3390 General works
3390.5.A-Z By region or country, A-Z
Customs relative to public and social life
For general works on the customs of a particular region or country, see D-F. For popular dramatic representations, broadcasts, motion pictures, the theater, etc., see PN1720+
For recreation, amusements, sports, games, dances, etc. see GV1+
3400 General works
Special events
Class here general works only; for specific types of special events, see the type of event, e.g. sports events, see GV, conventions and congresses, see AS
Including special events industry
3403 Periodicals
3404 Dictionaries and encyclopedias
3405 General works
3406.A-Z By region or country, A-Z
3408 Nighttime. Night life
Entertaining. Hospitality
Cf. BJ2021+ Etiquette of entertaining
Cf. GV1470+ Parties
Cf. TX731 Cookery
3410 General works. History
Geishas. Kisaengs
3412 General works
Biography

Customs relative to public and social life
Entertaining. Hospitality
Geishas. Kisaengs
Biography -- Continued
3412.5 Collective
3412.7.A-Z Individual, A-Z
3415.A-Z By region or country, A-Z
Town life
Cf. HT101+ Urban sociology
3420 General works
Fashionable life. High life
3430 General works
3433 Snobs
Dandies see GT6720
3440 Street life
3450 Street cries
For London cries see DA688
For New York City cries see F128.37
3452 Street decoration
Country life
Cf. HT401+ Rural sociology
Cf. S521+ Farm life
3470 General works
3471.A-Z By region or country, A-Z
3490 Mountain life
Court and castle life
Cf. GT5010+ Official ceremonies
Cf. GV1747 Court and state balls
3510 General works
By period
3520 Medieval
3530 Modern
By region or country
see classes D-F
3550 Castle life
Customs of chivalry
Cf. CR4501+ Heraldry
3600 General works
Minstrels. Troubadours. Minnesingers
Cf. ML182 Music history and criticism
Cf. PQ199 French literature
Cf. PR507 English poetry
3650 General works
3650.5.A-Z By region or country, A-Z
3660 Storytellers
Court fools. Jesters
3670 General works

Customs relative to public and social life
Court and castle life
Court fools. Jesters -- Continued
3670.5.A-Z By region or country, A-Z
Inns. Taverns. Hotels
Cf. GT2850+ Eating and drinking customs
Cf. GT2855+ Food and beverage customs
Cf. TX901+ Home economics
3770 General works
By period
3780 Medieval
3785 Modern
3801-3896 By region or country (Table G6)
Signs and signboards
Cf. HF5841 Advertising signs
Cf. HF5843+ Billboards
3910 General works
By region or country
United States
3911.A2 General works
3911.A3-Z By region or state, A-Z
Under each state:
.x General works
.x2A-.x2Z Local, A-Z
3911.112-.995 Other regions or countries (Table G2c modified)
Add country number in table to GT3911
United States
General works
see GV3911.A2
By region or state
see GV3911.A3+
Graffiti
3912 General works
By region or country
United States
3913.A2 General works
3913.A3-Z By region or state, A-Z
Under each state:
.x General works
.x2A-.x2Z Local, A-Z
3913.112-.995 Other regions or countries (Table G2c modified)
Add country number in table to GT3913
United States
General works
see GV3913.A2
By region or state
see GV3913.A3+

Customs relative to public and social life -- Continued
Festivals. Holidays
Including antiquarian, historical, and descriptive works
For local history, see D-F
For school exercises for special days see LB3525+
For production of (modern) amateur pageants and plays see PN3203+
Cf. BV30+ Church festivals
Cf. GV1748 Public balls
3925 Dictionaries. Encyclopedias
3930 General works
3932 Popular works
3933 Juvenile works
3935 Management of festivals
Public rejoicing. Spectacles. Fêtes
3940 General works
Processions. Pageants. Parades
3980 General works
4001-4096 By region or country (Table G6)
Carnivals. Mardi gras
4180 General works
4201-4296 By region or country (Table G6)
Harvest festivals
Including Oktoberfest
4380 General works
4401-4496 By region or country (Table G6)
Autumn festivals
4502 General works
4502.112-.995 By region or country (Table G2a)
Add country number in table to GT4502
Winter festivals
4503 General works
4503.112-.995 By region or country (Table G2a)
Add country number in table to GT4503
Spring festivals
4504 General works
4504.112-.995 By region or country (Table G2a)
Add country number in table to GT4504
Summer festivals
4505 General works
4505.112-.995 By region or country (Table G2a)
Add country number in table to GT4505

Customs relative to public and social life
Festivals. Holidays
Public rejoicing. Spectacles. Fêtes -- Continued
Fairs. Kermisses
Cf. HF5469.7+ Market fairs
Cf. HF5481 Street fairs
Cf. HV544 Charity fairs
Cf. S550+ Agricultural exhibitions. State fairs. County fairs
Cf. T391+ World's fairs
4580 General works
4601-4696 By region or country (Table G6)
4801-4896 By region or country (Table G6)
Special days and periods of time
Cf. TT900.A+ Decorations for special events
Cf. TX739+ Cookery for special occasions
New Year's Day. New Year's Eve
Cf. BV135.N5 Religious observance
4905 General works
4908 Special customs: New Year cards
4915 Twelfth Night. Epiphany
Cf. BV50.E7 Religious observance
4925 Valentine's Day
Spring see GT4995.V4
4930 Holy Week
Easter
Cf. BV55 Religious observance
4935 General works
4935.4 Easter Bunny
4935.5 Easter eggs
4945 May Day
Including maypoles
4965 Halloween
4975 Thanksgiving Day
Cf. BV75 Religious observance
Cf. E162 Colonial United States
Cf. F7 Colonial New England
Christmas
Cf. BV45+ Religious observance
4985 General works
4985.5 Juvenile works
By region or country
Prefer classification by special custom below
United States
4986.A1 General works
4986.A2-Z By region or state, A-Z

Customs relative to public and social life
Festivals. Holidays
Special days and periods of time
Christmas
By region or country -- Continued

4987.112-.995	Other regions or countries (Table G2b) Add country number in table to GT4987
	Special customs
4988	Christmas decorations Cf. TT900.C4 Handicrafts
4988.5	Advent calendars
4988.7	Christmas greens
4989	Christmas trees
4989.5	Crèches Cf. N8065 Religious art
4990	Pistol shooting
4992	Santa Claus
4995.A-Z	Other days, A-Z
4995.A4	All Souls' Day
4995.A53	Saint Andrew's Day
4995.A6	April Fools Day
4995.A8	Ascension Day
4995.A98	Autumnal equinox
4995.B74	Saint Brigid's Day
4995.C36	Candlemas
4995.C6	Corpus Christi
4995.D5	Dingaan's Day
4995.D65	Saint Dominic's Day
4995.F6	Fools, Feast of
4995.G4	Saint George's Day
4995.G76	Groundhog Day
4995.J35	Saint James' Day
4995.J6	John the Baptist's Day
4995.J66	Saint Joseph's Day
4995.L8	Saint Lucy's Day
4995.M3	Saint Martin's Day
4995.M53	Saint Michael's Day
	Midsummer's Day see GT4995.S85
4995.N5	Saint Nicholas Day
4995.P3	Saint Patrick's Day
4995.P45	Pentecost. Whitsunday
4995.P48	Saint Peter's Day
4995.P8	Purim
	Spring see GT4995.V4
4995.S73	Saint Stephen's Day
4995.S85	Summer solstice. Midsummer
4995.V4	Vernal equinox. Spring

Customs relative to public and social life
Festivals. Holidays
Special days and periods of time
Other days, A-Z -- Continued
Whitsunday see GT4995.P45
4995.W55 Winter solstice
Official ceremonies of royalty, nobility, etc.
For works on the official ceremonies of individual countries, see D-F
Cf. CR3499+ Titles of honor, rank, precedence, etc.
Cf. GT5350+ Customs of royalty and nobility
5010 General works
5020 Heralds, trumpeters, etc.
5030 Triumphs. Triumphal entries
Cf. DG89 Military and naval antiquities
Coronations
5050 General works
(5051) By region or country
see D-F
5070 Marriages
Cf. GT2660+ Marriage customs
5080 Baptisms
5090 Visits of royalty, etc.
5150 Customs relative to use of trees and plants
Cf. GR780+ Folklore of plants
Cf. GT4989 Christmas trees
Cf. GT5897+ Cultivated plants
Cf. SD363+ Arbor Day
Customs relative to use of flowers, leaves, etc.
Cf. GR780+ Folklore of plants, language of flowers
Cf. SB449+ Use of flowers in decoration
5160 General works
5164 Herbs
5168 Violets
5170 Customs relative to use of precious metals
Customs relative to transportation and travel
Cf. BJ2137 Etiquette of travel
Cf. G149+ Voyages and travels
Cf. G540+ Seafaring life
Cf. GT6490 Customs relating to wayfarers
Cf. HE1+ Transportation
5220 General works
By period
5230 Ancient
5240 Medieval
5250 Modern through 1800
5260 1801-

Customs relative to transportation and travel -- Continued

5265.A-Z By region or country, A-Z

Vehicles. Chariots. Cars

5280 General works

5283.A-Z By region or country, A-Z

Sleighs. Sleds

5285 General works

5286.A-Z By region or country, A-Z

Customs relative to special classes. By birth, rank, etc.

Cf. CR3499+ Titles of honor, rank, precedence, etc.

Cf. GT1710+ Costumes of special classes

Cf. HT641+ Sociology

5320 General works

Special groups

Royalty

For the customs of royalty in particular countries, see D-F

Cf. GT3510+ Court life

Cf. GT5010+ Official ceremonies

Cf. JC375+ Theory of kingship

5350 General works

By period

5360 Ancient

5370 Medieval

5380 Modern through 1800

5390 1801-

Nobility

For the customs of the nobility in particular countries, see D-F

Cf. HT647+ Sociology

5450 General works

By period

5460 Ancient

5470 Medieval

5480 Modern through 1800

5490 1801-

Burghers

5550 General works

By period

5560 Medieval

5570 Modern through 1800

5580 1801-

Peasants

Cf. HD1521+ Agricultural laborers (Economic history)

5650 General works

By period

5660 Medieval

5670 Modern through 1800

5680 1801-

GT

Customs relative to special classes. By birth, rank, etc.
Special groups
Peasants -- Continued
5690.A-Z By region or country, A-Z
Customs relative to special classes. By occupation
Cf. HT675+ Sociology
5750 General works
By period
5760 Ancient
5770 Medieval
5780 Modern through 1800
5790 1801-
Agriculture and hunting
Cf. GN406+ Primitive customs
Cf. GT3470+ Country life
Cf. SK1+ Hunting sports
5810 General works
By period
5820 Ancient
5830 Medieval
5840 Modern through 1800
5850 1801-
By region or country
United States
5855 General works
5856.A-Z By region or state, A-Z
5856.112-.995 Other regions or countries (Table G2b)
Add country number in table to GT5856
Domestic animals and cultivated plants
5870 General works
Domestic and otherwise useful animals
Cf. SF1+ Animal culture
5880 General works
Horses and riding
Including costumes
5885 General works
5888 Harness, bits, spurs, etc.
Cf. SF92 Use on farms
Cf. TS1030+ Leather industry
5889.A-Z By region or country, A-Z
5890 Dogs
5895.A-Z Other animals, A-Z
5895.C37 Cattle
5895.E43 Elephants
5895.M84 Mules
Pigs see GT5895.S95
5895.R4 Reindeer

Customs relative to special classes. By occupation
Agriculture and hunting
Domestic animals and cultivated plants
Domestic and otherwise useful animals
Other animals, A-Z -- Continued
5895.S5 Sheep
5895.S95 Swine
Cultivated plants
Cf. GT5150 Customs relative to the use of plants
Cf. SB1+ Plant culture
5897 General works
5899.A-Z Individual plants, A-Z
5899.B36 Bamboo
5899.H38 Hay
5899.M54 Millets
5899.R5 Rice
5899.R66 Root crops
5899.S5 Sisal hemp
5899.W5 Wheat
Fishing
5904 General works
5904.5.A-Z By region or country, A-Z
5905.A-Z Individual fishes, A-Z
5905.S53 Sharks
Industries. Trades
Including costumes
Cf. GN429+ Primitive industries
Cf. HD9000+ Economic history
5910 General works
By period
5920 Ancient
5930 Medieval
5940 Modern through 1800
5950 1801-
5960.A-Z Special, A-Z
5960.B34-.B342 Bakers (Table G16)
5960.B8-.B82 Building trades (Table G16)
5960.F57-.F572 Fire fighters (Table G16)
5960.G55-.G552 Glass workers (Table G16)
5960.L55-.L552 Loggers (Table G16)
5960.M5-.M52 Miners (Table G16)
Miners, Salt see GT5960.S35+
5960.P43-.P432 Peddlers (Table G16)
5960.S35-.S352 Salt workers (Table G16)
5960.S45-.S452 Servants. Domestics (Table G16)
5960.T2-.T22 Tailors (Table G16)
5960.T36-.T362 Tattoo artists (Table G16)

Customs relative to special classes. By occupation
Industries. Trades
Special, A-Z -- Continued
5960.T54-.T542 Tinkers (Table G16)
5960.W43-.W432 Weavers (Table G16)
Commercial occupations
Cf. HF1+ Commerce
6010 General works
Special
6060 Street vendors
Professions
Including costumes
6110 General works
Church, clergy
see subclasses BR-BX
(6230) Law. Judges, lawyers, etc.
see class K
Medicine. Physicians, surgeons, etc.
see R707+
(6380) Apothecaries. Pharmacists
see RS122.5
Soldiers
see class U
6390.A-Z Other professions, A-Z
Customs relative to other classes
6490 Wayfarers
Outlaws. The underworld
Cf. HV6201+ Criminal classes (Social pathology)
6550 General works
By period
6560 Ancient
6570 Medieval
6580 Modern through 1800
6590 1801-
6601-6696 By region or country (Table G6)
Prosecutions and punishments
Cf. HV8497+ Penology
6710 General works
6715 Prosecutions and punishments of animals
Cf. HV4701+ Protection of animals
6720 Dandies. Dandyism
For the biography of dandies see CT9985+
6730 Physically abnormal people
Cf. GN69+ Giants and dwarfs (Physical anthropology)
Cf. GV1834.7+ Side shows
Cf. QM690+ Teratology
6735 Redheads

Customs relative to other classes -- Continued

6737	Blondes
6739	Brunettes
	Miscellaneous implements, utensils, etc., illustrative of former customs
7050	General works
7055.A-Z	By region or country, A-Z
7070.A-Z	Special, A-Z
7070.A93	Axes
7070.D5	Distaffs
7070.K66	Knots and splices
7070.L6	Locks
7070.M4	Measuring instruments
7070.M67	Mortars and pestles
	Pestles see GT7070.M67
	Splices see GT7070.K66

Recreation. Leisure
Including amusement in general, play, etc.
Cf. BV1620+ Recreation in the Church
Cf. GN454+ Cultural anthropology
Cf. GR887 Folklore
Cf. HT281 Urban sociology
Cf. HT469 Rural sociology
Cf. LB1137 Play in education
Cf. LB3031 Recreation in the school management
Cf. LC5201+ Adult education
Cf. NX1+ The arts
Cf. TT1+ Handicrafts
Cf. Z1003+ Books and reading

1 Periodicals. Serials
3 Societies
4 Congresses
Collected works (nonserial)
7 Several authors
8 Individual authors
9 Questions and answers. Quiz books
11 Dictionaries. Encyclopedias
12 Directories (General and international)
For individual regions or countries see GV51+
Philosophy. Relation to other topics
Cf. GV706+ Philosophy of sports
14 General works
14.3 Relation to character and character building
Relation to Christian life see BV4597+
14.35 Relation to ethics
For ethics of leisure only see BJ1498
14.4 Relation to psychology
For the psychological aspects of special topics, see the topic
For the psychology of games see GV1201.37
Cf. BF717 Play (Developmental Psychology)
14.45 Relation to sociology
Study and teaching. Research
14.5 General works
14.6 Audiovisual aids
Museums. Exhibitions
14.7 General works
14.8.A-Z By region or country, A-Z
Under each country:
.x *General works*
.x2A-.x2Z *Special. By city, A-Z*
History
Cf. GV571+ History of athletic sports
15 General works

History -- Continued
Ancient. Classical games, etc.
Cf. GV213 History of physical training
Cf. GV573 History of athletic sports
17 General works
19 Oriental
Greek
21 General works
23 Olympic games
Cf. GV721.18+ Olympic revivals
24 Pythian Games
Roman
31 General works
33 Chariot racing
34 Circus
35 Gladiators, etc.
38 Celtic
41 Medieval
Modern
45 General works
47 State policy, finance, etc.
By region or country
Including history, conditions, policy, finance, calendars, etc.
America
Cf. E59.G3 Games of Indians
51 General works
United States
53 General works
54.A-Z By region or state
54.A1-.A195 By region
54.A11 New England
54.A13 Southern States
54.A135 Tennessee Valley
54.A14 North Central States
Including Great Lakes region and Old Northwest
54.A17 West (U.S.)
54.A18 Pacific Coast
54.A19 Pacific Northwest
54.A2-.W By state, A-W
Under each state:
.x *General works*
.x2A-.x2Z *Local, A-Z. Including regions, counties, river valleys, cities, etc.*
e.g.
54.H3-.H32 Hawaii
Canada
55 General works

History
Modern
By region or country
America
Canada -- Continued
56.A-Z Local, A-Z
Latin America
57 General works
Mexico
58.A1 General works
58.A2-Z Local, A-Z
Central America
59 General works
60.A-Z By country, A-Z
West Indies
61 General works
62.A-Z Local, A-Z
South America
63 General works
Argentina
65 General works
66.A-Z Local, A-Z
Brazil
67 General works
68.A-Z Local, A-Z
Chile
69 General works
70.A-Z Local, A-Z
71.A-Z Other South American regions or countries, A-Z
Under each country:
.x General works
.x2A-.x2Z By state, province, etc., A-Z
.x3A-.x3Z By city, A-Z
Europe
73 General works
Great Britain
75 General works
76.E-.W By division
England
76.E5 General works
76.E6A-.E6Z By region, county, etc., A-Z
76.E7A-.E7Z By city, A-Z
Northern Ireland
76.N6 General works
76.N7A-.N7Z By region, county, etc., A-Z
76.N8A-.N8Z By city, A-Z
Scotland

History
Modern
By region or country
Europe
Great Britain
By division
Scotland -- Continued

76.S4 General works
76.S5A-.S5Z By region, county, etc., A-Z
76.S6A-.S6Z By city, A-Z

Wales

76.W3 General works
76.W4A-.W4Z By region, county, etc., A-Z
76.W5A-.W5Z By city, A-Z

Ireland

76.5 General works
76.6A-.6Z Local, A-Z

Austria

77 General works
78.A-Z Local, A-Z

France

79 General works
80.A-Z Local, A-Z

Germany

81 General works
82.A-Z Local, A-Z

Former East Germany

82.5 General works
82.6A-.6Z Local, A-Z

Greece

83 General works
84.A-Z Local, A-Z

Italy

85 General works
86.A-Z Local, A-Z

Low Countries

87 General works

Belgium

89 General works
90.A-Z Local, A-Z

Netherlands

91 General works
92.A-Z Local, A-Z

History
Modern
By region or country
Europe -- Continued
Russia. Soviet Union. Russia (Federation)
For individual former Soviet republics in Europe see GV118.A+
For individual former Soviet republics in Asia see GV133.A+
93 General works
94.A-Z Local, A-Z
Scandinavia
95 General works
Denmark
97 General works
98.A-Z Local, A-Z
Finland see GV118.F55+
Norway
99 General works
100.A-Z Local, A-Z
Sweden
101 General works
102.A-Z Local, A-Z
Spain
103 General works
104.A-Z Local, A-Z
Portugal
105 General works
106.A-Z Local, A-Z
Switzerland
107 General works
108.A-Z Local, A-Z
Balkan States
109 General works
Bulgaria
111 General works
112.A-Z Local, A-Z
Romania
115 General works
116.A-Z Local, A-Z
Former Yugoslavia
117 General works
117.5A-.5Z Local, A-Z

History
Modern
By region or country
Europe -- Continued
118.A-Z Other European regions or countries, A-Z
Under each country:
.x *General works*
.x2A-.x2Z *By state, province, etc., A-Z*
.x3A-.x3Z *By city, A-Z*
e.g.
Czech Republic
118.C9 General works
118.C92A-.C92Z By state, province, etc., A-Z
118.C93A-.C93Z By city, A-Z
Finland
118.F55 General works
118.F552A-.F552Z By state, province, etc., A-Z
118.F553A-.F553Z By city, A-Z
Asia
119 General works
China
121 General works
122.A-Z Local, A-Z
India
123 General works
124.A-Z Local, A-Z
Japan
125 General works
126.A-Z Local, A-Z
Indonesia
126.5 General works
126.6.A-Z Local, A-Z
Iran
127 General works
128.A-Z Local, A-Z
(129) Soviet Union in Asia. Siberia
see GV93
(130.A-Z) Local
see GV94
Turkey. Asia Minor
131 General works
132.A-Z Local, A-Z
Israel
132.5 General works
132.6.A-Z Local, A-Z

History
Modern
By region or country
Asia -- Continued
133.A-Z Other Asian regions or countries, A-Z
Under each country:
.x *General works*
.x2A-.x2Z *By state, province, etc., A-Z*
.x3A-.x3Z *By city, A-Z*
e.g.
Korea
133.K8 General works
133.K82A-.K82Z By state, province, etc., A-Z
133.K83A-.K83Z By city, A-Z
134 Arab countries
Africa
135 General works
South Africa
137 General works
138.A-Z Local, A-Z
Egypt
139 General works
140.A-Z Local, A-Z
Tunisia
141 General works
142.A-Z Local, A-Z
Morocco
142.5 General works
142.6.A-Z Local, A-Z
143.A-Z Other African regions or countries, A-Z
Under each country:
.x *General works*
.x2A-.x2Z *By state, province, etc., A-Z*
.x3A-.x3Z *By city, A-Z*
e.g.
Angola
143.A5 General works
143.A52.A-Z By state, province, etc., A-Z
143.A53.A-Z By city, A-Z
Ethiopia
143.E8 General works
143.E82.A-Z By state, province, etc., A-Z
143.E83.A-Z By city, A-Z
Australia
145 General works
146.A-Z Local, A-Z
New Zealand

History
Modern
By region or country
New Zealand -- Continued
149 General works
150.A-Z Local, A-Z
Pacific islands
157 General works
158.A-Z By island or group of islands, A-Z
For Hawaii see GV54.H3+
Recreation personnel
160 Recreation as a profession
Biography
For biographies within special recreational subjects, see the subject
Collective
161 General works
163 Women
165.A-Z Individual, A-Z
166 Volunteer workers
General works, treatises, and textbooks
171 American, through 1975
173 English, through 1975
174 American and English, 1976-
177 French
179 German
181 Other (not A-Z)
181.15 Pictorial works
181.18 Interpretation of cultural and natural resources
181.2 Program handbooks
Class here comprehensive guides offering suggestions and ideas for special programs, activities, parties, games, fun, etc.
Cf. GV181.43 Program planning
Cf. GV1199+ Games and amusements
Addresses, essays, lectures see GV191
181.3 General special (Special aspects of the subject as a whole)
Recreation leadership
181.35 Study and teaching
181.4 General works
181.42 Leisure counseling
181.43 Program planning and supervising
181.46 Recreation surveys
Class here works on methodology only
For results of surveys of activities, see the activity
For results of particular surveys by country see GV51+
Administration of recreation services. Community recreation
181.5 General works

GV

Recreation leadership
Administration of recreation services. Community recreation -- Continued
181.55 Evaluation of services
181.6 Finance
Cf. TH4711 Construction of recreation buildings
Recreational areas and facilities. Recreation centers
Cf. GV401+ Sports facilities, playgrounds, etc.
Cf. HN41+ Community centers, social centers
Cf. HS2581 Country clubs
Cf. HT485 Social centers in the country
Cf. HV4175+ Social settlements
Cf. LC223 Schools as community centers
Cf. NA6800+ Recreation buildings (Architecture)
Cf. SB481.A1+ Parks and reserves
Cf. SK351+ Wildlife management areas
182 General works
By region or country see GV51+
Personnel see GV160+
182.15 Financial and business aspects
182.2 Public relations
Cf. GV714 Sports
182.3 Facility planning. Standards
182.4 Maintenance and repair
182.5 Equipment and supplies
Including catalogs
Recreation for special classes of persons
182.8 Families
182.9 Children
For works discussing the significance of play in the life of the child see HQ782
Cf. GV1202.92+ Games and amusements
Cf. RJ242 Children in hospitals
Youth see GV1+
Students see LB3608
183 Girls and women
183.2 Gay men. Lesbians
People with disabilities
Cf. GV445 Physical training
183.5 General works
183.6 Children with disabilities
Cf. LC4026 Games for children with disabilities
183.7 People with mental disabilities
For children with mental disabilities see GV183.6
183.9 People with social disabilities
For children with social disabilities see GV183.6
Blind see HV1765+

Recreation for special classes of persons -- Continued
Invalids, Games for see GV1231
Invalids, Recreation therapy for see RM736.7
Mentally ill see RC489.R4
Industrial workers see HD7395.R4
Military personnel (Armed Forces) see UH800+
184 Older people. Retirees
Special occasions
186 Vacations
Cf. G149+ Voyages and travel
Cf. HD5260+ Labor economics
Cf. LC5701+ Vacation schools
Leisure industry
188 General works
188.3.A-Z By region or country, A-Z
191 Addresses, essays, lectures. Anecdotes. Humor. Miscellanea
Cf. GV707 Sports
Outdoor life. Outdoor recreation
Cf. GT2955+ Picnics
Cf. QH81 Nature books. Outdoor books
Cf. RA604 Public health aspects
Cf. SF308.5+ Riding. Horsemanship
Cf. SH401+ Angling
Cf. SK1+ Hunting sports
Cf. SK650+ Wildlife-related recreation
191.2 Periodicals. Societies. Serials
191.22 Congresses
Collected works (nonserial)
191.24 Several authors
191.25 Individual authors
191.3 Dictionaries. Encyclopedias
191.35 Directories
Class here general directories or general directories of the United States
For directories of other regions, countries, states, etc. see GV191.42.A+
191.355 Computer network resources
Including the Internet
Study and teaching. Research
191.357 General works
191.358.A-Z By region or country, A-Z
191.36 History
By region or country
United States
Including works treating United States and Canada together
191.4 General works
For directories of the United States see GV191.35

Outdoor life. Outdoor recreation
By region or country
United States -- Continued
191.42.A-Z By region or state, A-Z
Canada
191.44 General works
191.46.A-Z By region or province, A-Z
191.48.A-Z Other regions or countries, A-Z
Biography
191.5 Collective
191.52.A-Z Individual, A-Z
191.6 General works
191.62 Juvenile works
191.623 Equipment and supplies
191.625 Safety measures
Works for special groups
191.63 Children
191.635 People with disabilities
Including children with disabilities
191.64 Women
Outdoor recreation resources planning and management
Including conservation
Cf. GV770.7+ Water sports facilities
Cf. QH75+ Nature conservation
Cf. SB481.A1+ Parks
By region or country see GV191.4+
191.66 General works
191.67.A-Z Special types, A-Z
191.67.F6 Forest recreation
191.67.R36 Rangeland recreation
Water-oriented recreation
Including public access to bodies of water for recreational use
Cf. GV770.7+ Water sports
191.67.W3 General works
By region or country see GV191.4+
191.67.W5 Wilderness recreation
Cf. GV200.5+ Wilderness survival
Cf. QH75+ Nature conservation
Camping
Including camping for individuals or small groups
191.68 Periodicals. Societies. Serials
By region or country see GV191.4+
191.7 General works
191.72 Campground construction and maintenance
Cf. GV198.L3 Layouts, buildings, etc., for organized camps

Outdoor life. Outdoor recreation
Camping -- Continued
191.74 Sanitation
191.76 Equipment and supplies
191.78 Safety measures
Summer camps. Organized camping
For camps operated by special youth societies or organizations see HS3250+
Cf. SH405 Fishing resorts
192.A1 Periodicals. Societies. Serials
192.A2 Congresses
192.A5-Z General works
192.2 Juvenile works
Biography
192.5 Collective
192.7.A-Z Individual, A-Z
192.8 History
By region or country
United States
193 General works
194.A-Z By region or state, A-Z
Under each state:
.x General works
.x2A-.x2Z Individual camps. By name, A-Z
195.A-Z Other regions or countries, A-Z
Under each country:
.x General works
.x2A-.x2Z Individual camps. By name, A-Z
197.A-Z Special types of camps, and camps for special groups, A-Z
197.A34 Aged. Older people
Boy Scouts see HS3313.Z65
Church camps see BV1650
Computer camps see QA76.33
197.D3 Day camps
Fresh-air fund see HV931+
197.G5 Girls
197.H3 Handicapped. People with disabilities
Jewish see BM135
Music camps
see MT
Older people see GV197.A34
People with disabilities see GV197.H3
197.S3 School camps
Cf. LB3481+ Open-air schools
Sports camps see GV711.7+
198.A-Z Special topics, A-Z

Outdoor life. Outdoor recreation
Camping
Summer camps. Organized camping
Special topics, A-Z -- Continued

198.A38 Accreditation
Administration see GV198.M35
198.C6 Counselors
198.D4 Decoration
198.F6 Food
Cf. TX823 Camp cookery
198.L3 Layouts, buildings, facilities, etc.
198.M35 Management
198.M38 Marketing
198.P74 Psychological aspects
198.R4 Recreational programs
Including campfire programs
Cf. GV1202.C36 Campers' games
Cf. GV1217 Scouting games
198.S2 Safety measures
Cf. RC88.9.C3 First aid in injury
198.S3 Sanitation
Cf. TD931 Sanitary engineering
Theatricals see PN3156
198.V63 Vocational guidance

Trailer camping. Recreational vehicle camping
Cf. GV1020+ Touring
Cf. TX1100+ Mobile home living

198.5 Periodicals. Societies. Serials
198.54 Dictionaries. Encyclopedias
198.56 Directories
Class here general directories or general directories of the United States
For directories of other regions, countries, states, etc. see GV198.65.A+

By region or country
Class here works on the technical aspects of trailer camping in particular places
For works of description and travel, see D-F

United States
198.6 General works
For U.S. directories see GV198.56
198.65.A-Z By region or state, A-Z
198.67.A-Z Other regions or countries, A-Z
198.7 General works
198.9 Ice and snow camping
198.92 Swamp camping
Low-impact camping

Outdoor life. Outdoor recreation
Camping
Low-impact camping -- Continued
198.93 General works
By region or country see GV191.4+
Farm vacations, dude ranches, etc.
Cf. SF308.5+ Riding. Horsemanship
198.945 Periodicals. Societies. Serials
By region or country
United States
198.95 General works
198.96.A-Z By region or state, A-Z
Under each state:
.x General works
.x2A-.x2Z Individual ranches or farms. By name, A-Z
198.97.A-Z Other regions or countries, A-Z
Under each country:
.x General works
.x2A-.x2Z Individual ranches or farms. By name, A-Z
198.975 General works
Canoe cruising and camping see GV789+
Hiking. Pedestrian tours
Cf. G504 Hitchhiking
Cf. GV502 Exercise walking
Cf. GV855+ Cross-country skiing
Cf. GV1044+ Bicycle hiking
Cf. GV1071 Walking matches
Cf. RA781.65 Walking for health
199 Periodicals. Societies. Serials
By region or country
Class here works on the technical aspects of hiking, climbing, etc., in particular places
For works of description and travel, see D-F
For Alps see DQ820+
United States
199.4 General works
199.42.A-Z By region or state, A-Z
Under each state:
.x General works
.x2A-.x2Z Local, A-Z
199.44.A-Z Other regions or countries, A-Z
Under each country:
.x General works
.x2A-.x2Z Local, A-Z
199.5 General works

Outdoor life. Outdoor recreation
Hiking. Pedestrian tours -- Continued
199.52 Juvenile literature
For special classes of persons
199.53 Older people
199.54 Children
199.58 Women
By region or country see GV199.4+
Backpacking
Cf. SH446.B3 Backpack fishing
199.6 General works
By region or country see GV199.44.A+
199.62 Equipment and supplies
199.7 Packhorse camping
For breakdown by region or country see GV199.4+
Cf. SF309.28 Trail riding
199.75 Llama pack camping
For breakdown by region or country see GV199.4+
199.77 Goat pack camping
For breakdown by region or country see GV199.4+
Mountaineering
Cf. GV854.9.S56 Ski mountaineering
199.8 Periodicals. Societies and clubs. Serials
Collected works (nonserial)
199.82 Several authors
199.83 Individual authors
199.85 Dictionaries. Encyclopedias
199.87 Directories
199.89 History
By region or country see GV199.4+
Biography
199.9 Collective
199.92.A-Z Individual, A-Z
200 General works
200.15 Equipment and supplies
200.18 Safety measures
200.183 Search and rescue operations
200.19.A-Z Special topics, A-Z
200.19.K56 Knots
200.19.P78 Psychological aspects
200.19.R34 Rappelling
200.19.S63 Social aspects
Alpine scrambling
200.195 General works
By region or country see GV199.4+
Rock climbing
200.2 General works

Outdoor life. Outdoor recreation
Mountaineering
Rock climbing -- Continued
By region or country see GV199.4+
Equipment and supplies see GV200.15
200.23.A-Z For special classes of persons, A-Z
200.23.C35 Children
200.25 Free climbing
Ice and snow climbing
By region or country see GV199.4+
200.3 General works
200.35 Canyoneering
For breakdown by region or country see GV199.4+
200.4 Orienteering
Wilderness survival. Desert survival. Jungle survival
Cf. TL553.7 Survival after airplane accidents
200.5 General works
Study and teaching. Research
Cf. GV192+ Organized camping
Cf. LB1047 Outdoor education
Cf. LB3481+ Open-air schools
200.52 General works
Outward bound schools
By region or country
United States
200.53 General works
200.54.A-Z By region or state, A-Z
200.55.A-Z Other regions or countries, A-Z
200.56 General works
Caving. Spelunking
Cf. GB601+ Caves. Speleology
200.6 Periodicals. Societies. Serials
Biography
200.615 Collective
200.616.A-Z Individual, A-Z
200.62 General works
200.63 Cave diving
200.64 Prusiking
200.645 Search and rescue operations
By region or country
United States
200.65 General works
200.655.A-Z By region or state, A-Z
Under each state:
.x *General works*
.x2A-.x2Z *Local, A-Z (Including caves)*

Outdoor life. Outdoor recreation
Caving. Spelunking
By region or country -- Continued
200.66.A-Z Other regions or countries, A-Z
Under each country:
.x *General works*
.x2A-.x2Z *Local, A-Z (Including caves)*
Physical education and training
Cf. BV4598 Physical education and Christianity
Cf. RA780.5+ Personal hygiene
Cf. RM719+ Mechanotherapy: Massage, exercise, etc.
201 Periodicals. Serials
Societies. Clubs. Turnvereins, etc.
Cf. GV391 Organization of athletic clubs and societies
Cf. GV563 Sports clubs and societies
202 International
203 United States
204.A-Z Other regions or countries, A-Z
Under each country:
.x *General works*
.x2A-.x2Z *Local, A-Z (Including regions, provinces, river valleys, cities, etc.)*
.x3A-.x3Z *Special societies, etc. By name, A-Z*
205 Congresses
Collected works (nonserial)
206 Several authors
206.5.A-Z Individual authors, A-Z
207 Dictionaries. Encyclopedias
Communication of information
207.3 General works
207.4 Documentation
208 Directories
Philosophy. Relation to other topics see GV342+
History
211 General works
By period
213 Ancient
215 Medieval
217 Modern
By region or country
For individual schools see GV367.A+
America
221 General works
United States
223 General works

Physical education and training
History
By region or country
America
United States -- Continued
224.A1A-.A1W By state, A-W
e.g.
224.A1H3 Hawaii
224.A2-Z By city, A-Z
Canada
225.A1 General works
225.A2-Z Local, A-Z
Latin America
226 General works
Mexico
227.A1 General works
227.A2-Z Local, A-Z
Central America
228 General works
229.A-Z By country, A-Z
West Indies
230 General works
231.A-Z Local, A-Z
South America
233 General works
Argentina
235 General works
236.A-Z Local, A-Z
Brazil
237 General works
238.A-Z Local, A-Z
Chile
239 General works
240.A-Z Local, A-Z
241.A-Z Other South American regions or countries, A-Z
Under each country:
.x General works
.x2A-.x2Z By state, province, etc., A-Z
.x3A-.x3Z By city, A-Z
Europe
243 General works
Great Britain
Including England
245 General works
246.A-Z By division, A-Z
Northern Ireland
246.N6 General works

Physical education and training
History
By region or country
Europe
Great Britain
By division, A-Z
Northern Ireland -- Continued

246.N7A-.N7Z By state, province, etc., A-Z
246.N8A-.N8Z By city, A-Z
Scotland
246.S4 General works
246.S5A-.S5Z By state, province, etc., A-Z
246.S6A-.S6Z By city, A-Z
Wales
246.W3 General works
246.W4A-.W4Z By state, province, etc., A-Z
246.W5A-.W5Z By city, A-Z
Ireland
246.5 General works
246.6.A-Z Local, A-Z
Austria
247 General works
248.A-Z Local, A-Z
France
249 General works
250.A-Z Local, A-Z
Germany
Including former West Germany
251 General works
252.A-Z Local, A-Z
Former East Germany
252.5 General works
252.6.A-Z Local, A-Z
Greece
253 General works
254.A-Z Local, A-Z
Italy
255 General works
256.A-Z Local, A-Z
Low Countries
257 General works
Belgium
259 General works
260.A-Z Local, A-Z
Netherlands
261 General works
262.A-Z Local, A-Z

Physical education and training
History
By region or country
Europe -- Continued
Russia. Soviet Union. Russia (Federation)
For individual former Soviet republics in Europe see GV288.A+
For individual former Soviet republics in Asia see GV303.A+

263 General works
264.A-Z Local, A-Z
Scandinavia
265 General works
Denmark
267 General works
268.A-Z Local, A-Z
Norway
269 General works
270.A-Z Local, A-Z
Sweden
271 General works
272.A-Z Local, A-Z
Spain
273 General works
274.A-Z Local, A-Z
Portugal
275 General works
276.A-Z Local, A-Z
Switzerland
277 General works
278.A-Z Local, A-Z
Balkan States
279 General works
Bulgaria
281 General works
282.A-Z Local, A-Z
Romania
285 General works
286.A-Z Local, A-Z
Former Yugoslavia
287 General works
287.5.A-Z Local, A-Z

Physical education and training
History
By region or country
Europe -- Continued
288.A-Z Other European regions or countries, A-Z
Under each country:
.x *General works*
.x2A-.x2Z *By state, province, etc., A-Z*
.x3A-.x3Z *By city, A-Z*
e.g.
Czech Republic
288.C9 General works
288.C92A-.C92Z By state, province, etc., A-Z
288.C93A-.C93Z By city, A-Z
Poland
288.P6 General works
288.P62A-.P62Z By state, province, etc., A-Z
288.P63A-.P63Z By city, A-Z
Asia
289 General works
China
291 General works
292.A-Z Local, A-Z
India
293 General works
294.A-Z Local, A-Z
Japan
295 General works
296.A-Z Local, A-Z
Iran
297 General works
298.A-Z Local, A-Z
(299) Soviet Union in Asia. Siberia
see GV263
(300.A-Z) Local, A-Z
see GV264
Turkey. Asia Minor
301 General works
302.A-Z Local, A-Z
303.A-Z Other Asian regions or countries, A-Z
Under each country:
.x *General works*
.x2A-.x2Z *By state, province, etc., A-Z*
.x3A-.x3Z *By city, A-Z*
e.g.
Indonesia
303.I5 General works

Physical education and training
History
By region or country
Asia
Other Asian regions or countries, A-Z
Indonesia -- Continued

303.I52A-.I52Z	By state, province, etc., A-Z
303.I53A-.I53Z	By city, A-Z
	Israel
303.I75	General works
303.I76A-.I76Z	By state, province, etc., A-Z
303.I77A-.I77Z	By city, A-Z
	Korea
303.K6	General works
303.K62A-.K62Z	By state, province, etc., A-Z
303.K63A-.K63Z	By city, A-Z
	Taiwan
303.T28	General works
303.T282A-.T282Z	By state, province, etc., A-Z
303.T283A-.T283Z	By city, A-Z
304	Arab countries
	Africa
305	General works
	South Africa
307	General works
308.A-Z	Local, A-Z
	Egypt
309	General works
310.A-Z	Local, A-Z
	Senegal
311	General works
312.A-Z	Local, A-Z
313.A-Z	Other African regions or countries, A-Z *Under each country:* *.x — General works* *.x2A-.x2Z — By state, province, etc., A-Z* *.x3A-.x3Z — By city, A-Z*
314.A-Z	Indian Ocean islands, A-Z
	Australia
315	General works
316.A-Z	Local, A-Z
	New Zealand
319	General works
320.A-Z	Local, A-Z
	Pacific islands
327	General works

Physical education and training
History
By region or country
Pacific islands -- Continued
328.A-Z By island or group of islands, A-Z
For Hawaii see GV224.A1H3
Biography
Cf. GV697.A+ Athletes
331 Collective
333.A-Z Individual, A-Z
341 General works, treatises, and textbooks
341.4 Popular works
341.5 Juvenile works
Philosophy. Relation to other topics. Methodology
Cf. BV4598 Christian life
342 General works
342.22 Relation to psychology. Psychological aspects
342.27 Relation to sociology. Social aspects
342.5.A-Z Special methods, A-Z
342.5.S7 Statistical methods
343 Addresses, essays, lectures
343.3 Anecdotes. Humor. Miscellanea
343.5 Organization and administration
Cf. GV713 Athletic events
344 Safety measures. Accident prevention
Cf. RC86+ First aid in illness and injury
Cf. RC1200+ Sports medicine
Cf. RD92+ Emergency surgery
Cf. RD101 Fractures and dislocations
345 Value of physical training in schools and colleges
346 School athletics. Intramural and interscholastic athletics
Cf. LC2580+ Student-athletes
College athletics. Intramural and interscholastic athletics
For programs in individual sports, see the sport
Cf. GV691+ Sports in individual colleges
Cf. GV710 Intramural sports (General)
347 General works
350 Financial and business aspects
350.5 Recruitment
By region or country
United States
351 General works
351.3.A-Z By region or state, A-Z
351.5.A-Z Other regions or countries, A-Z
Coaching see GV711

Physical education and training -- Continued
Study and teaching. Research
Class here works on the training of teachers of physical education
361 General works
362 General special
e.g., Women teachers
362.5 Examinations, questions, etc.
History see GV211+
Methods of teaching
363 General works
364 Audiovisual aids, motion pictures, television, etc.
364.3 Music in physical education
By region or country
For individual schools see GV367+
United States
365 General works
365.3.A-Z By region or state, A-Z
365.5.A-Z Other regions or countries, A-Z
Individual schools
Cf. GV691+ Sports in individual schools and colleges
367.A-Z American. By name, A-Z
368.A-Z Other. By name, A-Z
Museums. Exhibitions
381.A1 General works
381.A2-Z By region or country, A-Z
Under each country:
.x General works
.x2A-.x2Z Special. By city, A-Z
391 Organization of athletic clubs and societies
Physical education facilities. Sports facilities
For facilities of individual sports, see the sport
Cf. GV743+ Athletic and sporting goods
401 General works
Gymnasiums
Cf. BV1645 Church gymnasiums
403 General works
405 Planning. Design
Including architecture
Cf. NA325.G9 Roman gymnasiums
Cf. TH845+ Construction of buildings
407 Furniture
Equipment and supplies
409 General works
410 Catalogs
Athletic fields. Playing fields
411 General works

Physical education and training
Physical education facilities. Sports facilities
Athletic fields. Playing fields -- Continued
413 Planning. Design. Location
Special structures
Including sports arenas, coliseums, field houses, stadiums, spectator stands, etc., for multiple use or single sports
Cf. NA6860+ Architecture
415 General works
416.A-Z Individual. By city, A-Z
e.g.
416.N48 New York. Yankee stadium
Playgrounds. Play spaces
Cf. LB3251+ School playgrounds
421 Periodicals. Societies. Serials
423 General works
424 General special
Including adventure playgrounds
424.5 Playgrounds for preschool children
425 Planning. Design. Location
425.5 Construction
426 Apparatus
Including climbing structures, mystery boxes, sculpture, etc.
426.5 Equipment and supplies
427 Management
Physical fitness centers
428 General works
428.5 Management
428.7 Personal trainers
By region or country see GV429+
By region or country
United States
429.A1 Periodicals. Societies
429.A2 General works
430.A-.W By state, A-W
431.A-Z By city, A-Z
Under each:
.x General works
.x2A-.x2Z Individual facilities. By name, A-Z
Individual stadiums see GV416.A+
433.A-Z Other regions or countries, A-Z
Under each country:
.x General works
.x2A-.x2Z By state, province, etc., A-Z
.x3A-.x3Z By city, A-Z

Physical education and training -- Continued
435 Physical measurements
Including anthropometric manuals and tables
Cf. LB3421+ School children
Physical tests, etc. Fitness tests
Including tests for motor ability, physical aptitude, capacity, and efficiency; achievement scales and standards, etc.
436 General works
Evaluation of performance
436.5 General works
436.6.A-Z Individual tests, A-Z
436.6.E87 Eurofit
436.6.T47 Test of Gross Motor Development
436.7.A-Z By region or country, A-Z
437 Clothing for athletics and gymnastics
Cf. GV441 Dress for women and girls
Diet see TX361.A8
Physical education and training for special classes of persons
438 Individuals
Women and girls
Cf. GV464 Gymnastics for women
Cf. GV482 Exercises for women
Cf. GV709+ Sports for women
439 General works
441 Dress
443 Children
Class here general works on the physical education of children at the elementary level
For education at the secondary and higher levels see GV201+
For physical education programs of particular places or school systems, any level see GV221+
Cf. BV1640 Physical culture for the young in the Church
Cf. GV464.5 Gymnastics for children
Cf. GV709.2+ Sports for children
Cf. HV9083 Physical education for juvenile delinquents
444 People with social disabilities
445 People with disabilities
Cf. HV1767 Physical education for the blind
447 Older people
Employees see HD7395.P45
Sailors see V260+
Soldiers see U320+
Nudism. Sunbathing
450 General works

Physical education and training
Nudism. Sunbathing -- Continued
Nudist camps. Nude beaches
By region or country
United States
451 General works
451.2.A-Z By region or state, A-Z
451.3.A-Z Other regions or countries, A-Z
451.4 General works
452 Movement education
Cf. BF295+ Movement, Psychology of
Gymnastics. Gymnastic exercises
Biography
460 Collective
460.2.A-Z Individual, A-Z
461 General works
461.3 Juvenile works
461.5 Psychological aspects
461.7 Coaching
462 Circuit training
463 Exercises for grace and expression
Including Delsarte system, etc.
463.3 Rules, records, etc.
463.5 Gymnastics for men
464 Gymnastics for women and girls
464.5 Gymnastics for children
465 German
467 Swedish
468.A-Z In special institutions. By name, A-Z
469 Young Men's Christian Association
470.A-Z Special topics, A-Z
470.O73 Organization and administration
471.A-Z By region or country, A-Z
Calisthenics. Group exercises
Including physical fitness programs
For physical fitness centers see GV428+
For exercise for health on the part of individuals see RA781
Cf. GV838.53.E94 Aquatic exercises
Cf. GV1798+ Gymnastic dancing
Cf. M1993 Musico-calisthenics
481 General works
481.2 Psychological aspects
481.4 Physical fitness training as a profession
482 Exercise for women
For exercise for pregnant women see RG558.7
482.5 Exercise for men

Physical education and training
Gymnastics. Gymnastic exercises
Calisthenics. Group exercises -- Continued

482.6 Exercise for older people
482.7 Exercise for people with disabilities
483 School exercises
484 Balls
Cf. GV496 Medicine ball
485 Bar bells
487 Dumbbells
488 Flags
489 Free exercises
490 Hoops
Indian clubs
491 General works
493 Fancy club swinging
494 Jogging
Cf. RM727.J64 Therapeutic use
495 Marching and drill (nonmilitary)
Cf. GV1797 Fancy drills
Cf. UD310+ Military marching
496 Medicine ball
497 Poles
498 Rope jumping or skipping
499 Roundel
501 Setting-up exercises
Cf. U320+ Military exercises
501.5 Step aerobics
502 Walking
Cf. GV199+ Walking as recreation
Cf. GV1071 Race walking
Cf. RA781.65 Walking for health
503 Wands
Cf. MT733.6 Baton twirling
Tai chi. Tai ju quan
504 General works
504.6.A-Z For special classes of persons, A-Z
504.6.A35 Aged. Older people
504.6.C44 Children
Older people see GV504.6.A35
505 Other special exercises (not A-Z)
Including stretching, posture control, etc.
508 Development of special parts of the body
Including face, neck, arms, etc.
Reducing exercises for individuals see RA781.6
510.A-Z By region or country, A-Z
Heavy exercises

Physical education and training
Gymnastics. Gymnastic exercises
Heavy exercises -- Continued

511 General works
512 Balance beam
513 Balancing apparatus
Chest weights see GV547.6
Horse
517 General works
518 Pommel horse
519 Buck
521 Long
523 Side
525 High kick
527 Horizontal bars
529 Jumping exercises
Cf. GV1073+ Sports
Parallel bars
535 General works
536 Uneven parallel bars
537 Pyramids and Roman ladders
539 Rings
541 Rope climbing, pole climbing, ladders
543 Rowing machines, etc.
544 Stationary bicycles
545 Tumbling and mat work
Weight training. Weight lifting. Body building
Biography
545.5 Collective
545.52.A-Z Individual, A-Z
546 General works
546.2 Juvenile works
Weight lifting
546.3 General works
546.4.A-Z Special topics, A-Z
546.4.P78 Psychological aspects
546.4.R34 Refereeing
546.4.S74 Stone lifting
Bodybuilding
546.5 General works
Contests, competitions, etc.
546.55 General works
546.56.A-Z Individual, A-Z
546.6.A-Z For special classes of persons, A-Z
546.6.A35 Aged. Older people
546.6.B68 Boys
546.6.C45 Children

Physical education and training
Gymnastics. Gymnastic exercises
Heavy exercises
Weight training. Weight lifting. Body building
For special classes of persons, A-Z -- Continued
Older people see GV546.6.A35
546.6.W64 Women
Weight training equipment
547 General works
547.3 Barbells
547.4 Dumbbells
547.6 Chest weights
548.A-Z Special machines. By name, A-Z
548.N38 Nautilus
548.U54 Universal
Acrobatics. Trapeze work. Rope and wire walking
Cf. GV854.9.A25 Ski acrobatics
Biography
550 Collective
550.2.A-Z Individual, A-Z
551 General works
Acrobatics
552 General works
553 Hand balancing, triple somersault, etc.
555 Trampolining
Sports sciences
Cf. GV436+ Physical tests, etc.
Cf. GV706.4 Sports psychology
Cf. RC1200+ Sports medicine
557 Periodicals. Societies. Serials
557.5 Congresses
558 General works
Sports
Cf. GR887 Folklore
Cf. GV199.8+ Mountaineering
Cf. RC88.9.A+ First aid
Cf. RC1200+ Medical and physiological aspects of individual sports
Cf. SF277+ Horse racing, riding, and driving
Cf. SF294.198+ Horse sports
Cf. SF424 Dog sports
Cf. SF439.5+ Dog racing
Cf. SH401+ Angling
Cf. SK1+ Hunting
Cf. U327+ Military sports
Cf. V267+ Navy sports

Sports -- Continued

561 Periodicals. Serials

Cf. GV741 Sporting annuals

563 Societies. Clubs. Leagues

For clubs for individual sports, see the sport

For clubs in individual countries see GV581+

For programs of special sports events see GV721+

Cf. GV202+ Physical education societies

Cf. GV391 Organization of athletic clubs and societies

Collected works (nonserial)

565 Several authors

565.2 Individual authors

567 Dictionaries. Encyclopedias

567.3 Directories

Philosophy. Relation to other topics see GV706+

Communication of information

567.5 General works

568 Information services

568.3 Computer network resources

Including the Internet

Study and teaching see GV201+

568.5 Sports collectibles

Museums. Exhibitions

568.69 General works

568.7.A-Z By region or country, A-Z

Under each country:

.x *General works*

.x2A-.x2Z *Individual. By name, A-Z*

History

571 General works

By period

Preliterate see GN454+

573 Ancient

575 Medieval

576 Modern

By region or country

For sports in individual schools and colleges see GV691+

America

581 General works

United States

583 General works

584.A-Z By region or state, A-Z

584.5.A-Z By city, A-Z

Canada

585 General works

585.3.A-Z By province, A-Z

Sports
History
By region or country
America
Canada -- Continued
585.5.A-Z By city, A-Z
Greenland
585.7 General works
585.73.A-Z By state, province, etc., A-Z
585.75.A-Z By city, A-Z
Latin America
586 General works
587-588.5 Mexico (Table G8)
Central America
589 General works
590.A-Z Individual countries, A-Z
590.B44 Belize
590.C67 Costa Rica
590.G82 Guatemala
590.H65 Honduras
590.N53 Nicaragua
590.P53 Panama
590.S24 El Salvador
West Indies
591 General works
592.A-Z Individual countries, A-Z
592.C82 Cuba
592.D65 Dominican Republic
592.P83 Puerto Rico
592.T74 Trinidad and Tobago
South America
593 General works
595-596.5 Argentina (Table G8)
597-598.5 Brazil (Table G8)
599-600.5 Chile (Table G8)
601.A-Z Other South American regions or countries, A-Z
Under each country:
.x General works
.x3A-.x3Z By state, province, etc., A-Z
.x5A-.x5Z By city, A-Z
Europe
603 General works
Great Britain
Including England
605 General works
605.2 Scotland
605.3 Wales

Sports
History
By region or country
Europe
Great Britain -- Continued
605.5 Northern Ireland
605.6.A-Z By county, A-Z
605.7.A-Z By city, A-Z
Ireland
606.5 General works
606.53.A-Z By state, province, etc., A-Z
606.55.A-Z By city, A-Z
607-608.5 Austria (Table G8)
France
609 General works
610.A-Z By state, province, etc., A-Z
610.5.A-Z By city, A-Z
610.55 Colonies (General)
611-612.5 Germany (Table G8)
Including former West Germany
Former East Germany
612.6 General works
612.63.A-Z By state, province, etc., A-Z
612.65.A-Z By city, A-Z
613-614.5 Greece (Table G8)
615-616.5 Italy (Table G8)
Low Countries
617 General works
619-620.5 Belgium (Table G8)
621-622.5 Netherlands (Table G8)
Russia. Soviet Union. Former Soviet republics
623 General works
(624-624.5) Local
see GV624.62, GV624.75, etc.
Russia (Federation)
624.6 General works
624.62.A-Z By republic, oblast', krai, etc., A-Z
624.625.A-Z By city, A-Z
Belarus
624.7 General works
624.75.A-Z Local, A-Z
Moldova
624.8 General works
624.85.A-Z Local, A-Z
Ukraine
624.9 General works
624.92.A-Z By province, A-Z

	Sports
	History
	By region or country
	Europe
	Ukraine -- Continued
624.925.A-Z	By city, A-Z
	Baltic States
	Estonia
624.93	General works
624.935.A-Z	Local, A-Z
	Latvia
624.94	General works
624.945.A-Z	Local, A-Z
	Lithuania
624.95	General works
624.955.A-Z	Local, A-Z
	Scandinavia
625	General works
627-628.5	Denmark (Table G8)
629-630.5	Norway (Table G8)
631-632.5	Sweden (Table G8)
633-634.5	Spain (Table G8)
635-636.5	Portugal (Table G8)
637-638.5	Switzerland (Table G8)
	Balkan States
639	General works
641-642.5	Bulgaria (Table G8)
645-646.5	Romania (Table G8)
	Yugoslavia
647	General works
647.3.A-Z	By republic, province, etc., A-Z
647.3.M65	Montenegro
647.3.S37	Serbia
647.5.A-Z	By city, A-Z
	Bosnia and Hercegovina
647.52	General works
647.57.A-Z	By city, A-Z
	Croatia
647.6	General works
647.65.A-Z	By city, A-Z
	Macedonia (Republic)
647.7	General works
647.75.A-Z	By city, A-Z
	Slovenia
647.8	General works
647.85.A-Z	By city, A-Z
	Albania

Sports
History
By region or country
Europe
Balkan States
Albania -- Continued

647.9 General works
647.93.A-Z By district, A-Z
647.97.A-Z By city, A-Z
648.A-Z Other European regions or countries, A-Z

Under each country:

.x	*General works*
.x3A-.x3Z	*By state, province, etc., A-Z*
.x5A-.x5Z	*By city, A-Z*

648.C9-.C95 Czech Republic
648.E852-.E8525 Europe, Eastern
648.F32-.F325 Faroe Islands
648.F5-.F55 Finland
648.H8-.H85 Hungary
648.I2-.I25 Iceland
648.P6-.P65 Poland
648.S4-.S45 Slovakia

Asia

649 General works
651-652.5 China (Table G8)
653-654.5 India (Table G8)
655-656.5 Japan (Table G8)
657-658.5 Iran (Table G8)
(659-660.5) Soviet Union in Asia

see GV660.6+ GV662.6+

Central Asia

660.6 General works

Kazakhstan

660.62 General works
660.625.A-Z By city, A-Z

Kyrgyzstan

660.63 General works
660.635.A-Z By city, A-Z

Tajikistan

660.64 General works
660.645.A-Z By city, A-Z

Turkmenistan

660.65 General works
660.655.A-Z By city, A-Z

Uzbekistan

660.66 General works
660.665.A-Z By city, A-Z

Sports
History
By region or country
Asia -- Continued
661-662.5 Turkey. Asia Minor (Table G8)
Caucasus
662.6 General works
Armenia
662.62 General works
662.625.A-Z By city, A-Z
Azerbaijan
662.63 General works
662.635.A-Z By city, A-Z
Georgia (Republic)
662.64 General works
662.645.A-Z By city, A-Z
663.A-Z Other Asian regions or countries, A-Z
663.B3-.B35 Bangladesh (Table G9)
663.B95-.B955 Burma. Myanmar (Table G9)
663.C93-.C935 Cyprus (Table G9)
663.I5-.I55 Indonesia (Table G9)
663.I8-.I85 Israel (Table G9)
663.K6-.K65 Korea (Table G9)
Including South Korea
663.K7-.K75 Korea (North) (Table G9)
663.L4-.L45 Lebanon (Table G9)
663.M4-.M45 Malaysia (Table G9)
Myanmar see GV663.B95+
663.N35-.N355 Nepal (Table G9)
663.P25-.P255 Pakistan (Table G9)
663.P45-.P455 Philippines (Table G9)
663.S33-.S335 Saudi Arabia (Table G9)
663.S56-.S565 Singapore (Table G9)
663.S72-.S725 Sri Lanka (Table G9)
663.T3-.T35 Taiwan (Table G9)
663.T5-.T55 Thailand (Table G9)
663.Y46-.Y465 Yemen (Table G9)
664 Arab countries
Africa
665 General works
South Africa
667 General works
667.3.A-Z By state, province, etc., A-Z
667.5.A-Z By city, A-Z
Egypt
669 General works
669.3.A-Z By state, province, etc., A-Z

Sports
History
By region or country
Africa
Egypt -- Continued

669.5.A-Z By city, A-Z

Morocco

671 General works

671.3.A-Z By state, province, etc., A-Z

671.5.A-Z By city, A-Z

673.A-Z Other African regions or countries, A-Z

673.A44-.A445 Algeria (Table G9)

673.A54-.A545 Angola (Table G9)

673.B45-.B455 Benin (Table G9)

673.B55-.B555 Botswana (Table G9)

673.C85-.C855 Côte d'Ivoire (Table G9)

673.E6-.E65 Eritrea (Table G9)

673.E7-.E75 Ethiopia (Table G9)

673.G5-.G55 Ghana (Table G9)

673.I743 Islands of the Indian Ocean

673.K4-.K45 Kenya (Table G9)

673.L5-.L55 Lesotho (Table G9)

673.L75-.L755 Libya (Table G9)

673.M3-.M35 Madagascar (Table G9)

673.N34-.N345 Namibia (Table G9)

673.N63-.N635 Nigeria (Table G9)

673.R95-.R955 Rwanda (Table G9)

673.S38-.S385 Senegal (Table G9)

673.S45-.S455 Seychelles (Table G9)

673.S52-.S525 Sierra Leone (Table G9)

(673.S6-.S65) South Africa

see GV667+

673.S8-.S85 Sudan (Table G9)

673.T34-.T345 Tanzania (Table G9)

673.T8-.T85 Tunisia (Table G9)

673.U33-.U335 Uganda (Table G9)

673.Z33-.Z335 Zambia (Table G9)

673.Z55-.Z555 Zimbabwe (Table G9)

Indian Ocean islands

674 General works

674.5.A-Z By island or group of islands, A-Z

675-676.5 Australia (Table G8)

679-680.5 New Zealand (Table G8)

Pacific islands

687 General works

688.A-Z By island or group of islands, A-Z

689 Communist countries

Sports
History
By region or country -- Continued
689.2 Developing countries
Individual schools and colleges
For general college athletics see GV347+
Cf. GV367+ Schools of physical education and training
691.A-Z American. By name, A-Z
693.A-Z Other. By name, A-Z
Biography of sports personalities
Including spouses and families
For biography in individual sports, see the sport
Cf. CT9997.A1+ Strong men
697.A1 Collective
697.A2-Z Individual, A-Z
General works
701 American, through 1975
703 English, through 1975
704 American, and English, 1976-
705 Other languages (not A-Z)
705.3 Pictorial works
705.4 Juvenile works
Philosophy. Relation to other topics
706 General works
706.2 Relation to anthropology
706.3 Relation to ethics. Fair play. Sportsmanship
706.32 Relation to race and discrimination
706.34 Relation to nationalism
706.35 Relation to politics. Sports and state
706.4 Relation to psychology. Sports psychology
706.42 Relation to religion
706.45 Relation to scholastic achievement
706.5 Relation to sociology
706.55 Relation to success
706.7 Relation to violence. Violence and sports
706.8 General special (Special aspects of the subject as a whole)
707 Addresses, essays, lectures. Anecdotes. Humor.
Miscellanea
Sports for special classes of persons
708 Individuals
708.5 Older people
708.8 Gay men. Lesbians
Women
For biography of women athletes see GV697.A+
Cf. GV439+ Physical training for women
709 General works
709.14 Coaching

Sports
Sports for special classes of persons
Women -- Continued
709.18.A-Z By region or country, A-Z
Children
For sports for youth see GV561+
For juvenile delinquents see HV9083
709.2 General works
709.24 Coaching
People with disabilities
Including wheelchair sports in general
For individual wheelchair sports, see the sport
For wheelchair basketball see GV886.5
Cf. GV722.5.S64 Special Olympics
709.3 General works
709.4 Coaching
Minorities
709.5 General works
709.55 Indians
709.6 Jews
709.7 Travelers. Deck sports
Cf. GV1099 Shuffleboard
Cf. GV1206 Games for travelers
710 Intramural sports (General)
Cf. GV346 School athletics
Cf. GV347+ College athletics
711 Coaching
711.5 Training and conditioning
Sports camps
For camps of individual sports, see the sport
711.7 General works
By region or country see GV581+
Athletic contests. Sports events
Including sports tournaments
712 General works
713 Organization and administration
Cf. GV343.5 Physical education and training
714 Public relations
714.5 Mascots
715 Spectators. Spectator control
716 Financial and business aspects
717 Betting
Cf. GV1301+ Games of chance
Cf. SF331+ Horse racing
Corruption in sports
For corruption in individual sports, see the sport
718 General works

Sports
Athletic contests. Sports events
Corruption in sports -- Continued
718.2.A-Z By region or country, A-Z
Special contests and events
International
721 General works
Olympic games (Modern revivals)
Class here comprehensive works on the Olympics as well as works specifically on the Olympic Summer Games
For Olympic games in ancient Greece see GV23
For Special Olympics see GV722.5.S64
For Olympic winter games see GV841.5+
For horse events see SF294.85
Biography of trustees, etc.
721.18 Collective
721.2.A-Z Individual, A-Z
721.3 International Olympic Committee
721.4.A-Z National committees. National teams. By country, A-Z
e.g. United States participation, Russian participation
721.5 General works
721.52 Pictorial works
721.53 Juvenile works
721.6 Philosophy. Ethics. Olympic ideal
721.7 Anecdotes. Humor. Miscellanea
721.75 Posters. Collectibles
721.8 Rules, records, etc.
721.9 Facilities
721.92 Olympic torch
722 Individual contests. By year
Subarrange by author
722.5.A-Z Other contests and events, A-Z
722.5.A43 Alberta Games
722.5.A47 All Africa Games
722.5.A7 Asian Games
722.5.B32 Balkanski igri
722.5.B7 British Commonwealth Games
722.5.C35 Canada Games
722.5.D48 Deutsches Turnfest
722.5.E76 ESPN X-Games
722.5.E9 European Athletic Championships
722.5.G3 GANEFO Games (Games of the New Emerging Forces)
722.5.G36 Gay Games
722.5.G66 Goodwill Games
722.5.G73 Grandfather Mountain Highland Games

Sports
Athletic contests. Sports events
Special contests and events
International
Other contests and events, A-Z -- Continued

722.5.H36 Hamahaykakan khagher
722.5.H54 Highland Games
IAAF see GV722.5.W57
722.5.I29 Inter-Allied Games
722.5.I34 International Games for the Disabled
722.5.I38 International Sports Competition
722.5.I42 International Stoke Mandeville Games
722.5.I5 Internationaler Sportkongress
722.5.J48 Jeux du Québec
722.5.J78 Juegos Deportivos Bolivarianos
722.5.J8 Juegos Deportivos Centro-Americanos y del Caribe
722.5.M3 Maccabiah Games
722.5.M43 Mediterranean Games
722.5.N67 Nordic Games
Olympics, Senior see GV722.5.S46
Olympics, Special see GV722.5.S64
722.5.P3 Pan American Games
Pan-Armenian Games see GV722.5.H36
722.5.S27 Saskatchewan Games
722.5.S42 SEA Games (South East Asian Games)
722.5.S46 Senior Olympics
South East Asian Games see GV722.5.S42
722.5.S6 Spartakiads
722.5.S64 Special Olympics
722.5.T9 Työväen Urheiluliitto
722.5.U5 Universiade
722.5.W55 Western Canada Summer Games
722.5.W57 World Cup (IAAF)
722.5.W58 World Festival of Youth and Students for Peace and Friendship
722.5.W594 World Master's Track and Field Championship
722.5.W6 World University Summer Games
722.5.W65 World Youth Games
723.A-Z National contests. By name, A-Z
725.A-Z Local contests. By name, A-Z
731 Rules (Collections)
For rules for individual sports, see the sport
733 Professionalism in sports
Professional sports (General)
For individual sports, see the sport
By region or country see GV581+
734 General works

Sports
Professional sports (General) -- Continued
734.3 Vocational guidance
734.5 Sports agents
735 Umpires. Sports officiating
741 Sports records and statistics. Champions
Including sporting annuals
For records of individual sports, see the sport
Mass media
742 General works
742.3 Radio and television broadcasting
742.34 Sports video
Sports journalism see PN4784.S6
Biography of sports writers, broadcasters, promoters, etc.
742.4 Collective
742.42.A-Z Individual, A-Z
Sports facilities, playing fields, etc. see GV401+
Athletic and sporting goods, supplies, etc.
Cf. HD9992+ Sporting goods industries
Cf. TS1017 Athletic shoes (Manufactures)
Cf. TS2301.S7 Manufacturing industries
743 Periodicals. Societies. Serials
744 Directories
745 General works
747 Catalogs
749.A-Z Special equipment, A-Z
749.B34 Balls
749.M6 Mouth protectors
749.S64 Shoes
Including sneakers
Sports clothing see GV749.U53
749.U53 Uniforms. Sports clothing
For uniforms of individual sports, see the sport
Cf. GT1855 Sports clothes
749.5 Endurance sports
For individual sports, see the sport
Cf. GV1060.73 Triathlon
749.7 Extreme sports
Air sports
Cf. TL500+ Aeronautics
750 Periodicals. Serials
751 Societies. Clubs
752 Dictionaries
History
753 General works
754.A-Z By region or country, A-Z
755 General works

Sports
Air sports -- Continued
756 General special
757 Addresses, essays, lectures. Anecdotes. Humor. Miscellanea
Airplane flying
Cf. TL721.4 Private flying
758 General works
Racing
Cf. TL721.5+ Air meets
759 General works
759.2.A-Z Special races, A-Z
759.2.G67 Gordon Bennett Cup Race
759.2.N37 National Championship Air Races (Reno, Nevada)
759.2.P74 Powder Puff Derby
759.2.S35 Schneider Trophy
Models
Cf. TL770+ Model airplane construction
760 General works
761 Competitions
761.5 Racing
761.6.A-Z Special races, A-Z
761.6.W35 Wakefield International Cup
Balloon flying
762 General works
762.5.A-Z By region or country, A-Z
763 Racing
Gliding and soaring
Biography
763.85 Collective
763.86.A-Z Individual, A-Z
764 General works
765.A-Z By region or country, A-Z
766 Racing
Kiteflying
Cf. TL759+ Aeronautics
767 General works
768.A-Z By region or country, A-Z
769 Competitions
Parachuting. Skydiving
Biography
769.5 Collective
769.52.A-Z Individual, A-Z
770 General works
770.2.A-Z By region or country, A-Z
770.23.A-Z Skysurfing
770.25 Parakiting

Sports
Air sports -- Continued
770.27 Bungee jumping
Water sports
Cf. GV191.67.W3+ Water-oriented recreation
770.3 Periodicals. Societies and clubs. Serials
770.4.A-Z By region or country, A-Z
770.5 General works
770.6 Safety measures
Water sports facilities
Including resources, planning, etc.
770.7 General works
By region or country see GV770.4.A+
Boats and boating (General)
771 Periodicals. Serials
775 General works
775.3 Juvenile works
By region or country
United States
776.A2 General works
776.A3-Z By region or state, A-Z
Under each state:
.x General works
.x2A-.x2Z Local, A-Z
776.112-.995 Other regions or countries (Table G2c modified)
Add country number in table to GV776
United States
General works
see GV776.A2
By region or state
see GV776.A3+
777 Societies and clubs
Cf. GV822.8+ Yacht clubs
777.3 Anecdotes. Humor. Miscellanea
777.4 Boats and equipment (General). Catalogs
777.5 Seamanship. Boat handling
Cf. VK541+ Merchant marine
777.55 Safety measures. Rescue work
Cf. VK200 Merchant marine
For special classes
777.56 Children
777.57 Women
777.58 People with disabilities
777.6 Small boats. Dinghies
Cf. GV811.6 Dinghy sailing
777.7 Boat living
Cf. GV836 Houseboating

Sports
Water sports -- Continued
780 Rafting
Including tubing, use of inflatable boats
Cf. GV790.3 Inflatable canoes
By region or country see GV776.A2+
Canoeing
Including kayaking
781 Periodicals. Serials
782 Study and teaching
Biography
782.4 Collective
782.42.A-Z Individual, A-Z
783 General works
784 Anecdotes. Humor. Miscellanea
784.3 Juvenile works
784.55 Safety measures. Rescue work
785 Societies and clubs
786 Racing
788 White-water running
Sea kayaking
788.5 General works
By region or country see GV776.A2+
Cruising. Tripping
789 General works
790 Camping
790.3 Inflatable canoes
For special classes of persons see GV777.56+
Cf. GV780 Inflatable boats for rafting
By region or country see GV776.A2+
Rowing
Cf. GV543 Rowing machines
790.6 Periodicals. Serials
Biography
790.9 Collective
790.92.A-Z Individual, A-Z
791 General works
793 Societies and clubs
College, school, and club rowing
By country
795 England
796 United States
797.A-Z Other countries, A-Z
Special races
England
798 Henley regattas
799 University boat races (Oxford and Cambridge)

Sports
Water sports
Rowing
College, school, and club rowing
Special races
England -- Continued

800.A-Z Other English races. By place, A-Z

United States

801 New London

Including all Harvard-Yale races

803 Poughkeepsie

804 Saratoga

805.A-Z Other races. By place, A-Z

806.A-Z Other countries. By country, A-Z

At individual institutions

807.A-Z American. By institution, A-Z

e.g.

807.C6 Cornell

807.H3 Harvard

807.5.A-Z Other. By institution, A-Z

e.g.

807.5.E8 Eton

807.5.O9 Oxford

Sailing (General)

Including yacht sailing

810 Periodicals. Serials

810.5 Societies and clubs

810.8 Study and teaching

Biography

810.9 Collective

810.92.A-Z Individual, A-Z

811 General works

811.12 Pictorial works

811.13 Juvenile works

811.2 Sailboat catalogs

811.3 Maintenance and repair

Equipment and supplies

811.4 General works

811.45 Spars, rigging, sails

811.5 Handling and maneuvering

811.53 Safety measures. Rescue work

811.55 General works

Multihull sailboats

811.57 Catamarans

811.58 Trimarans

811.6 Small boats. Dinghies

811.63.A-Z Other special craft, A-Z

Sports
Water sports
Sailing (General)
Other special craft, A-Z -- Continued
811.63.S64 Sunfish
811.63.W56 Windsurfers. Windsurfing
811.65 Sailboat living
811.66 Sailing on land. Sand yachting
Sailboat racing see GV826.5+
811.7.A-Z Other special topics, A-Z
811.7.P75 Psychological aspects
Yachting
For yacht sailing see GV810+
For motor yachting see GV833.5+
Cf. VM331+ Yacht building
811.8 Periodicals. Serials
Societies and clubs for yacht sailing see GV822.8+
812 History
Biography
812.4 Collective
812.5.A-Z Individual, A-Z
813 General works
813.2 Pictorial works
813.3 Juvenile works
By region or country
814 Great Britain
815 United States and Canada
817.A-Z Other, A-Z
819 Anecdotes. Humor. Miscellanea
821 Illustrations of yachts
822.A-Z Individual yachts. By name, A-Z
Including illustrations, cruises, etc.
Societies and clubs
822.8 General works
823.A-Z Individual societies and clubs. By name, A-Z
Yacht lists, annuals, etc.
825 General works
826 Flags, codes, etc.
Yacht racing
Including sailboat racing
For motorboat racing see GV835.9
826.5 General works
826.7 Rules. Records. Programs
Races, regattas, etc.
827 General works
828 Measurement of yachts
America's cup

Sports
Water sports
Yachting
Yacht racing
Races, regattas, etc.
America's cup -- Continued
829 General works
830 Individual races. By year
Subarrange by author
832 Other races (not A-Z)
833 Model yacht racing
Cf. VM332 Model yacht construction
Cf. VM359 Toy and model boat construction
Motorboats and motorboating. Launches
Cf. VM340+ Motorboat construction
833.5 Periodicals. Serials
Societies and clubs
833.8 General works
834.A-Z Individual societies and clubs. By name, A-Z
835 General works
By region or country
United States
835.18 General works
835.2.A-Z By region or state, A-Z
835.3.A-Z Other regions or countries, A-Z
835.7 Anecdotes. Humor. Miscellanea
835.8 Outboard motorboating
835.9 Motorboat racing
835.93 Model motorboat racing
835.94 Personal watercraft racing
836 Houseboats and houseboating
Cf. VM335 Houseboat construction
836.15 Pontoon boating
Swimming, diving, lifesaving
836.2 Periodicals. Serials
836.25 Societies and clubs
836.3 Dictionaries. Encyclopedias
836.35 Study and teaching. Research
836.4 History
837 General works
For special classes of persons
Children
837.2 General works
837.25 Infants
837.3 Older people
837.4 People with disabilities
837.5 Women

Sports
Water sports
Swimming, diving, lifesaving -- Continued

837.6 Juvenile works
837.65 Coaching
837.7 Training
Biography
837.9 Collective
838.A-Z Individual, A-Z
838.4.A-Z By region or country, A-Z
838.5 Rules, records, etc.
838.52.A-Z Individual strokes, A-Z
838.52.B33 Back stroke
838.52.B73 Breast stroke
838.52.B87 Butterfly stroke
838.52.C73 Crawl
838.52.S54 Side stroke
838.53.A-Z Special topics, A-Z
838.53.E93 Examinations
838.53.E94 Exercises
838.53.F65 Floating
838.53.K52 Kicking
838.53.L65 Long distance swimming
838.53.M35 Management
838.53.M43 Medley swimming
838.53.O35 Officiating
838.53.P75 Psychological aspects
838.53.S24 Safety measures
838.53.S63 Social aspects
838.53.S75 Starts and turns
838.53.S85 Swimming pools
Cf. RA606 Sanitation
Cf. TH4763 Swimming pool construction
838.53.S95 Synchronized swimming
Swimming see GV836.2+
Diving
838.58 Study and teaching. Research
838.6 General works
838.613 Juvenile works
838.62.A-Z For special classes of persons, A-Z
838.62.M45 Men
838.62.W65 Women's diving
Biography see GV837.9+
838.63.A-Z By region or country, A-Z
838.64 Rules, records, etc.
838.65.A-Z Individual dives, A-Z
838.65.J32 Jack-knife

Sports
Water sports
Swimming, diving, lifesaving
Diving
Individual dives, A-Z -- Continued
838.65.S84 Swan dive
838.67.A-Z Special topics, A-Z
Administration see GV838.67.O73
838.67.O73 Organization and administration
838.67.P75 Psychological aspects
838.67.S34 Safety measures
838.67.S65 Springboard diving
838.67.T73 Training
Submarine diving. Skindiving. Scuba diving
Including underwater spear fishing
Cf. GV200.63 Cave diving
838.672 General works
838.673.A-Z By region or country, A-Z
838.6735.A-Z For special classes of persons, A-Z
838.6735.C45 Children
838.674.A-Z Special topics, A-Z
838.674.R43 Recreational dive industry
838.674.S24 Safety measures
Lifesaving
Cf. RC87.9 Artificial respiration
Cf. RC88 Restoration from drowning
Cf. VK1300+ Lifesaving services
838.68 Study and teaching. Research
838.7 General works
Biography see GV837.9+
Life guards
838.72 General works
838.73 Certification, examinations, etc.
838.74 Training
838.75 Drowning prevention
838.76 Survival swimming
Water polo
839 General works
Biography see GV837.9+
Surfing. Surf riding
839.5 General works
By region or country
United States
839.6 General works
839.65.A-Z By region or state, A-Z
839.66.A-Z Other regions or countries, A-Z
839.7.A-Z For special classes of people, A-Z

Sports
Water sports
Surfing. Surf riding
For special classes of people, A-Z -- Continued
839.7.W65 Women
840.A-Z Other water sports, A-Z
For biography see GV837.9+
Angling, fly casting, etc. see SH401+
840.B37 Barefoot waterskiing
840.J4 Jet skiing
840.J6 Jousting
840.K49 Kite surfing
840.K53 Kneeboarding
840.S5 Skiing
(840.S78) Submarine diving. Skindiving
see GV838.672
(840.S8-.S82) Surfing. Surf riding
see GV839.5+
840.W34 Wakeboarding
Winter sports
840.7.A-Z By region or country, A-Z
841 General works
841.15 Juvenile works
841.2 Winter sports facilities
Winter Olympic games
841.5 General works
842 Individual contests. By year
Subarrange by author
843 Iceboating
Curling
845 General works
845.5.A-Z By region or country, A-Z
Biography
845.6 Collective
845.62 Individual, A-Z
Ice hockey
846 Periodicals. Societies. Serials
846.5 History
Biography see GV848.5.A+
847 General works
847.2 Addresses, essays, lectures
847.23 Pictorial works
847.25 Juvenile works
847.3 Psychological aspects
847.4 Financial and business aspects
847.45 Trading of players
847.5 Rules. Records. Programs. Schedules

Sports
Winter sports
Ice hockey -- Continued

847.6 Hockey cards
847.7 International contests. Stanley Cup
847.75.A-Z In special institutions, A-Z
847.8.A-Z Special leagues, conferences, etc. By name, A-Z
848.A-Z Individual clubs, teams, etc. By name, A-Z
848.2.A-Z Tournaments and special games, A-Z
848.2.B42 Beanpot
848.25 Coaching
848.3 Training
848.35 Safety measures
848.4.A-Z By region or country, A-Z
Biography
848.5.A1 Collective
848.5.A2-Z Individual, A-Z
848.6.A-Z For special classes of persons, A-Z
848.6.A35 Aged. Older people
848.6.C45 Children
848.6.G56 Girls
Older people see GV848.6.A35
848.6.W65 Women
Other special topics
848.7 Offensive play
(848.73) Masks
see GV848.78
Defensive play
848.75 General works
848.76 Goalkeeping
848.78 Masks
848.79 Sticks
Other related games
848.8 Broomball
Ice skating
Cf. GV858.2+ Roller skating
848.9 Directories
(848.95) Juvenile works
see GV850.223
849 General works
849.112-.995 By region or country (Table G2c)
Add country number in table to GV849
Biography
850.A2 Collective
850.A3-Z Individual, A-Z
850.15 Insignia, buttons, pins, etc.
850.2 Rules, records, etc.

Sports
Winter sports
Ice skating -- Continued
850.223 Juvenile works
For special classes of persons
850.224 People with disabilities
850.3 Speed skating
Figure skating
850.4 General works
850.45 Pair skating. Ice dancing
Events and competitions
850.5 General works
850.55.A-Z Special, A-Z
850.55.I25 Ice Capades
850.55.W37 Walt Disney's World on Ice
850.6 Judging. Officiating
850.7 Facilities. Ice rinks
852 Equipment and supplies
Including skates, costumes, etc.
852.3.A-Z Other special topics, A-Z
852.3.P75 Psychological aspects
852.3.S63 Social aspects
852.5 Skate sailing
853 Snowshoeing
Skiing. Downhill skiing
854.A1 Periodicals. Societies. Clubs
854.A2 Directories
854.A3-Z General works
854.1 History
Biography
854.2.A1 Collective
854.2.A2-Z Individual, A-Z
854.3 Anecdotes. Humor. Miscellanea
854.315 Juvenile works
For special classes of persons
854.32 Children
854.33 People with disabilities
854.34 Women
Ski resorts
Including design, planning, resources, etc.
854.35 General works
By region or country see GV854.4+
By region or country
United States
854.4 General works
854.5.A-Z By region or state, A-Z
854.6.A-Z By resort, A-Z

Sports
Winter sports
Skiing. Downhill skiing
By region or country -- Continued

854.7 Switzerland
854.8.A-Z Other regions or countries, A-Z
Under each country:
.x *General works*
.x2A-.x2Z *Local, A-Z*
854.85 Training. Conditioning. Exercises
854.87 Rules, records, etc.
854.875 Competitions. Special events
854.88 Alpine combined contests
854.89 Nordic combined contests
854.9.A-Z Other special topics, A-Z
854.9.A25 Acrobatics
Cf. GV854.9.F74 Freestyle skiing
854.9.B5 Biathlon
Cf. GV1177 Rifleshooting
Cross-country skiing see GV855+
854.9.D78 Dry slope skiing
854.9.E6 Equipment and supplies
854.9.F74 Freestyle skiing
Cf. GV854.9.A25 Acrobatics
854.9.G7 Grass skiing
854.9.J8 Jumping
854.9.M65 Monoski skiing
854.9.P75 Psychological aspects
854.9.R3 Racing, Downhill
854.9.S55 Ski lifts
854.9.S56 Ski mountaineering
854.9.S6 Slalom
854.9.S63 Social aspects
854.9.T44 Telemark

Cross-country skiing
855 Periodicals. Societies. Serials
855.2 History
Biography see GV854.2.A+
855.3 General works
855.35 Juvenile works
855.4 Competitions. Special events
855.45 Rules, records, etc.
For special classes of persons
855.47 Children
855.5.A-Z Special topics, A-Z
855.5.E67 Equipment and supplies
855.5.P78 Psychological aspects

Sports
Winter sports
Skiing. Downhill skiing
Cross-country skiing
Special topics, A-Z -- Continued
855.5.R33 Racing
855.5.S34 Safety measures
855.5.S53 Skating
855.5.T73 Training
855.5.W39 Waxes. Waxing
By region or country see GV854.4+
856 Bobsledding. Tobogganing. Sledding
Including coasting
Snowmobiling
856.4 Periodicals. Societies. Serials
856.5 General works
By region or country
United States
856.6 General works
856.65.A-Z By region or state, A-Z
856.7.A-Z Other regions or countries, A-Z
Racing
856.8 General works
856.9.A-Z Special races, A-Z
856.9.E23 Eagle River Derby
857.A-Z Other winter sports, A-Z
Automobile racing on ice see GV1029.9.I25
857.S47 Skibobbing
857.S48 Skijoring
Cf. SF425.85.S57 Dog sports
857.S5 Sleighing
857.S57 Snowboarding
(857.S6) Snowmobiling
see GV856.4+
Roller skating
Biography
858.2 Collective
858.22.A-Z Individual, A-Z
859 General works
859.3 Juvenile works
859.4 Facilities. Rinks
859.45 Equipment and supplies
Including skates
859.5 Roller disco
859.6 Roller derbies
859.7 Roller polo. Roller-skate hockey
In-line skating

Sports
In-line skating -- Continued
859.73 General works
For special classes of persons
859.76 Women
859.762 Mountainboarding
859.77 Scootering
Skateboarding
859.8 General works
Biography
859.812 Collective
859.813.A-Z Individual, A-Z
859.82 Street luge racing
Ball games
861 General works
861.112-.995 By region or country (Table G2d)
Add country number in table to GV861
Baseball
862 Periodicals. Societies. Serials
862.3 Dictionaries. Encyclopedias
Communication of information
862.4 General works
862.44 Information services
862.47 Computer network resources
Including the Internet
History
862.5 General works
862.6 America
United States
863.A1 General works
863.A2-Z By region or state, A-Z
Under each state:
.x *General works*
.x2A-.x2Z *Local, A-Z*
863.112-.995 Other regions or countries (Table G2d modified)
Add country number in table to GV863
United States
General works
see GV863.A1
By region or state
see GV863.A2+
Biography
865.A1 Collective
865.A2-Z Individual, A-Z
e.g.
865.G4 Gehrig, Lou
865.R8 Ruth, George ("Babe Ruth")

Sports
Ball games
Baseball -- Continued

867 General works
867.3 General special
867.4 Pictorial works
867.5 Juvenile works
867.54 Anthropological aspects
867.6 Psychological aspects
867.64 Social aspects
Offensive play
867.7 General works
868 Base running
868.4 Home runs
869 Batting
869.2 Designated hitters
Defensive play
869.5 General works
870 Fielding
870.5 Shortstop
871 Pitching
872 Catching
873 Anecdotes. Humor. Miscellanea
Leagues, clubs, etc.
Cf. GV880.5 Little League baseball
875.A1 General works
875.A15 American League of Professional Baseball Clubs
875.A3 National League of Professional Baseball Clubs
875.A35 International League of Professional Baseball Clubs
875.A4-Z Individual clubs and other leagues. By name, A-Z
e.g.
875.A56 All-American Girls Professional League
875.C37 California League
875.I43 Indianapolis ABC's
875.N4 New York Yankees
875.P43 Peoria Chiefs
875.W3 Washington Senators
875.12.A-Z In special institutions, A-Z
875.2 Insignia, buttons, pins, etc.
875.3 Baseball cards
875.5 Coaching
875.6 Training
875.65 Safety measures
875.7 Managing
875.8 Baseball signs and signals
876 Umpiring
877 Rules, records, etc. "Guides"

Sports
Ball games
Baseball -- Continued

877.5 Corrupt practices
878 All Star Baseball Game
878.2 East-West All-Star Game
878.3 College World Series
878.4 World Series
878.5 Caribbean World Series
878.6 Junior World Series
878.7 JUCO World Series
879 Scoring, scorebooks, schedules, etc.
879.5 Baseball fields
879.7 Equipment
Including uniforms
880 Financial and business aspects
880.15 Collective bargaining
880.17 Strikes and lockouts
880.2 Trade unions
880.22 Scouting
880.25 Draft
880.3 Trading of players
For special classes of persons
Children and youth
880.4 General works
880.5 Little League baseball
880.6 Pony League
880.65 Youth league baseball
880.7 Women
(880.8) Youth league baseball
see GV880.65
Softball
Biography see GV865.A+
881 General works
881.15 Juvenile literature
881.2 Rules, records, etc.
Special classes of persons
881.25 Older people
881.3 Women
881.35 Youth league softball
Individual clubs and leagues see GV875.A4+
881.4.A-Z Special topics, A-Z
881.4.B37 Batting
881.4.C6 Coaching
881.4.P57 Pitching
881.4.T72 Training
881.4.U47 Umpiring

Sports
Ball games
Baseball
Softball -- Continued
By region or country
see GV863+
Other related games
881.5 T-ball
881.55 Indoor baseball
881.6 Halfrubber
881.7 Finnish baseball
Basketball
882 Periodicals. Societies. Serials
883 History
Biography
884.A1 Collective
884.A2-Z Individual, A-Z
885 General works
885.1 Juvenile works
885.13 Anecdotes. Humor. Miscellanea
885.14 Pictorial works
885.15 Basketball cards
885.2 Officiating
Including biographical works
885.25 Scouting
885.3 Coaching
885.35 Training
Basketball camps
885.38 General works
By region or country see GV885.7+
Amateur
885.4 General works
885.415.A-Z Special leagues, conferences, divisions, etc. By name, A-Z
885.42.A-Z Individual clubs. By place, A-Z
885.43.A-Z In special institutions, A-Z
885.45 Rules. Records. Programs. Schedules
885.47 Managing
885.49.A-Z Tournaments and special games, A-Z
885.49.A15 AAAD Basketball Tournament
Professional
885.5 General works
885.513 Financial and business aspects
885.514 Draft
885.515.A-Z Special leagues, Conferences, divisions, etc. By name, A-Z
885.52.A-Z Individual clubs. By name, A-Z

Sports
Ball games
Basketball
Professional -- Continued
885.55 Rules. Records. Programs. Schedules
885.59.A-Z Championship contests, special games, etc., A-Z
By region or country
United States
885.7 General works
885.72.A-Z By region or state, A-Z
885.73.A-Z By city, A-Z
885.8.A-Z Other regions or countries, A-Z
Girls' and women's basketball
886 General works
(886.2) Coaching
see GV885.3
Basketball for children and youth
886.25 General works
886.3 Youth league basketball
886.5 Wheelchair basketball
887 Halfcourt basketball
Other special topics
887.5 Ability testing
887.7 Betting
887.75 Courts
888 Defensive play
888.2 Free throw
888.22 Inbounding
888.25 Moral and ethical aspects
889 Offensive play
889.2 Psychological aspects
889.23 Rebounding
889.24 Refereeing. Officiating
889.26 Social aspects
889.5 Korfball
889.6 Netball
Billiards and pool
891.A1 Periodicals. Societies. Serials
891.A3-Z General works
Biography
892 Collective
892.2.A-Z Individual, A-Z
893 Shots
894 Billiard parlors. Pool halls
895 Championship contests, etc.
897 Rules
898 Records

Sports
Ball games
Billiards and pool -- Continued

899 Tables, equipment, etc.
899.4.A-Z Special topics, A-Z
899.4.P78 Psychological aspects
900.A-Z Special forms, A-Z
900.A16 8-Ball
900.S6 Snooker

Bowling games
901 Periodicals. Societies. Serials
Biography
901.9 Collective
902.A-Z Individual, A-Z
902.5 General works
902.6 Equipment and supplies
Special games
Bowling. Tenpins
902.7 Collectibles
903 General works
903.5 Juvenile works
904 Anecdotes. Humor. Miscellanea
905 Rules, scores, etc.
906.A-Z Individual clubs, teams, etc. By name, A-Z
907 Bowling alleys
908.A-Z By region or country, A-Z
Bowls. Lawn bowls. Bowling on the green
Including indoor bowls
909 General works
910 Bowling greens
910.5.A-Z Other special, A-Z
910.5.B56 Bitlles
910.5.B63 Boccie
910.5.C35 Candlepins
910.5.D8 Duckpins
910.5.N5 Ninepins
910.5.P4 Petanque
910.5.R63 Road bowling
910.5.T43 Team bowling
910.5.W48 Wheelchair bowling

Cricket
911 Periodicals. Societies. Serials
913 History
Biography
915.A1 Collective
915.A2-Z Individual, A-Z
917 General works

Sports
Ball games
Cricket -- Continued
919 Anecdotes. Humor. Miscellanea
920.A-Z Special leagues, conferences, etc. By name, A-Z
921.A-Z Individual clubs. By name, A-Z
e.g.
921.C2 Cambridge University Cricket Club
921.F8 Free Foresters
921.M3 Marylebone Cricket Club
921.W3 Warwickshire County Cricket Club
923 Contests, etc.
924 Umpiring
925 Rules, records, etc.
926 Coaching
927 Playing fields
927.5.A-Z Other special topics, A-Z
927.5.B37 Batting
927.5.B67 Bowling
927.5.S63 Social aspects
927.5.W53 Wicket-keeping
928.A-Z By region or country, A-Z
For special classes of persons
929 Women
929.3 Children
Croquet
931 General works
933 General special
935 Roque
Football games
937 Periodicals. Societies. Serials
938 History
Biography (General)
Cf. GV942.7.A+ Soccer players
Cf. GV944.9.A+ Rugby players
Cf. GV946.5.A1+ Australian football players
Cf. GV948.4.A1+ Florentine football players
Cf. GV948.6.A1+ Gaelic football players
939.A1 Collective
939.A2-Z Individual, A-Z
940 General works
941 Dictionaries. Encyclopedias
Special games
Soccer. Association
Cf. GV1060.15 Motorcycle soccer
942 Periodicals. Societies. Serials
942.2 Dictionaries. Encyclopedias

Sports
Ball games
Football games
Special games
Soccer. Association -- Continued

942.3	Terminology. Abbreviations
942.4	Study and teaching
942.5	History
	Biography
942.7.A1	Collective
942.7.A2-Z	Individual, A-Z
943	General works
943.2	Anecdotes. Humor. Miscellanea
943.23	Pictorial works
943.25	Juvenile works
943.3	Financial and business aspects
943.4	Rules. Records. Programs. Schedules
	International contests
943.45	General works
	World Cup
943.49	General works
943.5	Individual contests. By year Subarrange by author
	Europa Cup
943.52	General works
943.53	Individual contests. By year Subarrange by author
943.54.A-Z	Other, A-Z
943.55.A-Z	Special leagues, conferences, etc. By name, A-Z
943.6.A-Z	Individual clubs, teams, etc. By name, A-Z
943.7.A-Z	In special institutions, A-Z
943.8	Coaching
943.9.A-Z	Other special topics, A-Z
943.9.A35	Ability testing
943.9.A57	Anthropological aspects
943.9.B43	Beach soccer
943.9.C64	Collectibles
943.9.D43	Defense
943.9.E65	Equipment and supplies Including uniforms
943.9.F35	Fans and spectators Including spectator control and hooliganism
943.9.G62	Goalkeeping
943.9.I6	Indoor soccer
943.9.O44	Offense
943.9.O45	Officiating
943.9.P7	Psychological aspects

Sports
Ball games
Football games
Special games
Soccer. Association
Other special topics, A-Z -- Continued

943.9.R43 Refereeing
Skill testing see GV943.9.A35
943.9.S63 Soccer fields
943.9.S64 Social aspects
Spectators and spectator control see GV943.9.F35
Supplies see GV943.9.E65
943.9.T7 Training
944.A-Z By region or country, A-Z
944.2 Soccer for children
944.5 Soccer for women

Rugby
944.8 Periodicals. Societies. Serials
944.85 History
Biography
944.9.A1 Collective
944.9.A2-Z Individual, A-Z
945 General works
945.2 Anecdotes. Humor. Miscellanea
945.25 Juvenile works
945.3 Financial and business aspects
945.4 Rules. Records. Programs. Schedules
945.5 International contests. Tournaments, tours, etc.
945.55.A-Z Special leagues, conferences, etc. By name, A-Z
945.6.A-Z Individual clubs, teams, etc. By name, A-Z
945.7.A-Z In special institutions, A-Z
945.75 Coaching
945.8 Training
945.85.A-Z Other special topics, A-Z
945.85.P75 Psychological aspects
945.85.S65 Social aspects
945.9.A-Z By region or country, A-Z
946 Rugby league football
Rugby union football
946.2 General works
By region or country see GV945.9.A+

Australian football
Biography
946.5.A1 Collective
946.5.A2-Z Individual, A-Z
947 General works
947.3 Individual clubs, teams, etc. By name, A-Z

Sports
Ball games
Football games
Special games
Australian football -- Continued
947.4.A-Z For special classes of persons, A-Z
947.4.C55 Children
Canadian football
For biography see GV939.A+
948 General
948.3 Individual clubs, teams, etc. By name, A-Z
Florentine football
Biography
948.4.A1 Collective
948.4.A2-Z Individual, A-Z
948.5 General works
Gaelic football
Biography
948.6.A1 Collective
948.6.A2-Z Individual, A-Z
948.7 General works
American football
948.8 Periodicals. Societies. Serials
948.85 Dictionaries. Encyclopedias
950 History
Biography see GV939.A+
950.5 Anecdotes. Humor. Miscellanea
950.6 Spectator's guides. How to enjoy the game as a spectator
Cf. GV1202.F34 Fantasy football
950.7 Juvenile works
951 General works
Strategies and techniques. Playbooks
951.15 General works
951.18 Defensive play (General)
951.2 Line play
951.25 End play. Pass receiving
951.3 Backfield play. Quarterbacking
951.5 Passing
951.7 Kicking. Punting
951.8 Offensive play (General)
951.85 Special teams play
951.9 T formation
951.95 Wingback formation
Variants, etc.
952 Touch football
952.2 Flag football

Sports
Ball games
Football games
Special games
American football
Variants, etc. -- Continued

952.4	Flag football for women
953	Six-man football
953.4	Selection of players. Scouting
953.5	Training
953.6	Safety measures
	Professional
	History
954	General works
954.2	Individual football seasons. By year Subarrange by author
	General works see GV954
954.3	Financial and business aspects
954.32	Draft
954.35	Officiating
954.4	Coaching
955	Rules. Records. Programs. Schedules
955.3	Football cards
955.5.A-Z	Special leagues, conferences, divisions, etc. By name, A-Z
956.A-Z	Individual clubs, teams, etc. By name, A-Z
956.2.A-Z	Special games, A-Z
956.2.S8	Super Bowl game
	Amateur
	History see GV950
956.3	Individual seasons. By year Subarrange by author
	General works see GV951
956.4	Financial and business aspects
956.6	Coaching
956.8	Rules. Records. Programs. Schedules
957.A-Z	Special games, A-Z
957.A7	Army-Navy game
957.B55	Blue-Gray game
957.C64	College All-Star Football Game
957.F54	Fiesta Bowl
957.O72	Orange Bowl game
957.R6	Rose Bowl
957.S45	Shrine Bowl of the Carolinas
957.S5	Shrine East-West game
957.S8	Sugar Bowl game
958.A-Z	In special institutions, A-Z

Sports
Ball games
Football games
Special games
American football
Amateur -- Continued
958.5.A-Z Special conferences, etc. By name, A-Z
959 Miscellaneous topics (not A-Z)
By region or country
United States
959.5 General works
959.52.A-Z By region or state, A-Z
959.53.A-Z By city, A-Z
959.54.A-Z Other regions or countries, A-Z
959.55.A-Z For special classes of persons, A-Z
959.55.C45 Children
959.6 Youth league football
960.A-Z Other football games, A-Z
960.B4 Beeball
960.F66 Footbag
960.K45 Kemari
Golf
961 Periodicals. Societies. Serials
961.3 Dictionaries. Encyclopedias.
962 Directories
For region or country see GV981+
962.3 Computer network resources
Including the Internet
962.5 Study and teaching
963 History
Biography
964.A1 Collective
964.A2-Z Individual, A-Z
e.g.
964.J6 Jones, Robert ("Bobby Jones")
965 General works
For special classes of persons
965.5 People with disabilities
966 Women
966.3 Children
966.5 Older people
967 Anecdotes. Humor. Miscellanea
967.5 Pictorial works
968 Juvenile works
969.A-Z Associations, clubs, etc. By name, A-Z
e.g.
Cf. HS2581 Country clubs

Sports
Ball games
Golf
Associations, clubs, etc. By name, A-Z -- Continued

969.R6 Royal and Ancient Golf Club of St. Andrews
969.W5 Western Golf Association
969.5.A-Z In special institutions. By name, A-Z
970 Tournaments, etc.
970.3.A-Z Individual tournaments. By name, A-Z
970.3.S72 St. Andrews Open
971 Scorebooks, scoring, rules, etc.
Special topics
Golf courses. Greens. Driving ranges
975 General works
By region or country see GV981+
975.3 Environmental aspects
975.5 Management
976 Equipment
977 Caddies
979.A-Z Other special topics, A-Z
979.B47 Betting
979.B86 Bunkers. Sand traps
979.C6 Coaching
979.D74 Drive
979.E9 Exercises
979.G7 Grip
979.H3 Hand action
979.P7 Professionals
979.P75 Psychological aspects
979.P8 Putting
Sand traps see GV979.B86
979.S54 Short game
979.S63 Social aspects
979.S9 Swing
979.T68 Training
979.T7 Trophies
979.W43 Wedge shot
By region or country
United States
981 General works
982.A-Z By region or state, A-Z
983.A-Z By city, A-Z
984 Great Britain
985.A-Z Other regions or countries, A-Z
986 Contract golf
987 Miniature golf
988 Hope (Game)

Sports
Ball games -- Continued
Lacrosse
Including box lacrosse

989	General works
989.13	Pictorial works
989.14	Juvenile works
989.15	Women's lacrosse
989.17	Lacrosse for children
	Tennis and related games
990	General works
990.3	Collectibles
990.5	Equipment
990.7	Rules
	Tennis. Lawn tennis
991	Periodicals. Societies. Serials
	Communication of information
991.2	General works
991.4	Tennis literature
991.5	Study and teaching
992	History
	Biography
994.A1	Collective
994.A2-Z	Individual, A-Z
	e.g.
994.L4	Lenglen, Suzanne
994.T5	Tilden, William
995	General works
996	Anecdotes. Humor. Miscellanea
996.3	Pictorial works
996.5	Juvenile works
997.A-Z	Clubs, facilities, etc. By name, A-Z
	e.g.
997.A4	All-England Club, Wimbledon, Eng.
997.R3	Racket and Tennis Club, New York
997.5.A-Z	In special institutions. By name, A-Z
998	Resorts
	By region or country see GV1002.95.A+
999	Tournaments, etc.
	e.g. Davis Cup, Wightman Cup
1000	Financial and business aspects
1001	Rules, scores, etc.
(1001.2)	By region or country
	see GV1002.95
1001.4.A-Z	For special classes of persons, A-Z
1001.4.A35	Aged. Older people
1001.4.C45	Children

Sports
Ball games
Tennis and related games
Tennis. Lawn tennis
For special classes of persons, A-Z -- Continued
1001.4.G57 Girls
1001.4.H36 Handicapped. People with disabilities
Including wheelchair tennis
Older people see GV1001.4.A35
People with disabilities see GV1001.4.H36
Special topics
1002 Tennis courts
1002.5 Other equipment
e.g. Balls, nets, rackets
1002.7 Singles
1002.8 Doubles
1002.9.A-Z Other special topics, A-Z
1002.9.C63 Coaching
1002.9.P75 Psychological aspects
1002.9.S34 Safety measures
1002.9.S47 Serve
1002.9.T7 Training
1002.9.T86 Two-handed strokes
1002.9.V65 Volley
1002.95.A-Z By region or country, A-Z
1003 Court tennis (Royal tennis)
1003.2 Paddleball
Racquetball
1003.32 History
1003.34 General works
1003.36 Rules, records, etc.
1003.38.A-Z For special classes of persons, A-Z
1003.38.C48 Children
1003.38.W66 Women
1003.5 Racquet (Rackets)
Squash
Biography
1003.6 Collective
1003.62.A-Z Individual, A-Z
1004 General works
1004.3.A-Z For special classes of people, A-Z
1004.3.C45 Children
1004.5 Squash tennis
Table tennis (Ping-pong)
1004.9 Periodicals. Societies. Serials
1005 General works
1005.15 History

Sports
Ball games
Tennis and related games
Table tennis (Ping-pong) -- Continued
Biography
1005.2 Collective
1005.22.A-Z Individual, A-Z
1005.3.A-Z Clubs, etc. By name, A-Z
1005.32 Organization and administration
1005.35 Tournaments, etc. By date
1005.4 Rules, records, etc.
1005.45.A-Z By region or country, A-Z
1005.5 Tamburello
1006 Paddle tennis
Including playground paddle tennis and platform paddle tennis
Paddleball see GV1003.2
Handball see GV1017.H2
Badminton
Biography
1006.5 Collective
1006.52.A-Z Individual, A-Z
1007 General works
1007.5.A-Z Special topics, A-Z
1007.5.C6 Coaching
1007.5.D67 Doubles
1007.5.S55 Singles
1007.6.A-Z By region or country, A-Z
1008 Battledore and shuttlecock
Polo
Cf. GV839+ Water polo
Cf. GV859.7 Roller polo
Cf. GV1017.W6 Wicket polo
Cf. GV1058 Bicycle polo
1010 Periodicals. Societies. Serials
Biography
1010.3 Collective
1010.32.A-Z Individual, A-Z
1011 General works
1011.6.A-Z By region or country, A-Z
Volleyball
1015 Periodicals. Societies. Serials
1015.15 Study and teaching
1015.2 History
Biography
1015.25 Collective
1015.26.A-Z Individual, A-Z

Sports
Ball games
Volleyball -- Continued

1015.3 General works
1015.33 Pictorial works
1015.34 Juvenile works
1015.35.A-Z Clubs, etc. By name, A-Z
1015.37 Tournaments, etc.
1015.39 Rules, records, etc.
1015.4.A-Z For special classes of persons, A-Z
1015.4.C55 Children
1015.4.W66 Women
1015.5.A-Z Special topics, A-Z
1015.5.B43 Beach volleyball
1015.5.B56 Block
1015.5.C63 Coaching
1015.5.D54 Dig
1015.5.O44 Officiating
1015.5.P37 Pass
1015.5.S47 Serve
1015.5.S48 Set
1015.5.S65 Spike
1015.5.T73 Training
By region or country
United States
1015.55 General works
1015.56.A-Z By region or state, A-Z
Under each state:
.x General works
.x2A-.x2Z Local, A-Z
1015.57.A-Z Other regions or countries, A-Z
Under each country:
.x General works
.x2A-.x2Z Local, A-Z
1017.A-Z Other ball games, A-Z
1017.A5 America
1017.B33 Battle ball
1017.B4 Belle coquette. Lawn billiards
1017.C4 Cercle
1017.C45 Changers
1017.C5 Chivalrie
1017.D5 Dix
1017.F5 Fieldball. Field handball
1017.H2 Handball. Fives
Handball, Team see GV1017.T4

Sports
Ball games
Other ball games, A-Z -- Continued

1017.H7 Hockey. Field hockey
Cf. GV846+ Ice hockey
Cf. GV1017.I53 Indoor hockey
Cf. GV1099 Ring hockey
1017.H8 Hurling
1017.I53 Indoor hockey
Jai alai see GV1017.P4
1017.K3 Kang
1017.L3 Lapta
Lawn billiards see GV1017.B4
1017.L48 Lawn tempest
Medicine ball see GV496
1017.M6 Minton
1017.N4 Newcomb
1017.N7 Nine pockets
1017.P3 Pato
1017.P4 Pelota. Jai alai
1017.P5 Pize-ball
1017.P7 Po-lo-lo
1017.P9 Pushball
1017.R34 Raga
1017.R6 Rounders
1017.R9 Ruse
1017.S2 Schlagball
1017.S3 School
1017.S45 Shinty
1017.S5 Silver chimes
1017.S58 Speed-a-way
1017.S6 Speedball
1017.S7 Sphero
1017.S8 Stoolball
1017.T24 Takraw
1017.T27 Balle au tamis
1017.T3 Tan-to
1017.T4 Team handball
1017.T7 Trapball
1017.W34 Wallyball
1017.W45 Wheelchair hockey
1017.W5 Wicket
1017.W6 Wicket polo

Sports -- Continued
Racing (General)
Cf. GV759+ Airplane racing
Cf. GV786 Canoe racing
Cf. GV795+ Rowing races
Cf. GV826.5+ Yacht racing
Cf. GV1029+ Automobile racing
Cf. GV1049+ Bicycle racing
Cf. GV1061+ Footracing
Cf. SF321+ Horse racing
1018 General works
1019 Speed records
Motorsports
Cf. GV1059.5+ Motorcycling
1019.2 General works
1019.5.A-Z By region or country, A-Z
Under each country:
.x *General works*
.x2A-.x2Z *Local, A-Z*
Automobile travel. Motoring
Cf. TL, Motor vehicles
Cf. GV198.5+ Trailer camping
1020 Periodicals. Serials
1021 General works
1023 Anecdotes. Humor. Miscellanea
Road guides, route books, etc.
Class here works on automobile travel only
For general descriptive works on travel in particular places, see D-F
1024 United States
1025.A-Z Other regions or countries, A-Z
1027 Clubs
Including the American Automobile Association, Touring Club Uruguayo, etc.
1028.A-Z Directories of owners. By place, A-Z
Automobile racing
Including Grand Prix racing
For model car racing see GV1570
1029 General works
1029.12 Pictorial works
1029.13 Juvenile works
1029.14 Financial and business aspects
1029.15 History
Special topics
1029.2 Rallies. Rallying
1029.3 Drag racing
1029.5 Karting

GV

Sports
Motorsports
Automobile racing
Special topics -- Continued

1029.6 Midget car racing
1029.7 Soapbox racing
1029.8 Sports car events
1029.9.A-Z Other, A-Z
1029.9.A88 Autocross
1029.9.D45 Demolition derbies
1029.9.D75 Drifting (Motorsport)
1029.9.D8 Dune buggy racing
Cf. TL236.7 Dune buggies (Motor vehicles)
1029.9.I25 Ice racing
1029.9.M83 Mud racing
1029.9.R35 Rallycross
1029.9.R63 Rockcrawling
1029.9.S67 Sprint cars
1029.9.S74 Stock car racing
1030 Rules. Records. Programs
1030.2 Cards, collectibles, etc.
Biography
1032.A1 Collective
1032.A2-Z Individual, A-Z
By region or country
For particular types of races in particular places see GV1029.2+
United States
1033 General works
1033.5.A-Z Individual races, events, racetracks, etc., A-Z
1034.112-.995 Other regions or countries (Table G2e)
Add country number in table to GV1034
1034.996 Truck racing
1037 All terrain vehicle racing
Cf. GV856.8+ Snowmobiling
Cf. GV1029.9.D8 Dune buggy racing
Cf. GV1060.12 Motocross
Adventure racing
1038 General works
1038.2.A-Z Individual races, A-Z
1038.2.R34 Raid Gauloises
Cycling. Bicycling
Cf. HE5736+ Bicycle transportation
Cf. TL400+ Cycles
1040 Periodicals. Serials
1040.5 History
1041 General works

Sports
Cycling. Bicycling -- Continued
1043 Anecdotes. Humor. Miscellanea
1043.5 Juvenile works
1043.7 General special
Bicycle hiking, touring, etc.
1044 General works
Tour guide books. Route books
Class here technical works only
For descriptive works of travel in particular places, see classes D - F
United States
1045 General works
1045.5.A-Z By region or state, A-Z
Under each state:
.x General works
.x2A-.x2Z Local, A-Z
.x3A-.x3Z Individual tours, events, etc., A-Z
1046.A-Z Other regions or countries, A-Z
Under each country:
.x General works
.x2A-.x2Z Local, A-Z
.x3A-.x3Z Individual tours, events, etc., A-Z
Clubs
1046.9 Collective
1047.A-Z Individual. By name, A-Z
e.g.
1047.L4 League of American Wheelmen
1047.W3 Washington Cycling Club, Chicago
1048 Training for cycling
Racing
1049 General works
1049.2.A-Z Special races, A-Z
Cape Rally see GV1049.2.M44
1049.2.F38 FBD Milk Rás
1049.2.G57 Giro d'Italia
1049.2.L57 Little Soo
1049.2.M44 Mediterranean. The Cape Rally
1049.2.P37 Paris-Roubaix
1049.2.R33 Race across America
1049.2.R34 RAGBRAI
1049.2.T68 Tour de France
1049.2.T69 Tour de Suisse
1049.2.T74 Tour Du Pont
1049.25.A-Z Special topics, A-Z
1049.25.C63 Coaching
1049.25.C67 Corrupt practices

Sports
Cycling. Bicycling
Racing -- Continued
1049.3 Bicycle motocross
Biography
1051.A1 Collective
1051.A2-Z Individual, A-Z
1053 Records, etc.
1054 Equipment, costume, etc.
1055 Safety measures
1056 All terrain cycling
By region or country see GV1045+
1057 Cycling for women
1057.2 Cycling for children
1058 Bicycle polo
1058.5 Railbiking
1059 Unicycling
Motorcycling
Cf. TL439+ Motorcycles
1059.5 General works
1059.513 Pictorial works
1059.515 Juvenile works
By region or country
United States
1059.52 General works
1059.522.A-Z By region or state, A-Z
1059.53.A-Z Other regions or countries, A-Z
Racing
1060 General works
1060.12 Motocross
1060.125 Minibike racing
1060.13 Racing on ice
1060.14 Sidecar racing
1060.145 Speedway racing
1060.1455 Supercross
By region or country
United States
1060.146 General works
1060.147.A-Z By region or state, A-Z
1060.148.A-Z Other regions or countries, A-Z
1060.149.A-Z Individual events, races, etc., A-Z
1060.15 Motorcycle soccer
1060.154 Stunt cycling
1060.155 Track days
Biography
1060.2.A1 Collective
1060.2.A2-Z Individual, A-Z

Sports
Motorcycling -- Continued
1060.4 Safety measures
Track and field athletics
For special contests and meets see GV721+
1060.5 General works
1060.53 Pictorial works
1060.55 Juvenile works
By region or country
United States
1060.6 General works
1060.62.A-Z By region or state, A-Z
1060.65.A-Z Other regions or countries, A-Z
1060.67 Rules, records, etc.
1060.675.A-Z Special topics, A-Z
1060.675.C6 Coaching
1060.675.O74 Organization and administration
1060.675.T7 Tracks
1060.675.T73 Training
All-round athletics
1060.7 General works
1060.73 Triathlon
1060.74 Tetrathlon
1060.75 Pentathlon
1060.77 Heptathlon
1060.79 Decathlon
1060.8 Women's track
1060.9 Track for children and youth
1060.93 Wheelchair track-athletics
Foot racing. Running
1061 General works
Biography
1061.14 Collective
1061.15.A-Z Individual, A-Z
1061.18.A-Z For special classes of persons, A-Z
1061.18.A35 Aged. Older people
1061.18.C45 Children
Older people see GV1061.18.A35
1061.18.W66 Women
By region or country
United States
1061.2 General works
1061.22.A-Z By region or state, A-Z
1061.23.A-Z Other regions or countries, A-Z
1061.4 Officiating
1061.5 Training
1061.6 Running shoes

Sports
Track and field athletics
Foot racing. Running -- Continued
1061.8.A-Z Other special topics, A-Z
1061.8.P75 Psychological aspects
Distance running
1062 General works
1062.5.A-Z Individual races, events, etc., A-Z
Cross-country runs
Cf. GV200.4 Orienteering
1063 General works
1063.2.A-Z Special topics, A-Z
1063.2.C62 Coaching
1063.5 Ride and tie racing
Marathon running
1065 General works
1065.17.A-Z Special topics, A-Z
1065.17.T73 Training
By region or country
United States
1065.2 General works
1065.22.A-Z Individual races, events, etc., A-Z
1065.23.A-Z Other regions or countries, A-Z
Under each country:
.x General works
.x2A-.x2Z Individual races, events, etc., A-Z
1066 Relay races
1067 Hurdle racing
1069 Sprinting
1071 Walking
Cf. GV199+ Walking as recreation
Cf. GV502 Exercise walking
Cf. RA781.65 Walking for health
Jumping
Cf. GV529 Exercises
1073 General works
Biography
1073.14 Collective
1073.15.A-Z Individual, A-Z
1075 High jump
1077 Broad jump. Long jump
1078 Triple jump. Hop, step, and jump
Vaulting
1079 General works
1080 Pole vaulting
1084 Wheelchair road racing

Sports
Track and field athletics -- Continued
Throwing games and sports
Cf. GV861+ Ball games
1091 General works
Weight throwing
1093 General works
Biography
1093.9 Collective
1094.A-Z Individual, A-Z
1094.3 Discus throwing
1094.5 Hammer throwing
1094.6 Javelin throwing
1094.8 Shot-putting
1095 Quoits. Horseshoe pitching
1096 Knife throwing
Cf. GV1150.7 Knife fighting
1097.A-Z Other throwing games, A-Z
1097.B44 Billions
1097.B65 Boomerangs
1097.B7 Brist
Darts see GV1564+
1097.F7 Flying discs. Frisbee (Registered trademark)
1097.F75 Foxtail
1097.R5 Ringtoss
1097.T66 Toobee
1097.U48 Ultimate
1098 Tug of war
1099 Other athletic sports
Including ring hockey, shuffleboard, stilt walking
1099.5 Buzkashi
Fighting sports. Martial arts
By region or country
United States
1100.A2 General works
1100.A3-Z By region or state, A-Z
Under each state:
.x *General works*
.x2A-.x2Z *Local, A-Z*
1100.112-.995 Other regions or countries (Table G2c modified)
Add country number in table to GV1100
United States
General works
see GV1100.A2
By region or state
see GV1100.A3+
1101 General works

Sports
Fighting sports. Martial arts -- Continued
1101.3 Pictorial works
1101.35 Juvenile works
1101.5 Weapons for martial arts
Martial arts schools
1102 General works
1102.2.A-Z Individual schools. By name, A-Z
1102.7.A-Z Special topics, A-Z
1102.7.A56 Anthropological aspects
1102.7.B73 Breaking
1102.7.H64 Holding
1102.7.K52 Kicking
1102.7.P75 Psychological aspects
1102.7.R44 Religious aspects
1102.7.S82 Striking
1102.7.S85 Study and teaching
1102.7.T7 Training
Animal fighting
1103 General works
1105 Bear and badger baiting
Bullfighting
Cf. SF199.F5 Fighting bull culture
1107 General works
1107.3 Dictionaries. Encyclopedias
1107.5 Pictorial works
Biography
1108.A1 Collective
1108.A2-Z Individual, A-Z
1108.2 Costume
Bull rings
1108.3 General works
1108.35.A-Z Individual, A-Z
1108.38 Rejoneo
1108.4 Running to the pens. El encierro
By region or country
1108.5 Spain
1108.6.A-Z Other regions or countries, A-Z
1108.7.A-Z Special topics, A-Z
1108.7.S65 Social aspects
Cockfighting see SF502.8+
1109 Dogfighting
Cf. SF428.85 Fighting dogs
Human fighting. Hand-to-hand fighting
Including self defense
Cf. GV35 Gladiators
1111 General works

Sports
Fighting sports. Martial arts
Human fighting. Hand-to-hand fighting -- Continued
For special classes of persons
1111.4 Self-defense for children
1111.45 Self-defense for people with disabilities
1111.5 Self-defense for women
Oriental hand-to-hand fighting
1112 General works
Biography
1113.A2 Collective
1113.A3-Z Individual, A-Z
1113.25.A-Z Special topics, A-Z
1113.25.T48 Throws
Jiu-jitsu. Judo
1114 General works
1114.2.A-Z For special classes of persons, A-Z
1114.2.W64 Women
1114.25.A-Z Special topics, A-Z
1114.25.R84 Rules
1114.25.T48 Throws
Karate
Cf. GV1142.6 Nunchaku
Cf. GV1150.6 Sai
1114.3 General works
1114.314 Coaching
1114.315 Rules
For special classes of persons
1114.32 Children
1114.33.A-Z Special topics, A-Z
1114.33.A58 Anthropological aspects
1114.33.T72 Training
1114.35 Aikido
1114.38 Escrima
1114.39 Hapkido
1114.4 Hwarangdo
1114.6 Jeet Kune Do
1114.65 Kickboxing
1114.68 Kuk Sool Won
1114.7 Kung fu. Kempo
1114.73 Ninjutsu
1114.75 Pencak silat
1114.8 San-jitsu
1114.9 Tae kwon do
1114.92 Taekkyon
Boxing. Prize fighting
Cf. HV6733 Gambling in prize fighting

Sports
Fighting sports. Martial arts
Human fighting. Hand-to-hand fighting
Boxing. Prize fighting -- Continued

1115	Periodicals. Serials
1116.A-Z	Rules and regulations. By country, A-Z
1116.2	Collectibles
1117	Clubs
1118	Dictionaries. Encyclopedias
	History
1121	General works
1123	England
1125	United States
1127.A-Z	Other regions or countries, A-Z
	Biography
1131	Collective
1132.A-Z	Individual, A-Z
	e.g.
1132.L6	Louis, Joe
1132.S95	Sullivan, John
1133	General works
1135	Anecdotes. Humor. Miscellanea
1135.5	Pictorial works
1136	Juvenile works
	For special classes of persons
1136.3	Women
1136.5	Moral and ethical aspects
1136.7	Financial and business aspects
1136.8	Social aspects
1137	Records. Programs. Schedules
1137.3	Refereeing. Judging
1137.6	Training
	Stick fighting
1141	General works
1141.2	Single stick, quarter staff, etc.
	Kendo
1141.3	Study and teaching
1141.5	History
	Biography
1141.7	Collective
1141.72.A-Z	Individual, A-Z
1142	General works
1142.4	Pictorial works
1142.6	Nunchaku

Sports
Fighting sports. Martial arts
Human fighting. Hand-to-hand fighting -- Continued
Fencing
Class here general works on western or European fencing including fencing with foils
Cf. PN2071.F4 Stage fencing
Cf. U850+ Swords and daggers (Military science)
1143 Periodicals. Societies. Serials
1143.15 Congresses
1143.2 Dictionaries. Encyclopedias
1143.4 Study and teaching
1143.6 History
Biography
1144 Collective
1144.2.A-Z Individual, A-Z
General works
1145 Early through 1800
1146 1801-1900
1147 1901-
1148 Pictorial works
Cf. N8217.F4 Fencing in art
1148.4 Addresses, essays, lectures
1149 Rules. Records, etc.
1149.5.A-Z By region or country, A-Z
1149.6.A-Z For special classes of persons, A-Z
1149.6.W65 Women
Special
Oriental fencing
1150 General works
1150.2 Iaido
1150.4 Naginata
1150.6 Sai
Dueling see CR4571+
Wrestling see GV1195+
1150.7 Knife fighting
1150.8 Spear fighting
1150.9 Sickle fighting
Shooting
Cf. SK37+ Hunting sports
1151 Periodicals. Serials
1152 Dictionaries. Encyclopedias
1153 General works
Biography
1156 Collective
1157.A-Z Individual, A-Z
e.g.

	Sports
	Fighting sports. Martial arts
	Shooting
	Biography
	Individual, A-Z -- Continued
1157.O3	Oakley, Annie
1158.A-Z	For special classes of persons, A-Z
1158.H36	Handicapped. People with disabilities
	People with disabilities see GV1158.H36
1158.W65	Women
1159	Coaching
1163	Clubs (Rifle, revolver, etc.)
1164	Shooting schools
	Contests
1167	International
	United States
1169	National. Interstate
1171.A-Z	Local, A-Z
1172.A-Z	Other regions or countries, A-Z
1173	Scores, scorebooks, rules, etc.
	Guns and pistols
	Cf. SK274+ Hunting guns
	Cf. TS535+ Gun making
	Cf. UD380+ Infantry firearms
	Cf. UE400+ Cavalry firearms
1174	General works
	Pistols and revolvers
	Cf. GT4990 Christmas shooting
	Cf. UD410+ Military science
1175	General works
1175.5	Fast draw shooting
1175.7	Safety measures
1177	Rifles
	Cf. GV854.9.B5 Biathlon
	Cf. SK274.2+ Hunting rifles
	Cf. UD390+ Military science
1179	Shotguns
	Cf. SK274.5+ Hunting shotguns
1180	Silhouette shooting
	Trapshooting
1181	General works
1181.3	Skeet shooting
	Archery
	Cf. SK36+ Bowhunting
1183	Periodicals. Serials
1184	Societies. Clubs
1184.5	Dictionaries. Encyclopedias

Sports
Fighting sports. Martial arts
Shooting
Archery -- Continued
1184.54 Study and teaching
1185 General works
Biography
1185.9 Collective
1186.A-Z Individual, A-Z
By region or country
1187 United States
1188.A-Z Other regions or countries, A-Z
1189 Juvenile works
1189.5 Bow and arrow making
1189.6 Bow tuning
1190 Crossbow shooting
1190.7 Quivers
Tournaments, jousts, tilts, etc.
Class here works concerned with modern revivals of the knightly sports
Cf. CR4553 Chivalry and knighthood
1191 General works
By region or country
1191.7 United States
1191.75.A-Z Other regions or countries, A-Z
1193 Pancratium
Wrestling
Including Greco-Roman wrestling
Cf. GV1114+ Jiu-jitsu
1195 General works
1195.3 Juvenile works
Biography
1196.A1 Collective
1196.A2-Z Individual, A-Z
1196.2.A-Z For special classes of persons, A-Z
1196.2.C45 Children
1196.25 Tournaments, matches, etc.
1196.27 Rules, records, etc.
1196.3 Coaching
1196.4.A-Z Special topics, A-Z
1196.4.C64 Collectibles
1196.4.H64 Holds
1196.4.S63 Social aspects
1196.4.T33 Takedown
1196.4.T7 Training
1196.5 Arm wrestling
1196.8 Inuit wrestling

Sports
Fighting sports. Martial arts
Wrestling -- Continued
1197 Japanese wrestling. Sumo
1197.5 Sambo wrestling
1198.112-.995 By region or country (Table G2c)
Add country number in table to GV1198
Games and amusements
Including both indoor and outdoor games and amusements
For indoor games and amusements alone see GV1221+
Cf. E59.G3 Games of Pre-Columbian Americans
Cf. E98.G2 Games of American Indians
Cf. GN454+ Games of preliterate peoples
Cf. GV191.2+ Outdoor recreation
1199 Periodicals. Societies. Serials
1200 History
1201 General works
1201.3 Anecdotes. Humor. Miscellanea
1201.34 Games and technology
1201.35 Symbolism of games
1201.37 Psychological aspects
1201.38 Social aspects. Relation to sociology
1201.39 Games for one
1201.4 Games for two
1201.42 Rules
1201.5 Hobbies (General)
For individual hobbies, see the topic
1201.6 Contests (General)
For individual contests, see the specific subject
For school prize competitions see LB3068+
1202.A-Z Games not otherwise provided for, A-Z
1202.C36 Campers' games
Cf. GV198.R4 Campfire programs
Cf. GV1217 Scouting programs
Carnival games see GV1835.2
1202.D72 Dreidel
1202.D74 Drinking games
1202.F33 Fantasy baseball. Rotisserie League Baseball
1202.F333 Fantasy basketball. Rotisserie League Basketball
1202.F34 Fantasy football. Rotisserie League Football
Fantasy games see GV1469.6+
1202.G46 Geocaching
High Fantasy see GV1469.62.H54
1202.L48 Letterboxing
1202.M67 Morra
Paintball see GV1202.S87
1202.S87 Survival Game. Paintball

Games and amusements
Games not otherwise provided for, A-Z -- Continued
1202.T7 Treasure hunting
Children's games and amusements
Cf. GV182.9 Recreation, play, for children
Cf. LB3031 School games
History see GV1200
1203 General works
1204.112-.995 By region or country (Table G2a)
Add country number in table to GV1204
Games for special classes of children
1204.997 Boys
Children with disabilities see LC4026
Children with mental disabilities see LC4611
1204.998 Girls
Invalids, Games for see GV1231
Mentally ill see RJ505.P6
1205 Children's parties
Including menus, decorations, costumes, games, etc.
For works consisting solely of party games see GV1202.92+
1206 Auto games. Games for travelers
1207 Chasing games, blindman's bluff, etc.
Counting-out rhymes see GR485
1211 Kissing games
1213 Marbles
1215 Singing and dancing games
Cf. GV1771 Play-party
Cf. LB1177 Songs, games, etc., in kindergarten
Cf. M1993 Action and drill songs in schools
Games of skill and action
1215.4 General works
1215.7 Jacks
1216 Yo-yos
1217 How to play Indians. Scouting games, etc.
Cf. GV198.R4 Campfire programs
Cf. GV1202.C36 Campers' games
1218.A-Z Other, A-Z
1218.B34 Balloons
1218.B6 Building with blocks, etc.
Cf. LB1139.C7 Child development
1218.C3 Card castles. Houses of cards
1218.C47 Circle games
Circuses, Children's see GV1838
1218.C63 Conkers
1218.C7 Cutting out pictures
1218.F5 Finger games

Games and amusements
Children's games and amusements
Other, A-Z -- Continued
1218.F55 Floral games
1218.H35 Hand games
1218.H6 Hopscotch
Houses of cards see GV1218.C3
1218.M3 Masks
1218.M52 Milkcaps
1218.P3 Paper work
1218.P34 Parachute games
1218.P5 Pinatas
POGs see GV1218.M52
1218.S5 Shadow pictures
1218.S8 String figures
Cf. GN455.S9 Ethnology
1218.T5 Tops
1218.T55 Toy soldiers
Cf. NK8475.M5 Decorative arts
Cf. U311 Military science
Toys
Cf. GN799.T7 Prehistoric toys
Cf. HQ784.T68 Child development
Cf. LB1029.T6 Educational toys
Cf. NK9509+ Decorative arts
Cf. TS2301.T7 Toy manufacture
Cf. TT174+ Handicrafts
1218.5 General works
Toy lending libraries
1218.6 General works
By region or country
1218.62 United States
1218.63.A-Z Other regions or countries, A-Z
Dolls
Cf. NK4891.3+ Decorative arts
1219 General works
1220 Dollhouses
Cf. NK4891.3+ Decorative arts
1220.7 Teddy bears
1220.8 Virtual pets
Indoor games and amusements
Cf. GV1470+ Party games and stunts
1221 Museums. Exhibitions
History
1223 General works
1225.A-Z By region or country, A-Z
General works

Games and amusements
Indoor games and amusements
General works -- Continued
1227 Through 1800
1229 1801-
1230 Design and construction of games
1231 Games for invalids, shut-ins, etc.
Cf. RJ242 Children in hospitals
1231.5 Play-by-mail games
Card games
1232 Dictionaries. Encyclopedias
History
1233 General works
1234.A-Z By region or country, A-Z
Collections of playing cards. Illustrations of old cards
Including playing card collecting
1235 General works
1236.A-Z Museum catalogs. By city and museum, A-Z
1239 Anecdotes. Humor. Miscellanea
General works
Including Hoyle's rules
1241 Through 1800
1243 1801-
1244 Juvenile works
1245 Ethics of card playing
1247 Card sharping. Beating the game. Gamblers' tricks
Cf. HV6708+ Criminology
Card tricks in parlor magic see GV1549
Cartomancy: fortune-telling by cards see BF1876+
1249 Euchre
Poker
Cf. GV1469.35.P65 Video poker
Biography
1250 Collective
1250.2.A-Z Individual, A-Z
1251 General works
1252.A-Z For special classes of persons, A-Z
1252.W66 Women
1253 Anecdotes. Humor. Miscellanea
1254 Tournaments
1254.5 Rules, etc.
1255.A-Z Special topics, A-Z
1255.P78 Psychological aspects
1257 Skat
1261 Solitaire. Patience
Whist
1271 Periodicals. Societies. Serials

Games and amusements
Indoor games and amusements
Card games
Whist -- Continued

1273 Congresses
Biography
1274.9 Collective
1275.A-Z Individual, A-Z
1277 General works
Bridge (Bridge whist)
1281.A1 Periodicals. Societies. Serials
1281.A4-Z General works
1281.5 Anecdotes. Humor. Miscellanea
1282 Auction bridge
Contract bridge
1282.2 Periodicals. Societies. Serials
1282.22 Dictionaries. Encyclopedias
1282.23 History
Biography
1282.25 Collective
1282.26.A-Z Individual, A-Z
1282.3 General works
1282.32 General special
Strategies and tactics
1282.4 Bidding
1282.42 Defensive play
1282.43 Doubles
1282.435 Dummy play
1282.44 End play. Squeeze
1282.46 Opening leads. Signals
1282.48 Slams
1282.5 Collections of games
For collections of games of an individual player see GV1282.26.A+
Tournaments
1282.6 General
1282.62.A-Z Individual, A-Z
1282.64 Rules, etc.
1282.7.A-Z Other specific topics, A-Z
Computer bridge see GV1282.7.D38
1282.7.D38 Data processing. Computer bridge
1282.7.P76 Programmed instruction
1282.7.P87 Psychological aspects
1282.8.A-Z Variant forms or games based on contract bridge, A-Z
1282.8.C55 Chicago bridge
1282.8.D86 Duplicate bridge

	Games and amusements
	Indoor games and amusements
	Card games
	Whist
	Bridge (Bridge whist)
	Contract bridge
	Variant forms or games based on contract bridge, A-Z -- Continued
1282.8.F59	Five-suit bridge
1282.8.G56	Ghoulie. Train bridge
1282.8.G68	Goulasch
1282.8.M55	MiniBridge
1282.8.T57	Three-handed bridge
	Train bridge see GV1282.8.G56
1282.9.A-Z	Other, A-Z
1282.9.S65	Solitaire bridge
1283	Duplicate whist
1285	Progressive whist
1287	Short whist
1289	Solo whist. Boston
1291.A-Z	Other varieties, A-Z
1291.A8	Auction whist
1291.B53	Bid whist
1291.D7	Drive whist
1291.L7	Living whist
1291.P8	Preference. Swedish whist
	Russian whist see GV1291.V5
1291.S6	Social whist
1291.T8	Triplicate whist
1291.V5	Vint. Russian whist
1295.A-Z	Other card games, A-Z
	Argentine rummy see GV1295.C2
1295.A8	Auction piquet
1295.B3	Baccarat
	Basket rummy see GV1295.C2
1295.B5	Bezique
1295.B55	Blackjack
1295.C15	Calypso
1295.C2	Canasta
	Cf. GV1295.S3 Samba
	Cinch see GV1295.P3
1295.C6	Cooncan (Conquian)
1295.C9	Cribbage
1295.E3	Ecarté
1295.F5	Five hundred
1295.F6	Football poker
1295.F7	Forty-five

Games and amusements
Indoor games and amusements
Card games
Other card games, A-Z -- Continued
Gin rummy see GV1295.R8
1295.H4 Hearts
High five see GV1295.P3
1295.H57 Hofämterspiel
1295.H6 Hollywood bridge
1295.J3 Jass
1295.L68 Lotería
1295.O4 Oklahoma
1295.O5 Ombre (Quadrille)
1295.P17 Panguingue (Pan)
1295.P3 Pedro (Cinch, High five)
1295.P6 Pinochle
1295.P7 Piquet
1295.R8 Rummy (Gin rummy)
1295.R9 Russian bank
1295.S3 Samba
1295.S4 Scopa
1295.S6 Solo-sixty
1295.S65 Spades
1295.T37 Tarot
Cf. BF1879.T2 Occult sciences
1295.T7 Tressette
1297 Game counters, score sheets, etc.
1299.A-Z Games with other than regulation cards, A-Z
1299.G2 Gaigle
1299.G84 Guiñote
1299.I7 Iroha karuta
1299.K34 Kahiko
1299.M3 Mah jong
1299.M6 Money game
1299.R6 Rook
Lotteries see HG6105+
Gambling. Chance and banking games
Cf. HV6708+ Criminology
1301 General works
1302 Probabilities, betting systems, etc.
1302.5 Internet gambling
1303 Dice and dice games
1305 Faro
1306 Keno
1307 Monte
1308 Trente et quarante. Rouge et noir
1309 Roulette

Games and amusements
Indoor games and amusements
Gambling. Chance and banking games -- Continued

1311.A-Z Other, A-Z
1311.B5 Bingo
1311.L6 Lotto
1311.P32 Pachinko
1311.P5 Pinball machines
1311.S56 Slot machines
1311.T73 Triboulet

Board games. Move games
For ancient Egyptian board games see DT62.B5

1312 General works

Chess
Cf. NK4696 Chessmen

1313 Periodicals. Serials
1314 Societies, clubs, etc.
1314.5 Dictionaries. Encyclopedias
1314.7 Philosophy

History
1315 Collected works (nonserial)
1317 General works
1318 General special

By period
1319 Origin
1320 Middle Ages through 1600
1321 1601-1850
1322 1851-

By region or country
United States
1323 General works
1325.A-Z By city, A-Z
1330.A-Z Other regions or countries, A-Z

Biography
1438 Collective
1439.A-Z Individual, A-Z
Also class here the collected games of individual players, treating such works as autobiographies, e.g.
1439.F5A3 Fischer, Bobby. Games of chess

Study and teaching
1440 General works
1440.5.A-Z By region or country, A-Z

General works
1442 Early to Philidor
1444 Philidor (1726-1795) to Tarrash, 1894
1445 1894-

Games and amusements
Indoor games and amusements
Board games. Move games
Chess -- Continued

1446 Chess for beginners. Juvenile works
1447 Miscellany and curiosa
1448 Psychology
1449 Anecdotes. Humor. Miscellanea
1449.3 Data processing. Computer chess
Strategies and tactics
1449.5 General works
Openings
1450 General works
1450.2 Individual openings (not A-Z)
1450.3 Middle games. Combinations
1450.7 End games. Studies
Problems
1451 General works
1451.2 Fairy chess
1451.3 Helpmate
1451.5.A-Z Moves of particular men, A-Z
1451.5.B57 Bishop
1451.5.K5 King
1451.5.K6 Knight
1451.5.P3 Pawn
1451.5.Q43 Queen
1452 Collections of games
For the collected games of an individual player see GV1439.A+
1455 Tournaments, matches
1456 Correspondence chess
1457 Rules, records, etc.
1457.5 Rating of chess players
1458.A-Z Variant forms or games based on chess, A-Z
1458.A7 Archchess
1458.C44 Changgi (Korean chess)
1458.C47 Chez game
1458.C5 Chinese chess
1458.H4 Hexagonal chess
1458.K74 Kriegspiel
1458.M5 Military chess
1458.M65 Mongolian chess
1458.Q32 Quächess
1458.S5 Shōgi (Japanese chess)
1458.T74 Tri-chess
1458.Y35 Yamagochi
Go (Game)

Games and amusements
Indoor games and amusements
Board games. Move games
Go (Game) -- Continued

1459	Periodicals. Serials
1459.2	Societies, etc.
	History
1459.3	Collected works (nonserial)
1459.32	General works
1459.33	General special
1459.35.A-Z	By region or country, A-Z
	Biography
1459.4	Collective
1459.42.A-Z	Individual, A-Z
1459.5	General works
1459.52	Beginners' manuals. Juvenile works
1459.54	Addresses, essays, lectures
1459.55	General special
1459.56	Anecdotes. Humor. Miscellanea
1460	Joseki
1460.2	Openings
1460.3	Middle games
1460.4	End games. Studies
1460.43	Tesuji
1460.5	Handicap games
1460.6	Problems, etc.
	Collections of games
1460.72	General works
1460.73	By individual player
1460.75.A-Z	Tournaments, matches, A-Z Including Meijinsen, Hon'inbo, etc.
1460.8	Rules, etc.
	Checkers. Draughts
1461	Periodicals. Societies. Serials
	Biography
1462	Collective
1462.2.A-Z	Individual, A-Z
1463	General works
	Strategies and tactics
1463.5	General works
1463.7	Openings
1463.9	End games
1464	Data processing. Computer checkers
1465	Collections of games
	Dominoes
1467	General works
1468	Domino bridge

Games and amusements
Indoor games and amusements
Board games. Move games -- Continued

1468.3.A-Z Variant forms or games based on dominoes, A-Z
1468.3.F65 Forty-two
1469.A-Z Other board games, A-Z
1469.A75 Armchair Gold
1469.A96 Ayo
1469.B2 Backgammon
1469.C5 Checker pool
1469.C66 Connection games
1469.D54 Diplomacy
Dungeons and dragons see GV1469.62.D84
1469.F34 Fanorona
1469.G72 Gomoku
1469.H48 Hex
1469.K45 Kensington
1469.K54 Kiela
1469.L45 Leela. Snakes and ladders. Chutes and ladders
1469.M35 Mancala
1469.M65 Monopoly
1469.O4 Omweso
1469.O75 Othello
1469.O78 Oware
1469.P17 Pachisi
Palladium see GV1469.62.P34
1469.P44 Pente
1469.P52 Pictionary
1469.R85 Rummikub
1469.R86 RuneQuest
1469.S6 Solitaire
1469.S84 Sugoroku
1469.S94 Swan
1469.T75 Traveller
1469.T76 Trax
1469.T77 Trivial Pursuit
1469.W63 Woaley

Computer games. Computer simulated games. Electronic games
Including Internet games
Cf. TL712.8 Computer flight games
Cf. U310.2 Computer war games

1469.15 General works
1469.16.A-Z For special classes of persons, A-Z
1469.16.W66 Women
1469.17.A-Z Special topics, A-Z
1469.17.S63 Social aspects

Games and amusements
Indoor games and amusements
Computer games. Computer simulated games. Electronic games

1469.18.A-Z Associations, clubs, etc. By name, A-Z
1469.2 Computer programs
1469.22 Adventure games
1469.23 Yahoo! games
1469.25.A-Z Individual games, A-Z
e.g.
1469.25.A45 Alone in the dark
1469.25.A56 Antagonists
1469.25.A75 Armored fist
1469.25.B34 Balance of power
1469.25.B48 Betrayal at Krondor
1469.25.B55 Blackthorne
1469.25.B87 Buzz Aldrin's race into space
1469.25.C37 Carmen Sandiego
1469.25.C44 Celtic tales
1469.25.C58 Civilization
1469.25.C64 Colonization
1469.25.C92 Cyberia
1469.25.D45 Decent
1469.25.D56 Discworld
1469.25.D66 Doom
1469.25.D72 Dragon lore
1469.25.E18 Earl Weaver Baseball Hall of Fame League
1469.25.E45 Empire Deluxe
1469.25.F55 Fleet defender
1469.25.F69 Forza motorsport
1469.25.H37 Harpoon Battlebook
1469.25.H43 Heaven & earth
1469.25.H45 Hell
1469.25.H46 Heretic
1469.25.H47 Heroes of might and magic
1469.25.K56 King's quest
1469.25.L43 Legend of Kyrandia
1469.25.L45 Leisure Suit Larry
1469.25.L54 LINKS
1469.25.L63 Lode runner
1469.25.M333 Madden NFL
1469.25.M34 Marathon
1469.25.M346 Marauder 2107
1469.25.M35 Marco Polo
1469.25.M36 Master of Orion
1469.25.M53 MicroLeague Baseball
1469.25.M55 MicroLeague Football

Games and amusements
Indoor games and amusements
Computer games. Computer simulated games. Electronic games
Individual games, A-Z -- Continued

1469.25.M56	Microsoft Golf
1469.25.M57	Might and Magic
1469.25.M65	Monty Python's complete waste of time
1469.25.M95	Myst
1469.25.O88	Outpost
1469.25.P34	Pagan
1469.25.P47	Perfect General
1469.25.P63	Police Quest
1469.25.P65	Populous
1469.25.P68	PowerHouse
1469.25.P75	Prince of Persia
1469.25.Q47	Quest for Glory
1469.25.R34	Railroad Tycoon
1469.25.R42	Rebel assault
1469.25.R45	Renegade
1469.25.R47	Return to Zork
1469.25.R64	RollerCoaster tycoon
1469.25.S425	Second Life
(1469.25.S43)	Sega genesis see GV1469.33
1469.25.S45	7th guest
1469.25.S52	Shadow of the Comet
1469.25.S55	Simlife
1469.25.S563	Sims
1469.25.S57	SimTower
1469.25.S65	Space quest
1469.25.S68	Star crusader
1469.25.S69	Star trek
1469.25.S72	Star trek, the next generation
1469.25.S75	Stunt Island
1469.25.S82	Subwar 2050
1469.25.S85	Super munchers
1469.25.S88	Super Star wars
1469.25.S95	System shock
1469.25.T54	Timelost
1469.25.T73	Treehouse
1469.25.U45	Ultima
1469.25.U54	Under a killing moon
1469.25.W55	Wing commander
1469.25.X36	X-COM Terror from the Deep
1469.25.X82	X-COM UFO defense
1469.25.X85	X-wing

Games and amusements
Indoor games and amusements
Computer games. Computer simulated games. Electronic games -- Continued

1469.27 Other individual games (not A-Z)

Video games

Cf. TK6681 Video game equipment

1469.3 General works

1469.32 Nintendo video games

Including Game Boy video games

1469.325 Sega Dreamcast video games

1469.33 Sega Genesis video games

1469.335 Sega Saturn video games

1469.34.A-Z Special topics, A-Z

1469.34.A97 Authorship, scenario writing, etc.

1469.34.C48 Characters

Cheating see GV1469.34.C67

1469.34.C65 Collectors and collecting. Collectibles

1469.34.C67 Corrupt practices. Cheating

1469.34.S52 Social aspects

1469.35.A-Z Individual games, equipment, etc., A-Z

1469.35.A16 1080 Degree Snowboarding

1469.35.A18 A-Train

1469.35.A33 Ace Combat

1469.35.A43 Albert Odyssey

1469.35.A48 Alundra

1469.35.A75 Army Men World War

1469.35.B33 Banjo-Kazooie

1469.35.B34 Batman & Robin

1469.35.B35 Battle Arena Toshinden

1469.35.B36 BattleTanx Global Assault

1469.35.B37 Battletoads

1469.35.B48 Beyond the Beyond

1469.35.B54 Blast Corps

1469.35.B56 Blood Omen

1469.35.B57 Blue Stinger

1469.35.B59 Body Harvest

1469.35.B63 Bomberman 64

1469.35.B64 Bomberman World

1469.35.B65 Boogerman

1469.35.B7 Brave Fencer Musashi

1469.35.B73 Breath of Fire

1469.35.B76 Brigandine

1469.35.B83 Bubsy Bobcat

1469.35.B85 Buck Bumble

1469.35.B86 Bugs Bunny, Lost in Time

1469.35.B88 Bushido Blade 2

Games and amusements
Indoor games and amusements
Video games
Individual games, equipment, etc., A-Z -- Continued

1469.35.C36 Carrier
1469.35.C37 Castlevania
1469.35.C45 Centipede
1469.35.C56 Chocobo's Dungeon
1469.35.C64 Colony Wars
1469.35.C73 Crash Bandicoot
1469.35.C74 Crazy Taxi
1469.35.C75 Critical Depth
1469.35.C78 Crusaders of Might and Magic
1469.35.D37 Dark Seed II
1469.35.D39 Dead or Alive
1469.35.D4 Deathtrap Dungeon
1469.35.D43 Deception
1469.35.D46 Destrega
1469.35.D54 Diddy Kong Racing
1469.35.D58 Dino Crisis
1469.35.D66 Donkey Kong
1469.35.D68 Doom 64
1469.35.D72 Dragon Force
1469.35.D725 Dragon Warrior
1469.35.D73 Dragon's Lair
1469.35.D84 Duke Nukem
1469.35.D95 Dynasty Warriors
1469.35.E72 Earthworm Jim
1469.35.E74 Ehrgeiz
1469.35.F4 Fear Effect
1469.35.F52 Fighter's Edge
1469.35.F54 Fighting Force
(1469.35.G34) Game Boy
see GV1469.32
1469.35.G36 GameShark
1469.35.G38 Gauntlet
1469.35.G44 Gekido
1469.35.G48 GEX
1469.35.G52 Ghost in the Shell
1469.35.G55 Global conquest
1469.35.G58 Glover
1469.35.G64 GoldenEye 007
1469.35.G73 Gran Turismo
1469.35.G738 Grand Theft Auto
1469.35.G74 Grandia
1469.35.G75 Granstream Saga
1469.35.H65 Hot Wheels turbo racing

Games and amusements
Indoor games and amusements
Video games
Individual games, equipment, etc., A-Z -- Continued

1469.35.H67 House of the dead
1469.35.H94 Hybrid Heaven
1469.35.J34 Jade Cocoon
1469.35.J42 Jedi Power Battles
1469.35.J48 Jet Force Gemini
1469.35.J52 Jet Moto
1469.35.J83 Juggernaut
1469.35.K35 Kagero: Deception II
1469.35.K37 Kartia
1469.35.K54 Killer Instinct
1469.35.K58 King's Field
1469.35.K62 Knockout Kings 2000
1469.35.L28 Legacy of Kain
1469.35.L32 Legend of Legaia
1469.35.L43 Legend of Zelda
1469.35.L45 Lemmings
1469.35.L67 Lord of the Rings
1469.35.L84 Lunar
1469.35.M35 Mario Party
1469.35.M36 Mario Tennis
1469.35.M37 Masters of Teräs Kasi
1469.35.M4 Medievil
1469.35.M43 Mega Man X
1469.35.M46 Metal Gear Solid
1469.35.M53 Micro Maniacs
1469.35.M54 Misadventures of Tron Bonne
1469.35.M57 Mission Impossible
1469.35.M65 Monkey Hero
1469.35.M67 Mortal Kombat
1469.35.M73 Ms. Pac-Man Maze Madness
1469.35.N3 NBA 2K
1469.35.N33 NBA JAM
1469.35.N335 NBA Live 2000
1469.35.N336 NBA Showtime
1469.35.N338 NFL 2K1
1469.35.N34 NFL Blitz
1469.35.N347 NHL 2K
1469.35.N35 Nightmare Creatures
1469.35.N36 Nights into Dreams
1469.35.N39 Ninja, Shadow of Darkness
1469.35.N83 Nuclear Strike
1469.35.O2 O.D.T.
1469.35.O47 Ogre Battle

Games and amusements
Indoor games and amusements
Video games
Individual games, equipment, etc., A-Z -- Continued

1469.35.O53 One
1469.35.P33 Pac-Man
1469.35.P34 Pac-Man World
1469.35.P37 Parasite Eve
1469.35.P47 Perfect Dark
1469.35.P63 Pokémon
1469.35.P636 Pokémon Stadium
1469.35.P64 Pokémon Yellow
1469.35.P65 Poker
1469.35.Q32 Quake II
1469.35.Q47 Quest 64
1469.35.R38 Rayman
1469.35.R43 Ready 2 Rumble Boxing
1469.35.R47 Resident Evil
1469.35.R53 Ridge Racer 64
1469.35.R58 Rival Schools
1469.35.R59 Road Rash Jailbreak
1469.35.R6 Rocket
1469.35.R64 Rogue Trip Vacation 2012
1469.35.R67 Rollcage
1469.35.R69 Royal Rumble
1469.35.R85 Rush 2
1469.35.S33 San Francisco Rush
1469.35.S43 Secret of Evermore
(1469.35.S45) Sega Saturn
see GV1469.335
1469.35.S47 Shadow Madness
1469.35.S48 Shadows of the Empire
1469.35.S54 Silent Hill
1469.35.S6 Sno-cross Championship Racing
1469.35.S62 Sonic Adventure
1469.35.S64 Soul Blade
1469.35.S643 Soul Calibur
1469.35.S645 Spacestation Silicon Valley
1469.35.S65 Spellcasting 101
1469.35.S66 Sports Car GT
1469.35.S664 Spyro 2:-Ripto's rage
1469.35.S67 Spyro the Dragon
1469.35.S7 Star Fox 64
1469.35.S72 Star Ocean
1469.35.S74 Street Fighter Alpha
1469.35.S93 Suikoden
1469.35.S957 Super Mario 64

Games and amusements
Indoor games and amusements
Video games
Individual games, equipment, etc., A-Z -- Continued

1469.35.S96 Super Mario Bros.
1469.35.S965 Super Mario RPG
1469.35.S98 Super Smash Bros.
1469.35.S983 Superman
1469.35.S984 Sword of the Beserk
1469.35.S985 Syphon Filter
1469.35.T3 Tactics Ogre
1469.35.T33 T'ai Fu
1469.35.T37 Tekken
1469.35.T63 Tobal No. 1
1469.35.T64 Tomorrow Never Dies
1469.35.T65 Tonic Trouble
1469.35.T66 Tony Hawk's Pro Skater
1469.35.T68 Toy commander
1469.35.T69 Toy Story 2
1469.35.T8 Turok
1469.35.T85 Twisted Metal 2
1469.35.T86 Twisted Metal III
1469.35.U54 Unholy War
1469.35.U72 Urban Strike
1469.35.V34 Valkyrie Profile
1469.35.V37 Vandal Hearts
1469.35.V49 Vigilance
1469.35.V52 Vigilante 8
1469.35.V548 Virtua Fighter 1
1469.35.V549 Virtua Fighter 2
1469.35.V55 Virtua Fighter 3
1469.35.V57 Virtual Bart
1469.35.V73 Vs.
1469.35.W37 War Gods
1469.35.W4 WCW Nitro
1469.35.W414 WCW/NWO Revenge
1469.35.W416 WCW/NWO Thunder
1469.35.W42 WCW vs. the World
1469.35.W54 Wild Arms
1469.35.W65 World Series Baseball 2K1
1469.35.W67 Worms Armageddon
1469.35.W73 Wrestlemania
1469.35.W736 Wu-Tang Shaolin Style
1469.35.W75 WWF Smack Down
1469.35.X25 X-Men
1469.35.X26 X-Men vs. Street Fighter
1469.35.X42 Xena, Warrior Princess

Games and amusements
Indoor games and amusements
Video games
Individual games, equipment, etc., A-Z -- Continued

1469.35.X45 Xenogears
1469.35.Y67 Yoshi's Story
(1469.35.Z44) Zelda II
see GV1469.35.L43
1469.37 Other individual games (not A-Z)
1469.4 Foosball
1469.45 Tabletop hockey
Fantasy games
1469.6 General works
1469.612 Rules
1469.62.A-Z Individual games, A-Z
1469.62.A24 Aberrant (Game)
Advanced dungeons and dragons see GV1469.62.D84
1469.62.A35 All flesh must be eaten
1469.62.A4 Amazing Engine (Game)
1469.62.A42 Amber
1469.62.A73 Aria
1469.62.A75 Armageddon
1469.62.A77 Ars Magica
1469.62.A93 Avant Charlemagne (Game)
1469.62.B36 BattleTech
1469.62.B54 Big eyes, small mouth
1469.62.C34 Call of Cthulhu
1469.62.C36 Castle Falkenstein
1469.62.C43 Champions
1469.62.C44 Changeling
1469.62.C45 Chill
1469.62.C47 Chronopia
1469.62.C89 Cyberpunk
1469.62.C92 Cyberworld
1469.62.D2 d20 modern (Game)
1469.62.D365 Dark ages: Inquisitor
1469.62.D367 Dark ages: Mage
1469.62.D37 Dark ages: Vampire
1469.62.D373 Dark ages: Werewolf
1469.62.D43 Deadlands
1469.62.D46 Demon (Game)
1469.62.D65 Don't Look Back
1469.62.D84 Dungeons and dragons
1469.62.E17 Earthdawn
1469.62.E45 Empire galactique
1469.62.E82 Exalted
1469.62.F32 Fading suns

Games and amusements
Indoor games and amusements
Fantasy games
Individual games, A-Z -- Continued

1469.62.F33 Faerie mound of dragonkind
1469.62.F56 Final Bug
1469.62.F65 Forge: Out of Chaos
1469.62.F72 Freebase
1469.62.F74 Freeway Warrior
1469.62.F77 Friends & Foes
1469.62.G85 GURPS
1469.62.G86 GURPS Dinosaurs
1469.62.G87 GURPS Goblins
1469.62.G88 GURPS Reign of Steel
1469.62.H45 Heroes Unlimited
1469.62.H54 High Fantasy
1469.62.H64 Hōl
1469.62.H85 Hunter
1469.62.I5 In nomine
1469.62.I53 Initial reaction (Game)
1469.62.I84 Island of Kesmai (Game)
1469.62.L43 Legend of the Five Rings
1469.62.L45 Legendmaker
1469.62.L57 Little fears (Game)
1469.62.L67 Lord of the Rings roleplaying game
1469.62.M29 Mage
1469.62.M34 Magic: The Gathering
1469.62.M42 Mecha (Game)
1469.62.M43 Mechanoids
1469.62.M45 Men in black
1469.62.M53 Middle-Earth
1469.62.M84 Mummy: the resurrection (Game)
1469.62.N48 NetRunner
1469.62.P34 Palladium
1469.62.P36 Paranoia
1469.62.P44 Pelicar
1469.62.P67 Portal
1469.62.P73 Prime Directive
1469.62.P75 Prince Valiant
1469.62.R34 Rifts
1469.62.R62 Robotech
1469.62.S36 Scorpion Swamp
1469.62.S46 Sentinels
1469.62.S5 Shades of nightfall
1469.62.S52 Shadowrun
1469.62.S56 Silver age sentinels
1469.62.S65 Sorcery

Games and amusements
Indoor games and amusements
Fantasy games
Individual games, A-Z -- Continued

1469.62.S656 Space: 1889
1469.62.S66 Spellfire
1469.62.S67 Sphere
1469.62.S69 Star Trek
1469.62.S7 Star wars
1469.62.T33 Tales from the Floating Vagabond
1469.62.T35 Talislanta
1469.62.T37 Tao Chi
1469.62.T47 Terminus V
1469.62.T66 Toon
1469.62.V34 Vampire
1469.62.W35 Warhammer
1469.62.W43 Werewolf
1469.62.W44 Westbrook
1469.62.W45 Whispering Vault
1469.62.W54 Willow
1469.62.W58 Witchcraft
1469.62.W7 Wraith
1469.63 Other individual games (not A-Z)

Parties. Party games and stunts
Including entertaining at home, church, school, etc.
Cf. GV1205 Children's parties
Cf. GV1746+ Dance parties
Cf. GV1838 Amateur carnivals
Cf. PN3151+ Amateur theatricals, etc.
Cf. PN6120.S5 Shadow pantomimes
Cf. SF427.45 Parties for dogs
Cf. TT900.P3 Party decorations
Cf. TX731 Cookery

1470 Periodicals. Societies. Serials
1470.5 Congresses
1471 General works
1472 General special
e.g. Observance of anniversaries (General)
1472.3.A-Z By region or country, A-Z
1472.5.A-Z Private entertainers, A-Z
Unless otherwise provided for
1472.7.A-Z Parties for special occasions, A-Z
1472.7.B33 Bachelor parties. Bachelorette
1472.7.B5 Birthdays
1472.7.C5 Christmas
1472.7.S5 Showers
1472.7.W38 Wedding anniversaries

Games and amusements
Parties. Party games and stunts
Parties for special occasions, A-Z -- Continued

1472.7.W4 Weekends
1473 Guessing games
1474 Adult party games
Instructive games
Cf. LB1029.G3 Games in education
1480 General works
Special topics
1483 Authors
1485 Geography
1487 History
1488 Letter writing
1489 Parenting
Puzzles
Including literary and mathematical games
Cf. PN6366+ Riddles, charades, etc.
Cf. QA95 Mathematical recreations
1491 Periodicals. Societies. Serials
1493 General works
1501 Form puzzles
1507.A-Z Other, A-Z
1507.A5 Anagrams
1507.A75 Autographs
1507.B5 Bible games and puzzles
1507.C45 Checkerboard puzzles
1507.C5 Cipher stories
1507.C68 Cross-sums
1507.C7 Crossword puzzles
1507.C8 Cryptograms
1507.D4 Detective and mystery puzzles
1507.D6 Div-a-let
1507.D65 Double-crostics
1507.I5 Impenetrable secret
1507.J5 Jigsaw puzzles
1507.K35 Kakuro
1507.K5 Kleine Bosco
Labyrinths see GV1507.M3
1507.L37 Lateral thinking puzzles
1507.M2 Matchstick games
1507.M3 Maze puzzles. Labyrinths
1507.P35 Pencil games
1507.P38 Personal name games
1507.P43 Philosophical recreations
1507.P47 Picture puzzles
1507.P5 Pinwheel puzzles

Games and amusements
Parties. Party games and stunts
Puzzles
Other, A-Z -- Continued
1507.P7 Political puzzles
1507.P9 Psychological recreations
1507.Q5 Quiz shows. Quiz books
1507.Q6 Quotation puzzles
Rubik's Cube, Rubik's Revenge, Rubik's Snake, etc. see QA491
1507.S3 Scrabble
1507.S7 Story games
1507.S83 Sudoku
1507.S9 Syzygies
1507.T3 Tangrams
1507.T47 Tic-tac-toe
1507.T5 Time games
1507.W8 Word games and puzzles
1507.W9 Word lists
1511.A-Z Other party games, A-Z
1511.B65 Booster game
1521 Miniature theaters
For marionettes, Punch and Judy shows, etc. see PN1972+
1525 Peep shows
Tricks, illusions, etc.
Cf. BF1403.2+ Occultism
Cf. Q164 Scientific recreations
1541 Periodicals. Societies. Serials
1542 Collected works (nonserial)
1542.5 Dictionaries. Encyclopedias
History
1543 General works
1543.3.A-Z By region or country, A-Z
Biography
1545.A2 Collective
1545.A3-Z Individual, A-Z
e.g.
1545.H6 Herrmann, Carl
1545.H8 Houdini, Harry
1545.R7 Robert-Houdin, Jean Eugène
1545.T5 Thurston, Howard
General works
1546 Through 1800
1547 1801-
1548 Juvenile works

Games and amusements
Tricks, illusions, etc. -- Continued
1549 Card tricks
Cf. GV1247 Card sharping, gamblers' tricks
Fortune-telling see BF1845+
1553 Second sight, mind reading, etc.
Shadow pictures see GV1218.S5
Slate writing see BF1343
1555 Sleight of hand
1556 Pocket tricks
1557 Ventriloquism
1558 Juggling
1558.5 Fire twirling
1559 Other tricks (not A-Z)
Including tricks with cigarettes, coins, hats, matchsticks, paper, rope, etc.
1560 Magic patents
1561 Magicians' supplies, etc.
Darts
Biography
1564 Collective
1564.2.A-Z Individual, A-Z
1565 General works
1570 Model car racing
Dancing
Cf. HV1664.D3 Education of the blind
Cf. ML3400+ Music
Cf. RC489.D3 Dance therapy
Cf. RJ505.D3 Dance therapy (Pediatrics)
1580 Periodicals. Societies. Serials
1583 Congresses
1585 Dictionaries. Encyclopedias
1587 Terminology. Abbreviations. Notation
1587.5 Directories
1587.8 Archives
Philosophy. Relation to other topics
1588 General works
1588.3 Relation to aesthetics
1588.4 Relation to education
Relation to ethics see GV1740+
1588.45 Relation to politics. Government policy
1588.5 Relation to psychology
1588.6 Relation to society
Study and teaching. Research
1589 General works
1589.4 Dance schools
1589.45 Dance recitals

Dance -- Continued
General works
1590 Early through 1850
1593 1851-1974
1594 1975-
1595 General special (Special aspects of the subject as a whole)
1596 Pictorial works
Cf. TR817.5 Dance photography
1596.5 Juvenile works
Cf. GV1799 Children's dances
1597 Dance as a profession
1599 Addresses, essays, lectures
1600 Dance criticism. Appreciation
History
General works
Early through 1850 see GV1590
1601 1851-
1603 General special
1605 Preliterate (General)
For particular ethnic groups in particular countries, see the country see GV1621+
By period
Ancient
1607 General works
1609 Oriental
1611 Classical
Cf. GV1783+ Revival of classical dance
1613 Other ancient. Egyptian, etc.
1615 Medieval
Modern
1617 General works
1618 15th-18th centuries
1619 19th-20th centuries
By region or country
America
1621 General works
North America
1622 General works
United States
1623 General works
1624.A-Z By region or state, A-Z
1624.5.A-Z By city, A-Z
1624.7.A-Z Special races or ethnic groups, A-Z
1624.7.A34 African Americans
Indians see E98.D2
1624.7.M49 Mexican Americans
Negroes see GV1624.7.A34

Dance
History
By region or country
America
North America -- Continued
Canada
1625 General works
1625.5.A-Z Local, A-Z
Latin America
1626 General works
Mexico
1627 General works
1628.A-Z Local, A-Z
Central America
1629 General works
1630.A-Z By country, A-Z
West Indies
1631 General works
1632.A-Z By country, A-Z
South America
1633 General works
Argentina
1635 General works
1636.A-Z Local, A-Z
Brazil
1637 General works
1638.A-Z Local, A-Z
Chile
1639 General works
1640.A-Z Local, A-Z
1641.A-Z Other South American regions or countries, A-Z
Europe
1643 General works
Great Britain
1645 General works
1646.A-Z By division, A-Z
1646.E6 England
1646.I8 Ireland
1646.S35 Scotland
1646.W3 Wales
Austria
1647 General works
1648.A-Z Local, A-Z
France
1649 General works
1650.A-Z Local, A-Z

Dance
History
By region or country
Europe -- Continued
Germany
Including former West Germany
1651 General works
1652.A-Z Local, A-Z
Former East Germany
1652.5 General works
1652.6.A-Z Local, A-Z
Greece
Cf. GV1611 Classical dance
1653 General works
1654.A-Z Local, A-Z
Italy
Cf. GV1611 Classical dance
1655 General works
1656.A-Z Local, A-Z
Low Countries
1657 General works
Belgium
1659 General works
1660.A-Z Local, A-Z
Netherlands
1661 General works
1662.A-Z Local, A-Z
Russia. Soviet Union. Russia (Federation)
For former Soviet republics in Europe see GV1688.A+
Cf. GV1699+ Siberia (Russia)
Cf. GV1700.2+ Former Soviet Central Asia
1663 General works
1664.A-Z Local, A-Z
Scandinavia
1665 General works
Denmark
1667 General works
1668.A-Z Local, A-Z
Norway
1669 General works
1670.A-Z Local, A-Z
Sweden
1671 General works
1672.A-Z Local, A-Z
Spain
1673 General works

Dance
History
By region or country
Europe
Spain -- Continued
1674.A-Z Local, A-Z
Portugal
1675 General works
1676.A-Z Local, A-Z
Switzerland
1677 General works
1678.A-Z Local, A-Z
Balkan States
1679 General works
Bulgaria
1681 General works
1682.A-Z Local, A-Z
Romania
1685 General works
1686.A-Z Local, A-Z
Former Yugoslavia
1687 General works
1687.5.A-Z Local, A-Z
1688.A-Z Other European regions or countries, A-Z
e.g.
Czech Republic
1688.C9 General works
1688.C92A-.C92Z Local, A-Z
Finland
1688.F5 General works
1688.F52A-.F52Z Local, A-Z
Hungary
1688.H8 General works
1688.H82A-.H82Z Local, A-Z
Asia
1689 General works
China
1691 General works
1692.A-Z Local, A-Z
India
1693 General works
1694.A-Z Local, A-Z
Japan
1695 General works
1696.A-Z Local, A-Z
Iran
1697 General works

	Dance
	History
	By region or country
	Asia
	Iran -- Continued
1698.A-Z	Local, A-Z
	Siberia (Russia)
1699	General works
1700.A-Z	Local, A-Z
	Other former Soviet republics (Asia)
1700.2	General works
	Armenia (Republic)
1700.23	General works
1700.24.A-Z	Local, A-Z
	Azerbaijan
1700.25	General works
1700.26.A-Z	Local, A-Z
	Georgia (Republic)
1700.27	General works
1700.28.A-Z	Local, A-Z
	Kazakhstan
1700.3	General works
1700.32.A-Z	Local, A-Z
	Kyrgyzstan
1700.4	General works
1700.42.A-Z	Local, A-Z
	Tajikistan
1700.5	General works
1700.52.A-Z	Local, A-Z
	Turkmenistan
1700.6	General works
1700.62.A-Z	Local, A-Z
	Uzbekistan
1700.7	General works
1700.72.A-Z	Local, A-Z
	Turkey. Asia Minor
1701	General works
1702.A-Z	Local, A-Z
1703.A-Z	Other Asian regions or countries, A-Z
	e.g.
	Burma. Myanmar
1703.B95	General works
1703.B952A-.B952Z	Local, A-Z
	Cambodia
1703.C3	General works
1703.C32A-.C32Z	Local, A-Z
	Indochina

Dance
History
By region or country
Asia
Other Asian regions or countries, A-Z
Indochina -- Continued
1703.I5 General works
1703.I52A-.I52Z Local, A-Z
Indonesia
1703.I53 General works
1703.I532A-.I532Z Local, A-Z
Israel
1703.I75 General works
1703.I752A-.I752Z Local, A-Z
Myanmar see GV1703.B95+
1704 Arab countries
Africa
1705 General works
Egypt
Cf. GV1613 Ancient Egyptian dance
1709 General works
1710.A-Z Local, A-Z
1713.A-Z Other African regions or countries, A-Z
Australia
1715 General works
1716.A-Z Local, A-Z
New Zealand
1719 General works
1720.A-Z Local, A-Z
Pacific islands
1727 General works
1728.A-Z By island or group of islands, A-Z
For Hawaii see GV1624.A+
1735 Apparatus and equipment
Ethics. Dancing and the Church
1740 Early works through 1800
1741 1801-
1743 National dances. Folk dances and dancing (General)
For individual countries see GV1621+
For special dances see GV1796.A+
Cf. GT3925+ Festivals, holidays (Manners and customs)
Cf. PN3203+ Spectacles, tableaux, pageants, etc.
Social dancing. Ballroom dancing

Dance
Social dancing. Ballroom dancing -- Continued
Balls. Dance parties
Including college proms, school dances, etc.
For local history, see Classes D-F
Cf. GV1757 Cotillion
Cf. PN1992.8.D3 Television dance parties
1746 General works
1747 Court and state balls, etc.
1748 Public balls
1749 Mask and fancy-dress balls
1749.5 Gay and lesbian dance parties
1750 Programs, german cards, etc.
1750.4 Ballrooms
1750.5 Discotheques
Dance halls
1750.7 General works
1750.8 Taxi dancing
Technique (General)
1751 General works
1753 General special
e.g. Revival of old dances
Study and teaching. Research
1753.5 General works
1753.7 Audiovisual aids
1754.A-Z Individual schools, A-Z
For individual countries see GV1621+
Round dances
1755 General works
1757 German. Cotillion
Special dances
1761 Waltz
Other see GV1796.A+
Square dances. Quadrilles. Country dances
By region or country see GV1621+
1763 General works
1767 Call books
Special dances see GV1796.A+
1768 Line dances
1771 Play-party
1779 Dance in motion pictures, television, etc.
Cf. PN1992.8.D3 Television dance parties
Theatrical dance
1781 General works
1781.2 Improvisation
1782 Production and staging

Dance
Theatrical dance -- Continued
1782.3 Safety measures. Accident prevention
Cf. GV1789 Ballet
1782.5 Choreography
Individual dances
Including choreography, history, notation, scores, etc.
1782.6 Collected
1782.62.A-Z Individual. By title, A-Z
Modern or expressionistic dance. Revival of classical dance
For individual countries see GV1621+
1783 General works
1783.2.A-Z Individual dances. By title, A-Z
1783.2.B87 Butō
1783.5 Religious dance
1784 Jazz dance
Incidental dances in specific dramas
see PA - PS, e.g., incidental dances in Shakespearean dramas, see PR3034
Biography
1785.A1 Collective
1785.A2-Z Individual, A-Z
e.g.
1785.D5 Diagilev, Sergei
1785.D8 Duncan, Isadora
1785.F63 Fonteyn, Margot, Dame
1785.L5 Lifar, Serge
1785.N6 Nijinsky, Waslaw
1785.P3 Pavlova, Anna
Dance groups or companies
1785.8 General works
1786.A-Z Individual groups or companies. By name, A-Z
Ballet
Cf. ML3465 Ballet music (History and criticism)
Dictionaries. Encyclopedias see GV1585
Biography see GV1785.A+
By region or country see GV1621+
1787 General works
1787.5 Juvenile works
1787.6 Addresses, essays, lectures. Anecdotes. Humor. Miscellanea
Technique
1788 General works
1788.2.A-Z Special topics, A-Z
1788.2.M46 Men's and boys' techniques
1788.2.P37 Pas de deux

Dance
Theatrical dance
Ballet -- Continued
Study and teaching. Research
1788.5 General works
1788.6.A-Z Individual schools, A-Z
1789 Safety measures. Accident prevention
1789.2 Equipment and supplies
Including costumes, slippers, etc.
Ballets
Cf. M1520+ Music scores
Cf. ML51+ Librettos
1790.A1 Collected
Class here individual ballets discussed collectively
1790.A3-Z Individual. By title, A-Z
e.g.
1790.G5 Giselle
1790.R4 Red shoes (Ballet)
1791 Buck and wing
1793 Clog-dancing. Jig. Step dancing
Tap dancing
1794 General works
1794.5 Jazz tap
1795 Miscellaneous theatrical dances (not A-Z)
1796.A-Z Special dances, A-Z
1796.A6 Allemande
1796.A65 Alsharqi
1796.A73 Anglaise
1796.B25 Bailecito
1796.B28 Basse danse
1796.B3 Beseda
1796.B4 Bharata Natyam
1796.B56 Bolangera
1796.B74 Break dancing
1796.C13 Calandria
1796.C14 Candombe
Cante hondo see GV1796.F55
1796.C145 Capoeira
1796.C16 Caroco
1796.C2 Cha-cha
1796.C39 Chamarrita
1796.C4 Charleston
1796.C43 Chhau
1796.C45 Chilena
1796.C47 Ch'ŏyongmu
1796.C57 Condición
1796.C6 Conga

Dance
Special dances, A-Z -- Continued

1796.C63 Conquista
1796.C64 Contràpas
1796.C68 Country swing
1796.C82 Cueca
1796.C84 Cumbia
1796.D34 Danza de las tijeras
1796.D57 Disco dancing
Cf. GV859.5 Roller disco
1796.E8 Escondido
1796.F28 Farandole
1796.F3 Farruca
1796.F35 Fātele
1796.F55 Flamenco. Cante hondo
1796.F6 Fox trot
1796.F7 Frevo
1796.H2 Halling
1796.H57 Hip-hop
1796.H72 Huapango
1796.H75 Huella
1796.H8 Hula
1796.H88 Hustle
1796.J37 Jarabe
1796.J6 Jitterbug
1796.J73 Jota
Kagura see BL2224.25.K3
1796.K34 Kanggang sullae
1796.K36 Karākaṭṭam
1796.K38 Kathak
1796.K58 Kōlāṭṭaṃ
1796.K6 Kolo
1796.K64 Kordax
1796.K7 Krakowiak
1796.K83 Kuchipudi
1796.L29 Ladjia
1796.L44 Lelê
1796.L5 Lindy
1796.M32 Manzai
1796.M33 Margamkali
1796.M336 Marinera
1796.M34 Mariquita
1796.M35 Matachines
1796.M36 Maxixe
Maypole see GT4945
1796.M45 Merengue
1796.M5 Minuet

Dance
Special dances, A-Z -- Continued

1796.M57 Moçambique
1796.M58 Mohiniyattom
1796.M7 Morris dance
1796.M87 Mussoll
1796.N33 Nācanī
1796.N4 Negritos
1796.N67 Nōrā
1796.O34 Odissi
1796.P24 Pajarillo
1796.P28 Pantsula
1796.P3 Pavan
1796.P46 Pinđin
1796.P49 Pla
1796.P54 Poi
1796.P55 Polka
1796.Q52 Quickstep
1796.Q54 Quilombo
1796.R25 Rāī
1796.R3 Rapper
1796.R6 Rock and roll
1796.R8 Rumba
1796.S23 Sajuriana
1796.S24 Salp'uri dance
1796.S245 Salsa
1796.S25 Samba
1796.S3 Sardana
1796.S39 Schuhplattler
1796.S395 Sega
1796.S45 Serimpi
1796.S5 Shag
1796.S54 Shishimai
1796.S57 Sinulog
1796.S85 Swing
1796.S9 Sword dance
1796.T17 Tambú
1796.T2 Tamunangue
1796.T3 Tango
1796.T32 Tarantella
1796.T47 Theyyam
1796.T62 Tondero
1796.T8 Turas
1796.T9 Two-step
Waltz see GV1761
1796.Z34 Zapin

Dance -- Continued
1797 Drills, parades, etc.
Cf. GV495 Marching (Calisthenics)
Gymnastic dancing. Rhythmic exercises
1798 General works
1798.5 Belly dancing
1798.6 Jazz exercise
1798.7 Pole dancing
Cf. PN1949.S7 Striptease
1798.8 Team aerobics
Dance for special classes of persons
1799 Children
1799.2 People with disabilities
1799.3 Older people
1799.4 Women
Circuses, spectacles, etc.
Circuses
1800 Periodicals. Societies. Serials
History
1801 General works
By region or country
1803 United States
1805.A-Z Other regions or countries, A-Z
1807 Museums. Exhibitions
1808 Vocational guidance
Biography
Including circus clowns
1811.A1 Collective
1811.A2-Z Individual, A-Z
e.g.
1811.B3 Barnum, P.T.
1811.F7 Fratellini Brothers
1811.H2 Hagenbeck, Carl
1815 General works
1816 Pictorial works
1817 Juvenile works
1818 Addresses, essays, lectures. Anecdotes. Humor.
Miscellanea
1819 Parades
1821.A-Z Individual circuses. Special shows, A-Z
Including circulars, programs, etc.
1821.A8 Astley's Royal Amphitheater of Arts
1821.B27 Barnum, P.T., firm
1821.B48 Big Apple Circus
1821.B78 Buckskin Ben's Wild West and Dog and Pony Show
1821.B8 Buffalo Bill's Wild West Show
1821.C46 Circo Bell's

Circuses, spectacles, etc.
Circuses
Individual circuses. Special shows, A-Z -- Continued

1821.C48 Circo di Paolo Rossi
1821.C52 Circo Garcia
1821.C525 Circul de Stat (Bucharest, Romania)
1821.C54 Circus Busch
1821.C56 Circus Roncalli
1821.C563 Circus Smirkus
1821.C564 Circus Strassburger
1821.C575 Cirque Bidon
1821.C577 Cirque d'Amiens
1821.C5773 Cirque d'Hiver
1821.C5777 Cirque royal (Brussels, Belgium)
1821.C578 Cirque du Soleil
1821.C58 Cirque Knie
1821.C584 Cirque Lamy
1821.C59 Cirque Pinder
1821.C6 Clyde Beatty-Cole Bros. Circus
1821.C7 Cristiani-Wallace Bros. Circus
1821.G72 Great Cole Younger and Frank James Historical Wild West (Show)
1821.G74 Great Wallenda Circus
1821.H3 Hagenbeck-Wallace Circus
1821.H69 Hoxie Brothers Circus
1821.J56 Jim Rose Circus Sideshow
1821.N38 National Pyongyang Circus
1821.P39 Pawnee Bill's Wild West (Show)
1821.P47 Pickle Family Circus
1821.R5 Ringling Brothers and Barnum and Bailey Circus
1821.S3 Schweizer Nationalcircus Knie
1821.S82 Staatszirkus der DDR
1821.T47 Théâtre Zingaro
1821.W65 Women's Circus (Footscray Community Arts Centre)
1821.Z5 Zirkus Nock

Equipment and supplies

1821.5 Costumes
1821.8 Tractors
1822 Trains
1823 Wagons

Management, conduct, etc.

1825 General works
1826 General special
1827 Collecting living animals for exhibition purposes
Cf. QL61+ Zoological specimens

1828 Clowning. Clown acts
For biography of clowns see GV1811.A+

Circuses, spectacles, etc.
Circuses -- Continued
Training of animals
Including stories about circus animals
1829 General works
1831.A-Z Special. By name of animal, A-Z
1831.B4 Bears
1831.C45 Chimpanzees
1831.D65 Dolphin
1831.E4 Elephants
1831.H8 Horse
1831.L5 Lions
1831.M65 Monkeys
1831.P6 Pigs
1831.S4 Sea lions
1831.S42 Seals
Racing of animals
1832 General works
1832.3 Bull racing
1832.4 Camel racing
Dog racing see SF439.5+
Horse racing see SF321+
1833 Wild West shows
For specific shows see GV1821.A+
Rodeos
Biography
1833.5 Collective
1833.6.A-Z Individual, A-Z
1834 General works
1834.3 Equipment and supplies
For special classes of persons
1834.4 Children
1834.43 Women
1834.45.A-Z Special events, A-Z
1834.45.B35 Barrel racing
1834.45.B75 Bronc riding
1834.45.B84 Bull riding
1834.45.C34 Calf roping
1834.45.P34 Pole bending
1834.45.S73 Steer wrestling
1834.45.T4 Team penning
1834.45.T42 Team roping
By region or country
United States
1834.5 General works

Circuses, spectacles, etc.
Rodeos
By region or country
United States -- Continued
1834.55.A-Z By region or state, A-Z
Under each state:
.x General works
.x2A-.x2Z Local, A-Z
1834.56.A-Z Other regions or countries, A-Z
Under each country:
.x General works
.x2A-.x2Z Local, A-Z
Carnivals. Side shows. Human abnormalities, wonders, etc.
Cf. QM690+ Teratology (Human anatomy)
Biography
1834.7 Collective
1834.72.A-Z Individual, A-Z
1835 General works
1835.2 Carnival games
1835.3.A-Z Individual carnivals, A-Z
By region or country
United States
1835.5 General works
1835.55.A-Z By region or state, A-Z
Under each state:
.x General works
.x2A-.x2Z Local, A-Z
1835.56.A-Z Other regions or countries, A-Z
Under each country:
.x General works
.x2A-.x2Z Local, A-Z
1836 Waxworks
e.g. Madame Tussaud's
Cf. NK9580+ Wax modeling
1838 Amateur circuses, carnivals, etc.
1839 Daredevils
Spectacles. "Son et lumière," etc.
For local history, see D-F
Cf. GT3925+ Festivals, carnivals, Mardi gras
Cf. PN3203+ Tableaux, pageants, "Happenings," etc. (Dramatic representation)
1841 General works
1843.A-Z Local. By city, A-Z
Amusement parks, amusement park resorts, etc.
1851.A3 Periodicals. Societies. Serials
1851.A35 History
1851.A4-Z General works

	Amusement parks, amusement park resorts, etc. -- Continued
	Biography
1852	Collective
1852.2.A-Z	Individual, A-Z
	By region or country
	United States
1853.2	General works
1853.3.A-Z	By region or state, A-Z *Under each state:* *.x* — *General works* *.x2A-.x2Z* — *Individual. By name, A-Z*
1853.4.A-Z	Other regions or countries, A-Z *Under each country:* *.x* — *General works* *.x2A-.x2Z* — *Individual. By name, A-Z*
	Amusement devices
1859	General works
1860.A-Z	Individual devices, A-Z
1860.F45	Ferris wheels
1860.M4	Merry-go-round
1860.R64	Roller coasters

Special category maps and atlases

Class here works which cannot be placed in any subject group but, because of special format or treatment, are to be separated from general maps and atlases

.A1 Outline and base maps. Plotting charts. Cities (Collective). Suburbs and city regions

e.g.

G3701.A1 Outline maps of the United States

G3704.A1 Cities and towns of the United States

G3804.N4A1 Suburbs, or area around New York City

.A15 Business districts, center, or downtown of cities

.A2 Index maps

Class here topographic map indexes only; class indexes of special subject maps with the subject, e.g. indexes to geological maps are classed in .C5

.A25 Digital cartographic materials

.A3 Aerial views. Bird's-eye view

.A35 Panoramas

.A4 Remote-sensing maps. Photomaps. Orthophotomaps. Pictomaps

.A43 Remote-sensing images

.A45 Anaglyphs and stereographs

.A5 Pictorial maps

.A6 Cartoon maps

.A63 Cartograms

.A67 Mental maps

.A7 Maps for the blind

.A8 Special geographical names

Class here works on place names of special historical, national, or religious significance, e.g. Christmas, Santa Claus, etc.

.A85 Biographical maps. Maps showing travels of individuals

Class maps showing special groups of people under the subject, e.g. actors are classified in G1 .E645

.A9 Special format

Class here postcards, business cards, placemats, games, mechanical devices, slides, transparencies, metal, stone, stationery, stick charts, fans, powder horns, clay tablets, cloth maps, glass, etc.

Mathematical geography

Class here works on aspects of cartography, surveying, and mapping

.B1 Astronomical observatories and observations

.B2 Movements of the earth

Including international date line, time zones

.B3 Geodetic surveys

Including triangulation networks, prime meridians, base-measuring

Mathematical geography -- Continued

.B5 Surveying. Extent of areas surveyed or mapped

.B52 Aerial photography. Status. Progress

.B7 Cartography

.B71 Globe gores

Class here pictures of globes or any two-dimensional representation of a globe

.B72 Projections

Class here maps whose purpose it is to illustrate a particular projection

.B8 Comparative area maps. Comparison diagrams

Class here works showing area comparisons by superimposition, distortion, etc., and composite drawings comparing mountain heights, river lengths, etc.

Physical sciences

Class here works on the distribution of natural phenomena of the earth, the atmosphere, and subsurface features

.C1 General

.C18 Relief models. Raised relief globes

.C2 Physiography. Geomorphology

Including relief features and bathymetry

.C21 Natural geographic regions. Geophysical divisions

.C23 Caves. Underground grottoes

.C28 Ground characteristics. Surface quality. Terrain studies. Slope

.C3 Hydrology. Hydrogeology

Cf. G1 .N44 Water utilities

.C31 Hydrographic surveys. Status. Progress

.C315 Drainage basins. Catchment areas

.C32 Floods

Cf. G1 .N22 Flood control

.C34 Ground water. Water table

.C35 Water composition and quality

.C36 Mineral waters

For spas, etc. see G1 .E635

.C37 Sea ice

.C38 Glaciers. Glaciology

Cf. G1 .C74 Icebergs

.C5 Geology

Cf. G1 .N24 Engineering geology

.C51 Geological surveys. Status. Progress

.C55 Dynamic and structural geology. Tectonics. Earthquakes (Seismology). Vulcanology

.C57 Stratigraphy and paleontology. Historical geology

.C58 Geochemistry

Physical sciences -- Continued

.C7 Oceanography

For characteristics and morphology of the ocean bottom see G1 .C2

For distribution of aquatic life see G1 .D1

For economic aspects of aquatic life see G1 .L1+

.C72 Temperature of ocean water

.C73 Salinity and density of ocean water

.C74 Icebergs

.C75 Ocean currents

.C76 Ocean tides

.C8 Meteorology and climatology. Climate classification systems

.C813 Climate regions

Class here works on climate zones, distribution of arid regions, deserts, permafrost areas, tundras, etc.

.C815 Weather forecasting

.C82 Atmospheric temperature

.C83 Insolation and radiation

.C84 Structure and mechanics of atmosphere. Atmospheric circulation. Wind systems

.C842 Atmospheric pressure. Surface winds

.C86 Storms

.C87 Atmospheric electricity

.C88 Atmospheric moisture and precipitation

.C882 Condensation. Dew. Fog. Frost. Cloud cover

.C883 Rain

.C884 Snow. Snowmelt

.C885 Hail

.C886 Droughts

.C887 Artificial precipitation. Rainmaking

.C9 Geophysics

.C92 Radioactivity

.C93 Terrestrial magnetism

.C95 Gravity

Biogeography

Class here works on the distribution of plant and animal life, exclusive of man and economic activities

.D1 General

Cf. G1 .L1+ Aquatic biological resources

.D2 Plant geography. Botany. Vegetation

.D4 Animal geography. Zoogeography

Including birds, insects, fish, etc.

For sport fishing and hunting see G1 .E63

.D5 Wildlife conservation and reserves. Wildlife refuges

Cf. G1 .G3 Conservation (General)

Human and cultural geography. Anthropogeography. Human ecology
Class here works that are concerned with man as a physical and social being

.E1 General
Including ethnology, tribes, ethnic groups, etc.
.E15 Archaeological sites. Cities and towns which are ruined, extinct, etc.
.E2 Population
.E24 Vital statistics. Population increase and decrease. Birth control
.E25 Statistical areas. Census tracts
.E27 Movement of population (Voluntary)
Class here works on emigration, immigration, nomadism, tribal migration, transhumance, etc.
.E272 Regulation. Quotas
.E29 Demographic aspects of disasters
For technical aspects, see special fields, e.g. G1 .C55 Earthquakes; G1 .C32 Floods; G1 .E59 Famine; etc.
.E3 Languages. Ethnolinguistics
.E4 Religions
.E42 Christianity
.E423 Ecclesiastical organizations, sects, denominations, administrative areas, etc.
.E424 Missions
.E43 Judaism
.E44 Islam
.E45 Hinduism
.E452 Brahmanism
.E47 Buddhism
.E5 Medical geography
.E51 Diseases
.E52 Medical professions
.E55 Public health
.E58 Hospitals. Clinics. Dispensaries
.E59 Nutrition. Malnutrition. Famine
Cf. G1 .E29 Disasters
.E6 Social and cultural geography. Civilizations
.E62 Customs and folklore
.E622 Social customs (Social and ethnic aspects). Eating and drinking habits. Clothing
For technical and industrial aspects see G1 .M1+
.E6225 Genealogy. Families
.E623 Heraldry
.E624 Social organizations

TABLES

Human and cultural geography. Anthropogeography. Human ecology

Social and cultural geography. Civilizations

Customs and folklore -- Continued

.E625 Social problems

Class here works on problems arising from the interplay of social forces, e.g. crime, narcotics traffic, slavery, race relations, school integration efforts, efforts at revamping educational systems, confrontations, demonstrations, etc.

.E627 Folklore. Mythology

.E628 Astrology

.E63 Recreation. Sports

Including recreational trails and specific recreational activities, e.g. hiking, camping, hunting, fishing, etc.

Class individual trails as geographic features

For historic trails see G1 .P25

.E635 Tourist maps. Tourism

.E64 Intellectual and aesthetic life. The arts

.E642 Crafts. Special interests. Hobbies

.E644 Architecture

.E645 Theaters. Drama. Motion pictures

.E646 Music

.E648 Painting and sculpture

.E65 Literature

.E655 Museums

.E67 Libraries

Class here works on the location and distribution of libraries, those outlining library area classification schemes, etc.

.E68 Education

.E7 Material culture

.E73 Housing. Shelter

Cf. G1 .E644 Architecture

.E74 Income. Income tax

.E75 Treasure troves

Cf. G1 .P57 Wreck charts

.E9 Slavery

Political geography

Class here works on boundaries, administrative and political divisions, sovereignty, spheres of influence, and national aspirations

.F1 General

.F2 International boundaries

.F3 Sovereignty

Class here works on occupation zones, occupied territories, territorial waters, etc.

.F33 Colonial possessions

.F35 Territorial expansion

Political geography
Sovereignty -- Continued
.F37 Flags. Military colors
.F5 International relations
Class here works on treaty enforcements, international cooperation (League of Nations, United Nations, Atlantic Pact, Marshall Plan, etc.)
.F55 Diplomatic and consular service
Class here works on location of embassies, legations, consulates, etc.
.F7 Administrative and political divisions
Class here works on political subdivisions, minor civil divisions of a political jurisdiction, congressional districts, and election districts
For courts and judicial divisions see G1 .F85
.F8 Government
.F81 Forms of government
Class here works on the distribution of governing systems within a given area
Departments, agencies, bureaus, commissions
see G1 .F7 or appropriate topical subdivision
.F85 Laws and law enforcement
Class here works on the location of courts, judicial divisions, penal institutions, legal societies, etc.
.F86 Concentration camps. Detention centers, etc.
.F9 Political campaigns. Election results. Votes in legislature. Political results
Economic geography
For works on the economic geography of the specialized fields of mines and minerals, agriculture, forests and forestry, fisheries, manufactures and processing, technology, engineering, public works, transportation and communication, and commerce and trade see subdivisions .H through .Q
.G1 General. Economic conditions
.G15 Economic planning
Cf. G1 .G45 Planning
.G16 Economic cycles. Business cycles
.G17 Economic assistance (Domestic)
For international economic assistance see G1 .F5
.G2 Economic regions. Economic spheres of influence
.G3 Natural resources. Conservation (General)
Cf. G1 .D4 Wildlife conservation and reserves
Cf. G1 .J4 Soil conservation
Cf. G1 .K3 Forest conservation
.G4 Land. Land use. Land capabilities and classification
.G44 Zoning

TABLES

Economic geography
Land. Land use. Land capabilities and classification -- Continued
.G45 Planning
Cf. G1 .G15 Economic planning
.G455 Urban renewal
.G46 Cadastral maps. Land ownership. Real property
.G465 Land grants
.G47 Real property tax. Tax assessment
For income tax see G1 .E74
.G475 Insurance. Fire protection
Class here works showing data specifically useful in determining fire and other property rates, etc.
.G5 Public lands
.G52 Parks and monuments
Class here works on cultural and historic monuments, parks, zoos, etc.
Individual parks are classed as regions
Cf. G1 .D5 Wildlife conservation and reserves
Cf. G1 .K1 Forests
.G54 Cemeteries
.G6 Ethnic reservations
.G7 Business and professional organizations
.G8 Labor
Class here works on the distribution of the labor force or individual skills, labor relations, employment, strikes, unions, etc.
Mines and mineral resources
Including mineral rights and leases
For "Rock hound guides" see G1 .E63
.H1 General
.H2 Metallic group
.H5 Nonmetallic group
Including works on hydrocarbons (General), e.g. coal and petroleum
.H8 Petroleum and natural gas
.H9 Coal. Lignite. Peat
Agriculture
.J1 General. Agricultural regions
.J15 Agricultural economics. Economic aspects of agriculture
.J2 Systems of agriculture. Agricultural methods. Farming techniques
.J3 Soils. Soil classification. Soil capability and utilization
Cf. G1 .N26 Soil mechanics

Agriculture -- Continued

.J4 Soil conservation. Reclamation. Irrigation. Erosion

Cf. G1 .C3 Hydrology

Cf. G1 .G4 Conservation (General)

Cf. G1 .N22 Flood control

.J48 Fertilizers

.J5 Animal husbandry. Livestock

.J6 Crops

.J61 Cereals

.J67 Forage crops. Legumes

.J7 Vegetables

.J73 Fruits. Nuts

.J77 Sugar and starch

Class here works on the distribution of crops specifically cultivated for the production of sugar and starch

.J8 Industrial agricultural products

.J82 Cordage and textile fibers

Including cotton, flax, hemp, etc.

.J84 Rubber, gum, and resin products

.J9 Other plants

.J912 Beverage plants

Including coffee, tea, etc.

.J92 Medicinal plants

.J93 Spices. Condiments

.J94 Tobacco

.J95 Floriculture. Nurseries

Forests and foresty

.K1 General

.K2 Distribution of forest areas and forest types

Class individual forests as regions

.K3 Conservation. Reforestation. Afforestation

Cf. G1 .G3 Conservation (General)

.K4 Silviculture. Tree farms

.K5 Agents of forest destruction. Forest fires

.K6 Lumbering. Exploitation

Cf. G1 .M4 Wood processing and manufacture

Aquatic biological resources

Class here works on the economic aspects of aquatic life, including aquatic vegetation, aquaculture, and pelagic mammals

.L1 General

For hunting or fishing as a recreational activity see G1 .E63

Cf. G1 .D1+ Plant and animal distribution

.L2 Fishing and fisheries. Fish hatcheries. Sea animal products

.L4 Aquatic vegetation. Aquaculture

.L5 Pelagic mammals. Sealing. Whaling

Manufacturing and processing. Service industries

.M1 General

TABLES

Manufacturing and processing. Service industries -- Continued

.M2 Mineral processing and manufacture

.M3 Chemical processing and manufacture

.M4 Wood processing and manufacture

.M5 Paper processing and manufacture

.M6 Fiber, textile, and hide processing and manufacture

.M8 Food and beverage processing and manufacture

.M9 Transport equipment manufacture

.M95 Service industries

Technology. Engineering. Public works

.N1 General

Including inventions

.N18 Engineering

.N2 Hydraulic engineering. Dams

Class individual dams as geographic features

.N22 Flood control

.N23 Civil engineering. Building and construction. Building materials

.N24 Engineering geology

Class here works showing distribution of geologic characteristics of an area as they relate to capabilities for, or limitations on, construction activity

.N26 Soil mechanics. Soil engineering

Class here works showing the distribution of soil characteristics as they relate to capabilities for, or limitations on, construction activity

.N3 Power

.N32 Steam. Geothermal steam sources. Thermoelectric power generation

.N33 Water power. Hydroelectric power generation

.N34 Wind power. Aeroelectric power generation

.N35 Nuclear power. Magnetohydrodynamics

Cf. G1 .C92 Radioactivity

.N36 Solar power

.N39 Utilities

.N4 Electric utilities. Service areas. Power lines

.N42 Gas utilities

.N44 Water utilities. Water storage, distribution, and purification plants

Cf. G1 .C3 Hydrology

.N46 Sewerage. Waste disposal

.N85 Pollution and pollution control

.N852 Air pollution

.N854 Pollution of land

Including soil pollution, despoliation of the land by billboards and by the accumulation of refuse such as abandoned motor vehicles, etc.

Technology. Engineering. Public works
Pollution and pollution control -- Continued
.N856 Water pollution
.N858 Noise pollution
Transportation and communication
.P1 General
.P15 Distances
.P19 Trafficability. Traffic feasibility surveys
.P2 Roads
For soil characteristics affecting road construction see G1 .N26
.P21 Traffic surveys
.P22 Bus routes. Truck routes
.P23 Traffic and parking regulations
.P24 Bridges and tunnels
.P25 Trails (Historic)
Class individual trails as geographic features
For scenic and recreational trails see G1 .E63
.P3 Railroads
.P33 Urban and interurban railroads
Including elevated railroads, street railways, trams, subways, etc.
.P4 Pipe lines
.P5 Water transportation. Nautical charts. Pilot charts
Class individual canals, lakes, etc. as geographic features
.P53 Inland waterways
Class here works on navigable lakes, rivers, canals, and protected inshore channels
.P54 Ocean routes. Shipping lines. Load line charts
.P55 Ports and port facilities
.P57 Wreck charts
Cf. G1 .E75 Treasure troves
.P58 Electronic navigation charts
Class here Consol, Decca, Loran, and other hyperbolic navigation charts
For regular chart series with electronic lattice overprints see .P5 and .P6
.P6 Air transportation. Aeronautical charts
.P61 Airports, landing fields, etc.
.P62 Air routes
.P7 Space transportation
.P75 Satellite tracks, etc.
.P78 Other transportation systems
Including conveyor belts, cable ways
.P8 Postal service. Postal zones. Zip codes
.P9 Communications
.P92 Telegraph

TABLES

Transportation and communication
Communications -- Continued
.P93 Submarine cables
.P94 Telephone. Area codes
.P95 Radio
.P96 Television
.P97 Dissemination of information. The press. Printing. Propaganda. Public opinion
Commerce and trade. Finance
.Q1 General
.Q2 Business statistics
.Q3 Movement of commodities
Class here works on trade routes, caravan routes, etc.
For maps and atlases which emphasize the carrier and show specific routes see G1 .P1+
Cf. G1 .Q5 Tariffs and other trade barriers
.Q4 Marketing
.Q42 Trade centers and trading areas
.Q44 Shopping centers. Shopping malls
.Q46 Retail sales outlets
.Q48 Fairs, exhibitions, etc.
Class individual fairs and exhibitions as regions, e.g. New York World's Fair, and Transpo '72
.Q5 Tariffs and other trade barriers
.Q8 Finance
Class here works on coins and currencies, foreign exchange credit, special types of financial institutions, individual financial firms, etc.
Military and naval geography
.R1 General
.R2 Military and naval districts and establishments. Troop disposition
.R22 Air Force
.R24 Army
.R26 Coast Guard
.R28 Navy
.R282 Marine Corps
.R3 Military operations. Strategy and tactics. War games
.R4 Defenses. Fortifications
.R5 Logistics
Class here works on military support systems, munitions, lines of communication, etc.
.R6 Civil defense

Historical geography

Class here maps and atlases that portray specific historical events, including disposition of troops, battle lines, or a series of events

A map or atlas, either contemporary or reconstructed, which gives only general geographical information about an area at the time of a given event or series of events is treated without subject subdivision

A chronological subdivision for an area, based on its own history, is to be preferred to any universal arrangement except that the following Cutter numbers are to remain constant throughout the schedule:

For examples of such arrangements, see G3201.S World history, and G3701.S United States history

.S1 General

.S12 Discovery and exploration

.S65 World War I

.S7 World War II

TABLES

Special category maps and atlases
Class here works which cannot be placed in any subject group but, because of special format or treatment, are to be separated from general maps and atlases

.A1 Outline and base maps. Plotting charts. Cities (Collective). Suburbs and city regions
e.g.
G3701.A1 Outline maps of the United States
G3704.A1 Cities and towns of the United States
G3804.N4A1 Suburbs, or area around New York City

.A15 Business districts, center, or downtown of cities

.A2 Index maps
Class here topographic map indexes only; class indexes of special subject maps with the subject, e.g. indexes to geological maps are classed in .C5

.A25 Digital cartographic materials

.A3 Aerial views. Bird's-eye view

.A35 Panoramas

.A4 Remote-sensing maps. Photomaps. Orthophotomaps. Pictomaps

.A43 Remote-sensing images

.A45 Anaglyphs and stereographs

.A5 Pictorial maps

.A6 Cartoon maps

.A63 Cartograms

.A67 Mental maps

.A7 Maps for the blind

.A8 Special geographical names
Class here works on place names of special historical, national, or religious significance, e.g. Christmas, Santa Claus, etc.

.A85 Biographical maps. Maps showing travels of individuals
Class maps showing special groups of people under the subject, e.g. actors are classified in G1a .E645

.A9 Special format
Class here postcards, business cards, placemats, games, mechanical devices, slides, transparencies, metal, stone, stationery, stick charts, fans, powder horns, clay tablets, cloth maps, glass, etc.

Mathematical geography
Class here works on aspects of cartography, surveying, and mapping

.B1 Astronomical observatories and observations

.B2 Movements of the earth
Including international date line, time zones

.B3 Geodetic surveys
Including triangulation networks, prime meridians, base-measuring

Mathematical geography -- Continued

.B5 Surveying. Extent of areas surveyed or mapped

.B52 Aerial photography. Status. Progress

.B7 Cartography

.B71 Globe gores

Class here pictures of globes or any two-dimensional representation of a globe

.B72 Projections

Class here maps whose purpose it is to illustrate a particular projection

.B8 Comparative area maps. Comparison diagrams

Class here works showing area comparisons by superimposition, distortion, etc., and composite drawings comparing mountain heights, river lengths, etc.

Physical sciences

Class here works on the distribution of natural phenomena of the earth, the atmosphere, and subsurface features

.C1 General

.C18 Relief models. Raised relief globes

.C2 Physiography. Geomorphology

Including relief features and bathymetry

.C21 Natural geographic regions. Geophysical divisions

.C23 Caves. Underground grottoes

.C28 Ground characteristics. Surface quality. Terrain studies. Slope

.C3 Hydrology. Hydrogeology

Cf. G1a .N44 Water utilities

.C31 Hydrographic surveys. Status. Progress

.C315 Drainage basins. Catchment areas

.C32 Floods

Cf. G1a .N22 Flood control

.C34 Ground water. Water table

.C35 Water composition and quality

.C36 Mineral waters

For spas, etc. see G1a .E635

.C37 Sea ice

.C38 Glaciers. Glaciology

Cf. G1a .C74 Icebergs

.C5 Geology

Cf. G1a .N24 Engineering geology

.C51 Geological surveys. Status. Progress

.C55 Dynamic and structural geology. Tectonics. Earthquakes (Seismology). Vulcanology

.C57 Stratigraphy and paleontology. Historical geology

.C58 Geochemistry

Physical sciences -- Continued
.C7 Oceanography
For characteristics and morphology of the ocean bottom see G1a .C2
For distribution of aquatic life see G1a .D1
For economic aspects of aquatic life see G1a .L1+
.C72 Temperature of ocean water
.C73 Salinity and density of ocean water
.C74 Icebergs
.C75 Ocean currents
.C76 Ocean tides
.C8 Meteorology and climatology. Climate classification systems
.C813 Climate regions
Class here works on climate zones, distribution of arid regions, deserts, permafrost areas, tundras, etc.
.C815 Weather forecasting
.C82 Atmospheric temperature
.C83 Insolation and radiation
.C84 Structure and mechanics of atmosphere. Atmospheric circulation. Wind systems
.C842 Atmospheric pressure. Surface winds
.C86 Storms
.C87 Atmospheric electricity
.C88 Atmospheric moisture and precipitation
.C882 Condensation. Dew. Fog. Frost. Cloud cover
.C883 Rain
.C884 Snow. Snowmelt
.C885 Hail
.C886 Droughts
.C887 Artificial precipitation. Rainmaking
.C9 Geophysics
.C92 Radioactivity
.C93 Terrestrial magnetism
.C95 Gravity
Biogeography
Class here works on the distribution of plant and animal life, exclusive of man and economic activities
.D1 General
Cf. G1a .L1+ Aquatic biological resources
.D2 Plant geography. Botany. Vegetation
.D4 Animal geography. Zoogeography
Including birds, insects, fish, etc.
For sport fishing and hunting see G1a .E63
.D5 Wildlife conservation and reserves. Wildlife refuges
Cf. G1a .G3 Conservation (General)

Human and cultural geography. Anthropogeography. Human ecology
Class here works that are concerned with man as a physical and social being
.E1 General
Including ethnology, tribes, ethnic groups, etc.
.E15 Archaeological sites. Cities and towns that are ruined, extinct, etc.
.E2 Population
.E24 Vital statistics. Population increase and decrease. Birth control
.E25 Statistical areas. Census tracts
.E27 Movement of population (Voluntary)
Class here works on emigration, immigration, nomadism, tribal migration, transhumance, etc.
.E272 Regulation. Quotas
.E29 Demographic aspects of disasters
For technical aspects, see special fields, e.g. G1a .C55 Earthquakes; G1a .C32 Floods; G1a .E59, Famine; etc.
.E3 Languages. Ethnolinguistics
.E4 Religions
.E42 Christianity
.E423 Ecclesiastical organizations, sects, denominations, administrative areas, etc.
.E424 Missions
.E43 Judaism
.E44 Islam
.E45 Hinduism
.E452 Brahmanism
.E47 Buddhism
.E5 Medical geography
.E51 Diseases
.E52 Medical professions
.E55 Public health
.E58 Hospitals. Clinics. Dispensaries
.E59 Nutrition. Malnutrition. Famine
Cf. G1a .E29 Disasters
.E6 Social and cultural geography. Civilizations
.E62 Customs and folklore
.E622 Social customs (Social and ethnic aspects). Eating and drinking habits. Clothing
For technical and industrial aspects see G1a .M1+
.E6225 Genealogy. Families
.E623 Heraldry
.E624 Social organizations

TABLES

Human and cultural geography. Anthropogeography. Human ecology
Social and cultural geography. Civilizations
Customs and folklore -- Continued
.E625 Social problems
Class here works on problems arising from the interplay of social forces, e.g. crime, narcotics traffic, slavery, race relations, school integration efforts, efforts at revamping educational systems, confrontations, demonstrations, etc.
.E627 Folklore. Mythology
.E628 Astrology
.E63 Recreation. Sports
Including recreational trails and specific recreational activities, e.g. hiking, camping, hunting, fishing, etc.
Class individual trails as geographic features
For historic trails see G1a .P25
.E635 Tourist maps. Tourism
.E64 Intellectual and aesthetic life. The arts
.E642 Crafts. Special interests. Hobbies
.E644 Architecture
.E645 Theaters. Drama. Motion pictures
.E646 Music
.E648 Painting and sculpture
.E65 Literature
.E655 Museums
.E67 Libraries
Class here works on the location and distribution of libraries, those outlining library area classification schemes, etc.
.E68 Education
.E7 Material culture
.E73 Housing. Shelter
Cf. G1a .E644 Architecture
.E74 Income. Income tax
.E75 Treasure troves
Cf. G1a .P57 Wreck charts
.E9 Slavery
Political geography
Class here works on boundaries, administrative and political divisions, sovereignty, spheres of influence, and national aspirations
.F1 General
.F2 International boundaries
.F3 Sovereignty
Class here works on occupation zones, occupied territories, territorial waters, etc.
.F33 Colonial possessions
.F35 Territorial expansion

Political geography
Sovereignty -- Continued
.F37 Flags. Military colors
.F5 International relations
Class here works on treaty enforcements, international cooperation (League of Nations, United Nations, Atlantic Pact, Marshall Plan, etc.)
.F55 Diplomatic and consular service
Class here works on location of embassies, legations, consulates, etc.
.F7 Administrative and political divisions
Class here works on political subdivisions, minor civil divisions of a political jurisdiction, congressional districts, and election districts
For courts and judicial divisions see G1a .F85
.F8 Government
.F81 Forms of government
Class here works on the distribution of governing systems within a given area
Departments, agencies, bureaus, commissions
see G1a .F7 or appropriate topical subdivision
.F85 Laws and law enforcement
Class here works on the location of courts, judicial divisions, penal institutions, legal societies, etc.
.F86 Concentration camps. Detention centers, etc.
.F9 Political campaigns. Election results. Votes in legislature. Political results
Economic geography
For works on the economic geography of the specialized fields of mines and minerals, agriculture, forests and forestry, fisheries, manufactures and processing, technology, engineering, public works, transportation and communication, and commerce and trade see subdivisions .H through .Q
.G1 General. Economic conditions
.G15 Economic planning
Cf. G1a .G45 Planning
.G16 Economic cycles. Business cycles
.G17 Economic assistance (Domestic)
For international economic assistance see G1a .F5
.G2 Economic regions. Economic spheres of influence
.G3 Natural resources. Conservation (General)
Cf. G1a .D4 Wildlife conservation and reserves
Cf. G1a .J4 Soil conservation
Cf. G1a .K3 Forest conservation
.G4 Land. Land use. Land capabilities and classification
.G44 Zoning

TABLES

Economic geography
Land. Land use. Land capabilities and classification -- Continued
.G45 Planning
Cf. G1a .G15 Economic planning
.G455 Urban renewal
.G46 Cadastral maps. Land ownership. Real property
.G465 Land grants
.G47 Real property tax. Tax assessment
For income tax see G1a .E74
.G475 Insurance. Fire protection
Class here works showing data specifically useful in determining fire and other property rates, etc.
.G5 Public lands
.G52 Parks and monuments
Class here works on cultural and historic monuments, parks, zoos, etc.
Individual parks are classed as regions
Cf. G1a .D5 Wildlife conservation and reserves
Cf. G1a .K1 Forests
.G54 Cemeteries
.G6 Ethnic reservations
.G7 Business and professional organizations
.G8 Labor
Class here works on the distribution of the labor force or individual skills, labor relations, employment, strikes, unions, etc.
Mines and mineral resources
Including mineral rights and leases
For "Rock hound guides" see G1a .E63
.H1 General
.H2 Metallic group
.H5 Nonmetallic group
Including works on hydrocarbons (General), e.g. coal and petroleum
.H8 Petroleum and natural gas
.H9 Coal. Lignite. Peat
Agriculture
.J1 General. Agricultural regions
.J15 Agricultural economics. Economic aspects of agriculture
.J2 Systems of agriculture. Agricultural methods. Farming techniques
.J3 Soils. Soil classification. Soil capability and utilization
Cf. G1a .N26 Soil mechanics

Agriculture -- Continued

.J4 Soil conservation. Reclamation. Irrigation. Erosion

Cf. G1a .C3 Hydrology

Cf. G1a .G4 Conservation (General)

Cf. G1a .N22 Flood control

.J48 Fertilizers

.J5 Animal husbandry. Livestock

.J6 Crops

.J61 Cereals

.J67 Forage crops. Legumes

.J7 Vegetables

.J73 Fruits. Nuts

.J77 Sugar and starch

Class here works on the distribution of crops specifically cultivated for the production of sugar and starch

.J8 Industrial agricultural products

.J82 Cordage and textile fibers

Including cotton, flax, hemp, etc.

.J84 Rubber, gum, and resin products

.J9 Other plants

.J912 Beverage plants

Including coffee, tea, etc.

.J92 Medicinal plants

.J93 Spices. Condiments

.J94 Tobacco

.J95 Floriculture. Nurseries

Forests and foresty

.K1 General

.K2 Distribution of forest areas and forest types

Class individual forests as regions

.K3 Conservation. Reforestation. Afforestation

Cf. G1a .G3 Conservation (General)

.K4 Silviculture. Tree farms

.K5 Agents of forest destruction. Forest fires

.K6 Lumbering. Exploitation

Cf. G1a .M4 Wood processing and manufacture

Aquatic biological resources

Class here works on the economic aspects of aquatic life, including aquatic vegetation, aquaculture, and pelagic mammals

.L1 General

For hunting or fishing as a recreational activity see G1a .E63

Cf. G1a .D1+ Plant and animal distribution

.L2 Fishing and fisheries. Fish hatcheries. Sea animal products

.L4 Aquatic vegetation. Aquaculture

.L5 Pelagic mammals. Sealing. Whaling

Manufacturing and processing. Service industries

.M1 General

TABLES

Manufacturing and processing. Service industries -- Continued

.M2 Mineral processing and manufacture
.M3 Chemical processing and manufacture
.M4 Wood processing and manufacture
.M5 Paper processing and manufacture
.M6 Fiber, textile, and hide processing and manufacture
.M8 Food and beverage processing and manufacture
.M9 Transport equipment manufacture
.M95 Service industries

Technology. Engineering. Public works

.N1 General
Including inventions
.N18 Engineering
.N2 Hydraulic engineering. Dams
Class individual dams as geographic features
.N22 Flood control
.N23 Civil engineering. Building and construction. Building materials
.N24 Engineering geology
Class here works showing distribution of geologic characteristics of an area as they relate to capabilities for, or limitations on, construction activity
.N26 Soil mechanics. Soil engineering
Class here works showing the distribution of soil characteristics as they relate to capabilities for, or limitations on, construction activity
.N3 Power
.N32 Steam. Geothermal steam sources. Thermoelectric power generation
.N33 Water power. Hydroelectric power generation
.N34 Wind power. Aeroelectric power generation
.N35 Nuclear power. Magnetohydrodynamics
Cf. G1a .C92 Radioactivity
.N36 Solar power
.N39 Utilities
.N4 Electric utilities. Service areas. Power lines
.N42 Gas utilities
.N44 Water utilities. Water storage, distribution, and purification plants
Cf. G1a .C3 Hydrology
.N46 Sewerage. Waste disposal
.N85 Pollution and pollution control
.N852 Air pollution
.N854 Pollution of land
Including soil pollution, despoliation of the land by billboards and by the accumulation of refuse such as abandoned motor vehicles, etc.

Technology. Engineering. Public works
Pollution and pollution control -- Continued
.N856 Water pollution
.N858 Noise pollution
Transportation and communication
.P1 General
.P15 Distances
.P19 Trafficability. Traffic feasibility surveys
.P2 Roads
For soil characteristics affecting road construction see G1a .N26
.P21 Traffic surveys
.P22 Bus routes. Truck routes
.P23 Traffic and parking regulations
.P24 Bridges and tunnels
.P25 Trails (Historic)
Class individual trails as geographic features
For scenic and recreational trails see G1a .E63
.P3 Railroads
.P33 Urban and interurban railroads
Including elevated railroads, street railways, trams, subways, etc.
.P4 Pipe lines
.P5 Water transportation. Nautical charts. Pilot charts
Class individual canals, lakes, etc. as geographic features
.P53 Inland waterways
Class here works on navigable lakes, rivers, canals, and protected inshore channels
.P54 Ocean routes. Shipping lines. Load line charts
.P55 Ports and port facilities
.P57 Wreck charts
Cf. G1a .E75 Treasure troves
.P58 Electronic navigation charts
Class here Consol, Decca, Loran, and other hyperbolic navigation charts
For regular chart series with electronic lattice overprints see .P5 and .P6
.P6 Air transportation. Aeronautical charts
.P61 Airports, landing fields, etc.
.P62 Air routes
.P7 Space transportation
.P75 Satellite tracks, etc.
.P78 Other transportation systems
Including conveyor belts, cable ways
.P8 Postal service. Postal zones. Zip codes
.P9 Communications
.P92 Telegraph

Transportation and communication
Communications -- Continued
.P93 Submarine cables
.P94 Telephone. Area codes
.P95 Radio
.P96 Television
.P97 Dissemination of information. The press. Printing. Propaganda. Public opinion
Commerce and trade. Finance
.Q1 General
.Q2 Business statistics
.Q3 Movement of commodities
Class here works on trade routes, caravan routes, etc.
For maps and atlases which emphasize the carrier and show specific routes see G1a .P1+
Cf. G1a .Q5 Tariffs and other trade barriers
.Q4 Marketing
.Q42 Trade centers and trading areas
.Q44 Shopping centers. Shopping malls
.Q46 Retail sales outlets
.Q48 Fairs, exhibitions, etc.
Class individual fairs and exhibitions as regions, e.g. New York World's Fair, and Transpo '72
.Q5 Tariffs and other trade barriers
.Q8 Finance
Class here works on coins and currencies, foreign exchange credit, special types of financial institutions, individual financial firms, etc.
Military and naval geography
.R1 General
.R2 Military and naval districts and establishments. Troop disposition
.R22 Air Force
.R24 Army
.R26 Coast Guard
.R28 Navy
.R282 Marine Corps
.R3 Military operations. Strategy and tactics. War games
.R4 Defenses. Fortifications
.R5 Logistics
Class here works on military support systems, munitions, lines of communication, etc.
.R6 Civil defense
History
.S1 General
.S12 Discovery and exploration
Including exploration of the West

History -- Continued
.S2 Colonial period
.S26 French and Indian War, 1755-1763
.S3 Revolution, 1775-1783
.S4 1783-1865
.S42 War of 1812
.S44 Mexican War, 1845-1848
.S5 Civil War, 1861-1865
.S55 1865-1900
.S57 Spanish American War, 1898
.S6 1900-1945
.S65 World War I
.S7 World War II
.S73 1945-

0.112	America
0.115	North America
	United States
0.12	General works
0.13.A-Z	By region or state, A-Z
0.15	Canada
0.155	Latin America
0.16	Mexico
	Central America
0.17	General works
0.18	Belize. British Honduras
0.19	Costa Rica
0.2	Guatemala
0.21	Nicaragua
0.215	Panama
0.22	El Salvador
	West Indies
0.23	General works
0.24	Bahamas
0.25	Cuba
0.26	Haiti
0.27	Jamaica
0.28	Puerto Rico
0.29.A-Z	Other islands, A-Z
	South America
0.3	General works
0.31	Argentina
0.32	Bolivia
0.33	Brazil
0.34	Chile
0.35	Colombia
0.36	Ecuador
0.365	French Guiana
0.37	Guyana
0.38	Paraguay
0.39	Peru
0.395	Suriname
0.4	Uruguay
0.41	Venezuela
	Europe
0.42	General works
0.425.A-Z	Special regions, international bodies of water, A-Z
	Great Britain
0.43	General works
0.44	England
0.45	Scotland

	Europe
	Great Britain -- Continued
0.46	Northern Ireland
0.465	Wales
0.467	Ireland
0.47	Austria
	Belgium see G2a 0.53
	Denmark see G2a 0.57
0.48	France
0.49	Germany
	Including West Germany
0.495	East Germany
0.5	Greece
0.51	Italy
	Low Countries
0.52	General works
0.53	Belgium
0.54	Netherlands
	Norway see G2a 0.59
0.55	Russia. Soviet Union. Russia (Federation)
	Cf. G2a 0.79 Russia in Asia. Soviet Union in Asia. Siberia
	Scandinavia
0.56	General works
0.57	Denmark
0.58	Iceland
0.59	Norway
0.6	Sweden
0.61	Spain
0.62	Portugal
	Sweden see G2a 0.6
0.63	Switzerland
	Balkan States
0.635	General works
0.65	Bulgaria
0.66	Romania
0.67	Yugoslavia
0.68.A-Z	Other divisions of Europe, A-Z
	Asia
0.69	General works
0.7	China
0.71	India
	Southeast Asia
0.72	General works
0.73	Vietnam
0.74	Indonesia
0.76	Philippines

TABLES

	Asia -- Continued
0.77	Japan
0.78	Iran
0.79	Russia in Asia. Soviet Union in Asia. Siberia
0.795	Taiwan
0.8	Turkey. Asia Minor
0.81.A-Z	Other divisions of Asia, A-Z
0.813	Arab countries
0.815	Indian Ocean
	Africa
0.82	General works
0.83	Egypt
0.84	South Africa
0.85	Algeria
0.86	Tanzania
0.87	Angola
0.88.A-Z	Other African divisions, A-Z
	e.g.
0.88.E7	Ethiopia
0.88.Z3	Congo (Democratic Republic). Zaire
0.88.Z36	Zambia
	Atlantic Ocean Islands
0.883	General works
0.8835.A-Z	Individual islands and island groups, A-Z
	West Indies see G2a 0.23+
	Indian Ocean Islands
0.884	General works
0.8845.A-Z	Individual islands and island groups, A-Z
0.885	Pacific Ocean
0.89	Australia
0.91	New Zealand
	Pacific Islands
0.97	General works
0.98.A-Z	Individual islands and island groups, A-Z
0.985	Tropics
	Arctic regions
0.99	General works
0.993	Greenland
0.995	Antarctic regions

0.112	America
	Class here works on the countries of the Western Hemisphere collectively. For works on an individual country, see the number or numbers for the country
0.115	North America
	Class here works on the countries of North America collectively. For works on an individual country, see the number or numbers for the country
0.15	Canada
0.155	Latin America
0.16	Mexico
	Central America
0.17	General works
0.18	Belize. British Honduras
0.19	Costa Rica
0.2	Guatemala
0.21	Nicaragua
0.215	Panama
0.22	El Salvador
	West Indies
0.23	General works
0.24	Bahamas
0.25	Cuba
0.26	Haiti
0.27	Jamaica
0.28	Puerto Rico
0.29.A-Z	Other islands, A-Z
	South America
0.3	General works
0.31	Argentina
0.32	Bolivia
0.33	Brazil
0.34	Chile
0.35	Colombia
0.36	Ecuador
0.365	French Guiana
0.37	Guyana
0.38	Paraguay
0.39	Peru
0.395	Suriname
0.4	Uruguay
0.41	Venezuela
	Europe
0.42	General works
0.425.A-Z	Special regions, international bodies of water, A-Z
	Great Britain

TABLES

	Europe
	Great Britain -- Continued
0.43	General works
0.44	England
0.45	Scotland
0.46	Northern Ireland
0.465	Wales
0.467	Ireland
0.47	Austria
	Belgium see G2b 0.53
	Denmark see G2b 0.57
0.48	France
0.49	Germany
	Including West Germany
0.495	East Germany
0.5	Greece
0.51	Italy
	Low Countries
0.52	General works
0.53	Belgium
0.54	Netherlands
	Norway see G2b 0.59
0.55	Russia. Soviet Union. Russia (Federation)
	Cf. G2b 0.79 Russia in Asia. Soviet Union in Asia. Siberia
	Scandinavia
0.56	General works
0.57	Denmark
0.58	Iceland
0.59	Norway
0.6	Sweden
0.61	Spain
0.62	Portugal
	Sweden see G2b 0.6
0.63	Switzerland
	Balkan States
0.635	General works
0.65	Bulgaria
0.66	Romania
0.67	Yugoslavia
0.68.A-Z	Other divisions of Europe, A-Z
	Asia
0.69	General works
0.7	China
0.71	India
	Southeast Asia
0.72	General works

	Asia
	Southeast Asia -- Continued
0.73	Vietnam
0.74	Indonesia
0.76	Philippines
0.77	Japan
0.78	Iran
0.79	Russia in Asia. Soviet Union in Asia. Siberia
0.795	Taiwan
0.8	Turkey. Asia Minor
0.81.A-Z	Other divisions of Asia, A-Z
0.813	Arab countries
0.815	Indian Ocean
	Africa
0.82	General works
0.83	Egypt
0.84	South Africa
0.85	Algeria
0.86	Tanzania
0.87	Angola
0.88.A-Z	Other African divisions, A-Z
	e.g.
0.88.E7	Ethiopia
0.88.Z3	Congo (Democratic Republic). Zaire
0.88.Z36	Zambia
	Atlantic Ocean Islands
0.883	General works
0.8835.A-Z	Individual islands and island groups, A-Z
	West Indies see G2b 0.23+
	Indian Ocean Islands
0.884	General works
0.8845.A-Z	Individual islands and island groups, A-Z
0.885	Pacific Ocean
0.89	Australia
0.91	New Zealand
	Pacific Islands
0.97	General works
0.98.A-Z	Individual islands and island groups, A-Z
0.985	Tropics
	Arctic regions
0.99	General works
0.993	Greenland
0.995	Antarctic regions

0.112	America
0.115	North America
	United States
0.12	General works
0.13.A-Z	By region or state, A-Z
0.15	Canada (Table G12)
0.155	Latin America
0.16	Mexico (Table G12)
	Central America
0.17	General works
0.18	Belize. British Honduras (Table G12)
0.19	Costa Rica (Table G12)
0.2	Guatemala (Table G12)
0.21	Nicaragua (Table G12)
0.215	Panama (Table G12)
0.22	El Salvador (Table G12)
	West Indies
0.23	General works
0.24	Bahamas (Table G12)
0.25	Cuba (Table G12)
0.26	Haiti (Table G12)
0.27	Jamaica (Table G12)
0.28	Puerto Rico (Table G12)
0.29.A-Z	Other islands, A-Z
	South America
0.3	General works
0.31	Argentina (Table G12)
0.32	Bolivia (Table G12)
0.33	Brazil (Table G12)
0.34	Chile (Table G12)
0.35	Colombia (Table G12)
0.36	Ecuador (Table G12)
0.365	French Guiana (Table G12)
0.37	Guyana (Table G12)
0.38	Paraguay (Table G12)
0.39	Peru (Table G12)
0.395	Suriname (Table G12)
0.4	Uruguay (Table G12)
0.41	Venezuela (Table G12)
	Europe
0.42	General works
0.425.A-Z	Special regions, international bodies of water, A-Z
	Great Britain
0.43	General works
0.44	England (Table G12)
0.45	Scotland (Table G12)

	Europe
	Great Britain -- Continued
0.46	Northern Ireland (Table G12)
0.465	Wales (Table G12)
0.467	Ireland (Table G12)
0.47	Austria (Table G12)
	Belgium see G2c 0.53
	Denmark see G2c 0.57
0.48	France (Table G12)
0.49	Germany (Table G12)
	Including West Germany
0.495	East Germany (Table G12)
0.5	Greece (Table G12)
0.51	Italy (Table G12)
	Low Countries
0.52	General works
0.53	Belgium (Table G12)
0.54	Netherlands (Table G12)
	Norway see G2c 0.59
0.55	Russia. Soviet Union. Russia (Federation) (Table G12)
	Cf. G2c 0.79 Russia in Asia. Soviet Union in Asia. Siberia
	Scandinavia
0.56	General works
0.57	Denmark (Table G12)
0.58	Iceland (Table G12)
0.59	Norway (Table G12)
0.6	Sweden (Table G12)
0.61	Spain (Table G12)
0.62	Portugal (Table G12)
	Sweden see G2c 0.6
0.63	Switzerland (Table G12)
	Balkan States
0.635	General works
0.65	Bulgaria (Table G12)
0.66	Romania (Table G12)
0.67	Yugoslavia (Table G12)
0.68.A-Z	Other divisions of Europe, A-Z
	Asia
0.69	General works
0.7	China (Table G12)
0.71	India (Table G12)
	Southeast Asia
0.72	General works
0.73	Vietnam (Table G12)
0.74	Indonesia (Table G12)
0.76	Philippines (Table G12)

TABLES

	Asia -- Continued
0.77	Japan (Table G12)
0.78	Iran (Table G12)
0.79	Russia in Asia. Soviet Union in Asia. Siberia
0.795	Taiwan (Table G12)
0.8	Turkey. Asia Minor (Table G12)
0.81.A-Z	Other divisions of Asia, A-Z
0.813	Arab countries
0.815	Indian Ocean
	Africa
0.82	General works
0.83	Egypt (Table G12)
0.84	South Africa (Table G12)
0.85	Algeria (Table G12)
0.86	Tanzania (Table G12)
0.87	Angola (Table G12)
0.88.A-Z	Other African divisions, A-Z
	e.g.
0.88.E7	Ethiopia
0.88.Z3	Congo (Democratic Republic). Zaire
0.88.Z36	Zambia
	Atlantic Ocean Islands
0.883	General works
0.8835.A-Z	Individual islands and island groups, A-Z
	West Indies see G2c 0.23+
	Indian Ocean Islands
0.884	General works
0.8845.A-Z	Individual islands and island groups, A-Z
0.885	Pacific Ocean
0.89	Australia (Table G12)
0.91	New Zealand (Table G12)
	Pacific Islands
0.97	General works
0.98.A-Z	Individual islands and island groups, A-Z
0.985	Tropics
	Arctic regions
0.99	General works
0.993	Greenland (Table G12)
0.995	Antarctic regions

0.112	America
0.115	North America
	United States
0.12	General works
0.13.A-Z	By region or state, A-Z
0.15	Canada (Table G13)
0.155	Latin America
0.16	Mexico (Table G13)
	Central America
0.17	General works
0.18	Belize. British Honduras (Table G13)
0.19	Costa Rica (Table G13)
0.2	Guatemala (Table G13)
0.21	Nicaragua (Table G13)
0.215	Panama (Table G13)
0.22	El Salvador (Table G13)
	West Indies
0.23	General works
0.24	Bahamas (Table G13)
0.25	Cuba (Table G13)
0.26	Haiti (Table G13)
0.27	Jamaica (Table G13)
0.28	Puerto Rico (Table G13)
0.29.A-Z	Other islands, A-Z
	South America
0.3	General works
0.31	Argentina (Table G13)
0.32	Bolivia (Table G13)
0.33	Brazil (Table G13)
0.34	Chile (Table G13)
0.35	Colombia (Table G13)
0.36	Ecuador (Table G13)
0.365	French Guiana (Table G13)
0.37	Guyana (Table G13)
0.38	Paraguay (Table G13)
0.39	Peru (Table G13)
0.395	Suriname (Table G13)
0.4	Uruguay (Table G13)
0.41	Venezuela (Table G13)
	Europe
0.42	General works
0.425.A-Z	Special regions, international bodies of water, A-Z
	Great Britain
0.43	General works
0.44	England (Table G13)
0.45	Scotland (Table G13)

TABLES

	Europe
	Great Britain -- Continued
0.46	Northern Ireland (Table G13)
0.465	Wales (Table G13)
0.467	Ireland (Table G13)
0.47	Austria (Table G13)
	Belgium see G2d 0.53
	Denmark see G2d 0.57
0.48	France (Table G13)
0.49	Germany (Table G13) Including West Germany
0.495	East Germany (Table G13)
0.5	Greece (Table G13)
0.51	Italy (Table G13)
	Low Countries
0.52	General works
0.53	Belgium (Table G13)
0.54	Netherlands (Table G13)
	Norway see G2d 0.59
0.55	Russia. Soviet Union. Russia (Federation) (Table G13) Cf. G2d 0.79 Russia in Asia. Soviet Union in Asia. Siberia
	Scandinavia
0.56	General works
0.57	Denmark (Table G13)
0.58	Iceland (Table G13)
0.59	Norway (Table G13)
0.6	Sweden (Table G13)
0.61	Spain (Table G13)
0.62	Portugal (Table G13)
	Sweden see G2d 0.6
0.63	Switzerland (Table G13)
	Balkan States
0.635	General works
0.65	Bulgaria (Table G13)
0.66	Romania (Table G13)
0.67	Yugoslavia (Table G13)
0.68.A-Z	Other divisions of Europe, A-Z
	Asia
0.69	General works
0.7	China (Table G13)
0.71	India (Table G13)
	Southeast Asia
0.72	General works
0.73	Vietnam (Table G13)
0.74	Indonesia (Table G13)
0.76	Philippines (Table G13)

	Asia -- Continued
0.77	Japan (Table G13)
0.78	Iran (Table G13)
0.79	Russia in Asia. Soviet Union in Asia. Siberia
0.795	Taiwan (Table G13)
0.8	Turkey. Asia Minor (Table G13)
0.81.A-Z	Other divisions of Asia, A-Z
0.813	Arab countries
0.815	Indian Ocean
	Africa
0.82	General works
0.83	Egypt (Table G13)
0.84	South Africa (Table G13)
0.85	Algeria (Table G13)
0.86	Tanzania (Table G13)
0.87	Angola (Table G13)
0.88.A-Z	Other African divisions, A-Z
	e.g.
0.88.E7	Ethiopia
0.88.Z3	Congo (Democratic Republic). Zaire
0.88.Z36	Zambia
	Atlantic Ocean Islands
0.883	General works
0.8835.A-Z	Individual islands and island groups, A-Z
	West Indies see G2d 0.23+
	Indian Ocean Islands
0.884	General works
0.8845.A-Z	Individual islands and island groups, A-Z
0.885	Pacific Ocean
0.89	Australia (Table G13)
0.91	New Zealand (Table G13)
	Pacific Islands
0.97	General works
0.98.A-Z	Individual islands and island groups, A-Z
0.985	Tropics
	Arctic regions
0.99	General works
0.993	Greenland (Table G13)
0.995	Antarctic regions

TABLES

0.112	America
	Class here works on the countries of the Western Hemisphere collectively. For works on an individual country, see the number or numbers for the country
0.115	North America
	Class here works on the countries of North America collectively. For works on an individual country, see the number or numbers for the country
0.15	Canada (Table G14)
0.155	Latin America
0.16	Mexico (Table G14)
	Central America
0.17	General works
0.18	Belize. British Honduras (Table G14)
0.19	Costa Rica (Table G14)
0.2	Guatemala (Table G14)
0.21	Nicaragua (Table G14)
0.215	Panama (Table G14)
0.22	El Salvador (Table G14)
	West Indies
0.23	General works
0.24	Bahamas (Table G14)
0.25	Cuba (Table G14)
0.26	Haiti (Table G14)
0.27	Jamaica (Table G14)
0.28	Puerto Rico (Table G14)
0.29.A-Z	Other islands, A-Z
	South America
0.3	General works
0.31	Argentina (Table G14)
0.32	Bolivia (Table G14)
0.33	Brazil (Table G14)
0.34	Chile (Table G14)
0.35	Colombia (Table G14)
0.36	Ecuador (Table G14)
0.365	French Guiana (Table G14)
0.37	Guyana (Table G14)
0.38	Paraguay (Table G14)
0.39	Peru (Table G14)
0.395	Suriname (Table G14)
0.4	Uruguay (Table G14)
0.41	Venezuela (Table G14)
	Europe
0.42	General works
0.425.A-Z	Special regions, international bodies of water, A-Z
	Great Britain

	Europe
	Great Britain -- Continued
0.43	General works
0.44	England (Table G14)
0.45	Scotland (Table G14)
0.46	Northern Ireland (Table G14)
0.465	Wales (Table G14)
0.467	Ireland (Table G14)
0.47	Austria (Table G14)
	Belgium see G2e 0.53
	Denmark see G2e 0.57
0.48	France (Table G14)
0.49	Germany (Table G14) Including West Germany
0.495	East Germany (Table G14)
0.5	Greece (Table G14)
0.51	Italy (Table G14)
	Low Countries
0.52	General works
0.53	Belgium (Table G14)
0.54	Netherlands (Table G14)
	Norway see G2e 0.59
0.55	Russia. Soviet Union. Russia (Federation) (Table G14) Cf. G2e 0.79 Russia in Asia. Soviet Union in Asia. Siberia
	Scandinavia
0.56	General works
0.57	Denmark (Table G14)
0.58	Iceland (Table G14)
0.59	Norway (Table G14)
0.6	Sweden (Table G14)
0.61	Spain (Table G14)
0.62	Portugal (Table G14)
	Sweden see G2e 0.6
0.63	Switzerland (Table G14)
	Balkan States
0.635	General works
0.65	Bulgaria (Table G14)
0.66	Romania (Table G14)
0.67	Yugoslavia (Table G14)
0.68.A-Z	Other divisions of Europe, A-Z
	Asia
0.69	General works
0.7	China (Table G14)
0.71	India (Table G14)
	Southeast Asia
0.72	General works

TABLES

	Asia
	Southeast Asia -- Continued
0.73	Vietnam (Table G14)
0.74	Indonesia (Table G14)
0.76	Philippines (Table G14)
0.77	Japan (Table G14)
0.78	Iran (Table G14)
0.79	Russia in Asia. Soviet Union in Asia. Siberia
0.795	Taiwan (Table G14)
0.8	Turkey. Asia Minor (Table G14)
0.81.A-Z	Other divisions of Asia, A-Z
0.813	Arab countries
0.815	Indian Ocean
	Africa
0.82	General works
0.83	Egypt (Table G14)
0.84	South Africa (Table G14)
0.85	Algeria (Table G14)
0.86	Tanzania (Table G14)
0.87	Angola (Table G14)
0.88.A-Z	Other African divisions, A-Z
	e.g.
0.88.E7	Ethiopia
0.88.Z3	Congo (Democratic Republic). Zaire
0.88.Z36	Zambia
	Atlantic Ocean Islands
0.883	General works
0.8835.A-Z	Individual islands and island groups, A-Z
	West Indies see G2e 0.23+
	Indian Ocean Islands
0.884	General works
0.8845.A-Z	Individual islands and island groups, A-Z
0.885	Pacific Ocean
0.89	Australia (Table G14)
0.91	New Zealand (Table G14)
	Pacific Islands
0.97	General works
0.98.A-Z	Individual islands and island groups, A-Z
0.985	Tropics
	Arctic regions
0.99	General works
0.993	Greenland (Table G14)
0.995	Antarctic regions

29-30	Canada (Table G10)
30.5	Latin America
31-32	Mexico (Table G10)
	Central America
33	General works
35-36	Belize. British Honduras (Table G10)
37-38	Costa Rica (Table G10)
39-40	Guatemala (Table G10)
41-41.5	Nicaragua (Table G11)
42-42.5	Panama (Table G11)
43-43.5	El Salvador (Table G11)
	West Indies
45	General works
47-48	Bahamas (Table G10)
49-50	Cuba (Table G10)
51-52	Haiti (Table G10)
53-54	Jamaica (Table G10)
55-56	Puerto Rico (Table G10)
57.A-Z	Other islands, A-Z
	South America
58	General works
58.5.A-Z	Special regions, international bodies of water, A-Z
59-60	Argentina (Table G10)
61-62	Bolivia (Table G10)
63-64	Brazil (Table G10)
65-66	Chile (Table G10)
67-68	Colombia (Table G10)
69-70	Ecuador (Table G10)
	French Guiana
70.5	General works
70.6.A-Z	Local, A-Z
71-72	Guyana (Table G10)
73-74	Paraguay (Table G10)
75-76	Peru (Table G10)
	Suriname
76.5	General works
76.6.A-Z	Local, A-Z
77-78	Uruguay (Table G10)
79-80	Venezuela (Table G10)
	Europe
81	General works
82.A-Z	Special regions, international bodies of water, A-Z
	Great Britain
83	General works
85-86	England (Table G10)
87-88	Scotland (Table G10)

	Europe
	Great Britain -- Continued
89-89.5	Northern Ireland (Table G11)
	Wales
90	General works
90.5.A-Z	Local, A-Z
	Ireland
90.7	General works
90.8.A-Z	Local, A-Z
91-92	Austria (Table G10)
	Belgium see G3 103+
	Denmark see G3 111+
93-94	France (Table G10)
95-96	Germany (Table G10)
	Including West Germany
96.5	East Germany
97-98	Greece (Table G10)
99-100	Italy (Table G10)
	Low Countries
101	General works
103-104	Belgium (Table G10)
105-106	Netherlands (Table G10)
	Norway see G3 115+
107-108	Russia. Soviet Union. Russia (Federation) (Table G10)
	Cf. G3 155+ Russia in Asia. Soviet Union in Asia. Siberia
	Scandinavia
109	General works
111-112	Denmark (Table G10)
113-114	Iceland (Table G10)
115-116	Norway (Table G10)
117-118	Sweden (Table G10)
119-120	Spain (Table G10)
121-122	Portugal (Table G10)
	Sweden see G3 117+
123-124	Switzerland (Table G10)
	Balkan States
124.5	General works
127-128	Bulgaria (Table G10)
129-130	Romania (Table G10)
131-132	Yugoslavia (Table G10)
133.A-Z	Other divisions of Europe, A-Z
	Asia
135	General works
137-138	China (Table G10)
139-140	India (Table G10)
	Southeast Asia

	Asia
	Southeast Asia -- Continued
141	General works
143-144	Vietnam (Table G10)
145-146	Indonesia (Table G10)
149-150	Philippines (Table G10)
151-152	Japan (Table G10)
153-154	Iran (Table G10)
155-156	Russia in Asia. Soviet Union in Asia. Siberia (Table G10)
	Taiwan
156.5	General works
156.52.A-Z	Local, A-Z
157-158	Turkey. Asia Minor (Table G10)
159.A-Z	Other divisions of Asia, A-Z
159.5	Arab countries
160	Indian Ocean
	Africa
161	General works
163-164	Egypt (Table G10)
165-166	South Africa (Table G10)
167-168	Algeria (Table G10)
169-170	Tanzania (Table G10)
171-172	Angola (Table G10)
173.A-Z	Other African divisions, A-Z
	e.g.
173.E7	Ethiopia
173.Z3	Zaire
173.Z36	Zambia
	Atlantic Ocean Islands
173.4	General works
173.5.A-Z	Individual islands and island groups, A-Z
	West Indies see G3 45+
	Indian Ocean Islands
173.7	General works
173.8.A-Z	Individual islands and island groups, A-Z
	Pacific Ocean
174	General works
174.25	Bering Sea
175-176	Australia (Table G10)
179-180	New Zealand (Table G10)
	Pacific Islands
192	General works
193.A-Z	Individual islands and island groups, A-Z
194	Tropics
	Arctic regions
195-196	General works (Table G10)

TABLES

	Arctic regions -- Continued
	Greenland
196.5	General works
196.6.A-Z	Local, A-Z
197-198	Antarctic regions (Table G10)

This table is no longer used. The subarrangement has been incorporated into the text of the schedule.

Add the appropriate number from this table to the first number of the classification number span to which the table applies

When the table is modified, the modification normally occurs in the use of locals

0	General works
	By period
1	Ancient
2	Medieval
	Modern
3	General works
4	15th-16th centuries
5	17th century
6	18th century
7	19th century
8	20th century
	Local
11.A-Z	By region, state, province, etc., A-Z
12.A-Z	By city, A-Z

1	America
	North America
2	General works
	United States
3	General works
	By region
5	New England
5.5	Middle Atlantic States
5.7	Middle West
6	Southern States
6.5	Appalachian Region
7	Central
8	West
9	Pacific States
10.A-.W	By state, A-W
11.A-Z	By city, A-Z
13	Canada (Table G15)
	Latin America
13.5	General works
14	Mexico (Table G15)
	Central America
15	General works
16	Belize. British Honduras (Table G15)
17	Costa Rica (Table G15)
18	Guatemala (Table G15)
19	Honduras (Table G15)
20	Nicaragua (Table G15)
21	Panama (Table G15)
22	El Salvador (Table G15)
	West Indies
23	General works
24	Bahamas (Table G15)
25	Cuba (Table G15)
26	Haiti (Table G15)
27	Jamaica (Table G15)
28	Puerto Rico (Table G15)
29.A-Z	Other, A-Z
	South America
30	General works
31	Argentina (Table G15)
32	Bolivia (Table G15)
33	Brazil (Table G15)
34	Chile (Table G15)
35	Colombia (Table G15)
36	Ecuador (Table G15)
37	Guianas (Table G15)

	Latin America
	South America -- Continued
38	Paraguay (Table G15)
39	Peru (Table G15)
40	Uruguay (Table G15)
41	Venezuela (Table G15)
	Europe
42	General works
	Great Britain. England (General)
43	General works
44.A-Z	England (Local), A-Z
45	Scotland (Table G15)
46	Northern Ireland (Table G15)
47	Wales (Table G15)
47.5	Ireland (Table G15)
48	Austria (Table G15)
48.5	Hungary (Table G15)
49	France (Table G15)
50	Germany (Table G15) Including West Germany
50.5	East Germany (Table G15)
51	Greece (Table G15)
52	Italy (Table G15)
	Low Countries
53	General works
54	Netherlands (Table G15)
55	Belgium (Table G15)
56	Russia. Soviet Union. Former Soviet Republics (Table G15) For former republics of the Caucasus see G6 74.5.A+ For former Central Asian republics see G6 75+
56.2	Russia (Federation) (Table G15) For Siberia see G6 85
56.3	Ukraine (Table G15)
56.35	Belarus (Table G15)
56.38	Moldova (Table G15)
	Baltic States
56.39	General works
56.4	Estonia (Table G15)
56.45	Latvia (Table G15)
56.5	Lithuania (Table G15)
	Scandinavia
57	General works
58	Denmark (Table G15)
59	Iceland (Table G15)
60	Norway (Table G15)
61	Sweden (Table G15)

	Europe -- Continued
62	Spain (Table G15)
63	Portugal (Table G15)
64	Switzerland (Table G15)
	Balkan States
66	General works
66.5	Albania (Table G15)
66.7	Bosnia and Hercegovina (Table G15)
67	Bulgaria (Table G15)
69	Romania (Table G15)
69.5	Slovenia (Table G15)
70	Yugoslavia (Table G15)
71.A-Z	Other European regions or countries, A-Z
71.A54	Andorra
71.A57	Alps
71.A73	Ardennes
71.C9	Czechoslovakia
71.F5	Finland
71.P6	Poland
71.5	Mediterranean Region
	Asia
72	General works
	Middle East
73	General works
73.5	Turkey. Asia Minor (Table G15)
74	Iran (Table G15)
74.5.A-Z	Other regions or countries, A-Z
74.5.A74	Armenia
74.5.C93	Cyprus
	Soviet Central Asia
75	General works
75.2	Kazakh S.S.R. Kazakhstan (Table G15)
75.25	Kirghiz S.S.R. Kirghizistan (Table G15)
75.3	Tajik S.S.R. Tajikistan (Table G15)
75.35	Turkmen S.S.R. Turkmenistan (Table G15)
75.4	Uzbek S.S.R. Uzbekistan (Table G15)
	South Asia
75.5	General works
76	India (Table G15)
76.2	Sri Lanka (Table G15)
76.3	Pakistan (Table G15)
76.4	Nepal (Table G15)
76.43	Bangladesh (Table G15)
	Southeast Asia
76.5	General works
	Indochina

Asia
  Southeast Asia
    Indochina -- Continued
77 General works
78 Thailand (Table G15)
78.2 Burma. Myanmar (Table G15)
78.5 Vietnam (Table G15)
79 Malaysia (Table G15)
80 Indonesia (Table G15)
81 Philippines (Table G15)
  East Asia
82 General works
83 China (Table G15)
83.5 Taiwan (Table G15)
84 Japan (Table G15)
85 Siberia (Russia) (Table G15)
86.A-Z Other Asian regions or countries, A-Z
Africa
87 General works
88 Egypt (Table G15)
89.A-Z Other regions or countries, A-Z
Australia
90 General works
91.A-Z By state or territory, A-Z
Pacific islands
95 General works
96.A-Z By island or group of islands, A-Z

1 General works. General history of cartography
2 Official works. Documents
3 Collective biography
  Cf. GA 281+, Biography of globe makers
 By period see G7 3.1+
History. By period
 Early to 500
3.1.A1 History. Collective biography
3.1.A3-Z Individual biography, A-Z
 Medieval (500 to 1500)
3.3.A1 History. Collective biography
3.3.A3-Z Individual biography, A-Z
 16th century
3.5.A1 History. Collective biography
3.5.A3-Z Individual biography, A-Z
 17th-18th centuries
3.6.A1 History. Collective biography
3.6.A3-Z Individual biography, A-Z
 19th-20th centuries
3.7.A1 History. Collective biography
3.7.A3-Z Individual biography, A-Z
4 Individual maps. By date or approximate date
  Subarrange: (1) by cartographer or title, (2) by author or editor
5.A-Z Local, A-Z

TABLES

1	General works
2.A-Z	By state, province, etc., A-Z
2.5.A-Z	By city, A-Z

.x	General works
.x3A-.x3Z	By state, province, etc., A-Z
.x5A-.x5Z	By city, A-Z

1	General works
2.A-Z	Local, A-Z

1	General works
1.5.A-Z	Local, A-Z

.A2	General works
.A3-.Z	Local, A-Z

.A1	General works
.A2-.Z	Local, A-Z

.A1	General works
.A2-.Z	Individual races, events, racetracks, etc., A-Z

.A2	General works
.A3A-.A3Z	Provinces, regions, etc., A-Z
.A4-.Z	Cities, towns, etc., A-Z

.x	General works
.x2A-.x2Z	Local, A-Z

INDEX

INDEX

B

E

I

J

INDEX

P

INDEX

T

INDEX

V

GPO U.S. GOVERNMENT PRINTING OFFICE: 2007–330–111/60007